Also by Andrew Peyton Thomas
   Crime and the Sacking of America
   Fighting the Good Fight (with Reggie White)

CLARENCE THOMAS

A BIOGRAPHY

Andrew Peyton Thomas

ENCOUNTER BOOKS
NEW YORK · LONDON

First edition published in 2001 by Encounter Books, an activity of Encounter for Culture and Education, Inc., a nonprofit tax exempt corporation.

Encounter Books website address: www.encounterbooks.com

Cover and text design © Ayelet Maida, A/M Studios.
Cover photograph of Clarence Thomas courtesy of the Archives of the Diocese of Savannah; U.S. Supreme Court columns © Jeremy Woodhouse, PhotoDisc.
Author photograph © Patricia Varela.
Photographs courtesy of the author, unless otherwise indicated.

Manufactured in the United States and printed on acid-free paper.
The paper used in this publication meets the minimum requirements of ANSI/NISO Z39.48-1992 (R 1997) (Permanence of Paper).

FIRST EDITION

LIBRARY OF CONGRESS CATALOGING-IN-PUBLICATION DATA
Thomas, Andrew Peyton.
    Clarence Thomas : a biography / Andrew Peyton Thomas.
       p. cm.
    Includes bibliographical references and index.
    ISBN 1-893554-36-8
1. Thomas, Clarence, 1948– 2. Judges-United States-Biography. I. Titles.

KF8745.T48 T48 2002
347.73'2634-dc21
[B]   2001040501

10 9 8 7 6 5 4 3 2

To Monica, Peyton and Nathan

Contents

I will restore your judges as in days of old,
your counselors as at the beginning.

Isaiah 1:26

Prologue

"Do you have anything you would like to say?"

It was an odd question coming from Joseph Biden, chairman of the Senate Judiciary Committee, who knew very well that the man seated before him, Clarence Thomas, had a great deal he wished to say. For the preceding two weeks, the Supreme Court nominee had agonized as he watched his enemies lay waste to his reputation. Anyone who knew Thomas came to realize that reputation was everything to him—the work of art he had sculpted, the summit he had climbed, the treasure he had stored up from years of public service. Thomas often spoke of his life and reputation as one and the same. Concern about his reputation was also his hubris; that Thomas cared so much about what others thought of him was a flaw of character. He would suffer mightily for this shortcoming. For these two excruciating weeks, the prideful man had wept over the destruction of his good name like a farmer mourning the devastation of his crops by a flood or hailstorm.

His appearance before the Senate Judiciary Committee on October 11, 1991, was an opportunity to salvage what remained of this prized asset. Thomas blamed the committee—or at least the Democrats who dominated it—for his tribulations. As he calmly took his seat before them, he looked hard at the Democratic senators seated at the right half of the rostrum. A navy blue, two-piece suit, starkly white shirt and crimson paisley tie did their best to contain Thomas's stocky frame. His wife, Ginni, sat behind him to his right, in a black-and-white checkered jacket that seemed emblematic of their interracial marriage. Next to Ginni was Thomas's longtime patron, Senator John Danforth. They were seated literally front and center in the crowded Senate Caucus

Room, whose abundant marble and chandeliers lent the occasion a sense of grandeur and pending history.

More Americans were watching the televised hearings than the baseball playoff game on the one network not showing the hearings live. For a political event in an increasingly apathetic republic, the size of the TV audience was astonishing. The real-life drama unfolding in Washington, D.C., was too riveting to miss. Indeed, the subject matter—occasionally prurient and always personal—was not very different from that of many of the daytime television programs that dominated the nation's airwaves in the afternoon.

Thomas's nomination to the Supreme Court had been, for him, an overwhelming experience. When he accepted the nomination outside President George Bush's wind-swept, ocean-side house in Maine, Thomas visibly gulped down the emotion of the occasion. Like most who rise to power, he had toiled for years in anonymity serving others of higher station—first Senator Danforth, and then the president. His opponents dismissed him as undeserving of the honor. Many of them— ironically, the most committed supporters of affirmative action—branded him a "quota nominee" because of his race. The charge deeply stung the sensitive man. Yet this accusation helped him in an important way, by underscoring the fact that he carried along with him the aspirations of the African-American people. Blacks responded to this invective by rallying around Thomas; while most disagreed with his opposition to racial preferences, most supported his nomination.

For three months, Thomas's astute political skills, honed during his years in the nation's capital, had allowed him to check his adversaries. A few days before this dramatic appearance, the Senate had stood poised to confirm him to the Court by a comfortable margin. Then came allegations of sexual improprieties on the job. The charges Anita Hill made against him were sufficiently shocking to throw the Senate proceedings into chaos.

Thomas's opponents, seeing Hill's accusations as their last realistic means of defeating his nomination, demanded that the Senate investigate them. The Judiciary Committee commenced hearings. Before rows of TV cameras and, consequently, the rest of the nation, Hill expanded on her allegations in graphic detail.

The crucial speech that Thomas would deliver in response to Hill's testimony was the culmination of his life and his struggles. All the racism and discrimination of his youth informed his response to the hearings—which, he believed, had a racial animus at their core. The injustices of Jim Crow visited upon his family and himself; a summer spent reading about lynchings; the repeated racial slights in an all-white high school: these scenes from the life of a black American were the lens through which Thomas viewed the hearings, the worst cataclysm of his life. He had dealt with adversity before in Washington, the result of his unorthodox views. He had complained bitterly of his run-ins with civil rights leaders and the numerous rough congressional hearings—his "whuppings," he had called them. Such training had prepared Thomas for this pivotal moment. To defend himself adequately, he had dismissed his unreliable advisers from the White House, falling back instead on his own instincts and judgment. Through a haze of sleeplessness and the churning of his stomach, he grappled for the right words.

The long, harsh plight of his race had steeled him further for this experience. For all the attempts of some civil rights leaders to portray Thomas as a turncoat to his people, few blacks, according to polls, accepted this characterization. He was too obviously one of them. He was drawn from their ranks—born into poverty under segregation, someone exuding the values and folkways of black folk. Many blacks, moreover, seemed to sense a racial undercurrent in the last-minute attacks on Thomas, which were mounted overwhelmingly by white feminists. In response to his nomination, a schism had emerged between blacks and white feminists, something unseen at the national level since Susan B. Anthony and her allies broke from Frederick Douglass and black civil rights leaders following the Civil War.

When they learned of Hill and her useful if reluctant testimony, feminist leaders and their allies in the Senate prodded her into the limelight and exploited her charges. They rightly perceived that Thomas was a closet foe of the Supreme Court's ruling in *Roe v. Wade*. Other opponents of Thomas feared him because he was an intellectually independent black man who, as such, endangered their power base.

The race-based antagonism behind the campaign to defeat Thomas was, to him, just as real as the horrors of the hooded nightriders and the "strange fruit" dangling from Southern trees. True, this effort lacked the spectacular violence that had stained the nation's history books: the torture, the summary executions, the theft of entire lives spent in vassalage. Yet Thomas perceived that what his experience lacked in blood, it made up for in instant mortification before a whole nation.

Earlier in the day, as Thomas sought to put his outrage into words, centuries of racial oppression flooded his mind. An old friend had called him the night before to talk about the hearings. Although the friend disagreed with Thomas's politics, he abhorred what was happening to him. The two black men agreed that his adversaries were capitalizing on and perpetuating the vicious stereotype—responsible for so much racial violence—of a sexually voracious black man who needed to be stopped.

As he paced in Danforth's Senate office before going out to meet the committee, Thomas latched onto a thought and a phrase. "This is a lynching," he told the senator. "This is a high-tech lynching." He made some notes before leaving for the Caucus Room.

Throughout his career, Thomas had reassured himself that race was not an impediment to his success. He had been right, up to then. But now these hearings showed that all his vast efforts to move beyond race, in both public and private life, ultimately had been in vain. Race and sex, the two most explosive issues of his day, had mixed to form a conflagration that threatened to consume his longstanding dream of becoming a justice of the Supreme Court.

As Thomas leaned forward into the microphone, he prepared to personify and articulate, perhaps for the only time in his life, the African-American experience. His fellow blacks were already united behind him. They would be even more firmly in his camp when he was finished.

PART ONE

Iron Sharpens Iron

Family Tree of Clarence Thomas

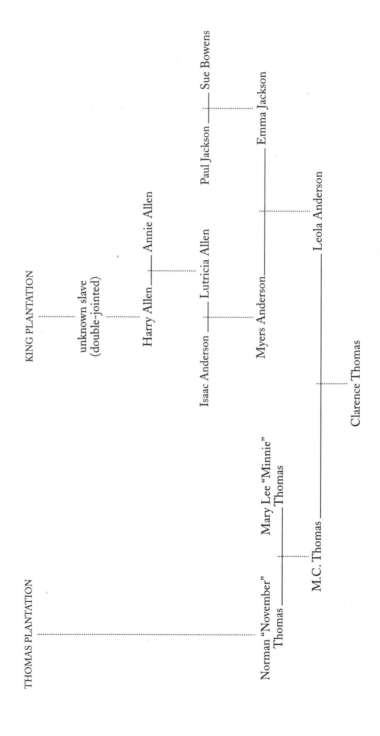

THOMAS PLANTATION

KING PLANTATION

unknown slave
(double-jointed)

Harry Allen —— Annie Allen

Paul Jackson —— Sue Bowens

Isaac Anderson —— Lutricia Allen

Myers Anderson —— Emma Jackson

Leola Anderson

Clarence Thomas

Norman "November" Thomas

Mary Lee "Minnie" Thomas

M.C. Thomas

CHAPTER ONE

Two Plantations in Georgia

"To understand," Frederick Douglass said, "a man must *stand under.*" Only by considering all the hardships a man has overcome in life, Douglass believed, can the rest of us judge him fairly. So it must be with Clarence Thomas. To understand how Thomas became one of the great intellectual and political rebels in American history, one must recall, in the context of his life, the unique evils that he and his fellow black Americans surmounted with such great struggle.

Thomas himself would eschew such an approach, but not for lack of respect for Frederick Douglass. Thomas often quotes Douglass, and a black-and-white portrait of the grizzled great man today peers over his shoulder from behind his desk in his Supreme Court chambers. Rather, Thomas, proudly independent to the point of vice, simply brooks no assessment of his life based on anything other than his own achievements. This policy is unduly modest, both toward himself and toward others of his race. Thomas's story cannot be fully comprehended, or his accomplishments given their full measure, without consideration of the broader history of racial injustice that forms the backdrop of his life and work.

"We Afro-Americans are like hunters on the trail of truth," Thomas once observed. "The prey we stalk is: Who we are, What we have been, What we will become as individuals and as a people." The dearth of recorded black family history is a large impediment to this historical quest. One of the great enduring offenses of American slave owners was their policy of forbidding slaves to chronicle their lineage—even while they and other white Southerners became famously obsessed with documenting every last twig of their own family trees. This crime against history robbed black Americans of the firm ancestral ties crucial for a fuller sense of continuity and tradition. Subsequent poor record keeping by Southern bureaucrats compounded this wrong.

And yet the trail of truth in Clarence Thomas's origins is discernible, and it leads unerringly through the heart of Georgia. His family story is but a tiny stitch or two in the tapestry of that state's history, but it provides the essential backdrop of Thomas's life. It also offers a reminder that Clarence Thomas's remarkable ascent in American government is not merely a tale of self-advancement, but a chapter in the continuing triumph of the African-American people, without whose sacrifices and sustenance Thomas would not be where he is today.

Clarence Thomas is a descendant of the African-American slaves emancipated from the Thomas plantation in Laurens County, Georgia, and from the King plantation in Liberty County, Georgia. His genealogy intertwines with the most sinister aspects of the nation's early history, a time when men could own other men and, ultimately, one-half of the nation made war on the other to bring this institution to a flaming end. Thomas's family bore the additional and great misfortune of living in Georgia, arguably the most racially oppressive corner of the entire slavocracy.

The black folk of Georgia resisted their fate with energy and ingenuity. W. E. B. Du Bois, the greatest of African-American scholars, noted this spirit when he wrote that Georgia was home to "a mass of peculiarly self-reliant black folk." Their stubborn assertiveness spilled over into the larger spectacle of American history, as the great black leaders born and nurtured in Georgia successfully championed the cause of all African-Americans.

Founded in 1732, Georgia was the only English colony in America that prohibited slavery from its inception. By 1750, however, so many slaves had been smuggled into Georgia that the colonial government finally bowed to popular will and repealed the ban. The government also, for good measure, clamped on a tough slave code modeled after that of South Carolina, where a slave revolt in 1739 triggered draconian criminal punishments and travel restrictions on its already shackled black residents.

Thomas's ancestors almost certainly came from the Atlantic shores of West Africa. The slaves at the King plantation, an estate built on rice production where his mother's ancestors lived, were overwhelmingly from this region, where the confluence of the sea and several West African rivers made the native people experts at cultivating rice. Amid the babble of tongues and kaleidoscope of customs and faiths transplanted to the Georgia coast, there was a common, ardent desire to recover the freedom many of them had only recently lost.

Some of the newly enslaved Africans resorted to the most direct expedient: suicide. One group of Ibos fresh from present-day Nigeria were delivered to St. Simons Island, some thirty miles from the King plantation, around the turn of the nineteenth century, and as soon as the opportunity presented itself, the chief of the tribe solemnly led his people into Dunbar Creek, where they drowned themselves. The point is now called Ibo Landing; local legend holds that it is haunted.

Many slaves escaped and ran away from Georgia, and then garrisoned themselves against their erstwhile owners. In 1681, black runaway slaves from South Carolina and English settlements in what later became the Georgia colony established Fort Mose, an outpost two miles north of St. Augustine, Florida. There they took up life among the native American Indians and at one point mustered a militia that fought off James Oglethorpe's English soldiers from Georgia. Other such "maroon" communities (from the Spanish word *cimarron*, meaning unruly) sprang up in the area. The ex-slaves in these societies subsisted on wild game and whatever they could grab in their raids on white villages.

During the Revolutionary War, Georgia's white leaders understandably were leery of providing arms to such a restive population. By the end of the conflict, Georgia and neighboring South Carolina were the only two states that did not permit blacks to serve as soldiers. The British exploited this disparate treatment, particularly in the southern theater of the war. They welcomed slaves into their ranks and enticed them with promises of freedom for services rendered. When the British captured Savannah, Georgia, in 1778, a former slave guided them into the city and a large contingent of black soldiers, comprising some 10 percent of the total British force, helped them take it.

Georgia's whites responded in kind. Between 1779 and 1788, the year after the Constitutional Convention in Philadelphia, Georgia was the only state that did not outlaw or suspend the slave trade. White landowners instigated hostilities against the Seminole Indians in Florida during the War of 1812 because of their refusal to return runaway slaves. Armed camps of former Georgia slaves conducted sorties out of northern Florida, killing whites and freeing slaves. From 1817 to 1818, between 400 and 600 runaway slaves joined the Seminoles in harassing Georgia plantations. Andrew Jackson grudgingly acknowledged their bravery and finally disengaged federal forces from the conflict, ending, for the time being, "this savage and Negro war."

Such insurrectionary battles were at the margins of early nineteenth-century life, however. In 1819, the United States acquired Florida from Spain, and with overwhelming force, the U.S. military methodically cleared the land of Indians and their fugitive neighbors. Until the Civil War, Georgia remained a nightmarish destination for blacks. Frederick Douglass wrote that the selling of a slave "to the State of Georgia was a sore and mournful event to those left behind, as well as to the victims themselves."

The Thomas plantation, near the geographical center of the state, was a microcosm of slave life in Georgia. Located in northern Laurens County, this tract of land fell just south of the "Fall Line," the jagged ancient shoreline that runs more or less diagonally from southwest to northeast across the middle of the state. The land south of the Fall Line is an ancient mixture of sand and clay originally deposited by the Atlantic Ocean before it ebbed to its current contour. The soil that remains is largely a loam-covered red piedmont clay. The consistency and nutrients of the soil make it hospitable for a valued commodity: cotton.

Part of the "plantation belt," the fertile crescent that sweeps down from Virginia south to Georgia and then edges west into east Texas, Laurens County offered pristine farmland to those early-nineteenth-century pioneers willing to fell and uproot enough trees to cultivate it. The brothers John and Peter Thomas arrived in the area around 1808 and claimed one of the county's richest bottomlands. Along the banks of Turkey Creek, amid a dense grove of cypress, birch and white oak trees, they built their first home and mill. Peter Thomas was one of the first five justices of the Laurens County Inferior Court, whose first term convened on April 25, 1808, in a small building next to the Thomas house.

In 1849, the Thomas family sold the property, including its slaves, to one of the more colorful personalities in Georgia history: George Michael Troup. The antique *Men of Mark in Georgia* informs posterity, "In the bright constellation of names which have illuminated the history of Georgia, there is none which shines with more effulgence than that of George M. Troup." In language evocative of Parson Weems, Troup is described as someone who, even as a child, was "tenacious of his honor, decided in character, and of unsullied reputation," and "never engaged in a senseless prank or a mischievous act." As an adult, the Southern aristocrat studied at Princeton, practiced law in Savannah, and married a cousin of Robert E. Lee. He subsequently enjoyed a phenomenal political career, including, in order, stints as a congressman, senator and governor. In 1823, he was the last governor of Georgia elected by the legislature; in 1825, he became the first elected by the people. The 1823 election capped off a ferocious and deadly campaign between the factions loyal to Troup and Matthew Talbot, himself a disciple of a local political boss named John Clarke. When the ballots were read aloud in the legislature and the roar of shouts and weeping died down, a locally famous Methodist preacher broke the silence by exulting, "O Lord we thank thee. The State is redeemed from the rule of the devil and John Clarke."

Troup was slender and of medium height. He walked with an erect military posture. His most distinctive physical features were his blazing red hair, sunken blue eyes, and a large, supple mouth which, a contemporary judge quipped, "nature had formed expressly to say 'Yazoo.'" Troup was an eccentric. He dressed in a blue coat with brass buttons, a buff vest and a fur cap, and he often wore summer outfits in winter and vice versa. When he was sworn into office as governor, he showed up before the legislature on a frigid November day wearing spring apparel: a round jacket of cotton cloth, a black cassimere vest, yellow nankeen trousers, silk hose, dancing pumps and a large white hat.

This odd bird, so haughty that he would not canvass for votes ("I have refused through life to electioneer and I am too old to do it now," he insisted during his gubernatorial campaign), was in one respect far ahead of his time. Advancing a theory of states' rights that would one day cleave the nation in two, Troup contended that all federal sovereignty flowed from the states. As governor, he threatened to take military action against the federal government when the administration of John Quincy Adams sided with Georgia's Indian tribes in a land dispute.

Troup retired from public life in 1833 and devoted himself to the plantations he owned in and around Laurens County. In 1849, he purchased the Thomas plantation, an estate of approximately 1,900 acres stretching from Turkey Creek on its western border some three and a half miles to the east. Troup already owned 300 to 350 slaves on his Laurens County plantations. (One was Isaac Jackson, who claimed to be George Washington's oldest surviving slave and who lived to be 112.) An estimated 200 slaves worked on the Thomas plantation.

The house that Troup obtained as part of the Thomas real estate crowned a gently sloping hill and enjoyed a literally commanding view of the slaves toiling in the cotton fields below. The structure was a typical Piedmont Plains plantation house: a "two-on-two" design with a complementary pair of rooms on either side of the house, both upstairs and downstairs, connected by two corresponding large halls. Slaves constructed the foundation and chimney with bricks made of red clay scooped from the ground and dried in the sun. Clapboard siding of native wood, most likely pine or cypress, covered the exterior. From a broad front porch, the standard architectural welcome mat of the South, Troup could view and acknowledge passersby traveling to and from Thomas Crossroads, the name by which the nearby intersection of former Indian trails had become known.

Troup traveled by wagon among his four plantations in the 1850s, as always an arresting sight. Decked out in his blue coat, its metal buttons reflecting sunrays as he passed over the rutted roads, Troup would tip his fur cap in friendly salute. He moved from plantation to plantation with a full entourage in tow, a caravan of wagons hauling slaves and household furnishings, horses and dogs neighing and barking along as part of the procession. Several states' rights parties, recognizing his early, prescient contributions to their cause, nominated him for president during the decade. He declined, citing failing health. George Michael Troup died in 1856 and was buried at Rosemont Plantation; his real estate and slaves passed to his daughter and grandchildren.

The master race he had served so ably mourned him in proportion to his deeds. A county was named after him. So was one of the squares in Savannah. (Clarence Thomas, a descendant of Troup's slaves, would grow up in a home two miles away from the memorial.) The Georgia Assembly commissioned a life-size portrait, which today hangs in a prominent corner of the Assembly's outer halls. Troup's visage is catty-corner to a portrait of Martin Luther King Jr., about one-quarter its size.

—∙—

W. E. B. Du Bois judged Liberty County, some 120 miles from where the Troup-Thomas plantation stood, "by far the most interesting black county in Georgia." Fanny Kemble, a nineteenth-century British actress and critic of slavery who married one of Georgia's wealthiest planters, chortled that given the slavery so prevalent there, the name "Liberty County" must be a "satirical title." The popularity of slavery in the county was not for lack of religious enlightenment. Liberty County had been founded in the 1750s by Puritans who were an offshoot of the hardy band that sailed from England and founded Dorchester, Massachusetts, in 1630. This group hopscotched down the Atlantic coast to establish Dorchester, South Carolina, in 1695, and Liberty County in the following century.

Wherever these Puritans came ashore, a local flowering of economic success was not slow in coming. These settlers were both a testament and a traveling road troupe for Max Weber's thesis on the Calvinist work ethic; their belief in thrift, private property, and the moral dignity of labor both condoned and increased wealth. Liberty County was one of the greatest showcases of these values. Out of a swampy terrain far more hospitable to mosquitoes and water moccasins than to men, these brave souls fashioned a miniature civilization envied throughout the South—a Plymouth Rock with slaves. Robert Manson Myers described this extraordinary elite in *The Children of Pride* as "sober, pious, God-fearing Calvinists.... No planting community could boast deeper religious convictions, higher intellectual cultivation, gentler social refinement, or greater material wealth."

Yet these devout Christians were forced to reconcile their faith with the profits drawn from a deeply sinful institution. They tried to thread this needle by becoming the most tolerant of slave owners and the most committed to teaching their human property the basics of Christianity. By 1770, whites had established a broad program for the religious education of the slaves in Liberty County. Charles Colcock Jones, who became known as the "Apostle to the Blacks," rode a circuit of some fifty plantations, preaching to the slaves after their daily labors had ended. Jones wrote a *Catechism of Scripture Doctrine and Practice*, taught in family and plantation schools in his absence. When the State of Georgia ordered these schools closed, the Puritans of Georgia ensured that their slaves received the same instruction in Sunday schools. Jones concluded that through these efforts, "Personal responsibility, freely admitted, engendered mutual respect and a most commendable degree of manliness" among the county's black residents.

Work reinforced this emphasis on individual responsibility. Slaves in Liberty County were required to perform a daily "task," which usually meant working a piece of land. After they finished this assignment, the rest of the day was theirs. They could hire themselves out to other planters or artisans, grow vegetables on plots of land next to their quarters, or engage in other commercial pursuits; and they were allowed to keep all or a substantial portion of what they earned from these entrepreneurial labors. In addition to making their existence less dreary, this practice offered slaves a personal incentive to work efficiently. Some were able to save enough money to buy their own land; and thanks to the toleration born of a guilty conscience, whites agreed to sell it to them. This policy of land ownership for slaves was incomprehensible and, indeed, anathema elsewhere in the South.

Liberty County "was not Tara," as one local historian hastened to note. Hard toil six days a week gave way to a ten-or-more-mile wagon ride on Sundays to the Midway Church, where services were a twelve-hour experience. Balls and other frivolities were rare, but the dividends of clean living were undeniable. Liberty County became one of the wealthiest rural communities in the antebellum South. In the decades after its founding, the little tidewater county produced many nationally recognized leaders of government, religion, education and science. Throughout Georgia and the South, it was said with admiration that the planter class of Liberty County "feared only malaria and a decline in the price of rice and sea-island cotton."

Sitting at the pinnacle of this privileged caste was the King family.

Of approximately a hundred plantations along the Liberty County coast in 1851, only six were larger than a thousand acres. One of these belonged to Roswell King Jr., whose wife, Julia, hailed from another prominent Liberty County clan, the Maxwell family. The King plantation covered much of Colonel's Island. The so-called island—it is really a saw-toothed peninsula—had been a Creek Indian settlement. Its name derived from the large number of colonels who subsequently resided there. A secondary barrier island nestled behind the much larger St. Catherines Island, which faces the sea and absorbs most of its force, Colonel's Island and its sandy bluffs jut into the coastal waterway that flows between the two islands and enables easy navigation along the coast.

The King plantation was part of Liberty County's rice empire. At Colonel's Island, swampland and bogs from the mainland merged with the alluvium of the low, flat peninsulas to form a prime area for growing rice. The Kings and neighboring planters bought or imported slaves with expertise in this specialized craft. To avoid contracting malaria, to which African blacks (conveniently enough) were genetically more resistant than whites, the local rice aristocracy entrusted the cultivation of this crop to the slaves while retreating to higher ground in the summer.

The King plantation house was a sizable two-story edifice constructed from the remains of a wrecked British ship that washed ashore nearby. The inventive Puritans put the flotsam to good use, making an ample veranda on the second floor directly above double front doors and an oversized front porch bracketing the ground floor. Plain white pillars supported the second story, and dark shutters for the windows lent the home a simple symmetry. By design, live oaks laden with Spanish moss partially obstructed the front view of the house.

In addition to tending to their holdings on Colonel's Island and nearby, the Kings supervised the massive estates of Pierce Butler in Glynn County. With over fifteen hundred acres and more than eight hundred slaves, Butler's plantations were one of the largest plantation systems in the nation. It was Butler who married Fanny Kemble in 1836 and brought her back home to nearby Darien, Georgia, where she tried to trade acting for a literary career by recording in her eloquent journal the atrocities of slavery and the paradoxical natural beauty of her new land.

It is to the feisty Kemble that posterity owes a fuller account of Roswell King. It was common knowledge, she wrote, that King had impregnated a Butler slave named Betty, wife of a fellow slave named Frank, the plantation's head driver. The son she bore resembled King, who kept her as a concubine.

Had this been widely known in Liberty County, King likely would have been ostracized. The same Puritan values that engendered wealth so predictably also publicly disdained the interracial congress that was one of the unacknowledged dividends of slave ownership elsewhere in the South. One Liberty County slave recounted that of 125 slaves at his Liberty County plantation, there "was but one mulatto." Antebellum census records speak of very few residents of mixed race. Du Bois similarly noted that in Liberty County, slaves' "family life was carefully protected," with the result that "mulattoes are rare in the county." Clarence Thomas one day would be teased mercilessly by his fellow black schoolchildren for the darkness of his skin. This pigmentation was, in fact, a backhanded compliment to the morals of the Liberty County Puritans.

The oldest known lineal ancestor of Clarence Thomas was a slave belonging to Roswell King. His name has been lost to history, but in the family's oral history he is remembered for one thing. "He was double-jointed," recalled Blanche Lambert, a relative of Thomas who was born in Liberty County in 1903. The family history suggests that his flexibility somehow rendered ineffective the traditional modes of corporal punishment employed against slaves. Because of this condition, his owners "couldn't rule him." As a result, Lambert said, this man was eventually sold to another plantation.

———

How did the slaves of the Thomas and King plantations live? The Thomas slaves undoubtedly suffered the worse conditions of the two groups, but neither was free of cruelty or deprivation. Masters in Liberty County who were less vigorous with the lash than proprietors elsewhere in Georgia nevertheless reaped the dividends of white-on-black violence outside their county. The family story of Thomas's ancestor at the King plantation indicates that even a relatively temperate owner in a progressive enclave of Puritans would not shy from torturing trouble-makers.

Babies of slaves experienced the injustices of the regime almost immediately. Their mothers were compelled to return to the fields as soon as they recovered from labor, usually within three weeks. It was left to the other children, ranging from four to ten years of age, to tend to them in a practice called "minding baby." When the sucklings cried for nourishment, their older siblings strained to carry them out to their mothers. After feeding, the babies were returned to their dirty cabins. John Brown, an escaped slave from Georgia, noted with understatement how babies "often come off poorly in consequence." Brown told of how he would often lay his little brother in the shade of a tree and then run off to play or nap. He would awaken to the sound of his brother's screams, and return to find the baby covered with ants or mosquitoes, or blistered from the sun, the tree's shade having moved away.

Families could be disbanded at the whim or financial exigency of the master. As the date of such sales approached, slaves would quietly gather and whisper among themselves about the pending heartbreak. Mothers kissed their children more often and cried over them discreetly. The night before Brown was sold for the first time at the age of ten, "the few things we had were put together that night, and we completed our preparations for parting for life by kissing one another over and over again, and saying good bye till some of us little ones fell asleep." At the auctions, slaves were forbidden to weep or display distress. Parents were told on pain of flogging not to hug their children good-bye. Often love and anguish overrode these rules, reducing the auction room, in Brown's words, to a "perfect Bedlam of despair."

Simply surviving to adulthood was no small milestone. Fanny Kemble told of one slave woman named Die who gave birth to sixteen children, fourteen of whom died young. Six perished *in utero:* four from miscarriages, one when she toppled over from carrying a heavy burden on her head, another when she was whipped while pregnant. Slave parents watched helplessly as owners or overseers beat their spouses or children. Youngsters not old enough to hoe or pick cotton, and unneeded for "minding baby," were sent to clean the yards, carry water to the fields, pick worms from cotton leaves, or stand amid the crops as "living scare-crows." They worked the same hours as the adults. Booker T. Washington said he could recall no period of his childhood devoted to play. Poor hygiene and general squalor fueled a high infant mortality rate.

Slave marriages were unrecognized by law and could be broken by lecherous masters at will. Kemble asserted, "it is notorious, that almost every Southern planter has a family more or less numerous of illegitimate colored children." Liberty County was a departure from this rule, yet even there, men such as Roswell King took advantage when their work led them outside the Puritan social orbit. When Kemble asked a female slave—"foolishly enough," she later admitted—whether she knew it was immoral to live with a man who was not her husband, the slave grabbed her wrist and replied: "Oh yes, missis, we know—we know all about that well enough; but we do any thing to get our poor flesh some rest from the whip; when he made me follow him into the bush, what use was there me tell him no? He have strength to make me." Kemble added, "I have written down the woman's words; I wish I could write down the voice and look of abject misery with which they were spoken."

There were other hindrances to slave marriages. Spouses frequently belonged to different owners. Kizzie Colquitt's parents lived on opposite sides of the Broad River in Georgia, and had to "cross the river to see each other." To discourage squabbling among married slaves, masters encouraged easy divorce. Kemble said that if the master "heard of any disagreement between a man and woman calling themselves married, [he would] immediately bestow them in 'marriage' on other parties, whether they chose it or not, by which summary process the slightest 'incompatibility of temper' received the relief of a divorce more rapid and easy than even Germany could afford."

As every morsel of food or pair of shoes given to slaves subtracted from the owner's profit margin, life's essentials were scarce. Slaves typically received a small amount of corn every week. They often transformed it into hominy, "hoe," and "Johnny-cake." Meat, usually bacon, was doled out to particularly industrious male slaves on rare occasions. Slave children dipped their spoons into a communal wooden food trough, where dirt often mingled with the meal. Such habits and the general lack of hygiene contributed to the pandemics of contagious diseases that periodically afflicted plantations in Georgia. Hunger was a slave's steadfast companion; at night, to relieve the day's biological cravings, slaves would wander into the master's house or other locations likely to yield scraps of food.

Twice a year, male slaves generally received for clothing thin cotton pantaloons and a shirt of the same material. Some were given "Georgia plains," a rough material of cotton and wool, dark blue or gray in color, that was exceedingly hot in the summer months and therefore often not worn. Female slaves were handed a light cotton shirt and petticoat, the latter held on by braces over their shoulders. This attire became tattered after days of working among the cotton fields, leaving the women with barely enough clothing to cover them "for purposes of the barest decency," according to John Brown. Charles Ball, another escaped slave from Georgia, reported that one of his former plantations along the Savannah River was an involuntary Valley Forge, where the slaves lacked shoes in winter and wore only a coarse blanket akin to a poncho.

Slave homes varied by location. At the Thomas plantation, they were one- or two-room cabins of hewn logs, some twelve by fifteen feet, their cracks dabbed with mud to block the wind. At the King plantation, the cabins were most likely built of pine or oak clapboards and tabby, a plaster formed from burned oyster shells, lime and sand. Many slave dwellings along the coast were small, rectangular huts, African in design, with dirt floors packed as hard as cement. Inside, there was typically a rough wooden table, perhaps a small bed with Spanish moss for a mattress, and several wooden spoons and dishes hung against the wall. Frequently, slaves simply slept on a heap of dirty cotton rags on the dirt floor.

When Clarence Thomas described himself as "a descendant of the slaves whose labors made the dark soil of the South productive," he did not give a full picture of the working lives of his ancestors. They would rise before dawn to begin their work; they would not stop to eat their first meal of the day until twelve or one o'clock in the afternoon. Their workday could run as long as eighteen hours. The Thomas slaves raised primarily cotton and corn. Every phase of the year entailed a different assignment. In January and February, they distributed manure across the fields; in March, they planted the seed; in the summer months, they weeded with hoes; in August through October, they picked bolls of cotton from the mature plants, often one hundred pounds a day. During the rest of the year, they removed seeds from lint and packed them into bags.

Like their fellow captives along the shoreline, the King slaves were rice-growing craftsmen on whom the local rice economy depended for survival. Rice could only be grown in a small strip of coastal land ten to twenty miles from the sea and near freshwater rivers. The land had to be close enough to the ocean for the tides to drain the rice fields daily, yet far enough that salt water did not enter the flooded squares and poison the rice. The slaves first cleared the swamps of prickly scrub palmetto trees and other tenacious native flora. They then built a series of dikes to separate the swampland into twenty-acre squares. The final product was a complicated system of canals, ditches and floodgates that opened and closed automatically with the tides. The soil on Colonel's Island was poor for growing anything but rice; the dark, grayish layers of sand, clay and sandy loam drained badly. Immersed up to their ankles in mud, contending with poisonous snakes that exerted claim over the same terrain, the slaves of the King plantation used hoes to cultivate the rice. When it was fully grown, they scythed off the stalks with rice hooks, set the harvested stalks out to dry, and gathered and bound the desiccated ones into sheaves. The white phobia about malaria and the expertise of the slaves combined to ensure them considerable autonomy, in contrast to their counterparts in Laurens County.

Slave owners hired overseers to run the plantations, mostly drawn from the lower classes and habituated to the violence that was the ubiquitous predicate of slavery. The overseers selected trusted slaves, known as "drivers" or "foremen," to manage the slave gangs. It was left to the overseers and their white subordinates, however, to mete out the terror essential for compliance with unjust rule.

Whippings were the basic staple of corporal punishment. At the Troup plantations in Laurens County, the main person to wield the lash was John A. Vigal, Troup's son-in-law. When Troup's daughter, Oralie, married Vigal, her new husband earned among the slaves the nickname "Marse Jack." Little is known of this man except through William Conway, a slave whom Troup gave to Oralie as a wedding gift. Conway's son, Oliver Edmund, remembered his father saying of Vigal, "Marse

Jack, he liked whippin'." Edmund related that Troup himself was considered a relatively moderate master, noting in support of this opinion that Troup disapproved of the beating of pregnant slaves. Such faint praise spoke lucidly of the horrors of the regime.

Eyewitnesses to cruel punishments at other Georgia plantations gave a fuller portrait of the times. Alexander Stephens, the Georgia politician who later became vice president of the Confederacy, related with disgust the whippings he saw. He noted how, to increase the humiliation, disobedient slaves were compelled to take off their pants and stretch out over a log before being beaten with a piece of buggy, or leather. Some slaves screamed horribly with pain, others evacuated their bowels. Pregnant women generally were not spared. They, like the men, were whipped with such implements as cowhide, bullwhips and paddles.

John Brown, who lived at a plantation approximately fifty miles from the Thomas plantation, said that his master's preferred lash was five bound hickory rods. On one occasion, he asked Brown irritably why he did not plow better. Brown sought to show him how the plough "ran foul":

> I stooped for this purpose, and was cleaning the dirt off from the share with my hands, when he viciously raised his foot, which was heavily shod, and unexpectedly dealt me a kick with all his might. The blow struck me right between the eyes, breaking the bone of my nose, and cutting the leaders of the right eye, so that it turned quite around in its socket. I was stunned for the moment, and fell, my mouth filling with blood, which also poured from my nose and eyes.... I have never been able to see so well since, and cannot now look long at print without suffering much pain. The letters seem cloudy. To this day my right eye has remained out of its proper place.

Charles Ball, whose plantation was just outside Augusta, observed his owner's new wife beat a slave girl severely for failing to keep her baby quiet. "I perceived by this, that my mistress possessed no control over her passions; and that, when enraged, she would find some victim to pour her fury upon, without regard to justice or mercy."

Ball told of an instance of "cat-hauling" inflicted on a slave in order to extract information from him about the theft of a pig. A "well-dressed gentleman" picked up a large, gray tomcat and placed it on the bare back of the prostrate slave, whom four other slaves were holding down.

The white man then dragged the cat by its tail down the black man's back. The cat scratched and bit off skin during its descent. To clean the wounds afterwards, the slave was given the standard, excruciating treatment: a washing down with salt water.

Brown's tale of the slave John Glasgow is so tragic that it would defy credence coming from a less reliable source. A free black sailor and a husband and father of two in Liverpool, England, Glasgow sailed for Savannah with a crew of English seamen in the early 1800s. Upon Glasgow's arrival in Georgia, the local authorities seized and incarcerated him until his ship had sailed off. He was sold into slavery for $350. His master, after three or four years, urged him to take a wife. Glasgow protested that he had one in England, the mother of his two children. For this protest and his assertion that he was a free man by birth, his master flew into a rage, flogged him mercilessly, and never forgave him. Glasgow finally agreed to take a new wife, but his misfortunes mounted as he found himself attracted to a woman on a nearby plantation that he was forbidden to visit. When Glasgow was caught sneaking off to see her, his owner sentenced him to "bucking." Glasgow was stripped naked, his hands were tied over his knees, and a stake was secured under his hams. For three hours, he was turned from side to side like a pig on a spit, as men thrashed him with willow switches and cowhide. His master looked on and laughed. When Glasgow still persisted in visiting the woman, he was given the "picket." He was hoisted by ropes above sharp stakes and beaten as he was suspended; when he rested, his feet came down on the stakes, upon which he was spun until his feet were impaled to the bone. After this half-crucifixion, Glasgow walked with a permanent limp. Eventually, he went insane.

Georgia slaveholders were not above assigning their slaves to Nazi-like experiments. Under the direction of a quack country doctor, John Brown was lowered repeatedly into a hole in the ground, up to his neck, right after a fire in the earthen oven was extinguished. After a short time, Brown fainted from the heat. The doctor noted the temperature when he fainted. After reviving, Brown would go off to finish his day's work. The same doctor later bled Brown every other day and applied blisters to his hands, legs, and feet, wounds which scarred him.

Some masters were worse than others. Brown allowed that there might have been kinder slave owners somewhere in the state: "I believe there are a few, though I never had the experience of them." Ball offered a more philosophical assessment: "The slave-holders are neither more nor less than men, some of whom are good, and very many are bad." Frederick Douglass, speaking of "the fatal poison of irresponsible power," put his finger on the problem when he observed that "slavery could change a saint into a sinner, and an angel into a demon." Even at her comparatively humane plantation, Fanny Kemble saw the wickedness of slavery advertised in the everyday facial expressions of the slaves. She spoke of "this pathetic expression of countenance in them, a mixture of sadness and fear, the involuntary exhibition of the two feelings, which I suppose must be the predominant experience of their whole lives, regret and apprehension, not the less heavy, either of them, for being, in some degree, vague and indefinite—a sense of incalculable past loss and injury, and a dread of incalculable future loss and injury."

Elderly slaves were worthless to their owners, and indeed a monetary drain. Many owners, according to Kemble, would systematically "work off (i.e., kill with labor) a certain proportion of their force, and replace them by new hands every seven years." A slave who survived into old age would find his last days spent alone in his cabin or on a dirt floor in an infirmary. A few sticks under his head served as a pillow. Virtually no light entered the building lest cold and pests enter with it.

Georgia's slaves struck what blows they could for freedom. Acts of passive resistance, such as malingering, along with more aggressive tactics, such as sabotage and arson, were some of the weapons in their arsenal. It was their faith, however, that sustained them. They commingled a religiosity native to Africa with the Christian principles they absorbed in Georgia. The mixture was an Afro-Christianity centered on exuberant worship services and moving spirituals. The Laurens County slaves would gather in the woods in "brush arbor" churches, where logs provided seats and the sky became a limitless cathedral. Kemble said of the slaves that they "have what a very irreligious young English clergyman once informed me I had—a *'turn* for religion.'"

Whites manipulated this religiosity to serve their own ends. Former slave Charles Coates remembered that one white preacher told the slaves to "be sure and get all them weeds out of that corn in the field and your master will think a heap of you." White ministers instructed slaves not to run away, steal, or talk back to their masters. But the slaves saw through these sermons. When the master at one Georgia plantation died, his slaves gathered around his body, shed false tears, and assured his bereaved mistress that the departed was surely looking down upon them from Heaven. Afterwards, they went outside and discreetly told one another, "Thank God, massa gone home to hell."

The African-American slaves of Georgia identified with the Israelites and held out hope of a similar deliverance from bondage. "We often waited until the overseer got behind a hill, and then we would lay down our hoes and call on God to free us," one Georgia slave recalled.

The slaves of the Thomas plantation, like their chained brethren throughout the South, sang spirituals in the cotton fields that carried a double meaning. Ada Snell, a descendant of slaves from an estate near the Thomas plantation, said "the songs that they were singing, the white persons there, landowners, were thinking that they were all talking about Heaven. A lot of that stuff, they were communicating with people in the other fields.... They would be telling them to meet down at the river to get away." Snell said there was also a subtext to the renowned hymn "Swing Low, Sweet Chariot": "When you swing down and swing low, we're going to get on and get away from here."

In 1857, the same year in which the U.S. Supreme Court handed down its *Dred Scott* decision, financially strapped Pierce Butler became solvent again by selling 429 of his slaves in the single largest slave auction in U.S. history. Butler's marriage to Fanny Kemble had ended in scandalous divorce (largely because of their vehement differences over slavery). Butler also had gambled away much of his estate. To liquidate these debts, Butler rounded up many of the slaves Roswell King had supervised on the vast Butler holdings in southeastern Georgia, then shipped them on railroad cars to Savannah. They were to be sold there at auction to the highest bidder. It is quite possible that some of Clarence Thomas's ancestors were among this ill-fated group.

The hardened characters who trafficked in slaves converged on Savannah from throughout the South to attend the sale. On the morning of March 2, they tottered out of the city's hotels and boarding houses, nursing and cursing hangovers as they headed off to the auction site, the Ten Broeck racetrack. Butler began the festivities by addressing the slaves. One last time, his human chattel gave him their respects: The men doffed their hats and bowed, the women curtsied. Butler bade them farewell, then joined the crowd and presided over their dispersal throughout the region.

Just as the auction began, an immense rainstorm slammed into Savannah. The wind blew the rain in diagonal sheets through the open side of the grandstand. The assembled merchants of men tugged at their hats and overcoats and squeezed into the crowded, dry space to evade the elements. The slaves, holding their small bags of belongings, were led in one by one to stand before the crowd. The auction catalog listed their names and descriptions:

> 111—Anson, 49: rice—ruptured, one eye.
> 112—Violet, 55; rice hand.
> > Sold for $250 each.
> > Or $500 for the pair.
> 345—Dorcas, 17, prime woman.
> 346—Joe, 3 months.
> > Sold for $1,200 each.
> > A new young mother and her baby, $2,400.

The bidders sauntered forward to examine the merchandise. They opened the slaves' mouths to inspect their teeth, pinched their muscles, and instructed them to bend and stoop. A reporter for the *New York Tribune*, who had impersonated a slave trader so that he could attend the event, later wrote:

> On the faces of all was an expression of heavy grief; some appeared to be resigned to the hard stroke of Fortune that had torn them from their homes, and were sadly trying to make the best of it; some sat brooding moodily over their sorrows, their chins resting on their hands, their eyes staring vacantly, and their bodies rocking to and fro, with a restless motion that was never stilled; few wept, the place was too public and the drivers too near, though some occasionally turned aside to give way to a few quiet tears.

Two of Roswell King's charges were too old to be of value: Betty, his concubine, and Frank, her husband. They were among the few who were not sold.

The auction carried over into the next day, March 3. The dark skies still drenched the site, the racetrack becoming a lagoon of mud and horse excrement. When the last slaves were sold, they stepped down haltingly from the auction block. At that moment, the rain stopped as abruptly as it had begun.

Champagne was served to the whites present. Butler was soon off to southern Europe for a vacation made possible by his new wealth.

Generations of black folk would refer to this event as "the weeping time." They would remember it as an occasion of summary family breakup on an unprecedented scale. They would remember it also as a time when the skies had opened and Heaven itself had wept for them.

––––

Four years later, the booming of the guns at Fort Sumter seventy miles to the north signaled an armed challenge to the white aristocracy of the South. Most of the residents of Liberty County opposed secession, but they threw in their lot with their fellow Georgians once the state resolved otherwise. The descendants of Peter Thomas and Roswell King enlisted and galloped off to glory. James A. Thomas, grandson of Peter Thomas, joined the Confederate army when he was sixteen (many years after the war, he was elected the national commander of the United Confederate Veterans). The Kings signed up for the Liberty Independent Troop.

For most of the war, both plantations and their residents tended to their crops and heard only news and rumors of conflict. An exception was on Friday, April 25, 1862, when federal gunboats floated unhindered in the Woodville River below the King plantation. A small detachment of Confederate troops took up positions on Colonel's Island to ambush and harass the Union invaders. The bluecoats responded by shelling the island with cannon fire for the better part of an hour. The cannonballs flew over the Confederates, crashing into trees and causing no casualties. The gunboats withdrew that afternoon.

Union vessels arrived in greater numbers and seized the outer islands off the Georgia coast, which very quickly became a magnet for slaves living on coastal plantations. The plantation of William King, Roswell King's son, hemorrhaged defections. In late December 1863, a twenty-seven-year-old slave named Cain led his young wife, Bella, their six-year-old son, Romeo, and ten other women and children out to the USS *Fernandina* in St. Catherines Sound. A few days later, Cain left the vessel to rescue his relatives from an estate near Sunbury; most likely, his destination was the King plantation. On January 7, he returned to the ship accompanied by a dozen more fugitive slaves.

Once they reached the terra firma of St. Catherines and the other barrier islands, the ex-slaves enjoyed the full fruit of their labors. They grew and sold vegetables and poultry to the U.S. sailors plying the nearby waters. The women washed the servicemen's uniforms. The new freemen shared intelligence information with federal forces. Many young blacks enlisted in the service. Schools were opened for black children and adults, with literate blacks and white naval personnel serving as teachers. Ministers formalized the ex-slaves' wedding vows. One minister found that the couples wanted this done in the most "public and solemn manner" possible. An estimated one thousand slaves escaped to these isles of freedom between December 1861 and October 1864.

It was by brute force that the white plutocrats of Georgia had maintained their regime; by like means would their world be smashed. The instrument of this reckoning, the man who drove the stake through the heart of Georgia and the Confederacy, was General William Tecumseh Sherman. From his vantage point in southeastern Tennessee, he recognized that Georgia lay defenseless to invasion. Protecting his lines of communication was among his most serious concerns; he solved this brilliantly by simply severing them. His army, Sherman decided, would live off the land by pillaging en route to the sea.

In May 1864, Sherman's forces descended into Georgia and laid siege to Atlanta. After the city fell, Sherman planned his final push to the Atlantic. On November 16, 65,000 Union soldiers marched out of Atlanta and pressed into the center of the state. The two wings of the army, oscillating along a sixty-mile front, were to converge at Milledgeville, Georgia's capital, forty-five miles northwest of the Thomas plantation. Sherman believed that with a policy of "liberal and judicious foraging" along the way, "I can make this march, and make Georgia howl!"

She still does. In Milledgeville, the locals have preserved immaculately and indignantly, in the plank floors of an Episcopal church, the telltale scuff marks of horseshoes, mementos of the time Sherman's men quartered their steeds there. Georgia's slaves remembered the crusade far more kindly. As it coursed through the countryside, the Union army acted as a massive vacuum of humanity, siphoning off black men and women who bolted from their plantations to join the jubilee caravan. Newly freed slaves joyfully pointed the Union troops toward smokehouses and lifted their wagons over potholes. Sherman's jolly foragers widely ignored his admonition to leave enough food behind for families. Once stripped of valuables, houses were set afire in a traditional sacking worthy of Caesar. Roadsides became depots of corn and sweet potatoes confiscated and, when judged superfluous, discarded in heaps. Soldiers on horseback trotted by with turkeys or other fowl swinging on both sides of their stallions like saddlebags. The black freemen who followed the procession offered their services in exchange for being a part of this grand act of leveling and liberation.

The right wing of Sherman's army touched both the Thomas and King plantations. Sherman assigned the job of guarding the right, or southern, flank of the Union army to General Hugh Judson Kilpatrick, a dandy and a notorious ladies' man. Kilpatrick's cavalry quickly put to rout the opposing Confederate cavalry led by Lieutenant General Joseph Wheeler. Laurens County natives remembered Wheeler's four thousand cavalry as more menace than defender: The official history of the county noted that the "hungry discouraged soldiers rode here and there pillaging the fields, seizing gathered crops, and taking every horse that was able to do heavy work and leaving old broken-down animals in their place." Other residents wisely buried their gold at the first signs of the Yankee onslaught.

Even as Sherman's legions were slicing through Laurens County, the slaves at one of Troup's former plantations did not realize they were free. After some time, recalled the son of a freed Troup slave, "a man came up and called them out of the field and told them they were free. Some of the masters hid in the woods three days after the slaves were free."

For Sherman, the march through Georgia was small sport, much like punching through a paper bag. The few armed provincials who resisted were easily swept aside. With this rolling success came a rising wave of black humanity seeking freedom, some twenty-five thousand strong. One Illinois artilleryman felt pity for the mushrooming parade of newly freed blacks. He remarked how their ranks grew "like a sable cloud in the sky before a thunder storm." He added, "They thought it was freedom now or never. . . . Let those who choose to curse the Negro curse him; but one thing is true . . . they were the only friends on whom we could rely for the sacred truth in Dixie." Entire black families joined the Union forces. Black women with babies draped over their arms or with little ones clinging to their skirts made haste after the advancing army. In their wake they left the "Burnt Country," a trail of ruin roughly as wide as the sixty-mile front. The most memorable totems of Union supremacy left behind in this streak of destruction were the ever-present, smoldering chimneys that stood as lonely, charred sentinels over scorched homes, as well as "Sherman neckties," iron rails pulled up from railroad tracks and twisted around trees to make them useless.

When Union forces reached the affluent farmlands of Liberty County, they encountered no resistance. On December 13, Kilpatrick's troopers cantered down the old Sunbury Road to lay claim to the Genesis Point Battery. That afternoon, approximately ten miles from the King plantation, one Union cavalryman called five-year-old James R. Morgan to his side. "Johnny," the soldier addressed him, "get me a piece of fire."

The boy compliantly returned with a glowing coal from his home's fireplace. He stood and watched as the soldiers rode off to Sunbury Church. They tore the wooden rails off a fence, stacked them under the stair steps, and ignited the pyre. The fire that engulfed the church informed the federal ships anchored in Ossabaw Sound that Sherman's army had reached the sea. The smoke was visible from the King plantation. The signal it sent to the residents of Colonel's Island, free as well as slave, was that the old order was no more.

Numerous plantation owners along the coast abandoned their homes, in the words of one local resident, "to the mercy of Yankees, Negroes, and Crackers." The whites who remained were subject to travel restrictions that once bound blacks under the old slave code: They were prohibited from moving without permit, while the former slaves were allowed to travel as they pleased. "There are to be *no more bondsmen and no more whippings,* the Yanks tell the Negroes here," wrote one Liberty County matriarch with evident dismay. When the Union troops finally departed Liberty County, leaving behind armed blacks patrolling the county's roads, another of the fallen white oligarchs commented, "Now for the first time we began to know fear of those who had formerly been our protectors."

Before Sherman pivoted and continued his march northward, he issued on January 16, 1865, his Field Order No. 15. This directive confiscated the sea islands south of Charleston and a swath of coastal land extending thirty miles inland from Charleston south to Florida, reserving the land for the newly liberated slaves. Blacks were to receive forty acres, clothing, seed and farm equipment. President Andrew Johnson countermanded this visionary policy six months after Lincoln's assassination. Unlike other black folk in the annexed strip, many blacks in Liberty County applauded Johnson's decision. Sherman and his men, unfamiliar with the peculiar folkways of Liberty County, were incredulous that blacks there had purchased their own land. The propertied blacks of the county inundated the local Freedman's Bureau with complaints about Sherman's order. Of the 44 claims filed against the federal government for wrongful confiscation in Liberty County, 27 were by blacks.

Clarence Thomas's ancestors do not appear to have been among this aggrieved class. But the Civil War and the issues that sparked it would become a subject of endless fascination to Thomas, and would provoke some of his most important works.

CHAPTER TWO

Furnaces of the Will

The black citizens of Georgia did not have to await Robert E. Lee's surrender to gain their freedom. As soon as Sherman's horses clattered past Thomas Crossroads, the emancipated men and women of the Thomas plantation had to create from scratch a system for putting food on their tables and building a community of freemen.

One of their first priorities was to shed the names imposed on them during slavery and choose their own. With considerable ingenuity they came up with new ones—their "entitles," they called them. In Laurens County, many former slaves used initials for first names. It was also commonplace to take the last names of masters, such as Troup or Cummings. Even then, many Laurens County blacks put their own individual stamp on the name, adding, for example, an "e" or "pe" to Troup for distinction. The ex-slaves of the Thomas plantation who took the surname Thomas were not, of course, adopting their masters' name, since the Thomas brothers had sold the property decades before. These black folk were rather naming themselves after the property itself, the only home they knew.

In time of war and resulting devastation, it was no simple matter to replace a centuries-old economic system, even a manifestly unjust and deficient one. When hostilities ended, planters lacked cash and former slaves needed food. The landlords offered their former slaves deferred pay in the form of a share of the crop grown on their land. This agreement gave landlords or merchants a lien on the tenant's share of the next crop, which was the tenant's collateral for the seed and goods needed to live until the crop was harvested. Such sharecropping soon became the norm at the Thomas plantation and throughout the state. By 1890, nine out of ten black farmers in Georgia were sharecroppers.

For those blacks who did not submit to this regime, peonage often became a surrogate for slavery. So it was that the freemen of Laurens County passed from slavery to sharecropping with only marginal improvement in their daily lives. They remained in the rough-hewn log cabins of slave times. As in the old regime, the work lasted from sunrise to sunset, and the women and children still worked the fields.

Racial violence assumed a different form in this era and was not entirely one-sided. In 1865, President Johnson repealed Sherman's Field Order 15 and commanded the new black landowners to vacate their farms along the coast. They responded predictably: the whites who went to reclaim their antebellum property found themselves, in the words of one observer, "surrounded by fierce black faces and leveled guns." Eventually, General Davis Tillson of the Freedmen's Bureau was constrained to send in federal troops to dispossess the blacks and enforce the white claims.

In the summer of 1866, Henry McNeal Turner, a black political leader and minister from Macon, spoke to a black civic organization in Greensboro, approximately ninety miles from the Thomas sharecropping land. He urged his fellow blacks to protect themselves and to retaliate against the white men who molested black women. Turner's lecture infuriated the whites of the town, who attempted to attack him. Blacks attending the meeting drew weapons in response and stopped the mob. "I never saw more firearms among one set of people in my life," Turner later said with satisfaction.

By 1868, the strife had become clearly political, as whites sought to ensure black inferiority through law and government. While under Union occupation, Georgia's whites had endured the grave indignity of watching blacks stand for and win elections. In 1868, blacks made up 49 percent of registered voters, and thirty-one blacks sat in the Georgia state legislature. Whites organized and retaliated: from August through October that year, there were thirty-one murders of blacks and many more vicious assaults across the state. In some counties, as the election approached, violence became a nightly expectation, with victims shot, hanged, or mutilated. The Ku Klux Klan became such an accepted part of Georgia society that it fielded a baseball team to play that of Mercer University (Mercer won).

In Laurens County, as throughout Georgia, the nightriders tried to intimidate blacks into staying away from the polls, an activity that whites saw as chivalry rather than crime. The official history of the county, published in 1941, records that after the Civil War, "white men would have had little trouble with former slaves had it not been for straggling Yankees who went through the county formenting [*sic*] dissatisfaction and strife among the negroes. So Laurens men organized a Ku Klux Klan and thus kept the negroes in hand."

On September 9, 1868, Georgia's white legislators succeeded in ousting from the state Assembly all black Republican legislators. Each displaced legislator was given one hour to speak before he was required to give up his seat. While some of the ejected members were obsequious, many were defiant. Turner showed predictable panache, saying, "I shall neither fawn nor cringe before any party, nor stoop to beg them for my rights. . . . I am here to demand my rights and hurl thunderbolts at the men who would dare to cross the threshold of my manhood."

Eventually, the Radical Republicans in Congress drew the line at such recalcitrance, and on December 22, 1869, Congress placed Georgia under federal military rule for a second time. This occupation, triggered by Georgia's unique intransigence against basic civil rights, happened in no other state. Congress also reseated the black representatives.

The following year, Georgia's whites, undeterred, finished what they had started. The week before Georgia's state elections, set for December 22–24, 1870, Klansmen galloped across the state again. This time, Democrats at last gained control of the legislature. The Klan's tactics came to be known as the "Georgia Plan," and were later copied in other states, most notably Mississippi.

With the political struggle finished, the Klan began to use terrorism for other ends. Fearing the educational and economic strides that blacks were making, the Klan fanned out across Georgia in the 1870s to whip black teachers and burn black schools to the ground. In one especially vicious incident in 1876, black ministers were lashed and one black schoolteacher had his teeth filed down to the gums. The history of Laurens County states that throughout the 1880s, "there was a latent fear of negro uprisings."

Law enforcement officials in Laurens County and throughout the state often were Klansmen themselves, or at best were indifferent to the violence. When blacks committed offenses against whites, on the other hand, "they were severely dealt with," according to Scott Thompson, an attorney and historian of Laurens County. His father-in-law retained for many years a photograph of the body of a black man who was accused of killing the sheriff of Johnson County (two miles north of the Thomas sharecropping land) in 1904. Authorities shot the suspect, put a noose around his neck, placed him on top of a pot-bellied stove, and kicked the stove out slightly. Then they lit the stove and set him aflame.

Lynchings were more common in Georgia than in any other state. Between 1882 and 1923, Georgia led the nation with 505 recorded lynchings. This number excludes the "legal lynchings" that resulted when an angry white community rushed a suspect through legal proceedings without due process of law. In Laurens County, there were only two lynchings in the 1880s—a low number compared with other counties. Many whites saw lynchings as a deterrent to rape, as they believed black men to be voraciously on the prowl for white women. This stereotype would still be strong a century later, and would give rise to Clarence Thomas's most memorable statement during his confirmation hearings for the Supreme Court.

By the turn of the century, this project of political and social oppression of blacks was complete. The black share of the vote fell to 18 percent in 1896, and dropped further in the early twentieth century after the imposition of literacy tests and other Jim Crow laws. The world into which Clarence Thomas's paternal grandfather was born was one in which, as Thomas himself put it almost a century later, black folk "persevered in the most inhuman conditions."

"My grandfather was raised by his grandmother, who, according to him, was freed from slavery at the age of nine," Thomas once said in a speech. This great-great-grandmother was named Annie. Born in 1856, she and her future husband, Harry Allen, grew up on the King plantation and labored there both before and after the war. During Reconstruction, the period that one Liberty County historian called the "black pioneer period," they and the other former King slaves scratched out an existence on a small parcel of land on Colonel's Island, growing rice and perhaps corn.

It appears that members of the King family harbored resentment toward the former slaves. James Audley Maxwell King, the son of Roswell King, ran the plantation land on Colonel's Island after the war, and complained to the family that the blacks on the island were no longer willing to work. One letter from a King family intimate in 1867 states that in response, "Audley is filling up the Island with white laborers, and is encouraged."

It was not until the 1890s that Harry and Annie Allen were forced to vacate the land. The reasons for this relocation are not clear. Blanche Lambert, a resident of Liberty County and distant relative of Clarence Thomas, stated that the owners of the land were "selling out." This transaction apparently was not related to the three hurricanes that successively pummeled the Georgia coast in the 1890s and wiped out the county's rice industry. Whatever the stimulus, a migration of entire families from Colonel's Island occurred at this time. The Allens brought with them a daughter, Lutricia, born on Colonel's Island.

Harry Allen purchased sixty acres off the old Sunbury Road, formerly part of the Seabrook plantation, on October 14, 1892. He bought the land for $65, including $11 cash at time of purchase. James and Charles Allen, his brothers, lived with Harry and his family. A century later, the property would pass to Clarence Thomas and two other relatives.

On these sixty acres of substandard cropland, the Allen family raised sugarcane, rice and sweet potatoes. They also fished and sold their catch to supplement their income. Fishing and net weaving were part of their African heritage; the fishing nets they painstakingly braided were taut seines with small, square holes. The seasons determined whether they worked by land or by sea: generally they tended the fields in the summer, and fished and crabbed in the winter. The expatriates of the King plantation successfully transplanted to the Seabrook area a tight-knit community. Neighbors thought nothing of helping other neighbors finish their row of crops at the end of the day.

The homes, appliances and apparel they constructed were a sturdy homage to what their descendants would call "the art of makin' do." For homes, they put up frames and clapboards of pine with corrugated tin roofs, then used flour paste and paper as rudimentary caulking to keep out the drafts. A peanut roaster might be made from tin cans, a pipe, and old sewing machine parts. The men were commonly attired in flannel shirts and suspenders. The women wore sensible cotton dresses permitting work in the fields, with handkerchiefs tied over the head to absorb perspiration and shield them from the sun.

Piety undergirded work and education. Like almost all of their neighbors, the Allens were Baptists. Two Baptist churches vied for loyalty and tithes. Sunbury Baptist Church was an offshoot of one of the first black churches in Savannah. The Allens attended the Palmyra Missionary Baptist Church, a half-mile down the road and some fifty yards from the Seabrook School.

As throughout Georgia, church services were the most important social events in the black community. Revivals had been a central feature of Southern life since shortly after John Wesley made Savannah his American parish. These provided both exciting entertainment for rural folk and a welcome supplement to the preachments of local pastors. Revivals roared through Sunbury and other nearby communities in tornadic fashion, usually just after the harvest in the fall, as minds became more open to things not of the earth. Baptisms were performed in Sunbury River, and were also a major occasion. A black preacher in a long, white robe led the initiates to the river. Their family and neighbors followed. The minister performed the rite when the tide was going out, so that the sins could be washed away from the community.

For less sublime entertainment, the residents of Sunbury and the Seabrook community attended dances on St. Catherines Island during the summer. They rowed out to the island by boat in the early evening and remained there, in the words of one Sunbury participant, to "dance till most daylight."

In this community, Lutricia Allen, the daughter of Harry and Annie, matured into adulthood. She was tall, dark, medium-sized, and "on the quiet side," according to one neighbor. She worked alongside her family on the Allen plot until shortly after 1900, then moved to Savannah and worked as a maid. In Savannah, Lutricia met a young man named Isaac Anderson and bore him a son, Myers Anderson. He would become the greatest influence on Clarence Thomas's life.

The summer of 1906 was an ominous time for Georgia blacks generally, and especially those in Atlanta. The Prohibition campaign picked up steam in the city, and many white advocates of the policy pressed into service the old cry "Keep whiskey from the Negro." Sam P. Jones, an evangelist second only to Billy Sunday in national notoriety, hosted a large revival in Atlanta, inveighing against, among other things, prostitution and Negro women. The state gubernatorial campaign which had just ended had been largely a competition in race-baiting.

On July 30, an Atlanta mob lynched a black man falsely accused of rape. The city's newspapers subsequently made a profitable crusade of decrying the "intolerable epidemic of rape" which they said was gripping the metropolis. Stories of "black fiends" deflowering white virgins became a running theme in Atlanta dailies into September.

In the early evening of Saturday, September 22, newspaper extras began hitting the streets, detailing further alleged interracial rapes. "THIRD ASSAULT" read one headline in large letters. At around 6:00 P.M., white men began to mill around on Peachtree and Decatur Streets, some declaiming against the reported wave of molestation. At about 8:30, one speaker ascended a dry goods box in the center of the crowd, near Decatur and Marietta Streets, and held aloft one of the newspapers.

"Are white men going to stand for this?" the man yelled.

"No! Save our women!" came the angry reply.

The cries from the crowd eventually turned more homicidal. Chants of "Kill the niggers!" began to fill the air. The outer fringes of the crowd tried out their growing aggression on nearby black pedestrians.

In an hour and a half, one hardware store downtown sold $16,000 worth of firearms. The Fulton County sheriff eventually halted the gun sales, but mainly to deny the weapons to blacks. He signed hundreds of gun-sale permits for "respectable citizens," meaning whites, even as he supervised the confiscation of firearms from legally armed, terrified blacks (he later "handled" two hundred rampaging white men by deputizing them). As police stood by or joined in the incipient riot, Governor Joseph M. Terrell refused to send out the state militia for several hours. By ten o'clock, more than ten thousand whites, many of them wielding guns, were scouring downtown Atlanta in search of blacks.

At the main entrance to the Piedmont Hotel, the hooligans dashed bottle after bottle on the head of one black man they had overtaken. Others stabbed him repeatedly with knives. When fifteen minutes of such torture did not kill him, men came forward with more knives and hatchets to finish the job. After they determined he was dead, one of his killers held up the "THIRD ASSAULT" newspaper over his corpse as a triumphal banner. Other revelers cut off his fingers and toes as souvenirs.

Members of Atlanta's upper crust exited a minstrel show downtown to enjoy a double feature of entertainment out on the sidewalks. As they stood in their bowler hats and flowing evening gowns, the hoodlums outside sought to amuse the upscale sidewalk galleries with their antics. They would release a black captive and give him a five-yard head start, then chase him down and slay him.

Lying in wait for streetcars became a lawful form of hunting for several hours. Gangs of white thugs looked for streetcars sputtering downtown to deposit new black targets. They then surrounded the cars and climbed into them "like rats," in the words of one observer, dragging men and women from the cars to flog them or finish them off.

Outnumbered and outgunned, black Atlantans nevertheless slowed the mob's progress by returning fire. Days before, many had heeded rumors of looming racial violence by purchasing firearms and stocking up on ammunition. One black mortician clandestinely arranged for a load of guns to be shipped down from Chicago in a casket. When the horrors of the evening erupted, cadres of black men took over houses and edifices with fields of fire for snipers. To protect one streetcar line, nine black men occupied a downtown building and halted traffic with repeated rifle fire for an hour.

The next day, Sunday, hats and caps from some of the victims were hung on the iron hooks of telephone poles in the city, each one of them presumed to represent a black murder victim from the night before. Whatever the purpose of this exhibition, which was strongly reminiscent of rows of heads atop pikes in Elizabethan England, blacks by this time had mobilized and were ready for the next clash. When he learned of the riots, the young W. E. B. Du Bois returned to Atlanta to guard his home, sitting on his front porch with a shotgun in his hands.

Order was not restored in the city for four more days. Official reports later said that 25 blacks died in the riots and 150 were seriously wounded. These same reports alleged that only one white was killed. Blacks knew the figures were absurdly low. Du Bois estimated that at least one hundred people died, "most of whom were Negroes, although a large proportion of both the dead and maimed were white, the exact number on either side being unknown." He credited an armed black counterattack for halting the destruction, and noted proudly, "The day when mobs can successfully cow the Negro to willing slavery is past. The Atlanta Negroes shot back and shot to kill, and that stopped the riot with a certain suddenness."

———

Fourteen months after the Atlanta Riots, on November 25, 1907, Norman Thomas, Clarence Thomas's paternal grandfather, was born near Lovett, a hamlet in Laurens County. His was one of the ten black families in Laurens County that had adopted the surname Thomas. They lived in an area at the far northern part of Laurens County, approximately eight miles from the edge of the old Thomas plantation and two miles south of the Johnson County line.

Nicknames were handed out liberally among blacks in the county. Ada Snell, a neighbor who was close to the Thomas family, described the custom as a "community thing." The nickname given Norman Thomas was odd indeed: November. The genesis of the nickname is not known; perhaps it was a childhood corruption of his first name. "When I was a little girl, I'd ask my grandfather, 'Why is his name November? Was he born in November?'" Snell recalled. November Thomas was always good-natured about his moniker, and indeed about life in general.

There was much about his upbringing that could have left him bitter. He was born into a sharecropping family and picked cotton by hand as a boy. In 1918, when November Thomas turned eleven, the boll weevil arrived from Texas and ravaged the crop on which the county's landlords and sharecroppers depended. In 1911, Laurens County produced over 60,000 bales of cotton annually, each bale weighing an average of 500 pounds. By 1918, the county's output had dwindled to a quarter that amount.

November Thomas also came of age during the height of organized racism in the county. By 1912, there were 2,500 black men of voting age in Laurens County, but only 54 were registered to vote. Peonage was commonplace. The years 1919–20 were the peak years of Klan activity in the county as well. "Sometimes the whites weren't as fair to the blacks as they should've been," Snell said. "The whites would tell them, 'You borrowed money from me during the year, you don't have money to get back.' Only when they'd take the cotton bales at night to sell them would they make money."

November Thomas grew to around five feet, eight inches in height, with a wiry frame and a dark complexion. He and his family lived near Lovett and worked for a landlord named Dennen Barron. Lonnie Thomas, an unrelated black man who knew both November and Barron, said that while Barron "didn't pay too much for the cotton," he was "all right" to work for. Three or four families raised cotton on his land, working near his cotton gin. Barron's brother Sam was known as a "liquor man," which suggests the Barrons may have been on the rougher side of the local social life.

November took for his first wife a woman named Mary Lee. She bore him five children—Mary Lee, Willie, Major, M.C., and Norman Jr.—before dying in 1932. November subsequently married another woman from the area, Juanita Hunter.

Life in Lovett exemplified the slow advances that Georgia's blacks had made in the half-century since emancipation. There was, at least, enough food to go around. Will Thomas, a black Thomas from the area born in 1889, stated he was "raised on red river peas and homemade meat. It wasn't fancy but I never went hungry." Canning was a frequent practice; delicacies from beets to pig's feet were preserved in this way. "They had good food because they were raising their own food," Ada Snell recalled. Relatives from Florida came north bearing oranges and other fruit. With pigs a favored livestock in Lovett, the meat served was most often pork chops, ham, bacon, spare ribs or chitterlings. Chicken, beef and ox-tail stew were occasional dishes. Collard greens, cabbage, green peas, black-eyed peas, fried tomatoes—a cornucopia of locally raised vegetables crowded the table.

From physical labor and an ample diet, the men and women grew stout and robust. "That's why you had the men who were so strong, because they had all that good food," Snell said. And indeed the black men of Laurens County would figure prominently in American athletics. Among them were the great boxer Sugar Ray Robinson (born Walker Smith Jr.); Quincy Trouppe, a renowned catcher in the Negro League; and Herschel Walker, the standout NFL running back (born two miles from Lovett). Clarence Thomas himself took much pride in his athletic ability as a young man and in the powerful physique he inherited from his father.

November Thomas lived in a "shotgun shack," so called because, as Ada Snell put it, "if you shoot a gun into the house, it would hit the front door and go straight to the back door." A person entering November Thomas's "straight little house" would have walked through a wooden door, entered a living room with an old potbellied stove or fireplace to give warmth, then two bedrooms in succession, and finally the kitchen in the back. Cardboard was used in lieu of plaster to fill the cracks. Wooden shutters, not glass, covered the windows, and blankets served as additional insulation in the windows during the winter. Dirt floors were common.

November was an affable man who took pride in his work and solace in his faith. "He didn't meet no strangers," recalled Lonnie Thomas, an unrelated neighbor. "You know, he met you, he acted just like he'd been knowing you all the time." He was also "strong-willed" and ever mindful of the value of labor and property. November's son M.C.'s most enduring memory of his father was that "he worked hard."

Ada Snell remembered her grandfather's stories about November and his solicitude for his livestock. "His hogs and cows and pigs would get out and he would have to go out and hunt them. Because when your cows got out of their domain, where they were supposed to be, and you didn't go out and seek them out, then people would just claim them. He would always go out and get them back in. November would go out and he would get his cows."

"Didn't everybody else do that?" Snell asked her grandfather.

"No," her grandfather replied. "It'd be cold. They wouldn't go out looking for no cows. But November would go out no matter how cold it was."

Ivalene Beacham, another neighbor, remembered November as "very dutiful about going to church. He was a church man." November was a deacon at Brown's Chapel, a local Baptist Church. For a time, he also attended the St. James C.M.E. Church near Lovett.

Evelyn Thomas, a cousin of Clarence Thomas's, said November "would always preach to us when he would come down, as far as doing the right thing, staying in school, that sort of thing—getting an education." She added, "He was very firm, but he was a happy person. He made you laugh. He spoke with authority, but he made you laugh."

November spoke decisively, with a weight and conviction rooted in his abiding faith in immutable principles. Abraham Famble, another of Clarence Thomas's cousins, described November as a "preacher-teacher," meaning that he taught as he preached. "He wasn't one of these preachers that bounce around. He was just a cool, calm, ol' preacher. Down to earth … And when he speaks, you listen."

More than one person who knew November Thomas said they thought of him many decades later as they watched Clarence Thomas during his confirmation hearings for the Supreme Court. Ada Snell "noticed the anger that he [Clarence Thomas] portrayed [*sic*]. I understand that November, he wasn't an angry man, but he could be provoked. And he would tell you what he thought. He wouldn't just sit back and not say anything."

The parallels that came to Evelyn Thomas's mind were even more direct. "I could remember watching the hearings, and that last speech he made [in response to Anita Hill's allegations] … I turned to my mother and said, 'That sounds just like his grandfather.'"

———

Clarence Thomas would share many of November's traits—good-natured but steely-willed, and given to flashes of anger. His other grandfather would mold him by example and training. Born, like November Thomas, in 1907, Myers Anderson joined a young family that soon would come apart. His own father, Isaac Anderson, would dissipate like mist in the collective memory of his family. "My daddy wouldn't even talk to me about him," recalled Leola Thomas Williams, Clarence Thomas's mother. Later in Myers' life, both she and her sons prodded him for details about his father. "But he didn't want to talk about it. So I don't know what bad blood there was."

Myers Anderson lived in Savannah for only a short time before his mother, Lutricia Allen, died. Isaac then sent him to live with his grandmother, Annie Allen, in Liberty County. His uncles, Charles and Jim Allen, later took over the responsibility of raising him. Their house was an early, informal sort of boys' town; they had taken in some of his cousins and had a family of about sixteen children in all. Anderson would later describe his Uncle Charles as a "hard man." With so many mouths to feed on so little income and land, he had to be.

Anderson soaked up the ethos of industry and simple virtues that were the Puritan residue of his rural life. He grew up working on the Allen farm, breaking the ground with a mule-drawn plow, putting his back into the indispensable drudgery of hoeing and harvesting. Uncle Charles taught him how to hunt and to catch crabs and oysters as part of the family's diversified self-employment. They also did "piece" work for nearby white families. Anderson attended the Seabrook School, but only through third grade; his uncles needed him for the farm. He attended Palmyra Baptist Church with them on Sundays, and likely was baptized before he set out on his own.

Anderson grew up to be a tall man of relatively light skin, his toils having hardened his body into a thin, taut frame of sinuous muscle. A photograph of him taken late in his life, after Clarence Thomas and his brother pleaded with him to pose for it, captured a man most notable for his broad nose and searing eyes.

At around the age of twenty, Myers Anderson began to display the independent streak that marked his life and career. Returning to the city of his birth, he took a job working in a lumberyard, fashioning dogwood into lumber. It was not long before he embarked on his own business, hauling wood, coal and ice in a pushcart along the city's cobblestone streets.

He also learned at around this time how to read. Like the Puritans of Liberty County, the Catholic Church in Savannah had a tradition of encouraging education among the city's black population. The nuns of St. Benedict's Church "taught my dad what he knows," Leola Thomas Williams said, most notably reading. Although a Baptist, Anderson was a man of iron loyalties, and he was so grateful for the kindness the Catholic Church had shown him that he "just went on and joined that church."

Anderson began seeing a woman of the Seabrook community named Emma Jackson. She was the daughter of Paul Jackson, described as a "tall, heavy fellow" of dark hue, about five feet, eight inches in height and well over two hundred pounds in weight—a brick house of a man. He lived at the Half Moon plantation, part of the old King plantation land on Colonel's Island, where he was caretaker for the landlord, George

M. Brown. Jackson oversaw the sharecropping on the property and ensured that Brown received the right amount of compensation from his sharecroppers.

Emma's mother, Sue Bowens, was also dark and of average height, weighing around a hundred pounds. John Stevens, a neighbor and cousin of Clarence Thomas, remembered her as "a very nice little lady—kind of a hard-working little lady." She toiled in the fields during the summer, tending to the peas, okra and sweet potatoes grown by the Bowens family. She also worked in an oyster and crab processing plant in Sunbury. Her job was to "shuck oysters," removing the oyster meat from the shell and discarding the latter into a large pile of disemboweled mollusks. She enjoyed the local parties and social events.

Her parents were not married when Emma Jackson was born in 1912. She was the first clearly illegitimate child in the Thomas family tree.[*]

This event became a cycle when Emma Jackson grew into a woman and gave birth to a daughter out of wedlock in 1929. Emma named her Leola Anderson, after her father, Myers Anderson, whom she never married. When Emma died in childbirth in 1933, Anderson did no

---

[*]Clarence Thomas has contended that the breakup of the black family is a very recent development. "I am tired of all this talk about the black family being destroyed by slavery," he complained in a 1986 speech. "There is no factual basis for this.... From 1890 to 1950, there was very little difference between black and white families. From 1950 to the present, things went haywire, with the rapid disintegration taking place after 1960."

Thomas's own family history is a tragic refutation of this analysis. While government statistics at the turn of the twentieth century must be taken with a grain of salt, Du Bois concluded, based on his analysis in 1900, that a clear and baneful trend was emerging in the black family. Whites and blacks had a similar marriage rate, he found, but the illegitimacy rate for blacks was 25 percent, compared with 10 percent for whites. He despaired of the debased "sexual mores" of the black community, but stressed, "All this, however, is to be expected. This is what slavery meant, and no amount of kindliness in individual owners could save the system from its deadly work of disintegrating the ancient Negro home and putting but a poor substitute in its place."

Du Bois traced these trends back to the practice of "taking up" with somebody under slavery instead of settling for a sham marriage that masters could ignore at will. "This widespread custom of two centuries has not disappeared in forty years," Du Bois remarked. "Here is the plague spot of the Negro's social relations, and when this inherited low standard of family life happens to be in the keeping of lustful whites, as it sometimes is, the result is bad indeed."

better for his daughter than his father had done for him. He sent Leola off to Pin Point, a black community of mostly fishermen and seafood-plant workers south of Savannah, where she lived with her Aunt Annie Devoe for several years. Later in her childhood, she was shuttled back to Liberty County to live with her grandmother, Sue Bowens. As she grew up, Leola gained the nickname "Pigeon." She attended the Seabrook School for a while, and enjoyed playing baseball with the other Seabrook children, using a ball made from rags. When Sue Bowens died, Leola was returned again to the care of Annie Devoe.

Myers Anderson's eventual wife, Christine Anderson, was a generous soul who treated his children and grandchildren as her own. Leola remembered Christine Anderson as "a loving person, a good mother" who treated her as a daughter.

—◆—

No documented lynchings occurred in Laurens and Liberty Counties during the 1940s. News of the racial violence elsewhere in the South—death throes of a system of segregation under increasing challenge in the postwar world—made the racial slights of the time seem bearable. Ada Snell recalled the blue-and-white Greyhound and red-and-white Trailways buses that passed on the nearby highway, and how blacks would have to sit in the back or stand up if the bus was full of whites. (As a student at Clark Atlanta University, Snell was one of the students who rode to Montgomery, Alabama, to participate in Martin Luther King Jr.'s bus boycott.) Evelyn Thomas reported that race relations in the county were "very separate." In the morning, as the black children of the area made their way to Mount Pullen Elementary School on Route 2, "the blacks walked and the whites rode the buses. To escape the rocks and the spitballs or whatever, we'd have to walk on hills so that they wouldn't throw the rocks or whatever on us."

Liberty County, for all its history of racial tolerance, was not above the fray. John Stevens said of the race problems of the day, "You had that all around Georgia. You could be hit or kicked by a white man anytime, and there wasn't nothing to it." He shuddered when recalling such events fifty years later—times he saw black men bloodied from beatings at the hands of whites. "A lot of people got killed around here," he said. "Some got missing, and you'd never see them again."

The African-Americans of Georgia fought this oppression with violence and revenge, but also through a distinctive—and protective—culture, one aspect of which was a separate language. Childhood friends of Clarence Thomas teased him about his "Geechee" accent, which he picked up during his summers in Liberty County. "Man, you're from the islands or something," they would say. Geechee is a dialect derived from Gullah, a language limited to the coasts of Georgia and South Carolina. This coastal zone became the "center of African linguistic survival" in America, noted historian John Blassingame. The autonomy granted slaves along the coast because of the threat of malaria meant little daily communication with whites, and this allowed them to fashion a new language from the polyglot, fusing elements of English and African tongues.

The name "Gullah" appears to come from "Angola," the homeland of many African slaves imported into the southeastern United States. Gullah is a patois of African words and English phrases forming a Creole language similar in rhythm and origin to that heard on the Caribbean islands. Even at the end of the twentieth century, elderly blacks could be found in Liberty County who spoke with the pleasing lilt of Jamaicans. Most of the vocabulary is derived from English, but the rules of grammar are largely African. A number of words in common usage today are from Gullah: *goober* (peanut), *yam, gumbo, juke* (as in jukebox). Geechee (the name is probably shortened from the Ogeechee River) is a variant of Gullah with similar intonations.

African practices suffuse other traditions of Georgia blacks, especially along the coast where Thomas was born and reared. Eugene Genovese concluded that in South Carolina and Georgia, "African influence has remained strongest." This influence is evident in a wide range of folkways and practices, including oral tradition, sculpture, pottery, basket weaving and grave decoration.

African trickster tales, adapted to the New World by Georgia slaves, are the most famous example of this heritage. In these stories, weaker people or animals defeat stronger adversaries by outsmarting them, and often through guile or magic as well. The heroic underdog is clever but ruthless, frequently self-centered, and willing to resort to crafty devices to vanquish his foe. The slaves of Georgia identified with these figures and lived vicariously through them. Joel Chandler Harris, a white journalist who wrote for the *Atlanta Constitution* in the late 1800s, debriefed Georgia's ex-slaves about these stories, then published and made them famous in a book of tales told by the fictional black character Uncle Remus. In these tales, characters such as Brer Rabbit, Brer Fox and other animals come to life as the proxies for master and slave, and later landlord and sharecropper. Brer Rabbit, the most memorable figure, is a cunning rabbit whose wits allow him to elude the many tricks and snares of predators.

The arts and crafts of blacks in tidewater Georgia also show a debt to Africa. The pottery often is molded into faces with bulging eyes and large, clenched teeth. Reptiles are a familiar African motif in pottery and sculpture. Baskets are intricately and tightly woven in the African manner from grass, pine straw and palm leaves, in patterns of concentric circles.

One of the more famous black American sculptors is Cyrus Bowens, a resident of the Seabrook community and a distant relative by marriage of Clarence Thomas. Bowens is remembered mostly for chiseling pieces of wood into distinctive grave markers, fluid figures of clearly African inspiration. One resembles a snake writhing, another appears to be a man with a head that looks like a ball. On Bowens' grave, in an African touch, a dolphin skull was placed atop the cross. At the time of Clarence Thomas's birth, rows of glasses, broken bottles, vases and other trinkets routinely rested on the graves in the cemetery next to the Palmyra Baptist Church—another old African tradition. Today, as if to ensure the permanent celebration of these customs, glass is encased in a headstone some twenty feet from the final resting place of Myers Anderson.

Most striking of all, perhaps, is the effulgence of creativity in the Georgia arts. White Americans know of this trait mostly from black music, which has become American popular music. The roster of great black musicians from Georgia is long and far out of proportion to the number of blacks there: James Brown, Little Richard, Otis Redding and Ray Charles lead the list. Clarence Thomas would grow up listening to their music, songs that subtly reaffirmed and transmitted their common cultural heritage.

"It's something about the clay we're molded out of here," Ada Snell speculated in jest as she sought to explain Georgia's disproportionate

influence on African-American history and culture. Blacks throughout the state responded to their oppression by taking up arms and fighting in large numbers for their freedom; using their autonomy along the
coast to preserve their African traditions; and clinging to the ways of
their ancestors with unusual devotion. In view of this history, it is not
surprising that Georgia has offered the nation its greatest black scholar
in Du Bois and its greatest black political leader in Martin Luther King
Jr. And in 1948, a boy was born in Pin Point, Georgia—into some of
the most malevolent conditions devised by man—who would also be
an heir to this extraordinary legacy. He would grow up to offer the
nation a new vision for racial unity so radical that even many of his fellow blacks in Georgia would wonder what had gotten into him.

PART TWO

The Roots of Rebellion

CHAPTER THREE

A Phoenix Rises in Pin Point

I n Pin Point, Georgia, births and weddings were cause for community celebration. They affirmed life and union, neither of which African-Americans ever had taken for granted. On June 23, 1948, the people of Pin Point were treated to one of each.

Like virtually all of the other residents of Pin Point, Leola Thomas was looking forward to attending the wedding of two townspeople later in the day. The nuptials of Jack and Patricia Luten went forward as planned, but Leola would not be there because early that morning, "Clarence decided he wanted to come."

Upon learning of Leola's labor, the women of Pin Point arrived at the house and huddled around her bed. Lula Kamp, a midwife, showed up shortly to coach Leola through the ordeal. The bedroom sweltered with the light and heat of the rising Georgia sun. Occasional brackish zephyrs from the saltwater marsh bordering the back yard wafted through the window but provided little relief. Throughout the day, the mounting wails of childbirth competed with the cawing of blue jays and mockingbirds in the motley forest of trees surrounding the house.

After fourteen hours of labor, Leola let out her final cries and exerted her last strong, youthful pushes. As the head and shoulders appeared, Kamp pulled the baby through.

Several months earlier, Leola's father, Myers Anderson, had stood before her, making faces and mumbling things to her belly. He subscribed to a superstitious maxim he had heard along the way, or perhaps invented himself: A baby will resemble whoever perturbs the child's pregnant mother. Myers' tense stare easily melted Leola to tears. By all appearances, his attempt to "will" Leola's second baby to be a boy was a success.

The baby would not be named after Myers, who would have to wait for a following grandson to receive this honor. Leola, in fact, had not picked out a name at all. Her cousin Annabelle Wiggins, who had been close to Leola's deceased mother, suggested the name Clarence. Leola deferred to Wiggins' recommendation without ever finding out the origins of the name. Like his mother but unlike his siblings, Clarence would not be given a middle name. His birth certificate stated with brutal simplicity the life into which he had been born: "Pinpoint, rural, boy, colored."

———

Clarence Thomas was the second child of M.C. and Leola Thomas. The vagaries of Georgia agriculture are the most likely explanation for why M.C. moved to the outskirts of Pin Point and came to know Leola. Life in Laurens County—which was hard enough for black folk under the best of financial circumstances—became unsustainable in the 1940s. The official history of the county notes almost casually that while before the Depression deer had been plentiful, there were none left in the country in 1941 (all of them having been hunted for food).

In 1942, November Thomas moved M.C. and the rest of his family to Savannah, finding both work and shelter southeast of the city, on the edge of Pin Point. The institution that employed him as a handyman and farmhand was the Bethesda Home for Boys.

George Whitefield, at the time the most famous man in the English colonies, established the Bethesda Home for Boys in 1740. A Christian minister who followed John Wesley and helped spur the Great Awakening in both England and America, Whitefield was the first great preacher of the modern tradition. (Lord Chesterfield praised him as "the greatest orator I ever heard, I cannot conceive of one greater.") His injection of passion and emotion into sermons electrified churchgoers, who were accustomed to services that sounded like seminars. Whitefield is believed to have preached more than sixteen thousand sermons in his thirty-two-year career.

When he was not exhorting his followers to greater brotherly love, Whitefield was overseeing a 640-acre plantation he owned in South Carolina—an estate that relied heavily on slave labor. This disconnect between Christian theory and practice was not lost on his fellow ministers, some of whom criticized him roundly. Whitefield recognized the

terrible abuses endemic to the institution. He urged fellow slave owners to be kind to their slaves, "for your Slaves, I believe, work as hard if
not harder than the Horses whereon you ride." In one letter, he even
ventured to write that "perhaps it might be better for the poor Crea-
tures themselves, to be hurried out of Life, than to be made so miserable, as they generally are in it. . . . I have wondered, that we have not
more Instances of Self-Murder among the Negroes, or that they have
not more frequently risen up in Arms against their Owners." Still, he
maintained his plantation to finance what he regarded as one of his
most important enterprises: starting an orphanage outside Savannah.
He hoped that orphan boys would learn self-sufficiency there by raising their own crops and livestock.

Two centuries later, the Bethesda Home for Boys enlisted the Thomas
family, descendants of Georgia slaves, to maintain the grounds and to
assist the agrarian efforts of its juvenile residents. The Thomases also
built cottages and, with the advent of the Cold War, a fallout shelter.
It was steady work and a considerable advancement from the hardscrabble life of sharecropping.

The property and landscape of the home were gorgeous. A large,
newly constructed red brick archway welcomed visitors entering from
Ferguson Avenue. A long driveway lined with live oaks led to Whitefield Chapel, a charming red-brick edifice with white shutters and half-
moon windows. Behind the cottages and horse stables, the property
gently sloped down to a large marsh known locally as Moon River. It
was a slice of classic, tidy Americana that otherwise, in all likelihood,
the Thomases never would have known.

Bethesda, the abbreviated name its neighbors gave the institution,
was only a short walk through the woods from Pin Point. Nine miles
southeast of Savannah, Pin Point was about half a mile long and pop-
ulated with perhaps two hundred people. Shaded by mammoth, old-
growth trees and freshened by marsh breezes, the tiny fishermen's village
was typically ten degrees cooler than Savannah. In the 1890s and early
1900s, the land at this former plantation site became available for sale
to blacks. A number of black families vacated nearby Skidaway and
Green Islands, where they were prohibited from buying real estate, to
buy plots in Pin Point. Other families came from Liberty County, row-
ing over in the bateaux they used for culling crabs and oysters from the
sea.

A later economic attraction—Pin Point's one and only industrial site—was the A. S. Varn and Son oyster and crab company. Its first processing plant in the town opened in 1926. This long, two-story building, which extended out to the water line of the marsh, constituted the Pin Point skyline. Its barn-red tin roof presided over a stark white structure; at its rear, a hillock of empty oyster shells descended down to the water's edge. The company sold "Pin Point Oysters" in cans (one of which would eventually sit on display in the den of Clarence Thomas's home in Virginia). The town's civic activities were centered on Pin Point Hall, a Spartan structure topped with corrugated tin, which the Brotherhood of Friendship Society put up in 1925.

Few residents owned automobiles, relying instead on walking for transportation. Foot trails of white sand and dirt wove throughout the town and surrounding woods—a web of manmade lanes that connected Pin Point and Bethesda physically as well as socially. Ferguson Avenue also ran between the two communities. The women of Pin Point often carried stacks of wood on their heads, in the African manner, from Bethesda for the wood heaters in their homes. Along this road and in the sylvan terrain that separated them, the residents of both communities met and mingled.

The orphans and the children of the groundskeepers, including the Thomases, played and socialized with the children of Pin Point—which was how M.C. Thomas met Leola Anderson. Leola attended an all-black public school on Montgomery Crossroads through the tenth grade. By then, she had grown to average height, with a dark complexion and her father's broad nose. She then began her years of work at the Varn company, where she mostly "picked crabs," removing the meat from the shells.

M.C., four years older then Leola, grew to a height of five feet, nine inches, about an inch taller than his father. M.C.'s most striking features were his strong, broad shoulders and muscular build. He had attended school through fifth grade in Laurens County, then dropped out to help his family raise and pick cotton. At Bethesda, he chipped in with the rest of the family in doing the daily chores at the institution.

M.C. and Leola were married on January 19, 1947, in Leola's home in Pin Point. He was twenty-one, she was seventeen. She soon bore him a daughter, whom Leola named Emma Mae after her mother.

The marriage was never close. M.C. did not take pains to hide his interest in other women and life outside Pin Point. He spent little time in his new home, frequently heading off on long trips with ambiguous destinations.

When he was around, the young family lived in a house belonging to Leola's Aunt Annie Devoe Crawford. The house had two bedrooms, a "family room," and a Jimbo iron heater. Uncle Charlie had built the house in the Liberty County way, with a corrugated tin roof and wooden siding caulked with a makeshift epoxy of flour and water. Newspapers provided both insulation and wallpaper. There was a dirt floor and no electricity or plumbing. Kerosene lamps along with several electric ceiling lights provided limited lighting. The Devoe household shared an outhouse with several neighbors.

Leola Thomas returned to her job at the Varn seafood company a month after Clarence was born in 1948. She was one of the plant's better workers, earning five cents a pound for picking crabs, shucking oysters, and chopping the heads off shrimp. Leola delegated her parenting responsibilities to Uncle Charlie Devoe and his wife, Maggie. The two watched Emma Mae and Clarence in shifts depending on who was not working at the time. As an adult, Clarence noted matter-of-factly that neither of his parents took much part in his upbringing: "Like so many black children, I was raised initially by relatives and finally by my grandparents."

In 1949, Leola learned she was carrying M.C.'s third child. She also became aware that M.C. had impregnated another woman in the area. Always a "wanderer," in the euphemistic phrase of the Thomas family back in Laurens County, M.C. began to feel even more trapped. To escape entirely the pressures of his home life, he decided shortly before his third child was born in 1949 to leave his family and start anew. He went to Savannah and caught a train for Philadelphia, where he began a succession of jobs in manual labor, including stints working in construction, digging ditches and installing pipe.

More than fifty years later, when M.C. was asked why he had left his family, the only explanation he could offer was, "I just wanted to get out of the country." He also agreed that he was "ready to see something new." Indifference to the welfare of his wife and children would become the pattern of his life.

The third Thomas child, Myers Lee, was born a few months after M.C. left, on November 3, 1949. None of the three children would ever truly know their father. Clarence would see M.C. only once during his childhood, when he was nine. Clarence would spend the rest of his life wondering how, "after creating his children," his father could have blithely "walked away."

From a purely statistical standpoint, M.C.'s departure should have doomed Clarence and his siblings to a life of poverty and antisocial conduct. Several factors prevented Clarence from sliding into the trap that captured so many of his childhood friends. One was his natural disposition. Born with an independent and reflective bent, Thomas was comfortable with solitude and the hours of lonely study necessary for self-education. He was also fortunate in the presence of a great-aunt, Maggie Devoe, who would influence his future profoundly.

Maggie was one of the town's most impressive residents. She could read and write, talents rare in the community. She was, moreover, a bright woman who enjoyed learning and encouraging others to learn. She possessed light skin, a noble nose worthy of a Roman senator, and stern, piercing eyes suggestive of a school-marm scrutinizing a pupil. She assumed the role of teacher to young Clarence.

Backing up Maggie was her husband, Charlie (Clarence's great-uncle), an industrious, diminutive man with a thin moustache and a strong bearing. He was "a hard man," one of his grandnephews said. "When he said something, you could stick a pin in it, because what he said, that's what he meant."

Charlie and Annie Devoe, Charlie's sister, did odd jobs for Richard Heard, an attorney who lived in a mansion on Ferguson Avenue across from Bethesda. The two also worked for a man named General Travers who lived on Lehigh Avenue, which traversed one end of Pin Point. These residences were about a mile from Pin Point. Charlie maintained the grounds of these properties and Annie worked as a maid, cooking and cleaning their houses.

When the Heard and Travers children finished with their books, which ranged in seriousness and utility from comic books to English texts, their parents often gave them to Charlie or Annie. These employers may have expected the Devoes to throw the books away or burn them; instead, this minor act of noblesse oblige (intended or not) set a poor black child on the road to Yale Law School. Lacking access to a library and the money to purchase books, Charlie and Annie recognized the value of these discarded items and took them home, where Maggie used them to teach Clarence how to read.

When Aunt Maggie thought he was neglecting his reading, she would summon Clarence from his outdoor play to attend to a higher priority indoors. "Come on in here, boy, and study," she would yell out the door. "Get a book or something and read it." When he learned to read by himself, Clarence would go in a corner and become immersed in the material. He also became fascinated with the newspaper insulation on the walls. What was meant as improvised shelter reinforced Clarence's love of the written word: He would stand and stare at the jumbled articles, trying to decipher the meaning of news from long ago.

After a while, his joy of reading and reflection set him apart from his young peers in the neighborhood. When his cousin Abe Famble would ask him to come out and play, often he would reply, "No, y'all go ahead. I ain't coming out. I'm reading today." His brother, Myers, was more likely to join the youngsters outside, even if it meant sneaking out of the house. Referring to his spells of reading and quiet, Famble recalled: "Clarence was always . . . a little different than we were."

When Clarence did play, Uncle Charlie confined him and his siblings to a zone around the house. "Clarence was under a close watch," Famble recalled. The Devoe house was thirty yards from the marsh, on the "marsh side" of Pin Point (as opposed to the side that backs up to the woods and toward Bethesda). Charlie allowed a play range of about 200 yards' radius from the back yard; the crab factory was about 500 yards away, allowing for backup patrol by Leola.

These boundaries restricted the children's movement but not their exuberance. Along the sand-streaked paths of Pin Point, Clarence first displayed and developed his athleticism, racing barefooted against Myers and cousins Famble, Isaac Martin, and "Little" Richard Wiggins. In front of the house, they played stickball. The boys of Pin Point called the game "half rubber." They cut a rubber ball in half and used it as a baseball; if one half was lost, a common problem of playing ball in the woods, the other half remained.

With no money for toys, Clarence and the other boys made their own. They would remove the spokes from an old bicycle rim, insert a straightened wire hanger into one of the holes, and run down the road, spinning the wheel alongside them. By poking holes in a row of large, cylindrical oilcans, running a wire hanger through them, and tying a string on the end, they would create a train. From a heap of parts, they would try their hand at constructing a complete bicycle.

Instead of toy guns, Clarence and the gang made "pluffers." First, a water hose was cut in half. After they had whittled a stick down to fit tightly inside the hose, the boys would take turns placing chinaberries inside. When they jammed the stick in rapidly, the contraption made a loud noise and discharged the chinaberry, which became a bullet of small fruit. When, in later experiments, one of the boys taped a broken bottle mouth onto the end of the hose, the resulting sound was like that of a small-caliber rifle.

Besides these games and reading, there was much else in this lush, paludal environment to occupy a boy who enjoyed his own company. As an adult, Clarence would well remember climbing trees to pick scuppernongs, the wild, amber-green grapes that grew throughout the region. Pin Point was something of a free-growing arboretum, perfect for a tree-climbing child. The wide variety of native coastal trees shooting up to the sky—palmetto trees along the banks of the marsh, majestic oaks and maples reaching out to the sun, magnolias with the sweet, short-lived scent of their white *grandiflora*—formed a massive canopy that blocked much of the direct sunlight above the village. Mistletoe and long, gray streamers of Spanish moss decorated the boughs like tinsel on Christmas trees. Swamp lilies floated nearby in the creek and marsh; red hibiscus, irises, and Southern blue flags splashed color throughout the landscape. One of Clarence's most distinct memories of childhood was simply sitting under the house and enjoying the feel of the cool earth.

Clarence sneaked outside Uncle Charlie's perimeter to catch minnows or tadpoles in the creek that ran through the woods. On one occasion, he and Abe Famble climbed the fence and went down to the marsh to indulge in a forbidden pastime, "crab bogging"—walking along the banks with a net and scooping up fiddler crabs out of the mud at low tide. Leola finally spied them from the Varn factory. "What are y'all boys doing down there?" she shouted. The fun ended as Abe was sent home and Clarence went off to face an uncertain punishment. When

Clarence, almost thirty years later, told an audience of young black men, "We have to stop tearing each other down like crabs in a basket," the unusual analogy was undoubtedly inspired by his childhood.

Clarence was not above other high jinks. He and Famble sometimes stole away to Frank English's little store on Ferguson Avenue. Knowing they had arrived penniless, an elderly worker there named Hazel might take pity on the two. "Oh, you come in the store today, you don't have no money, huh?" she would say good-naturedly. With a smile, she would give them some candy on the house. Other times, the boys would slip the candy into their pockets without permission and walk back chomping on pilfered Squirrel Nuts and Mary Janes.

There was a tall price to pay when parents or elders in the community uncovered such shenanigans. "These old folks were strict around here," Famble said. "If you would do something wrong, you would think, 'How did, before I get back home ... my mother or my father know that we did this?'" The children surmised that adults had a "secret code" for communicating such things. Wayward children usually received swift corporal punishment, often a "whupping" with a switch from a willow or other nearby tree.

Later on, Thomas would describe Pin Point as "a small community of blacks, most of whom are my relatives." Family ties overlay and reinforced the sinews of community. Religion was another important socializing force. Uncle Charlie took Clarence, Myers, and their cousins to prayer meetings every Tuesday and Wednesday night at Charlie's church, the Sweet Field of Eden Baptist Church. Charlie was a church elder, and he trained the boys on how to lead a devotional service. "They just taught us the fundamentals of being a good Christian, good boys," Famble said. "They taught us the wages of sin is death."

November Thomas bolstered these teachings as well. With his savings, he managed to purchase a comfortable, middle-class house on Montgomery Avenue. This house was close to the Montgomery Baptist Church, where he was a preacher. After M.C. deserted his family, November, like Uncle Charlie, became a surrogate father to Clarence, whom he saw weekly along with his other grandchildren. Often on Sundays, he invited Clarence and his kin over to the house for fried chicken, collard greens, and okra soup. Always well dressed and properly groomed, wearing overalls only if he was working in the yard,

November lived an orderly and relatively prosperous life very similar to that led by Myers Anderson. Clarence would remember Anderson throughout his life, deservedly, as his hero and the greatest influence on his life. Both grandfathers, however, set an example of hard work and self-discipline.

Over the years, as Clarence Thomas scrupulously thanked the numerous relatives and friends who had helped launch his career, his list of acknowledgments consistently would exclude Charlie and Maggie Devoe and November Thomas. Perhaps this was simply for lack of recall—the incomplete memories of childhood being a merciful boon to young parents whose errors abound in those trying years, but an injustice to the caregivers whose contributions in this period are usually forgotten. Or there may have been hidden animosities to explain this omission. Regardless, Clarence's profound love of English, industry, and religion started in Pin Point under the tutelage of these overlooked relatives.

In September 1954, Clarence stood at the end of Pin Point Road and awaited his ride to his first day of school. With him was his sister, Emma, who was starting second grade. Clarence grew excited as he glimpsed yellow school bus number 101 slowing to pick up the children of the marsh community. The driver of the bus was a familiar face, November Thomas. His career had evolved from sharecropper and farm hand to this position, which he took as seriously as everything else in his life.

"Mr. November," as the schoolchildren called him, enforced relative quiet among his exuberant young passengers. Too much chattering would cause him to pull over to the side of the road and deliver an impromptu sermon: "Didn't I tell y'all about making noise on my bus? I've got to concentrate on driving this bus! Y'all distracting me!"

Every day, his grandfather deposited Clarence at Haven Home Elementary School, a large school "built up like a hospital," as one alumnus described it, with vast oak trees on the grounds. Like all public schools in Georgia, Haven Home was racially segregated. Three months before Clarence's first day—on Monday, May 17—the Supreme Court had declared school segregation unconstitutional in *Brown v. Board of Education*. With a bigoted double entendre, white politicians throughout Georgia and the South branded the day of the decision "Black

Monday." Governor Herman Talmadge called the ruling "a mere scrap of paper" and vowed to fight desegregation to the death. Georgia passed new laws to entrench school segregation more deeply. Lawmakers made it a felony to teach a racially mixed class or to use tax money for integrated schools. *Brown* exerted no effect on Clarence's experience at Haven Home.

The school suffered from the very defects that *Brown* had condemned. There was insufficient heating. Books were old and in short supply. Students sat in rickety chairs. But at least Clarence's somewhat worn school attire did not attract attention, as most children were of like economic circumstances. He wore "ragged hand-me-downs" from relatives or from Bethesda: worn jeans, T-shirts, tennis shoes, bib overalls, and Sears and J. C. Penney brands. Going barefoot was commonplace for the children of Pin Point, as for many schoolchildren throughout the rural South.

One teacher at Haven Home observed something about Clarence that she thought striking. Dorothy Barnes-Pelote, who later became a state legislator, recalled the boy inspecting one of the towering ancient oaks on the property. "He was talking and pointing at the tree with his grandfather," she said, referring to Myers Anderson, who stood next to him. "This little boy was standing there and was concerned about the tree being so big. And his grandfather was explaining to him about the big trees. . . . He was very inquisitive about those trees."

Anderson saw the teacher and acknowledged her, shaking his head about the boy's curiosity. "I tell you, he really wants to know about that tree," Anderson explained. "He likes to ask questions. He really wants answers. He wants answers right now. He doesn't want to wait."

"He had the time to talk to him so compassionate," she said of Anderson. Finally, the grandfather nudged Clarence along. "Come on now. It's time for us to go," Anderson told him. He then led the boy to his fuel truck and drove off, and Clarence's school day ended, bracketed by grandfathers.

On a frigid afternoon a few months after school began, Mr. November drove Clarence, Emma and their classmates back home. It was unusually cold for the season—around October or November, as winter began to take over from fall. Big leaves speckled with crimson and orange tumbled from the trees along the route, fluttering down to a frozen ground.

Leola had left for work earlier in the day without getting a babysitter for Myers; the Devoes had been unable to watch him that day. The five-year-old was instructed to leave the house at a certain hour and walk down to the residence of Alethia Cruise, who often watched him and the other Thomas children when the Devoes could not. Myers was more rambunctious than Clarence, and he was in no hurry for adult supervision. He stayed behind in the house for some time and played with Little Richard. They happened upon some long stick matches used for lighting the wood heater. A curtain ignited. When Myers arrived at Cruise's house, he did not mention the havoc he had left behind.

After the bus dropped off Clarence and Emma, the two walked with the other children down the sandy dirt road. Somebody soon spotted them and ran up to give them the news that would abruptly alter Clarence's life: Their house was on fire.

Clarence, Emma and the rest of the children raced down the road toward the pandemonium. They saw smoke ascending and flames lapping up a side of the house. The people of Pin Point banded together to help subdue the blaze, pumping water from the yard into buckets and carrying them over to douse the flames. The Montgomery Fire Department responded slowly and incompetently; when the truck arrived, the water inside its tank was frozen. By then, the fire was largely contained, and the house already charred.

Though not entirely destroyed, the house was no longer habitable. Leola's children possessed literally only the clothes on their backs.

Frantically trying to cope with the new crisis, she made decisions that would have large consequences for the family. She formalized, for instance, what had been up to then an unspoken delegation to Aunt Annie of responsibility for rearing Emma. Leola told Emma she was "sickly" and required this care, which reduced Leola's childrearing responsibilities by a third. Leola decided to keep the boys, however. She would seek work and a new place to live in Savannah.

Leola ended up working for a white woman, who paid her $15 a week. "Like virtually every black woman in my family and my neighborhood, my mother was a maid," Clarence later observed. There was plenty of such work to be had in the city. She not only cleaned house but tended to the children of her employer, a nurse who worked nearby and who ultimately inspired Leola to become an aide at a local hospital.

The place Leola found for her shattered family was significantly worse than the Devoe house in Pin Point. Clarence later summed up the living conditions as "awful." The "tenement" she rented was a one-room flat that lacked electricity and adequate heating. The old gas stove worked only intermittently; the so-called icebox upstairs did not deserve the name. The kitchen floor was a roll of old linoleum laid on the bare ground. The dwelling had "outdoor facilities which were decrepit and rarely worked," Clarence later said, adding, "It didn't really matter because we were not used to such facilities anyway." These facilities were a common toilet that was always filthy, inside a rotted wooden structure that leaked sewage into the back yard.

In Pin Point, the food Clarence received had at least been filling and reasonably balanced. Soups with rice and greens, ham and chitterlings, and Hoppin' John dishes of cow peas and rice with hog jaw or tail were typical fare. In Savannah, his overwhelmed mother frequently provided the children with Kellogg's Corn Flakes floating in a sickly combination of water and evaporated PET milk. On other occasions, lunch and dinner consisted of the edges of bread Leola had trimmed in making hors d'oeuvres for her employer.

Leola left Clarence and Myers alone for hours. The two small boys fended for themselves during these long stretches of risky self-rule. Leola later claimed that she dropped the children off with her father and stepmother in the morning and picked them up at night. Clarence remembered differently: "I can remember spending countless hours alone, wandering the streets, or looking out the window on the dirt streets below."

Clarence sometimes awakened from his bed on an old loveseat (brother Myers slept in the bed with Leola) and watched the women of Savannah go to work. He observed them in the early morning and in the evening standing on street corners, waiting in the heat and humidity for the segregated buses to arrive, then crowding into the back of buses that lacked air conditioning. "They endured this to get home dead tired so they could raise *their* families, clean *their* houses, and cook *their* dinners," he recalled.

Clarence was supposed to attend the Florance Street School near their dwelling. He often played hooky, spending the day taking in the sights of his new city, walking about and shifting for himself.

Then, in the summer of 1955, Leola found another man. He made it clear, according to Clarence's later account, that he "didn't want children from the previous marriage around." So Leola packed up the two boys and sent them to live with their grandparents, Myers and Christine Anderson. In taking in the little boys, Myers Anderson followed the example of his uncle, who had done the same for him. He also may have felt remorse over his abandonment of Leola twenty years before. After father and daughter had come to an agreement, Clarence and Myers placed all their earthly belongings into two grocery bags, said goodbye to their mother, and left her.

Clarence would always speak of this event with great bitterness. In one speech, after discussing his upbringing, he plaintively asked his audience, "Why did my mother choose to marry someone who did not want two little boys?" Leola herself later offered conflicting explanations for her behavior. Clarence clearly did not believe them. In discussions with friends and subordinates, he spoke of this abandonment with "force and conviction and emotion," in the words of one.

Yet for all the pain of this parting, Clarence would later realize that the fire that destroyed his home and life in Pin Point and his abandonment by his mother fundamentally altered—and perhaps even saved—his life. Finding sanctuary in the household of Myers Anderson, Clarence would thereafter refer to himself as a "son of his grandfather." He would remember Anderson as the man who rescued him from a future in which he was "a statistic waiting to happen."

CHAPTER FOUR

The Strongest Man in the World

Clarence and Myers Thomas would come to call their grandparents "Daddy" and "Aunt Tina." The names were revealing. "Daddy" was the standard Southern word for father, even among adults. This name dispelled any question as to who had filled M.C.'s shoes. "Tina" was short for Christina. The title "aunt"—pronounced, in the black tradition, not like the insect but with the "a" sound in "father"—acknowledged that she was not a grandmother by blood. In fact, it bespoke a certain thoughtful diplomacy and decorum on her part in handling her relationship with the children.

The grandfather who became "the greatest single influence on my life" impressed his will on Clarence as soon as he moved in. There would be no more aimless and unattended wandering of the streets, no more hours frittered away watching the urban hurly-burly and skipping school. Clarence had entered an environment that revolved around work, education and faith, and a household immersed in rules, discipline, labor and learning to an extent remarkable even by the standards of the rigorous decade in which he came of age. His first year in Savannah had been one of almost boundless liberty, a reckless arrangement sanctioned by his parents. The remainder of his years in this city of quaint squares and omnipresent tradition would be just as extreme, but of the opposite quality—order.

The two Thomas boys became, in effect, the littlest employees of Anderson Fuel Company and its affiliate, the Anderson household. Anderson had started his company after striking out on his own and moving to Savannah to earn more money and assert his independence. The bigotry he encountered at the hands of his first employers during this time singed his substantial pride and further reinforced his yearning for self-employment. Anderson told two stories as to why he decided to go into business for himself, both of which involved prejudice. One was that a white co-worker saw him wearing a nice watch one day and forced him to give it to him. The other story held that Anderson had worked as a stable hand for a white family, and one of his duties was to lead the son around on his pony. When the son grew older, his father instructed Anderson to address the youngster as "Mister." Anderson walked off the job instead. Perhaps both stories were true; in any event, he decided he had had enough, and subsequently sawed the top off his old Model T and turned it into a delivery truck, thus commencing his fuel business.

The Anderson Fuel Company became a prosperous enterprise, as Clarence later noted with pride, "during the most repressive period of Jim Crow law and racial bigotry." Daddy sold and delivered fuel, mostly to fellow blacks: first wood, then coal, and later still fuel oil. He also delivered ice in the summer to offset the decline in sales during those months. His all-black Catholic parish bought blocks of ice from him to cool the iceboxes where the priests and nuns stored their milk and vegetables. Daddy later branched out into other concerns. After purchasing a machine that made cement cinderblocks, he built three small houses in east Savannah, living in one and renting out the other two. He and a friend, Sam Williams, opened a nightclub for blacks. Eventually, their landlord took over this business.

Forty-eight years old when he assumed responsibility for his grandsons, the energetic Anderson kept a demanding schedule and expected his grandsons to honor it too. He went to bed between eight and nine o'clock at night and rose between two and four in the morning, while it was still dark. The rule that he cited in support of this timetable—which he probably learned from his taskmaster uncle in Liberty County—was to be up "fo' day in the morning." Not once would Clarence see his grandfather sleep until dawn. If the weather was warm, Daddy would haul ice in the morning, then spend the rest of the day distributing fuel oil to customers. The boys helped out both with the business and with chores around the house, including yard work, painting, and washing Daddy's car and truck.

Daddy denounced idle time as the "devil's workshop" and did his best to banish it from the children's days. He warned his grandsons frequently that if they did not work, they would not eat. It was an admonition worthy of the Puritan scions of Liberty County, which was where he had learned this ethic. If the boys managed to sleep until seven or eight in the morning, Daddy would roust them by coming into the room and announcing, "Y'all must think y'all are rich!"

The sayings he bestowed on his grandsons were numerous and pungent. "Hard times make monkey eat cayenne pepper"; "If you make your bed hard, you lay [*sic*] in it hard"; "If you lie, you'll steal; if you steal, you'll cheat; if you cheat, you'll kill." They were steely apothegms for a life of self-mastery, and rules of conduct that he drilled into the boys until they became second nature. Clarence looked with awe upon this fierce, successful man and soaked up these precepts with little amendment: "His truths became the basis of my own." When Daddy spoke with his "deep baritone voice," "the whole house seemed to resonate." To Clarence, he seemed "the strongest man in the world."

Christine Anderson, a kind and taciturn woman who complemented a "tough-as-nails" grandfather, would become to Clarence "the heart and soul of my childhood." She would "slave away in the kitchen, clean house, cook and endure, so we could make it." Aunt Tina woke him up for school in the morning, greeting him with ironed shirts, a hot breakfast, lunch in a paper bag, and the stirring rhythms of gospel music from radio station WSOK. She ministered to his illnesses (Clarence did not see a doctor until he was fifteen), dispensing cod liver oil and castor oil "to clean us out," spider webs for bad cuts, and bacon and a penny for puncture wounds, typically gotten from stepping barefooted on nails. She also pitched in and helped the family business, answering the telephone and tending to some of the paperwork. For supper, she would routinely reserve for Clarence his favorite part of the chicken while eating only the neck or wing. Her most constant instruction to the children was, "Say your prayers."

One of Aunt Tina's other acts of grace was to intercede with her husband on matters of punishment. Sometimes Aunt Tina would seek a pardon or commutation for the boys, or she would give them a light spanking to spare them from a harsher rod at day's end. (Clarence said he "tasted the belt regularly," the belt being the normal instrument for "whuppings.") Aunt Tina's relative leniency did not lull her into winking at misbehavior. One time, a neighbor, Miss Gertrude, rode by on a bus and saw Clarence crossing East Henry Street before the light had changed. She stuck her head out the window and bellowed as she passed, "I'm gonna tell Teeny!" She made good on her threat, and Aunt Tina passed along the bad news to Anderson. Before rearing back with his belt, he gave Clarence his usual refrain: "This hurts me worse than it hurts you."

In exchange for following their grandfather's rules, Clarence and Myers enjoyed a vastly improved home life. The Anderson house was a six-room cinderblock structure in a black neighborhood on East Thirty-second Street. Past the front porch was a comfortable living room, which connected, through an archway—an intriguing touch to the simple Savannah abode—to the dining room and kitchen. A wood heater burned some of the Anderson company's inventory to warm the house in the winter. Clarence and Myers shared a bedroom and slept in twin beds; rosary beads and a picture of St. Christopher were the only wall decorations. For the first time in their lives, the boys had indoor plumbing. Floyd Adams, one of Clarence's childhood friends, noted that "when his grandfather took over, Clarence moved into what would be considered a fairly successful black middle-class family."

Their new, close-knit neighborhood embraced Clarence and Myers. Daddy's emphasis on politeness and neighborliness facilitated this acceptance. He enjoined the boys to "put a handle" on the names of grownups—Miss Mariah, Cousin Hattie, etc.—and to address them as "sir" or "ma'am." Two other standing rules were "Always say 'good morning'" and "Speak when spoken to." The two brothers were never permitted to debate an adult or to refuse to do an errand for a neighbor. The neighbors evidently caught wind of this, for Clarence was conscripted many times to walk to the store and purchase BC's, Goodies, or Stanbacks and a Coke for them.

"Boy, go get me a Stanback," was an especially common request from the hard-working women of the neighborhood. Clarence's frequent treks to the store to buy aspirin for them helped him to experience vicariously their daily travails in the work force. One especially influential group of employed women had custody of Clarence during a large part of his waking hours. They were the nuns of the Franciscan Order who lived down East Broad Street. They would wield more influence over the latter part of his childhood than anybody but his grandfather.

The three props supporting Clarence's development—work, education and faith—were a joint effort of Daddy and his adopted Catholic Church. His parish was St. Benedict the Moor, the first black Catholic parish in Georgia. St. Benedict the Moor was the son of African slaves who lived in Sicily in the sixteenth century. He was the obvious choice for a patron saint when the diocese established a parish in this black neighborhood on the south side of Savannah.

The parish supported a school, convent and church. The school was four stories high, made of common red brick, with long windows permitting plenty of sunlight. Across the street, a convent of like material and design housed the nuns who taught at the school. The convent was next to the church, a squat building of reddish-brown bricks with a simple arched roof and a belfry.

In September 1955, Clarence and Myers spent the first day of the school year at East Broad Street School, a public school in their neighborhood. From that day forward, Clarence never again attended a public institution. Daddy stressed the importance of education to his grandsons. He had been denied this great advantage in life; at the time, blacks in the Savannah area attended school for only seven years on average. He resolved that his grandsons would not be similarly deprived. To put his money where his mouth was, he enrolled them at St. Benedict.

Daddy gravitated to the school not only for the obvious religious reasons, but because of the uniforms and strict order maintained there. This schooling would cost him $30 a year in tuition, no small amount at the time. But the boys were given over to a brigade of teachers who were just as committed to stringent discipline as their grandfather: the Franciscan Sisters, who founded their mission in Savannah in 1878 and dedicated themselves to serving the black community. For this emphasis, they came to be known in the city and surrounding area as the "nigger nuns." Many came from Ireland. The black schoolchildren who grew to adore them tried to imitate their Irish accent. One of Clarence's classmates recalled the humorous sight of "little black kids in Savannah running around speaking with Irish brogues."

At a time when racism permeated every social setting in the city,

the Franciscan nuns, in Clarence's words, "accepted our equality without a Civil Rights Act, they accepted equality of education without
Supreme Court decisions, they lived in the inner city before we knew
it was the inner city." On one class trip, a bus driver announced that
nuns were permitted to sit in the front of the vehicle, but the children
had to sit in the back. "Where my kids sit, I will sit," the nun replied.
She went to the back and took a seat among her students. In less tolerant Augusta, where the sisters also taught black children, one of the
sisters was ejected from a bus after she insisted on sitting in the back
with one of her pupils. During citywide services at the Cathedral of St.
John the Baptist in Savannah, white worshipers were permitted to enter
first. The nuns always stood in a huddle with the black schoolchildren
at the bottom of the steps until it was their turn to go in together.

The nuns—"*our* nuns," Clarence later called them—invoked this
discrimination in the classroom to rile their students into working
harder—to "make us competitive," as one student said. They told their
pupils that white children thought they were smarter than black children. The students of St. Benedict responded with high performance
compared with schoolchildren in public schools, and with pride. They
boasted to the other children in the neighborhood of being able to recite
the Mass in Latin and of having white teachers.

The nuns practiced compassion backed by force: Students who judged
these women incapable of effectively administering corporal punishment learned in short order how wrong they were. Penalties came in
various forms, all of them stern. Clarence recalled the "swift tug of your
shoulder, being shaken, or the ruler in the palm of the hand." Other
infractions required "penance" ranging from standing in the corner,
writing something repeatedly, mopping floors, or pulling weeds in the
schoolyard. When one two-hundred-pound teenage student acted up,
the nun teaching his class commanded him to kneel in front of her. She
stood before him and slapped him in the face with all her might.

The daily class routine reflected this unyielding commitment to
order and hierarchy. The children lined up outside the school at 8:15
A.M., after the morning bells tolled, in a navy-blue wave of uniforms—
the boys with blue pants, white shirts and a tie, the girls with blue skirts
and a white blouse. After reciting the Pledge of Allegiance and singing

the national anthem, they strode slowly two by two into the school, keeping a wary eye out for pigeon droppings en route. Classes began promptly at 8:30. A crucifix hung prominently above the blackboard; a small American flag projected from the right. The school day began and ended with catechism.

Clarence would remember his grade school years as a succession of nuns. There was Sister Mary Dolorosa for second grade (a year which, understandably, he described as "a particularly difficult transition period"); Sister Mary Chrysostom in third grade ("drilled us endlessly on the multiplication tables"); Sister Mary Geraldine in fourth grade ("where long division and geography were major challenges"); Sister Mary Francis Paul in fifth grade; Sister Mary Katherine in sixth grade ("*wonderful* teacher but didn't hit very hard. We got away with a lot"); and Sister Mary Aquin in seventh grade ("*more than* made up for" the leniency of Sister Mary Katherine).

Then there was Mother Mary Virgilius Reidy, the principal of St. Benedict, whom Clarence referred to simply as "*my* teacher." Born in Ballmacelligott, Ireland, in County Kerry, Reidy joined the Franciscan Order and came to America in 1934. After teaching the black children of Augusta, she was assigned in 1958 to St. Benedict. With thin lips, pronounced high cheekbones, and bright blue eyes that could enflame on cue to compel obedience, the quick-witted and sharp-tongued Reidy cut a striking figure in Clarence's memory, and would have a major impact on his life.

The school curriculum stressed the basics. English, mathematics, history, geography, spelling and handwriting were the primary subjects. Handwriting was emphasized in first, second and third grades. From this careful attention to making letters and words, Clarence learned penmanship that Reidy later described as "good, firm handwriting that shows character." A reading program encouraged the students to read books outside the classroom and to "compete against themselves."

Daddy did his part by ensuring that his grandsons had near-perfect attendance and diligent study habits. He made it clear that "all illnesses would be presumed to be feigned." For further clarification and emphasis, he added, "If you die, I'll take you to school for two days to make sure you're not faking." During the nine years in which Clarence and his brother, Myers, lived with their grandparents, they missed one half-day of school. When the boys suggested that perhaps good grades might merit some reward on his part, Daddy scoffed: "If I pay the tuition, your job *is* to get the good grades."

With a curious intellect and the early stirrings of ambition, Clarence did not require much coaxing to succeed in school. Reidy classified him as a "B-plus student" and an "all-around good student." Reidy's evaluation of his academic performance squared with Clarence's self-critique: "I was never the best black student when I was in segregated schools—ever."

In eighth grade, Clarence was selected to serve as a crossing guard. Before and after school, he and the other crossing guards would assist their schoolmates in traversing busy East Broad Street. The guards were under the supervision of a Lieutenant Faulk, a Jewish policeman who outfitted the boys in hard hats and crossing-guard belts.

Clarence also became an altar boy. The altar boys often went to a nearby monastery on Saturdays, sitting on the front porch while a priest drilled them in Latin. They also were the pool of young men whence the church hoped to draw its future priests. As Clarence entered adolescence, these expectations hovered over him as he sought to decide his future career.

Daddy and Aunt Tina were "deeply religious," he recalled, and approved of his contributions to the church. "There's no problem that can't be solved by hard work and prayer," was one of Myers Anderson's oft-invoked pearls. He taught his grandsons that human rights came from God, not man, and that segregation and discrimination were evil because they violated this natural order.

—⌒—

As an adult, Clarence would find that the onset of winter reminded him of the many hours he spent "cloistered" with his grandfather in their oil truck early in the morning. Daddy later removed the heater from the truck so that the boys would not grow too comfortable and neglect their work duties. He also disabled the radio at one point to prevent them from playing the "terrible" rock-and-roll and rhythm-and-blues that were starting to dominate the airwaves.

When classes were dismissed at 2:30 P.M., Clarence and Myers made a beeline down East Broad Street back to their house. They were required to finish the mile walk home, strip off their uniforms and change into work clothes, and report for work by 3:00 P.M. Most afternoons were spent pumping heating oil out of the Anderson Fuel Company's tanker truck. They pulled down the heavy hose and dragged it into houses to fill the oil tanks while Anderson did the paperwork. When there were no deliveries to make, there was almost always work to be done at home or at the houses Daddy rented out—painting, roofing, plumbing, yard work. These work details filled most Saturdays as well. "He used to work Clarence like a dog," was friend Robert DeShay's blunt recollection of Anderson.

Daddy forbade his grandsons to use the word "can't" in his presence. The litany that followed every time they slipped was so predictable that the boys could, in Clarence's words, "lip-sync it on cue": "Old man can't is dead. I helped bury him." Clarence later said that he hated rushing home from school every day and not being able to play sports because of his work obligations. But he also observed of his grandfather: "I didn't know it, but each day he dragged us around, he was passing on our inheritance."

Daddy was a teacher as well as a taskmaster. Upon returning from one trip north to visit some relatives who resided in housing projects and lived off the dole, Anderson exclaimed, "Damn welfare, that relief! Man ain't got no business on relief as long as he can work."

Later in life, Clarence came back to the subject: "Daddy, why is it you never accepted welfare? You struggled out here with your oil business. We farmed to make ends meet."

His grandfather replied, "I never took a penny from the government because it takes your manhood away. Once you accept it, they can ask you whatever they want to. They can tell you whatever they want to. They can come into your home whenever they want to. They can tell you who can come and who can go, and I'd prefer to starve to death first."

After the family finished supper and Clarence washed the dishes, he was free to walk the three blocks to the Carnegie Library on East Henry Street. Carnegie's fortune was rarely put to better use than in constructing this unpretentious little red-brick rectangle of a library. This was the local "Negro library," as blacks were banned from the Savannah Public Library. This small warehouse of books and magazines, Clarence later said, "brought me into contact with heroes and villains, with hatred and with love." It became his refuge when he was angry with his grandfather or others, and the one place where he could stay out until nine o'clock at night.

Clarence sampled the periodicals to which the Carnegie Library subscribed. "I used to run to the library to flip through the pages and dream," he recalled. "I just remember the *New Yorker*. You know, what did I know about New York? But I said, One day, I'm going to be able to read this, be sophisticated enough to deal with these kinds of things." A black librarian at Carnegie, Mrs. Cameron, also took an interest in the inquisitive young man who was so often seated at one of her tables. She arranged for interlibrary loans from the whites-only public library to sate his appetite for more reading material.

Clarence and Myers received $2 a week in allowance from Daddy. While Myers saved up for a pair of new pants or shoes, Clarence spent his money on books. Often these were comic books, which he had relished since his earliest days of reading in Pin Point. The Two Gun Kid, Kid Colt, and the Rawhide Kid were some of his favorites. His interest in Westerns would become a lifelong literary obsession.

On weekends, when work was done, Clarence played football and basketball with the neighborhood kids. Roy Allen, a schoolmate and fellow altar boy, described him as an "intense and serious student, a voracious reader, a faster than average runner, a basketball player with such moves that, on the playground of St. Benedict the Moor Catholic Church, he was nicknamed Cousy, after the famous Celtic Star." In both schoolwork and play, "Cooz" was a "fiercely competitive guy" who "just plain hated to lose."

With his friends, Clarence roamed the neighborhood when he could escape his grandfather, frequenting the Dairy Queen, the confectionery, and the corner stores that "provided an endless supply of candy, ice cream, and other goodies." He also patronized the Eastside Theater at East Broad and Wynette Streets, the segregated theater where, for ten cents, he could watch both a Western and rats scuffling in the corner.

Some of the teasing by Clarence's peers reflected and abetted the climate of racism in the city. He liked being called "Cooz," but one childhood nickname that deeply stung him was ABC, which stood for "America's Blackest Child." The other black children of the neighborhood ridiculed him for his dark complexion, thick lips and short, curly African hair, which they called "nigger naps."

Anderson took pains to make certain that Clarence stayed in touch with the other side of his family. He and Myers visited Pin Point regularly, where they played with their cousins and visited November Thomas. "Clarence and Myers, they always would come back home to see their people," his cousin Abe Famble recalled. Clarence also occasionally visited the Thomas side of the family in Dublin, back in Laurens County. Ada Snell remembered him during these visits as "very intelligent. Highly intelligent."

The strongest ties, naturally, were to Anderson's native Liberty County. It is significant that Clarence would later say, "I grew up partially in Savannah and partially on a small farm outside Savannah." This farm was on the land near Sunbury that Anderson had inherited from his uncles. Clarence's attachment to this area began when he was in fourth grade. On Christmas 1957, "when all the other kids were running up and down the road and enjoying their toys, shooting firecrackers, and generally having a great time, my grandfather came to me and my brother . . . and said that he had work for us to do." Clarence and Myers

> piled into the 1951 Pontiac and rode. He took us to a field that had laid [sic] fallow for years and had grown up. He drove down the remnants of an old road. We made our way across the field to an old oak tree. He looked at it, surveyed it, paced pensively and announced that we would build a house there. And, he marked the spot.

Over the next five months, Daddy and his young helpers drove south of Savannah in their Pontiac along U.S. Highway 17, the Coastal Highway, past the shimmering bogs, stands of tall pine, and intermittent "Impeach Earl Warren" signs. Upon arrival, the boys mixed cement and carried cinderblocks to the foundation as Anderson assembled another of his cinderblock residences. On May 17, 1958, they finished the steps to the house.

Thereafter, and during subsequent summers, they began to farm. At first, Daddy plowed the soil with a horse and mule, the two boys trailing him. Later, he bought an old gray Ford tractor, which helped in removing logs and cutting hay. They cleared more land every year, making more room for crops and pasture. More structures were needed to support the operation, so up went barns and garages. The trio strung long ribbons of wire fence around the property. They worked from sunup to sundown, with up to ninety minutes set aside for lunch (the extended lunch hour owing to the short nap Daddy took after the meal). They grew sugar cane, beans, corn, watermelon, okra, tomatoes. Their menagerie of livestock expanded to include pigs, cows, chickens and ducks. Enveloped by the swampy humidity of Liberty County, they picked beans until their backs were numb with pain, and cut trees or bushes until their hands were a mass of blisters. More than twenty years later, when a co-worker offered Clarence some fresh vegetables from her garden at home, he grimaced as he recalled "all those chores" growing up in Liberty County. "If it doesn't come frozen or in a can," he declared, "I don't want to see it. I don't want it."

Many of the local children in Liberty County were relatives, and therefore instant playmates, of Clarence and Myers, whom they called by the nicknames "Boy" and "Peanut." Their sister, Emma, joined them in the country one weekend a month, and in some years for the entire summer.

During the same period, while Daddy was handing down the work ethic of Liberty County to his grandsons, others were learning of the area's unusual qualities. Martin Luther King Jr. heard of this unique pocket of the state and its reputation for industry and relative tolerance. From 1962 to 1964, as the Anderson grandchildren worked the land of their ancestors, the Southern Christian Leadership Conference (SCLC), under King's leadership, held citizen education workshops a few miles away at Dorchester Academy. Founded in the 1870s for the education of blacks in Liberty County and coastal Georgia, the academy hosted a retreat in January 1963 at which King and his followers prepared for the coming civil rights offensive in Birmingham, Alabama. By then, the storm clouds of three and a half centuries of racial oppression were clearing over Georgia and the rest of the South, and a racial caste system that decreed the Anderson grandchildren should confine their dreams to the sort of back-breaking enterprises in which they involuntarily invested their summers was headed for extermination.

———

Like other port cities, Savannah was a comparatively broad-minded place where the daily mixture of peoples dissolved much of the native prejudice. Savannah took Charleston, not Atlanta, as its model. The public squares with moss-covered oaks, charming Colonial-era homes, brownstones and historical monuments told of Savannah's status as Georgia's oldest and most European city. The city's whites were proud of their relative toleration, which included a certain amount of integration in housing. In many neighborhoods, for example, the front of a white family's house was called a street; the lane behind was called an alley. The white address might be 316 Smith Street, the black address 316 Smith Alley; and the children often played together in the back yard or the alley between them. They could not go to school together, however, or to any public accommodation in one another's company— just to mention a few of the social obstacles that would pry these children apart as they matured. As an adult, Clarence Thomas would denounce the discrimination of his youth with considerable emotion. He would describe this experience as a "nightmare," and refer to these times as "the agony of discrimination—the humiliation of prejudice."

Of the Savannah of his youth, Clarence recalled, "Segregation was written into the laws; it controlled almost every aspect of a person's existence—from maternity ward to burial site." Black residents of Savannah were excluded from "the best that society offered—the best libraries, the best schools, the best parks." Black parents trained their children from infancy in all the minutiae of segregated life; they were expected to run this gauntlet of do's and don'ts daily, without error, on pain of social humiliation or worse. His grandfather warned Clarence at an early age not to "look a white woman in the eye." Blacks could not swim in most public pools or walk across certain parks. There were "separate drinking fountains, riding at the back of the bus, rudeness in the stores. These things were as certain a part of life as the Savannah heat and humidity." There were exactly one black bus driver and one black policeman in the city. No blacks worked as clerks in the department stores downtown. If a department store served black customers, whites were free to cut in front of them in line. In some shops, blacks who tried on clothes or shoes were required to purchase them whether or not they fit.

"It was 'nigger' this and 'nigger' that," said W. W. Law, who at the time headed the Savannah chapter of the National Association for the Advancement of Colored People (NAACP). Even many houses of worship barred blacks, so that, in Law's words, "the Sabbath became a day of shame for the churches that closed their doors to the Negroes." The Savannah newspaper did not publish the scores from the sporting events of black schools. When a black citizen of Savannah died, the obituary ran in a separate section of the paper reserved for "Colored Deaths." Whites were interred in Laurel Grove North Cemetery, while blacks were buried in Laurel Grove South.

Wanda Lloyd, another black who grew up in Savannah in the same era, recalled:

> I come from a generation of black youths who never read a best seller because we didn't get them in our segregated library; who never saw a first-run movie because we weren't permitted as patrons in the whites-only movie houses. We lived just a few miles from the Atlantic, but I didn't see the Georgia coast until I was an adult. We weren't allowed on the beach.

This "most brutal experience," Clarence said, had a "devastating impact . . . on the lives of the people I knew and loved." Two incidents of discrimination that were seared deeply into his memory involved his beloved grandfather. One time, when the family was driving from Savannah to the farm in Liberty County, Daddy stopped for gasoline. He asked the attendant if Aunt Tina could use the restroom. The attendant said that she could not, as there was no "colored" restroom. Daddy "loudly and forcefully" told the attendant that if his wife could not use the restroom, he would not use their gas. He drove off and eventually pulled into a gas station that had a "colored" restroom.

On another occasion, this time on the farm, a white woman drove up to the house in a big Buick Electra. Working out in the fields, Daddy saw the car approaching as it churned up dust from the dirt road. He walked over to greet her. Meeting him, she called him "boy." Daddy looked around and saw his two grandsons had heard the slur. Clarence later remembered how the proud man had seethed, and marveled at "what must it have taken for him not only to take the insult but the stares from his kids seeing him being called a boy."

Daddy struck back with the means at his disposal. He joined the Savannah NAACP and donated fuel oil to the group. During the civil rights movement, he put his property up to bail the protesters out when protests occurred in Savannah. Though his grandparents "hated no one and were polite to whites," Clarence later said, "their attitude was not to rely on them for anything—and certainly not to put ourselves at their mercy."

Beginning in the late 1950s, civil rights advocates began to organize protests and resistance in Savannah. Mass meetings were held weekly on Sunday afternoons. The meeting site rotated among various black churches: the large hall in the First African Baptist Church downtown was a frequent gathering place; the Second Baptist and Bryan Baptist Churches also offered shelter to the movement. In addition, the Catholic Church provided succor. Thomas McDonough, the bishop of Savannah, worked with the city's political and business leaders to encourage peaceful desegregation (McDonough was instrumental in securing the employment of the one black policeman in the 1950s). He also cajoled the parishes to fully desegregate their schools. On May 1, 1960, more than 2,500 people of diverse denominations entered the St. Piux X High School auditorium for the weekly Sunday meeting to plan civil rights protests in the city.

By then, Savannah was in the throes of a massive campaign to get rid of Jim Crow. In June 1961, downtown merchants gave in to demands for desegregating the lunch counters. However, the city's power structure—known informally as the "House of Lords"—held the line on segregation in other public accommodations, such as hotels, theaters and restaurants. Hosea Williams, a chemist who was vice president under W. W. Law at the NAACP, decided that things should move faster and formed the Savannah chapter of the SCLC. He organized thousands for a downtown march in the summer of 1963 to demand full desegregation, and was sentenced to sixty-five days in jail for his troubles. As the summer wore on, riots flared up; bricks were thrown; the Sears, Roebuck and the Firestone stores were burned. Finally, Savannah's business elite capitulated. In January 1964, King came to the city to celebrate the relatively hasty downfall of Jim Crow there. Eight months later, while seven-eighths of Southern public accommodations remained segregated, King declared Savannah the most desegregated city in the South.

Daddy supported these protests with his money and membership, but left it at that; he was no street-walking radical. Perhaps he believed that he could do more good for the cause by bankrolling it than by being arrested and depriving his household of its breadwinner. He had a good deal to lose from collaborating with the movement at all.

In November 1961, Clarence took the entrance exam for St. Piux X High School. When he learned he had finished sixth on the exam, the thirteen-year-old concluded, rightly, that he "had done quite well compared to the other students." But his eighth-grade teacher, Mother Virgilius Reidy, was less impressed. "You're just lazy," she told him after hearing the results. "You're just wasting all your God-given ability."

For some reason, this largely *pro forma* kick-in-the-pants made an extraordinary impression on Clarence. Never again would he be content with second place.

When he enrolled at St. Pius X, trading his navy blue uniform for the standard gray slacks, burgundy jacket, and tie of his new school, Clarence redoubled his efforts to excel. Sister Mary Genevieve was his homeroom teacher in room 9A during his freshman year; Sister Mary Thaddeus taught him in tenth grade. Most memorable of all the faculty was Father Timothy Dwyer, "who called everyone 'curly.'"

Clarence played basketball for the St. Pius team. He joked of entering high school as a "formidable physical specimen" of five feet, two inches, and ninety-eight pounds. Orion Douglass, a classmate, remembered dryly that he played for the school's team, the Crusaders, "without distinction."

Daddy had joined the Catholic Church out of gratitude for helping him learn to read. Clarence, in like spirit, decided to discharge his debts to his grandfather and his church simultaneously by becoming a priest. He broached the subject of the priesthood with his family and friends knowing he was in for some ribbing. When visiting Pin Point, Clarence told his cousin, Abe Famble, in a very serious tone of voice, "I think I'm going into the priesthood."

"Man, you're gonna be a priest? All this life out here in this world and you're gonna be a priest?"

"Yeah," Clarence replied, "I think that's what I want."

"Well, good luck to you then," Famble chuckled. "That's your bag. I'm gonna have fun."

Lester Johnson, a friend and fellow black parochial student, responded with equal candor when he heard the news: "I might be able to take all the whites, but what about having a life with no girls? Now, that's a serious problem."

"That may be a disadvantage," Clarence told Johnson, "but there are a couple of big advantages. It's a good education and it's free."

Clarence left St. Pius in 1964 for the St. John Vianney Minor Seminary. In the autumn of 1964, along with Richard Chisholm, another black teenager, he knelt at the minor seminary's altar as part of the investiture ceremony. A diocesan publication noted that "the determined gait of Clarence Thomas ha[d] lost nothing of its buoyancy." Father Kevin Boland, a priest at the minor seminary, gave the homily, emphasizing in his native Irish lilt the need for priests in the diocese and the glories of being called to the vocation. As the sign of the cross was made for the final time, the Anderson trinity of work, education and faith seemed to be fusing perfectly in the young black man from Pin Point with the long, purposeful stride.

CHAPTER FIVE

Black Spot on the White Horse

St. John Vianney Minor Seminary, which Clarence Thomas's friends unkindly dubbed "the cemetery," was located on the Isle of Hope. The optimistic name is a misnomer. Like many of the small fingers of the Georgia coast projecting into the Atlantic, the Isle of Hope is really an isthmus that the tides occasionally separate from the mainland. The seminary on this pocket of pine-topped coastline was only a few miles down Skidaway Road from Pin Point.

The Benedictines had established a presence in the area in 1877, erecting a monastery and beginning to serve the needs of newly emancipated blacks along the Atlantic seaboard. Their efforts complemented those of the Franciscan Sisters, who began their mission in Savannah a year later. In the 1950s, the Diocese of Savannah selected the Isle of Hope as the site for a new high-school, or minor, seminary. Throughout the United States, the Catholic Church was embracing the notion that young men considering the priesthood should be segregated during the high-school years into their own little universe, a minor seminary fairly close to home. On the Isle of Hope, a collection of cottages that had housed displaced persons after World War II beckoned for conversion. The minor seminary that blossomed from this refurbishing was named after St. John Vianney, a nineteenth-century French priest who, after canonization, became the patron saint of priests engaged in parish work.

St. John's, as its residents called it, opened its doors to these youngest seminarians in September 1959. The stated "Philosophy of Education" of the institution limned the values that undergirded the course of studies:

> Man is made to the image and likeness of God. God has endowed man with a certain nature. The development of this nature belongs to the

process of education.... This program of education is based on the fundamental fact that truth is one, that it is perpetual, and that it never changes.

Thomas began his studies at St. John's in September 1964 as the only black in his class and one of two in the school. (A year later, Richard Chisholm, the other black seminarian, dropped out.) Merely departing from his home and family entailed an emotional vertigo. Magnifying this upheaval was the fact that this was, as Thomas recalled, his "first opportunity to associate with white people" other than the Franciscan nuns. "It probably was a culture shock," said Betty Purdy, a secretary at the seminary. Some of the white students were from the rural patches of south Georgia and had never attended school with blacks. Kevin Boland, a priest and teacher at St. John's who later became bishop of Savannah, described Thomas as a "real trailblazer" for toughing it out in this lonely environment.

The seminarians resided in a large, barracks-type common room whose cinderblock construction was reminiscent of the homes Daddy had built. The students slept in double bunk beds; their bedspreads were blankets of thin, plaid wool. Each resident had a small dresser for his belongings. Ping-pong and pool tables, a concession to leisure, took up some space on the checkered linoleum floor. The large windows looked out onto thick woods.

Morning prayers and meditation began at 6:20, and Mass at 6:40. After breakfast, the students performed domestic chores—dusting, cleaning, taking out the trash, washing dishes. Classes began at 8:30. The students broke at 12:20 for ten minutes of "recreation," ten minutes to visit the Blessed Sacrament, and then lunch. Classes ended at 3:30. Recreation followed, including what the seminary called "league sports" between little squads of seminarians. After study hall, the rosary, supper, and a final, short recreation period, the pupils studied until night prayer and spiritual reading at 8:50. Lights were out at 9:30. Classes were held six days a week.

The clergy also regulated the seminarians' spare time. Newspapers and magazines were censored. Television could be watched only at certain times. On Sunday afternoons, the young men were, in the words of one faculty member, "free within reason to walk around the grounds." They could not, however, leave the property except on Thursday afternoons. Before dismissing the students for vacation, the priests would enjoin them to avoid "mixed company," as women were called.

Coats and ties were the required, standard attire. Thomas's wardrobe was more limited and dowdier than that of his better-off white classmates. Some of his pants were too short; one loud plaid sports coat made a regular appearance.

Thomas benefited from a demanding core curriculum: three years of religion, Latin, English, music and physical education. There was a miscellany of other subjects as well—courses in geometry, algebra, physics, art, German, chemistry. The academic rigors, he said, "initially seemed crushing." Three years of Latin were required (as a result, Thomas would have to repeat the tenth grade). Thomas said later, "Latin was a demon to be subdued and Latin class—well, that was a daily confirmation hearing."

In his pedestrian wooden desk with the requisite pencil-holder slot at the top, facing the blackboard and crucifix above it, Thomas sat in class—quietly. His teachers remembered him as a young man of few words, at least in the classroom, and considered his silence somewhat peculiar.

When he transferred to St. John's, Thomas was, he later admitted, "self-conscious." He was so mindful of his Geechee accent that he would sometimes correct himself mid-sentence. As a result, he subsequently said, "I just developed a habit of listening." When called upon in class, his teachers noted, Thomas was prepared and sharp. He also became less tightlipped with time. Still, his marks for leadership were the lowest he received for any category of personal conduct while at St. John's. His speechlessness became as much a pattern in his academic performance as high grades. When thrust into a new and challenging environment, Thomas took the route of least peril: silence.

Racial tensions probably contributed to this reticence. "Each day I had to prove not only my equality but the equality of all blacks," Thomas said. One somewhat murky incident at the beginning of his tenure set the tone for his experience:

> I remember being called in the first report period—we got report cards every six weeks—and all but told that I was inherently inferior. Therefore, I had to work harder. I knew that it was a way of downgrading me, but in fact it spurred me on. I did not think anybody should get away with calling me "inherently inferior." So I performed very well.

He quickly earned a reputation for exemplary study habits. Father Coleman remarked to Sister Mary Virgilius, who was monitoring her former student's progress, "Clarence knows how to study." Thomas supplemented his formal studies with often-furtive leisure reading. Several times, he was caught and admonished for reading in the bathroom after the lights-out curfew. He then pestered his mother for a flashlight during a visit home. After she supplied him with one, Thomas propped it on his knee under his blanket so that he could continue reading in the dark.

It was in sports—the daily recreation periods—that Thomas most stood out. He had inherited a powerful, naturally muscular build from his father. He dominated in all the sports offered by the school: football, basketball, baseball and track. Although only five feet, nine inches tall, Thomas could dunk a basketball. The seminary held a multi-day athletic competition between the four classes of students. When the students posed for a group photo at the end of one such contest, Thomas had more blue ribbons pinned to his chest than any other seminarian.

Thomas also wrote for the student newspaper, the *Pioneer*, and eventually became co-editor. His first article, published in the September-October 1966 issue (and apparently the first thing he ever published), was entitled "A Freshman's Thoughts." It was an account of the investiture of the newest class of seminarians and a ceremony preceding it. The article cited Robert Frost's poem "The Road Less Traveled," the first of many occasions in Thomas's life when he would fondly invoke Frost's famous ode to loners. The article also ended with a sentence that displayed some panache: "The entire chain of events was concluded in a fashion befitting it—Benediction."

Thomas's offering in the next issue was more thoughtful. It was his first written analysis of race relations in America, the subject that would become his burning professional passion. It was written against the backdrop of a civil rights movement jolted by the emergence of Stokely Carmichael's call for Black Power (and the exclusion of whites from the Student Nonviolent Coordinating Committee) and Huey Newton's Black Panther Party. These developments made Thomas's analysis of recent events in the struggle for equality—in a newspaper for an all-white school—a revelation. The essay was entitled "It's About Time":

Is it disastrous or auspicious? Well, looking back, I notice that the violence and hatred which developed from the acquisition of equality of all races seem to indicate that a disaster has gripped our country. Just to keep the records straight, I don't believe that one race is more to blame than the other. There are times when one ethnic group provokes the other until there is a violent eruption of anger and, consequently, more melees, picketing, and rioting.

But why can't black and white live in harmony? This is quite a question. I am sure that some Stokely Carmichael's [*sic*] would quite readily assert that if there were fewer George Wallace's, race [*sic*] could live together with no friction, while the George Wallace's would, of course, pay the same compliment to their accusers. These conclusions do not offer a solution, but on the contrary, make matters worse.

I think races would fare better if extremists would crawl back into their holes, and let the people, whom this will really affect, do just a little thinking for themselves, rather than follow the Judas goats of society into the slaughter pens of destruction. True, the intellectuals must start the ball rolling, but ignorance in the intelligentia [*sic*] is not unheard of.

It's about time for the average American to rise from his easy chair and do what he really and truly believes God demands of him—time to peel off the veil of hate and contempt, and don the cloak of love (black for white and white for black).

In addition to showing a distinctive language of self-expression, the article was notable in several respects. The eighteen-year-old Thomas mentioned for the first time a mistrust of intellectuals as a class. The piece also demonstrated a talent of sorts for telling both sides what they wanted to hear. In this vein, the "Judas goats of society" reference was an intriguing metaphor in both phrasing and calculated ambiguity. Thomas wanted to get along with his classmates and to make his way in the world, but he was not willing to disavow the rightful grievances of his race. His solution was to blame the problems on "extremists" and to exhort all to practice love—an approach at once Christian and, to some degree, intellectually evasive.

Drama and community outreach were two of Thomas's other extracurricular pursuits. Thomas was a member of the St. John Bosco Players, the school's theatrical troupe. He assisted backstage with production and also performed in some of the plays. In the Christmas passion play, he portrayed Simon of Cyrene, the African who helped Christ carry the cross to Calvary. He was the obvious choice for such a role, which may have made the selection uncomfortable for him.

Thomas was also an assumed and willing participant in Project Sandfly. Every Wednesday afternoon, six seminarians traveled to a nearby black community, Sandfly, a coastal hamlet very similar to Pin Point. A program offered by the seminary in imitation of Head Start, Project Sandfly provided supplementary education for children of the town through seventh grade. Thomas and classmate Randy Barnes taught the sixth and seventh graders.

On Thursday afternoons, Daddy picked up Thomas and took him back home to visit his family. Although such trips were a welcome break from the school routine, these afternoons often amounted to impressments into service for Anderson Fuel Company. Thomas frequently worked in his grandfather's coal yard or engaged in other helpful pursuits; idle time was still discouraged. Daddy drove Thomas back to the school grounds in the evening.

During vacations and the summer months, Thomas enjoyed riding in his cousin Isaac Martin's red 1963 Ford Coupe. Together, they would venture out to the movies or the beach, which had been desegregated. Such reunions always offered opportunities for teasing Thomas about the course he had chosen. His friends were merciless: "Man, what are you hanging around that 'cemetery' for?" "Don't you like girls?" "You must be funny." "You ain't got no clothes, nothing."

His concentration on his studies paid off. Through all three years at St. John's, Thomas maintained an A average (92 on a scale of 100). He was strong in all courses. His lowest grade was 87 in history and in algebra during his sophomore and junior years; his highest, in senior chemistry, was 96. In his senior year, he earned straight A's. Thomas thrived in competition, and he was peaking at the right time.

To the right of Clarence Thomas's senior picture, a strikingly handsome photograph of the young man, were several arcane references to inoffensive inside jokes, suggesting the students accepted him as a peer. There was the phrase "Mmwuaahaahaa," evidently referring to his booming, infectious laugh. Other, more scrutable comments were "Bob Hayes' idol" (Hayes, the great track star and football player of the day, was one of Thomas's heroes); "blew that test, only a 98" (in fact, it was the highest score he ever received on an exam at St. John's); and "likes to argue."

Still, Thomas felt isolated at St. John's. His years there, he said, were "difficult and lonely." After a while, he accepted the "loneliness that came with being 'the integrator,' the first and the only." Even so, during his time on the Isle of Hope, he considered himself a "stray dog." The photographs from *The Grail*, the school yearbook, would bear this out. One shows him sitting alone, as business editor of *The Grail*; it was the only picture during his three years at the school for which Thomas smiled broadly.

His usual mask of grim resolve was Thomas's answer to an environment he perceived as hostile. He felt himself being peppered regularly with racial slights and pettiness. For the first time in his young life, Thomas believed, "my inherent equality was directly challenged." Later on he explained:

> Growing up, we knew it [prejudice] was there all along. But we never had to come face to face with it 24 hours a day. You didn't have to meet it in the shower. You didn't have to meet it in the bathroom. You didn't have to meet it in the classroom. You didn't have to meet it walking down the street. You didn't have to meet it on the ballfield. When I went to the seminary, it was the first time in my 16 years that I had to face this daily.

Some of the insults were relatively benign. One classmate, Mark Everson, said Thomas was teased about his shoes, which he said were "more acceptable in a black school." At mealtime, Thomas's fellow pupils teased him by acting as if he had a "contagious disease." Thomas also bristled at a comment written in his yearbook in 1965: "After maintaining close to an A average and establishing myself as the best athlete in the school, a white student wrote in my yearbook: 'Keep on trying Clarence, one day you will be as good as us.'" On at least one occasion, when the lights went out at 9:30, a fellow student yelled out, "Smile, Clarence so we can see you." Thomas said later, "The statement wasn't the bad part, it was no one saying, 'Shut up.'"

The jibes and mistreatment escalated as Thomas surpassed the other students in schoolwork and athletics. "Many of my classmates would stop talking to me," he said. "Some would walk on the other side of the street to avoid me. The students temporarily discontinued awards, like Athlete of the Year, that I was likely to win." Thomas received a statue of Saint Jude as a trophy for winning the annual Latin bee, and placed it on his bureau in the open dormitory room where the seminarians slept. He recalled:

> A few days later, I looked over and saw the head was broken off, lying there right next to the body on my bureau, where I'd be sure to see it. I glued it back on. After another few days, it happened again. So I got more glue—put it on real thick—and fixed it again. Whoever was breaking it must have gotten the message: I'd keep gluing it forever if I needed to.

As this brash, strong-willed young black man outperformed his white classmates, jealousy combined with prejudice to create an intimidating and hostile environment. The harder Thomas tried, the more he outdistanced his peers—and the more he stirred up these toxic passions.

This disgruntlement with Thomas flared up starkly one evening on the basketball court. The students who did not have kitchen duty typically played basketball after supper. The unwritten code was that the students would shoot baskets to choose up sides; the person who made the first basket could pick the members of his team. One spring evening, Thomas and six other classmates assembled on the court. Thomas made his first shot. The other six walked to the other end of the court and huddled in conversation. They opted to play three on three instead, excluding Thomas from the game. "That walk back from the basketball court into the seminary was my loneliest walk," he later remembered.

Thomas responded by withdrawing further from his classmates. On those Thursday afternoons when his grandfather did not come by, Thomas stayed behind at the seminary instead. His public reason was that the theaters were still segregated, and eating at a restaurant with whites would have made everybody uncomfortable. More likely, he had come to feel that he just did not fit in. As he explained later, "I was referred to, not too politely, as the black spot on the white horse."

The most menacing act of bigotry directed at Thomas occurred in the classroom. One student slipped Thomas a folded note. On the outside a message was written: "I like Martin Luther King." Inside, the note said: "Dead." This sanguinary sentiment was an eerie premonition of an event that, a few years later, would end King's life and change Thomas's life fundamentally.

Thomas did not speak with others about his ordeal at the school, although he certainly had numerous opportunities to do so. His proud grandfather took him to the local NAACP meetings at 4 P.M. on Sundays to update the gathering on the progress in his education. When W. W. Law called upon him to speak, Thomas felt "scared to death." But he also remembered "feeling the pride they showed for me as I was coerced into telling them how well I was doing academically." Law would "publicly and effusively encourage me to redouble my efforts in school, even while applauding me for doing well." Elderly folks in the audience shouted words of encouragement. "Keep it up, boy, keep it up," they exclaimed. "Things are going to work out. The Lord will help you."

Years later, former students and teachers at St. John Vianney did not recall many of the slights that Thomas had logged mentally with great care, and which he would mention freely when interviewed about his days in the seminary. "I don't remember any problem or hearing anything racially in the one year we overlapped," said John Lyons, one of the few students who went on to become a priest. "... To my knowledge, he was well accepted, well liked by everyone there." Mark Everson, editor in chief of *The Grail,* allowed, "Some of the students were openly racist. Most of us were just insensitive." Father Fitzpatrick insisted, "It was a small school, and if something like that was going on, we would have known about it." Father Boland observed that the students spoke to spiritual directors weekly, so Thomas could have confided in him or his pastor at St. Benedict's.

That the instructors at St. John's were unaware of their students' rude antics is surprising only to those who have never attended school. It was not hard-core bigotry that Thomas encountered, but the comparatively mild taunting that was the echo of the South's surrender. Yet it was enough to overwhelm a young man cultivating an immense pride and concern for reputation.

In response to his ill-treatment, the teenage Thomas recoiled, stewed and rebelled. "I decided then and there," he said, "at the ripe old age of sixteen, that it was better to be respected than liked." Self-education through reading had long been his trusted portal to freedom. "Instead of just languishing in the classics or continuing to have a steady diet of philosophers, Catiline or Cicero, I got into some of the black writers in an effort to understand precisely what was going on. And the more I read, the angrier I got."

When asked two decades later which author had most influenced him, Thomas named Richard Wright as "number one, *numero uno*. Both *Native Son* and *Black Boy* really woke me up." The impressionable young man committed to memory a number of passages from Wright's work. *Native Son*, Wright's classic novel, tells the story of Bigger Thomas (a namesake antihero for the young seminarian), a black man who resorts to violence in response to racial oppression. *Black Boy*, Wright's autobiography, is an account of a life committed to such values, specifically through Wright's eventual turn to Marxism. The former book reinforced Thomas's wrath toward racism and his aversion to intellectuals; the latter deepened his race-based anger and stimulated his interest in writing. Both works extolled self-worship, racial bitterness, and hostility toward religion, notions that were at war with Thomas's planned profession.

As Thomas communed with Wright, the plight of blacks became an "all consuming interest" for him. He spent much of one summer in the newly desegregated Savannah Public Library reading accounts of lynchings from the prior century. "As I read, I seethed with anger and simmered with bitterness," he recalled. "I could feel myself falling prey to the sweet sounds of vindictiveness."

Robert Frost's poetry also affected Thomas and helped to offset Wright's anger. "Two roads diverged in the woods and I—I took the one less traveled by, and that has made all the difference": the words offered great solace to the brooding teenager. He explained that Frost's poem "helped me during my high school days as I fought to harness the anxieties of Richard Wright's Bigger Thomas; reconcile Christianity and segregation, and educate myself in a seminary which was all white—except for me."

But now Thomas was undergoing a full-fledged "crisis of faith" that would deepen as he entered full manhood. Wright and the bigotry of his classmates assailed his pride and inflamed his sense of injustice. Of his years at St. John's, he explained:

> It was there that I failed to understand why there could be segregated
> churches when my religious values and the teachings of the Catholic
> Church stated that all of us were created equal and were equal in the
> eyes of God. And, we were all his children. I could not understand why,
> when we attended white Catholic churches, we could only receive com-
> munion after the white communicants had done so. I could not under-
> stand why the Catholic Church would suffer and permit segregation
> in its schools, in its parishes and in its churches. I could not understand
> why the Church did not speak out against something so obviously
> immoral, wrong and in violation of our own religious beliefs.

Thomas's mounting frustration with the church tugged against his gratitude to his grandfather, who had made what Thomas later termed a
"tremendous financial sacrifice" in sponsoring his education at the seminary. Freedom beckoned, but how could he back out of the deal?

In his last year at St. John's, the faculty offered their sober judgments
about which of the young men should continue studying for the priesthood. They gathered quarterly in the faculty lounge (known among the
students as "the Kremlin," so off-limits was it) to discuss the seminarians' progress. Thomas was a standout who had excelled in almost everything he attempted. He was extraordinarily mature and well-mannered.
And, despite Richard Wright, he remained deeply spiritual, if less enam-
ored of organized religion.

Not surprisingly, the faculty voted to recommend him to the diocese as a candidate for the priesthood. Father Coleman also recommended Thomas to a college seminary, Immaculate Conception, a
Benedictine institution in remote northwestern Missouri. Presiding
over a small diocese, Bishop McDonough himself approved the letters
of petition and endorsed Thomas's candidacy. Immaculate Conception
accepted him, and, in the spring of 1967, he began to prepare mentally
for the journey. Thomas was the first in his family to graduate from
high school.

Thomas recognized later, after the bitterness had subsided, that his
experience at St. John Vianney had its rewards. The years on the Isle
of Hope "helped me to learn to live with white people.... I understood
that it was not easy to walk into a dorm room and feel the antagonism
of the other seminarians. And it instilled confidence in me." St. John's
would close its doors forever the following year, as the Catholic Church
abandoned its experiment with minor seminaries. Thomas would carry

with him a solid high-school education, a mounting wrath toward racism, and a growing feeling that by signing up for the priesthood, he had made an enormous mistake.

CHAPTER SIX

Dreams Denied

"Left my home in Georgia, headed for the Frisco Bay ..." Thomas was not going all the way to the West Coast, but Otis Redding's new hit song, "Sittin' on the Dock of the Bay," understandably struck a chord with him as he left the Peach State for the cornfields of Missouri in August 1967. After emotional goodbyes to family and friends, he climbed aboard the Nancy Hank, the train that ran between Savannah and Atlanta. From Atlanta, he took his first airplane flight to Kansas City.

The two-hour drive north from Kansas City to Immaculate Conception Seminary led Thomas over the gently undulating farmlands of northwest Missouri. In the mid-nineteenth century, European immigrants, mostly Irish and German, began to pour into the area and plant corn in its unusually fertile soil. Swiss priests were not far behind the immigrants. They journeyed from the Swiss Abbey of Engelberg to establish a Benedictine presence in the area and minister to the local Catholic diaspora. They founded a little town, Conception, and erected a monastery. In 1886, the monks established Conception Seminary College at the burgeoning site. Five years later, a consortium of farmers, contractors and monks finished construction of a gorgeous church of similar red-brick exterior. In 1941, Pope Pius XII designated the church a minor basilica.

Like all other Benedictines, the clergy cloistered at Conception Abbey followed the ancient Rule of St. Benedict, who called his followers to a life of *ora et labora*, "prayer and work."

Thomas's ride to tiny Conception that Sunday in August led him past man-height stalks of corn, occasional farmhouses, and finally to the Basilica of the Immaculate Conception, which, like the rest of the abbey, was built on a low hill. It was as if Divine Hands had lifted up a nineteenth-century brick Catholic church, of the style normally found in large Eastern cities, and plunked it down in the middle of a pasture.

The building was laid out to appear from the sky as a giant red cross. Inside the structure were twenty-two Beuronese murals depicting the lives of Saints Mary, Benedict and Scholastica, painted by the founding monks as they stood on wooden scaffolding. Above the murals was a high ceiling of dark green vaults with a pattern of gold crosses. Adorning the apse was a large painting of Mary surrounded by a mandorla, twelve stars, and a moon entwined with a snake; the picture represented her triumph over Satan. Monastic choir stalls made of oak were situated between parishioners and the altar. In these seats of honor and worship, the monks gathered six times a day for prayer.

Upon his arrival, Thomas reported to St. Benedict Hall, the dormitory that housed the freshmen. It was a humble structure whose plain façade of red and black bricks was interrupted only by a front door and intermittent dual storm windows. The accommodations were similarly unpretentious. Thomas's room offered two of everything, as if Noah had done the interior designing: two twin beds, hardback wooden chairs, built-in desks with Formica tops and white bookshelves, closets with varnished wooden shelves. A blown-particle ceiling with occasional shiny speckles, a communal bathroom, and a crucifix on the wall were some of the few features that the roommates would have in common.

Jim Kopp was unpacking when Thomas entered their room. They immediately exchanged greetings and, as Kopp recalled, started "trading bios on each other." Kopp was one of about a dozen students who had graduated from St. John's Minor Seminary in Kansas City. Later in the day, after initial conversation with Thomas, Kopp would go down the hall to check in with other members of the Kansas City contingent. One was Tom O'Brien, who would be Thomas's best friend at Conception. Although O'Brien, like Kopp, had worked alongside blacks and could cite some other, limited interracial experience, he and his comrades were, in his words, "virgins in terms of diversity." As Kopp and his friends talked of their new abode, O'Brien recalled, "the issue was, Oh my gosh, we have a black guy in our class."

Thomas had learned survival techniques back on the Isle of Hope; here, instead of withdrawing from the alien surroundings and snapping at his gawking colleagues, he embraced them. "He was just so funny,"

O'Brien said of his first impressions of Thomas. "There just seemed to be so much energy coming from the guy." O'Brien saw that unlike most young men of his age, Thomas already was "pretty at ease with himself." He was also "mature—past a lot of the insecurities" that the others still were feeling. The thicker skin he had grown at St. John Vianney served him well during this time of adjustment. By the time the freshmen all gathered that first evening for orientation, Thomas was already making friends.

There were over four hundred students at the seminary. Candidates for the priesthood were required to complete eight years of formal education—four years of undergraduate study and four of theology. There were sixty-two students in the freshman class, 60 percent of them graduates of minor seminaries, the new "feeder schools" for collegiate seminaries. The men of the freshmen class came from as far away as Central America. Three were black. One of these, Dorick Wright, graduated from the seminary and eventually became a monsignor in his native Belize. There was also one distinctive gang known as "the Georgia boys"—Thomas and six of his classmates from Savannah.

"The aim of Immaculate Conception Seminary," declared the seminary bulletin, "is to educate men to be cultured Christian gentlemen, who as priests will serve the Church of today spiritually, intellectually, and socially in a Christ-like manner." This broad training entailed 16 to 18 hours of demanding classes per semester. Thomas studied American history, English, French, Latin, music, natural science (physics and biology), and religion ("Introduction to Christian Life"). It was the most competitive academic environment he had yet faced.

"Clarence was a very smart individual," Kopp said of his first-semester roommate. "Classes where I was an average student, Clarence was above average." And Thomas was not outshining mere dolts. As O'Brien observed, "The books were important to all of us. Of the eleven guys we took up there [from Kansas City], there were a ton of strong students. . . . There was a lot of competition about grades."

Thomas was especially strong in English, French and philosophy. Particularly in philosophy, O'Brien remarked, "you could see how bright he was. He was able to make the move from A to B to C to D." In this coursework, Thomas was first exposed to St. Thomas Aquinas, the greatest Catholic philosopher, who would influence Thomas through his notion of natural law. Reconciling the Judeo-Christian tradition and Aristotle, Aquinas held that mankind is subject to natural, unchanging laws decreed by God. Humans violate these divine rules at the risk of unhappiness on earth and perdition hereafter. Aquinas and the natural law tradition began to put intellectual muscle on the beliefs Clarence Thomas had absorbed from his grandfather.

Theological injunctions against gambling did not dissuade Thomas and O'Brien from having a standing $1 bet each semester as to who would receive the better grades. "He won a buck and I won a buck," O'Brien recalled. "That was big money for us." O'Brien said Thomas was in the top third of their class.

Although well prepared, Thomas remained quiet in the classroom, answering questions if called upon but rarely volunteering information or opinions. Kopp said that while he "wasn't outgoing," he was sufficiently assertive that "his viewpoints would always be known." Benedict Neenan, another classmate, reflected, "He was pretty quiet, except when he laughed. And he laughed easily."

Indeed, it is a tribute to Thomas's sociability that his laugh, not his race, became his most noted characteristic. "Everybody had their signature," Kopp recalled of his classmates. For one seminarian, it was his habit of mooching half of a cookie sent from home, then returning some time later and asking for the other half as well. For Thomas, it was his laugh. For this eruption of mirth, he seemed to summon his entire, considerable energy and vitality. He would often lean back, his body convulsing, his lips receding to reveal almost all of his teeth and a sizable crescent of gums. Then came the artillery: a series of booming emissions that sounded like a WAA-WAA-WAA! One person compared the effect to a woofer pounding in a stereo speaker.

The social tempests spinning across the nation in the late 1960s did not pass over this pastoral corner of the Midwest. As the academic year unfolded, the freshman seminarians learned through the media how fundamentally their society was being challenged and remade. In early 1968, the Tet Offensive in Vietnam invigorated college antiwar protests and helped bring to an end President Lyndon Johnson's ambitions for a second full term. Then came what for a time looked like a possible revolution in the streets as the war dragged on. Television and radio beamed into Conception, Missouri, images and sounds of a society discarding settled norms and customs and experimenting with possible replacements.

Some of the most profound upheaval was occurring within the Catholic Church itself. The Second Vatican Council, or Vatican II, had convened for the last time in 1965. The reforms it inaugurated were still being implemented throughout the church when Thomas arrived at Conception. The Benedictine priests and monks were some of Vatican II's most ardent proponents. Their order had figured prominently in the liturgical reform movement, especially in Europe, over the prior century. Now that Rome finally had blessed their efforts, the clergy of Conception joyfully set about exploring the limits of this new liberty.

Benedict Neenan, a classmate of Thomas's and subsequently president and rector of Conception Seminary, described Conception at the time as a "liturgically innovative place" that embraced the "progressive" ideas emanating from the Holy See. But Neenan acknowledged that this revamping of liturgy and accompanying doctrine was "very unsettling for a seminarian." During this period, the Catholic liturgy changed from Latin to vernacular. The priest no longer looked at the altar affixed to the back wall of the church; now he turned and faced the people. The laity became far more involved in the Mass and church services. The notion of the church as a hierarchical entity gave way to a sense that, in Neenan's words, "we are all the church."

One of the more tangible signs of this revolution was the change in the dress code at Conception. The year before Thomas arrived, the graduate students, or theologians, were required to wear a cassock except when working or involved in recreation. Beginning in the 1967–68 school year, suit and tie were acceptable. The cassock—that basic uniform of the priest—became exceptional and, by implication, something of a curiosity.

Conception also carried out Vatican II's Decree on Priestly Training. This decree encouraged seminaries to develop those qualities that "especially contribute to dialogue with men." Conception, accordingly, initiated a Contemporary Man Lecture Series. In March 1967, Michael Novak delivered a lecture representative of this approach on the unthreatening topic "The Church in the Modern World." The following year, the topics of the lecture series had evolved into one comparable to a college speakers' program at a liberal arts college. These talks addressed such subjects as "A Contemporary Understanding of the Latin American Situation"; "Sex Education" and "Sex before Marriage?" (punctuated by a sly question mark); and "Loneliness and the Fear of Self-Expression."

Mass began to sound less like a somber European affair filled with organ music and Gregorian chants and more like a bluegrass festival. The services conducted at Conception, in Neenan's words, relied on "a lot of guitars, a lot of folksy experiments with prayer, a lot of banners. A lot of it was insipid but we thought it was great because it was new." Gregorian chanting was going the way of the cassock: "There wasn't a lot of love for it." Kopp recalled, "We started having smaller liturgy services where we didn't worry about clothing, the vestments the priests would wear. People would talk about their lives. . . . We were experimenting."

But the inventive Benedictines of Conception were simultaneously witnessing, and by some accounts contributing to, a threat to their own *raison d'être*. Paradoxically, just as the church was granting its seminarians more freedom than ever, Neenan recalled that "the whole seminary system began to collapse." Of the sixty-two young men in Thomas's class, only three would be ordained as priests. "We were going through a very liberal time" in the church, Kopp recalled. The dual experience of Vatican II and the sixties' counterculture administered, in his words, a "double dose" of liberalism to the seminarians.

Thomas had arrived at Conception already uncertain about his future and his church. Such broad invitations to question the creed in which he had grown up further corroded his tenuous convictions. Still reeling from the prejudice he had experienced at St. John Vianney and Richard Wright's exhortation to atheism and debauchery, Thomas noted, his "faith slowly eroded during the first year of college seminary."

When it came to the "work" requirement of the "prayer and work" regime, Thomas needed little coaxing. Earning the $550 for tuition every semester was a constant preoccupation. Paying jobs at Conception were reserved for needy students. Thomas met that criterion easily, and secured a work/study job at the newly christened John F. Kennedy Recreation Center and swimming pool. Even so, O'Brien recalled, "Clarence was the brokest guy I ever knew."

Sports again became an outlet for him. He faithfully used the weightlifting equipment at the recreation center. Thomas possessed a classic hourglass physique of the Charles Atlas mold, with a twenty-eight-inch waist that led O'Brien to wonder "if he had room for a spleen in there." O'Brien noted, "When he had his shirt off playing basketball, the rest of us looked scrawny."

Conception had three playing fields for baseball, soccer and football. O'Brien judged that Thomas had "the best arm of anybody I ever saw." Once, O'Brien measured off the distance Thomas threw a football: seventy-five yards. Thomas's skills in basketball were less legendary. The seminary patched together a team that played the tiny colleges in the area. O'Brien, who went on to coach high-school basketball, said, "He may have been 'Couz' down in Georgia, but we didn't trust him out at point guard.... He was the worst shooter. For a little guy, a guard, he couldn't shoot to save his soul." Still, as at St. John Vianney, Thomas was the star athlete at the annual athletic competition, which was called May Day at Conception. Out of all the four hundred students there, he won the most combined individual and team points, making him the best athlete in the school.

Liberated from the stifling prejudice and resentments he had endured in south Georgia, Thomas flourished in his new relationships. Like the other freshmen, he spent his share of time in the TV room, playing practical jokes and munching popcorn with his colleagues. After years of alienation on the Isle of Hope, Thomas finally had found a predominantly white institution where he felt that he fit in. Neenan thought Thomas "consciously worked" at assimilating—and succeeded. Neenan compared him favorably with his own black roommate, who was quick to yell prejudice.

He was almost universally liked. Kopp could not recall anybody who did not accept him. O'Brien remembered one group, however, that never really socialized with Thomas: his fellow travelers from Savannah. "Clarence way overshadowed, in terms of his popularity, his academics, his athletic achievements ... the group that he came with," O'Brien recalled. And O'Brien noticed something else: "I saw some quiet resentment there."

During the fall semester, as one weekend of potential release approached, Thomas contrived an unusual way to earn some spending money. As he dined with his classmates, he announced, "I can eat anything."

Kopp, intrigued, dared him. "I can fill this glass with something you can't eat," he said.

"Five bucks," Thomas replied.

Kopp accepted.

Kopp and his compatriots gleefully dumped into a glass two entire pepper shakers, a salt shaker, milk, potatoes, gravy, green beans, and other morsels off their plates. Thomas drank the disgusting cocktail down to the last drop. "And," O'Brien remembered, "he came home with me that weekend. He had five bucks."

Tom O'Brien became Thomas's closest friend at Conception. Thomas rode home with him to Kansas City half a dozen times during the academic year. During one of these visits to Kansas City, O'Brien took Thomas out for a night on the town that proved unexpectedly memorable. They went to a hangout called Shakey's, a pizzeria across the state line in Kansas that was always packed on Saturday nights with eighteen- to twenty-year-olds seeking 3.2 percent beer. The two were fortunate enough to find a booth unoccupied. O'Brien ordered a pitcher of the treasured, low-proof brew.

It never arrived. They waited as the other teenage revelers around them were served. Finally, a manager walked over to their booth.

"We've had complaints about you guys being too loud and out of control," the manager told them. "You'll have to leave."

"That couldn't be us," O'Brien replied. "We just got here."

"I'm not going to argue about this," the manager said. "We've had complaints. You'll have to leave."

"No, it can't be us," O'Brien insisted. "I've been coming here for a long time—"

The manager cut him off. "If you want to argue, I'll call the police and you can spend the night in jail."

At that point, O'Brien finally caught on. He realized that he had never seen a black person at Shakey's before.

As O'Brien prepared to make an ugly situation even worse, Thomas grabbed his arm. "Forget it, man," he told him. "Let's go."

As they strode out to the car, words escaped O'Brien. He was amazed at how calmly Thomas had handled the situation. "I realized it was just another day in the office for him," he said.

The O'Brien household itself narrowly averted becoming a potentially worse scene. O'Brien and Thomas arrived one weekend to find that the living room had been cordoned off with tape. They could hear conversation in the room, but they honored the tape and went on to Tom's room. O'Brien later learned that Aunt Minnie, a family matriarch from Natchez, Mississippi, was in town. To prevent her from seeing Thomas and possibly sputtering racial epithets in shocked response, O'Brien's mother had isolated Aunt Minnie in the living room.

Even at Mass, Thomas was not safe from perceived racial affronts. One Sunday, a monsignor in the Kansas City diocese gave the homily. He was, in O'Brien's words, "pretty right-wing." The sermon meandered into an endorsement of George Wallace, the barely repentant arch-segregationist governor of Alabama then beginning his insurgent campaign for president. A year after the monsignor's sermon, Thomas was still smarting. In a letter to O'Brien, he said he could not respect "anyone who calls himself a Christian and a George Wallace supporter."

In March 1968, the kind monks running the seminary made what O'Brien called the "immense mistake" of inviting the girls' choir from St. Teresa's Catholic High School in Kansas City. Fifty girls descended on the all-male enclave to perform on Friday and Saturday nights. The hymns they offered up to God reminded their hosts that they were men.

The seminarian in charge of hospitality asked Thomas, O'Brien and their classmates if they would be willing to help with hospitality. O'Brien recalled that he and Thomas "volunteered pretty easily." On a beautiful, seventy-degree spring day, the two priests-in-training set their sights on a couple of especially lovely members of the choir. They met them and paired off in the student union that afternoon. Thomas's choice was a beautiful African-American girl named Monique. The foursome strolled around the pond—Lake Lockjaw, the residents unromantically called it. By the time Monique and her friend returned to Kansas City, Thomas and O'Brien had their telephone numbers. They had also arranged for a rendezvous the following weekend.

The next Saturday, after Thomas and O'Brien managed a ride to Kansas City, O'Brien called to check in with his date for the evening. He was crestfallen when he "got the 'Dear John' thing" over the phone. Thomas had more success when he called Monique. Even though his date had cancelled on him, O'Brien was determined to be a "team player." He told Thomas after receiving the bad news, "That doesn't keep me from being your chauffeur tonight."

Monique lived on the east side of Kansas City. To reach her residence, O'Brien had to drive through one of the city's tougher ghettoes. Thomas expressed some concern along the way about the neighborhood. O'Brien cracked, "What are you worried about? I'm the one who should be worried."

Soon the blighted area was behind them and a cul-de-sac of beautiful homes unexpectedly appeared. They found the address and drove up to the property. Thomas tried to talk O'Brien into coming to the front porch with him. No such luck; he was on his own.

Thomas walked gamely to the house and rang the doorbell. The door opened and a man appeared.

"What do you want?" asked Monique's father.

"I'm here to pick up Monique," Thomas declared.

Her father stared for a moment. "Wait here," he said. He slammed the door.

"Monique!" Her father's yelling could be heard from the street. An argument ensued.

The door opened, revealing Monique's father once again. He pointed to Thomas. "You, come in."

Thomas stepped inside without offering resistance.

More angry words flew from the father. Finally, the door opened again. Thomas sprang out of the house.

"Let's go, man," Thomas urged O'Brien after reaching the car.

O'Brien punched the accelerator and sped off.

It turned out that Monique had misled Thomas about something important—her age. Her father, a prosperous physician, informed Thomas that the young lady who looked and represented herself as eighteen was actually a high-school freshman.

Other members of the Conception Seminary freshman class met with more success in their courtships. Several of the Kansas City freshmen began dating members of the St. Teresa choir. At least two ended up marrying the girls they met that March afternoon.

Thomas corresponded with Monique for some time after their contretemps. Age and distance conspired to thwart any romance that might have blossomed. "I often wonder," O'Brien reflected many years later, "if the guy who threw him out of Shakey's, or Monique's dad, ever realized that the guy they did that to was Clarence Thomas."

———

A month later, the magical spring was shattered. On April 4, Thomas learned that Martin Luther King Jr. had been assassinated in Memphis.

In the hours thereafter, a nebulous incident in a seminary stairwell brought Thomas's ongoing "crisis of faith," in his words, "to a boiling point." He would recount the story many times, publicly and privately, over the years: "I was following a classmate up the stairs in our dormitory at Immaculate Conception Seminary. Someone yelled out that the Reverend Martin Luther King had been shot. His words, without seeing me, were 'That's good, I hope the s.o.b. dies.'"

This celebration of King's death, Thomas said, was the final straw in his losing struggle to retain his vocation. He explained: "It was this event that shattered my faith in my religion and my country.... This was a man of God, mortally stricken by an assassin's bullet, and one preparing for the priesthood had wished evil upon him." As a result: "The division between what the Church preached was moral and right and what the Church practiced, what I saw in the seminary, was too great a chasm. I left the Church. I could not understand how someone could love the God whom he had never seen and hate his neighbor whom he always saw."

He related a slightly different version of what happened that day to his old chemistry teacher at St. John Vianney, Sister Mary Carmine Ryan. Soon after he left Conception, Ryan said, "I recall his telling me that the day after Martin Luther King was assassinated in Memphis, he [Thomas] had walked into a common TV room in the seminary and heard one of the seminarians say, 'I'm glad they shot that nigger.' He said the other seminarians sitting in the room didn't seem to disagree with the remark. He left the room and soon after left the seminary."

When Thomas's classmates heard of this incident more than two decades later, the common reaction was incredulity. "Most of my class-mates here were baffled," said Benedict Neenan. "With blacks in our class and our school, I think it would've been considered very unusual and very wrong. And I can't imagine anyone saying that to Clarence." He noted that many students and alumni went to Kansas City to march for civil rights, and Selma before that. "If that were ever said publicly, a lot of people would've jumped on him," he insisted. For that matter, "Clarence could've beaten the pud out of any of them. I wouldn't have said anything like that in front of Clarence Thomas in those days."

Thomas did not mention the incident to anybody at the time. He never told Jim Kopp, his roommate during his freshman year, to whom he remained close. Nor did he confide in his best friend at the semi-nary, Tom O'Brien. O'Brien, in fact, was with Thomas when they learned of the assassination. They ran together downstairs to the common room in St. Benedict Hall to watch televised news of the assassination. "I was sitting with him then.... I think I would've noticed the n-word." He also did not recall hearing the "s.o.b." remark. (On the other hand, the event may have taken place later, when Thomas was alone, as some-body announced the news to passersby in the stairwell.)

"I wonder if that's what really jolted him from that career course," observed Neenan decades later, after having the benefit of years of expe-rience in running the seminary himself. "Sometimes, if people are in a seminarian course and want to leave, they latch onto something that gives them permission to leave." Such "permission" is a strong, psycho-logically acceptable excuse for releasing the seminarian from his career track. Besides, Neenan added, "the likelihood of Clarence becoming a priest under any circumstances was very slim at that time." The class before Thomas's yielded 12 to 15 ordained priests; the 62 in his class offered only 3. Thomas's "decision to leave the seminary was very typ-ical," Neenan said.

Sister Ryan agreed. "Actually," she observed, "as with many other boys at the time, I think the incident was just one part of his finally finding out that he probably didn't have a priestly vocation all along."

Thomas's fidelity to the church had been deteriorating for years. The racism surrounding the King assassination certainly contributed to this erosion; but racism may also have provided a convenient escape hatch as well. Regardless, by courting Monique, Thomas revealed an estrangement from his professed calling that predated any harsh words from fellow seminarians. His decision to leave the seminary no doubt had at least as much to do with a girl named Monique as with a man named Martin.

Hard feelings abounded among Conception alumni when their alma mater's name surfaced for its brief moment of fame during Thomas's Supreme Court fight. That this proudly progressive Benedictine institution had become synonymous with racism was, to them, bewildering and heartbreaking. The alumni association took the step of issuing a press release in response to Thomas's testimony to the Senate. It stated in part: "While we deeply regret that a racist remark apparently was made in the presence of Judge Thomas on the day of the assassination of Dr. Martin Luther King, Jr., the sentiment it expressed was not the attitude of the majority of seminary faculty and students."

At both St. John Vianney and Conception Seminary, Thomas left behind him a swirl of recriminations about racism suffered in silence at the time of his studies. His failure to complain while he was a student does not establish that the events did not occur. Indeed, his deep-seated yearning for privacy and his desire to be accepted fully explain such quiescence. His numerous references to the King incident over the years, even privately among friends, suggest that some sort of disturbing event did occur after the assassination. The details, however, remain hazy. Along with his divorce from his first wife and Anita Hill's allegations against him, the King episode would become one of the three most perplexing in his life.

———

Thomas knew he was not meant to be a priest, yet he had made a pledge to his grandfather that he felt trapped him. The prejudice he had experienced exacerbated matters. "I was disenchanted with my church and my country," he noted later. "I was tired of being in the minority, and I was tired of turning the other cheek."

"How could I stay there when the world seemed to be disintegrating around me? It all seemed so pointless." Thomas's point of reference was his namesake character in *Native Son*. "Just as Richard Wright's Bigger Thomas had been consumed by the conflagration of prejudices, stereotypes, and circumstances beyond his control and understanding, I felt myself being similarly consumed."

In May, as the semester drew to a close, Thomas went to O'Brien's room. "Can I talk to you a minute, man?" he said. He asked O'Brien to follow him to his room. Once alone, Thomas told him he was not returning to Conception. There were tears in his eyes. "I've run into too many rednecks," Thomas said.

The first signs of extremism in Thomas's temperament emerged at this time. Thomas decided not only to leave the priesthood, but the Catholic Church altogether.

His new freedom carried responsibilities—namely, deciding what to do with the rest of his life. Thomas dreamt of becoming a writer. He toyed with transferring to the University of Missouri to study journalism. Ultimately, he decided to go home. He resolved to attend Savannah State College, a traditionally black institution where his brother, Myers, eventually enrolled.

Thomas surely sensed the reckoning awaiting him back in Savannah. The news of his career decision did not please Daddy. The tension in the house was unbearable, and it was a matter of time until the proud grandfather and the proud grandson he had reared in his image parted company. "After a minor dispute over an unrelated matter," Thomas said, "he simply told me that since I was man enough to make such important decisions, I was man enough to take care of myself." Daddy asked him to leave his house.

Myers Anderson had offered Thomas far more than nature intended grandfathers to give. He had become a surrogate father and, even more, a personal hero. Daddy had provided him a daily inspiration and model of conduct during his youth—no small advantage in life. But Daddy was also a businessman; his underling had backed out of an agreement. The two would go their separate ways carrying the feelings typical of such a falling-out, the patron accusing the protégé of ingratitude, the protégé feeling that his patron was overbearing and unreasonable.

"In the years which followed," Thomas recalled, "I often asked, as Nina Simone sings: Why? (The king is dead!)" The lugubrious melodies of the "High Priestess of Soul," who had recently become a Black Power exponent, deepened Thomas's funk. More mundane concerns pressed in upon him as well. He supported himself by making bags for Union Camp Corporation in Savannah.

Thomas told Sister Ryan of his decision to leave the seminary. She encouraged him to apply to a northeastern college that was actively recruiting black students: Holy Cross in Worcester, Massachusetts. Two of his black classmates from Savannah parochial schools already were attending the college. One was Robert DeShay, a close friend. Ryan simultaneously lobbied DeShay to send Thomas an application form for the college. When DeShay mailed him the form, Thomas decided to fill it out.

The death of Martin Luther King now would touch Thomas profoundly a second time. The assassination deeply shook the faculty and administrators of Holy Cross. Having graduated fewer than twenty black students from 1843 to 1968, the college resolved to increase vastly their black recruitment efforts. Within days of King's death, Holy Cross established a Martin Luther King scholarship fund. The leading clergy at the college began to drive to major cities in the northeast, as well as Chicago and Detroit, to recruit students from inner-city high schools personally. They also urged their few black students to talk up Holy Cross during their visits home for the holidays. The Worcester paper reported these efforts with a headline that, to many whites in the city, sounded ominous: "2 City Colleges Recruit Negroes."

Early in the summer of 1968, Thomas received an acceptance letter from Holy Cross. At the time, the letter seemed "meaningless" to him. He had no idea how he could pay the $2,850 for tuition, room and board, so he decided to inquire about financial aid. He called information in Massachusetts and asked for Holy Cross College in "Worchester," Massachusetts. The operator informed him that it was pronounced "Woostah." Thomas spoke to someone in financial aid who told him that with a package of scholarships, loans and work-study, he could meet the expenses. The Martin Luther King scholarship fund was quickly put to important use.

Thomas would depart for this new Catholic institution "with no hope in my religion, no faith in my country, and no desire to be in a predominantly white school again. But, in so many ways, I had no place else to go." It was August 1968. Thomas was finally ready to enter the sixties.

PART THREE

Heretic

CHAPTER SEVEN

Years of Rage

With a chicken sandwich for lunch, $100 hidden in a pair of red socks, and a suitcase laden with books instead of clothing, Thomas boarded a train with his friend Robert DeShay in Savannah in August 1968 and headed north. In what had become the archetypal black journey north, his father had taken the same route and mode of transportation to Philadelphia nineteen years before. But the freedom M.C. sought up north was, in Clarence's view, at the expense of his family, and destructive. His son desired only the intellectual and economic liberty that came from higher education. The only casualty of Clarence's journey out of Georgia would be his poverty.

After spending a few days with DeShay's uncle in White Plains, New York, Thomas and DeShay climbed aboard a Silver Eagle Trailways bus for the final segment of the journey to Holy Cross. As the bus streaked through Connecticut, the driver mentioned New Haven to the south, describing it, memorably to Thomas, as "the home of Yale University." Night fell that Sunday before the two Georgians pulled into Worcester. When the bus passed Holy Cross on the way to the bus depot, Thomas recalled, "My heart pounded with apprehension, anticipation and hope." Illuminated by the lights of the campus, Holy Cross was, to him, "a shining light on a hill."

Founded by Jesuits in 1843, the college was an outcropping of attractive red-brick buildings terraced halfway up the hillside, later christened Mount St. James. The original plan was for the college to crown the crest of the hill. The draft horses used for the construction vetoed these designs, as they could not (or would not) carry their burden of bricks and mortar that high. Even at a reduced elevation, the college enjoyed a panoramic view of Worcester below and Mount Wachusett twenty-five miles to the north. Merely walking to and from classes and dormitories required excellent cardiovascular conditioning; all Holy Cross students were, by definition, mountaineers.

Thomas and DeShay stepped off the bus into a city that was a blue-collar manufacturing hub in the region. Located in the center of New England, and with approximately 175,000 residents, Worcester was ethnically diverse but racially uniform. Large numbers of Irish, Italian, and even Swedish-Americans formed most of the population, along with some old Anglo-Saxon families still in the area. In the poorer sections of Worcester, many enviously referred to the students at Holy Cross as "fools on the hill."

Except for a small influx of Puerto Ricans, who performed agricultural work in the surrounding farms, Worcester's population was almost completely Caucasian. Less than two percent of Worcester's citizens were black. Bill Russell and other black players for the Boston Celtics were outspoken about the prejudice they were then encountering in Boston. Black students at Holy Cross believed that Worcester, a microcosm of Boston in essential respects, was even worse in this regard. Many longtime residents resented the new minority recruitment efforts and scholarships offered by area colleges. Crystallizing this attitude was an exchange between one Holy Cross student and William Loeb, arch-conservative publisher of the *Manchester Union Leader*, just across the Massachusetts line in Manchester, New Hampshire. The student wrote a letter to the editor denouncing a recent editorial, which had contended that New England colleges should cease "importing" black students and their "problems" into the region. Loeb stood by his editorial, saying local academia should desist from the "importation of black people who have proven time and time again that they are not capable of being assimilated into a community." Loeb argued, "It isn't their fault. And, it isn't the fault of the white population. They are just so far apart that they don't mix successfully." When one of the few black residents of Worcester saw a young black man walking up the hill to Holy Cross, he approached him near the entrance gate to ask if he was, in fact, a student. When the student assured him that he was, the man broke down in tears, saying he had never before seen a black student there.

Holy Cross had become a stronghold of second- and third-generation Irish Catholics, many of whom preferred to keep things that way. The news of Martin Luther King's death, for example, triggered a scene at

Holy Cross reminiscent of Thomas's experience at Conception: One white student was overheard announcing in a dormitory that "Martin Luther Coon" had been assassinated. On the first day of school, one white roommate candidly informed his new black roommate, "I am a racist," then brandished a hunting knife in front of him. Another white student tore a poster of Huey Newton off the door of a black student's room and spewed assorted slurs. The leader of a student social committee balked at inviting black women to campus mixers, saying he did not want "jigaboo women overrunning the halls."

Perhaps because of such incidents, the college mailed letters to the homes of white students, just before a small wave of new black recruits arrived at Holy Cross, to inquire whether they would object to a black roommate (no similar letters were dispatched to black students about white roommates). One student at the time said of Thomas's incoming class, "I think the guys who solicited for the Martin Luther King Scholarship Fund had a lot of guts."

Thomas described his early days at Holy Cross and Worcester in Hobbesian terms as "lonely, miserable, and cold." Massachusetts was, to him, like "a cold, isolated foreign country." He never felt more like a country bumpkin than right after he purchased the Sunday edition of the *New York Times* from a store in Worcester. After flipping through it, he returned to ask the clerk where the comics section was.

Thomas was one of twenty-eight new black students who enrolled at the college in 1968. His roommate in Room 233 of Hanselman Hall was John Siraco, who had transferred there from Northeastern University and was majoring in biology. Thomas found him a "superb" roommate, a "model student and an outstanding person." Thomas recalled that Siraco's "side of the room was always neat, he had excellent study habits, he never patronized me." They became good friends.

Thomas worked his new dormitory, as at Conception, like a politician, making friends with people of diverse backgrounds rapidly and easily. He met many other students by working as a waiter in Kimball Hall, the campus cafeteria. Thomas, clad in a white jacket, placed large trays of food on the ends of the tables; the students then scooped and divvied up the contents themselves while the other student waiters conversed among themselves before and after serving the food. Thomas was the only collegian who tried to get to know the townspeople also

employed at the cafeteria. His unusual amiability toward the "little people" he met along the way in his academic and professional career would
prove a striking feature of his personality.

No longer in the service of grandfather or church, Thomas began
to assert his independence. Father John Brooks, the academic vice president and dean at the time, judged Thomas a "very independent" soul.
Jaffe Dickerson, a fellow black student, put it this way: "You had a left
view, a right view, a center view and then you had 'Cousy's' view"
(Thomas's nickname from the Savannah basketball courts had followed
him north).

The unconstrained Thomas also exhibited a sometimes-abrasive
pride. Eddie Jenkins, a black classmate and friend, recalled, "He had
this personality he could switch on you in a second. He would come
across like he was very country, and within a split second he could show
you his intellect. He prides himself on doing that, on being under-
stated." Another classmate, Malcolm Joseph, spoke of first impressions
that were somewhat less flattering. "Oftentimes, when speaking with
Clarence," he observed, "there would be a certain tension. The tension
derived from the fact that he was always in a certain sense probing and
challenging. And for some people in some environments, that might
be viewed as either threatening or even arrogant when in fact, if you
were to know him, that's not the case." Others over the years would
drop Joseph's last qualification and describe Thomas as quarrelsome
and brusque.

Even among fellow blacks of modest means, Thomas was deprived.
"I didn't know I was poor until I got to New England," Thomas later
remarked of his arrival at Holy Cross. About a third of the students
were from prosperous families; the vast majority were middle-class.
Richard Leon, a white student from Boston who became a friend, said
that Thomas was "among the poorest of the blacks." Thomas's brother,
Myers, had given him a pair of Army boots and jeans as a going-away
gift to college. He wore these and other inexpensive duds—including
Army surplus fatigues and khakis—throughout his Holy Cross years.

African-Americans constituted a little over 1 percent of the Holy
Cross student population, and Thomas quickly became one of the dominant members of this small community. "The biggest thing that shocked
me was the differences in the brothers from New York, Philly and D.C.,"

he recalled. "There was a world of difference. Nothing like those of us who came from Savannah, Ga., even though we were the sort of city slicker type." When the black students decided it was time to form a Black Students' Union shortly after Thomas arrived, they elected him secretary-treasurer. Thomas insisted he was elected to the position merely because he could "type and edit" the BSU's new constitution.

The call to Black Power and separatism resonated with the angry young black men at Holy Cross. "If social integration was the rallying cause of ten years ago," a reporter for the Holy Cross student newspaper, the *Crusader*, noted in 1969, "racial independence and pride have taken its place." Father Brooks recalled that the black students "tended to band together, live together. They were quite isolated, actually." Black students defended their attitudes with in-your-face candor. "We don't have to mix with whites; why should we?" one told the *Crusader*. "We think differently, and like different things. When we want to relax, we stick together."

For all his fury at past racial effrontery, as well as his sympathy for the Black Power movement, Thomas led a one-man campaign against such attitudes. Matters came to a head in the spring of 1969 when the BSU debated whether to seek a black corridor in one of the dormitories. The BSU explained to the newspaper that the black corridor would permit a more "relaxed atmosphere," one "free from the tensions that they feel inevitably result from inter-racial contact." On March 20, 1969, the BSU took up a resolution to demand that the administration set aside a black corridor.

Thomas argued that blacks had come to Holy Cross to get to know white people and to understand their culture. If the black students of Holy Cross wanted to isolate themselves, he told them, they should transfer to Howard University, the historically black university in Washington, D.C. Self-segregation meant turning their backs on "the real world."

The BSU voted 24 to 1 in favor of the black corridor. Thomas was the lone holdout. The college approved the BSU's request on April 18, designating for that purpose the fourth floor of Healy Hall, named after Bishop James A. Healy, the first black Catholic bishop in the United States and the valedictorian of the first graduating class of Holy Cross in 1849. Thomas, in the end, was not willing to divorce himself from his black classmates, and before the fall semester of 1969 began, he struck a compromise. He would move onto the black corridor, but would bring along his white roommate.

———

In his correspondence with Tom O'Brien back in Missouri, Thomas gave regular updates on his grades. "I rarely got a letter when he didn't mention academic progress and books," O'Brien said. "He was always upfront in his progress." Thomas shared that he maintained a 3.7 grade-point average during his sophomore year.

Thomas discovered that his years of exacting Catholic education had been a boon. "I had been well prepared in my seminary studies," he realized, "with four years of Latin and two of German and French and a solid background in mathematics, philosophy and English." He decided to major in English, entertaining visions of becoming a journalist.

One English course damaged Thomas's grade-point average but added a new figure to his pantheon of personal heroes. "Readings in Renaissance Prose" introduced him to Cavendish's *Life and Death of Cardinal Wolsey* and Roper's *Life of Sir Thomas More*. Thomas was moved by the courage More demonstrated in instructing his executioner, "Pluck up thy spirits, man, and be not afraid to do thine office." Thomas received a C+ for the course, one of his lowest grades, but thereafter he said he sought to emulate More. A quarter-century later, Thomas still was affected. "In this era when dead white men have fallen in disrepute," he said in a speech a quarter century later, "I look back on the character and stature of Thomas More as a model."

Even with such saintly inspiration, Thomas could not muster much courage in the classroom. His professors recalled that he rarely raised his hand but was prepared when called upon. Thomas later gave conflicting explanations for his muteness in class. "I didn't want anyone to see my blackness," he told one friend years later. "I wanted them to judge my work." More credible was his subsequent admission that he feared saying something that would make him look foolish.

In his second year at Holy Cross and junior year of higher education, Thomas emerged from his books long enough for a fateful romantic encounter. On Friday nights, students from nearby, all-female Catholic colleges arrived by bus for mixers at the Holy Cross field house. Black students tended to avoid the events. "What are we expected to do at white mixers?" one black student asked. "Sure white girls will come up and talk to us, but it's usually for the sake of saying she talked to a real Black student."

Based on the letters he received from Worcester in 1969, O'Brien concluded that Thomas then "was pretty much in search of the mother of his children." A lack of dating during his years in the seminary may also have reinforced in Thomas a prideful fear of rejection that made normal romantic overtures difficult. His friends japed him mercilessly. "What woman would want this man anyway?" they would say. "He's got boots on, he's got nappy hair, he's into books and Black Power."

In the fall of 1969, a friend, Eddie Jenkins, introduced him to a young black woman from Worcester with the ominous name of Kathy Ambush. She was one of five children of Nelson Ambush, a dental technician in Worcester, and Shigao Ambush, a homemaker of Japanese descent. Although Episcopalian, Nelson had enrolled Kathy and her twin sister in Catholic schools after concluding the public schools were "going downhill."

Kathy had graduated from Marian Central Catholic High School in Worcester, then attended tiny Anna Maria College, a Catholic school in the woods outside the nearby hamlet of Paxton, Massachusetts. In October 1969, the campus unrest bubbling throughout the Ivy League universities in the region suddenly came to little Anna Maria. On October 15, the administration agreed to a moratorium day, a trend then sweeping academia. Classes were suspended to allow students and faculty to discuss the Vietnam War and other controversial issues. Kathy Ambush participated actively in this panel discussion, and asserted herself generally in the weekly school assemblies held in the campus auditorium. One high-ranking official at Anna Maria recalled that Ambush was "very forthright" and "highly spirited" in these gatherings. Standing up amidst the crowd, Ambush "would ask questions which threw everybody," the official said—questions challenging the policies of the Anna Maria administration. The official concluded that this ability to "ask a pointed question required a certain amount of aggressiveness."

When Thomas met her, Ambush was a diminutive figure, dark and slightly overweight. Her eyes showed her Asian parentage. A large, rounded Afro made her head appear the shape of an almost perfect sphere. Thomas saw a soul mate in this assertive young woman. Jenkins said, "I remember him coming back a week after the first date, saying he was in love."

———

Thomas's politics, inchoate when he arrived at Worcester, found homeostasis after his flirtation with black power, finally settling into the typical campus liberalism of the day. He would later say of his Holy Cross years, "I was truly on the left. . . . there was nobody on the other side of me." Not only that, "I was never a liberal . . . I was a radical." This was the hyperbole of nostalgia and self-dramatization.

During Thomas's time at Holy Cross, a significant cadre of students thought highly of the violent Marxism of Che Guevara and other guerrilla movements in Latin America and Africa. The Red Book of Mao Tse-tung earned some space on dormitory bookshelves. The I.R.A. even had a following. Thomas, in contrast, was remembered, in the words of one black classmate, as a "moderate liberal." In November 1968, he voted for Hubert Humphrey for president over Richard Nixon and the unspeakable George Wallace. Thomas's individualism and belief in private property, among other characteristics, thwarted any serious flirtation with the far left.

There was one other thing impeding such a commitment. His religious faith, though buffeted, was not snuffed out. On January 17, 1969, Thomas wrote Tom O'Brien and reported that he had "transcended" the racial indignities suffered in Missouri and was attending Mass again. "Maybe someday I'll go back to the sacraments," he added.

Even as the last months of a tumultuous decade flew by, Holy Cross remained, in the fall semester of 1969, much as it always had been. Dick Leon described the college at the time Thomas arrived as a "clean-cut, Catholic, all-male community" where longstanding rules for clean living still were enforced. Each dormitory housed a priest who resided there not merely for ornamental reasons, but to lead nightly group prayers and to deter mischief. Students leaving for the weekend were required to sign out. Parietal hours were enforced: Women were permitted in the dormitories only if there was a football game that Saturday, and then only from noon until 6 p.m. By resisting the fads—if with diminishing resolve—the embattled Jesuit institution stood several years behind the times.

The campus protests that started at the University of California-Berkeley in 1964, and subsequently upended one Ivy League college after another throughout New England, did not arrive at Holy Cross until just after Thanksgiving 1969. The Revolutionary Students' Union (RSU), an affiliate of Students for a Democratic Society, announced at that time that it intended to obstruct recruitment efforts at Holy Cross by "military, para-military agencies and corporate agencies whose workers were at the time on strike." Fearing a "serious confrontation," in the words of the vice president of student affairs, the administration prevailed upon two Marines to postpone their scheduled visit to the college.

This success emboldened the protestors to broaden their demands. They vowed to the campus newspaper that they would "block activities" involving "any recruiters having anything to do with human oppression." On December 1, the faculty senate responded by affirming the college's policy of granting access to all corporate and military recruiters wishing to interview students at Holy Cross. Assured of their right to meet with students on campus, representatives of General Electric (GE), an important military contractor, made arrangements to conduct interviews there nine days later.

At 8:30 A.M. on December 10, college officials escorted two GE recruiters into the Hogan Campus Center. A few minutes after 9:00, approximately fifty-four supporters of the RSU congregated in the hall in front of the interview room. Students and professors gathered in counter-protest. Soon the two throngs were shouting at each other. When Donald T. McClain, dean of men, tried to escort a student into the interview room, the RSU demonstrators turned their backs and locked arms to block them. Chants went up from the RSU faction: "Workers, yes! GE, no!" and "Workers, yes! Scabs, no!" McClain attempted twice to lead the student into the room. Both times, the RSU forces repelled them.

McClain returned a few minutes later with two more students. The chants began anew, this time accompanied by shouts from the counter-protestors: "Freedom, yes! Students, yes!" McClain asked for silence.

He told the RSU faction that they were violating the rights of the students who wished to be interviewed. As a result, McClain said he would refer the matter to the college judicial board for potential disciplinary action. In the meantime, however, he would ask the GE recruiters to postpone their interviews and leave campus. Before McClain retreated for the last time, he and two assistants identified seventeen students who were violating the college's accessibility policy.

One of the seventeen dropped out of school; the others, four of them black, faced a trial before the college judicial board. It began on December 18 and lasted about two hours. Ted Wells led the defense of the black students. In a performance that foreshadowed the brilliant legal career that lay ahead of him, Wells noted that the college had charged 4 of the 5 black students who participated in the protest, but only 12 of the 49 white protestors. Wells condemned the administration for the racism implicit in such disparate treatment. He warned that the Black Students' Union would take action "commensurate with the situation" if the four blacks were not granted amnesty.

Although closed to the student body, the proceedings were broadcast over the campus radio station, WCHC. After the trial concluded, the board, recognizing the stakes of the occasion, deliberated for twelve and a half hours.

That evening, the black students of Holy Cross also met and mulled things over. Sequestered in a room at the Hogan Campus Center, they debated the BSU's response to various possible verdicts by the board. Malcolm Joseph recalled, "We had some very radical black students at Holy Cross at the time." One of these students, a troubled young man who later ended up committing suicide, proposed taking up arms against the administration, as black student radicals had at nearby Cornell University.

A well-modulated baritone voice then filled the room. Although reticent in the classroom, Thomas was vocal and opinionated in the company of his fellow black students. He said firmly that it was important not to break any laws. Violence was not an option. The students agreed, and moved on to other topics. The shadow of the Black Panthers thus passed by Holy Cross.

The students then considered other possible responses to a guilty verdict. Many felt that the best tactic was to walk out of school en masse.

Thomas again spoke out in the negative, saying, in what one classmate described as a "long dissenting opinion," that they had come to Holy Cross to obtain an education, and they should finish their studies. This time, the other members of the BSU rejected his view overwhelmingly. If the four black students on trial did not receive amnesty, they resolved, they would strike.

At 3:30 A.M. the following day, the judicial board announced its decision: all sixteen students were to be suspended for the second semester. A few minutes after WCHC announced the ruling, the station carried the BSU's response: The college's black students would pull out of Holy Cross later that morning.

Thomas had passionately opposed a walkout on prudential grounds that could have been scripted by his grandfather. He had already left one institution of higher learning under a cloud, and quitting was not in his nature. But racism had dented his pride since his days on the Isle of Hope, and like the other black students, he regarded the disparate punishment as a serious injustice. Above all, he was not willing to alienate himself from his black classmates or to abandon friends in time of need. Robert Bliss, one of the four black students suspended, concluded that Thomas decided to leave with the other BSU students as "an act of solidarity with black classmates who felt aggrieved by the college."

"As I packed all my belongings that night," Thomas later remembered, "I teetered precariously over the abyss." He augured that the black students "were doomed." Thomas simply "wanted to go home." But what would he tell his grandparents who had suffered far more indignities than he had, and who had made it clear, in any case, that he was not welcome back home? For Thomas, the decision to leave Holy Cross was freighted with uncertainty and the very real prospect of homelessness.

Several hours later, the black students met again, this time at Kimball Hall, where they shared a last breakfast of pancakes and doughnuts. Afterwards, they picked up their suitcases and trudged up the steep stairs from Kimball Hall to the Hogan Campus Center.

News of the imminent walkout had electrified the campus, drawing a huge crowd. At ten o'clock, the black students arrived—a train of exotics with goatees and Afros, wearing suits and long, thin ties, who strode up to the stage and sat behind folding tables. Wells, the handsome, light-skinned mastermind of the occasion, took a seat next to

Arthur Martin, the chairman of the BSU, whose high cheekbones, angular face, goatee, and wire-rimmed glasses combined to make him look like the director Spike Lee two decades ahead of his time.

Before approximately six hundred people assembled in the ballroom, Wells announced the BSU's decision. Afterwards, the students behind him raised their clenched fists in a Black Power salute. Then, one by one, they tossed their student ID cards onto the table. Thomas, with his luggage in hand, took his turn. As the black students marched out of the ballroom, some of the white students took up the chant, "Strike! Strike! Strike!"

The walkout knocked the administration back on its heels. P. Michael Saint, then the editor of the student newspaper, the *Crusader,* thought the strategy "brilliant." The college, whose emissaries had driven all over the Northeast and industrial Midwest to recruit black students, now watched the fruit of their considerable labors simply walk away in a public relations nightmare.

The BSU members dispersed into various short-term dwellings throughout the area. Many went to stay with black students at nearby Clark University; others remained with well-wishers in Worcester. By this time, Thomas had come to know Kathy Ambush and her family well enough that he was permitted to stay with them.

The president of Holy Cross, Father Raymond J. Swords, consulted a prominent civil rights leader in Worcester. John F. Scott, Chairman of the Worcester Advisory Committee on Human Rights, agreed to serve as mediator between the college and the black students. Scott recommended that the college accept the BSU's position and grant amnesty to the students. Swords, seeing his administration completely outmaneuvered, eventually acceded to the BSU's demands.

At around 6:30 P.M. on Sunday, December 14, Swords walked into the same ballroom where Wells and his BSU brigade had executed their strategy and read a speech that represented complete surrender: "Upon the recommendation of Dr. John F. Scott, chairman of the City of Worcester's Human Rights Committee, whom both the Black Students' Union and I agreed to accept as arbitrator, I am granting amnesty to the sixteen students whose suspension from the College because of their involvement in the General Electric Co. incident was previously announced." He also declared that classes would be suspended the following day, December 15, so that all students could participate in a "day of discussion" concerning the recent events.

Clarence Thomas, BSU secretary-treasurer and journalist-in-training, wrote an apologia for the walkout that the *Crusader* published later in the week. It was one of the more fascinating pieces he ever wrote. Referring to the "black exodus" of the past weekend, he began the article with the deep conviction that henceforth would distinguish his prose: "Amid the confusion that Holy Cross found itself caught up in this weekend, the black students became more aware of themselves as black men." He continued with a fervid, occasionally rambling defense of their actions, including at times a cadence and high-flown terminology suggestive of the Black Panthers and other activists of the left:

> The walk-out itself resulted from a blatant manifestation of attitudes that were previously concealed in articulate justifications and rationalizations. No particular individual or individuals are objects of the accusing finger; yet, some have been, and are, by coincidence, more prominent in the recent culmination of 400 years of the inhuman tradition of permitting and apathetically foisting upon the black man a role that lies some place between animal and human.

Thomas dismissed the rumor that the walkout had been a bluff, noting that the black students "did not entertain hopeful thoughts of returning." But these fears of never going back to Holy Cross "were easily outweighed by the importance of the action itself—an action for liberation." By shaking off the "social shackles of racism" in defense of "the black brothers," the participants in the walkout had "demonstrated that nothing is more important than being the black men that they are." Moreover:

> For the black students this Exodus is one more step in the direction of complete liberation from the slavery that whites—whether knowingly or otherwise—persist in foisting upon the black man.... Whether or not the blacks went home or not does not really matter. They were willing to forget Holy Cross and make new futures. The blacks acted as men, and that was all that counted. They did not plan to compromise manhood for a "good" education, and didn't.
>
> If a compromising ultimatum had been issued, there was but one answer: forget it!

Despite the awkward last sentence, Thomas's article showed an emerging writing style: powerful, blunt assertions flowing from ardor of purpose. The emphasis on manhood was notable and predictable given his personality, upbringing, and all-male surroundings. Notably absent from the composition was any recitation of the BSU's rationale for the walkout, i.e., the unequal treatment accorded the four black defendants.

The BSU was now the most powerful student group at Holy Cross. Virtually nothing they requested was denied. Wells led the negotiations, which resulted in a steady stream of additional concessions from the administration.

The BSU meetings on Sunday nights became lengthy digressions on the Vietnam War, national civil rights concerns, and other, more global issues. In these meetings, Thomas delighted in playing devil's advocate and, in classmate Eddie Jenkins' words, "arguing for arguing's sake." On issue after issue, he would be the lone voice opposing 30 to 40 black students. Some of these provocations were clearly facetious; Thomas, Jenkins believed, enjoyed the opportunity "just to show his intellect."

If he delighted in vexing the other students, there was a serious analytical thread woven throughout his arguments. "Remember why we're here" was Thomas's frequent, didactic riposte. They were attending Holy Cross, above all else, to gain an education and to advance their careers. For insisting on this focus, and for opposing some of the BSU's steps toward racial separatism, Thomas sparred often with Wells. Both were intelligent, articulate and forceful, and their debates featured a clear philosophical divide. As Jenkins described it, "this was W. E. B. versus Booker T.," an allusion to the most famous rift in African-American thought.

Those were "my radical days," Thomas would later say of his years at Holy Cross. He also referred to this time as "my rebellious stage." His passions no longer checked by external authority, his anger at past racial mistreatment still smoldering, Thomas latched onto much of the militant rhetoric and causes of the era. He sometimes signed his letters, "Power to the People." Once critical of Stokely Carmichael in his high school newspaper, he now praised him and saw much to admire in the Black Panthers. The group, he felt, "offered, for some of us who were young and hot-blooded and ill-tempered, another way" of combating bigotry that was more aggressive than the prescriptions of the NAACP. On the other hand, the Panthers' call for violence and Marxism-Leninism conflicted with his respect for order and property; there he drew the line. He observed:

> ... those who beckoned us to collective action and ethnic nationalism planted their ideological seeds in minds made ready by pain, frustration, and the blatant lies of our so-called free society. We were sitting ducks for a call to arms and action—to fight fire with fire—blows with blows—hatred with hatred—irrationality with irrationality—power with power. We burned with the zeal of youth to obtain compensation for past wrongs and retribution for indefensible ills.

After one of its members visited a free breakfast program run by the Black Panthers in Oakland, the BSU initiated a similar program in downtown Worcester. Once a week, Thomas and Siraco rose from their beds at 5 A.M. The metal heater on their wall creaking as it strained to emit sufficient heat, the two roommates dressed, Thomas leaving his Afro and goatee uncombed and throwing on his fatigues and combat boots. In a church basement in a poor neighborhood, they cooked and served breakfast for needy children, and then tutored them. Since the black population in Worcester was miniscule, most of the impoverished children benefiting from the program were white.

Rebellious and contrarian by nature, Thomas was in his element during an era he would look back on as "tumultuous." For all his later disgust with the sixties, Thomas's temperament made him well suited for the era. His headwear advertised his politics: Sometimes he wore a leather beret imitative of Huey Newton; other times it was a blue denim hat with sloganeering buttons such as Muhammad Ali's "No Vietnamese ever called me 'Nigger.'" Thomas had a "crummy" draft number, according to Tom O'Brien, but his student deferment and curved spine ("amazing-looking," in O'Brien's description) would keep him out of harm's way. He enjoyed late-night discussions about Nixon, Spiro Agnew and other "right-wing extremists," as he then called them, and the war in Southeast Asia.

The rush of new ideas left many young minds spinning. Thomas was sober enough to pick through the competing notions and begin to assemble, plank by plank, his own working personal philosophy. He read the leading existentialist philosophers of the day, including Sartre and Camus. The figure who most influenced him was Malcolm X.

Thomas first read the *Autobiography* shortly after arriving at Holy Cross. He listened to records of Malcolm's speeches on Siraco's phonograph, and would retain these recorded speeches well into adulthood. What attracted him was Malcolm's bitter rejection of condescending whites and of compromising "Negro 'leaders,' so-called." Malcolm's stirring call for manhood and self-reliance also resonated.

Black Muslims, too, fascinated Thomas because of their belief in self-help. A significant number of black students converted to Islam during this time. There was a mosque in Worcester, but it was small enough that prayer meetings often were in members' houses. These defections from Catholicism represented a further blow to the Jesuit character of Holy Cross, the tradeoff being that students were exposed to a more ecumenical environment. Thomas held the Muslim students in high regard and engaged in a regular dialogue with them.

When Thomas returned to visit his family in Savannah—carrying books in his suitcase to the exclusion of clothes—he proselytized his grandfather in his new creed. Thomas informed his grandparents he "had discovered our oppressed and victimized status in society." He predicted that "the revolution was imminent and that we all had to stick together as black people." Thomas would vividly recall years later the frustration on Daddy's face when he returned home from college and questioned whether there was anything such as a right and a wrong.

Both the content and deliverer of this message did not go over well in the Anderson household. "Needless to say," Thomas said, "relations were quite strained, and our vacation visits were somewhat difficult."

—

By the fall of 1970, Holy Cross was no longer the traditional Jesuit institution that Thomas had entered two years before. Long hair was a direct and unmet challenge to the canons of the *ancien régime*. The sexual revolution crept in, as the old parietal policy—which banned women from the dormitories except during limited daylight hours—was no longer enforced. The *Crusader* began to feature advertisements with unclothed women barely covering their breasts. At the beginning of the semester, the dean of students held a large meeting with the resident assistants, upperclassmen paid to help oversee the dormitories. By then, Thomas and Dick Leon, a white fellow student and friend, both had risen to this status. "Gentlemen," the dean said, "don't worry about enforcing parietal rules or marijuana. They'll be so pervasive that you won't be able to enforce it. You should worry about hallucinogenic drugs." This slide could only have further demoralized young men such as Thomas who were struggling with their Catholic faith.

Thomas later observed of this time:

> It seemed that no tradition was so time-honored it couldn't be changed or eliminated.... All authority was questioned and challenged. So much that had been taken for granted in the past was now criticized and challenged—from dress codes to values and mores. Suddenly, little if anything was sacred, perhaps with the exception of our self-centered notion of autonomy—which we mistook for freedom. We were pulling away from the cultural mooring that had previously provided stability, structure, and civility—even as imperfections abounded. Major portions of our time and energy (intellectual and otherwise) were spent supporting and reinforcing the effort to rip away the cultural and moral strictures that we felt were too confining. It seemed that we constantly engaged in an odd sort of narcissism and permanent temper tantrums.

Still years from embracing such an analysis, Thomas began his senior year at Holy Cross immersed in the politics of anger. Indeed, one day he would look back and refer to his college days overall as "years of rage." The invasion of Cambodia and the shootings at Kent State University several months earlier had reenergized the antiwar movement, of which Thomas remained a member. Unknown vandals painted a large peace sign on the roof of the Air Force ROTC building.

Yet Thomas was starting tentatively to reexamine some of his political and philosophical assumptions. The prior spring, he had attended a demonstration in Cambridge, Massachusetts, to free certain "political prisoners." At one point, he found himself wondering what he was doing there. "It was intoxicating to act upon one's rage, to wear it on one's shoulder, to be defined by it," Thomas later recalled. "Yet, ultimately, it was destructive, and I knew it." He worried that he might suffer the fate of Bigger Thomas. While still in a "nihilistic fog," he realized that he was approaching a crossroads: "Do I believe in the principles of this country or not?"

For social outings, the black students typically left campus. Father Brooks and another official persuaded the administration to procure a bus for the Black Students' Union for this purpose. "That bus was what got the black students connected to the rest of the world," classmate Eddie Jenkins said. On weekends, black students would drive in from nearby colleges, or the BSU bus would carry the blacks of Holy Cross to parties thrown by black students at Boston University, Wellesley College, or elsewhere.

Thomas usually sat out these events. "Cooz never liked to socialize," recalled Lester Johnson, a childhood friend from Savannah who also came north to Holy Cross. "He'd like to come around the dormitory and talk, but usually he'd stay on campus when we'd party. He was always about business." Thomas usually declined invitations from Siraco and others to parties and other social functions. He was virtually a teetotaler. When, twenty years later, Thomas informed the press that he had taken a few puffs of a marijuana joint during this period, his classmates were dumbfounded ("Those were several puffs I never saw," Jenkins remarked).

This complex young man, sometimes eristic and belligerent, other times subdued and antisocial, was sensitive enough to pen some verse in these years. In his senior year, the campus was gripped by debate over whether to admit women. When female black students from Wellesley were scheduled to visit Holy Cross on an experimental co-ed basis, Thomas wrote a poem for the occasion. "Is You or Is You Ain't a Brother?" urged his classmates to treat black women with respect. He particularly exhorted them not to greet the visiting Wellesley sisters with entreaties to sexual immorality. Any student who failed to show such respect, the poem asserted, was not a real brother. Thomas also prevailed upon the BSU to pass rules concerning proper conduct when women were guests on weekends, a code governing such things as bathrooms, dress, and foul language.

His zest for sports was undiminished, even after his self-esteem in that area had taken a bit of a beating. Thomas had not panned out as a serious collegiate athlete. He had been a member of the Holy Cross track team his junior year and had enjoyed a moment of glory. At the Boston College Relays in the spring of 1969, he was a member of a three-man long-jump team that won their event after a Yale jumper stumbled on his final leap (Yale otherwise was poised to win). Most of Thomas's athletic attention then was channeled into weightlifting and intramural contests. At the time, lifting weights was uncommon and viewed as "odd," according to Leon, who worked out with Thomas. The five-feet, nine-inch Thomas weighed 155 to 160 pounds, yet could bench-press an astonishing 275 pounds.

Thomas needed recreation as a diversion, and not simply from academics. The fall of 1970 was a depressing time for him, the result of a cruel joke by his black classmates. When the BSU held its annual election of officers, almost everyone assumed that Ted Wells would be elected chairman. A natural leader, Wells, according to Jenkins, "should've been elected unanimously." But the overwhelming consensus among BSU members, he recalled, was that Wells "had taken on a lot of power. And a lot of people thought that Ted was getting big-headed." Several hatched a scheme to teach Wells a lesson by denying him this prize, and in a humiliating fashion: by working to elect his intellectual nemesis, the lone wolf of the campus black assembly, in his place. They nominated Clarence Thomas for chairman.

After Thomas won the vote, the group was noticeably stunned, and remorse soon set in. They had made their point; now they needed to dethrone unceremoniously their iconoclastic leader. Discussion ensued. One member, Skip Hartwig, finally moved for reconsideration of the vote.

To a young man who rarely spoke in class to avoid this very sort of public spectacle, such a hoax election was mortifying. And yet Thomas found it within himself to make a gesture of statesmanship. With no outward show of embarrassment, Thomas told the members, "Just do what you got to do. We're just fighting among ourselves." Then he, too, joined the vote in favor of the motion for reconsideration. In the second vote, Wells was elected unanimously.

For all his good sportsmanship, this election appears to have precipitated Thomas's flirtation with leaving Holy Cross that fall. All his years spent up on lonely, frozen Mount St. James had led to this—a public embarrassment by the same black classmates whom he had joined, despite strong philosophical objections, on a perilous walkout less than a year before. There may well have been other emotions battering his resolve to finish what he had started at Holy Cross. Thomas later told a Holy Cross alumni publication that he went so far as to begin packing: "I had my trunk all packed. I had decided that it was true, what the other blacks had been saying: that Holy Cross was a crusher, that it would break your spirit."

Father Brooks now played a decisive role in Thomas's life. A native of West Roxbury, the young Brooks had a florid Irish complexion, bright brown eyes beneath horn-rimmed glasses, and an easy, frequent smile that was just starting to crease his face with crow's feet, the indelible sign of a sunny disposition. Brooks had served as an informal counselor and shepherd to the scores of new black students he had done so much to attract to Holy Cross. Thomas came to Brooks that fall and told him that he was considering leaving the college. Brooks recalled that "the whole race issue was part of it." Thomas mentioned specifically that he was weary of the "complaining among the brothers and fighting among themselves."

Brooks tried to lift his spirits. "Things aren't as bad as they look," he pointed out. Besides, Thomas had come there for an education, and was very close to receiving his degree. Thomas recalled that Father Brooks was "very understanding and sensitive about my feelings. He looked after me." Thomas knew, of course, that he needed an education to accomplish his career objectives, and that he was tantalizingly close to receiving his degree. He decided to stay.

First a seminarian, then an aspiring journalist, Thomas was now thinking about going to law school. He consulted his best friend, Gil Hardy, who was pondering the same thing. A native of Philadelphia, Hardy was the opposite of Thomas in many obvious respects. Light-skinned and slender, Hardy's "personality type was very different from Clarence's," according to Malcolm Joseph. Although a straight-A student, Hardy was "very unassuming" and almost never discussed his grades. Another adjective that pops up repeatedly from former friends and intimates of Hardy is "warm." Hardy lacked the rough, combative edges of his good friend from Savannah.

His grades, Thomas realized, might give him entrée to top-flight law schools. When he started sending in applications, he aimed high.

Thomas was also considering other profound issues. After dating Kathy Ambush for more than a year, he had fallen in love. They were birds of a feather temperamentally; both had brash and fiery streaks alongside quiet and reflective spells. Since meeting Thomas, Ambush had remained very active in the new Black Students' Union at Anna Maria. Like Thomas, she was accustomed to attending a high school and college with very few blacks, with all the anxieties that came from such extreme minority status. A photo of the Anna Maria Black Students' Union in the 1971 annual shows eight female black students, the majority of whom look quite stern—in marked contrast to the giddy white students whose smiles brighten the other pages of the volume. Thomas and Ambush in 1970 were kindred, rough-and-tumble spirits in a revolutionary cause, integrators with chips on their shoulders. He was grateful to have found someone who would love him because, and not in spite of, the sandpaper of his personality.

The Ambush family welcomed Thomas into their home and family. Thomas and other black students at Holy Cross who could not afford to travel home for the holidays were invited over to the Ambush compound on Lovell Street for turkey dinners and televised football games. During the school year as well as the summer of 1970, when Thomas stayed in Worcester to work as an assistant to a surveyor, he often visited the Ambushes. Sometimes, he would help Nelson Ambush with trimming the hedges. Thomas's distinctive laugh was commonly heard reverberating up from the basement, where the Ambush pool table provided another small arena for his competitiveness. Tom O'Brien found that there was a "real sense of peace" suffusing Thomas's letters to him after Ambush accepted his proposal for marriage.

Neither knew where they would be a year later until Thomas started to hear back from law schools. Thomas and a white friend, Brian O'Connell, kept tabs on each other to see who would be the first accepted. Both applied to Harvard, Yale and the University of Pennsylvania. A month before O'Connell learned that Harvard had accepted him, Thomas received an acceptance letter from New Haven. Acceptance letters from Harvard and the University of Pennsylvania followed.

Thomas ended up choosing Yale, he later explained, because the school offered a "substantial grant" and, more vaguely, because of the "kind of program offered there." Thomas did not boast of his acceptance to Yale—Siraco said, in fact, "you had to pry it out of him"—but Holy Cross showed no such reserve, proudly putting out a press release about Thomas's accomplishments to the alumni newspaper. Thomas told college officials that after graduating from Yale, he planned to return to the South "to begin helping some people." Even so, he would be no standard-issue civil rights lawyer. Leonard Cooper, a black classmate and friend, said that the former "moderate-liberal" was drifting away. Cooper noticed, "As time went on he was moving more toward the right."

Thomas graduated from Holy Cross *cum laude* on June 4, 1971. The students, garbed in graduation robes, assembled on Fitton Field, the college football stadium, under sunny skies. For Holy Cross, the class of '71 included by far the most impressive group of black graduates they would send forth into the world. Alongside Thomas were Ted Wells, who became one of the top attorneys in New York and active in the national Democratic Party; Stanley Grayson, managing director of Prudential Securities in New York; Malcolm Joseph, a colonel in the Air Force and a physician stationed on Air Force Two (Vice President Walter Mondale would be his most famous patient); and Eddie Jenkins, who soon after graduation was playing in the NFL for the Miami Dolphins (he became a member of their undefeated 1972 team, which won the Super Bowl). Thomas's poverty and the loose fashions of the day prompted him to wear beneath his graduation gown a pair of raggedy jeans and his familiar Army boots.

The next day, June 5, Thomas and Kathy Ambush were married at All Saints Episcopal Church in downtown Worcester, the Ambushes' family church. Of English revival Gothic design, the church offered soaring Gothic arches and stone gargoyles hunched on the belfry to serve as additional, silent witnesses to the occasion. Gil Hardy stood by Thomas's side as best man. DeShay and Joseph Wilson, also of Holy Cross, served as ushers. Karen Ambush, Kathy's twin sister, was maid of honor; another sister, June, and a cousin were bridesmaids. In a small news item about the wedding, the Worcester newspaper described Thomas as the "son of Mr. and Mrs. Perry Ling of Savannah, Ga." M.C. Thomas had slipped so far from his son's life that he did not earn a mention. In contrast, Thomas made sure that his grandparents were named.

Kathy's birthday was the next day, June 6. There would be no real honeymoon for the young couple. Thomas was too poor and too anxious to be on his way to New Haven.

CHAPTER EIGHT

The Monkey on His Back

By the time Thomas arrived in the summer of 1971, Yale too had experienced its radical moment. The arrest and trial of Bobby Seale and the other members of the so-called New Haven Nine the year before had set off campus demonstrations that culminated in violence and a moratorium on classes. Around the edge of campus, the Black Panthers sold newspapers advising readers on the use of firearms, which could be employed to "Off the pigs!" Although founded by the same busy Puritan colony that had sent out a tendril to Liberty County, Georgia, Yale had become a cauldron of racial animosities and far-left politics when Thomas and his new wife drove south from Worcester and set up their modest household just off campus.

Thomas and Kathy moved into a small, Yale-owned apartment on Prospect Street less than a mile from the law school. They lived on the upper floor of one of the simple, two-story, red-brick rectangles that provided student housing in the little Esplanade Apartments complex.

In a season that should have been rapturous for the couple, something greatly disturbed Thomas, possibly regrets about the marriage. He described the summer of 1971 as "perhaps one of the most difficult of my life." In the years to come, he gave only a few ambiguous details about the source of his malaise:

> It was clear to me that the road to destruction was paved with anger, resentment and rage. But where were we to go? I would often spend hours in our small efficiency apartment in New Haven pondering this question and listening to Marvin Gaye's then new album, "What's Going On?" To say the least, it was a depressing summer.

Thomas had received a summer grant from the Law Students' Civil Rights Research Council, and spent most of his summer days working at the New Haven Legal Assistance Office. Located in an older, predominantly Italian section of New Haven, the storefront legal aid office exposed him for the first time to the law and the legal problems of the poor. Landlord-tenant disputes, consumer issues, and other matters dull but crucial to his clientele filled his days.

When classes commenced in September, Thomas entered a marvelous structure notable for its combination of traditional architecture and whimsical decorations. Inspired by the English Inns of Court, Yale had placed its law school in a single building, of the design known as Collegiate Gothic, with early Renaissance and modern Gothic influences. The exterior was of pinkish-red brick and seam-faced granite, with light gray limestone trim, and slate and copper roofing. Abundant kaleidoscopes of stained-glass windows featured judges and lawyers in costume and miscellaneous symbols of law, justice and criminal punishment. The façade was studded with fanciful stone sculptures ranging from a laurel wreath to a ball and chain to a patrol boat chasing a rum runner. Entering off Grove Street, Thomas stepped below Gothic arches and a stone figure depicting the lawyer as bulldog, its exaggerated eyes and long mouth begging for a punch line from a deranged cartoonist. Farther below, under the stone balconies at the second-floor level, were two adversaries: a Puritan with a Bible faced off against a man with a whiskey bottle and playing cards. The latter would be a fitting encapsulation of the temptations that would assail both Yale and Thomas during the three years he would spend there.

He did not exactly blend in with the environment. He was one of only twelve blacks in his class, and his attire did little to make him less noticeable; at Yale, he shed his fatigues for a more agrarian look—a set of bib overalls. His teachers and fellow students would disagree over his headgear years later: Some said he wore a wool cap, others a floppy-brimmed denim hat. He may well have worn both. He also donned suspenders from time to time, perhaps an homage to his grandfather. The combat boots remained in service as well. The attempt to look "like someone who might have come out of the cornfields in Georgia" was, his teacher Quentin Johnstone thought, a way of informing others that "he was a Southern kid and by God, that's the way it was."

The work ethic learned from Myers Anderson never served Thomas better than during his three years at Yale. He rose early, spent his entire day at school, and went home after midnight. This regimen could not have pleased his young wife, but Thomas was determined to succeed in this great academic challenge. Again, the library became for him a den of self-preparation. Over the entrance to the library was the inscription *Prudentis est Petere Fontes,* which was Sir Edward Coke's counsel, "It is wise to go to the sources." Thomas would go to the sources that had never failed him—the books and the library—in preparing daily for class. The Black Panthers or their sympathizers had tried to burn the library down the year before; their failure was Thomas's gain. He typically stayed there until the library closed at 10 P.M.

Thomas concentrated on business law—such subjects as accounting, antitrust and tax law. He said later that he avoided more theoretical courses in favor of learning the nuts and bolts of the law, particularly law with commercial applications. "He wanted to get an education," recalled John Marini, a co-worker in Washington with whom Thomas subsequently shared some of his experiences at Yale. Marini said that Thomas "knew that a lot of these guys [professors in theoretical courses] were substituting their views for rigor." They spent a good deal of class time "just talking about the Vietnam War and stuff like that." Despite his continuing sympathy with such views, Thomas wanted to ensure the best investment possible for the large student loans that would indenture him for almost two decades.

True to the pattern of his earlier school years, Thomas was among the quieter students at Yale. Johnstone evaluated his class participation in familiar, diplomatic terms: "He wasn't a particularly aggressive student, but his views did become known." He frequently sat in the back row of the lecture hall or at the end of a row to be less conspicuous to the instructor. As throughout his academic career, Thomas was quite prepared if called upon. The initiative, however, lay with the professor.

Thomas said he earned "good grades" at Yale, an evaluation endorsed by the faculty. There was no class ranking at Yale, an arrangement that, in Professor Quentin Johnstone's words, meant "there's less push for top grades than there might be at other places." Still, Thomas "performed very well," according to Johnstone, known as one of the toughest graders at Yale at the time.

His academic work compared well with that of other Yale Law students who would one day become household names. The faculty would remember Bill Clinton, a year ahead of Thomas at Yale, as brilliant.

Thomas's most distinctive memory of Clinton was that he never went to class. That Clinton nevertheless reaped excellent grades must have been especially galling to the studious Thomas. On the other hand, Thomas's academic performance was very similar to that of Clinton's classmate and future wife, Hillary Rodham, who "wasn't even the best woman student from Wellesley in her class," in the words of Guido Calabresi, a law professor and later dean of Yale Law School. Calabresi observed that Thomas and Rodham "were both excellent students and had the same kind of reputation" among the faculty. Another Yale Law student who would figure prominently in Thomas's life matriculated three years after he graduated. Anita Hill was remembered as not on the "same level" with Thomas and Rodham. One professor, comparing her performance with Thomas's, remarked, "She was a solid student . . . but a little less imaginative. It's the difference between a student who will get nice solid B's and a student who will occasionally maybe get a lower grade but who will occasionally get A's—and real ones."

Such comparisons could be made readily because of Yale's small student body. Even so, when one news organization canvassed two hundred Yale Law alumni for their recollections of Thomas twenty years after he enrolled there, most did not remember him. Of those who did, the most common description of him—numbering in the dozens—was "retired and quiet." Those who spent time with him, however, tended to say he was "argumentative and independent." One classmate and close friend of Thomas, Frank Washington, recalled, "We used to say, 'Clarence is just Clarence.'"

Thomas's pride grew more eccentric during the Yale years. Nothing exemplified this quality better or more visibly than his decision to hang a Confederate flag on the wall of his apartment alongside a Pan-African flag. Harry Singleton, another close friend of Thomas, judged the Confederate flag "a shocker, a means of engaging people in debate." Rufus Cormier, a fellow black student, attributed this to Thomas's "sense of the outrageous."

Although remembered by some as a loner, Thomas's paradoxical sociability enabled him to make many friendships easily—friendships that, in many cases, would endure a lifetime. James A. Thomas, then dean of admissions and the most prominent African-American in the law school administration, observed that "Clarence wandered pretty well among the students. He had friends among the black students and among the non-minority students." Thomas became a stalwart member of the so-called breakfast club, a group of black students who met at 7 A.M. in the law school dining hall. This was his first exposure to the upper crust of American society, especially wealthy blacks. One was Lovida Coleman, the daughter of William Coleman, the prosperous attorney and later secretary of transportation. In these sometimes-raucous conclaves, Thomas would end his contributions by saying, presciently, "Thomas, J."—in the manner of a Supreme Court justice signing off on an opinion.

Thomas met two other black men at Yale—Harry Singleton and Frank Washington—and formed a threesome they called "the triumvirate." Together, they constituted a full 25 percent of the blacks in their class. Thomas introduced himself to them in the registrar's office during their first day at Yale. Singleton's father was a janitor and his mother a maid; Washington was also of modest circumstances. The three shared a common belief in individual responsibility, a cardinal principle instilled by the hard-working men and women who reared them. Throughout their first year they spent large amounts of time together, often drinking beer and Boone's Farm jug wine and holding forth on Vietnam, civil rights, and the Watergate scandal.

Thomas signed up for intramural athletics and played on an all-black intramural football team. Again showing his high-caliber arm, Thomas "could just about throw the ball the length of the field," said one classmate. Sometimes, he overthrew his receiver by 30 to 40 yards. Chivalry fell prey to competitiveness on the field, as Thomas did not hesitate to throw a hard spiral even to Lovida Coleman when she joined in. "Clarence has only one speed," Coleman explained. "I give him credit for throwing it to a woman. Most men wouldn't have." Thomas did not make the *Yale Law Journal,* which was edited by the elite law students at Yale. But when it came time for the journal to match up against its archrival, the *Harvard Law Review,* in a football game, the editors unabashedly recruited Thomas.

A grant from a civil rights fund compensated him for his work at the New Haven Legal Assistance Office during the summers of 1971 and 1972. He also volunteered at the center during all three years of law school. The clients were mostly New Haven residents receiving welfare. In addition to tenant and consumer issues, Thomas also did some basic criminal defense work. Frank Cochran, the managing attorney at the small, neighborhood office, said Thomas was a "quick learner." He was "very well organized and the kind of person that you were able to trust to do the work well." Antonio Califa, a Yale Law student who worked in the office with Thomas, said he remembered Thomas coming into the office wearing his customary overalls. Not surprisingly, his common touch gave him excellent rapport with the clients. Califa had the impression during those years that Thomas was "very liberal."

Actually, Thomas's views had started to change before he even arrived at New Haven, but it was at Yale that he began decisively cutting his ties to the left. What radicalized him was the school's affirmative action system—and more precisely, the implied inferiority that came with it.

Yale Law School first instituted an affirmative action program in 1969. Whereas Holy Cross had earmarked scholarship money for minority students, Yale gave preferences in the admissions process itself. Admission to Yale was the real prize, for once there, students almost always went on to graduate, and Yale Law graduates almost never failed to become wealthy, powerful, or both. At first, Yale set aside up to 10 percent of the places in the entering class for members of minority groups, who would compete against each other, rather than whites, for those slots. Seven years after Thomas entered Yale, the U.S. Supreme Court struck down such quotas as unconstitutional. Calabresi could not say whether Thomas would have been admitted to Yale if not for this program. But Frank Washington, one of the triumvirs, said that Thomas "clearly recognized that affirmative action had helped us get to Yale."

Thomas supported the drive for more black students and professors at Yale. The unofficial black table at Yale's dining hall was the site of many mealtime conversations devoted to lamenting the decreased enrollment of blacks in Yale's '74 class (the numbers dropped from more than 20 blacks in the class of '73 to 12 blacks and 1 Hispanic in Thomas's class). The Black Law Students' Association, which Singleton chaired and which counted Thomas as a member, lobbied Yale to recruit more black students and professors. "The students called into question our admissions criteria, asserted that tests didn't test, that grade point averages didn't predict success, that life experience and diversity were more important," said Abraham S. Goldstein, then dean of the law school.

While sympathetic, Thomas avoided a leadership role in these efforts. "Clarence always professed concern and interest," Singleton remembered. "But his time to participate in protests and that sort of thing was severely limited." Thomas publicly (and perhaps reflexively) supported affirmative action at the breakfast club and elsewhere; to do otherwise carried the very serious risk of ostracism from the small, close-knit platoon of black students at Yale. But privately, and in discussions with his closest friends, he began to voice doubts. The stimulus for this reevaluation was an event so jarring and traumatizing that it began to dislodge him from his commitment to liberalism generally.

Thomas would later say that the worst experience of his life was when whites at Yale told him he was admitted there only because of racial quotas. This is an extraordinary statement, all the more puzzling because the specifics of these incidents are lacking. The one exception was the occasion when Lovida Coleman and other black students dined with a law professor opposed to affirmative action. "I remember having lunch with a law professor who said there weren't any minorities at Yale qualified to be there," Coleman reported—an allegation she considered "outrageous and untrue." The professor was almost certainly Ralph K. Winter, a conservative who served on the admissions committee.

Upon hearing of this slight, Thomas boiled with anger. Ricky Silberman, who later became a close friend of Thomas, said that at Yale, Thomas "began to see his own accomplishments questioned. He began to believe he was being viewed by people not so much as a good law student going on to practice tax law, but as a black law student who must be there as a result of affirmative action and would certainly never do anything but practice civil rights law." Although he knew affirmative action had aided him, "Clarence did not like what he felt was the stigma of affirmative action," according to Henry Cornelius Terry, a fellow black law student. "He felt that people would assume that we were not as good as others." Thomas's acceptance of affirmative action faded as he felt the sting of such assumptions.

Thomas was the first to acknowledge that he was not part of the academic crème de la crème. "I was never the number one student," he admitted frankly in later years. "I was never the extraordinary student. I was kind of the guy who worked hard and did well, and sometimes very well." What he would not accept, even into later adulthood, was that but for affirmative action, he would not have been admitted to Yale Law School.

He became convinced that the whites around him pitied rather than respected him. "You had to prove yourself every day because the presumption was that you were dumb and didn't deserve to be there on merit," he said. "Every time you walked into a law class at Yale it was like having a monkey jump on your back from the Gothic arches. . . . The professors and the students resented your very presence."

With such white-hot rhetoric against his would-be patrons, Thomas took a page out of Malcolm X's diatribes against white liberals. Philip Lyons, later a Thomas intimate, recalled, "Intellectually, he spoke about how troubling it was for well-meaning white liberals to give their condescending opinions at the time." Thomas complained about the "insufferable condescension of some of the white liberals there." Jeffrey Zuckerman, a fellow Yale Law graduate and, later, a co-worker of Thomas's, also remembered that white liberals provoked his ire. "They just assumed he wasn't smart. And this really grated on him. . . . He deeply resented this, because he could never prove otherwise."

This was the rub. Thomas hoped to prosper as an attorney; this meant applying to such places as Yale; yet Yale had an affirmative action policy that virtually advertised the inferiority of its minority students. Thomas grew to despise this tradeoff—though, notably, never enough to drop out of Yale in protest. His resentment of this stigma grew to become what Thomas later called the "monkey on my back."

The question of whether Yale would have admitted Thomas but for affirmative action would dog him the rest of his life. Jeffrey Zuckerman defended him as comparable to his peers. Noting Thomas's ability to fashion his own philosophy from competing principles, as well as the obstacles he had overcome in life, Zuckerman noted, "To me, the ultimate test of intelligence is the ability to think creatively for yourself. . . . There's a certain intelligence in being able to read stuff, understand it, explain it to other people. Beyond that, is being able to take all those things that you've read and have an original thought." By these measures, Thomas was indeed highly qualified. But in arguing that these less traditional standards for admission were more appropriate than factors like LSAT scores, such defenders would find themselves embracing a position not very different, in essential respects, from that at the core of the Yale affirmative action policy.

Thomas realized that affirmative action could only have aided him vis-à-vis white applicants; the lone remaining question was how much. Having learned of the full price of admission—the cloud that hovers over a black man's Yale law degree—he suffered grave second thoughts. For voicing such apostasy in later years, Thomas would be called a hypocrite; and to some extent, having knowingly benefited from affirmative action, he was. Yet the prospect of such ad hominems was not sufficient to deter him from reconsidering his philosophical moorings. He began to pull away from the liberalism that had given birth to affirmative action, and sought comfort instead in the philosophy of black self-help enunciated by Booker T. Washington and, in his own, homespun way, Myers Anderson.

Many of Thomas's colleagues at Yale never noticed his shift to the right. He voted for McGovern in 1972, and in the words of one observer, he was remembered as part of the "liberal mainstream" at Yale. Nonetheless, he had embarked on a conversion experience which Harry Singleton summed up this way: "He came into law school espousing liberal views from his freewheeling, unattached undergraduate days. But he became more conservative as he went through the process of legal education."

Thomas did not identify himself as a conservative. He never joined, for example, Singleton and other conservative students who called themselves "Winter's Warriors," a clique named after Professor Winter and a takeoff on the liberal "Nader's Raiders." Still, the change of heart was noticeable to those close to Thomas. When he and Kathy returned during vacations to her home in Worcester, he would argue vigorously over politics with Lenny Cooper, who was in his final year at Holy Cross. Cooper observed that "you could see where he was going" politically, as Thomas shared his disenchantment with the Black Panthers and campus protestors. By then, Thomas was already expressing regret over his participation in some of the actions taken by the Holy Cross BSU. He was also criticizing leading black political figures such as Jesse Jackson.

Singleton believed that Thomas's "real transformation to a 'conservative,' if you have to label him, took place during the last part of his tenure at the law school, when he was in Missouri, and then was really complete when he came to D.C. to work on [Senator John Danforth's] staff." In their conversations at Yale, Singleton and Thomas saw eye to eye on the importance of individual liberty, responsibility and self-reliance. Like Singleton, Thomas had concluded that government assistance in the form of transfer payments was authorizing an entire class of people to systematically "ri[p] off the government." They shared the view that "[t]here's no mythical man forcing you to put drugs in your veins," and "[t]here's nobody making you have babies that you can't take care of." Thomas later explained, "I never gave up my grandfather's ideals, and when my left-wing opinions began to clash with those ideals, I began to move away from the left."

A moral or spiritual reformation did not attend this political metamorphosis. Thomas did not return to the Catholic Church. As the Yale years went by, he grew further alienated from his childhood creed and Christianity generally. He admitted, "I wandered aimlessly through the desert of moral relativism. I did it my way. . . . The anchor of my upbringing, the tugging of my religious values, never ceased, but I resisted. My rational capacity justified—and, I wandered." Richard Wright was still wrestling with his soul.

The most palpable evidence of Thomas's spiritual drift was his frequenting of pornographic movie houses in New Haven during these years. Supreme Court decisions in the 1960s had punctured the dike of laws and customs that had long suppressed published and filmed pornography. As a new, profitable industry took shape and its products cascaded over the land, college towns such as New Haven became cutting-edge markets. Few young men of Thomas's generation and subsequent cohorts would enter adulthood without ever having observed pornographic material. That Thomas, a former seminarian and a newlywed, would indulge in such conduct is illuminating only to the extent that it serves as a guidepost for how estranged he had become from his traditional Christian underpinnings. The Thomas of later years was ashamed of this conduct in his early twenties, conduct which he came to regard as dishonorable.

The summer following the second year of law school was crucial for law students seeking to line up employment after graduation. Large law firms throughout the country, but especially the Northeast, would court recruits from prestigious law schools such as Yale. Despite his political change, Thomas still aspired to become a civil rights lawyer back in Savannah. During his second year at Yale, Thomas contacted Bobby Hill, a flamboyant black legislator and nationally known civil rights lawyer, about the possibility of a summer job at his small Savannah firm. Hill was and would remain, in Thomas's words, one of his "heroes."

As the summer approached and Thomas did not hear back from Hill, a black classmate at Yale, Meredith Jones, contacted one of the partners she knew at Hill, Jones & Farrington. She told Fletcher Farrington, "There's a really good student up here who wants to work for you this summer, but he hasn't heard from you."

The firm finally responded and asked Thomas to work as a summer clerk. Farrington believes that Hill, Jones & Farrington was the first racially mixed law firm in Georgia. Jones and Farrington, a white good ol' boy from Alabama who became a civil rights attorney with the Justice Department, enjoyed a national reputation in civil rights law and managed to recruit high-quality law students from top schools. Thomas accepted the firm's offer. He and Kathy moved south into his grandfather's house for the summer (his grandparents spent the summer in Liberty County).

"It was an extremely busy summer," Farrington recalled. The firm was located in a lovely two-story house built in approximately 1914 on East Thirty-fourth Street. Behind it was a quaint carriage house. Thomas was stationed mostly upstairs in the library, where he would sit at a big mahogany table with enormous legs that once had served as a counsel table in a federal courtroom.

One of Thomas's main projects was a real estate transaction on Hilton Head Island, South Carolina. The island was part of the coastal zone that General Sherman evanescently allotted to emancipated blacks after his march to the sea. Over a century later, blacks were almost exclusively the landowners on Hilton Head. Most owned heirs' property, the same title that Myers Anderson's family held in their land in Liberty County. To force sales of the property, developers fastened upon the old stratagem of buying a small portion of the heirs' property—such as a

$^1/_{132}$ interest in twenty acres—and then filing suit to obtain what was known as a partition. When the judge deemed a partition of such a small size impractical, he would order the sale of the property at auction. The developer could end up owning the entire tract. The system was ripe for abuse and manipulation at the expense of the small class of propertied black residents of the island.

The client who retained Hill, Jones & Farrington owned a $^1/_8$ interest in a ten-acre plot next to the Palmetto Dunes Resort. The resort wanted to buy the land; the client wanted to ensure that the resort paid a fair price. The case entailed numerous car trips from Savannah to the island. "There were no thorny legal issues involved," Farrington recalled. The case was nevertheless an "administrative nightmare." Thomas had to search titles, identify the heirs—40 to 50 in total—and obtain their signatures. The work was as dry as it comes in the law, but Thomas impressed the firm by doing a meticulous job.

On one of the many automotive trips to Hilton Head in Farrington's '71 Audi, Thomas began to talk freely with Farrington about his family. "The two things I remember," Farrington said, "were his unhappiness or dissatisfaction that his sister was on welfare, and the glow that he projected when he talked about his grandfather."

Thomas worked on other cases that were less tedious. One client was especially notorious. He assisted with a preliminary hearing on behalf of Carl Junior Isaacs, who along with three other defendants was charged with six counts of murder. On May 14, 1973, five members of the Alday family were shot to death in their mobile home in Donalsonville, Georgia, in nearby Seminole County. A sixth victim, Mary Alday, was abducted, raped, then shot to death. Hill was locally famous for his criminal practice and for being a staunch opponent of the death penalty. He won few friends in Georgia by taking on the defense of the alleged mass murderer. Isaacs ultimately was convicted of all six counts of murder and handed six separate death sentences.

More than twenty years later, when Isaacs' case finally wound its way through the serpentine appeals process up to the U.S. Supreme Court, Thomas was then a justice. Because of his earlier role in the defense of Isaacs, he felt obliged to recuse himself from the case. The Court ended up denying relief for Isaacs. His former client said of Thomas, "He was on the good side of the track in the case. Now the world has flipped upside down. I wish he'd remember what it was like to face the death penalty in Georgia."

Thomas's stellar performance at Hill, Jones & Farrington earned high praise from the firm's partners. Yet Thomas did not quite fit in with the erstwhile hippies who stood to become his bosses in Savannah. "My perception of Clarence was that he was very bright, he was very focused, he was not cut out of the same cloth as the rest of us," said Farrington. Thomas, he observed,

> had very strong intense feelings about his family situation. And I think not necessarily politically but personally and socially, Clarence was always a very conservative person. He believed in going to church, doing the right thing. I'm sure that his upbringing and Catholic schooling had something to do with that. . . . I didn't regard him as a particularly religious person. He just had old-fashioned social ideas, old-fashioned in the good sense—you pay your bills, go to church, go to school.

To Farrington and others at the firm, "heavy-duty partying" was routine and "raising hell was a way of life." Marijuana was a staple, if off-site; spirits flowed freely after hours on the premises. "When we cut loose, we probably committed some misdemeanors—maybe even felonies back then," he acknowledged. But "Clarence just wasn't a part of that. He was always serious and always focused on what was in front of him." Thomas was not a scold, however. "If he found [those practices] offensive, he didn't say so. He seemed to be, Live and let live."

After Thomas concluded his clerkship, the firm offered him a full-time job upon graduation. The starting salary would have been $17,500—not a mountain of cash but no pittance either, considering the city and the area of law. Thomas declined their offer. While Thomas suggested that he was interested in returning to Savannah, he indicated that Kathy was not. Thomas would later say cryptically that his goal of returning to Savannah to practice civil rights law "didn't work out."

Thomas had concentrated in commercial law in law school, suggesting he already may have been considering a career in the corporate world. The prospect of becoming a highly paid corporate lawyer would long tug at him, but he had not made the right career moves to position himself well for this objective. Thomas never seemed to realize that he had made a huge mistake by working only for a small civil rights firm in Savannah in the critical summer before graduation. Once Kathy soured on Savannah, he was left with no clerkships at other firms and, as a result, no job offers. He was stuck.

Thomas still hoped to return to Georgia, "if for no other reason, after spending six years in college and law school in the Northeast, I was dying for some decent southern cooking on a regular basis." He interviewed with the major Atlanta law firms, but none would hire him. Thomas became "disillusioned and angry," in his own words. Compounding these employment worries was the fact that Kathy was pregnant with their first child. She had left college without obtaining her degree in sociology, and would be staying at home with their child; the family depended on him for their income.

Desperate, Thomas resorted to looking outside his home state. He interviewed with firms in Washington, D.C. He "couldn't get a job" there, either. This futile job search yielded a "bitter and fruitless harvest." His ego ravaged, Thomas saved the "barren husk of rejection letter after rejection letter" for a lifetime of brooding.

Thomas completed his senior essay for Professor Johnstone, who had given him a poor grade in one of his earliest courses at Yale. Rather than avoid Johnstone thereafter, Thomas took additional classes from him, and wrote his dissertation under Johnstone's direction. Thomas and Gil Hardy worked together on the project, the hopeful thesis of which was that bar exams should be repealed. Johnstone gave them a grade of honors, the highest grade given in the school.

As the fall of 1973 continued to bring in the hard rain of rejection letters, Thomas finally heard of a solid prospect. John Danforth, a Yale Law alumnus and Republican attorney general of Missouri, had called Professor Calabresi to ask for the names of students who might be interested in coming to work for his office. Heir to the Ralston Purina fortune, Danforth was a tall, intelligent patrician distinguished by a large, handsome nose and a baritone voice as resonant as Thomas's. He later recalled, "I was really trying to find good African-American lawyers. . . . I went up to Yale Law School for that purpose." Calabresi asked one of his students, Rufus Cormier, if he knew of any potential candidates.

Thomas's plight was known to his friends at the law school, including Cormier. A black, former All-American football player from Southern Methodist University who would become the first black partner at a major law firm in Texas, Cormier asked Thomas if he was interested. Finding out that he was, Cormier passed along the word to Calabresi, who then phoned Danforth. Calabresi's main worry was that Thomas seemed too left-wing for the Republican attorney general.

Danforth flew out to New Haven and interviewed Thomas and several other law students in the faculty lounge. He was forthright with his young recruit, telling him that he didn't know how it was to be black and poor, since he was neither. "If you come to work for the attorney general's office in Missouri," he added, "I will promise you more work and less pay than anybody else who has interviewed with you at Yale Law School." Thomas later would speak of Danforth as an earnest politician "whose sales pitch was nothing more than 'I will treat you the same as everyone else' and whose vision was 'Clarence, there is plenty of room at the top.'" At this point in his life, Thomas's state of mind was such that when he heard the latter statement, he could only muster the inward response, "Yeah, right."

The two discussed the work at the attorney general's office. Thomas mentioned his time at Conception and his familiarity with Missouri. He impressed Danforth sufficiently that Danforth offered him a job on the spot. For all his desperation, Thomas had a few more questions that needed to be answered. He said he would first like to travel out to Missouri and visit the office.

In the spring of 1974, Thomas flew to Jefferson City, Missouri. On a lovely spring day, he toured the attorney general's office, met and spoke with some of the attorneys, and went out to lunch with some of Danforth's senior staff. He struck up a conversation about sports with Michael Boicourt, one of the attorneys Danforth asked to attend the lunch.

"He interviewed us—we didn't interview him," was the summary of Alex Netchvolodoff, Danforth's chief aide. Thomas had one overriding issue: He desired more and tougher cases than the other attorneys. "He wanted to know whether we were going to give him the tough cases, a caseload larger than others," Netchvolodoff said. Having received adequate assurances that he would indeed have an opportunity to excel in the office, Thomas accepted.

"I accepted that offer because of the *man*," Thomas would later state in reference to Danforth. He clearly found Danforth a refreshing change from his other interviewers, but it certainly helped Danforth's cause tremendously that the job offer he extended was the only one Thomas received, aside from the spurned overture from Savannah.

As Thomas finished his last semester at Yale and prepared for the journey west, Kathy gave birth in February 1974 to a son, whom they named Jamal Adeen Thomas. Jamal is Arabic for "handsome." Thomas would later say of the Muslim name, "That was my wife's and my way of striking out." Thomas would occasionally take the baby with him to the library. Friends called Jamal "the dude." Thomas would employ the corporal punishment and stern disciplinary techniques he had learned from his grandfather in rearing Jamal.

As graduation approached, classmates with better job offers could not resist rubbing it in. Some smirked at Thomas and implied that he had "wasted all that money and all that time at Yale Law School to go to Jefferson City, Missouri." Others looked at him "with pity."

Thomas would remain bitter about his difficulty in finding a job. He once said, "I couldn't get a job out of Yale Law School. That's how much good it did me. I ought to send them that degree back, too, while I'm at it." On another occasion, when an interviewer asked him about his Yale Law days, Thomas said, "That's not a resume highlight for me." Thomas left New Haven with a "swirling combination of frustration, of some disappointments, of some anxiety about the future, and some anxiety about how I would repay my student loans, how I would feed a young child, where I would live."

www.encounterbooks.com

Please add me to your mailing list.

Name

Company

Address

City, State, Zip

E-mail

Book Title

ENCOUNTER BOOKS

900 Broadway

Suite 400

New York, New York 10003-1239

CHAPTER NINE

Apostle to the Rednecks

Thomas's wishful dissertation at Yale had not swayed the Missouri State Bar. The first order of business after graduating from law school was a summer of preparing for the bar exam.

He did not lack lodging, thanks again to assistance from Danforth. In the spring, Danforth had found himself seated at a luncheon next to Margaret Bush Wilson, then the head of the St. Louis branch of the NAACP. Danforth mentioned during conversation that Thomas would be joining his staff. He said he would like to introduce the two of them.

"Well, that is fine," Wilson said.

"And he is black," Danforth added.

"Well, that is great," she replied wryly.

"Do you happen to know a place where he can live?" Danforth asked. "I don't think Jefferson City is the most exciting place in the world to spend the summer."

Wilson thought for a moment. She mentioned that her son was not returning home for the summer. Thomas, she said, could stay with her.

This kind arrangement meant that Thomas would have to leave Kathy and Jamal behind temporarily in New England, but the economics of the offer made it hard to quibble with. Thomas moved in to Wilson's home in St. Louis in June, and stayed there for two months, sleeping in her son's bedroom, until he completed the bar exam.

In August, Thomas, Kathy and Jamal rumbled into Jefferson City in what one friend called an "old, broken-down Volvo that worked mostly when he [Thomas] pushed it." About thirty thousand people lived in Jefferson City, a river town whose homes and businesses dot the hills that undulate from the Missouri River. Jeff City, as the locals call it, is in the center of the state—as befits a state capital—and within the swath of mid-Missouri known to political scientists as "Little Dixie."

A slave and border state during the Civil War (occupation by Union troops prevented the state from seceding), Missouri was still balkanized into county-by-county zones that voted Democratic or Republican depending largely on whether the gray or the blue controlled it during the war. The residents of Jefferson City and the surrounding area spoke with an accent reflective of the geography, one that blended a Midwestern twang with a Southern drawl. Thomas would find the folkways and values there similar to those he had grown up with. In later years, he quipped, "If you ever want to be deprogrammed from any kind of a cult, go to Jeff City."

The Thomas family took up residence in the upstairs portion of a two-story, older brick house on Adams Street eight blocks from the capitol. The house was near the railroad tracks that ran along the Missouri River, and only a few blocks from the mammoth stone walls that formed the perimeter of the Missouri State Prison. The apartment they rented had two bedrooms, a living room and a kitchen. Thomas normally walked to work, climbing the sizable hill on which Adams Street runs—a significant feat in the winter—and then turning right onto High Street.

The crew of lawyers Thomas joined considered themselves an anointed band out to reform a backward state government. When Danforth ran for attorney general in 1968, every one of Missouri's state officers was a Democrat, an electoral hegemony that dated back to Reconstruction. Drawing on his personal fortune, Danforth took on the incumbent Democratic attorney general, Norm Anderson, a classic good ol' boy. Danforth offered no real agenda or reason for change except for the rallying cry, "I Dare You," his challenge to the one-party state to elect a Republican and invigorate political competition. It was an embarrassingly simple strategy, but it worked. Danforth pulled off a stunning upset by winning 52 percent of the vote.

When he was elected, Danforth later admitted, "I had no idea what the attorney general's office was." Thirty-two years old and suddenly in power, Danforth resembled the Robert Redford character in the movie of the same era, *The Candidate*, wondering what he was supposed to do after the election. Danforth decided that his "main goal" would be to "try to create a really good law office." He set out to do this by

ending the patronage hiring practices at the attorney general's office
and bringing in idealistic, mostly young lawyers of high quality.

The office Danforth reformed became, person for person, one of
the most remarkable Republican farm teams ever assembled. Out of an
office of 30 to 35 attorneys would emerge not only Danforth, whose
phenomenal political career was only beginning, but also Christopher
"Kit" Bond, who later became governor and U.S. senator; John Ashcroft,
who followed Bond's trajectory and eventually became U.S. attorney
general; E. Thomas Coleman, a future congressman; D. Brook Bartlett,
a federal judge; Alfred Sikes, future chairman of the Federal Communications Commission; and one Clarence Thomas.

The office was loosely structured, with Danforth delegating a great
deal of responsibility and autonomy to the attorneys. A chief counsel
presided over each of the three divisions in the office—criminal, civil
and opinions. Given the smallness of the office and the egalitarianism
of the times, it was understood that this was no feudal hierarchy. Danforth himself made the rounds occasionally to give pats on the back.
Mostly, he left his attorneys to their own devices.

The attorney general's office was located on parts of the first and
second floors of the Missouri Supreme Court building. The three-story
building was of French Renaissance architecture and constructed in
patriotic hues: starkly red bricks, white stone Ionic pillars, and a roof
of blue slate tiles. Across the street was the state capitol, a huge gray
edifice modeled after the U.S. Capitol and overlooking the Missouri
River. The sturdy, red-brick Catholic Church standing nearby no doubt
pricked Thomas's conscience from time to time.

The attorney general represented the state of Missouri in almost all
of its legal business. Among his responsibilities was handling the appeals
of all felony criminal convictions in the state. Rookies in the office were
required to do a stint in the criminal division. On Thomas's first day of
work, Preston Dean, the head of the criminal division, took him around
and introduced him to some of his new colleagues.

Once again, Thomas found himself, in his words, "the integrator."
He was, by everyone's recollection, the first black attorney ever to work
for the Missouri Attorney General's Office. Thomas became an ambas-
sador for the creed of integration articulated by King, a creed now fully

embodied by the young Yale Law graduate who owed so much to the slain leader. With the interracial friendships and racial bonhomie he cultivated in his years in Jefferson City, Thomas would leave behind a trail of improved race relations in the office and social circles in which he moved.

"We were young, pro–civil rights people anxious to accept him," explained Dick Weiler, an attorney in the office. "And . . . he went out of his way to be accepted." One way Thomas worked to facilitate this acceptance was to downplay his connection to Yale. Prior to his arrival, the attorneys in the office were exclusively graduates of the University of Missouri and St. Louis University law schools. Thomas avoided discussing his law school years, lest he ruffle the egos of colleagues lacking an Ivy League diploma. Weiler recalled, "I don't think he talked to anybody about Yale Law School, all that stuff." Very quickly, Thomas would be considered "one of the guys."

Thomas's apparel, dictated by his finances, still left a good deal to be desired. The standard men's wear for the office was coat and tie (coats could be shed inside one's own office). "Initially, Clarence probably didn't have clothes that were as nice as the other guys'," attorney Mike Boicourt observed. He recalled in particular one "obnoxious sports coat." Plaid and "pretty loud," with a "bunch of maroon in it," the coat provoked so many catcalls that Thomas finally began to leave it at home in his closet. With a young family and substantial student debts, Thomas would struggle sartorially for years.

He had accepted the position of assistant attorney general knowing his compensation would be, in his words, "$11,000 a year and all the gruel I could eat." It turned out that even the work environment was dour. The impressive exterior of the supreme court building hid the rundown conditions inside. Paint was peeling off the walls. The basement was subject to flooding. The offices themselves were, in one attorney's words, "rabbit warrens," perhaps five feet by ten feet in size. An old rumor held that a former state supreme court justice had once raised chickens there.

Thomas's office, one of the warrens, was in the basement. He was given a metal desk, a metal filing cabinet, an uncomfortable little desk chair, and another government-issue chair for entertaining a visitor. The office had no window. Photos of Kathy and Jamal sat on his desk.

It was in this little space of his own that the first black attorney in the history of the office made a statement that would preclude him from being stereotyped. As soon as he moved in, Thomas unfurled the Confederate flag that once decorated his New Haven apartment and displayed it on his office wall. The flag was an attention-getter. Like Thomas's friends at Yale, Neil Bernstein, a fellow attorney, observed, "He did it obviously to provoke."

"This is a reminder that I shouldn't be pigeonholed," Thomas told Dick Weiler, interpreted the flag as "a symbol of his individualism." Bernstein said, "When asked why he'd put it up, his basic argument was, they [the Confederates] were honest about their attitudes on race. That made life a lot simpler than people who aren't honest about it."

Years later, Thomas mentioned the flag to a co-worker in Washington, Michael Middleton. "Yeah, I flew the flag," Thomas told him, chuckling. "I wanted to shake things up. I was the only black guy there. You know, let's see what these mid-Missouri rednecks have to say about this."*

After passing the bar exam, Thomas was sworn in as a practicing attorney on September 14, 1974. Three days later, he argued his first case before the Missouri Supreme Court. Inside a courtroom of dark wood paneling, he rose from his chair behind a long wooden desk to defend his new client, the State of Missouri. Thomas admitted that he was "absolutely scared beyond belief."

For the first seven months, Thomas's practice, in his words, was "almost exclusively" briefing and arguing appeals in criminal cases before the three state courts of appeals and the supreme court. He also occasionally appeared in circuit courts throughout the state on related criminal matters. His caseload, as requested, was staggering: He oversaw

---

*Others had a different recollection of the flag. S. Joel Wilson, another attorney and friend of Thomas, said Thomas had a miniature desk flag that was actually the Georgia state flag, which incorporated the Confederate flag. Thomas apparently used this smaller flag later in his time at the attorney general's office, perhaps because the full-size flag proved too much of a shocker. There were too many people who saw the full-length rebel flag—both at Thomas's apartment at Yale and in his office in Jefferson City—for history to absolve Thomas of this provocation. Bernstein was adamant: "It wasn't there to show he loved Georgia, where he came from." Thomas wanted to provoke an argument and make an impression. He succeeded at both.

several hundred cases at a time. This practice was appellate rather than trial; he never would participate in a jury trial. But an appellate practice was ideal for an intellectually curious young lawyer who, as his high-school yearbook announced, "loved to argue."

One of Thomas's first cases would be among his more memorable. In *Missouri v. Torrence*, Vernon Torrence appealed his convictions for rape and sodomy. The victim had been driving down Prospect Avenue in Kansas City with her three-year-old son seated next to her. This was in a predominantly black area of the city, a fact Thomas would have known from his experiences there. She stopped for a traffic light. Torrence opened the passenger door and jumped in. He placed a can opener to her son's side and ordered her to drive. Torrence threatened to kill them if she did not comply.

At an intersection, Torrence unzipped his pants and ordered the woman to "play" with his genitals. After protesting, she obeyed. He then ordered her to continue driving, then to pull into an alley. Once they were parked behind a building, he forced her to perform oral sex upon him. He subsequently raped her as well.

After reentering the vehicle, he commanded her to drive to another location, where he raped and sodomized her again. Then he told her to get up and dress and drive him to another location, where she let him out. The victim later positively identified Torrence as the perpetrator.

On appeal, Torrence argued that the testimony about the second rape and sodomy should not have been admitted into evidence in his trial. He claimed that the second round of atrocities constituted separate and distinct crimes for which he was not charged. Torrence sought to avail himself of the general rule that evidence of other crimes cannot be introduced against a criminal defendant to prove his guilt.

Thomas, representing the state, contended that the entire series of events constituted one transaction in the eyes of the law. He argued that an exception to the general rule applied, i.e., one that permits the introduction of evidence showing that the other crimes were part of a common scheme or plan so interrelated to the first rape and sodomy that proof of one tends to establish proof of the other. The trial court, he argued, ruled correctly in holding that the second rape and sodomy were part of the *res gestae,* or the admissible facts of the case.

On February 3, 1975, the court of appeals came down on the side of the state and its young attorney, holding that the "evidence points to but one conclusion—that defendant exercised power and control over [the victim] to effect but one design and plan, namely, to make ... the victim of sexual excesses." While the term "sexual excesses" was an infelicitous description of a crime spree reminiscent of the recent, controversial movie *A Clockwork Orange,* the court agreed that the separate offenses were "manifestations of this one common design and plan," and therefore admissible. The court upheld Torrence's convictions.

On the same day the court handed down its decision in *Torrence,* it gave Thomas another victory in *Missouri v. Collins.* The defendant, Manny Collins, shot Thurlow Johnson once and attempted to shoot him a second time. The second shot misfired, however, allowing Johnson to flee to safety. Upon arrest, Collins admitted to shooting Johnson and expressed his resolve to finish Johnson off if given the chance. He was convicted of assault with malice aforethought.

Collins asserted in his appeal that the state did not prove a knowing and voluntary waiver of his *Miranda* rights. Thomas noted on behalf of the state that the officers had complied with *Miranda:* a police officer read Collins his rights and Collins acknowledged that he understood them. Noting that the state's evidence on this point "was unimpeached," the court of appeals affirmed the conviction.

In oral argument, Thomas stood and projected a "wonderful, deep voice," said Boicourt. He also did not display much nervousness. As Mike Boicourt put it, Thomas "wrote well, spoke well, thought well on his feet"; he learned by immersion and did not flounder. Thomas would come away from these criminal cases with a good understanding of appellate practice and a deeper horror of crime and its ravaging effects on the black community.

———

As he racked up victories in the courtroom, Thomas also was becoming one of the most popular members of the attorney general's office. His exuberant personality attracted co-workers; he diligently developed these relationships into friendships. Mike Boicourt was one who fell under the spell of this charisma. Boicourt was a stout good ol' boy from nearby Mexico, Missouri. Six feet, five inches tall, with blue eyes and a thick moustache, Boicourt played freshman basketball for the University of Missouri before going on to law school. He introduced Thomas to one of his passions, cigars. The two smoked their stogies in their offices and while they were out on the town. Thomas henceforth became a stubborn aficionado of cigars—even as smoking later fell into wide disfavor—for over twenty years.

Dick Weiler was another colleague who became a friend. This friendship, more than any other in Missouri, demonstrated the range of Thomas's relationships. Weiler, who had blue eyes, strawberry blonde hair and a florid complexion, was a quadriplegic as a result of having contracted polio at the age of fifteen. Undaunted, he graduated from the University of Missouri Law School with honors. Thomas and Weiler hit it off and soon became almost daily lunch companions. After Weiler moved to the Jefferson Building, Thomas would come over and join him in the building's cafeteria (already, Thomas was revealing his preference for cheap, government-subsidized lunches, notwithstanding his later libertarianism). Other times, they would eat in Weiler's office or outside the building. The topics of their lunchtime discussions meandered from office gossip to sports to philosophy to personal ambitions. Thomas traveled occasionally on weekends to Weiler's nearby forty-acre hobby farm, where they and other friends from the office watched fish splashing and jumping in the pond.

Thomas said that when he met Weiler, he was, at first, "*very* uncomfortable." Thomas explained, "He was there—he was in a wheelchair—he wrote with his mouth—he was my friend." A friendship grew because they had much in common otherwise. "I had grown used to being stared at because I was black. But, now we were being stared at because he was in a wheelchair. I was used to being excluded from places because of my color, but not because there were too many steps to carry Richard up." To Thomas's awe, Weiler rarely complained about any of this.

Another fellow attorney with whom Thomas did not get along as well was John Ashcroft, who graduated from Yale and the University of Chicago Law School before returning to Missouri to launch a political career. It began inauspiciously with a losing bid for Congress in 1972. Later appointed state auditor, he then lost his bid for reelection in November 1974. Danforth hired him for the attorney general's office after his defeat. For a time, Ashcroft and Thomas both represented the department of revenue.

Ashcroft pursued a friendship with Thomas, but in this he enjoyed no better success than he had in politics. Thomas had many other colleagues with whom he shared more interests. Thomas viewed Ashcroft, correctly, as a politician-in-training who was holding down his position only until he could run for office again. Others in the office realized that Ashcroft was being groomed to succeed Danforth. Accordingly, many courtiers would drop by Ashcroft's office to compliment a memorandum he had written or otherwise flatter him. When the bootlickers arrived, Thomas would leave the room.

Ashcroft also had the misfortune of meeting Thomas at a time when he was moving further from his faith. Neil Bernstein described how "Ashcroft would come in and gleefully report having gone to a revival the night before and all the souls he had saved." This was not what Thomas cared to hear at this point in his life. He repeatedly declined invitations from Ashcroft for him and Kathy to come over for dinner. Thomas, Boicourt recalled, "was afraid they might have to pore over the Bible and sing hymns afterwards."

Thomas also had a mischievous streak, and would, in Boicourt's words, try to "rile up" Ashcroft from time to time. Although nobody remembered him using profanity in Ashcroft's presence, Thomas would tease Ashcroft with such queries as, "How do you have time to write this brief if you have to sing in the choir every night?"

It was only fair that at times, the mischief was turned on Thomas. Soon after he joined the office, Thomas, Weiler and another attorney, Charlie Blackmar, were telling stories in Weiler's office "like kids around a campfire," said Weiler. Blackmar, a fourth-generation lawyer and native of Missouri, began talking about snakes. Weiler recalled: "I don't like snakes. I could tell Clarence really didn't like snakes. The tales kept getting taller." Finally, Blackmar moistened his index and middle fingers and struck them on the back of Thomas's neck to imitate a snakebite. "Clarence just about cleared my desk," Weiler recalled, and simultaneously "let out a yawl" that resounded throughout the office.

When Thomas splurged and went out to eat, he sometimes joined Boicourt and Weiler for Chinese food from the Kai Min Chinese restaurant on Broadway, where Thomas carried Weiler's wheelchair up a flight of steps. The gang might also meet at Weiler's apartment. "He was the first guy to fall asleep on my couch," Weiler remembered. As Thomas dozed off, one of the fellows would smear up his glasses. Thomas sometimes even tagged along on Boicourt's dates.

Once a month, Boicourt would drive thirty miles north to Columbia, the home of the University of Missouri. He took Thomas to several football and basketball games. They also frequented assorted "watering establishments," Boicourt recalled. Kathy "trusted I wouldn't get him in trouble very much." Thomas often spent the night at Boicourt's place afterwards.

Boicourt took the opportunity to introduce Thomas to some of his "redneck friends." One was a goliath of six feet, nine inches and 280 pounds who taught in a state prison, and called Boicourt by the nickname "Boris." This man would offer a stiff challenge to Thomas's faith in racial integration. When Boicourt and Thomas would enter Harpo's, a favored drinking establishment in downtown Columbia, the friend would announce in a loud voice, "Here comes Boris and his nigger again."

Thomas's reaction to this mistreatment offered a fascinating window into his soul and his future. He did not demand that they leave, nor did he lecture the man. Instead, he laughed. As the slurs kept coming, so did Thomas's laughter. As he made his way in the heart of a state where such language was common, Thomas responded by turning the other cheek.

Thomas's forbearance won a convert to King's dream. "He just charmed him," Boicourt said, adding that his big friend "asks me about Clarence to this day. He says he's the best man he ever met."

On those weekend nights when they did not make the pilgrimage to Columbia, Boicourt frequently drove Thomas and Joel Wilson around in his Cadillac Seville. They traveled on the many two-lane roads that snaked through the surrounding countryside, passing through sleepy little towns along the way. After a while, they would pull over and stop, then gaze at the woods and the stars unobstructed by city lights. They puffed on "good American" cigars, in Boicourt's words, as they chewed over the issues of the moment. Then they would climb back into the smoke-filled car and drive some more. The eight-track tape player offered background music for such tours. One of the group's favorite tapes was a Ray Charles album featuring his versions of classic country-and-western songs. Given the interracial social dynamic within the car, it would have been hard to select a more fitting soundtrack for these occasions.

Boicourt concluded from these outings that "maybe Clarence missed some of the exuberance of youth, having to work so hard to get where he was." He added, "I don't mean sowing any oats. The idea of having a beer, going out, was fun to him. I don't think he'd done very much of that."

Thomas went out of his way to meet and know all of the lower staff in the attorney general's office. "He would've known everybody by name, whether he be a janitor or a marshal," Boicourt remembered "—no matter what their color." The clerical staff especially liked Thomas: "The secretaries—they all loved him."

At the same time, Thomas's pride was as ardent and unyielding as ever. Christmas 1974 brought an example of this quality that stood out in Danforth's memory. Thomas spent his first Christmas Eve in Jefferson City without Kathy and Jamal, who were back east visiting her family. The reasons for this odd separation were and remain unclear. When Danforth learned that Thomas had stayed behind, he invited him over to his home for a holiday dinner.

Thomas declined. Danforth said he "press[ed] the invitation." Thomas declined again. Danforth concluded Thomas was reluctant to accept because he felt Danforth was "feeling sorry for him." One thing Thomas would never tolerate, Danforth learned, was being "an object of pity." Danforth kept after him until Thomas finally relented. He came over for Christmas turkey, but under protest, insisting all the way that he did not want them to feel sorry for him. "That's really telling, you know," Danforth remarked. "That's Clarence."

In September 1975, a friend told Thomas about a book review he had just read in the *Wall Street Journal.*

"Clarence, there's another black guy out here who is as crazy as you are," he told Thomas. "He has the same ideas that you have. There are *two* of you!" He struggled, however, to recall the name of the author. "I can't remember his name. It's *Sowl* or *Sool* or *Sail* or something."

The book was *Race and Economics* by Thomas Sowell. The reviewer, Michael Novak, hailed the work as "brilliant" and "the most important book on politics and race in years." After reading the review, Thomas bought the book.

Reading *Race and Economics*, Thomas said, was "like pouring half a glass of water on the desert. I just soaked it up." He also described the work as "intellectual manna." The book would become one of the intellectual cornerstones of Thomas's philosophy.

Sowell was an economist who had earned degrees from Howard, Harvard and the University of Chicago. With such credentials, his writings carried intellectual weight—and they would need it, for his views were not only unorthodox but utterly explosive in the academic world of his day. Sowell started the book by explaining the basic thrust of his argument: "Race makes a difference, in economic transactions as in other areas of life. There has been a tendency to pass over this unpleasant fact, or else to deal with it in purely moral terms."

Sowell, whose emphasis was on the materialistic and secular, disputed the assumption that racial progress was inevitable. He found that history "gives little support to the view that time automatically erodes racial aversions, fears and animosities, or even tames the overt behavior based on such feelings." Sowell sought to make headway against these ancient resentments by demonstrating that they were economically foolish. Races and ethnic groups, he contended, are endowed with certain traits that grant them comparative economic advantages over other groups.

Candidly addressing the economics of slavery, Sowell found the institution economically ruinous to the South in the long run. Slavery made the South "a *permanently* less hospitable place for learning and intellectual life—which meant an enduring economic handicap for the whole region." Blacks born in the United States were economically disadvantaged because they were "denied the more basic opportunities to fully develop their abilities themselves." Black immigrants from previously slaveholding nations in Latin America and the West Indies fared better because they had been permitted, under their old regimes, to learn economic self-sufficiency. West Indian blacks, for example, "even under slavery ... had direct personal responsibility for an important part of their own well-being, and also acquired experience in economic activity on their own, since they cultivated their individual plots without supervision and were usually allowed to sell any surplus in the market." This environment "permitted and fostered more self-reliance, more economic experience, and more defiance of whites."

Much of the book was devoted to an examination of the distinguishing traits of immigrant peoples. Like African-Americans in the 1970s, Sowell noted, immigrants traditionally suffered from broken homes, high crime and infant-mortality rates, and youth gangs. Sowell thought that immigrants were able to climb out of their initial conditions through hard work and self-help. The Irish progressed more slowly than the Italians, he concluded, because the Italians were more likely to decline charity.

Echoing the conclusions of Harvard professor Edward C. Banfield, Sowell blamed poverty not on its "various 'causes,'" but on the lack of a "*future* orientation—a belief in a pattern of behavior that sacrifices present comforts and enjoyments while preparing for future success." The groups who were future-oriented—"the Jews, the Japanese-Americans, and the West Indian Negroes, for example—all came from social backgrounds in which this kind of behavior was common before they set foot on American soil."

Charitable organizations and government programs often did more harm than good. "Ethnic minorities have never seen social reformers as these reformers have seen themselves," Sowell wrote. "In both the nineteenth and twentieth centuries, ethnic minorities have often rejected the outside missionaries as dilettantes, slummers, ideologues, moral imperialists, or hopelessly uncomprehending human beings." For Thomas, this passage read as if Bigger Thomas escaped the gallows and became a fellow at the Hoover Institution.

Sowell did not go so far as to offer a social philosophy of his own. Instead, he criticized the "disasters in the social reforms of recent years" and recommended alternative principles in piecemeal fashion. "One need only mention Urban Renewal, public housing projects, welfare, or inner city schools to realize that the 'experts' have produced more than their share of disasters," Sowell remarked. He rejected such government aid, noting that government and bureaucracy are more likely to discriminate than businesses in the free market because they lack a profit incentive (discrimination is not profitable, Sowell contended). Without spinning a full theory of social reform, Sowell made it clear in which direction American society should be headed: less government and more self-reliance by its citizens.

Here, Thomas found a sophisticated worldview he could adopt virtually without alteration. Sowell was advocating the beliefs and values of Thomas's own grandfather. The primacy of education, free enterprise and individual initiative stood in stark contrast to the standard intellectual dogma of the day, which emphasized government assistance, collectivism and affirmative action.

He immediately set out to meet his new hero. "I called UCLA, where he was—the word I got was nobody knew who he was," Thomas recalled. Then he learned that Sowell had moved to Stanford. At that point, Thomas "bugged him. I know I bugged the man." The notoriously prickly Sowell did not return Thomas's calls.

Eventually, a friend noticed that the elusive guru was scheduled to speak at Washington University in St. Louis. He was to be part of a conference at the law school, and was to debate then-Professor Ruth Bader Ginsburg. Thomas left work early to make it to the conference. He approached Sowell and asked him to autograph his copy of *Race and Economics*. Thomas made such an impression on the aloof Sowell that not only did they stay in touch, but a genuine friendship blossomed.

"When I read *Race and Economics*, it really moved me back to an approach that was consistent with my own predisposition and my own background," Thomas observed of this critical turn in his thinking. He was beginning to identify more explicitly with conservatism. In 1976, he registered to vote in Missouri as an independent (as appropriate a label for Thomas's politics as could be devised). That year, he voted for Gerald Ford for president.

The liberal of Holy Cross and, to a diminishing extent, Yale moved farther to the right during his years in Jefferson City—so much so, in fact, that Danforth would remember Thomas as "the most conservative person in the office." Danforth himself was a member of the more liberal-moderate wing of the Republican Party, then under the leadership of Nelson Rockefeller. Thomas never fell within that group.

Thomas became a vociferous critic of the liberal remedies proposed in Congress and the federal courts to ameliorate race relations. He fulminated against the civil rights agenda of most black politicians and interest groups such as the NAACP: busing, quotas, affirmative action. He argued with Boicourt over busing, which had flared up into a deeply divisive issue in many of America's major cities. Boicourt thought busing a commendable policy; Thomas condemned it, saying it sent the wrong message to young blacks—that they had to sit next to whites in class in order to learn.

The young black attorney was "frustrated and disappointed with race relations generally," Dick Weiler said. He remained a "big, big follower of Martin Luther King," one committed to seeking a way to "blend together" the races and to dissolve old hatreds. He spoke often of the values ingrained by his grandfather and the nuns.

Roe v. Wade, the 1973 Supreme Court decision that legalized abortion, had placed abortion rights at the center of national politics. On this issue, Thomas was still anchored to the values of his youth. He discussed abortion a good deal with Mike Boicourt, who was working on several cases in which the state was defending statutes restricting the right to an abortion (and he would go on to be the lead counsel in the landmark abortion case *Webster v. Reproductive Health Services,* handed down by the Supreme Court in 1989). Because of his views, Boicourt was "ambivalent" about his work on these cases. Thomas, on the other hand, made it clear that he was anti-abortion. As part of these conversations, Boicourt and Thomas discussed *Roe.* Boicourt said years later that he could not remember what Thomas's views were.

Weiler and Thomas had become good friends, and Weiler was sensitive to Thomas's impatience with his criminal cases and preference for civil work. Weiler invited him to come over to the civil division and inherit Weiler's area of practice: representing the department of revenue, which was responsible for collecting corporate, income and sales taxes and for motor vehicle licensing.

The subject matter of Thomas's caseload would change from gore to money, a change that suited him fine. He won most of the cases he took to court. One of his more important victories was in *McKay Buick v. Spradling.* Missouri's automobile dealers had lobbied successfully for a flat tax on new motor vehicles, used motor vehicles and parts. The attorney general's office had issued an opinion declaring this new tax scheme unconstitutional. Motor vehicles are property, Danforth's office reasoned, and the state constitution mandated that all property taxes be *ad valorem,* or based on the value of the property. The dealers sued. On November 10, 1975, the Supreme Court agreed with Danforth and Thomas and struck down the new tax as unconstitutional.

This success in *McKay Buick* helped to offset one of Thomas's few losses, which the high court announced the month before. In *L&R Distributing v. Missouri Dept. of Revenue,* the state sought to apply a sales tax to pinball machines and other coin-operated amusement devices. This move came on the cusp of the video game craze in the 1970s, and a windfall of potential revenue stood to be gained. Unfortunately for Thomas, the Supreme Court held that the machines were exempt from the tax.

Thomas's chief glory in the courtroom would not come until 1976. That year, the state court of appeals took up *Missouri ex rel. Dyke v. Spradling.* The department of revenue had decided in 1973 to issue randomly all noncommercial motor vehicle license plates except for official or historic vehicles. The idea was to accommodate the expected surge in vehicle registrations in the coming years. But this reform stood to liquidate an important perk of a small but politically influential elite: people who held low-numbered license plates. These plates, which Thomas would later describe as "similar to vanity plates," became "a sign of status and were often displayed by those who were politically well-connected."

Danforth understood well the political damage he would sustain if he pressed forward with the appeal. At one point in the litigation, he walked to Weiler's office and said, "This isn't making me very popular. I'd be a lot better off if you lost this. But you go ahead." Thomas importuned Danforth to stay the course. He argued persuasively there was no property right to certain numbers in a government-issued license plate.

Years later, Thomas would proudly recount how the court of appeals, "accepting my argument," found there was no property right to the low-numbered plates. The court held "there is no statutory provision expressly establishing property or personal rights in the license numbers to which relators claim a right." The court went on to employ language that Thomas would cherish: "To recognize a personal right in these numbers ... would be to exalt the vanity of these holders of low numbers over the public interest and welfare." By the same reasoning, the court pointed out, any holder of any other number "which happened to appeal to him" could also insist on retaining it indefinitely. The court upheld the department's policy.

The ringing decision pleased Thomas immensely. Weiler said he and Thomas considered the case "our blow against wealth and privilege."

As Thomas ended his second year at the attorney general's office, he had established his reputation as a young attorney with solid prospects. The record he compiled was impressive: 30 wins and 6 losses in cases before the supreme court and the court of appeals.

Things were not going as well in the Thomas household as they were in the courtroom. While they were in New Haven, Kathy had stayed at home to concentrate on rearing Jamal. Upon their move to Jefferson City, she returned to college. Perhaps she merely decided that domestic life was not for her; or she may have sensed the need to obtain her degree for financial security. The profound yearning for privacy she shared with her husband would leave such questions unanswered. She attended Lincoln University, a small, all-black college in Jefferson City founded by Union soldiers after the Civil War. Weiler said Thomas was enthusiastic about her enrollment there. Thomas himself had become essentially the general counsel for Lincoln University, as he represented Lincoln at the attorney general's office.

"Kathy was a very private person," said Weiler. "I don't know if anybody [from the attorney general days] can tell you anything about her." Friends who dined at the Thomas place found her very quiet and reserved. In these spells of silence and her zeal for privacy, she was very much like the man she had fallen in love with. She began to work outside the home in addition to attending Lincoln. She held down a part-time job for the Bicentennial Commission, helping to coordinate Missouri's participation in the celebration in 1976. Jamal was placed in day care starting when he was two years old.

Thomas later recalled that he would walk to work "before dawn, so that I could put a full day's work in, and still be with my son in the evenings." (It is noteworthy that Thomas did not mention his wife as a reason for returning home at night.) In rearing Jamal, he fused the steel discipline of Myers Anderson with his own giant ambitions. He read to him and had him performing pushups by the age of three. When asked whether he wanted Jamal to be president or a professional football player, Thomas replied, "Both."

On the Fourth of July, 1976, the Thomas family and Weiler drove to Faurot Field, the University of Missouri football stadium in Columbia, to watch the fireworks. Jamal sat behind the wheel.

"Kid wants to be a truck driver," Thomas remarked.

Weiler could sense where this was going. "Clarence, you need to let up on this kid. You want him to be an All-American and a Rhodes scholar in his junior year." Thomas laughed heartily as usual. These were expectations that no son could live up to. Still, Thomas saw no reason for his son—and, through him, his father—not to reach for the sky.

In November 1976, Danforth was elected to the U.S. Senate. His departure reminded Thomas that it was time for him to seek other opportunities as well. "Once Jack left, he didn't see any reason for being there," Weiler said of Thomas. He could have had a position in Danforth's office in Washington, but he was, in his own words, "financially strapped—in fact, desperately so."

Thomas decided he needed to parlay his experience at the attorney general's office into a better-paying job. "It's time to pay off my loans," he explained to friends.

CHAPTER TEN

Money Isn't Everything

When Thomas sought to switch to corporate law, he applied at large law firms in Missouri's two biggest cities, Kansas City and St. Louis. But he also learned of an enticing opportunity to work for a major corporation in St. Louis. Monsanto was exceptional in that it maintained a sizable stable of "in-house" attorneys, at a starting salary higher than that of any law firm in the state.

Monsanto, moreover, was looking with a very narrow focus. Ned J. Putzell Jr., vice president and general counsel for Monsanto, recalled he was "looking for minority members to put into my law department." He explained: "I had a large number of lawyers there, and I wanted diversity as well. And I set about looking for a female lawyer and a black lawyer, and I ended up hiring both."

An intriguing man in his own right, Putzell grew up a Republican in heavily Democratic Louisiana, then attended Harvard Law School and joined a Wall Street law firm upon graduating. The Second World War intervened, and his charismatic boss at the firm, "Wild" Bill Donovan, persuaded Putzell to follow him to work for the Office of Strategic Services. He served at the OSS headquarters in Washington, coordinating information on the office's clandestine operations (the OSS gathered intelligence and conducted unconventional warfare behind enemy lines). After working for a company in Montana, Putzell settled in St. Louis and rose to prominence in Monsanto, one of the city's major corporations.

Thomas arrived at Monsanto in early January 1977. Wearing one of his better suits, he interviewed with Putzell in the C building. "I was impressed with his background, his origin and what he'd made of himself," Putzell later said. "He was talking about antitrust law at the time. And having spent a lot of time in that field myself, I was also interested in how he talked on that subject. He seemed to be a personable, low-key guy." A conservative Republican, Putzell also was pleased to note that he "didn't seem to be carrying any kind of torches."

Another interviewer that day was Richard Duesenberg, a Monsanto attorney who later succeeded Putzell as general counsel. He said he was "impressed" with Thomas's preparation for the interview. Thomas had ferreted out that Duesenberg previously had been a law professor and had written on the Uniform Commercial Code. Thomas arrived at the interview prepared to discuss some of the finer points of the UCC, as well as a professor back at Yale Law School who was a specialist in the field. After the interview, Duesenberg said to himself, "Here is a fellow who really came ... prepared."

Thomas's day of interviews in the Monsanto law department left behind a string of good impressions. After learning of these good reviews, Putzell extended Thomas a job offer, which he accepted.

For a young attorney trying to maximize his income, it was the best job in town. Larry Thompson, an attorney who joined Monsanto in 1974, said that the company "paid more money than any other job offer I had in St. Louis from law firms." Monsanto offered $20,000 a year, at a time when law firms in St. Louis were paying $14,500. Thompson observed, "Monsanto was considered to be, at the time, the plum position in Missouri in terms of pay."

In January 1977, Thomas moved his family to St. Louis and joined a legal staff of over fifty attorneys. Monsanto's large, verdant grounds, appropriately referred to as a "campus," sprawled over both sides of Lindbergh Boulevard near Creve Coeur, an affluent suburb fifteen miles west of downtown St. Louis. Thomas moved into a comfortable office with glossy new furniture and company-provided artwork on the walls. The rebel flag would be unfurled no more.

Monsanto's newest assistant general counsel learned in short order why good corporate lawyers earned so much. While representing the Missouri Department of Revenue had hardly been titillating, it was a fast-paced life compared with the tedium of corporate practice at Monsanto. The company's primary business was manufacturing pesticides, herbicides and other chemicals to aid farmers and agricultural concerns in their ceaseless battle against the organisms that humans presumptuously lump together under the name "pests." The company relied on its lawyers mostly to look over or write contracts and to provide advice on legal issues that might arise. The lawyers were divided into "business groups," or units of attorneys responsible for handling certain areas of the law.

Thomas's group drafted and reviewed contracts and advised corporate managers on matters such as antitrust and product liability concerns. He helped to coordinate the registration of Monsanto pesticides and herbicides with federal agencies, and dealt with liability issues concerning the transportation and disposal of hazardous waste. He was involved in registering herbicides with the Environmental Protection Agency (EPA). One that later stood out in his mind was the Monsanto herbicide Roundup, which became one of the company's best-known products.

Joining the corporate law world spurred Thomas to study the art of acquiring wealth and nurturing successful relationships. His reading interests changed. Books on relatively airy topics of social justice gave way to such works as *Winning through Intimidation, Dress for Success,* and *How to Be Assertive.* Of this time, Thomas would later say that he and his profit-motivated new friends "thought that we could conquer the world if armed with enough energy, intellect, and how-to books."

One partner in these pursuits and much else was Larry Thompson, who would become one of Thomas's closest friends. Thompson was born in Hannibal, the hamlet in northeast Missouri along the Mississippi River known as the home of Mark Twain. His father had worked on the railroad, his mother as a housewife and maid. Like Thomas, he had attended an all-black school. After *Brown v. Board of Education,* the schools in Hannibal desegregated, but Thompson and many other black children in the area continued to attend the all-black grammar school because of the high quality of instruction there. The teachers were black, "old-fashioned," and "tough," Thompson recalled, and the school became a magnet for local blacks seeking a better education. In an incident curiously similar to the scolding of Thomas by Sister Virgilius at around the same time, Thompson recalled that when he finished in second place in a seventh- or eighth-grade spelling bee, "the teacher really gave me hell for doing a poor job." Thompson went on to graduate from the University of Michigan Law School.

Thomas had met Thompson in the summer of 1974 at the bar review course in St. Louis. As Thompson remembered, "There weren't that many black people, so you had that sort of natural attraction." Afterwards, Thompson went to work at Monsanto—becoming the corporation's first full-time black lawyer—while Thomas moved to Jefferson City. They did not reconnect until Thomas joined Monsanto and was introduced to his new colleagues at a luncheon. "We reacquainted ourselves and became good friends," Thompson said.

Thompson would recall that "some of the fondest conversations, wide-ranging conversations, that I ever had with anyone" were with Thomas at a Chinese restaurant in nearby University City, Missouri. Usually twice a week, the two lunched together, sharing their professional dreams, hopes for their families, and politics and beliefs.

The Thomas and Thompson families lived close to each other in townhouses in University City and got together regularly. Their sons, Jamal and Larry Jr., were close in age and played together while Kathy and Linda, Thompson's wife, cooked or talked. The two men enjoyed "hanging out" and watching sports on television.

Thomas still kept in touch with Father Brooks back at Holy Cross. Brooks traveled to St. Louis once a year to visit the Holy Cross alumni club in the city, and saw Thomas there during these trips. In 1978, Brooks was instrumental in arranging for Holy Cross to extend Thomas the highest compliment it could bestow on an alumnus: asking him to serve on the college's board of trustees. A photograph of Thomas taken at the time of his appointment shows a young man in a dapper suit, with a wide silk tie fashionable in the late 1970s, stylish black-rimmed glasses, and a very broad smile.

Service on the board required trips to Holy Cross for the board's meetings. Brooks recalled that at the meetings Thomas advocated his stern egalitarianism, insisting that everyone be held to the "same standards of excellence." He also met with members of the Black Students' Union, and, in Brooks' words, became "a kind of role model." Thomas encouraged them to study diligently and make the most of their opportunity at Holy Cross.

When Thomas learned of the high failure rate for black students at Holy Cross—over 60 percent—he was appalled. "We brought in valedictorians . . . and kids from the top twenty percent of the classes of the inner cities' public schools," he noted. "My question to the faculty and the administration was: Why are we bringing in these bright kids and turning them into anti-social people?"

Living in St. Louis spurred Thomas to ponder more deeply the nation's racial divide. In the old federal courthouse downtown, which stood high upon a bluff above the Mississippi River, a federal court had ruled on the freedom of the escaped slave, Dred Scott, and initiated a case that would become one of the most famous decisions of the U.S. Supreme Court. In Thomas's day, the St. Louis public schools were embroiled in federal litigation over the extent and duration of desegregation efforts. Thomas later commented on how the desegregation cases in St. Louis and the false premise on which they were based hardened his conviction that exposure to white students was not essential for academic success by blacks.

In their discussions of race relations, Larry Thompson said that Thomas "was always more versed in the philosophical thoughts than I was. His views were more advanced, and he was more articulate about those kinds of things, and I think was more serious than I was in that stuff." The two young attorneys were conservatives of the Booker T. Washington mold. "We were always amazed at the monolithic thinking in the African-American community, and how that was not good. And we were always amazed, we could see through some of those so-called leaders at that time."

Jesse Jackson had started Operation PUSH, which was targeting major corporations with boycotts if they did not embrace affirmative action. Thomas thought racial preferences unnecessary and counterproductive. "He talked about changing the way our people thought," Thompson recollected. "That was a clear dream. He talked about a time when we would not be so foolish to be enslaved by just one particular view, or leaders who were clearly captured by one political party." They both believed that schoolchildren should not be taught to regard themselves as victims. "And in fact, what we were taught was that the world isn't nice, and if you wanted to succeed, you had to be better than the other people."

Thomas subsequently observed of the era:

In the 70's . . . the mood of the civil rights movement changed. People were realizing that the major civil rights legislation of the 60's were [*sic*] not getting results fast enough to right the injustice of centuries of discrimination. Civil rights advocates wanted more government action; action that would result in drastic change in perhaps a decade, and rid the country of racial prejudice. Needless to say, such drastic change takes drastic measures. The question of the day was: "What action do we take?" The result was a quest for racial integration with the intention that racial integration would result in racial harmony and an end to discrimination. Unfortunately, the concept of racial balance and proportionate representation often supplanted the concept of racial integration and racial desegregation.

These policies, Thomas concluded, "caused several unintended and unwanted social problems on the *individual* level. For example, white workers with seniority who felt that their jobs were in jeopardy because of affirmative action, were convinced that the government was only playing a numbers game and that in the urgent quest for an end to racial injustice, the government was inspiring reverse discrimination, and only seeking balanced numerical results."

Thomas saw these policies "undermine public confidence in the efforts of the civil rights movement." He grew frustrated that unscrupulous leaders were exploiting the black community, in his view, by teaching them that they were victims. His belief in self-help and individual initiative was stronger than ever; his own new prosperity had shown there was a way out.

———

Thomas's interest in politics was common knowledge among his business-minded colleagues at Monsanto. It was also clear that he was growing bored solving other people's legal problems while the world was waiting to be saved from the likes of Jesse Jackson.

After a while, Thomas made less of an effort to obscure his dissatisfaction with the work he was given. He would blurt out to Thompson such things as, "This was a stupid assignment." Duesenberg carried the overall impression that Thomas "had ... a healthy irreverence for corporate America." Given that he was working in the very heart of corporate America, such a remark is telling.

Thomas and Thompson both had their gripes about the company, each with his own source of irritation. Thompson recalled, "I was talking about money. Because I wanted to make a lot of money." Yet "Clarence really never talked about that stuff. I mean, he talked about ideas and philosophy. And while I was frustrated with Monsanto because I didn't think I was advancing enough monetarily, he was frustrated with Monsanto . . . because it was too barren from a philosophical or idea standpoint. He wasn't doing enough to sort of change the world."

Eventually, both of these young men with options tired of hearing their own complaints. With Thomas's encouragement, Thompson started to look at firms in Atlanta—the same firms that had turned Thomas down in his fruitless last year at Yale. Thompson obtained a position at one of Atlanta's blue-chip firms and left Monsanto in 1978.

Before Thompson left, Thomas had begun to recite to him a refrain that would become a mantra for that time in his life. As for the work at Monsanto, he told Thompson, "I've got better things to do with my life, buddy."

Those "better things" involved politics and government. No city beckoned to someone with such interests more than Washington, D.C., and no man was better able to accommodate this change in career than Thomas's old patron, John Danforth. After Danforth and Thomas went down their separate professional paths in early 1977, they did not remain in contact. As a result, when he sought to approach Danforth about a job, Thomas was forced to enlist help from others who still remained close to the senator. The person who knew Danforth the best was, unfortunately, also Thomas's employer.

Aware of the risk, he went ahead and approached Ned Putzell. "He expressed an interest in going to Washington, and asked me if I could help him," Putzell later said. He then "made a few phone calls" on Thomas's behalf. Putzell knew Danforth's brother Bill and was able to get word to Danforth of Thomas's wish to return to his employ. Putzell gave Thomas a strong recommendation, saying Monsanto "had a high regard for him."

Thomas left Monsanto and St. Louis in August 1979. Almost two decades later, he stated:

> I made a decision when I was in the early part of my career not to ever work for money. I would never take a job for money, never switch jobs for money. So often we think, "I can make 15 or 20 percent more if I move over here." But that would mean either that I wasn't working for something that was meaningful to me, or if I was working for someone meaningful, that it was for sale.

The Senate Judiciary Committee once asked Thomas, among a long list of personal questions, what he had done in his career to "serv[e] the disadvantaged" through legal pro bono work (the canons of legal ethics ask attorneys to give back to the community through pro bono service to indigent clients or through public interest work). Such a question would have been well directed to many of Thomas's liberal colleagues from Yale, who went on to prosperous careers on Wall Street without paying much mind to such strictures. Thomas's reply summed up well the decision he made when he came to the fork in the road in St. Louis: "I consider my government service to be in the nature of 'pro bono' work, and an opportunity to make a contribution."

CHAPTER ELEVEN

The Coattails of St. Jack

The next year and a half would be among the more eventful seasons in Thomas's life. He arrived in the nation's capital a lowly staffer for a little-known, first-term senator. Soon he would be hurtling down a fast track to power.

In the late summer of 1979, Thomas moved into Room 239 of the Russell Senate Office Building, sharing office space with four other staffers. Of all the congressional office buildings where he might have been quartered, none was more likely to inspire a reverence for the Senate and its traditions. Bounded by Constitution Avenue, Delaware Avenue, First Street and C Street N.E., which formed a trapezoid around it, the Russell building was the first Senate office building. Built at the turn of the twentieth century, it featured the Beaux Arts style of architecture popular in the day. Many Doric columns and pilasters gave an austere regularity to the exterior of bright white marble and limestone. Inside, equally lovely if more downtrodden, staircases of white marble led staffers between floors. Thomas could add little grandeur to the accommodations; he settled for decorating his office space with pictures of Corvettes.

The new title he received was legislative assistant. Within Danforth's office, he was responsible for all matters involving energy, the environment, public works and the Department of the Interior. He advised Danforth on related legislation. These areas of public policy were not exactly of sizzling interest to most budding policy wonks, but the Organization of Petroleum Exporting Countries (OPEC), a cartel of oil-producing countries mostly in the Middle East, helped to make things more interesting by raising oil prices during this time and driving the American economy into a deep recession.

"It was a great job," Thomas concluded years later. "There wasn't much money involved, but we had a heck of a time. The great thing about that job was that you were not the principal, but you got to see the principal and you got to work with all the issues. There was just so much to get involved with." The "principal" was, of course, Danforth. A graduate of both Yale Law School and Yale Divinity School, Danforth was an ordained Episcopalian minister as well as a politician, and he preached occasionally at one of Washington's most highbrow Episcopal churches. For this avocation and his rectitude, Danforth's colleagues in the Senate began to refer to him as "Saint Jack." His emphasis on ethics imbued the office. Whenever the merits of proposed legislation or policies were discussed, Thomas recalled with admiration, Danforth's bottom-line query of his staffers was, "What is the right thing to do?"

Danforth, in turn, remembered Thomas as "clearly the most popular person in the office." J. C. Alvarez was one Danforth staffer charmed by the forceful young black attorney. For all of Danforth's early commitment to affirmative action, several of his white staffers did not refrain from questioning openly and crassly the qualifications of the minorities he hired. Like Thomas, Alvarez had sterling academic credentials, including a bachelor's degree from Princeton and a master's from Columbia. Yet she found herself mocked by certain colleagues, who said she was hired only because she was Hispanic.

One rude staffer also confronted Thomas with such resentments. The nature of the questioning suggested more a jealousy of his Yale Law degree than anything else, but the assault on Thomas's qualifications nevertheless carried racial overtones. "Let's face it," the staffer told Thomas. "The only reason you are here is because you went to Yale, and the only reason you got into Yale was not because of your ability, but because of affirmative action."

In response, Thomas drew a deep breath that, in Alvarez's words, "filled out his broad shoulders." He looked at the staffer and gave a reply that seemed both practiced and effective: "You know, I may have been lucky enough to get in, but I was smart enough to get out."

The people he met and relationships he cemented while on Danforth's staff would become linchpins of his political success. One admirer was a new Republican senator from Utah named Orrin Hatch, who remembered him as a "terrific" staffer—"very bright, very articulate, very principled." Thomas also mentioned to his friend Eddie Jenkins that he had developed "a very good relationship" with the former director of the Central Intelligence Agency, George Bush, a Republican who was preparing to run for president in 1980 against Ronald Reagan, the former governor of California.

As a new political era began to dawn, the thirty-one-year-old staffer was discovering that an accomplished black Republican could all but name his price in Washington. Harry Singleton, one of Thomas's closest friends from Yale, once acknowledged that he and Thomas recognized the glut of civil rights lawyers who were Democrats, and the concomitant opportunities for blacks who became Republicans. "Clarence and I and a bunch of us figured that out a long time ago," he said. "That's when we decided to switch." Thomas had a somewhat different tale. He later told another acquaintance from his Yale days, Fletcher Farrington, that when he arrived in Washington, he sought out both Democrats and Republicans about his future prospects. The Democrats did not talk to him, but the Republicans did.

Two friends from Holy Cross, Eddie Jenkins and Gil Hardy, were practicing law in Washington during Thomas's time with Danforth. When the three of them ventured out to parties in the city, Jenkins recalled, Thomas still showed his trademark reserve in large gatherings. "Clarence would come in real quiet. He wasn't really interested in partying. We always ended up on the porch outside, smoking cigars, and talking about life and politics. He didn't seem that interested in socializing in a large group." Thomas was, however, meeting people with political connections. "He asked me if I'd consider being a Republican," Jenkins recounted. "I said, 'No.' He said, 'You know, you'd be a Republican if you had some money.'"

On one occasion, the normally precocious Thomas showed remarkable indiscretion in revealing his dreams to strangers. Shortly after beginning his second tour of service with Danforth, he shared lunch with a reporter for Danforth's hometown newspaper, the *St. Louis Post-Dispatch*. As they dined at a Capitol Hill café, Thomas blurted out his ultimate career goal at the time. "I want to be on the Supreme Court," he told her. This statement was extraordinary for a multitude of reasons, not the least of which was the fact that he would say such a thing, out of the blue, to a reporter covering his boss. Yet the brash plan made sense. He was not the typical politico, but an attorney who had actually practiced law seriously in the hinterlands and still thought of himself primarily as a lawyer. What better aim for an attorney than a seat on the nation's highest court?

Shortly after Thomas arrived in Washington, Chris Brewster, another Danforth aide, gave him a copy of the *Lincoln Review,* a policy journal for black conservatives. As he had with Sowell, the self-confident Thomas wasted no time in trying to make the acquaintance of the journal's editor, Jay Parker. Thomas called him and said, "I wasn't aware there was someone else like me out there"—an exaggeration, given his relationship with Sowell and others. Parker invited the eager Thomas to dine at the old Duke Ziebert's restaurant. He and Thomas promptly became not only ideological comrades but good friends.

During this time, Thomas commuted from a low-rent apartment in Bethesda, Maryland, a suburb of Washington. The apartment complex was known as a way station for transient bureaucrats. Jamal was enrolled in preschool in Maryland and Kathy was working. In his spare time, Thomas began to train for a marathon.

Ronald Reagan's landslide victory in the 1980 election gave Republicans the presidency and Thomas his greatest professional opportunity since his acceptance by Yale. "As soon as that election was over," Danforth remarked, "I knew it was, 'Goodbye, Clarence.'" Danforth thought that the new administration would seek diversity in its appointments. Moreover, "Clarence was really unusual. He was an African-American conservative. I knew that it was going to be 'bye-bye.'"

Thomas was not yet visible to the Reagan team. Sowell, Thomas's hero and friend, would remedy this. Shortly after the election, Sowell called Thomas to invite him to a conference of independent-minded blacks that was to convene in San Francisco in December. Sowell expressed the hope that from the meeting would sprout an organization to counter the "consistently leftist thinking of the civil rights and black leadership." Thomas believed that this congress of iconoclastic black thinkers and policymakers would appeal especially to those who felt that "black Americans were being fed a steady diet of wrong ideas, wrong thinking and certainly nothing approaching pluralism." Also, scouts for the incoming administration would be there, and it was a great place to be seen. Thomas flew out to San Francisco with both intellectual and professional goals in mind. He arrived, he said, "bubbling, bursting with excitement. I could hardly contain myself."

The Black Alternatives Conference, as it was formally called, was held at the Fairmont Hotel high atop Nob Hill. Among the one hundred black thinkers and their supporters gathered from across the country were people who would become famous in Republican circles: Sowell, Walter E. Williams, Henry Lucas Jr., Clarence M. Pendleton Jr. Economist Milton Friedman, one of Sowell's colleagues from the Hoover Institution, also was present. Tony Brown taped his weekly PBS television show at the conference. A young black reporter named Juan Williams covered the event for the *Washington Post*. He reported that at the conference, black conservatives, "who have thought of themselves as the outcasts or the minority within a minority, had finally found a home." Thomas echoed these words. "For those of us who had wandered in the desert of political and ideological alienation," he recalled, "we had found a home, we had found each other. For me, this was also the beginning of public exposure that would change my life and raise my blood pressure—and anxiety level." This would not be the last time he would complain about the predictable consequences of the "public exposure" he was beginning to court.

Thomas was part of a symposium on education. The topic of his discourse was "Being Educated Black." He related many of the details that would become some of the more familiar aspects of his life story: attending the black parochial schools of Savannah and the critical boost this education had given to him despite segregation. He also shared his growing certitude that the nation was erring terribly in trying to abolish all-black education to promote integration. Speaking of St. Pius X High School, Thomas said, "The interesting thing about the school is this: as a result of racial integration, as a result of the requirement that all high schools be integrated in the city of Savannah, they closed down St. Pius X High School because there was no cross-integration from the white community, and approximately 300 students who could afford to go to St. Pius X High School were put out." Thomas concluded, "I think we had some very intelligent people who were displaced to what I would consider inferior schools."

Thomas shared some of the racial taunting he endured at the minor seminary. He noted how "I was referred to, not too politely, as the black spot on the white horse." Yet this discrimination, he said, had urged him to work all the harder. "At that time there was no mercy shown to blacks and there were no changes made in the curriculum. We were simply required to go on and perform as the other students." He also spoke of the dismal experience of many black students at Holy Cross during his time on the board of trustees.

In a discussion with Juan Williams after his presentation, Thomas spoke candidly and at length. One riff he delivered went right to the heart of the Fairmont Conference's differences with the civil rights establishment: "I'm tired of blacks being thought of only as poor people, people on welfare, people who are unemployed. That's the only way the Jesse Jacksons and the other black leaders talk about black people. To them, we're all a monolith. Well, they are not talking for the 80 to 90 percent of black people in this country who have never been on welfare or in jail."

Thomas then said a couple of things he would very much regret. In offering an example of the destructiveness of the welfare mentality, he needed look no farther, in his eyes, than his own sister, Emma Mae Martin. Before he could take it back, he ungraciously made her a topic of the conversation. "She gets mad when the mailman is late with her welfare check," he said. "That is how dependent she is. What's worse is that now her kids feel entitled to the check too. They have no motivation for doing better or getting out of that situation."

It was a ready but careless example. His sister had received government assistance while she sought to rear her four children alone, after her husband deserted her, and while simultaneously taking care of ailing Aunt Annie Devoe. Her acceptance of welfare under these circumstances was hardly grasping, especially since she also continued to work steadily thereafter. Emma Mae later was gracious enough to insist that her brother's comments were "blown out of proportion" by the media, and that no ill will lingered over the remarks. But a public airing of such familial discord was unseemly, and in his only public follow-up to the issue, Thomas later described his comments about his sister as "accurate, but unfortunate."

Thomas also impetuously made a career pledge to Juan Williams that he would soon break. He explained that throughout his career, he had refused to work on so-called black issues. In Danforth's office, for example, the areas of public policy for which he was responsible excluded any civil rights matters, lest his colleagues think he had obtained his position because of his race. Then, in a comment that would prove deeply ironical, Thomas observed, "If I ever went to work for the EEOC or did anything directly connected with blacks, my career would be irreparably ruined. The monkey would be on my back again to prove that I didn't have the job because I'm black. People meeting me for the first time would automatically dismiss my thinking as second-rate."

Thomas had captivated Williams. His subsequent article in the *Post* became, for the young, unknown Danforth staffer, an advertisement for employment in the new administration. Williams concluded his article with the observation:

> While the black conservatives like Clarence Thomas point out that not all blacks are poor or in jail, their challenge will be to remember that a disproportionate number of blacks are poor and are in jail. This country is not yet so sophisticated that blacks, even black Republicans, can say it makes no difference what color an American is. But thanks to Clarence Thomas and other black Republicans like him, new approaches to stagnant problems are being discussed for the first time since Martin Luther King Jr.

Juan Williams said years later that he came away from the Fairmont Conference viewing Thomas as "the most interesting of a very self-important crowd, because he was so brutally candid." This judgment shone vividly in the article, which became a minor sensation back in Washington. Thomas recalled: "All of a sudden my views, or at least the journalistic synopsis of my views, are in a major paper, the *Washington Post*. I wasn't used to this kind of thing. I never ran for office. I rarely raised my hand in college." His profile raised, Thomas spent a good deal of time ducking from hostile fire. The "resulting outcry," Thomas said, damaged his relations with fellow staffers on Capitol Hill. Black Republicans with whom he had worked became "distant and some were even hostile." The letters to the editor of the *Post* "castigated and ridiculed me." A group called the Black Women's Agenda invited him to a panel presentation, where he received a memorable scolding from Congressman Harold Washington of Illinois.

One of the more attentive listeners at the conference was Edwin
Meese. An affable man with full blonde eyebrows, ruddy complexion
and a ready smile, Meese was, like Thomas, a Yale-educated attorney.
He had served Reagan while he was governor of California, and was
the director of transition for the new administration, in charge of filling it with new faces ready to implement the Reagan mandate. Meese
already knew Jay Parker and had asked him to assist with the transition effort. He requested specifically that Parker make recommendations regarding the U.S. Equal Employment Opportunity Commission
(EEOC). Parker asked his protégé, Thomas, to write a memorandum
outlining issues for the EEOC to take up under the new administration.

This two-page memo, dated December 22, 1980, began with a typically bold proclamation. "The Civil Rights Act of 1964," Thomas
declared, "does not authorize the Equal Employment Opportunity
[Commission] to require affirmative action." He went on to offer a
compact, lucid explanation of the central problems that would confront
the EEOC:

> EEOC, however, encourages employers to implement voluntary affir-
> mative action programs. EEOC takes the position that Congress intended
> to encourage voluntary affirmative action. Thus, EEOC provides a pro-
> cedure for voluntary compliance, which is similar to the mandatory
> plans under Executive Order 11246. The employer is required to con-
> duct a self-analysis which is primarily a statistical determination of the
> under-representation (or under-utilization) of minorities and women
> in the workforce. A finding of such under-representation should result
> in a numerical timetable to eliminate such under-representation.
>
> There is no requirement of a determination that the under-repre-
> sentation results from discrimination. Rather, the EEOC assumes that
> under-representation results from discrimination. However, there appears
> to be little evidence that under-representation always occurs as a result
> of racial discrimination in the workforce. Ironically, even a court must
> find intentional discrimination by a specific employer before imposing
> an affirmative action plan.
>
> It appears that the EEOC has made little effort to validate the assump-
> tions underlying affirmative action and has not evaluated the effects of
> affirmative action on the lot of minorities, especially those who are dis-
> advantaged. ... Affirmative action theoretically is designed to com-
> pensate minorities and women for this past discrimination and give
> them an opportunity to participate in the workforce. The former objec-
> tive is statutorily supportable only with a specific finding of racial

discrimination, while the latter is laudable, but does not appear to have been quantified beyond mere representation. There appears to have been little effort made to determine whether disadvantaged minorities and women have actually been helped as a result of affirmative action. Nor does it appear that there has been any determination that the inadequacies which resulted in the disadvantage have been removed or whether they can be remedied by mere inclusion in the workforce.

Thomas concluded by proffering several recommendations:

1. EEOC's top priority should be the vigorous and expeditious enforcement of the anti-discrimination provisions of the Civil Rights Act of 1964.
2. EEOC should determine whether employment-based approaches such as affirmative action are, in fact, addressing the problems of past discrimination.
3. EEOC should re-examine the assumptions underlying affirmative action, with special emphasis on determining whether there are non-employment and non-race-related causes of under-representation of minorities and women in certain areas.

While laden with legalese, the memo faithfully recited the main conservative objections to affirmative action and quotas. The federal government, through the EEOC, was encouraging employers to hire more minorities so that their work force would have a percentage of minorities proportionate to that of the overall population. The EEOC was fighting such "under-representation" without proof that these employers were actually discriminating against minorities. From the tone and thrust of the memo, Thomas gave every appearance that he agreed with these criticisms of affirmative action and quotas.

The decision to extend a job offer to Thomas came from the Justice Department. The new attorney general, William French Smith, was a congenial lawyer and longtime friend of Reagan from California. Because of Smith's penchant for delegating, William Bradford Reynolds, the man tapped to be assistant attorney general for civil rights, would hold considerable power. When Thomas's name came up as a potential civil rights appointee, Reynolds was asked to give, as he put it, a "thumbs-up or thumbs-down."

Thomas seemed perfect for a position at the Department of Education. The administration needed a loyalist to head the department's Office of Civil Rights. The new secretary of education, Terrel Bell, knew of Thomas and thought well of him. So did the department's general counsel, Dan Oliver. Danforth also gave Thomas a strong endorsement. When Reynolds was consulted about Thomas, he recalled, "I had no hesitation to give Clarence a thumbs-up."

The only thing that lay between Thomas and a position of prominence in the new administration was his pride. In early 1981, when administration officials first asked him about accepting the position of assistant secretary for civil rights at Education, Thomas declined. He later said he felt "insulted." He had refused civil rights work at the Missouri Attorney General's Office and at Danforth's office in Washington, seeking to avoid being "pigeonholed" as a token black doing the predictable black portfolio.

Eventually, he had a change of heart:

> When I was asked to go to the Department of Education as well as come here [the Equal Employment Opportunity Commission], you're dang right I was insulted. What other reason besides the fact that I was black? But then I had to ask myself, if you don't do it, what are you going to say about these issues in the future? If you had an opportunity to get in there and you didn't do it, what standing do you have to complain? As one friend put it to me, "Clarence, put up or shut up." And I wasn't going to shut up.

This self-analysis deleted far too cleanly the decisive role that ambition played in his thought processes. He had come to Washington with dreams that were at once gigantic and possible. Any young man who would announce to a reporter that he was aiming for a seat on the Supreme Court was not going to toil as an anonymous congressional staffer for long. Still, Thomas would later admit that by going back on his vow not to accept a civil rights post, he had "eaten crow."

As Thomas pondered his proliferating career options, his home life began to unravel. Thomas and Kathy had grown apart—friends would call it a "mismatch of ambitions"—as she obtained her degree and returned to work, and he sought work in a conservative Republican administration. Both had been liberal campus activists when they met and fell in love. Time had driven an ideological wedge between them. They separated in January of 1981—a curious date, given that it coincided with the inauguration of Reagan and the beginning of the administration that was making overtures to Thomas. They would reconcile briefly in the summer, then separate permanently in August.

Thomas moved out of their apartment in Maryland. He and Jamal moved in for a time with Gil Hardy. Thomas later confided that it was during this time, when he and his son were sleeping on Hardy's floor, that he decided he would not live that way anymore. He decided to take the job at Education if it was offered formally.

As one important woman began to exit his life, another entered. Gil Hardy had come to know a young lawyer—a fellow black Yale Law graduate—whose life, like Thomas's, also was on the rocks. Anita Hill hailed from the small town of Morris, Oklahoma, south of Tulsa. She was descended from a line of blacks who had packed their wagons and moved from the South into the former Indian territory in search of a better life. Her family tree, like Thomas's, had many broken homes in it; but Hill's own parents, unlike Thomas's, were married and had raised thirteen children together. The family chopped and picked cotton and lived in a home similar to Thomas's in Georgia—no electricity or running water, tar paper for insulation.

Hill had excelled in school. She was valedictorian of her class at Morris High School, then a standout at Oklahoma State University. From there, she made the leap to Yale Law School. As a student at Yale in 1978, Hill met Gil Hardy when he interviewed her for a summer position at his D.C. law firm, Wald, Harkrader and Ross. She accepted, then clerked for the firm in the summer of 1979. A full-time job offer followed, which she accepted in the spring of 1980.

She was a naturally beautiful woman blessed with large, expressive eyes, high cheekbones and a dazzling smile. Yet things did not pan out for Hill at her new firm. The transition from student to full-time employee is a difficult and unnatural one for many; new lawyers learn that success is no longer predicated on the relatively objective merits of grades, but on office politics and relationships. She did not play the game well. When the firm expanded to include a new floor in their building, which faced Eighteenth and M Streets in the northwest quadrant of the city, Hill and four other associates gullibly volunteered to take the offices. Hill later noted that they "were content with [their] separate space," but the tradeoff was that the gang of four was "away from much of the goings-on" in the firm.

This estrangement grew worse. Hill received little substantive work from the firm's partners. Her "main project" there was helping a partner prepare his contribution to a banking law manual. This generated no billable hours, for which clients compensated the firm. Billable hours, Hill recognized, were "the key measure of accomplishment in the law firm." This was true of any law firm, but especially the cutthroat, money-centered environment of corporate law. Soon, the partner left the firm, taking the project with him. Hill continued to flounder. Minor projects came her way, ones which, she said, "required little ongoing contact with specific partners."

Several attorneys with the firm expressed dissatisfaction with her work. One judged it shallow, and concluded she did not write well. Another recalled, "Sometimes I would ask her to do something, and get no response at all. Just a blank look." One partner told her of his concerns and suggested that she look for employment elsewhere.

Hill said she did not encounter "overt discrimination" at the firm, but blamed prejudice nonetheless for her professional tailspin there. She described this bias vaguely as "[t]he kind so ingrained as to be unconscious but whose cumulative effect can be as devastating as anything made blatant." She realized she was not doing well at the firm, certainly not well enough to remain on the partnership track. As a result, she sought out the man who had recruited her for the firm, Gil Hardy, to ask for some career advice.

Hardy lived in the same apartment building as Hill in the Adams-Morgan section of the city. Sometimes, they walked to work together. She spoke to Hardy about "the disappointments of my first few months." Hardy then mentioned his friend Clarence Thomas, who, he said, was expecting an appointment to the Reagan administration.

A few weeks later, Hardy invited Hill to a get-together in his apartment a few floors below hers. Thomas was living with Hardy at the time, and Hardy introduced the two. Hill would say later that Thomas struck her as "sincere, if a little brusque and unpolished"—a common reaction. Thomas, for his part, would recall that his most distinct memory of Hill would be that she had bad breath. They argued over politics. A liberal, Hill criticized the idea of "trickle-down economics," the economic theory which held that cutting taxes for the wealthy would ultimately enrich the poor as well. Thomas insisted that much of Reagan's rhetoric would not become policy—a belief he would reiterate for some time.

All in all, it was an inauspicious start to a relationship. Moreover, it was an oddly pugnacious way for Hill to seek a job from Thomas. Fortunately for her, Thomas enjoyed the company of assertive women. A few weeks later, shortly after President Reagan announced his intention to nominate Thomas for the position of assistant secretary for civil rights at DOE, he offered Hill a job as an attorney assistant.

This first step into higher office would prove a metaphor for Thomas's life and career. He had obtained a powerful and impressive position for a man of his age. Yet he also brought with him a young staffer with a larger chip on her shoulder than any he had labored beneath during his angriest days at Holy Cross. As Thomas began his rise in American government, triumph and tragedy would clasp hands and follow behind him, whispering portents then inaudible to the young man on his way up.

PART FOUR

The Man

CHAPTER TWELVE

Call It Stormy Monday

The Office of Civil Rights in the U.S. Department of Education was a double provocation to the conservatives who dominated the incoming Reagan administration. Established by President Jimmy Carter and a Democratic Congress, the department had spun off from the erstwhile Department of Health, Education and Welfare, a behemoth that was the very embodiment of Great Society liberalism. Reagan viewed the new department as a further distension of an already unwieldy federal bureaucracy. During the campaign, he pledged to seek its abolition.

The Office of Civil Rights (OCR) was offensive to conservatives for other reasons. While conservatives challenged the very existence of the Department of Education, they questioned the aims of its unit for civil rights enforcement. OCR was responsible for safeguarding the civil rights of students at educational institutions that received federal financial support. Mostly, these rights arose from Title VI of the Civil Rights Act of 1964 and other federal civil rights statutes established in the 1970s. The office investigated complaints of discrimination and conducted inquiries to monitor compliance with civil rights laws. OCR referred violations to the Department of Justice for litigation and potential termination of federal funding. Within this broad ambit fell a myriad of public policy concerns, from desegregation at Southern colleges to bilingual education to special education of disabled children in elementary and secondary schools.

Under Carter, OCR had pursued a liberal civil rights agenda. State colleges and universities in the South were pressed to increase the percentage of students who were black. Affirmative action and racial quotas were encouraged accordingly. Reagan had run for president on a platform of eliminating such racial preferences. Indeed, Theodore White, the presidential historian, judged that popular resentment over racial preferences was one of the main shifts in public opinion that helped to sweep Reagan into office. The new president would charge his civil rights team with implementing his designs. William Bradford Reynolds at the Justice Department was the de facto leader of this team. The administration assumed that Thomas would be the prime agent of such change at Education.

Thomas joined OCR in May 1981, and formally began serving as assistant secretary of education for civil rights on July 3 after his confirmation. The office he inherited was massive, boasting a $44 million annual budget and 1,023 employees, 20 percent of the entire Department of Education.

Virtually all of these career employees were hostile to the new administration, and therefore to Thomas. "Everybody in the place was a liberal Democrat," recalled Michael Middleton, who had worked at OCR since its formation. Thomas and Terrel Bell, the secretary of education, decided they could not simply dump overboard what limited institutional knowledge they found at the new unit. As a result, the vast majority of the OCR staff—much of it shifted over from Health, Education and Welfare—survived the transition. Thomas sought to cull the best of the Carter team and convert them to his own brigades, counting on their desire for continued employment to ensure fealty.

Mike Middleton would become his closest adviser. A light-skinned, genial black man with penetrating eyes, Middleton was roughly the same age. A native of Jackson, Mississippi, he too had grown up in the segregated South in the 1950s and 1960s. Unlike Thomas, he had a responsible father—a military officer and third-generation Episcopal priest. A civil rights lawyer with the federal government since 1971, Middleton had served Thomas's predecessor as chief deputy assistant secretary.

From the outset, Thomas displayed notable political savvy. Middleton came away from his initial conversations convinced that Thomas was not a hard-charging conservative committed to overturning the old order. In fact, Thomas was deliberately ambiguous about his own beliefs and goals. "He gave me the impression that he was reluctant to make some of the dramatic turnarounds that the Reagan administration had been promising their constituency," Middleton said of their discussions. Middleton concluded Thomas was hesitant to execute these changes "because once he found himself in position to make those changes, he feared they would have a damaging effect on the civil rights community." Having obtained his position by assuring the administration of his opposition to racial preferences, Thomas indicated to Middleton that he would not be as gung-ho as they had supposed.

Thomas also admitted frankly his ignorance of civil rights law. He shared with Middleton what his co-workers back in Jefferson City knew well: that he had avoided civil rights work after Yale "because he didn't want to be pigeonholed as a black man in civil rights." Thomas said he needed guidance in managing the agency, and he asked Middleton to stay on as his chief deputy assistant and general counsel. He made the offer more enticing by asking Middleton to serve as a "sounding board" and devil's advocate to prepare him for the debates that were sure to come with the White House over civil rights policy.

Another top lieutenant who was likewise a holdover from the Carter administration was Antonio Califa. A Mexican-American from a ranching family in Texas, Califa had known Thomas at Yale when both served in the New Haven Legal Assistance Office. As deputy director for litigation enforcement and policy at OCR, Califa, like Middleton, possessed institutional knowledge and a strong background in civil rights law.

Thomas rounded out his staff with a small coterie of friends and associates from outside OCR. One was Carlton Stewart, a black friend and attorney from Georgia. Stewart, said one co-worker at OCR, was "sort of a henchman or sidekick. He would go around and talk to people, apparently gathering information." Although he "didn't have any obvious function" in the office, the co-worker added, "that's not unusual at that level of the federal government." Thomas knew Stewart would be loyal to him. In an adverse environment such as OCR, that was qualification enough.

Thomas believed he could rely on Anita Hill in the same manner, although he knew from their first, tempestuous meeting at Gil Hardy's apartment that they did not see eye to eye philosophically. Hill was a Democrat and, by her own admission, someone who "would not pass the administration's litmus test" if selected for a political position. But Thomas found a home for the feisty castaway from corporate law as a Schedule A attorney. Schedule A employees were career employees who

enjoyed the full protection of the federal civil service rules; they could
be dismissed only if their employer showed good cause. In the easygoing federal bureaucracy, managers rarely even attempted to meet this
high burden, with the result that few Schedule A employees were ever
let go. Schedule C employees such as Thomas, on the other hand, could
be discharged at the whim of the president or his delegate. (All employees of the federal government understood this distinction; all became
well versed in the nomenclature of employment classifications, for on
such distinctions hinged their economic livelihood.) Having secured
for her a coveted Schedule A position, Thomas carved out a niche for
Hill in the office. He would assign her "special projects."

Initial impressions of Hill were mixed but largely favorable. Thomas
took her around the office to introduce her. When he brought her to
Middleton's office, he told Middleton a little about her background and
said that a good friend at a law firm had referred Hill to him. Hill
seemed a little nervous—"probably first-day job jitters," he said. In Middleton's view, she went on to perform her job ably. Califa remembered
her as "down-to-earth" and "very quiet." Califa also found that "she
wasn't fully occupied. I don't know if Clarence didn't give her enough
to do. But she didn't seem to be very busy." Indeed, Califa thought her
"significantly less busy than other people in the office. But," he added,
"it may not have been her fault." Creating a job for Hill turned out to
be easier than keeping her busy; Thomas struggled to rustle up enough
work for her.

His staff patched together from Carter appointees and personal loyalists, Thomas turned to the largest issue confronting the agency: desegregation. "Within a month of taking that job," Thomas reflected, "I was
terrified by the possible effects of the desegregation effort on black colleges." He learned that the Carter administration had been cajoling
Southern states to unify their white and black college systems. While
this sounded in theory like the very fulfillment of King's dream, Thomas
feared that in practice, this would mean the death of historically black
colleges founded by such men as Booker T. Washington, which had
been the centers of African-American learning and culture for over a
century. To simply dissolve them, Thomas thought, was folly. He
explained:

I refused to pursue desegregation policies which penalize black colleges. They were *not* the ones doing the discriminating.... I approached enforcement with great care. I insisted that the state plans have as a major objective the enhancement of black institutions. This means better libraries, better programs, upgraded faculty and more funds. In that way, equality of educational opportunity was best realized.

Thomas was also critical of bilingual education and what he considered to be its divisive effects on American society. Still, Califa (who called this area "my baby") recalled that Thomas "didn't really make any effort to change [it]." But he was disturbed at "the festering wound of miseducation and undereducation taking place in grammar schools, the overrepresentation of blacks in educable mentally retarded classes and underrepresentation in math, science, and languages." Thomas judged this trend "devastating. It steers children away from the course that leads to the many opportunities that are available and toward a life of unemployability."

The most maddening item on his agenda was a juridical black hole called *Adams v. Bell.* In 1970, black students attending racially segregated public schools in seventeen states filed suit alleging that the Department of Health, Education and Welfare was not enforcing Title VI. To resolve the matter, the Carter administration in 1977 entered into a consent decree, and in so doing, effectively ceded to the federal courts the right to run the civil rights arm of HEW. The consent decree imposed strict time limits for the agency to process discrimination charges. As a federal court of appeals later stated, the case ultimately "expanded to colossal proportions: the litigation came to encompass enforcement by units of the Department of Education and the Department of Labor of four civil rights measures as they pertain to the education systems of all fifty states." Twenty years after the case began winding its way through the federal judiciary, a federal appeals court would dismiss the consent decree for improperly encroaching upon the powers of the executive branch. The case would become Thomas's worst professional bugbear.

Even the sympathetic liberals who served at OCR "hated the time frames," according to one attorney in the unit. The consent decree consumed virtually every hour of every employee's workday at OCR. Worse still from their standpoint, the decree imposed strict time limits on them—something that they, like almost all federal employees, were not used to and did not much care for. OCR had fifteen days to acknowledge a complaint, ninety days to investigate, ninety days to negotiate a settlement, and thirty days to commence enforcement. The office devised elaborate statistical systems to generate regular reports for the court. Officials in the Carter administration eventually concluded that OCR could not comply with the time limits the administration had agreed to. By the end of 1980, OCR met the deadlines for compliance reviews in only about 5 percent of its cases and for complaint investigations in about one-third of its cases.

One of Thomas's first priorities was to order the staff to conduct an "Adams Time Frame Report" to determine whether the office was complying with the time limits. He discovered in the process that approximately 95 percent of staff time was dedicated exclusively to obeying the consent decree. The office was investigating such issues as disparate punishment of black students in public schools, denial of female access to certain vocational programs, and disabled students' alleged lack of access to catheterization at certain institutions. He made the *Adams* situation one of Anita Hill's "special projects," asking her to review and monitor the agency's progress. He also made it his own abiding concern. Thomas admitted he was "scared to death" at what he had uncovered; he knew a showdown with the courts was imminent.

Shortly after his arrival at OCR, the plaintiffs in the *Adams* litigation filed a motion asking the judge overseeing the case to find Thomas in contempt for the department's failure to meet the time frames. Thomas's deposition testimony in the case was blunt and extremely humbling. He stated that despite a good-faith attempt to comply with the consent decree, it was impossible for his office to meet the time frames. He added that the consent decree was sapping him and his agency of the time and energy necessary to do much of anything else in regard to civil rights.

The plaintiffs' attorney asked: "But you're going ahead and violating those time frames, isn't that true? You're violating them on compliance reviews on all occasions, practically, and you're violating them on complaints most of the time, or half the time, isn't that true?"

"That's right," Thomas replied.

"So aren't you, in effect, substituting your judgment as to what the policy should be for what the court order requires? The court order requires you to comply with this 90-day period. Isn't that true?

"That's right."

"And you have not imposed a deadline [for an agency review of non-compliance with the decree]. Is that correct?"

"I have not imposed a deadline."

"And meanwhile, you are violating a court order rather grievously, aren't you?"

"Yes."

Thomas ended up admitting that the Department of Education violated the applicable time frames "in compliance reviews on all occasions, practically."

His candor, combined with the timing of the motion, induced the judge not to hold him in contempt. Judge John Pratt ruled, "We are reluctant to find the defendants in contempt for a variety of reasons, not the least of which is that they arrived on the scene relatively late and the motion to hold them in contempt was filed within a matter of just a few months after they came aboard." Thomas escaped with only a scolding. He came away from the experience with his pride a bit frayed and his commitment to judicial restraint strengthened.

As the seasons changed, Thomas alternately drove or sloshed through ice and snow on foot from his efficiency apartment less than a mile from the office. He rented a place in the Capitol Park Towers at 301 G Street S.W. In the early morning, he emerged from the austere modern high-rise, exited onto G Street, then walked along Fourth Street for three blocks to 330 C Street S.W. The Department of Education building was a dour rectangle of tan bricks and unimaginative design, so rundown that the ceiling leaked in places. Thomas was given a corner office on the third floor, where he could enjoy through the Venetian blinds a view of C Street and a variety of other, similarly constructed government rectangles. Outside one door was his secretary, Diane Holt, in her own vestibule/office. Beside her were Anita Hill's quarters.

Sometimes, Thomas would bring Jamal into his office. Jamal lived with Thomas during the summer, then with Kathy the rest of the year.

One day during this time, Thomas drove his small blue sports car, a Fiat Spider, to work. As the day went on, a blizzard gathered and Thomas offered Tony Califa a ride home. He thought he would spare Califa from the elements; he also had a good deal on his mind and felt like talking.

As they drove through the snow-covered city, leaving in their wake dual tracks of gray and brown mush, Thomas shared with Califa his frustrations with his home life. Thomas seemed to sense a kind soul in him, or at least somebody who would listen.

"Some people just aren't cut out to be part of a family," Thomas told him. "To mow the grass," that sort of thing. Thomas made it clear that this was not something he felt cut out to do.

Califa observed, "That was the time when he seemed very, very sincere. It was like he had this shell around him, but when he chose to break out of it, he broke out of it with a vengeance."

Thomas's reflections on married life suggested a man who either was rationalizing a doomed relationship or, more likely, very much meant what he said. That the eldest son of M.C. Thomas second-guessed his marital situation was predictable. Clarence Thomas was extraordinary in many ways, but in at least this respect, he was the son of his father.

———

Even as Thomas looked down the barrel of a contempt citation from a federal judge, his professional woes were only beginning at OCR. His tenure became even rockier as he found himself increasingly at loggerheads with the White House.

Thomas met regularly at the White House and Justice Department with the other captains of the administration's civil rights policy. His boss, Brad Reynolds, was frequently at the center of these meetings. Another important voice belonged to Michael Horowitz, general counsel for the Office of Management and Budget. A graduate of Yale Law School and a former professor at the University of Mississippi Law School, Horowitz, a self-described "classic neoconservative," became a player in civil rights policy because of his background in civil rights law and his commitment to abolishing racial preferences.

In one meeting, Reynolds proposed a direct legal challenge to court-ordered busing. He contended it was time to "go to court and tell the court it's time to let these schools out of the penalty box and hand it back to the educators and let the educators devise what could or should be done." Although he had long assailed busing in private conversations, Thomas now argued, according to Reynolds, "You can't just turn it back over to the educators without some constraints. There needed to be some part of the policy that put some shackles on the school board so they couldn't just have free rein and walk away from all their responsibilities."

Even so, Reynolds left the meeting believing that their disagreement was merely "a matter of degree," and that Thomas was in accord with his position that "the busing remedy had been an abject failure in most jurisdictions." Still, after years of complaining about busing and finally acceding to a position of high federal power, Thomas had been given the chance to do something about the problem. And he had balked.

"Clarence was very guarded at the beginning," Horowitz recalled. He attributed much of this to the fact that Secretary Bell "had less in common with Ronald Reagan's governing philosophy than anybody with any authority in the Reagan administration. Clarence was new to the game and was also acting as a lawyer defending his client." Horowitz added, "We had between us a sort of classic and healthy tension that always exists between agency officials and people who work in the White House." Already, however, Thomas was showing reluctance to be a point man for more controversial measures. Only later would his careful acts of political self-protection become enough of a problem to prompt the White House to take action.

Thomas trod slowly through these political and personal minefields. He recognized very well the consequences of allying himself too firmly with the administration's civil rights policies. "He didn't want to be the guy who shut all those activities down that were designed to help black people," Middleton remembered. In such event, the black community would not only look askance at Thomas, but thoroughly ostracize him. During his time at the Department of Education, Middleton recalled, Thomas "would defend many of the traditional civil rights approaches" in his meetings with Reynolds, Horowitz and other officials. Indeed, "What I was impressed with there [OCR] was that he did not seem to have a strong political agenda."

Other administration officials began to discern what Middleton already saw—namely, that Thomas was hedging on these issues out of self-preservation. Thomas would come back from these high-level meetings and share with Middleton how he had acted "as a lawyer." He would argue that "the court has already made an argument on this [policy]" and therefore the administration should leave well enough alone. But of course, the mere fact that the courts had ruled one way or another did not settle the question forever. The core principle behind Thomas's legal opinions and actions at this time was the assertion of his own sovereignty.

Thomas's political judgment came to the fore in other ways. Far more than any other high-ranking official, Thomas realized that the administration's tin ear on civil rights policy was destroying Reagan's credibility in the black community. Some of this ill will, Thomas felt, was simply a result of poor public relations. He later said of his first year in the Reagan administration: "The emphasis in the area of civil rights and social policies was decidedly negative. In the civil rights arena, we began to argue consistently *against* affirmative action. We attacked welfare and the welfare mentality. These are positions with which I agree. But, the emphasis was unnecessarily negative."

The problem quickly became much more than that. A series of missteps by the administration genuinely embarrassed Thomas. On June 30, 1981, an article appeared in the *Washington Post* stating that the White House was delaying taking a position on whether to seek an extension of the Voting Rights Act. The administration's main concern was whether Southern states still should be required to obtain "preclearance" from the Justice Department before making any changes to their local voting laws. Democrats in Congress and liberal civil rights organizations did not have to work hard to portray this as opposition to blacks' right to vote.

The administration ended up beating a retreat. Exactly a year later, Reagan signed an extension of the act. "But by failing to get out early and positively in front of the effort to extend the act," Thomas noted, "we allowed ourselves to be put into the position of opposing a version of the Voting Rights Act that was unacceptable, and hence we allowed the perception to be created that this administration opposed the Voting Rights Act, not simply a version of it."

Civil rights leaders exploited this debacle to foster the image of an administration, as Thomas put it, "hell bent on returning blacks to slavery." Blacks associated with the administration were becoming unwelcome at African-American social events in Washington. Thomas lamented years later that during this time, a "very good friend" of his complained that he was attacked in these circles simply for being Thomas's friend. At one get-together, the friend and his date were so harassed that they felt obliged to leave.

As 1982 began, Thomas spearheaded a public relations initiative that he hoped would burnish the administration's image. On January 5, OCR issued a press release announcing Thomas's request that the Justice Department begin enforcement proceedings against the State of Alabama for failing to desegregate its institutions of higher public education. This was not a particularly bold stroke; a federal court had ordered the Department of Education to take such legal action if Alabama failed to achieve compliance with Title VI by December 31, 1981. Thomas was scarcely spoiling for another fight with a federal judge. Just before Christmas, Thomas had written Governor Fob James of Alabama concerning the state's plan, noting that it contained only "vague commitments to consider undertaking unspecified steps some time in the future." Historically black colleges in Alabama were still 88 percent black, while state schools remained overwhelmingly white; state resources also were not apportioned equally. The press release stated that OCR's investigations "revealed continuing vestiges of unconstitutional segregation." The media noted that this was the first time since Reagan's inauguration that the Department of Education had refused to accept a state's settlement plan for desegregating its colleges and universities.

Thomas could not even enjoy the week. Two days later, the administration stumbled into its biggest public relations disaster yet in the realm of civil rights. On January 8, the Reagan administration announced that it was revoking the Internal Revenue Service's twelve-year-old policy of denying tax exemptions to private educational institutions that discriminate against minorities. The president and his top advisers believed that the IRS had exceeded its lawful authority in depriving such

schools of tax-exempt status. From a political standpoint, the repeal of
the IRS policy would aid financially many institutions whose adherents
were becoming reliably Republican. The foremost beneficiary of the
new policy was Bob Jones University, the South Carolina school that
barred interracial dating based on a bizarre Gnostic interpretation of
the Bible.

The following Monday morning, at a meeting with administration
officials, Thomas warned his colleagues of the damage the Bob Jones
issue was causing. He predicted the new tax policy "would be the undoing" of those like him who were trying to attract blacks to the Republican Party. By then, the firestorm touched off by the announcement
was already engulfing the White House. The following day, the administration backtracked somewhat. It announced that it would submit legislation to Congress to prohibit tax exemptions for schools that
discriminate against blacks. But until the legislation passed, the IRS
would continue to grant the exemptions.

A front-page article in the *Post* later that month described the Bob
Jones flap as "perhaps . . . the most embarrassing action of [Reagan's]
first year as president." The following year, the U.S. Supreme Court
dealt the administration another setback. In an 8–1 ruling, the Court
struck down the administration's new policy, holding that public policy barred tax exemptions for racially discriminatory schools. A mortified Thomas publicly distanced himself from the affair. In an interview
with *U.S. News and World Report,* he branded the case a "fiasco." He
reflected on another occasion, "The winds were not taken out of our
sails until early 1982 when we changed positions in the Supreme Court
to support a tax exemption for Bob Jones University." He added,
"Although the point being made in the argument that the administrative and regulatory arm of government should not make policies through
regulations was a valid one, it was lost in the overall perception that the
racial policies of Bob Jones University were being defended."

Throughout OCR, the common touch Thomas displayed with lesser
employees now became an enormous managerial asset. Even for the
most hardened liberal veterans in the office, it was difficult to dislike
him entirely. When he struck up a conversation, smiles swept over his
face early and often. His large, rounded cheeks would rise up to swell
his cheekbones, long dimples forming vertically beneath them. Two

rows of large, well-formed, pearly-white teeth were the only early warning of the ensuing, charming guffaw. Middleton marveled at Thomas's
"engaging" manner and sense of humor, and saw these qualities as two
of the most basic reasons for his success at Education.

But it was more than mirth that made Thomas a rising star. His
ability to motivate people and inspire loyalty proved to be the greatest
talent he brought to the administration; and management was, after all,
what the executive branch was ultimately about. Middleton summed
up Thomas's contributions: "Paper moved; he set deadlines; he managed well.... He was forceful in trying to find problems from an efficiency standpoint and a public policy perspective."

For all his natural friendliness and skills as a manager, he had to
reckon with the political realities of his position. A man sensitive enough
to write poetry at Holy Cross felt keenly the deep philosophical schism
separating him from others in the office. He described himself as "isolated" during his time at OCR. Thomas enjoyed, perhaps too often, the
privacy of his office and the stillness of his own thoughts. Middleton
and Califa both remembered him as "aloof" on occasions. "He was not
always chatty," Middleton said. By contrast, his predecessor, Cindy
Brown, "was much more engaged with her people." But Brown did not
have to govern employees who thought her political mandate repugnant. "He knew he was in a situation where people disagreed with his
philosophies and approaches," Middleton said. "And he did have to
work with a large group of ... liberals. He walks in the door and they
believe he's come in to destroy everything they've done."

Thomas went to considerable lengths to overcome this hostility. He
had little trouble making inroads with the clerical and blue-collar staff;
they became, as it were, his natural constituency. The attorneys and
holdover managers were far tougher nuts to crack. He would initiate
or join conversations to "break the ice" and "show he was a regular person," Middleton recalled. The lack of social grace that some had noticed
since his days at Holy Cross became more evident in this challenging
environment. "He seemed at times to be uncomfortable in terms of how
to act," Middleton said. "Sort of not knowing quite how to fit in with
this group." But these were cavils for a young man placed in such inhos-
pitable terrain.

In his conversations with Califa, Thomas let his guard down even more, sharing many private thoughts. "He told me once that his favorite character in fiction was Darth Vader," Califa said, referring to the villain in the movie *Star Wars*. "I looked at him, and I said, 'Darth Vader?' He said, 'Yeah, he's strong and he's tough.'" Like the rebel flag, this statement may have been intended to provoke. If so, it succeeded— Califa remembered it well twenty years later.

Thomas also could be abrasive. Califa recalled, "He'd say something and I'd say, 'Well, I hadn't really thought of it that way before.' And he'd respond by saying, 'Well, you could fill this whole room with things you know nothing about.'" Califa thought him "socially a bit off," as well as "very unhappy" about his marital situation. "He's the kind of person, at that time, who would derive pleasure from putting somebody else down." When Califa saw Thomas at a restaurant years later, he seemed very different—far more smooth and diplomatic.

Anita Hill, unlike Thomas, fit in well, at least ideologically. Finally among like-minded, liberal attorneys working for civil rights and the government, she was in her element. Thomas gave her almost no casework, sending her special projects instead. Her "two major projects" at OCR, in her words, were an article she ghostwrote for Thomas on minority academic achievement and organizing a seminar on "high-risk" students. Neither required very much work, leaving her with much time on her hands. Some of this was spent in "bull sessions" about the issues of the day. In her discussions with Thomas, he recalled, Hill would become "a bit irate" on the issue of quotas, about which she was "adamant." Thomas would argue with Hill over the importance of *Brown v. Board of Education* and its proper place in the civil rights movement, invoking the research of social scientist William Julius Wilson in contending that economic development, rather than racial discrimination, was thwarting black progress. Hill believed racial discrimination still was a major obstacle, and that economics "was secondary."

After a while, Hill's work product and surliness began to grate on Thomas and her other colleagues. Thomas concluded that her work "wasn't spectacular." He also judged her "immature and very ideological." Diane Holt, Thomas's secretary, said that Hill was "always like a spoiled brat," frequently "pouting" and "always wanting to have her own way." When she failed to win over an opponent in one of these office debates, "she just walked away."

Years later, Hill would acknowledge (perhaps unwittingly) just how disengaged she was from her work at OCR. During this time, she attended a reception in which she noticed a person with an obvious air of importance. She walked up to him and introduced herself. She then said, "Excuse me, but I didn't catch your name." "To his considerable amusement," Hill recalled, the man informed her that he was Secretary Bell. "I had not a clue as to who he was," Hill explained.

Thomas sometimes wished he were as anonymous. The constant denunciations from civil rights groups stung his ego. At OCR, he revealed himself to be thin-skinned and deeply sensitive to public criticism. "He really does not like criticism," Middleton said. "That was his thing with the civil rights community."

Middleton remembered an occasion when Benjamin Hooks, executive director of the NAACP, requested a meeting with Thomas. "I don't want to meet with him," Thomas responded.

Middleton was bemused. "Clarence, you have to," he said. "You have to talk to him—those interest groups."

Thomas was indignant. "All they're going to do is come here and criticize me and say I'm being used by the Republicans. That I'm not a real brother. I don't want to hear that. You meet with them." Eventually, Thomas relented.

It quickly became evident that Thomas wished to serve prominently in government but without the unpleasantness of public scrutiny. These two goals were incompatible, as were so many others in his galaxy of aspirations. More than most other high-ranking officials, he squirmed when placed under the media's microscope. The Juan Williams article that reported his remarks about his sister's dependence on welfare "embarrassed" him, according to Middleton. But that coverage was only a friendly prelude to the buzz saw he ran into upon joining the Reagan administration.

"The cacophony of harangues and criticisms were [*sic*] continuous and deafening," Thomas complained years later. He summarized the media's treatment of him as: "Here's a strange black. Let's go see if he has two heads and a tail." He concluded that the Washington press corps, which was overwhelmingly liberal and critical of the administration's policies, looked upon black conservatives as "mere curiosities." He blasted the media as "recklessly irresponsible in printing unsubstantiated allegations that portrayed us as anti-black and anti–civil rights." He recounted one ongoing dialogue with a particularly partisan reporter:

> ... on numerous occasions, I have found myself debating and arguing with a reporter, who had long since closed his notebook, put away his pen, and turned off his tape recorder. I remember one instance when I first arrived at the Department of Education, a reporter, who happened to be white, came to my office and asked: "What are you all doing to cut back on civil rights enforcement?" I said, "Nothing! In fact, here is a list of all the things we are doing to enforce the law properly and not just play numbers games." He then asked, "You had a very rough life, didn't you?" To this, I responded that I didn't; that I did, indeed, come from very modest circumstances but that I had lived the American dream; and that I was attempting to secure this dream for all Americans, especially those Americans of my race who had been left out of the American dream.

Thomas concluded this anecdote with eloquent self-pity: "Needless to say, he wrote nothing. I have not always been so fortunate."

One reporter with the *Legal Times* interviewed Thomas early in his tenure under Reagan. She commented insightfully on his unusual bundle of traits: "Although he has an appealing sense of humor and can be disarmingly candid, he is tightly wound. His reaction to criticism from the civil rights community is a blend of shock, outrage, and hurt feelings."

Thomas's beliefs crystallized most fully on the subject of welfare. His position was brave and well ahead of its time. Thomas, according to Middleton, believed that the welfare system "lulls people into total dependence on government. There are some people who don't get jobs so they have marginal subsistence on government handouts." Welfare, Thomas reasoned, was "detrimental to people because it sucked out of them any motivation, any ambition." Thomas's solution was "to cut it off and force people to work and learn and pull themselves up by their bootstraps." Thomas, in other words, proposed the abolition of welfare several years before the publication of Charles Murray's *Losing Ground,* the first major work to seriously suggest this policy (so radical was this notion even then that Murray proffered the idea merely as a "thought experiment" rather than a "blueprint for policy").

Thomas's courage did not move Middleton to reconsider his position. "Well, Clarence," he responded, "even if you're right, you must recognize that there are millions of babies, black babies, who depend upon that welfare system for the milk that they drink every day. And if you cut it off today, without some policies or programs in place, you really are putting a generation of our children at serious risk for the purpose of forcing their parents to get up and go to work. And I'm not willing to sacrifice a generation of black kids for this theoretical experiment."

This pathos did not sway the grandson of Myers Anderson. "Well, if that's what it takes to get us off our behinds and get motivated and go to work, I'm willing to do it," Thomas replied.

"You can't tinker with it," he insisted of welfare. "We've been tinkering with it for twenty years. We've just got to shut it down."

As Thomas prevailed upon his deputy to see the merits of his philosophy, he also tried to persuade him to become a Republican. "On several occasions, he told me I could advance my career if I became a Republican," Middleton said. Thomas insisted, "All you gotta do is go downtown and register as a Republican. These guys are beating the bushes for qualified black Republicans." It was solid, practical advice that Middleton declined to follow.

In the course of these and other discussions, Thomas reiterated his dream of one day being appointed to the Supreme Court. In one conversation, as he and Middleton mulled over the latter's career opportunities, Thomas "indicated that [the Supreme Court] was one of his goals and that he was positioned to do it." As Middleton explained, "He was in a position to make a name for himself and move on. And the ultimate thing for a lawyer is a seat on the Court." Thomas "recognized the fact that the person who would fill [Thurgood] Marshall's seat would most likely be black. He was the highest-ranking black person in government at the time with a law degree and support from a powerful senator."

Soon, a ladder extended from the sky to lift Thomas to the next stop in his political career. During the transition, he had advised Meese and the transition team on the EEOC, but had not been offered the job of EEOC chairman. He had no management experience at that point, and EEOC, in size and power, dwarfed OCR. Instead, the Reagan administration, after offering the job to a number of other blacks, made another poor decision related to civil rights by selecting one William Bell to head the agency.

Bell's qualifications for the job were negligible (he owned a one-man "consulting firm" in Detroit with an annual income of $7,000). The civil rights furies began to descend in November 1981, claiming that Bell was unqualified to run an agency with a budget of $140 million and a staff of 3,376. Thomas privately agreed, and had urged the administration not to select Bell. Soon after the first negative news articles about Bell began to appear, the administration decided to put the nomination on hold and not seek his confirmation.

Thomas, in the meantime, was acquiring managerial experience. Meese continued to think highly of him and serve as his advocate. "He had both good judgment and he also had a maturity of thinking," Meese said. Even Thomas's cautiousness could be a great boon in a manager; he would be unlikely to make major errors by acting impetuously. Most important of all, the open EEOC job was becoming a major political embarrassment.

In early February 1982, Thomas emerged from a meeting with Pendleton James, the Reagan administration's director of personnel. In the meeting, Thomas learned that the president wished to nominate him to be chairman of EEOC. "My reaction was to very calmly panic," Thomas would later say of the occasion. By contrast, Califa remembered that when Thomas was tapped for the EEOC, "he was really, really happy." Thomas summoned his senior staff for a meeting and informed them of the president's decision. Throughout the meeting, Califa observed, Thomas was "just smiling and happy." Soon afterward, Anita Hill asked Thomas to take her with him. He agreed, and Hill, according to Diane Holt, seemed "pretty excited" about the new job. On February 13, the front page of the *New York Times* carried a large story on Thomas's appointment, and alongside it a picture of Thomas beaming with a large smile of undeniable sincerity.

After he learned of Thomas's appointment to EEOC, Larry Thompson wrote to congratulate his old friend from Missouri. "I will never doubt you again," the note read. Thomas treasured it.

CHAPTER THIRTEEN

A New Sheriff in Town

O n his first day of work for EEOC, Clarence Thomas secured a taxi
to shuttle him to his new office. His destination was scarcely a
landmark; both he and his driver, Thomas remembered, "had a hard
time finding the agency." Eventually, they found the address—2401 E
Street N.W.—and pulled up alongside a high-rise, tan-brick government building that looked almost as if two Department of Education
buildings had been stacked one atop the other like Lego blocks. The
complex was called Columbia Plaza. Situated near the State Department in the Foggy Bottom section of Washington, the building offered
a picturesque view of the Kennedy Center to the west and the Potomac
River flowing lazily behind it.

The security guard in the ground floor proved his mettle by detain-
ing Thomas for a while until his credentials were found to be in order.
When he finally was admitted to his new office, Thomas found his
quarters to be completely bereft of essentials such as pencils and writing pads. Most conspicuously and ominously, there was no chair. It was
customary for government employees to raid the offices of their newly
departed colleagues for desirable furniture and other such community
property. To pick over the chairman's office, however, was another matter entirely. It was an indication of anarchy. Moreover, as one of Thomas's
co-workers at EEOC noted, this theft was likely meant to send him a
message.

Thomas was handed the reins to an agency with vast powers over
the American workforce and economy. The commission was the chief
entity in the federal government responsible for the enforcement of civil
rights. EEOC enforced Title VII of the Civil Rights Act, which prohibited employment discrimination based on race, color, religion, sex,
or national origin. Subsequent federal legislation broadened EEOC's

mandate, making it responsible for combating discrimination based on age and disability. All companies with more than fifteen employees were obliged to follow EEOC guidelines on the hiring, training and promotion of employees. EEOC also assessed the affirmative action plans of all federal agencies pursuant to Executive Order 12106.

Federal law provided that a person who suffered discrimination in employment first file a charge of discrimination with EEOC. The agency investigated the complaint before the employee would be vested with a right to file suit for civil rights violations. EEOC could dismiss the complaint, mediate or settle the dispute, issue a right-to-sue letter allowing the party to file a private lawsuit, or file suit itself. If EEOC investigators recommended that the agency initiate litigation, the district office would have to concur, then refer the case to the national office in Washington. The legal staff at the national office would review the case and, if they judged it meritorious, place it on the agenda for a full meeting of the commission. The five commissioners would vote on proposed litigation and settlements of suits already filed. One of the commissioners was chairman, and as such, was also responsible for running the agency.

Thomas's predecessor, the chairman of EEOC under President Carter, was Eleanor Holmes Norton. A black woman with a hard, self-righteous demeanor, ever-pursed lips, and a more or less permanent scowl, Norton was an unswerving advocate of broadened racial preferences in employment. Under her leadership, EEOC focused almost exclusively on plying employers to expand their affirmative action programs. In exchange, EEOC would offer to settle discrimination claims against them. Norton had little patience for the pesky details of administration, or for finding lieutenants who were any differently inclined. As a result, according to one senior official in the EEOC, "there was not any attention given to what was happening in support and administrative areas in the agency."

"I found an agency in shambles," Thomas remembered. The Norton regime had neglected to track properly the streams of money coursing through EEOC. "We didn't know from one day to the next how much money we had on hand," he recalled. The agency was unsure how much money it owed to outside parties for the prior fiscal year, which had closed out eight months earlier. Similarly, it was not certain of its current obligations. Over $1 million had been given in outstanding travel advances to employees, an absurdly and suspiciously high figure. For almost nine hundred contracts—some awarded as far back as fiscal year 1974—the agency could not confirm whether the contracted work or services ever had been performed. The automated payroll system was so larded with erroneous and outdated information that the agency continued to issue checks to former and deceased employees.

The working conditions did not inspire high performance. The General Service Administration, following an inspection, declared the office space at EEOC "environmentally unsound." Walls were green with the verdure of flourishing mold and mildew. Some were also pocked with holes, yet another sign that the natives were restless. Carbon monoxide wafted up from the garage, causing headaches and light dizziness in some employees by the end of the day. The roof and ceiling did not protect from precipitation. Fleas, in contrast, found comfortable housing in the musty carpeting. The agency's management information system depended on, in Thomas's words, "two antiquated computers, located in different areas, both of which were cooled only by electrical fans rather than a properly controlled air conditioned environment." These computers "spent much of their lives in downtime because they became overheated"—a common problem, as temperatures in the rooms where they were stored sometimes topped a hundred degrees.

The agency was not even discharging its most basic legal duties effectively. Thomas learned of a huge backlog of cases that had built up under the prior administration. Nobody knew just how big it was. It took a month before his subordinates could give Thomas an estimated tally: 12,000 cases pre-1979. EEOC received approximately 3,000 cases a year; it disposed of about 1,000 annually, ensuring that the backlog steadily worsened. Some employees had taken to hiding case files above the ceiling tiles in the building to help them meet their already low work quotas. The chaos was such that EEOC literally could not put together an agency telephone directory. The various offices were so decentralized, the autonomous units so scornful of the other fiefdoms, that they would not cooperate even to this limited extent.

Harsh external evaluations of EEOC descended on the agency before Thomas had even found his chair. Thomas arrived just after the Office of Personnel Management released a report taking the agency to task for improperly classifying and assessing the performance of its employees. The most thoroughgoing critique came from the General Accounting Office, an arm of the Democrat-controlled Congress, which essentially declared the entire accounting system at EEOC "unreliable." Loans were not recorded properly; receivables were not collected; money from one fiscal year was improperly used to purchase goods and services for past or future years. Perhaps most ominously, GAO noted that federal laws had been violated, and that the agency had lent or granted funds to private persons based on "questionable authority."

The first meeting of the commission under Thomas's watch came before the month was over. It was short. Thomas handed a copy of the agenda for the meeting to the other four commissioners. He took a long look around the room. Then, he stood up and announced that the meeting was adjourned. The abrupt exercise was meant to demonstrate that although Carter appointees still dominated the commission, he also wielded some power—such as the right to call and to terminate commission meetings. It was a heavy-handed beginning for a young man trying too hard to make a point. Still, the point was made.

One of his first major personnel decisions was equally dramatic. His emergency task force recommended eliminating the position of executive director, averring that there was no need for such an "intervening political level" between the chairman and the office directors. Excising this position, of course, would enhance the power of these latter officials, who made up much of his task force. Thomas would make the first of several bold staffing decisions by endorsing the abolition of this position, dismissing its current occupant, Edgar Morgan, and assuming the responsibilities himself.

Thomas hired Diane Holt as his secretary and three individuals as special assistants on his personal staff. Carlton Stewart and Anita Hill followed him from Education. He also lured J. C. Alvarez, his former co-worker on Danforth's Senate staff, over to EEOC to serve as his third special assistant. Rose Jourdain, a liberal holdover from the Carter era, was retained as a speechwriter. Thomas also brought over Mike Middleton to serve as associate general counsel and oversee the trial division of EEOC's litigation department.

His personal staff left much to be desired. Stewart became the head special assistant, whose actual job duties remained amorphous to all but (presumably) Thomas. It was generally understood that he dealt primarily with matters "political." As for Hill, Thomas would later proudly tell a reporter, "the first person I hired, a black woman, Anita Hill, is still with me." Hill recalled that her "primary duties were to be the liaison to the Office of Congressional Affairs and the Office of Review and Appeals, so that I reviewed a number of the cases that came up on appeal, to make certain our office had been given proper consideration." She also "acted as a liaison to the press sometimes for the chairman's office, through Congressional Affairs and Public Relations." She continued to pick up some special projects from Thomas as well. All in all, she acknowledged, things at EEOC were "much busier" than they had been at OCR.

It quickly became apparent that at EEOC, Hill no longer was Thomas's protégé or special project from Yale. Confronted with an administrative crisis at his new agency, Thomas concluded that he needed to surround himself quickly with "an experienced EEO staff." The career bureaucrats on whom he relied in this time of crisis were "much more mature" than his crew at Education. "As a result," he said, Hill "did not enjoy that close a relationship with me, nor did she have her choice of the better assignments, and I think that as a result of that there was some concern on her part that she was not being treated as well as she had been treated prior to that." The "relationship was more distant. And our contacts less frequent."

Soon, Hill faced stiff competition for the chairman's time and good opinion from another woman on Thomas's personal staff. Allyson Duncan was what Hill might have become years later with comparable experience and dedication to her post. She had grown up in a middle-class black family in Durham, North Carolina. After graduating from Duke Law School, she clerked on the prestigious U.S. Court of Appeals for the District of Columbia Circuit, then joined EEOC as a staff attorney. A light-skinned black woman with a gentle but serious mien and liberal politics, Duncan came to Thomas's attention soon after he began his search for talented, experienced guides in the labyrinthine agency. Soon she became one of the most respected lawyers in the agency, handling the appeals from trials across the country involving the agency.

Shortly after his ascent to the chairmanship, Thomas invited Duncan into his office to interview her for a position on his staff. She remembered that they quickly "got into an argument about adverse impact." Thomas was critical of recent court decisions stating that civil rights plaintiffs could prove a *prima facie* case of discrimination by showing that the percentage of minorities at the plaintiff's employment site was significantly smaller than the percentage of minorities in the nearby population. A business that, for example, had a workforce that was only 10 percent black when the surrounding population was 50 percent black would be required to prove that it was not discriminating. Duncan politely but firmly shared her disagreement with Thomas over the issue. She left the interview thinking not only would she not receive the special assignment to his office, but "I probably wouldn't have a job" at the agency. When Thomas nevertheless offered her the position, she accepted; she said later that the offer "amazed" her. Like Thomas's other co-workers over the years, she would learn that he thrived on such philosophical debates, and that he admired assertive men and women who held their own and deepened his understanding of an issue.

Duncan and Hill became locked in a zero-sum game: As Duncan's portfolio expanded, Hill's shrank. Duncan reviewed cases that were coming up for a vote by the commission, making recommendations to Thomas. This had formerly been Hill's duty. Duncan also coordinated relations with other federal agencies, and even wrote speeches. As Thomas learned of Duncan's worth, more work headed her way. She became overwhelmed, she said.

> And at one point, it did seem to me as though I was handling every substantive piece of research that came in the office. And when you think about it, I had been at the EEOC at least long enough to know the law. And I had a pretty good work ethic. Carlton did not. I can't speak to Anita because I didn't really know her then. And he [Thomas] sent out a division of authority list that showed the three of us. And under mine, he had, "Anything that requires analysis." And I think he was a little frustrated with the organization and stuff. So I started getting more and more stuff. I got to work more and more closely with him. And at one point told him ... I said, "I can't take on—you've got to spread this out a little bit." I said, "Please give that one to Anita."

There was a dark side to Thomas's budding adeptness at managing and inspiring people. Like the good acolyte of Sowell that he was, he believed that competition brought out the best in people—or at least their best efforts. Thomas was not above deliberately tweaking the egos of his subordinates to inspire such competition. Duncan thought that his "division of authority list" was such an attempt. In this tiny organizational chart, he assigned "political stuff" to Carlton Stewart and "anything that requires analysis" to Allyson Duncan. Duncan said she could not remember what was assigned to Hill. Clearly, however, it was the crumbs. Duncan inferred that "when he wrote something like that, he was goading Anita and Carlton a little." She judged this a "dig" at her two co-workers and a calculated attempt to motivate them. "He could pit people against one another," she recalled. Duncan herself would suffer this fate when Thomas subsequently brought in a competitor to Duncan, Bill Ng.

Between his emergency task force and personal staff, Thomas gathered around him a motley group of varied talents. Alvarez remarked that Thomas would "surround himself with all types of people, from the book-smart people to the people with experience about those specific issues. He always wanted to be sure not just to get the facts, but to get some real-life perspective so that he could make the right decision." In the agency's financial department, the backwater sector that rose to prominence through epic mismanagement, Thomas came to rely particularly on Willie King. She had earned a footnote in the history of the civil rights movement when, as a secretary for the Southern Christian Leadership Conference, she had typed Martin Luther King Jr.'s letter from Birmingham Jail. She was memorialized as Willie Mackey—her maiden name—when Taylor Branch wrote of her falling asleep at her typewriter in his celebrated history of the civil rights movement, *Parting the Waters*. Willie King joined EEOC in February 1966, right after the agency was formed. After the Thomas era began at EEOC, she was promoted to financial manager and charged with getting to the bottom of the agency's financial woes.

Under the Norton regime, Willie King said, "we kept slippin', slippin', slippin'. When some of the employees tried to bring this to the attention of the powers that be, they were dealt with." After Thomas's arrival, she informed him that she had identified over three thousand errors in the agency's financial records. Thomas instructed her and her staff to document every problem they encountered. Afterwards, a timetable was established in which these errors were to be corrected. Thomas began to base his performance ratings of managers in part on how well they tracked and husbanded their funds.

Overall, Thomas found an agency that lacked an infrastructure of basic principles of accountability. He tried to rectify this by articulating, at the outset of his chairmanship, four cardinal rules of sound management:

> First, agency goals and objectives had to be established and tracked during the fiscal year.
> Second, the objectives had to be consistent with the agency's internal resource allocations.
> Third, to ensure their priority, the objectives had to be explicitly included in individual S.E.S., merit pay, and general staff performance agreements.
> Fourth, managers and staff had to be delegated enough responsibility to be able to initiate and complete the objectives.

Then came what he christened the "five element performance management system." The first of these elements was the adoption of a mission statement. As he lamented years later, "It may sound like I am espousing classroom public administration dictum, but I thought it was a sad commentary that an agency, 18 years old, had never developed a succinct mission statement capturing the essence of why it was created in the first place." In August, the commission approved a mission statement: "To ensure equality of opportunity by vigorously enforcing federal legislation prohibiting discrimination in employment through investigation, conciliation, litigation, coordination, regulation in the federal sector, and through education, policy research and provision of technical assistance." It was clumsy and bureaucratic, but so was the agency it was written to govern—and, from Thomas's standpoint, at least it was a start.

The other four elements of the Thomas "performance management system" were more straightforward. EEOC established a "formal agency goals-and-objectives system" for the ten headquarters offices across the country. Thomas met quarterly with the office directors to review their progress. The agency and its employees entered into "performance agreements," linking job performance reviews to employees' compliance with the new goals of the agency. Because the federal government could not simply discharge lackluster employees, these agreements were the best strategy Thomas could muster for making his subordinates hew to the new, more professional standards. Thomas sought to buy more computers—then coming into vogue—to allow the agency's management information system to track more accurately the status of EEOC's cases. Finally, he advocated more training for employees. Soon, at his insistence, the training budget more than doubled.

Notably, this burst of practical innovation came from a man who just as easily could have expounded intelligently on economics or political philosophy. Thomas quickly demonstrated a rare capacity to combine an intellectual, "big picture" understanding of the major issues of the day with attention to detail in the discharge of humdrum daily duties. He seemed to delight in learning about the mechanics of a hapless, foundering bureaucracy and making it work more smoothly, soaking up the tedious arcana of federal personnel rules along the way. Just as rare was the fact that unlike his predecessors, he actually cared about how well the commission fulfilled its mandate.

—

The congenial Thomas temperament again aided him immensely in bringing a hostile agency to heel. William Bradford Reynolds especially appreciated Thomas's success at winning converts, having struggled to do the same thing in a similarly chilly environment at the Justice Department. "I'd go over to see Clarence and we'd walk down to the cafeteria," Reynolds said. Throughout this ideologically "entrenched" office, Reynolds would observe en route to lunch one "remarkable" scene after another. "Everybody, from the damn messenger boy to staff, legal staff people, to the commissioners," would stop and greet Thomas as if saluting a rock star or triumphant gladiator.

Thomas came to know virtually every worker in the building. He learned their names, family histories, and the ups and downs of their lives. He roamed the hallways to meet and greet, stopping and chatting along the way, and visited nearby government cafeterias and lunch places frequented by the employees. Jeffrey Zuckerman, another attorney who later worked for Thomas, marveled at his conviviality. "He played, you know, the I'm-just-a-homeboy-from-Pin-Point kind of thing around the EEOC to his advantage," he remembered. "Every secretary in the place loved him." And because secretaries typed the reports and memoranda that were the synapses of the agency's collective nervous system, "that's how he could find out what was going on in his own agency." The overwhelming majority of secretaries and other blue-collar workers there were black. "To a lot of them," Zuckerman said, "he was the son they dreamed they had ... a guy who'd come out of their life and made it. And to see that he didn't turn on them, and came back and talked to them," forged between the leader and his flock an abiding loyalty.

One person Thomas came to know especially well was James Randall, the driver of his government-owned limousine. One of the perquisites of the chairmanship was a chauffeur-driven limousine to transport Thomas to and from work and his official functions. Conveniently enough, his Fiat Spider was recalled shortly after he joined the EEOC; he ended up using the money to pay for Jamal's private school education. Thomas enjoyed long conversations with Randall, who would tell him about life in Washington fifty years before. Randall, said Armstrong Williams, later a top Thomas aide, was a "God-fearing man" who, under Thomas's reign, "could never be late."

The employees in the agency's financial department saw a good deal of him for obvious reasons. "First of all, you'd hear a laugh—a hearty laugh," said Willie King. This was akin to the distant rumbling of a welcome thunderstorm on the Midwestern horizons—the full treatment was soon to follow. Thomas would bound down the hallway with his long, vigorous, purposeful strides, and soon would be upon them. "And he'd start saying to us, 'How's it going? What do you need to do your job?'" Thomas and King, both natives of Georgia, would swap stories about their grandparents and growing up amid the cotton fields. Football inevitably became a staple of his conversations with the men. Eventually, he would follow up with questions such as, "Is Willie treating you right?"

With his rumbling low voice, maturity, and fine sense of humor, Thomas exerted himself forcefully and with good results in meetings. "He was an imposing figure," said Mike Middleton. "He projected himself as an imposing figure. And it worked for him. I have to admire him for that. He could get a room full of fifteen high-level government officials, generally white, and he'd breeze in at the head of the table with that voice and that booming laugh and he would clearly take control of the room and get what he wanted to get done, done.... He would stick a big cigar in his mouth, rear back in his chair, and bark out orders."

Thomas was much less effective in delivering formal speeches than he was in speaking extemporaneously or to small groups. Two journalists who reviewed videotapes of his earliest speeches at EEOC said they showed "an ungainly young man going through a kind of professional adolescence." He typically read his speeches "awkwardly, without polish, his language stiff." While his voice and other gifts naturally commanded an audience's attention, formal oratory was not his forte.

His mind on the agency and other concerns, Thomas "wasn't a clothes person," according to one of his aides. He favored dark blue business suits, the standard-issue apparel of a conservative administration, but purchased them from department stores rather than upscale boutiques that were beyond his price range. "He'd wear the same suit with a different tie for three days," Armstrong Williams said. "He's like a 'bama,' a country person." Willie King described his attire as "tacky almost, conservative—not flashy. He doesn't spend a lot of money on clothes." He often wore suspenders under his jacket, which he would shed and hang up once in his office. Photos from the time show him wearing silk ties with equidistant dots, which were then in style. Perhaps as homage to Malcolm X, he grew a moustache and goatee. His thick, black-framed glasses were much like those popularized by the rap group Run DMC several years later.

His sense of decorum led him to insist on being called "Mr. Chairman" or "Chairman Thomas," not his first name. None but his most intimate advisers were permitted to call him "Clarence." This was not an ego trip: He scrupulously referred to Eleanor Holmes Norton as "Ms. Norton" (although never "Chair Norton") even as everybody else called her "Eleanor."

The more abrasive features were still there, all the better to ensure that he remained interesting. One civil rights activist told a reporter, "Clarence is like a 1960s student who's filled with anger and not really directed anywhere. He's a very complicated, conflicted individual." Thomas himself told a journalist in a moment of petulance, "I don't fit in with whites, and I don't fit in with blacks. We're a mixed-up generation—those of us who were sent out to integrate society.... If it were not for [the] few friends I have who do not give a damn about this stuff, this place could drive me insane."

Even as he charmed hundreds of previously hostile employees, Thomas relished long bouts of solitude. He admitted on one occasion, "my personality and style of operating approaches that of a *monastic recluse.*" This flip side of his soul, the side that had inclined him to the priesthood for a time, led some to regard Thomas as reserved. Others perceived social awkwardness, another observation about him that recurred occasionally. When Allyson Duncan heard years later of Anita Hill's allegations that Thomas often entered her office for private conversations, this did not jibe with her recollections. "When Anita talked about him coming to her office, he didn't come out of his sanctum much. He just didn't chat much."

Duncan recalled one occasion, approximately two months after she began working for him, when she joined Thomas for lunch in the cafeteria. "It was just painful," she said. "I just kept trying to think of things to say. His first words were, 'What are the major issues confronting the EEOC?'" She groaned inwardly. "I was not at ease with him," she stated. Thomas did not seem to her to be particularly warm—"he was not a warm-fuzzy person"—yet she recognized that he had parachuted into a very difficult situation. "He was feeling his way," she allowed. "He was very young. . . . He came into this bureaucracy that didn't welcome him with open arms. In retrospect, I can understand it."

Thomas also was preoccupied with something foreign to him: a love life. He was separated from Kathy but not divorced. Nevertheless, he began to date other women. One was Lillian McEwen, a black woman who worked for Democratic senator Joseph Biden and who was a friend of Anita Hill. He also became involved romantically with a Hispanic woman shortly after joining EEOC. These relations were inconsistent with his marital vows, and the guilt over this period in his life would well up inside him and burst forth years later during the confirmation hearings for the Supreme Court. He would then conclude, as he suffered what he regarded as a public death, that he was being punished for these years of "dating" and other sins.

As crime rates began to rise precipitously in the early 1980s, and as the order in his own life eroded, Thomas sought to make law enforcement the central precept of his new agency. To him, EEOC was above all a law enforcement agency. Congress had created it not to lobby for affirmative action, he reasoned, but to bring to justice violators of the nation's civil rights laws. He discovered that the ethos of the EEOC, after so many years of leadership committed to different priorities, was hostile to this mission.

The problem lay in the Norton-inspired system of "rapid charge" of cases. "My predecessor was faced with a significant backlog," Thomas remarked years later, a backlog "which had received considerable congressional, media, and public attention. She developed a system to specifically address the backlog and to rapidly dispose of new cases. In essence, the system *forced* settlement between the charging party and the employer prior to investigation of the case." About 50 percent of EEOC's charges were settled in this manner. The commission, the employer and the employee signed a "no-fault settlement agreement" disposing of the case. Often, the agreement mandated merely that the employer purge the charging party's file of information related to the charge and give a neutral employment reference. In an attempt to reduce the backlog, cases were given short shrift, and, Thomas observed, "frivolous and meritorious charges received the same treatment."

This system of bartering civil rights for short-term administrative expediency shocked Thomas's sensibilities. The former assistant attorney general, who had cut his teeth in the law doing criminal work, found the arrangement deeply offensive. "I am a strict law and order man," he declared. He denounced "law breakers" and pledged to hold them to account henceforth. "I refuse to preside over a system which places a premium on quick resolution at the expense of someone's legal rights— to let a law breaker off without sufficient punishment; to let a victim suffer without sufficient relief," he observed. The numbers bore out his concerns. Out of 2,500 charges brought in one year, only 300 to 400 were actually brought before the full commission for possible litigation.

Thomas devoted himself to transforming the EEOC from an advocate of social engineering to a professional law enforcement agency. In this vein, he persuaded the commission to adopt a new policy: The commission would consider for possible litigation every case in which it issued a "reasonable cause determination" or "letter of violation"—in short, in every case in which the complaint was found to have merit. Thomas stressed that the agency intended "to litigate, to enforce our findings—no matter how small the case is." He urged this policy shift both to serve the victims of these civil rights violations and to enhance the overall credibility of the agency. He believed generally that "civil rights statutes will not be respected until the linkage between right and remedy is firmly established and the connection between transgressor and punishment is reaffirmed."

Thomas also made it a calling to seek treble damages for civil rights violations. "I am appalled at the fact that there are greater penalties for breaking into a mailbox than there are for violating someone's basic civil rights," he remarked. He wanted EEOC's laws "to have at least as much teeth as the antitrust laws." Treble damages for Title VII violations, he believed, "just might do a lot" to eradicate discrimination. Eventually, this vision would become law—and would mark a major change in the civil rights universe.

Years later, Thomas was still grumbling over the invective that civil rights organizations hurled at him in the wake of these changes. "As you can expect, the criticism from the civil rights community was fast in coming," he recalled. He listed some of the allegations that came within earshot: "'This was nothing but a smoke screen.' 'This was a ploy.'" The frivolousness of some of these aspersions dumbfounded him. "We are being told to bypass fighting *obvious* discrimination so that we can have the time and resources to fight imagined discrimination," he observed. Indeed, these groups soon were chiding Thomas and EEOC for filing too *many* lawsuits, instead of large class-action claims more likely to generate affirmative action plans.

Thomas reported the flak he was taking in his new position to his grandparents when he visited them in Georgia. He recalled that when he "started feeling sorry for myself" in the face of this resistance and anger, Daddy said, "Son, you've got to stand up for what you believe in." Thomas would fondly quote this epigram thereafter.

During his visit, he and his grandparents, who were Democrats, discussed the coming 1982 elections. They asked why he was a Republican. He thought a bit, then responded: "You all made me become Republican." He said they "looked at him in total disbelief." Then, Thomas said, he explained his reasoning:

Aunt Tina and Daddy, remember those summers when you told me that working all day in the fields would teach me how to work. Remember when you told me that it wasn't right to beg as long as I could work and get it myself. Remember when you all would get up at 3 and 4 o'clock in the morning to work. I bet you thought I didn't hear you. Remember when you told me that if I ever amounted to anything it would be by the sweat of *my* brow and *my* elbow grease. And, remember when you said you would rather starve than have anyone give you something—as long as you could work for it. You thought I wasn't listening—but I was listening.

I went on to tell them that I embraced the values they taught me: individual effort, individual freedom and unlimited opportunity. Politically, I had no choice: the only party *openly* standing for these values was the Republican party. Needless to say, they voted Republican.

Shortly after the next year began, Thomas spotted an article in the *Washington Post* that intrigued him. The article, which appeared in the Style section on January 15, 1983, recounted a moving speech that the comedian Richard Pryor had delivered in Washington in commemoration of Martin Luther King Jr.'s birthday. Pryor had given the speech at, of all places, the U.S. Department of Agriculture. The reporter noted—helpfully for Thomas—that the person responsible for booking Pryor's speech was an Agriculture Department employee named Armstrong Williams. A handsome and glib African-American, Williams came from South Carolina, and his political mentor was Strom Thurmond, the state's senior U.S. senator. By attracting one of the most prominent comedians of the day to such an event, Williams had shown he would be a prime asset to any administrator seeking to make a name for himself.

The following Monday morning, January 17, Thomas called Williams at the Agriculture Department and asked him to come to his office. In their meeting, which became a job interview, Thomas asked Williams a series of pointed questions that served as a clever sales pitch.

"Do you have a mentor over at the Department of Agriculture?" he asked.

"No," Williams answered.

"Do you work directly for the Secretary of Agriculture?"

Again, the answer was "No."

And on it went. "He was very direct, very clear," Williams recalled.

"He said, 'Don't be fooled. The EEOC isn't Agriculture. We're in the dungeon.'" But with Williams' contacts in the entertainment world, Thomas said, more publicity and prominence soon would come. Williams began work at the EEOC before the month was out. Thomas gave him the job title "confidential assistant"—in retrospect, a humorous sobriquet for a man who would become a notoriously voluble media figure.

Thomas could look back on his first year at EEOC with growing pride. The agency had closed out almost 60 percent of its backlogged contracts. Through an "aggressive debt collection program," EEOC had reduced its outstanding travel advances from $1.2 million to $200,000. Under Thomas's leadership, EEOC had been streamlined to prevent it from "falling into the trap of excessive organizational units with over-graded positions." The agency had restored lost grades for most of the sixty downgraded staffers by assigning the cashiered employees "more meaningful responsibilities" and "holding them accountable for meeting those expectations." Renovations of EEOC's headquarters were approved. Several field offices were consolidated. A new computer center was under construction.

Thomas's operational reforms and his transformation of EEOC to a professional law enforcement agency would prove his two greatest contributions to the agency. By the end of his first year, he was well on his way to accomplishing both. This was not the stuff of headlines, however. "Doesn't sound very exciting—does it?" he once said to an audience as he enumerated the problems he had confronted and tamed. "And because it is *not* exciting you won't read about it and I won't be invited to discuss these changes on *Good Morning America* or the *Today Show*. In fact, these are the boring time-consuming factors that make an organization work. These are the aspects of a manager's job that politicians, interest groups and news media could not care less about."

CHAPTER FOURTEEN

Turkey Shoot

Having laid down basic standards of accountability at EEOC, Thomas now sought to make them stick. As one of the more notorious havens of inept and indolent employees within the federal government, EEOC had come to be known among other federal employees as the "turkey farm." Norton's neglectful tenure had not helped matters. By the time Thomas arrived, EEOC had become an unofficial dumping ground for some of the worst of the worst in the federal personnel system, a sort of penitentiary for substandard employees—except that there were no guards, and everyone went home at night reasonably well paid.

One EEOC employee who became famous within the agency right before Thomas's arrival exemplified this state of affairs. First, she was caught falsifying her time records in order to embezzle $4,000 for work not performed. Instead of being sent to jail, she was given a thirty-day suspension. Subsequently she became the toast of the agency and received a cash award when she brokered a peace accord among factions in the agency that previously had refused to share their telephone numbers with each other. From her efforts, the agency telephone directory was born.

Improving the quality of service at the agency was not simply a matter of dismissing poor employees and hiring new ones. Federal law prohibited Thomas from taking this commonsense step, one that any private business would have favored. Federal employees who became part of the civil service could be dismissed only for cause, and then only after their managers had complied with an exhausting code of statutes and regulations. If managers wished to discipline an employee, they had to counsel the employee first and give him a chance to correct his deficiencies. If they then decided to try to discharge the employee, they had to inform him of their intention in advance. The employee had a right to counsel and an array of other liberties to wield against his managers in a mini-trial conducted by a hearing officer. After all of this, the employee still could file a discrimination complaint or do any number of other things to stymie management. Enacted with the good intention of protecting employees from political coercion, the civil service rules had become, by the early 1980s, a shelter for poor employees that even the hardiest managers could rarely penetrate.

Imposing a Liberty County work ethic on such a restive population was a tall order. Thomas made it clear from the beginning of his tenure that for all his warmth and good cheer, he would not permit anything to stand in the way of performance and results. Mike Middleton observed: "He doesn't suffer fools. A person who screws things up can quickly be dismissed by him." While saying that Thomas "was like a father" to him, Armstrong Williams admitted that Thomas was a relentless disciplinarian. "When I'd mess up, sometimes he wouldn't talk to me for a week. He'd ice me for a week," Williams said. "Then he'd call down and say, 'Have you learned your lesson?'" Middleton likewise noticed "a coldness in him once he made the decision not to use you or not to appoint you to this or to give you this work." Of Thomas's talent for awing sluggards into mending their ways, Williams observed, "They knew he was crazy, that he'd get rid of them if he wanted to."

Typically, the first item on Thomas's daily agenda was a staff meeting that started right on time. "If he said we had a meeting at 7:00, you can't walk in at 7:02," Williams said. Then would follow "the walk." At 8:00 A.M., Thomas would tell Williams, "Come on, buddy. Let's go." Thomas and Williams would prowl the halls and offices to ensure that his people were manning their stations. "I like to walk 'em and shock 'em and see if they're lollygagging," he explained to Williams. People knew that he meant it, too—that he would find a way to hold them accountable if they fell short of his standards. "He'd fire your butt in a heartbeat," Williams said. Throughout EEOC, Williams observed, there was no doubt about Thomas's authority and ability. Quite simply, "He was the man."

At 9 A.M., Thomas would slip outside the front door and stand near the entrance to the building, sipping his morning Diet Coke as he conducted an informal survey of employees who were arriving late. Thomas also lunched outside regularly, permitting him to mingle with the employees and to monitor who was taking excessively long lunch breaks.

Unions and antiquated laws that tied his hands felt his wrath. He blasted the "totally *obstructionist* attitude of our union, and the give-away contract which our predecessors locked us into," paying high wages for employees who, he felt, were often undeserving. "Nor have I mentioned a civil service system which prevents us from terminating those who should be terminated and from hiring those whom we *need.*" Thomas was appalled at the poor work ethic he found almost everywhere he turned. In one speech, he hammered his point home: "I cannot convey to you the tremendous frustration of chairing commission meetings week after week, to review poor quality work, brought to us in an untimely manner—and damn little of it."

One subordinate who fell from grace was Frank Quinn. The long-time supervisor of EEOC's office in San Francisco, Quinn was, in Thomas's eyes, one of a number of regional supervisors who were not up to the job. In the spring of 1983, Thomas decided to transfer Quinn and eight other senior executives in the agency to lesser posts. Right before Thomas executed his plan of sending Quinn to Montgomery, Alabama, Quinn's luck turned in a strange way. An article ran in *Newsweek* questioning why the number of discrimination cases filed under Thomas's watch had plunged. Quinn was quoted as suggesting that EEOC headquarters in Washington was "spiking" recommendations from the field. Shortly after the article came out, Quinn learned of his transfer to Alabama. He went to court and, citing the article, argued retaliation. A federal judge scotched the transfer. Soon thereafter, Quinn retired.

In an agency stocked with liberals, the order of the day was competence, not ideology. One aide recalled that Thomas was fond of saying, "'I don't care if somebody is white, black, or green.' And it was clear that he really didn't." In his years at EEOC, Thomas would assemble a team of all races and hues, faiths and creeds. His cell of reformers was a "Rainbow Coalition" of the sort which Jesse Jackson, then a presidential candidate, aspired but failed to create. "I'm prejudiced in only one way," Thomas told one lieutenant. "I hire smart people. That's the only way I discriminate."

As he amassed this brain trust, he was not above using his position to preach to the unconverted. A couple of times, Thomas invited his friend Tom Sowell to lecture to his senior staff. Sowell published a new book in 1983, *The Economics and Politics of Race: An International Perspective,* an elaboration on *Race and Economics,* the book that had captivated the young Thomas. Indeed, for the next two decades Sowell would publish a new book every couple of years that rewrote and expanded on his 1975 classic. *The Economics and Politics of Race* explored the extent to which distinct individual and social traits among races and ethnic groups persisted across the globe. Sowell's presentations to Thomas's staff were major events that provoked lively discussion.

Thomas's reforms bore good fruit throughout the agency. As of September 30, the case backlog had been pared down from over 10,000 charges to only 782. During his first sixteen months at EEOC, he reported, "I have seen a continuing flow of discrimination charges filed with the EEOC.... An alarming number of these charges have merit." The new policy requiring full commission review of all meritorious claims meant these claims would not be shoveled out the door. An enormous surge in the workload of the commissioners followed. But by the end of September, the commission had authorized 112 new cases for litigation and had won more than $433 million in awards for charging parties. Thomas also had managed to automate the agency and develop and purchase a central data system without any additional funding for the purpose.

For the first time in years, the agency was operating effectively.

———

Even as the administration and EEOC staff members took notice of these improvements, Thomas still had not received the recognition he most craved. Myers Anderson was even stingier with his praise than the grandson who idolized him. He was a hard man who still had not quite overcome his hurt feelings over Thomas's decision not to join the priesthood. As Thomas did his best to stamp his grandfather's work ethic on an entire federal agency, Daddy still held back his full blessing.

Daddy, Thomas recalled, "never seemed to be satisfied with anything I did—not my academic or athletic honors—not my graduation from college or law school." Finally, his grandfather said the words

Thomas had hoped to hear since his departure for Holy Cross. In February 1983, apparently after Thomas raised the subject, Daddy said of the life Thomas was leading: "I am satisfied." This meager praise, Thomas later said, was "the single most important recognition I have received."

His grandfather was in the last days of his life. He dispensed his homespun advice liberally now, as if recognizing that the end was nearing. "I have done all I can do, it's up to you young ones now," he told Thomas. Among his last words was a saying that was unoriginal but, given the source, uniquely compelling to Thomas: "Stand up for what you believe." Daddy suffered a stroke and died on his farm near Sunbury on March 30.

Thomas's brother, Myers, was living in Connecticut and working as an accountant when he called to deliver the news. "It was the worst news I had heard in my life," Thomas said. "I found myself growing angry with him for bringing such bad news. Then, I refused to believe him. It was only when I actually saw the lifeless body of my grandfather that I began to try to accept the truth."

The funeral was held on April 4 at St. Benedict Church in Savannah, the house of worship that had framed Daddy's thoughts on eternity. The funeral bulletin distributed to the attendees misidentified his grandson as "Clearance Thomas of Washington, D.C." Myers Anderson was buried later in the day in the old cemetery next to Palmyra Missionary Baptist Church near his farm, amid the African-inspired glass and other devotions to the departed that adorned the graves at the site.

"No levee or dam could hold back the flood of tears," Thomas said of this time. He "cried like a baby without shame, without control, and without remorse. The starch of independence washed from my body—I drooped now in a raglike posture." In the days and weeks following this crushing experience, "I had reached the nadir, the bottom of the bottomless pit of endless wandering in an aimless existence. This was the dark night of my soul." More than two years later, as he wrote a speech recounting this loss, "the tears of grief and agony streamed down my face."

A little over a month after Daddy's death, Thomas suffered another blow. Christine Anderson—Aunt Tina, the grandmother who complemented his grandfather's fierceness with kindness and occasionally shielded Thomas from Daddy's fury—passed away as well. Another heartrending funeral led her to a final resting place beside her husband.

The deaths of his grandparents greatly shook Thomas, both emotionally and spiritually. As a result, he told a religious gathering some years later, "I turned where the hopeless and the lonely turn—to God. I fell on my knees—begged for his forgiveness—asked for his help and his guidance." These events also led him to reexamine his life and to recognize more fully his shortcomings. "My strong will and my intellect had dominated and I was drowning in the confusion of their work product," he came to realize.

Thomas found comfort in a passage from Scripture. "I remember reading a quote from Isaiah that: 'Those who hope in the Lord will renew their strength. They will soar on wings like eagles; they will run and not grow weary, they will walk and not be faint.'" The recent movie *Chariots of Fire* had popularized the quotation; whether he learned of it through random reading is uncertain. Clearly, it bolstered his soul: "This hope has been the sweet nectar to renew my strength."

The trauma of his grandparents' deaths tugged him closer to the faith he had drifted away from. On his way to work, Thomas began to ask Mr. Randall to stop at a Catholic church. There, he would pray for a few minutes. He still was not prepared to attend church regularly. "God is all right," he told a reporter at around this time. "It's the people I don't like." This comment, an attempt at cleverness, undoubtedly was both insincere and intended to provoke. Thomas, in fact, was edging back toward the faith he had left behind at Conception.

After his grandfather's death, Thomas invoked his memory to bid defiance to his unremitting critics. "When the civil-rights people indict me," he told a reporter, "the man they are indicting is that man. Let them call him from the grave and indict him."

The organizational chaos sowed by his predecessors at EEOC left Thomas very little time to mourn. Back at the turkey farm, a crisis was brewing involving one of the more prominent members of the flock. In less than a year of working at EEOC, Anita Hill had managed to alienate herself from almost all of her colleagues. Worse still from the standpoint of professional longevity, she had added little value to Thomas's shop. She had ceded work to Allyson Duncan and was largely without clear responsibilities. Her downward spiral was becoming obvious.

Thomas judged her work "good." But such a modest appraisal was insufficient to earn the chairman's time and attention. "The problem," Thomas explained about her efforts, "was that—and it wasn't a problem—was, it was not as good as some of the other members of the staff." More to the point, "There was sort of a pecking order and I don't think that she, in that role, at EEOC was very high on the pecking order because of experience." Middleton, who was sympathetic to Hill, said, "I do remember Anita complaining about her status at EEOC. That he wasn't relying on her at EEOC like he had at Education. She wasn't getting the work she wanted." Middleton concluded, "Anita was probably given duties that she didn't think were commensurate with her skills."

Hill was suffering from the professionally fatal infirmity of high ambition saddled with indolence. Thomas thought Hill was not knowledgeable about Title VII and "didn't try to take her time and learn from the bottom up. She wanted to start at the top and stay at the top, and I had other people at the top." Duncan believed Hill did a "good job," but added, "I thought she was hampered understandably by her lack of background in Title VII matters." She made little effort to become familiar with the law. One of Hill's assignments was to review the EEOC's position on sexual harassment, namely, whether the agency should recommend that sexual harassment become a cognizable claim under Title VII. Eight years later, when she aired allegations of sexual harassment, she would remember so little of Title VII—even after teaching civil rights law following her stint at EEOC—that she would have to consult other lawyers to become conversant in the relevant law.

What work came her way seemed to overwhelm her. Andrew Fischel, one of Thomas's closest advisers at EEOC, judged that "the job was too challenging" for Hill. "There was a lot of pressure. She did not work well under pressure." Her temper would simmer as the stack of documents in her in-box grew. Yet at the same time, she complained about not receiving good assignments.

Thomas remembered Hill as an "aggressive debater. She stood her ground. When she got her dander up, she would storm off." Others simply saw this quality as belligerence. Once, when a bigwig from another agency attended a meeting and referred to her as "Anita," she shot back, shades of Sidney Poitier, "Call me Ms. Hill!" One EEOC staffer who witnessed this cringed. "She chilled the entire room. This was a woman who took no crap from anybody, no matter how powerful they were." Williams agreed, saying, "Anita did not take any prisoners."

J. C. Alvarez, a fellow special assistant, also grew to dislike Hill. She was, in Alvarez's estimation, "very strong-willed, she liked to do things her way. . . . [S]he kind of had her own agenda, her own way of doing things. So, no matter what the rest of the team was doing, she was going to do it Anita's way."

Hill tried to polish her image by suggesting that she still enjoyed a special relationship with Thomas. She would "tout the fact that she had worked with him before," Alvarez noted. "You know, when we would get into debates on how we were going to handle an issue, she would say, 'Well, I know how he thinks, I know how he likes his papers written or I know the position he wants to take,' or something like that. That was something she always sort of held out in front of everyone at the staff, that she had this sort of inside track to him." Willie King concurred. "Anita appeared to be a very frustrated person who was vying for a lot of attention. She felt she'd earned his attention. She became more frustrated when his attention became more divided." King recalled occasions when Hill went into commission meetings and made a major production out of arranging his papers. "She'd say, 'The chairman wants it like this. What do you have for him?'" She used officiousness to try to convey authority: "She'd say, 'I know how he wants it.' She was trying to make herself important." After a while, "we just got to the point that we'd disregard her."

King's overall assessment of Hill was harsher still. "I felt that she just was not all there. There was something missing. She was strange." King concluded that Hill "had a loose screw. There was something that just didn't come off right, like the position she was in. She was different from the other special assistants I've been used to throughout the history of the agency."

When Thomas decided he needed a legal counsel position on his personal staff, the Vesuvius inside Hill began to rumble. Hill and Duncan were the obvious candidates. But Duncan's superior experience, intellectual and legal sophistication, and work ethic meant that the outcome of the unfolding melodrama was predestined and obvious to all but Hill. Although Duncan said she did not sense the one-sided competition coming from Hill, others in the office felt it acutely and saw the unpleasantness to come.

Adding fuel to this volatile situation was Thomas's practice of openly favoring some employees over others to foster competition. A later special assistant to Thomas, Sukari Hardnett, agreed: "Clarence would pit people against one another." Hardnett subsequently witnessed Thomas do so between Duncan and another employee, Thomasina Rogers. "And he might have done that with Anita Hill and Allyson," she believed.

In or around March 1983, it became clear even to Hill that the legal counsel job would be handed to Duncan. "I thought Anita was gonna croak," King recalled with a chuckle. Soon thereafter, Hill was hospitalized for stress-related symptoms. When Duncan officially was tapped for the promotion, Hill began refusing to attend meetings. She would fling puerile comments at Thomas or others, such as, "I'm as smart as her" or "If you've got her, why do you need me?" Things came to a head when Duncan told Hill that her work was not up to standards.

Hill's relationship with Thomas also deteriorated visibly. Thomas noticed that she became "very bitter" when he criticized her work as not being sufficiently analytical. Unknown to him, she responded by keeping a log tracking her work, a standard move for a federal employee considering filing a grievance in the civil service process or a lawsuit in the courts.

Her ambitions checked at EEOC, Hill set her sights elsewhere. She prevailed upon Thomas to help her seek a job of prominence at the Justice Department. In one of his meetings with William Bradford Reynolds at around the time of Duncan's promotion, Thomas raised the issue with Reynolds. "Anita Hill was ... interested in moving up," Reynolds recalled. "And Clarence did not have a spot for her to move to, and did not really feel that she deserved to be promoted."

This was hardly a ringing endorsement of an employee, but Thomas pressed on. He asked Reynolds if there was a position available involving litigation in the civil rights division. Thomas made it clear that Hill was interested in more than an "administrative job."

Although he did not have a high position to offer her, Reynolds agreed to meet with Hill. At the meeting, Hill expressed her desire to join the civil rights division and to litigate cases. Almost two decades later, Reynolds stated, "I have a very vivid recollection of me sitting in my desk and her sitting in a chair actually on that side [pointing to his left] of the office and saying what a wonderful employer [Thomas] was. And how much she liked it" at EEOC. His impression was that she felt "Clarence Thomas could walk on water." While some of Hill's commentary may have been normal puffery for a job interview—Hill undoubtedly was shrewd enough not to berate Thomas in front of Reynolds—it is notable that she hid her animosity toward Thomas so effectively and audaciously.

Finally, opportunity knocked. Charles Kothe, the dean of the law school at Oral Roberts University in Tulsa, Oklahoma, had invited Thomas to speak at the law school in April. ORU was the eponymous creation of Oral Roberts, a nationally televised evangelist based in Tulsa who became best known for his declaration several years later that if his followers did not mail in enough donations, the Lord would strike him down and "call him home" (bumper stickers soon appeared throughout Tulsa reading, "Send Oral to Heaven in '87"). Tulsa was less than an hour's drive north of Hill's hometown, so she took advantage of the federally sponsored travel to fly back with Thomas and visit her family after the seminar.

At a luncheon sponsored by ORU, Hill and Kothe dined together and talked. At one point, he asked her a question that, as she put it, seemed to come "just out of the blue."

"How would you like to come home and teach?" he asked.

"I would like it," was Hill's frank reply.

After a press conference following the luncheon, Kothe informed Thomas of his idea regarding Hill. He asked what Thomas thought.

"Well, if that is what she would like to do, I would be all for it," Thomas said.

"Well, do you think she would make a good teacher?" Kothe asked.

Thomas's response helped to clinch the deal. "I think she would make a great teacher," he told the dean.

Formal letters of recommendation to Kothe soon followed. On May 13, Gil Hardy wrote a letter to Kothe advocating for Hill. Thomas penned his letter on May 31, offering careful and highly measured praise for Hill. "Overall," Thomas wrote, "her work product during the past two years has been of high quality. Moreover, the improvement in her work during this period has been exceptional." Thomas said that her analytical skills—which he had criticized both directly to her and implicitly through the office organizational chart—had "sharpened." He added, "While we have disagreed on the positions to be taken in particular matters, she is able to support her positions and we are able to resolve the disagreements professionally." Thomas toned down the assessment he had given Kothe in Tulsa, saying that Hill would be a "worthwhile"— not, as he had said in person, a "great"—"addition to your teaching staff." Nevertheless, ORU soon made Hill a formal offer. She accepted and left EEOC in July.

Hill later wrote that she cried on the flight from Washington to Tulsa. If so, it is hard to understand why. She did not lose anything in salary or income by moving to Tulsa. The cost of living in Tulsa was so much lower that, in effect, she had received a substantial pay raise. She would be less than an hour's drive from her family. Of course, ORU was not Yale; she would have to work her way up if she desired a prestigious career in academia. But for a young lawyer who was floundering badly in her second job in three years, the ORU position was an extraordinary opportunity and a stroke of good fortune.

Thomas and his erstwhile protégé from Yale parted company, he thought, on good terms. He had found a good home for Gil Hardy's charge back in her native state. The law professorship was the position of prominence she had sought without success in Washington. Armstrong Williams saw things differently. Hill had left the agency under a cloud of failure—failure she blamed not on herself, but on Thomas. Williams warned Thomas, to no avail, "This woman is your mortal enemy, and will do anything to destroy you."

⌒

As Hill headed west, Thomas confronted other professional troubles. The case of *Williams v. City of New Orleans* became a major focus of his energies. The New Orleans Police Department had signed on to a plan to promote equal numbers of black and white policemen until 50 percent of officers at all ranks were black. Thomas, at the urging of his team of EEOC attorneys, endorsed the plan. As the case went on appeal to the Fifth Circuit, Thomas agreed that EEOC should write an amicus, or friend-of-the-court, brief in support of the city's plan.

When Brad Reynolds and Michael Horowitz learned of this brief, they were furious. Reynolds and the Justice Department argued that by federal statute, their agency possessed exclusive authority to file briefs for the federal government in public-sector cases. On March 16, Theodore B. Olson, head of Justice's Office of Legal Counsel, sent Thomas a legal opinion stating that EEOC lacked the authority to appear before the Fifth Circuit in *Williams* or any other public-sector case. On March 21, Thomas fired back his own memorandum, asserting the agency's authority to participate as a friend of the court.

Finally, Horowitz and the White House intervened, coming down hard on the side of Justice. Thomas was called to a meeting with Meese and Attorney General Smith and instructed not to file the brief. A spokesman from the Justice Department explained that the federal government needed to speak with "one voice" in its litigation. Thomas was reduced to sending a meek, follow-up letter on April 5 pledging that EEOC would not file a brief. He asked merely and in vain that Justice's brief reflect the views of the commission.

Thomas told a reporter later in the year that the flap over the *Williams* case was "the only conflict at any time" he had had with the administration. This was an overstatement. It was merely the worst internal conflict Thomas had endured; there were plenty of other squabbles.

For all his private bombast against civil rights liberals, the Clarence Thomas of Reagan's first term was a very cautious and moderate figure in public. Charles Fried, who served as a consultant to the White House Office of Policy Development, was alike in his moderation. A professor at Harvard Law School and, subsequently, solicitor general under Reagan, Fried was an amiable man and moderately conservative lawyer with a rapid, sharp smile and a genial demeanor that allowed him to navigate the hostile ideological waters of Harvard. Fried joined Thomas as part of an administration task force that reviewed civil rights policies. The task force, which included Reynolds and Horowitz, met in the Executive Office Building next to the White House. "There were some very hard-edged views expressed in those meetings," Fried recalled—hardly surprising, given the presence of Reynolds and

Horowitz. Fried remembered, however, that "Clarence was always a voice of experience, common sense, moderation.... We were all pretty convinced that there needed to be significant changes. But he was always a more moderate tone and a more practical tone."

Reynolds and Horowitz, on the other hand, were growing concerned about Thomas's reluctance to fight for the administration's civil rights policies. This rift came to the fore at a public forum in August. Thomas appeared on a National Urban League panel in New Orleans with Reynolds and Mary Frances Berry, a liberal former member of the U.S. Civil Rights Commission. Juan Williams, who covered the event for the *Washington Post,* reported that Thomas "offered little if any support for Reynolds' contention that the Justice Department is vigorously enforcing the nation's laws against racial discrimination." Saying the administration must get "its own house in order," Thomas tossed populist bromides out to the crowd like so many fistfuls of candy. "We cannot expect to be effective in enforcing the . . . laws in the private sector if we do not do all we can to comply with those laws ourselves," he said, basking in applause in the manner of Louisiana's own Huey Long. Reynolds responded with a loyal defense of Reagan's civil rights policies: "We are not a special-interest law firm.... We cannot condemn practices of discrimination against black police officers in Nassau and Suffolk counties, N.Y., or Milwaukee, Wis., and ignore the claims of unlawful discrimination by Hispanics, females and white officers challenging a promotion quota that favors blacks." Although he privately agreed with such sentiments, Thomas remained unwilling to affirm his accord in public.

Privately, Reynolds and Horowitz were more blunt with their rebellious colleague. During lunch at the White House mess, Reynolds loudly cajoled Thomas to speak out against affirmative action publicly. Thomas responded by pulling out the race card: "Don't tell me what to do, Brad. All I *have* to do is die and stay black."

Horowitz also urged Thomas to carry the administration's banner on civil rights. He pressed him repeatedly to be a "more overt change agent," only to encounter, again and again, "a cautious resistance." Horowitz ultimately concluded that Thomas was placing his own career aims above loyal execution of administration priorities. At one point, he snapped, "Clarence, what are you saving yourself for?"

Thomas later sounded off about this pressure. During the first Reagan term, he said, "the hounds were snapping at our heels." He recalled:

> Some people appeared to want us to change every policy which they found objectionable over night—if not sooner. Others wanted me to proclaim my opposition to quotas loudly, using the strongest rhetoric. Be out front—throw yourself in front of a train to show how strongly you *feel*. Well, there is a problem with that: Unless you are Superman— you only get one shot at the train.

This self-lamentation was wonderful rhetoric, but it rested on a false analogy: There was no train that was going to destroy Thomas's career if he opposed racial preferences. Indeed, his career was soaring precisely because of his opposition to such policies; he would have endeared himself further by voicing those views publicly; his career would rise or fall based largely on his commitment to this cause. Thomas preferred, however, to play the martyr:

> The administration's attitude for the most part was supportive—they looked at me as you would look at a terminally ill relative or a friend destined for certain disaster. You see your friends and relatives peering in at you and whispering behind your back, "Isn't it too bad! Who would have thought it would come to this. And he was such a nice person."

Thomas continued to exchange fire with other administration officials in the press. In remarks amplified by the *New York Times* in June, Thomas bemoaned the pervasive public perception that the Reagan administration did not enforce civil rights laws. The "perception problem out there" was so strongly ingrained, Thomas said, that he had found some employers were surprised to learn they would be penalized for violating civil rights laws.

Reynolds and the Justice Department crossed swords with Thomas the following month over the mandatory federal affirmative action plans. Attorney General Smith, at Reynolds' urging, informed EEOC that Justice would not comply with a twelve-year-old executive order requiring agencies of the federal government to set goals for the hiring of minorities and women. On July 21, Smith submitted Justice's affirmative action plan to EEOC without any such goals. He explained, "Such goals often become, in fact, quotas. . . . That is discrimination and that is wrong." On September 6, EEOC rejected Justice's plan as unsatisfactory, saying it failed to properly set standards for determining whether minorities and women were underrepresented. Thomas even leaked his rejection letter to Smith to the press before Justice had received it. In response, Reynolds, one reporter noted, "took a slap at Thomas." Reynolds told the press, "As is customary with the EEOC, they have apparently communicated with the press before communicating with the attorney general."

In October, Thomas added his voice to the shower of denunciations then descending on Interior Secretary James Watt, who had described the membership of a coal commission as "a black, a woman, two Jews and a cripple." Thomas told an audience in Cleveland that Watt's comments revealed a broader problem in Washington: "People are not treated as individuals, but as representatives of constituent groups." This reproach was relatively gentle for Thomas, perhaps because so many others had pounced on Watt already. Again, however, Thomas did not miss the opportunity to clearly separate himself from another administration misstep in the realm of civil rights.

Most biting of all were comments Thomas made to Juan Williams at around this time, but not published until years later. Thomas openly agreed with the single worst calumny hurled by liberal civil rights groups at the Reagan administration. "Yes, there are a lot of racists in the Administration," Thomas told him. "So what? . . . I prefer dealing with an out-and-out racist anyway to one who is racist behind your back." Thomas offered no evidence to back up such an outlandish claim. It was the height of self-service for him to grant such aid and comfort to the administration's most bitter enemies. But it sounded good, and Thomas went with it.

His comments on racial preferences during this time were in line with this public posture. They reflected not so much anguish over choosing the right policy as an elaborate and ultimately unsuccessful attempt to shuck and jive to avoid being pinned down one way or the other on the highly charged issue. In this, as in so many of Thomas's other actions and statements during the first Reagan term, he showed a keen survival instinct worthy of comparison to some of the more successful politicians in the nation's capital.

When he accepted the post at EEOC in 1982, Thomas had publicly criticized "over-reliance on quotas"—but not quotas per se. Indeed, he represented at the time, "I do not believe there should be a wholesale abandonment of numerical devices." Several months into the job, Thomas told a reporter from *Business Week* that while he was no fan of hiring quotas, he believed "you do need to use numbers and timetables to measure progress." Still, "where you might need them for a big AT&T, you may not need them for a smaller business." *Business Week* sought to sum up Thomas's amorphous views by reporting that Thomas believed "minorities and women sometimes need help in catching up with other workers, so some affirmative action is desirable."

By March 1983, Thomas still was vaguely and nominally in favor of racial preferences—just enough, he seemed to hope, to avert total ostracism from the black community. "I tend to think that actions short of quotas are more acceptable remedies," he told *U.S. News and World Report.* "For example, after determining the number of minority people in his region, an employer might set out to recruit, train or fill jobs with a certain goal or time frame in mind. From a remedial standpoint, that seems appropriate in specific instances." Yet an employer should not be penalized if he falls short of this goal, Thomas argued, "because he has done everything he realistically could do." This reasoning was specious: Hiring goals that could be ignored with impunity were not quotas at all, but feckless aspirations. But the reporter left it at that.

In this interview, Thomas made other curious assertions. He claimed "there really isn't any such thing as reverse discrimination," saying that whites can file suit under Title VII just like other groups when they unfairly lose a job to a minority. This statement both undercut administration policy—Reagan had been elected in part by denouncing reverse discrimination—and overlooked the fact that some whites had sued successfully for such discrimination, most notably the plaintiff in the *Bakke* case. When the reporter asked if Thomas believed, as the Heritage Foundation recently had argued, that affirmative action caused "racial bitterness," Thomas replied, "I don't know of a study that has been done that supports a theory that affirmative action causes that kind of resentment." This was both evasive and inaccurate. In fact, one of the professional passions of his friend Tom Sowell was documenting this very sort of racial resentment the world over. It was at around this very time that Sowell came to EEOC to lecture Thomas's staff on his findings regarding international ethnic tensions related to affirmative action. *The Economics and Politics of Race*, published that year, asserted

that "Preferential treatment of various racial and ethnic groups has produced political resentments and a growing racist extremist fringe in the
United States."

Thomas's speeches betray a similarly dishonest attempt to have it
both ways on affirmative action. In March, he declared: "Although my
commitment to individual rights causes me to raise questions about the
effectiveness of group remedies, with the exception of quotas, I support
many affirmative action remedies. I support these remedies because the
remedies which are truly necessary to make individual rights a meaningful reality are not yet on the books." Yet he also conceded, "A policy which awards different rewards and benefits to different groups
cannot command public respect, and will, in the long run, damage the
civil rights of all."

Other times, he seemed to be trying just to wish the whole issue
away. "A good deal of the confusion caused by the debate can be
explained by the fact that many minorities and women view criticism
of affirmative action as *prima facie* evidence of insensitivity toward issues
of discrimination and civil rights," Thomas said peevishly in one speech.
"Further misunderstanding and confusion about affirmative action are
also caused by the fact that the debate over affirmative action is being
waged in moral terms." He continued with prose that improved in syn-
tax but degenerated in intellectual candor:

> In a debate appealing to morality, all efforts to include minorities and
> women in the mainstream of society are lumped indiscriminately together
> as affirmative action; and, depending upon one's point of view, branded
> as right or wrong. A debate where issues are drawn in terms of right
> and wrong has the unfortunate effect of polarizing the parties involved
> in the debate, thus preventing meaningful communication between the
> parties and hardening the opposing positions to the point where it
> becomes "us against them." There is no hope of meaningful discussion
> or dialogue at this point.

Elsewhere, Thomas condemned the discussion over affirmative action
and racial quotas as "divisive" and a "red herring." He insisted that "the
issue is not who is right or wrong but how we can effectively ensure
that all persons have equal opportunity in and access to the employment arena."

Thomas simply was not willing to speak candidly about racial preferences, even though his opposition to them was the principal reason he had been hired. Perhaps some of this was a product of genuine uncertainty. Middleton said that Thomas realized he had "lots of friends and relatives who have benefited from those programs. He himself has benefited from them." While "he probably thought it was a good idea to [abolish them] intellectually," Middleton said, Thomas "didn't want to be marked as the man who did it if it didn't work out right." More important, he simply was not willing to incur the enmity of virtually all African-Americans by spearheading the assault on policies that had become a political touchstone of their community. Middleton observed simply, "He didn't want to be known as the up-and-coming superstar who shut down affirmative action."

Did the Thomas of the first Reagan term qualify as a conservative? For all his waffling, Thomas publicly flashed his ideological credentials at the appropriate occasions. "As you all know, I am a conservative," he told one audience in Kansas City. He did express discomfort at being called a "black conservative," and on this designation he quoted Sowell: "at least it was better than being labeled a transvestite." Years later, however, the enigmatic Thomas would disclaim the "conservative" label. He told one audience of collegians, "I really don't refer to myself particularly as a conservative. I was defined as that to be dismissed."

Most Thomas intimates detected a philosophy that was then in flux. "I was more conservative than he was," said Armstrong Williams. "Thomas was an evolving conservative. . . . He was amazed at what a pure conservative I was." Thomas would exclaim in his philosophical chats with Williams, "Dag, man, you're more conservative than Ronald Reagan," or "Man, you sound like Brad Reynolds." ("Dag" was an intriguing interjection.)

"Clarence was not a conservative when I met him," recalled Ricky Gaull Silberman, whom Reagan appointed as an EEOC commissioner in 1983. "I'd call him a freethinker."

Reynolds described the Clarence Thomas of the first Reagan term as a "libertarian." Libertarianism is a philosophy that stems from the writings of the nineteenth-century British philosopher John Stuart Mill, who advocated expansive individual rights and personal sovereignty vis-à-vis government and society. In the late twentieth century, American conservatism was an uneasy amalgam of Judeo-Christian tradi-

tionalism and libertarianism, a blend that Reagan championed to good
electoral effect. The unifying principle was opposition to an overweening
federal government and the militant socialism of the Soviet Union.

Thomas found much to his liking in libertarianism. Thomas,
Reynolds said, believed "very strongly in individual rights. He felt that
freedoms of individuals were unduly trounced upon by government.
And I think that that guided his thinking for a considerable period of
time in the administration." Reynolds contrasted his own views with
those of Thomas:

> My view was that if you live in an ordered society, that there are cer-
> tain individual rights that necessarily are surrendered to some extent in
> order to allow a democratic process to govern itself. And therefore I did
> not feel as strongly as he felt that the individual's assertion of rights was
> so totally sacrosanct and protected, as he thought it should be. . . . I feel
> there's far too much government intrusion [on individual rights], but I
> think I stop short of where Clarence would go.

Thomas found support for this "libertarian strain," as Reynolds
termed it, in writings he started to devour at around this time. Ayn
Rand was an intellectual who smartly promoted her ultra-libertarian
philosophy through novels. *Atlas Shrugged* and *The Fountainhead* featured heroic, solitary characters battling big government and excessive
regulation that crimped individuality and self-expression. The characters often were largely mouthpieces for her viewpoints, and the writing did not earn critical acclaim as top-tier fiction. But she became
enough of a cultural figure to appear on the *Tonight Show* and to see
The Fountainhead made into a 1949 movie starring Gary Cooper and
Patricia Neal. That book became one of Thomas's favorites; he would
show the filmed adaptation to his EEOC staff—during the lunch hour,
so as not to consume government time—as what one aide called "sort
of a training film."

By the early 1980s, Thomas was well on his way to fleshing out his
own conception of conservatism. "In my view," Thomas explained at
the time,

> a conservative is a person who seeks to advance and preserve the fun-
> damental values of this country—the fundamental values which built
> this country, the fundamental values which make the country great and
> the fundamental values which make this country unique. A great and

> overriding tradition of this country is the respect for the preservation of individual rights. This means that individuals [are] to be judged on the basis of individual merit and individual conduct; individuals are not to be judged on the basis of accidents of birth or conditions which are immutable and over which they have no control.

This individualistic message was a patriotic celebration of the rights-centered American experiment.

These beliefs were starting to forge an early philosophy of law. Predictably, his thoughts coalesced around notions of individual rights. Reynolds held many conversations with Thomas in which he outlined this legal philosophy of robust individualism. "In the First Amendment area," Reynolds recalled, "it is generally recognized that even though you have free speech rights, you can't yell fire in a crowded movie theater. I think Clarence was of the view that free speech would permit you to yell fire in a crowded movie theater." This was a view, Reynolds added, that Thomas tempered over time. Thomas also was a strong advocate of greater property rights and of striking down many governmental regulations as "takings" of property that violated the Fifth Amendment. "I think he was one of the ones that early on, was sort of way out in front in saying that government takings of property had gotten, sort of gone overboard, and there were such things as regulatory takings, and there ought to be redress when the regulations are written by the EPA [Environmental Protection Agency] or other people in such a way as to deny individuals their property rights. Whether it's air space or tangible property."

Thomas also strongly endorsed a right to life for the unborn, a view which Reynolds shared. The two discussed *Roe v. Wade*, the landmark abortion rights case. Reynolds said, "I know we discussed it. I think that he thought little of *Roe v. Wade*." Reynolds explained:

> I don't want to say that he thought that the decision was constitutionally bankrupt. But I will say this, that I know I think that today. I thought that then. And there were a number of people in the administration that thought that. And Clarence was never one to jump in and say, I think otherwise. I don't think he ever sort of took that issue on. He didn't have to, so he didn't. But I think that on, from a scholarly standpoint, we were talking about constitutional law, constitutional issues, and Supreme Court decisions. It was clear he didn't think much of it.

Thomas limned a similar philosophy in his talks with Armstrong Williams. They discussed *Roe v. Wade,* which both of them opposed. "He would also talk about where the Supreme Court would've erred on some of these decisions," said Williams. "He thought they weren't interpreting the Constitution but trying to make law. And that's not the proper role for a judge."

In speeches, Thomas revealed the extensive thought he had given to the Constitution's treatment of blacks and racial issues generally. "Our country was born during a long tradition of slavery and human bondage," he explained, "and although our venerable Constitution was framed with ambitions of 'human equality,' the term 'human' connotated [*sic*] white, literate, property-owning males." He noted frankly the prejudices that colored the worldview of the Framers of the Constitution:

> Our founding fathers, though worthy of endless emulation, were victims of the times in which they lived; hence, our own Constitution, the highest form of law in the land, and the greatest document of guaranteed civil rights—was tainted by a deeply rooted history of prejudice. Blacks in the Constitution, for example, were assigned a fractional status of other "free" persons, and were guaranteed none of the basic rights extended to other citizens.

In other addresses, Thomas discussed the *Dred Scott* case. He decried the Supreme Court's holding that "there was no conflict between slavery and the Declaration of Independence." Already, Thomas was seeking a way to legitimate the American experiment for black Americans, whose rights the Framers had negotiated away. He believed he saw such a basis for legitimacy in the "all men are created equal" language of the Declaration of Independence. Later, he would read the works of scholars who pursued this thesis more exhaustively. But by 1983, he had already arrived at this essential principle by himself.

——

With his emergence as a minor public figure, Thomas found that greater public scrutiny was part of the bargain. As his privacy slowly melted with each public appearance and newspaper article, Thomas grew more uncomfortable. His relationship with the media remained tense. In a speech to the American Newspaper Publishers Association in 1983,

Thomas took the opportunity to get some things off his chest. He began by declaring he would not "stand here and take a defensive posture about the press coverage of me." He then proceeded to do exactly that. "Suffice it to say that I have been zapped . . . and people are surprised to learn upon meeting me that I am not *the* Clarence Thomas they read about."

Williams noted an aspect of his personality that became more pronounced in public gatherings. He described Thomas as "painfully shy" at receptions and public galas. "During those days, Thomas didn't meet and greet people." At functions, Thomas would often skulk in the back of the hall or room. He may have been merely weary from the crush of public burdens for the day; on the other hand, such behavior is consistent with the ways of a "backbencher" at Yale who preferred a quiet place out of sight. Shyness would help to explain the awkwardness that people sometimes noted in his demeanor when he was thrust into the limelight.

There was another peculiar quality, but likewise something hardly unique to Thomas: a resentment of lighter-skinned blacks. Several black co-workers detected in Thomas some such resentment toward them or others of lighter hue. Middleton, whose light complexion had led his peers in Mississippi to call him a "yellow nigger," recalled, "He would actually express his lack of appreciation for light-skinned blacks. And I think it came off as we had benefited from that." Indeed, as Sowell and others noted, after the Civil War, light-skinned blacks enjoyed certain economic advantages and tended to constitute the upper social echelon of the black population, in part because they were disproportionately freed before the Civil War and allowed to develop economically before other blacks. The more likely source of Thomas's resentment was the teasing he suffered as a child for his dark skin and African features. He was slow to forgive and forget, and the pangs of childhood embarrassment still were felt.

—

Shortly after the new year began, Thomas saw an article in the January 19, 1984, issue of the *Washington Post* that perturbed him. On the front page of the Style section, an article described how William J. Bennett, chairman of the National Endowment for the Humanities, had announced the day before that his agency would follow the lead of the Justice Department and refuse to set numerical goals for women and minorities employed by his agency. Citing his belief in "human equality," Bennett wrote Thomas a letter informing him of this decision. The letter was made available to the press. Bennett explained, "To believe in human equality and equal liberty can mean nothing less than to treat white and black, male and female, Jew and Gentile as morally equal."

Thomas was offended less by the views than by the fact that they had appeared in the newspaper before he had received a copy of the letter. Such umbrage was hypocritical, of course—Thomas had done precisely the same thing to Reynolds and the Justice Department a few months before. Nevertheless, "Clarence felt strongly that that was not the way a team plays," Jeff Zuckerman recalled. For a long time, Bennett and Thomas were "not friendly" as a result. Eventually, things were patched up, according to Thomas, after Bennett apologized to him. But for over two years, Zuckerman said, "Clarence would have nothing to do with Bill Bennett."

Insubordination was an even worse affront. David Slate, the general counsel for EEOC, learned this belatedly after taking issue publicly with Thomas's management style. Like Thomas, Slate was a presidential appointee confirmed by the Senate. But he lacked the clout at the White House that Thomas, for all his run-ins with the administration, possessed by virtue of his position and higher profile. In February 1984, Slate wrote a memorandum to the other EEOC attorneys, in which he argued that Thomas's decision to require agency lawyers to report the average time they spend on cases was "unfair" to attorneys and complainants. Thomas contended that he was simply trying to find out, as a good manager should, how busy his employees were. On February 8, an article by Juan Williams appeared in the *Washington Post* that quoted from the memorandum. The article repeated the memorandum's allegation that thousands of cases had been "curtailed, closed ... settled prematurely and for inadequate relief" because of Thomas's policies. When, in an interview, Williams pressed Slate for specifics, he could not quantify how many cases he thought had been improperly dismissed or processed.

Slate refused to rescind his memo. The core of his argument was, as Thomas repeated to others, "I'm a presidential appointee like you."

Thomas then was off to the White House. "He goes or I go," Thomas told the administration. Slate was soon on his way to private practice.

Public upbraiding from Congress also nettled Thomas. Part of his job was testifying at congressional hearings and listening to liberal Democrats rail against his leadership, the administration's policies, and the direction of the agency. While unpleasant by their very nature, such experiences were especially harsh for a man of Thomas's profound pride and longing for privacy. "You could always tell when he was going to the Hill," said one aide, Clint Bolick. "He would get quiet and moody. He would say he was going to be taken out to the woodshed and get his whupping." In March 1984, Thomas finally had had enough. He refused on one occasion to testify before the House Government Operations subcommittee on the issue of wage discrimination. After this caused a small uproar, he admitted that his nonappearance "may not have been the appropriate step." He explained, unconvincingly, that he did not attend because he lacked sufficient guidance about what he would be asked.

The tenderness within the proud warrior showed in an incident several days after he played hooky from the congressional hearing. On March 16, Thomas was walking down Seventeenth Street when a black man asked him for alms. The man was one of the many thousands of vagrants who began to populate the nation's urban streets in the 1980s. Thomas asked the man some questions about his background.

The man replied, "I've been out here for seven years, and there ain't nothin' left for me. Just lost my job in a car wash. Don't know where I'm gonna go next."

Thomas gave him a dollar and his card and asked him to call him. The man called the next day when Thomas was unavailable, and never called again.

Thomas concluded, based on this and other experiences, that the so-called homelessness of the time was a result of pathologies that "will not be easily solved." His efforts toward this one man, he realized, had not altered this truth. Still, he had tried.

In 1984, Thomas's marriage officially ended. He had filed for an uncontested divorce in D.C. Superior Court in August 1983. The case was dismissed on a residential technicality—not a promising sign for an attorney who wished to be a Supreme Court justice. Kathy then took the initiative, filing for a no-fault divorce in Montgomery County, Maryland, on May 22, 1984. On July 16, the divorce was granted.

The breakup of the marriage appears to have been by mutual desire. Their "mismatch of ambition," as one friend had put it, became accentuated as their political views diverged and Kathy pursued a career. Sixteen years later, the man who had introduced Thomas and Kathy at Holy Cross, and who has kept in touch with Kathy in the years since the divorce, observed that she "does not appear to be a scorned woman." Kathy could not have approved of his "dating" while they were married; in fairness to Thomas, however, her own conduct during this time is unknown. Their joint obsession with privacy—one of the common traits that bound them together in marriage for thirteen years—will likely forever keep the reasons for their parting away from the prying eyes of historians. The only interview Kathy ever gave to the press was to her hometown newspaper in Worcester, Massachusetts, in 1991. She said of Thomas, "He has been a wonderful friend."

The divorce caused Thomas more guilt. Allen Moore, a friend from Senator Danforth's staff, recalled, "I spent many hours talking with him as it [the marriage] broke apart. He was tormented both about breaking his wedding vows and about the impact of the divorce on his young son. He sought me out for advice because I was a divorced father with two well-adjusted children."

The end of his marriage to Kathy was arguably the only major failure he had experienced in his life. He took it hard, as one would expect of a man who proudly held himself to the highest personal standards. In so many other ways, Thomas had beaten the odds by overcoming the broken and chaotic home of his youth. In this instance, he succumbed to statistical probabilities. By the standards of the ages, his divorce was a grave moral failing; by the standards of his day, it was routine.

CHAPTER FIFTEEN

Running for a Second Term

House Speaker Thomas "Tip" O'Neill, Ronald Reagan's main political antagonist in the 1980s, coined one of the great American political sayings: "All politics is local." EEOC offered its own peculiar testimony to the accuracy of this aphorism. The agency was a political domain whose leaders, whether they liked it or not, were required to attend to the distinct hopes and goals of their constituent interest groups. The chairman was constrained to act as both chief executive officer and political dealmaker. This was particularly the case if a chairman such as Clarence Thomas was trying to implement a new vision for the agency. Thomas, as a result, sought to build unity among his fellow commissioners and, to a lesser extent, various pressure groups. In doing so, he endorsed certain policies and pronouncements that, years later, he would have preferred to forget.

By 1984, two of the five EEOC commissioners were Hispanic. The following year, another commissioner resigned, making the Hispanic bloc a full 50 percent of the commission. One of these two commissioners, Fred Alvarez, was described by a senior EEOC staffer as a "very bright, committed liberal." The other, Tony Gallegos, was "monomaniacally concerned with Hispanic issues" and made decisions based on racial grounds. "If a case came up with a Hispanic plaintiff, Tony would pay attention," the staffer explained. "If not, there were fewer commissioners." Thomas was attuned to the nation's political trends; one of these, the growing clout of Hispanics, arrived at EEOC decades before other public officials were forced to reckon with it. Thomas paid heed.

As the Hispanic influence on the commission grew, so did the frequency of Thomas's public references to the Hispanic community. In his speeches throughout 1984, Thomas enumerated the programs EEOC was devoting to Hispanics. It was a "major concern," he stated, that the commission was "failing to fully serve a significant sector of our population." He informed one crowd that as part of an "urgent study," EEOC had conducted hearings in cities across the country to determine "why the number of Hispanic charges has been so low." He announced that the commission had conducted a broader study of EEOC's services to the Hispanic community over the prior year. EEOC had opened an extension office in East Los Angeles, "the heart of L.A.'s Hispanic community," and had launched TV and radio announcements in Spanish and English tailored to Hispanics.

At a time when the White House was twisting his arm to condemn affirmative action publicly, Thomas instead took credit for expanding affirmative action for Hispanics at EEOC. "When I first came to EEOC," Thomas related, "I discovered that at the EEOC headquarters, there was not a single Hispanic working in the senior executive service—the highest career service level in the federal government." In recounting how he addressed this imbalance, Thomas offered an apologia for affirmative action that any liberal attorney in the agency would have lauded. "This was a problem because *enforcement* of the law can only be as effective as the people *enforcing* the law.... These people must be representative of the varied and diverse segments of our constituency." He was proud to note, "During my time at the commission, I have appointed three Hispanics to the senior executive service in headquarters." The chairman concluded, "To champion the cause of equal employment opportunity elsewhere, without first trying to put our own house in order, would be the ultimate hypocrisy."

Thomas paid homage to his other interest groups. For American Indians, he noted that EEOC had started a "Tero Program" specially designed to protect their employment rights. From Alaska to Puerto Rico, he spoke to audiences in honor of Asian Pacific American Heritage Week, the rights of elderly and disabled workers, and other special interests. It was terrific training for a rising political star.

Thomas also ran the commission meetings with comparable political deftness. Prior to commission meetings, he read the case materials thoroughly, then met with his staff. He enjoyed presiding over an exuberant debate by his staff members, who argued their positions on the upcoming cases and issues. The commission meetings were closed to the public. Those privy to the meetings noted certain leadership qualities in Thomas. He was relatively active in speaking at the meetings, but less so than Silberman or Alvarez. One staffer noted, "He would be more prone to make a joke than to really wade into the battle." He was careful not to cut off his fellow commissioners in mid-speech, seeking instead to facilitate a vigorous dialogue.

On most matters, he did not canvass for votes on the commission. Already, Thomas was comfortable being a dissenter: It was not unusual for him to be on the short end of a 4–1 or 3–1 commission vote. Sometimes, the lone wolf surprised even his staff with his votes.

In his speeches, Thomas also asserted a fair measure of intellectual freedom. One in particular from this period stands out. On June 17, 1984, Thomas gave an extraordinary speech in honor of Father's Day that would be forgotten, and that would escape the eyes of historians for almost two decades. In terms of condensed wisdom, creative structure, pith and rhythm, it is one of the very few addresses Thomas delivered that belong in the upper echelon of late-twentieth-century American oratory.

By this time, Thomas was the primary caregiver for Jamal, and would soon receive full custody. In rearing Jamal with a delicate balance of love and discipline, he was living up to the high example set by his grandfather. Throughout, the speech is quite clearly the distillation of extensive personal reflection.

"What is a father, a grandfather?" Thomas began, notably giving a grandfather co-equal status with a father.

> He is a setter of standards. He is a maker of dreams. He is a demander of hard work, of honest work, of the *best* his child can do.
>
> He is an answerer of questions, who is not ashamed to say he doesn't know.
>
> He is a setter of direction, who helps put the first steps on the way.
>
> He is the lion of children's safety and he is the sheep of their peace.
>
> He provides and protects and he loves and he gives and he is wise because he has lived in a world where he must be wise to survive.
>
> His is the hand that gives discipline. His is the hand that helps heal.
>
> He is tough when necessity demands toughness. He is gentle when life demands love.
>
> He is the setter of rules, because he knows the "why" of those rules.
>
> He is the teller of truth because he knows the truth must be told.
>
> He is the holder of confidence because he can always be trusted.

He is patient when circumstance demands patience and understanding, and when all else seems to have failed, he is a mender of life's
broken pieces.

He is always there to be turned to and is turned to because he is
strong.

Father is a word, in all its translations, honored by every people on
earth. It means the founder, the originator, the leader. We address our
Lord as our Father. . . .

It is a title, not a hereditary title, but a title that must be earned and
re-earned. It is a title of love.

Thomas went on to chastise "absentee fathers." Noting that at the
time, 56 percent of all black children were born out of wedlock, he
reproached those who "strut rapping of their 'cool' life," who "by their
own selfishness and immaturity ruin the young lives of their children,"
and who "breed poverty by breeding those they do not love and cannot
or will not support." For those parents who ignore their children out of
indolence or pleasure, Thomas had a message: "I want to tell her [a
mother on welfare] to turn off *Dallas, Dynasty* and *All Those Other Folks'
... Children* [referring to the soap opera *All My Children*] when her own
child needs help with his or her homework."

The solution to the problems besieging the black community, Thomas
concluded, was religion, education and self-discipline. "I *believe* that
the salvation of our race lies in the moral and spiritual force of the
church, in the education and training of our youth and the strength *and
the will* of black men."

In his peroration, he shared his own travails in rearing Jamal. He
did so knowing that his marriage was nearing official dissolution, and
things would only become more difficult for him. He then closed by
placing these challenges in cosmic perspective:

As a father—as a black man, I too know the midnight moments of
soul searching. I too have gotten on my knees and asked: "Lord, how?"
But He has always been with me. And He has shown me the way.
The way of my Father in Heaven. The way of my grandfather on
earth.
Happy Father's Day.

Thomas was about to receive an intellectual gift from an unlikely source.
For two years, he had relied on the experienced staff at EEOC to exe-

cute his reforms. He was now ready for greater intellectual stimulation and diversity. He also needed a top conservative aide to reassure Reynolds and Horowitz of his ideological bona fides, thereby keeping the "hounds" at bay.

He found the right candidate for this mission in a bookish, sharp-tongued New York lawyer named Jeffrey Zuckerman. Zuckerman had attended the City College of New York, then Yale Law School (he graduated two years before Thomas, but neither man remembered the other). After a stint at a Wall Street law firm, Zuckerman decided to pursue his longtime interest in civil rights law. He read an article about Michael Horowitz, whose background reminded him of his own, and dropped him a note. The two met, and Zuckerman mentioned his interest in practicing law with the federal government.

"Brad Reynolds and Michael Horowitz had been pushing on Clarence from the day he was nominated to get to work on reversing policy at the EEOC," Zuckerman recalled. Thomas, of course, had deferred, saying that the management problems at EEOC took precedence over policy matters. He frequently recited his inability even to find his chair when he arrived at the agency. This was manifestly an evasion for a man not anxious to take on racial preferences. After a while, it became an old song.

After EEOC filed its amicus brief in the *Williams* case, Reynolds and Horowitz, in Zuckerman's words, "went bonkers" and urged Thomas to "bear down." Finally, at the beginning of 1984, Thomas told them that the agency was running well enough that he could turn to other issues. He let them know he was in need of somebody to be his point man on policy.

Horowitz sent over Zuckerman's resumé. Normally a White House recommendation would have made a wonderful introduction. However, as Zuckerman put it, "Clarence and Michael did not have a very warm and fuzzy relationship." Thomas interviewed Zuckerman under protest.

Behind a desk of polished oak, flanked on each side by a flag—one Old Glory, the other the "Don't Tread on Me" flag from the Revolution—Thomas asked Zuckerman, "Why do you want to be involved in civil rights?"

Zuckerman told him he did not care for busing and quotas. Thomas replied, "I agree with that, but I don't believe you can make a policy out of two negatives."

Zuckerman then gave a lengthier critique of racial preferences and overall civil rights policies in America. He credited Thomas Sowell for enlightening him on these issues. Zuckerman did not know that Sowell was a friend and mentor of Thomas. Only after the conversation ended, and Thomas was leading Zuckerman out of his office, did Zuckerman see two photographs that had been hanging on the wall previously out of sight: one of Myers Anderson, and one of Thomas Sowell.

Thomas later invited Zuckerman back for a second interview. From these talks, he gained a higher comfort level with a candidate he had presumed to be a Horowitz mole. Thomas wasted little time in offering Zuckerman a job, proposing to name him as his chief of staff. This was strictly an honorific; in fact, no employees would report to Zuckerman. Instead, his fellow Yalie would become Thomas's top policy adviser, a sort of "big-picture thinker." Zuckerman accepted the position and joined the agency in the late summer.

In August, Thomas and Armstrong Williams attended the Republican National Convention in Dallas. "I told him we had to go," Williams said. Although Thomas preferred returning to his room by 8 P.M., Williams insisted that they mingle with the convention goers. A *Washington Post* reporter doing a story on black Republicans spotted Thomas and asked for his thoughts on the convention. Thomas praised the "great" treatment he had received. While the reporter was interviewing Thomas, a white conventioneer with camera in hand walked up to Williams and asked him to pose for a picture. Williams humored the man. The reporter noted that after the "evidently satisfied" man departed, Thomas said, "He's going to prove to his friends there are some black people here." Thomas then "laughed and laughed."

As Reagan campaigned from coast to coast, his dark pompadour bobbing energetically as he spoke of the nation's renewed optimism, few political observers doubted that he would win four more years from the voters. Thomas played a bit role in the campaign. He spoke to black groups—not a choice assignment, given the friction between blacks and the administration—where he promoted the creation of enterprise zones, or designated areas (typically blighted urban centers) that would qualify for reduced taxes. Reagan had come to know Thomas, to a degree, during the first four years of his administration. Meese recalled that Thomas "had a good rapport with Reagan. There weren't too many occasions for direct contact, meetings, things like that." Nevertheless, "The president thought very highly of him." Thomas, for his part, was in awe of Reagan. He told Dick Weiler back in Missouri that "being in a room with Reagan was a unique experience. He thought Reagan had the most commanding presence of anyone he knew."

By October, as Reagan's reelection neared, Thomas's rhetoric took on a more iron, conservative cast. His speeches were notable most of all for expressing a stiffened stance against racial preferences. On October 22, he told one audience, "I am deeply troubled by the rise of a new form of racism—no less pernicious than the old—which ascribes the success of any minority group member or woman to quotas, and denies the possibility of merit-based success. And I am even more troubled by the mounting evidence that the 'goals and timetables' approach to affirmative action has had disastrous consequences for the intended beneficiaries." He noted recent studies showing that these preferences were counterproductive for African-Americans.

On the eve of the election, Thomas took a free shot at the leadership of the old-line civil rights organizations. Instead of working together to promote constructive change, Thomas told Juan Williams, their modus operandi was to seek out the media and "bitch, bitch, bitch, moan and moan, whine and whine." Thomas added, "That doesn't help anything." With this volley, Thomas simultaneously endeared himself to White House hard-liners and vented his frustration at civil rights leaders and the media. He regarded the last of these as generally an uncritical megaphone for these liberal leaders and their invective.

On November 6, Reagan crushed his opponent, Walter Mondale, winning forty-nine states and the largest Electoral College total ever. Soon after the election, Thomas began to hear rumors that top administration officials—presumably Horowitz—would seek to replace him as chairman or, at minimum, not nominate him for a second term. This could not have been shocking news. His refusal to advocate a rollback of liberal civil rights policies had been a major bone of contention since he began his service in the administration.

Horowitz was determined to make the second term more productive than the first in tackling racial preferences. He focused on Executive

Order 11246, the directive that established goals and timetables for affirmative action hiring by federal agencies and by private contractors doing business with the federal government. Horowitz wanted it repealed. Brad Reynolds recalled, "And there was a division very clearly within the administration between those who wanted to basically pull down that executive order in its entirety, and say you can no longer have the federal government assigning minority contracts by race." The Department of Justice, Reynolds said, "was leading the charge to rewrite the executive order."

Meanwhile, Reynolds noted, "there were those who felt this was a political fireball. And were we to do that, it would cripple the ability of the administration to do anything else for the last two, three, four years." Not surprisingly, Thomas was in this group. Reynolds remembered that Thomas wanted to strike a compromise. Thomas argued "there were ways in which to modify that executive order so as to leave room for some contracting that would give a nod to minority groups, but not have it quite as overt as it is. But I think that he was more inclined to side with those who said, leave this one alone, than he was to take it on."

Thomas's latest equivocation did not sit well with Horowitz. "Mike Horowitz was on this project with a vengeance," Reynolds said. "And anybody who might suggest that this was not a good idea tended to be painted with a black hat on by Mike, and anybody who said it was a good idea had a white hat on."

Later in November, Horowitz called a meeting to discuss the priorities of the second term in regard to civil rights policy. Reynolds and Thomas were two of the invitees. Horowitz later explained, "I regarded myself as a major enforcer to ensure ultimately single legal positions" for the administration. "Everybody else was going to victory parties" while he and a few others were preparing initiatives for the second term. At this meeting, Horowitz laid down the law on behalf of the White House.

"Look, we have an opportunity," Horowitz told the assembled. "There's a honeymoon phase when a president is elected." Horowitz envisioned revoking the executive order and finally taking decisive action to eradicate racial preferences in the law. According to Reynolds, "Mike Horowitz let it be known that this is the way things are gonna be, and should be, and everybody'd better be on board, and anybody who's at all squishy on this, raise their hand and get off the ship." Thomas, Reynolds noted, "was more reluctant to push that than others." But Horowitz stood firm. Indeed, he made it clear that Reynolds would be the administration's spokesman on civil rights, so that the administration at last would speak with "one voice" on the subject. This designation was a bitter blow to Thomas's pride, but a concession that Horowitz insisted on.

After the meeting, Thomas returned to his office and told Middleton about what had occurred. "The decision has been made," he told his longtime aide. Middleton observed, "And when that decision was made, apparently Clarence made the decision to stop debating that issue [racial preferences] and go ahead and do what he thought was probably appropriate anyway, but was reluctant to commit himself to." Thomas informed Middleton solemnly that he was "not going to stand in the way of the mandate the administration had gotten from the reelection." He said he also had accepted the White House's coronation of Reynolds as the administration's spokesman on civil rights. There would be no more long "bull sessions" with Middleton pondering civil rights policies. He gave Middleton the clear impression that he would execute the administration's plans to dismantle affirmative action and racial preferences.

Middleton told Thomas, "If that's what you've decided, you should give me time to find another job." Thomas gracefully consented to his old colleague's last request. Middleton said his departure "was a mutually understood decision that my conscience wouldn't allow me to do what he needed me to do. I simply could not be in a position where I had to aggressively undo things I'd spent ten years building up." At around Christmas time, Middleton moved to St. Louis, where he served as EEOC's district director until the following September. Afterwards, he joined the faculty of the University of Missouri Law School. Middleton said that he and Thomas "parted friends."

Thomas's reward for such loyalty to his employers would be continued, rapid ascent in the federal government. When a *Washington Post* reporter asked him in January 1985 about highlights of his tenure thus far, Thomas replied tellingly, "Survival."

By then, the press was speculating that Thomas was positioning himself to promote his career in the administration. *Legal Times,* a newspaper widely read by the nation's lawyers, noted that Thomas had been, up to that point, an "enigmatic figure" who had "seemed to shun publicity." Yet the reporter stated, "He has been making the news with his attacks on the use of statistics in discrimination cases. Some observers, in and out of the commission, have concluded that he's angling for reappointment when his term expires in July 1986."

In response to this suggestion, Thomas protested too much. "I'm not going to lobby for this job," he told the reporter. "This job has kicked my ass, and you can quote me on that." Even so, the reporter dutifully noted, "he does not rule out a second term."

The constituent interest groups soon noticed a shift in policy and agency direction. "In his first two years, Thomas was really the only strong voice in the administration for continuing civil rights enforcement," said a spokesman for the Women Employed Institute. "He was fighting Brad Reynolds tooth and nail on every policy decision." She noted that "With President Reagan's reelection, somehow we had a conversion of Clarence Thomas."

The worst omen for liberal civil rights activists came in December 1984, in the form of a front-page article in the *New York Times.* Thomas was then recovering at home from surgery recently performed on his leg. He had forbidden Williams to allow any employees to visit his hospital room or send flowers or cards. Williams attributed this instruction to proud self-protection, saying, "He was afraid people wouldn't send flowers or cards or call." The article, which appeared on December 3, was entitled "Changes Weighed in Federal Rules on Discrimination." Its lead sentence read, "Federal officials have begun an extensive review of whether to change the guidelines used to detect patterns of discrimination in employment against blacks, women and Hispanic Americans." Thomas was quoted as saying he had "serious reservations" about the policy. Accompanying the article was a photo of him with an appropriately serious countenance.

"If a predominantly white college, such as Georgetown University, has a black basketball team, you can't automatically assume that there was discrimination against whites," Thomas told the reporter. He said EEOC had relied too heavily on statistics in the past, and that reviewing the guidelines will be "the No. 1 item on my agenda." This was a front-page advertisement for reappointment as chairman, and it was noticed.

The call to decision that Horowitz and the White House issued in November also seemed to energize Thomas as a speaker. Since the beginning of his public service, Thomas had inserted, with obvious relish, a certain number of caustic statements into his speeches, statements clearly intended to provoke. But these were used sparingly out of political caution. Newly liberated, Thomas began to declaim freely his views on the hot-button issues of the day.

In a speech to the National Chamber Litigation Center on January 17, he took up the vast array of social ills afflicting the black community. "My proposition is that in the last twenty years, we comfortable people, in the name of fairness and generosity, have ravaged their lives," he said of African-Americans.

> How can this be, when the last twenty years have been an explosion in spending on behalf of such people? To see why, let us begin by ridding ourselves of a curious condescension that takes hold whenever middle-income people talk about what the government is doing for low-income working people. They count up the extra income in food stamps or housing subsidies or the welfare check, and judge fairness in terms of increase in the dollar total—when it would not occur to them to measure their own lives in such terms.

He deplored the surge in drug-related crime then gripping the nation's ghettoes, and argued that the nation would act more expeditiously if this criminality were plaguing society's upper crust:

> People who live in the ghetto fear for themselves and their children too. But they have no option about where to live. They cannot afford to move away from troubles: they must endure them. Do you know what happened to the crime problem in their neighborhoods in the last twenty years? It went through the roof. Yes, we affluent people have our tales of being mugged or burglarized that we tell one another at cocktail parties. But the increased risks are nothing compared to the increased risk run by people in poor neighborhoods.

Yet the maverick of Pin Point—the man who simultaneously flew the rebel flag and venerated Malcolm X—still thought for himself. As he advanced the conservative case on these painful social issues, Thomas was deeply sympathetic to a cause on the left. He had grown up under the care and example of women who worked outside the home: his mother, her aunts, and his extended family and community in Pin Point and Savannah. The right of women to be free from predatory male behavior on the job was something he firmly championed. This right lay at the conjunction of several principles to which he subscribed ardently: individual rights, social order, proper decorum around women. The young man who had authored "Is You or Is You Ain't a Brother?" at Holy Cross to encourage good male conduct during parietal hours grew into a law-enforcement official who believed the federal courts should recognize in the law a right to be free from sexual harassment in the workplace.

In 1985, the Supreme Court agreed to hear the case of *Meritor Savings Bank v. Vinson.* The case centered on whether sexual harassment was a form of sexual discrimination outlawed by Title VII of the Civil Rights Act. Charles Fried, who by then had risen to solicitor general, recalled, "There were views within my office across the spectrum of inclinations that really we should urge the Supreme Court not to endorse that jurisprudence and not to see harassment as part of Title VII. That it was a stretch and an exaggeration and not really a proper interpretation."

Thomas had learned his lesson about filing amicus briefs, but he was resolute in his conviction that Title VII should be construed as prohibiting sexual harassment. He decided to take the extraordinary step of meeting with Fried personally, on behalf of EEOC, to lobby him and the Justice Department in favor of this view. "Clarence came himself, which is very unusual," Fried said. "Because it's usually on these things the general counsel. And he made a very strong presentation on two points: first, that sexual harassment in the workplace was a significant impediment to women's opportunities in the workplace, and second, that it is practicable to enforce rules against it because his agency had been doing it for years."

Thomas's forceful presentation carried the day. "As a result, clearly as a result of his intervention, we came in on that side," Fried remembered. The administration argued in favor of including sexual harassment under the aegis of Title VII. The following year, the Supreme Court agreed and wrote this doctrine into law.

Even after three years of hard-nosed management at EEOC, personnel challenges still cropped up regularly. One that arose in 1985 would trail Thomas for the rest of his career. In March 1984, Thomas offered the post of director of public affairs to Angela Wright. A beautiful black woman with long, wavy hair and a voluptuous figure she accentuated with flattering apparel, Wright was, in Willie King's words, a "had-to-hire" when she arrived at Thomas's doorstep. She had worked for Democratic congressman Charlie Rose of North Carolina in the late 1970s. Rose fired her for storming out of the office while yelling about some manner of unfair treatment, then not returning for the rest of the day.

Her next stop was the Republican National Committee. There, her bizarre conduct included telling male co-workers that she enjoyed walking around her house in the nude. She was soon off to work for a federal agency, Aid for International Development (AID), which managed the U.S. foreign aid program. At AID, she locked horns with her supervisor, Kate Semerad, who in obedience to the civil service rules tried to counsel her about arriving to work punctually and improving her work performance. For her trouble, Semerad sowed hostility, as Wright became, in Semerad's words, "more and more belligerent." The spoiled beauty flung accusations at Semerad, alleging that she was fostering "racial tensions" and "steadily persecuting the minority members" of her staff who did not display a "slave-like obeisance." Wright's vendetta grew into an unsuccessful attempt to torpedo Semerad's Senate confirmation for a higher position in the agency. In the meantime, Wright found an important ally outside the agency in Phyllis Berry Myers at EEOC, who took a liking to the high-spirited woman and fellow black Republican. She helped to arrange Wright's subsequent hiring by Thomas.

Wright's tenure at EEOC was rocky. She dressed provocatively and had a sailor's mouth, which she unleashed even on journalists. Wright would "curse the press out on the phone," recalled Diane Holt, Thomas's secretary. Cursing to the press was a privilege reserved for the chairman alone. Thomas learned of Wright's ways and was not happy. Armstrong Williams added, "I remember a situation where Angela Wright was giving a seminar, something in Texas, and she got upset and started using expletives. It got back to him." Thomas also took exception when he heard that Wright had referred to a top EEOC administrator, John Seale, as a "faggot."

In February 1985, less than a year after joining Thomas's staff, Wright wore out her welcome in spectacular fashion. Thomas had called a press conference to announce an EEOC initiative, and Wright was supposed to invite all the commissioners. She forgot one: Tony Gallegos. As one senior EEOC staffer recalled, Thomas had been "trying to build rapport with" Gallegos. He was part of the Hispanic bloc on the commission, which Thomas had been courting assiduously with greater affirmative action and outreach. All these efforts were for naught in the wake of what one EEOC official termed Wright's "huge faux pas." Pamela Talkin, later a top aide to Thomas, said of Gallegos, "This guy was left out by accident but took it personally." Another EEOC staffer recounted, "I remember going into the room and somebody saying, 'Where's Tony?' It was just horrible."

That did it for Thomas. Wright was a political appointee and as such not covered by the civil service rules; she was therefore fair game for prompt dismissal. "I was there when he fired her," Armstrong Williams said. Fifteen years later, Williams still was struck by the ruthless manner with which he dispatched her.

Thomas and Williams sauntered down the hall to Wright's empty office at 6:20 P.M. Thomas wrote a message on a piece of paper and taped it to her chair. It read: "You're fired."

"You can't do that," Williams said.

Thomas would not budge. "I've told her. I've given her chances."

Williams warned him about the likely public relations fallout.

"I could care less about P.R.," Thomas snapped. "I'm trying to run an agency, and I'm not dealing with incompetence."

When Wright arrived the next morning, "she flew into my office," Williams said, thinking he had had something to do with the note. She then sought out Thomas. In his office, she encountered cold steel. He shared with Wright his displeasure at her failure to invite Gallegos to the press conference. That debacle, he explained, was the culmination of too many miscues. "Pack your bags and leave," he told her.

The dismissal letter he wrote Wright was less blunt. Dated March 1, her final day of employment, Thomas informed her simply that her services "are no longer needed." On the bottom half of the letter, in large letters over an inch in size, Wright scrawled, "Thank you!"

"He had a right to fire her," Williams asserted. "But it's the way he fired her. It was so cold."

On the same day that Thomas released Wright, the professional guillotine also descended on his liberal speechwriter, Rose Jourdain. Shortly thereafter, Thomas was proudly telling audiences, "There was a time when I employed speech writers to draft speeches for delivery to audiences such as this. But, that time has long since passed. Though many have tried, others simply cannot put words into my mouth."

Ironically, at around this time, Anita Hill, newly ensconced in academia, came to call with grant requests. Zuckerman said she had been phoning Thomas and "bugging" him for a research grant or contract from EEOC. Remembering the quality of Hill's work while she was under his supervision, Thomas was not agreeable to this. When Thomas learned that Zuckerman had known her slightly through the Washington-area Yale Law School alumni association, he asked his titular chief of staff to call her and give her the bad news.

"You already told her no," Zuckerman said. "What do you want from me?"

"She's not taking no for an answer from me," Thomas replied. "Maybe she'll take no for an answer from you."

Zuckerman then phoned Hill and told her, with his best New York verve, "We just don't have money for that kind of stuff." Having finally met her match, she accepted his explanation with relative docility.

Not long after this exchange, Hill returned to EEOC to see her old office, where Zuckerman now was quartered, and to visit Thomas. Zuckerman judged that she was "quite delighted to be back in the chairman's office, visiting with the chairman."

———

As the first year of Reagan's second term progressed, Thomas began to hit his stride philosophically in his public addresses. He was still on a tear about racial preferences. In a speech to the Southwestern Legal Foundation in Dallas, he noted his fear that affirmative action and racial preferences might incite racial or ethnic conflict "à la India and Malaysia."

This was Sowell's thesis, one that Thomas disclaimed any knowledge of two years before but now freely endorsed.

The downside to racial preferences, he reasoned, remained what it always had been: the presumption that minorities were intellectually inferior. This tradeoff had grated on him since Yale; now he ripped into these "obnoxious assumptions" openly. "My friends, I will not concede my intellectual inferiority or my son's for socio-economic gain. . . . For me, this concession has been, and always will be, too great a price to pay."

In June, he returned home to Savannah to deliver the commencement address at Savannah State College. He saw himself not only as a native son but as a forerunner.

"Today I stand before you as one who had the same beginnings as yourselves—as one who has walked a little farther down the road, climbed a little higher up the mountain," he told the graduates. "I come back to you, who must now travel this road and climb this jagged, steep mountain that lies ahead. I return as a messenger—a front-runner, a scout. My friends, what lies ahead of you is even tougher than what is now behind you."

He exhorted his fellow natives of the Georgia coast to do better by their race:

> We procreate with pleasure and retreat from the responsibilities of the babies we produce. We subdue, we seduce, but we don't respect ourselves, our women, our babies. How do we expect a race that has been thrown into the gutter of socio-economic indicators to rise above these humiliating circumstances if we hide from responsibility for our own destiny. The truth of the matter is we have become more interested in designer jeans and breakdancing than we are in obligations and responsibilities.

He concluded with an appeal to patriotism. This was becoming a Thomas trademark, one reflecting his efforts to reconcile the justice of the American experiment with the horrors that largely defined the African-American experience. He noted that America was "the greatest country on earth—it does have more freedoms than any other nation. It is the richest and the most powerful country. All of this is true, and makes me proud, but how are we black Americans to feel when we have so little in a land of so much." He quoted from Frederick Douglass's

chilling blast against American despotism, "What to the Slave is the
Fourth of July?" and invoked the great man's luminous prose: "For it is
not light that is needed, but fire; it is not the gentle shower, but thunder. We need the storm, the whirlwind, and the earthquake. The feeling of the nation must be quickened; the conscience of the nation must
be roused; the propriety of the nation must be startled; the hypocrisy
of the nation must be exposed; and its crimes against God and man
must be denounced."

Thomas's tour of the old Savannah neighborhood was depressing.
He found his old red-brick schoolhouse boarded up and gathering
pigeons. The convent across the street that once housed his heroic nuns
had become a halfway house, full of the female casualties of a dissolv-
ing culture. This development drew from him the bitter comment, "Perhaps that is considered progress."

Back in Washington, other battles awaited. Early in 1985, Thomas
had told the press that he wanted EEOC to reject the notion of comparable worth. This policy, advocated by feminist interest groups, held
that federal law should require employers to pay men and women the
same wages for "comparable" jobs whose "worth" was to be determined
by the government. On June 17, the commission voted unanimously to
reject the policy, stating that Title VII did not encompass such pay-
equity cases.

Reynolds and the White House were urging another major project:
a radical overhaul of the Uniform Guidelines on Employee Selection
Procedures (UGESP). Issued jointly in 1978 by EEOC and several other
federal agencies, UGESP required that any prerequisite for employment
(physical or written tests, interviews, performance evaluations, etc.) not
yield a pool of employees very different from the percentage of minorities and women who applied for the jobs. UGESP mandated that the
federal government follow the "⁴/₅" or 80 percent rule: The hiring rate
for minorities and for women must be no less than four-fifths or 80
percent of the hiring rate for white men. If the employer failed to meet
this threshold, discrimination would be presumed as a matter of law,
based on adverse impact. The employer then would have the burden of
proving that the prerequisite for employment causing this disparity—
the physical test, for example—was a valid predictor of performance on
the job. Federal agencies followed the 80 percent rule, and the federal

courts deferred to UGESP as an authoritative interpretation of the Civil Rights Act.

Thomas knew the UGESP review would be a donnybrook, and he took his time in ordering it. He directed Zuckerman to analyze UGESP and make recommendations about reforms. However, Thomas put the brakes on actually drafting any proposed changes. He would not take this fateful step for over three years. Even then, he would allow the controversial revisions to languish.

Opposition from business interests doomed the race-related initiative dearest to the hearts of the Reynolds-Horowitz camp. By mid-August, the White House sent up a trial balloon in the press about a possible rewriting of Executive Order 11246. This was the presidential directive that established mandatory goals and timetables for federal hiring and contracts. Reynolds, now working under Meese, the new attorney general, authored a draft of the modified executive order which would have made affirmative action hiring voluntary. The leak of these draft revisions to the press, observed one newspaper, "touch[ed] off an uproar among civil rights groups."

Two months later, at a Cabinet council meeting, Meese finally had an opportunity to set the revised executive order before the president for his signature. Reagan was philosophically opposed to racial quotas, which is what the executive order effectively decreed. At the meeting, Meese counted among his allies Thomas; Clarence Pendleton, the African-American chairman of the Civil Rights Commission; and William Bennett, the new secretary of education, who was represented by his chief deputy. Leading the opposition was William Brock, secretary of labor. The National Association of Manufacturers and other business groups had been busy lobbying for the status quo. Indeed, a survey by *Fortune* magazine in September had found that "persuasive evidence indicates that most large American corporations want to retain their affirmative action programs, numerical goals and all"; the policies, *Fortune* found, kept civil rights groups from surrounding them with picket signs and had good "business value in customer relations" with minorities and women.

When the executive order came up for discussion, rhetorical bedlam broke out. Brock and other Cabinet secretaries denounced the plan. Meese spoke in favor. Pendleton, a flamboyant personality who regularly made the papers with his uninhibited comments, declared at one point, "Mr. President, give me my freedom!"

Reagan, presiding over a badly split Cabinet, decided to think things over. The issue soon perished. But Meese noted and appreciated Thomas's quiet support.

The revolution continued at EEOC. Clint Bolick, who was hired as a special assistant to Ricky Silberman, enlisted for a tour of duty. Highly intelligent and tenaciously opposed to racial preferences, Bolick had practiced law with the Mountain States Legal Foundation in Denver, a conservative public-interest law firm, and with the Civil Rights Division of the Justice Department. Bolick noted that at the time of his hiring in 1985, Thomas "was, in those days, referred to as the 'other Clarence'; the main Clarence being Clarence Pendleton, the chairman of the U.S. Civil Rights Commission." Pendleton, or "Penny" as his friends called him, was "a total lightning rod" who easily attracted publicity, occasionally to his regret and Thomas's minor envy.

Before he began working at EEOC, Bolick wrote an op-ed article for the *Washington Times* that had sat in a pile at the newspaper for several months. The *Times* finally published it a few days before he was set to join EEOC. It was a stinging critique of the civil rights establishment.

When she saw the article, Silberman panicked. She told Bolick, among other things, "When you listed the new leaders of the alternative civil rights movement, you didn't even mention Clarence Thomas."

"Well, Ricky, I don't even know who he is," Bolick admitted.

On Bolick's first day of work, Silberman introduced him to Thomas. Bolick remembered being "terribly embarrassed over my horrible gaffe."

Thomas finessed the issue impressively. He told Bolick, "Hey, I loved that line in your article about the civil rights establishment ceding the claim to moral leadership. And I just used it in a speech."

"Don't worry," Bolick quipped. "If anyone asks, I'll tell them I stole it from you." And that, Bolick noted, was the first time he heard "The Laugh."

Bolick later learned that Thomas had told Silberman he would hire Bolick as a speechwriter, based on his article, if she decided not to hire him as a special assistant.

Thomas's quest to infuse a more stringent work ethic throughout the agency was a harsh and sometimes messy business. "Some heads are gonna roll!" Thomas occasionally roared as he waltzed through the halls with attorney Johnny Butler. In July, he proved yet again that he was serious. The press learned that he and Butler had transferred, demoted and discharged "at least a dozen long-time commission personnel," wiping out the entire supervisory staff of the legal services division of the legal counsel's office in Washington. Since federal attorneys lacked civil service protection, Thomas could take fast and untrammeled action. He transferred the head of the appellate division to the trial division; he terminated another senior supervisory attorney pursuant to federal regulations after he declined Thomas's offer of a transfer to Detroit. Still another attorney, who had failed to meet Thomas's new quota for filing a certain number of discrimination suits a month, was reprimanded. (He subsequently sued Thomas and Butler.) Thomas also contracted out some clerical and investigative work; the private sector, he concluded, could only be an improvement.

Such a strong personality was bound to engender some enemies. One of the more articulate and credible to emerge was Sukari Hardnett. She was part of a social circle of black Washington professionals that included Thomas and two of his old friends from Holy Cross, Gil Hardy and Eddie Jenkins. Even with these friendships of long standing, Thomas did not quite fit in with the group, Hardnett observed; both his politics and his personality drove a wedge. She described Thomas harshly as "a social misfit." "It was a joke that Clarence was strange," she said. "It was a standing joke, he danced to the tune of a different drummer."

Thomas also could be abrasive and bossy with his best friend, Hardy, a bumptiousness which Hardy endured but which made Hardnett and others cringe. "Gil had such an easy personality," she said. "Clarence would often be rude and nasty to Gil, and he would tolerate that from Clarence, and none of the other people would." The clique vacationed one summer on Martha's Vineyard *sans* Thomas; he was not invited.

Hardnett's presence on Thomas's personal staff began in September 1985, when he promoted her from the office of review and appeals to special assistant. Hardnett was thirty-five, a beautiful, light-skinned black woman with long, flowing hair, slender figure, and large brown eyes. Her portfolio was an indeterminate assortment of assignments that Thomas made daily and seemingly in ad hoc fashion.

In the mornings, Thomas often asked Hardnett to accompany him to buy coffee from a nearby deli. Along the way, "he would just kind of babble on about all kinds of things." He shared the ups and downs of his dealings with his loyal secretary, Diane Holt. "She'd better get her act together," he warned at one point after he had criticized Holt's work performance. "She did," Hardnett noted, as Holt was later promoted to a higher personnel grade. The topics were "whatever came to his mind. He talked about himself a lot"—a phenomenon in Washington scarcely limited to the chairman of EEOC.

He enjoyed teasing Hardnett about her antipathy toward Ed Meese. "I'm going over to see your boy, Ed Meese, today," he once joked.

"You mean the pig?" she responded harshly.

Not one to impose his views on subordinates tyrannically, Thomas shrugged off the attack. Hardnett recalled, "He'd just look at me—just like, 'Well, that's your opinion.'"

She, like others, saw certain traits in Thomas that distinguished him as a man at home in politics and the nation's capital. Like many of his former colleagues, she discerned that Thomas "liked attention." Hardnett also noticed that he had another problem common in Washington: a tendency to stretch the truth: "The truth or reality existed for him at the time, whatever the moment was." Hardnett allowed, "I guess maybe that's what's typical of politicians." Like other ex-aides, Hardnett remembered that he could be extraordinarily "cold" to associates who had fallen out of favor. Hardnett said he "did a turncoat" on Allyson Duncan after using her to gain an understanding of the agency.

Thomas's attraction to Hardnett made his relationship with her even more complex. They were of almost the same age, intelligent and upwardly mobile. Both had attended Catholic schools; she described herself as "a Southern conservative morally." Yet his vast pride gave him a dread of female rejection. "Clarence has a strange relationship with females," Hardnett said. "Clarence was not the kind of person to just go out and overtly chase a lot of women. I don't know if his ego would've been able to stand the rejection." This fear of rejection would be overlooked when Anita Hill later alleged that Thomas had repeatedly made unsuccessful (and therefore, for him, humiliating) advances toward her.

"He would call me at home or look around the office to find me because he wanted someone to go to lunch with," Hardnett added. Not lacking for male attention, she found such treatment disconcerting. "It was clearly embarrassing to me to say, 'I'm going to the library,' and he'd go around the commission looking for me." Yet she bore little lasting resentment over this very minor abuse of power by Thomas. "I'm not saying Clarence is an all-bad person, because I don't believe that," she stated. He was simply "looking for a Mrs. Thomas."

A proponent of affirmative action, Hardnett eventually realized that whatever vague duties she had on Thomas's staff were being put to the service of undoing racial preferences. Two years later, she transferred from Thomas's staff down to the general counsel's office. Eventually, she would become an attorney in private practice—and would play a cameo role in a national drama.

On June 23, as Thomas was "glumly" celebrating his thirty-seventh birthday, his precocious and plucky son Jamal asked him, "Dad, what are you going to do next?" Thomas recalled that he gave his son "my most penetrating stare and replied: 'Maybe I ought to start thinking about that.'"

Thomas acknowledged in a remarkably self-effusive speech a month later that he had indeed been giving the question some thought. "[T]here is only one question *I* have: What am I going to do next," he told a gathering of EEOC employees in Tulsa. "I guess the answer is that I really haven't given my future much thought."

The spur for this reflection was the announcement on Thomas's birthday that David Stockman, the director of the Office of Management and Budget, was resigning to become a top executive at a Wall Street banking firm. Thomas noted that he would leave for "an annual income of up to a million dollars." He and Stockman, Thomas noted, were almost the same age and had served in the administration about the same length of time.

Still, as envious as he was of Stockman for cashing in, Thomas realized that his interests lay in government service. He enjoyed a $71,000-a-year salary, not a bad annual haul for a public servant. He drove a black sports car, a Camaro IROC-Z, thus fulfilling another dream. And he stood out as the administration's second-highest-ranking African-American.

Thomas let it be known to the White House, as his first term neared expiration, that he was interested in serving another stint as EEOC chairman. His decision puzzled some of his friends. "This is really not a good job," his old patron, Senator Danforth, told him candidly. "You can't make people happy in this job. You're bound to make everybody mad. It is not what I would call a good career path for you. Why would you want it again?"

Thomas replied, "Because I have to finish the job."

Thomas's explanation to Dick Leon, his old friend from Holy Cross who was now practicing law in Washington, was almost identical. Over lunch at a restaurant in the Watergate Hotel, Leon asked him about his position. Thomas complained that he felt "under siege" from Congress, and he explained to Leon—who was largely unfamiliar with politics—why the Reagan administration's policies were so unpopular among black congressmen, and why, as a result, he was "persona non grata" with the Congressional Black Caucus. When Leon asked him why he did not leave all that unpleasantness behind and seek employment elsewhere, Thomas told him, "I have a job here to get done."

Two acts of fealty followed and helped to cement his reappointment. First, he changed his voter registration, at last, from independent to Republican. This was a relatively minor matter in the scale of things; the timing, however, suggests some external prompting. Second, and far more bracing for Thomas, he unambiguously went on the written record, once and for all, in favor of repealing Executive Order 11246 and racial preferences generally.

At some level, Thomas undoubtedly knew he had benefited from racial preferences at every stage of his career. From his admission to Yale Law School—perhaps the single biggest leap—to Danforth's race-based recruitment drive to Monsanto's search for a black lawyer to his meteoric promotions in Washington: all were premised largely on race. That he had excelled in these roles once given the chance did not change the fact that but for his race, he probably never would have received those opportunities. Thomas realized that by turning on affirmative action, particularly at this point in his career, he would open himself to charges of hypocrisy and set himself adrift from the other members of his race.

He took this momentous step in a letter to President Reagan dated

February 6, 1986. "It was good seeing you this morning at the National Prayer Breakfast," he began in a somewhat breezy opening sentence. He then led directly to the crux of the matter:

> My task at this moment is a difficult one. I must urge you to issue a revised Executive Order which makes it clear that at least this Administration is opposed to preferential treatment under *any* guise, and no matter how palatable it is made or whether it is called quotas or goals and timetables. I urge you to do this not because it is politically feasible or because it is the easy thing to do, but because it is the *right* thing to do. Even though we have not done enough to eliminate the many other preferences in our society, I believe that race and sex preferences are particularly dangerous. And, as is clear from the experiences of other multi-ethnic and multi-racial societies which have codified preferential policies, such policies are social time bombs.

Then Thomas laid bare the fears that had deterred him from saying this previously:

> I am fully aware of the potential, negative political consequences of taking such an action. I am also aware that upon writing this letter, I do tremendous harm to my personal well-being and aspirations. I certainly alienate myself further from my race. The latter is clearly the most *painful.* Although I often prayed that "this cup pass from me," this is clearly my cross to bear. This is a deeply personal decision to stand up for what I believe is right.

He concluded with an allusion to the constant needling he got from the Reynolds-Horowitz faction. He said he hoped the letter would "put an end to the unnecessary bickering within the Administration, and permit us once and for all to set a *positive* agenda to address the seemingly countless problems facing minorities."

This correspondence to Reagan, the most extraordinary letter by Thomas to find its way into the public domain, was remarkably self-engrossed for a letter to a president. His frankly expressed concern that the correspondence might subvert his "aspirations" confirmed his abiding desire for self-preservation, and how profoundly this motivation had influenced his public policy statements previously. Thomas's fear of alienation from his race is notable, reasonable and prescient. This letter also contained Thomas's first recorded invocation of Jesus' words from Gethsemane and a self-comparison to Christ's ordeal.

Two weeks later, Thomas gave a speech across town at an EEOC symposium at Georgetown Law Center that offered a similar glimpse into his soul. He would repeat a variation of this speech to several other crowds over the course of the year. It was a chest-thumping oration that showcased the liberated Thomas, now free of ideological self-restraint and feeling his oats. The first stop on this speaker's circuit was the home turf of Eleanor Holmes Norton, Thomas's predecessor-turned-law-professor and the progenitor of most of his continuing management woes. He did not let this opportunity go to waste.

He began by stating his preference that his agency be "a serious force" instead of a "bumbling idiot." He boasted to his assembled subordinates, "I have no time to waste on losing propositions or useless projects.... The naysayers and detractors have had their say, but now I have the *team,* and *we* will have the final say."

Thomas pilloried those who still desired large class-action lawsuits instead of individual relief. Norton was undoubtedly in the crosshairs of this remark: "This would be a wonderful approach for law professors and think tanks *but* charging parties want justice from us—not law review articles and arcane legal theories. They want us to roll up our sleeves and fight the wrongs done to them *today*—not sit back in professional poses, puffing arrogantly on our pipes and spewing forth reams of intellectually entertaining theories."

Throughout, Thomas made clear his longstanding disdain for intellectuals and academics. "We cannot gain credibility as a law enforcement agency if we act like a law school," he told the audience. "We are here to deal with reality—not ghosts, goblins, gnomes, or gremlins." No line better crystallized the address than this: "My friends, this is an enforcement agency—not a candy store."

He had honed his critique of racial preferences into something genuinely eloquent:

> I am black. I am part of the grand experiment, having started by competing against the odds and succeeding; then having my personal achievements inextricably woven in the whole cloth of racially preferential social policies.... I have been both deterred and preferred by racially conscious policies. I have been the guinea pig for many social experiments on minorities. To all who would continue these experiments, I say please "no more." Please leave me alone.

The speech ended with a reference to the wellspring of his opposition to race-based policies: his pride. "My friends, I will not concede my intellectual inferiority or my son's for socio-economic gain. We are not objects of charity and refuse to be treated as objects of disdain."

—◦—

While Thomas shuddered at the memory of his previous confirmation hearings, the coming round of hearings for reconfirmation promised to be by far the most contentious and probing he had endured. This was not only because of the record he had developed at the agency; he could also survey the growing trail of political carcasses strewn on Capitol Hill from recent, failed nominations.

The president and Congress were in the midst of an intense power struggle. The primary casualties of this conflict were people nominated by the president to high office subject to Senate confirmation. Many of these nominees came away from the experience with their reputations destroyed.

Mutual frustration by the two dominant political parties fueled this acrimony. The presidency appeared to have become the eternal preserve of Republicans. Because of their near-unanimous support from Southern and Western states in presidential elections, Republicans were thought to have an electoral "lock" on the presidency. They had won four out of the past five presidential elections, and had barely lost the fifth following the Watergate scandal. Republicans, in turn, regarded the Democrat-controlled Congress as "election-proof" and beyond their reach. They pointed to certain institutional advantages exploited by the Democratic majority: gerrymandering, franking privileges, and the overwhelming power of incumbency generally. Neither political party had fully accepted its limited role, yet both knew the recent history, and so clung all the more tenaciously to what power it had.

The system of checks and balances between the three branches of government was an untidy business—so much so that this constitutional phenomenon came to be known and denounced by politicians of the time as "gridlock." Such clashes were the predictable collisions of two opposing political parties and the branches of government they dominated. In the 1980s, the most arresting arena for such battles was the Senate confirmation process; and the worst duels came over presidential nominees whose prospective jobs dealt with the judiciary. The judicial branch might be theoretically nonpartisan, but since the 1960s, it had become a center of rights-based liberalism. The Supreme Court and federal judges had imposed by judicial ruling sweeping changes on American society that could not have been enacted through legislation. These rulings touched and inflamed the most visceral social issues of the day: abortion, criminals' rights, affirmative action, the size and scope of government. Liberal political and opinion leaders knew that the judiciary, whose members had lifetime tenure, was a far more reliable and impregnable power base than Congress. Through their allies in the Senate, they defended this power with few scruples.

Their first ideological victim was William Bradford Reynolds. Meese wished to promote him to associate attorney general, which required Senate confirmation. Reynolds, unlike Thomas, had bravely carried spears for the administration on its most controversial civil rights policies. He would pay a high personal price for this loyalty.

Reynolds' confirmation hearings in the summer of 1985 were a sort of Fort Sumter in the coming cultural war over legal and judicial nominees. The civil rights groups that mobilized to defeat him charged failure to enforce vigorously the nation's civil rights laws; but their real issue with him was his opposition to racial preferences. On June 27, the Senate Judiciary Committee narrowly rejected his nomination. In a striking sign of appreciation for his loyal service, President Reagan personally criticized the committee's vote. "Let me emphasize that Mr. Reynolds' civil-rights views reflect my own," he stated. "That some members of the committee chose to use the confirmation process to conduct an ideological assault on so superbly qualified a candidate was unjust and deeply wrong." When the news of Reynolds' demise was announced on the floor of the NAACP convention in Dallas, the crowd cheered lustily and at length. From a political standpoint, those cheers, and Reynolds' fate, vindicated Thomas's prudent caution over the prior four years.

The casualties mounted. Michael Horowitz had angled for an appointment to the prestigious U.S. Court of Appeals for the District of Columbia Circuit. A coalition of the many liberal interest groups he had offended banded together and shot him down. He withdrew his name from consideration in February 1986.

Later in the year, the Senate Judiciary Committee voted down

Jefferson Beauregard Sessions III in his bid to become a federal judge. Democrats decried his insensitivity to civil rights concerns. Meese called Sessions the "unfortunate victim" of a "smear" campaign based on distortions of his record. Democrats attacked the qualifications of another conservative Republican judicial nominee, Daniel Manion, the son of a leader of the John Birch Society, who went through a bruising struggle before being confirmed by a close margin.

Closer to home for Thomas, Reagan had nominated Jeff Zuckerman to become the new general counsel of EEOC. His hearings became a meat grinder. Senator Howard Metzenbaum of Ohio took the lead. Metzenbaum was a highly partisan liberal with a reputation for shady ethics and bare-knuckled political tactics. With pale skin, thinning white hair carefully slicked back, and piercing eyes, Metzenbaum held, in Zuckerman's estimation, "a special animus toward Jews who were conservative."

In May 1986, Zuckerman met with Lowell Weicker, a liberal Republican senator from Rhode Island and a swing vote. Zuckerman remembered that Weicker "basically just said, 'I hear you're a racist. You have problems with black people.'" Even the tough New York façade crumbled at this insult. "I actually started to cry," Zuckerman said of the meeting. "Tears welled up in my eyes." A few days later, the Senate Labor and Human Resources Committee voted down Zuckerman by a 10–5 vote. Zuckerman left to practice law at the Federal Trade Commission two months later.

Thomas was fast becoming the last man standing. For years, he had carefully positioned himself on the issues—generally out of self-preservation, but nonetheless with a display of uncommon political adroitness. Now, all the implicit accusations of cowardice and self-service from Reynolds and Horowitz seemed trivial, having exploded with the first whiff of grapeshot. Thomas had indeed "saved" himself. From the standpoint of conservatives, it was a very good thing that he had.

Thomas's political skills stood out starkly when compared, for example, with those of his friend, Clarence Pendleton, the chairman of the U.S. Civil Rights Commission. A flashy, boisterous man who enjoyed a good off-color joke, Pendleton delighted in talking tough. Most famously, he made headlines, and many lasting enemies, for deriding the comparable-worth doctrine as "looney tunes." Though Thomas knew this was politically foolish, still he could not help but resent some-what Pendleton's higher profile; "Penny" was doing what Thomas longed to do, if only he were willing to throw caution to the wind. Thomas complained publicly and often about how frequently he was confused with Pendleton, saying the two names and agencies are "just inter-changeable—like spare parts." And yet Thomas had thrived politically while Pendleton had seen his career go up in smoke after needlessly antagonizing the entire civil rights establishment and influential black journalists with his free-flowing commentary.

At this point, even Thomas's past waffling on affirmative action became an asset. An early clue to his ambitions and thought processes came in the *Legal Times* interview he granted at the end of 1984. When asked what he thought of a 1979 Supreme Court case upholding affir-mative action, Thomas said that the case "is the law. I feel very strongly about that, when something is the law." The reporter, Kim Masters, noted rightly and insouciantly, "But he refuses to say whether he agrees with the ruling. 'You're asking me a question that I'm not going to answer, but I will tell you that . . .' he tapers off. Then he resumes, 'I'll just leave it there. There are some things that are tough.'" The reporter judged him, quite properly, to be "elusive" on the subject of goals and timetables. Thomas already was thinking ahead. This interview fore-shadowed his strategy for reconfirmation two years later.

Thomas went into his confirmation hearings battle-tested from many previous congressional hearings. He had appeared before the Sen-ator Labor and Human Resources Committee numerous times to defend his record at EEOC. Thomas had shown himself, time and again, to be a worthy match for Metzenbaum in particular. Dan Quayle, who then served on the committee, remembered Thomas as "very articulate." "The liberal Democrats in particular didn't like him as a witness because he was so effective. They tended not to show up" when he testified. Even in his scrimmages with the cunning Metzenbaum, Quayle noted, Thomas tended to come out ahead: "I can remember in some of the hearings, Metzenbaum would start to go after him. Clarence always had his facts together, he came back and he was not a shrinking vio-lent. Part of Metzenbaum's tactics was intimidation, and Clarence wasn't one to back down."

The groups arrayed against Thomas included the National Women's

Law Center, National Women's Political Caucus, the National Organization for Women (NOW) Legal Defense and Education Fund, and the Women's Legal Defense Fund. While the NAACP and black organizations did not support Thomas, neither did they campaign against him vociferously in the manner of the feminist lobbies.

The predominantly black work force at EEOC voted with their feet. On July 23, the day Thomas was scheduled to testify, the cadres of loyalists from EEOC queued up to enter the committee room in the Dirksen Senate Office Building. This sign of support was scarcely mandatory; indeed, the employees had to deduct this time from their annual vacation leave. So numerous and ardent were his admirers that the line into the hearing room snaked through the corridors of the Dirksen Building.

Senator Orrin Hatch, who had come to know Thomas when he was an aide to Danforth, was chairman of the Senate Labor and Human Resources Committee. He began the hearings by commending Thomas for cleaning up EEOC and for an "incredible job" overall.

Soon it was Metzenbaum's turn. The first sentence of his prepared statement was a song to himself. The senator trumpeted his role in fighting "for the enactment of Fair Employment Practices Commission legislation in the Ohio General Assembly" years before. He then questioned why Thomas sat before him without support from civil rights organizations. "To me it is rather significant, and I would think to the nominee himself it would be particularly significant, that we are conducting a hearing today in connection with his renomination, and to the best of my knowledge, nobody—nobody—in the American civil rights community will be here urging the confirmation of the nominee." Metzenbaum wondered if this did not send "a strong message to the nominee himself." Did not this absence of support lead Thomas to ask himself: "What is there about me that causes the civil rights community not to be here, supporting my nomination? Does the whole army march to a different drumbeat than that which I play?"

Thomas saw that Metzenbaum had not only fluffed his own feathers inappropriately, but had foolishly presented himself as a superior civil rights pioneer to a black American who had grown up under Jim Crow. When his chance to speak came, Thomas could not resist departing from his prepared remarks to put Metzenbaum squarely in his place:

I find . . . amazing the talk about commitment. Senator Metzenbaum mentioned his efforts in the Ohio Legislature. Well, all I have to offer is the fact that I grew up under segregation. I attended school under segregation, and I was the only black in my high school for 2 years of high school. And I am not used to walking in step with anybody because I was the only one of my kind, normally, wherever I was.

This was a public dressing-down to which Metzenbaum was not accustomed, and which he would never forget. He evened things up a bit during his questioning of Thomas, noting that recent Supreme Court decisions had upheld the constitutionality of voluntary affirmative action. Would EEOC pursue goals and timetables as a result? Metzenbaum wondered.

In a remarkable political pivot, Thomas said that his agency would do just that. "That is no problem," Thomas said. He explained, "I mean, the law is the law, and I have said clearly . . . that when the Supreme Court ruled, that was the end of it."

Metzenbaum pressed further. "Do you have any further reservation with respect to the use of goals and timetables as an appropriate remedy for the EEOC to seek?"

"Senator," Thomas responded, "I think again, the Supreme Court has ruled, and as far as I am concerned, that is that. Whatever reservations I have are purely personal, and they are subversive literature at this point."

"Did I hear you use the words, 'subversive literature'?" Metzenbaum asked.

"Dissenting opinions, according to J. Willie Moore, are nothing but subversive literature."

It was a good line, but Metzenbaum detected Thomas's dodge. Simply because affirmative action was legal did not mean, *ipso facto*, that it was correct public policy. He followed up by asking Thomas about his "moral and ethical opposition" to the practice.

This was now the "law of the land," Thomas insisted. "Whether I like it or not, I am to abide by it. I take an oath to enforce the law, and I enforce it aggressively."

The old pro would not settle for this. "Let me then ask you categorically, will EEOC make a clear statement, commitment to goals and

timetables as one form of relief in order to dispel the confusion resulting from its waffling on this issue in recent months?"

Finally cornered, Thomas relented. "EEOC will make a clear statement to our people that goals and timetables are one form of relief available under Title VII, consistent with the Supreme Court."

Senator Paul Simon also aimed some sharp questions at Thomas.
A bow-tied, slow-talking former journalist from Illinois, Simon was an
odd fit in the Senate. But he knew what he believed: He was an aggressive liberal who stood his ground.

Again, however, Thomas was no pushover. When Simon read from
a letter from the NAACP criticizing him, Thomas interjected midway
through: "Do they give you any facts, Senator?" Later, Simon unfairly
tried to dismiss Thomas's fundamental reforms at EEOC as "the nuts
and bolts things," saying they were "things that your administrative
assistant ought to be doing."

Thomas would not let his four years of unrequited toil be swept aside
so easily. He replied, "If you are going to run this agency, the person
who heads the agency has to run it. That is something that we should
have learned from the 21-year history of EEOC.... Until you have that,
you have nothing but a promise."

And so it went: Thomas took some blows and delivered some of his
own, showing fancy political footwork throughout. He also lobbied the
committee members behind the scenes, privately promising to send
them reports twice a year on the number and types of cases in which
EEOC used goals and timetables.

The critical move, however, was his flip-flop-flip on affirmative
action. He was personally opposed to affirmative action, he said, but
the Supreme Court's recent rulings made him duty-bound to use such
remedies in cases before the commission. This was illogical but politically smart. The chief counsel to the Democrats on the Senate Labor
and Human Resources Committee admitted to the press that given
Thomas's new position on goals and timetables, "There were no substantive grounds on which to oppose the nomination." Metzenbaum
and Simon were the only votes in opposition to Thomas's reconfirmation. He passed out of committee on a vote of 14 to 2 on August 6, and
soon thereafter was granted a second term. Caution, it turned out, had
its advantages.

CHAPTER SIXTEEN

Thomas Becomes a Conservative

"The best thing that can be said about the confirmation process is, 'It's over,'" Thomas remarked. His depiction of this relatively minor scuffle as the "nightmare of reconfirmation" showed that he had lost neither his penchant for exaggeration nor his thin skin. The swearing-in ceremony that followed offered little emotional ointment for these abrasions. The ceremony was an Armstrong Williams production, and Williams billed it as precisely that. The programs printed for the event bore the prominent advertisement, "Armstrong Williams Presents Clarence Thomas's Second Swearing-In." One high-level EEOC employee described the scene as "surrealistic." The festivities were held on the fifth floor of EEOC's headquarters. A band played in one room— "like a bar mitzvah"—but to no audience. "No one went in there because it was so odd."

The investiture itself was no less afflicting. Williams prevailed upon Senator Strom Thurmond to do the honors. Meese and Reynolds attended as well. Although the three dignitaries stayed for only a few minutes, this brief period was pregnant with discomfort for the man of the hour. Thurmond welcomed Thomas to Washington—despite the fact that Thomas had worked there for seven years. The senator vainly sought out Thomas's better half. "Where's your wife? Where's your wife?" Thurmond wailed in his Southern accent. "Your wife should be here." This was grating enough for a man still sensitive about his recent divorce; worse still, his new romantic interest, a white woman named Virginia "Ginni" Lamp, was standing nearby.

The ceremony reached its low point when Reynolds spoke. He raised his glass to propose a toast to the chairman. The words he uttered were well intended but hurtful. "It's a proud moment for me to stand here,"

Reynolds said, "because Clarence Thomas is the epitome of the right kind of affirmative action working the right way."

Some of Thomas's aides and co-workers looked down. Others shook their heads. Thomas visibly flinched. A reporter present, Juan Williams, noted of the remark, "Reynolds had dismissed him as affirmative-action hire and thought it a compliment." Williams observed that Thomas "showed a look of cold hurt—a look of disgust." Thomas stared off elsewhere, his arms folded, perhaps girding himself against further blows.

A few days later, Thomas was asked about Reynolds' comment. Thomas waved his hand, "as if swatting away the memory." "I can't pay no attention to Brad," he said. Privately, one friend recalled, Thomas was "furious" about Reynolds' remark. The whole occasion was "exquisitely painful," said one participant. Armstrong Williams left the agency and his vague job duties shortly thereafter.

Thomas rose above these and preceding indignities. This was a conservative administration that had bestowed many blessings on him. Moreover, from a philosophical standpoint, he was becoming, ever more firmly, one of the team.

His second term as EEOC chairman featured a philosophical quickening. He began the term a man with conservative impulses inculcated by his grandfather and, to a lesser degree, the nuns and black community of Georgia. His philosophy also showed streaks of libertarianism, as well as some of the dying embers of liberalism (in the form of his ambivalence toward affirmative action). In the latter half of the 1980s, Thomas's views would grow to become more in step with orthodox, Reagan-style conservatism. The philosophy that congealed in his mind was the product of hour after lonely hour of consulting great literature as well as the dictates of conscience. Another important influence was his staff. He surrounded himself with several conservative special assistants who aided him in this process of self-education. Their catechizing helped to lay the intellectual foundation for the professional opportunities and challenges that lay ahead.

Before Zuckerman departed, he located for Thomas's staff a conservative voice that he hoped would offset the liberal din. Ken Masugi was a Japanese-American from the Claremont Institute in Southern California and editor in chief of the *Claremont Review of Books,* an obscure quarterly journal familiar to Zuckerman and other conservatives. He was an unabashed intellectual; when Thomas later traveled with him, he joked that Masugi treated him to a "night on the town in the used bookstores." When Zuckerman first sought him out, Masugi was nonplussed. "The people who reported to me about [Thomas] weren't that flattering about him," Masugi recalled. "They didn't think he was that aggressive a conservative." Moreover, the notion of working for EEOC "just sounded so dull and so bureaucratic."

The interview changed his mind. "I met Thomas and I was really blown away by him," Masugi later said. Thomas told him that he had read a package of articles and materials by Masugi that Zuckerman had prepared. He said he was "very impressed," and offered Masugi a job.

"Come to work for me and we'll have great fun for a year, maybe two," Thomas told him. After that, Thomas said, he planned to return to the private sector.

"I have to run the agency," Thomas explained when Masugi asked about his job duties. "I have to testify before Congress. I have to give speeches. I don't have time to think. I want you to think."

"Well, think about what?" Masugi asked.

"I want you to think about the moral crisis of the age and the political crisis," Thomas said. "I want you to relate the two."

This was obviously a sweeping mandate, and Thomas endeavored to explain himself further. "I went to Yale," Thomas said. He noted the many other EEOC staffers who had attended Ivy League and other premier institutions. "You don't learn anything in law school. It's just a trade school. There's so much else I need to know."

"Basically," as Masugi put it, "it was an invitation for me to be his tutor."

Masugi joined Thomas's staff as a special assistant in June 1986. In reality, he would serve as a docent of prevailing conservative thought and a sort of connoisseur of periodical literature. Masugi recommended to Thomas various books and articles that he thought had merit, and wrote Thomas memoranda on current affairs or issues that he believed would pique his interest. One such memo that stood out in Masugi's memory criticized *Brown v. Board of Education* for its reliance on social science instead of eternal principles of equality and justice.

Masugi also wrote speeches, articles and letters to the editor, and served generally as court tutor. The Thomas-Masugi tandem targeted conservative journals in particular. "He liked my way to get into print," Masugi remembered. Letters to the editor offered a relatively easy way for Thomas to increase his public profile, and always on his own terms. Masugi wrote only about a dozen speeches for Thomas but many more letters. Before he drafted a letter, Masugi would meet with Thomas and discuss the subject matter; Thomas generally had "very strong views," Masugi found. Even after these consultations, Thomas edited the writings freely and adapted them for use in other documents or projects he was working on.

Masugi later brought in reinforcements. He mentioned to Thomas the work of another Claremont alumnus, John Marini, a professor of politics at the University of Dallas who had written on separation of powers and American constitutionalism. Masugi gave Thomas one of Marini's articles lambasting Congress, a theme bound to score points with the harassed chairman. He jotted a note back to Masugi: *"Ken* I *really* [underlined three times] like this! We need to talk to Marini ASAP."

Thomas wished to hire Marini immediately, and he asked Masugi to call Marini for him. "I've been reading your stuff," Thomas told Marini after he came on the line. He then offered a variation of the same self-deprecating story he had shared with Masugi. "I graduated from Yale Law School, but I'm uneducated. I don't have the time to get the kind of education you've gotten over many years. I'd like for you to come out and work for me as a special assistant." Marini consented and soon thereafter moved to Washington.

The two Claremont friends worked out a division of labor for speechwriting. Masugi wrote on natural rights and broader social issues, Marini on separation of powers and the agency's relationship with Congress. Philip Lyons, who subsequently joined Thomas's staff, said of Marini that he "had an extraordinary ability to capture the cadence of [Thomas's] speech." At the same time, however, Marini "fed his worst instincts about Congress. For [Thomas] to hear that, after being raked over the coals by Congress, that probably was not what he needed to hear." Thomas appreciated the sentiments, however. He even allowed Marini, after he finished jogging, to take showers in the private washroom adjacent to the chairman's office.

Thomas also recruited superior managers for the agency. In early

September 1986 he hired a new chief of staff. Pamela Talkin had served as a special assistant for fellow commissioner Fred Alvarez during Thomas's first term. In 1985 she returned to San Francisco to work for another agency. "About Labor Day of '86, I got a call from Clarence Thomas out of the clear blue," she recalled. Thomas told her that he had been reconfirmed for a second term. He also mentioned that his former chief of staff, Zuckerman, had just suffered a "pretty brutal defeat" in his attempt to become general counsel for the commission. He hoped to fill Zuckerman's slot with someone possessing managerial experience. Although he knew she was a liberal Democrat, Talkin said, "He wanted someone who didn't have a political agenda, who knew how to run an investigative law enforcement agency."

With the agency now on a better footing, Thomas finally could risk handing over the daily reins of management to somebody else. Talkin would not only run the agency effectively, but serve as a close adviser and ideological contrast. "I have a very strong ego," he cautioned her when she joined his staff. "I have strong opinions. I need someone who can pull me back from the edge." Thomas also believed he would benefit from a chief of staff with "different political views." Thomas and Talkin were a year apart in age, and thus shared many generational experiences. "We listened to the same music," Talkin said. Thomas's musical tastes were encyclopedic, in fact. "He liked everything. He liked classical music, jazz, old-time rock-and-roll from the fifties and sixties, when we grew up. He liked country music." When Tracy Chapman, a black female singer with doleful lyrics, came out with her first, self-titled album in 1988, Thomas recommended it to Talkin and even made a duplicate cassette tape for her.

The staff Thomas gathered about him was extraordinarily diverse. While chairman of EEOC, Thomas hired a total of 49 people who reported directly to him. These were directors of headquarters offices, special or executive assistants, and personal support staff. Of these, 26 were women (53 percent of the total) and 33 were minorities (67 percent). Of his 29 special and executive assistants, 14 were women, 15 were black, 1 was Hispanic, and 2 were Asian. Ten of the eleven people on his personal support staff were black.

Staff meetings in Thomas's second term became a grand intellectual mixer. Aside from the weekly meetings dedicated to EEOC matters—

which often involved fascinating and complex legal and constitutional issues—Thomas called a special staff meeting every few weeks to discuss current events or some topic that was on his mind. "Some of these were broader than EEOC matters," Marini recalled; accordingly, these sessions were questionable from a strictly managerial perspective. Yet he basked in such colloquies. Thomas later reflected that these discussions, which occurred in an "often difficult political environment," were "an intellectual oasis, a refuge of civility and intellectual honesty." In the privacy of this sanctum, Thomas could argue and play devil's advocate with abandon. "The unfettered exchanges were liberating," he later said.

The topics varied. Sometimes, when he returned from Capitol Hill following a rough hearing, Thomas would summon his aides and give them a debriefing/catharsis. "He'd get beaten up by some guys," Masugi remembered, and then "he'd hash over what had happened." Masugi recalled another meeting when "he went on about abortion." "How do you justify the termination of life?" Thomas asked his staff. Philip Lyons, who before coming to EEOC had worked for federal agencies and leaders in both houses of Congress, described Thomas as "the most intellectually open official I've worked for." The full ideological spectrum was represented in these meetings: "He had everything from left-wing liberal to creationist conservative on his immediate staff. And he loved to bounce ideas off us and hear our arguments." Over this raucous assemblage, with feisty liberal Brooklyn natives squaring off against hard-boiled conservatives of the Claremont school, Thomas presided in all his glory—expostulating, nodding with approval, roaring with his booming laugh. The only rule he laid down for such conclaves was that nobody was permitted to hold hard feelings afterward.

Thomas also soaked up new ideas through a program of constant reading. Marini described him as a "pretty voracious reader" who solicited a wide array of ideas. During his second term at EEOC, he read a number of books that molded his thought. One was Alexis de Tocqueville's *Democracy in America*, a nineteenth-century work that explained the distinctively American character then emerging in the new nation. Another classic of conservative literature ingested during this period was Friedrich Hayek's *The Road to Serfdom*, which argued that government control of the means of economic production was the basis of totalitarianism. Masugi and Marini stoked Thomas's interest in the *Federalist Papers*. He also enjoyed *Modern Times,* a best-selling history of the 1920s through the 1980s by British historian Paul Johnson. Talkin remembered that Thomas read extensively about Lincoln and the Civil War.

These mental exertions were born of curiosity and intellectual rigor. "Thomas is a very thorough, very systematic kind of thinker," Marini observed. "He likes to work these things out." If Masugi or Marini quoted from one of these works, Thomas "wouldn't just read the quote. He'd ask you for the book. He'd read the book." These books and their central ideas became the building blocks of his personal philosophy.

Before leaving EEOC, Zuckerman had done Thomas one other great, albeit unforeseen, service. In May, as his nomination was pending before the Senate, Zuckerman was scheduled to attend a panel discussion in New York sponsored by the Anti-Defamation League. The topic, Zuckerman recalled, "was quotas, timetables, the usual thing." At the same time, he had been trying to set up an appointment with Senator Lowell Weicker to discuss his nomination. When Zuckerman finally was able to earn a place on Weicker's calendar, he found that the appointment conflicted with the ADL roundtable.

Zuckerman asked Weicker's office if the meeting could be rescheduled. Weicker's staffer, he recalled, "basically said, 'This is the only time in the history of the universe you can have this meeting.'" Zuckerman was caught in the middle; the ADL was the only mainline civil rights organization supporting his nomination. When Zuckerman called the ADL to inform them of the conflict, they were blunt. "This creates a problem for us," they told him. "You owe us. The way you satisfy the debt is, you get the chairman to come instead of you."

He dutifully related the conversation to Thomas, who, after some good-natured kidding, allowed himself to be conscripted into going as Zuckerman's substitute.

While the symposium itself was forgettable, this business trip would prove the most important of Thomas's life. Also on the panel was Virginia Lamp, a young representative of the U.S. Chamber of Commerce. She was twenty-nine, with limpid blue eyes, a softly chiseled nose and short red hair. She was also white, a native of Omaha, Nebraska. Her father was an engineer, her mother a Republican activist who once ran for the state legislature and served as a delegate to Republican national conventions. Ginni, the name by which all her friends knew her, became involved with the Young Republicans and student government while in high school.

After getting her B.A. and later her law degree from Creighton University in Omaha, Ginni moved to Washington to join the staff of Nebraska congressman Hal Daub in 1981. She later became a spokesman for the U.S. Chamber of Commerce. Clint Bolick met her while with the Mountain States Legal Foundation, which had joined forces with the Chamber to combat comparable worth. Ginni was the Chamber's leading representative on the issue, and she and Bolick worked together closely in a number of strategy sessions and other common efforts. "I just thought she was an absolute superstar—bright, articulate, attractive, passionate, sweet," Bolick recalled. At the time she met Thomas at the Anti-Defamation League colloquium, Ginni was seriously considering running for Congress.

She was recovering from a very painful experience in her private life as a result of her involvement with an organization called Lifespring, which styled itself as a self-improvement program. As Ginni became immersed in the group, she found some of its sessions objectionable and strange. At one, the song "The Stripper" was played as people disrobed to reveal bathing suits and bikinis. At other meetings, overweight people were teased, and members quizzed each other with sexual questions. With the help of a counselor in Connecticut, she broke away from the group in 1985 and joined the Cult Awareness Network.

After the conference, she and Thomas struck up a conversation, then shared a taxi ride to the airport. En route, Ginni asked him how he withstood all the abuse that came his way for being a prominent black conservative. Such sympathy was music to Thomas's ears. He provided music for hers when he reached into his pocket and pulled out a copy of a favorite prayer, which, he told her, he read when times got tough. They also learned that they shared an appreciation for Ayn Rand.

Ginni volunteered to find "one of my black female friends" for him to date. "And I meant it," she later recalled. "I was going to set him up. I thought he was a great eligible bachelor."

The next day, Zuckerman asked Thomas about the conference. Thomas gushed over his conversation with Ginni. "He was very intellectually smitten," Zuckerman said.

Shortly after returning to Washington, Thomas called her up and invited her to lunch. Ginni accepted, and soon was overwhelmed. "Once I got to know him, I was like a pool of butter," she said. "I was in love with this man."

Her romance with Thomas grew into one of her first serious relationships. Thomas, for his part, was no Lothario. Armstrong Williams noted that he disliked dancing and barhopping, and could "bore women to death." Three months after meeting Ginni, Thomas took Ricky Silberman to lunch at Clyde's in Georgetown and told her, "I want you to know that I'm in love." He broke the news to Armstrong Williams somewhat differently. "You need to have a seat," Thomas told him. "I think I've fallen in love with someone who just happens to be white."

As more people learned of their relationship, the reaction was in keeping with the racial realities of the day. "I was a little startled at first that my daughter was interested in a black man," Donald Lamp said of hearing about Ginni's deepening relationship with Thomas. "She was 30 years old, it was her decision. But ten minutes after I met him, his color made no difference. He's the greatest guy you ever did see. He is really an impressive person." Ginni's Aunt Opal also weighed in on her niece's selection, with less sophistication. She said of Thomas: "He treated her so well, all of his other qualities made up for his being black." Among staffers for Nebraska's congressional delegation, word spread as well. "There were some raised eyebrows that she was dating this black man," one of them acknowledged.

Any unpleasantness this issue stirred up, however, often seemed less imposing than the troubles that continued to undermine Thomas's relations with the White House. He contributed to the tension by asserting his independence yet again in a speech to the National Press Club. For two weeks before the November 19 speech, Masugi sent Thomas memoranda about welfare's erosion of the black family and other social ills in the black community. Such an inventory of the black community's shortcomings was becoming trite, not to mention a convenient excuse for many conservatives to write off the inner city as a unique tangle of pathologies. Thomas's editing of Masugi's draft speech telegraphed his intention to use the speech to launch a broadside against the Republican Party generally. He had never fully subordinated himself to the administration; he had toed the line on affirmative action, under pressure, but his pride would not allow him to be reduced to a flack. In his speech, he criticized the administration for "blatant indifference" to blacks. He explained that he was expressing this view publicly "because apparently privately it's not heard." The administration's clumsiness in dealing with the black community and civil rights issues, he added, "is probably my biggest frustration, those four years I've been here."

The following month, a major administration initiative on social policy came to fruition, one in which Thomas had played an important hand. The White House Working Group on the Family issued its report. The group's mission, as Thomas later explained it, was "reviewing federal statutes to assess their impact on the American family and making recommendations on how to strengthen the family." Members of the panel included chairman Gary Bauer, the under secretary of education; William Kristol, chief of staff and counselor to William Bennett, the secretary of education; and Terry Eastland, director of the Office of Public Affairs at the Justice Department. Thomas was "tasked," as he put it, with overseeing portions of the report dealing with black self-help and the status of the black family. If he regarded such a race-oriented assignment as an affront, he appears to have kept it to himself.

"The family needs help!" the report cried out on page two. Within only a few years, the truth and urgency of this visionary proclamation would become common wisdom. The document was a diagnosis of the decline of the American family and a cogent, wide-ranging manifesto for social conservatism, asserting that "private choices have public effects.... It simply is not true that what we do is our business only. For in the final analysis, the kind of people we are ... is the sum of what millions of Americans do in their otherwise private lives." The report noted the rise in drug use, illegitimacy, divorce, pornography and abortion, and recommended "A Pro-Family Policy" premised on the notion that the rights of the family "are anterior, and superior, to those of the state." The report called for an end to "the abrasive experiments of two liberal decades," including judicial activism, the coining of new, socially corrosive rights by judges.

In February 1987, the *Atlantic Monthly* published a lengthy article on Thomas by Juan Williams. Thomas had begun meeting with Williams soon after he was appointed to EEOC. Armstrong Williams said it took him two months to talk Thomas into doing the interview, as he was still "bitter" about Juan Williams' past reporting of his sister's welfare dependency (even though Thomas himself had raised the issue). Juan Williams noted that his series of interviews with Thomas took place because "Thomas thought that the conversations would be advantageous to him." Relating many details of Thomas's life and background that Thomas would not mention in subsequent interviews, Williams unwittingly became, in the process, an informal Boswell to someone now regarded as a rising political star.

Assessing Thomas's politics, Williams wrote that the EEOC chairman "stands in the tradition of Booker T. Washington." He also compared Thomas to Malcolm X and noted Thomas's affection for him. Thomas asked Williams, "Where does he [Malcolm X] say black people should go begging the Labor Department for jobs? He was hell on integrationists. Where does he say you should sacrifice your institutions to be next to white people?"

Thomas shared his anger at the presumption of intellectual inferiority that was the handmaiden of affirmative action. He directed his ire specifically at the cloud of suspicion that he believed hovered over his Yale law degree. "This thing about how they let me into Yale—that kind of stuff offends me," he said. Williams ascertained that Thomas held a dim view of the future of race relations in America: "It is unlikely that whites will ever fully accept blacks as equals, in his opinion, and so blacks should prepare to do for themselves by making black schools into rigorous training grounds, by investing in black businesses, by working for black corporations, and by living in black neighborhoods." Some of this reflected Thomas's past. "He has too many scars from episodes in which, in the name of integration, he was the only black."

Williams could not help but recognize Thomas's intense dedication to his job: "As I discovered in a series of interviews spanning Thomas's nearly five years in office, Thomas does take seriously the stated responsibilities of his position." Yet he "walks a lonely road, not really agreeing with conservatives or liberals." Williams described him as "something of a black nationalist, as well as a sad, lonely, troubled, and deeply pessimistic public servant." Years later, Thomas would compliment Williams for capturing in his article the "loneliness and the solitude and the despondent nature that can come about when it all seems to be to no end and no avail."

Thomas began to receive other favorable publicity in his second term. In an editorial in August 1987, the *Washington Post* declared, "The EEOC Is Thriving." The editors explained in an unexpected tribute, "Under the quiet but persistent leadership of Chairman Clarence Thomas," the number of cases filed by EEOC had soared. Thomas, they noted, had advocated greater funding for EEOC to ensure its effectiveness. They concluded that "legislators who care about civil rights enforcements have a special obligation to sustain an agency doing this work and enjoying, to an unusual degree in these times, the support and encouragement of the administration."

In the same month, Thomas hired another special assistant, bringing to three the number of conservative intellectuals on his staff. Masugi brought to Thomas's attention the published work of Philip Lyons. A graduate of the University of Chicago, Lyons then was working at the U.S. Civil Rights Commission. He had written on the baleful effects of affirmative action and double standards in hiring practices. Soon thereafter, he found himself being interviewed by Thomas—an interview "in which [Thomas] did most of the talking." From "the tension in his face and expression," Lyons discerned that the notion that "blacks needed extra points in hiring angered him terribly."

"C.T.," as Lyons and others called Thomas, "wanted me to revise the entire [Uniform Guidelines on Employee Selection Procedures]," he recalled. For his first six weeks, Lyons "crashed" on this project, overhauling the uniform guidelines from top to bottom consistent with the goal of phasing out quotas. This was an enterprise that Zuckerman also had undertaken, but to no avail; Lyons' effort would end in comparable frustration. Thomas hoped to disseminate the revisions at the same time the nation would be distracted by the Supreme Court confirmation hearings for Judge Robert Bork. Thomas, Lyons remembered, believed that "all the people who would've gone ballistic over the uniform guidelines now would've been preoccupied with another event. . . . C.T's thinking was, we could slip these changes through unnoticed." This was wishful thinking, and Talkin, among others, talked him out of it. "You'll lose this, and you'll lose a lot of political capital," she admonished him. The UGESP revisions were shelved.

Lyons accepted the demise of his efforts with equanimity. "He loved them. He loved the changes," Lyons recalled. "But they went nowhere." Lyons later could look back and see the political prudence behind Thomas's decision. "I don't think he'd be on the Supreme Court today if he'd spent his political capital on that," he concluded.

——

Thomas had told a reporter in 1984, "You don't see anyone trying to integrate marriages, do you? That would solve everything." Exactly one year and one day after their first date, Thomas and Ginni would do their part to test this hypothesis, standing before a crowd of well-wishers in St. Paul's United Methodist Church in Omaha on May 30, 1987, and exchanging marital vows.

The couple had so much in common, and fell in love so fast, that the relatively rapid wedding was not much of a surprise to those who knew them. They referred to each other as his or her "best friend." Thomas, ever the formalist, insisted on calling her Virginia, even though none of her relatives or friends did so (perhaps he was still, in his own way, following Myers Anderson's instruction to put a "handle" on names).

Thomas asked his son Jamal to be his best man. While seemingly sentimental, this was arguably an insensitive request, since the young man was being asked to give away his father to a second wife. Jamal at first wondered if things would "work out" with his future stepmother. But Thomas had already shown himself a far better parent than his parents had been for him, and Ginni, for her part, was a far more loving stepparent than the ones Leola had brought home to her sons thirty years earlier. After the marriage, Jamal told friends Ginni was "cool."

Thomas moved out of his rented home in Prince Georges County, Maryland, and Ginni sold her condominium. They bought and moved into a modest two-story, three-bedroom house in Kingstowne, Virginia. Ginni led them to a nearby church, Truro Episcopal Church in Fairfax, Virginia. It was not very Episcopalian: The style of worship was "charismatic," featuring parishioners speaking in tongues, and the church leadership preached a social conservatism and opposition to abortion at odds with the prevailing creed in most other Episcopal churches. But for the first time in the better part of two decades, Thomas began to attend church regularly. Alex Netchvolodoff, a friend from the Missouri Attorney General's Office and, later, Senator Danforth's office, said that Thomas's second marriage sparked a "reawakening of his faith." Previously, Thomas had observed, "I was not yet ready for organized religion." This changed when Ginni came into his life.

The rest of his belief system was ripening as well. When Marini arrived at EEOC in early 1987, he concluded that Thomas's views were still in flux. Thomas at that point "didn't have a principled defense of conservatism." What Thomas did possess, something he would never negotiate away, was the cache of values inherited from his grandfather. In essence, Thomas's court tutors fleshed out Daddy's philosophy. "What we were telling him in a way was why his grandfather was a good man," Marini explained. As a result of these efforts and his own reflection, "He was becoming more conservative."

The sinews of thought Thomas used in weaving together his conservatism came from variegated sources. He found pearls of wisdom in the books he treasured, the people he admired, and, eventually, in the outlook of a newly syndicated radio host named Rush Limbaugh. The most celebrated conservative book of the 1980s also struck a chord, Allan Bloom's *The Closing of the American Mind.* Bloom argued that moral relativism had infected American higher education, and accordingly all of society, with destructive results for academia and the nation's soul. The middle third of the book was a relatively dense discussion of modern philosophy, which Thomas, like some other readers, found "boring." Thomas relished other parts of *Closing,* however, especially Bloom's discussion of racial separatism on campus, a trend that Thomas had fought without success two decades before at Holy Cross. Thomas praised the book in speeches for offering "a rewarding, reassuring attack on the moral relativism that typifies and corrupts our age." He added, "I heartily approve of his critique of black studies and the debilitating effects of preferential treatment on black students, especially those at elite universities."

Thomas's reading tastes were eclectic, but reflected some common themes. He enjoyed cowboy novels by Louis L'Amour; the celebration of the lonely individual triumphing over lawbreakers held great appeal. Except for novels by Ayn Rand and L'Amour, however, Thomas read little fiction; like other men of action, he had little time for literature that did not instruct.

Clint Bolick, who went on to become one of the nation's leading libertarians, summed up the one-of-a-kind philosophy Thomas was developing. "If you want to discern Clarence Thomas's philosophy," he advised, "connect the dots between Richard Wright, Ayn Rand, Tom Sowell, Malcolm X, and Louis L'Amour. And there are probably only a handful of people who can see a very logical line there. . . . It is a real, rugged individualism backed by a very strong moral code of conduct toward other human beings." Bolick added, "I think that if Clarence had been alive at the time of the Revolution, he would've flown the flag that bore the inscription, 'Don't Tread on Me.'" Indeed, just such a flag stood behind Thomas's desk at EEOC—flags having become for him a primary mode of self-expression.

Yet this libertarianism coexisted with a religious-based morality. "By the same token, he's very much a believer in the golden rule, and that a society of individuals requires a very strict moral code—one that cowboys in Louis L'Amour novels live up to," Bolick said. Libertarianism and religion were largely antithetical. Bolick believed, "You can be a religious libertarian, but most libertarians tend not to be." Masugi saw the tension in these viewpoints and tried to address them. "He really thought Ayn Rand, that this was really great stuff. He was also really religious. He realized that didn't quite square." In one of his tutorial memos, Masugi gave a no-holds-barred critique of *Atlas Shrugged*. He denounced it as "terrible literature, dubious morality, bad politics." Masugi remembered Thomas as being "a bit chastened." Masugi observed: "That libertarian argument is always very attractive to him. But I think his religious convictions kept him from accepting that completely."

Thomas emerged from the 1980s with his own carefully crafted system of thought. It had several pillars. One was distrust of government. "Based on my experience and my education, if I had to summarize the task of government in a phrase, I would have to say that government's task is to allow citizens to be self-governing," he told the Cato Institute, a libertarian public policy organization, in April 1987. Masugi recalled that Thomas "was so suspicious of bureaucracy, just from his own experience." The discrimination and injustice of Jim Crow framed his view of government; the disaster he inherited at EEOC and Congress's self-interested machinations further ingrained this distrust. "Now from this experience you would correctly infer that I am deeply suspicious of laws and decrees," he noted after discussing his segregated childhood. "Government does have necessary functions to play, but the most important thing it can do is respect peoples' freedoms." He emphasized the right to "control of one's property and livelihood" and the "ability to debate and deliberate about the issues, but also moral self-government."

Economic liberty was another important plank in his thought. Again, he invoked the experience of Myers Anderson as the basis for his worldview. His grandfather, Thomas noted often in speeches, was able to overcome racism "because there was at least some economic liberty, some economic freedom, even though political and social freedom were denied." The influence of Hayek showed in his attack on Marx in one speech in 1987. "The attack on wealth," Thomas explained, "is really an attack on the means to acquire wealth: hard work, intelligence, and purposefulness. And that in turn is an attack on people like my grandfather."

Yet he was no shill for big business. Indeed, Masugi recalled Thomas condemning large corporations and their lobbies for their political cowardice, and for "caving in" to new regulations generally. He disapproved of using the federal tax code to encourage certain behavior. "One of the things he always harped on was how he thought it was wrong to use the tax code to institute social change," Masugi said. He criticized the interest deductions available for mortgages but not for other loans, viewing this system as slanted against the poor and minorities.

In the ideal society envisioned by Thomas, all laws orbited the individual. "Everything that I do and say flows from my commitment to the rights of the individual," Thomas once said. This seems like hyperbole until one considers that he once asked his staff to calculate the number of times the term "individual" appeared in Title VII of the Civil Rights Act. They came back with a number he cited with some frequency: 27. "I personally continue to adhere to the principle that individuals should be judged on the basis of individual merit and individual conduct," he said, confirming the core of his opposition to racial preferences. "No one should be rewarded or punished because of group characteristics." He noted that the antislavery movement and civil rights movements were "founded on the sanctity of the individual and the God-given rights of the individual."

Even so, he recognized that the minting of too many rights eroded social order and depreciated the more fundamental rights he revered: "Today, there appears to be a proliferation of rights—animal rights, children's rights, welfare rights, and so on." Thomas preferred the approach of Tocqueville, an emphasis on certain primary liberties central to the American personality. Under this regime, Thomas believed, freedom would become "a teacher of a way of life."

These views came together effectively in several speeches in this time. In a speech to the Cato Institute in Washington, he highlighted his differences with libertarians generally and with certain libertarian scholars then ascendant. Thomas began by taking issue with the very name of the group. He questioned their reliance on *Cato's Letters* for their mission, and their related belief that civil and economic liberties had shrunk since the American Revolution. Thomas pointed out, "the history of freedom in America is not as simple as that statement implies. By excluding the massive fact of slavery, it misunderstands the nature of the social problems and the civil and economic liberties it seeks to protect." The rest of the speech was devoted to the reconciliation of liberty with individual responsibility, a theme that sparkles through his subsequent public addresses and that largely defines his subsequent public career.

Thomas also spoke out against the type of judicial activism advocated by some libertarian scholars. Several such theorists had urged the federal courts to strike down laws and regulations that impeded economic liberties. He criticized "the current eagerness of some libertarians to develop a jurisprudence which justifies judicial activism by the courts to strike down laws and regulations concerning economic and business activity." He observed: "Do such people really think such a powerful court would stop at striking down only those laws? That defies reality."

Thomas's speech to the Heritage Foundation two months later was every bit as uncompromising. The Heritage Foundation was a traditional conservative organization, one firmly allied to the Reagan conception of conservatism. In this setting, Thomas changed his message to exhort conservatives to welcome blacks to their ranks. He argued,

"Conservatives must open the door and lay out the welcome mat if there is ever going to be a chance of attracting black Americans.... Conservatives must show that they care.... Conservatives must understand that it is not enough just to be right." It could be argued that Thomas adumbrated "compassionate conservatism" more than a decade before it came into broad currency.

What would become the most controversial portion of the speech was not recognized as such at the time: Thomas's brief treatment of the right to life. Thomas remarked, "Heritage trustee Lewis Lehrman's recent essay in the *American Spectator* on the Declaration of Independence and the meaning of the right to life is a splendid example of applying natural law." He explained:

> This approach [basing a political regime on natural law] allows us to reassert the primacy of the individual, and establishes our inherent equality as a God-given right. This inherent equality is the basis for aggressive enforcement of civil rights laws and equal employment opportunity laws designed to protect individual rights. Indeed, defending the individual under these laws should be the hallmark of conservatism rather than its Achilles heel.

While not asserting that judges should recognize a right to life in the Constitution—a ruling that would effectively overturn *Roe v. Wade*—Thomas came fairly close. He would later struggle to squirm away from this bold language.

Thomas propagated his beliefs in various publications as well as in speeches. With a stable of conservative writers at his disposal, he sent forth numerous missives in the form of newspaper and magazine articles and letters to the editor. Starting in February 1987 and continuing over the next three years, Thomas published 10 articles in law reviews and other journals of opinion and 55 letters to the editor. In one 29-month period, he unloaded 43 letters to the editor, from major papers like the *New York Times, Wall Street Journal* and *USA Today* and magazines such as *Time* and *National Review* to small ethnic papers such as the *Richmond Afro-American.* His articles ranged broadly in subject matter. In a 1987 article in the *Yale Law and Policy Review,* Thomas defended EEOC's emphasis on individual remedies instead of class-action relief in the enthusiastically titled article, "Affirmative Action Goals and Timetables: Too Tough? Not Tough Enough!" The following year, he reviewed Clint Bolick's new book on civil rights in an issue of the conservative journal *Policy Review.*

Thomas granted another illuminating interview in this time. The November 1987 issue of *Reason,* a libertarian magazine, carried an interview of Thomas that focused on the philosophical rather than the personal. Thomas's answers were remarkably candid and lucid. When asked "Why do you think that this agency [EEOC] should exist in a free society?" Thomas did not simply laugh off such a radical question. Instead, his answer showed remarkable depth of thought:

> Well, in a free society I don't think there would be a need for it to exist. Had we lived up to our Constitution, had we lived up to the principles that we espoused, there would certainly be no need. . . . Unfortunately, the reality was that, for political reasons or whatever, there was a need to enforce antidiscrimination laws, or at least there was a perceived need to do that. . . . [I]f I had to look at the role of government and what it does in people's lives, I see the EEOC as having much more legitimacy than the others [agencies], if properly run.

When the interviewer asked him whether a private employer who is racist has the right to hire whomever he wishes, Thomas replied:

> I guess theoretically, you're right. You say, it's my property and I can do as I damn well please. I'm able to choose my wife, I can choose my employees. . . . I think, though, that we've embodied the principle of nondiscrimination because we don't have a homogeneous society. And the problem is that we had state-imposed racism in our society. We had segregation and slavery that was state-protected, state-imposed, state-inflicted. The state can't undo the harm that was done, but I feel very strongly that if there is any role for the state, it is to protect us from others.

Politically, this was a clever answer. The reasoning, however, disintegrated with any analysis. By this measure, if slavery and segregation had been enforced privately, instead of by the state, racial discrimination in employment would be acceptable today. Thomas undoubtedly recognized this rhetorical train wreck but chose to ignore it, trying instead to sidestep a tough question.

The interviewer did not let up. He noted that while "it's clearly immoral to do that, but should it be illegal?"

"I'm torn," Thomas responded.

"Would you describe yourself as a libertarian?" the interviewer asked.

"I don't think I can," Thomas said, pulling back from the edge. "I certainly have some very strong libertarian leanings, yes. I tend to really be partial to Ayn Rand, and to *The Fountainhead* and *Atlas Shrugged*. But at this point I'm caught in the position where if I were a true libertarian I wouldn't be here in government." Thomas did describe himself as a Republican, but said he was uncomfortable with the term "conservative"—a complaint he would reiterate later in life despite his earlier avowal of such credentials.

Thomas had not given up on his dream of becoming a writer. He discussed possible books with both Masugi and Lyons. Following one such conversation, Masugi sent Thomas a memo stating, "If you were to do a book, the following would be obvious divisions and chapters." Masugi's outline of chapter topics constituted an intriguing book proposal:

Natural law
Higher law calling
Basic education through grandfather
Libertarians vs. conservatives
Education employment
Family policy
Welfare

Blacks and foreign policy
Blacks and GOP
The black establishment
Blacks and the Constitution
Blacks and conservatives
The courts

Experiences:
 Congress
 "the most dangerous branch"

Education

EEOC
1. administrative reform
2. quotas, goals, and timetables
3. civil rights enforcement in the Reagan administration

Conclusion:
 The future of America

Thomas similarly enlisted Lyons to ponder a possible book project. Thomas had expressed irritation with theorists such as Arthur Jensen who were asserting a substantial hereditary basis for the IQ gap between blacks and whites. He wanted Lyons to help him write a book on the parallels between racists on the right and the left. "He felt it was racist for people to argue that blacks had been so damaged by discrimination that they were in fact not as capable intellectually and volitionally," Lyons said. By the time Thomas left the agency, Lyons had written five chapters.

Thomas's plan was to publish the book under his own name. This arrangement was questionable for any number of reasons, not the least of which was that it amounted to a significant misuse of staff time. Thomas's departure from EEOC brought Lyons' project to an end; Lyons ended up publishing part of the work in a political science review. Several years later, a work entitled *The Bell Curve* was published, exploring many of the same themes. It became a huge bestseller and further confirmed Thomas's remarkable sense of timing and feel for the public mood.

The public policy issue that loomed above all others in Thomas's career was race. As a patriot, he wished to synthesize his love of country with the African-American experience, which in many ways was hostile to such nationalism. He sought to bridge this gap by combining natural law with a heightened appreciation for a sometimes overlooked founding document, the Declaration of Independence.

In the context of political theory, natural law held that people possess certain rights, as human beings, that government and other people cannot rightly infringe. The Declaration of Independence reflects this view by stating that Americans are "endowed by their Creator with certain unalienable rights." The Bill of Rights grew out of this natural law tradition.

In applying natural law to the American regime, Thomas drew upon his Catholic upbringing and education, the writings of the Framers, and a philosophy of right learned from mostly libertarian authors such as Rand. Masugi and Marini also helped him to formulate his views on the subject. Stanley Grayson, one of Thomas's friends from Holy Cross, once joked, "I've interpreted natural law as the law according to Clarence." This was not far from the mark.

In a series of speeches in 1987, Thomas outlined his understanding of natural law and its relationship to individual rights. "[W]here is natural law today?" Thomas asked in one speech. "Is it gone, along with the segregated schools, buses, and drinking fountains of my youth?" He pointed out the connection between churches and the civil rights movement, a tie that existed because of the "higher law" that white supremacists violated. Thomas noted that natural law allows society to place firm limits on governmental action and to ensure individual autonomy. "This approach allows us to reassert the primacy of the individual, and establishes our inherent equality as a God-given right.... This inherent equality is the basis for aggressive enforcement of civil rights laws and equal employment opportunity laws designed to protect individual rights. Indeed, defending the individual under these laws should be the hallmark of conservatism rather than its Achilles heel."

Some months later, Thomas ventured his own theory. "With my personal experience in mind, I would like to use this occasion to present a sketch of a theory of natural law, which would unite both libertarian and conservative principles. I doubt that what I will say will be anything new, but I think it is important to present a coherent, principled basis for approaching current political and ethical questions." He set forth three elements of natural law theory governing economic relations: (1) "the common sense of the free market"; (2) the right to the fruits of one's own labors; and (3) the "dignity of labor." These were quite obviously the condensed, tightly reasoned thoughts of Thomas, not merely the suggestions of staffers.

Years before Thomas met Masugi or Marini, he sensed that the Declaration of Independence might prove to be, in the eyes of blacks, the cornerstone of legitimacy for the American political regime. In one speech in April 1983 he spoke of his "enduring hope that this country will live up to the principles enunciated in the Bill of Rights and the Constitution of the United States: that all men are created equal and that they will be treated equally." Garry Wills won the Pulitzer Prize several years later for making a similar argument, noting that Lincoln in the Gettysburg Address altered the meaning of the Declaration of Independence—and the American experience—by invoking its "all men are created equal" principle as a *post hoc* rationale for racial equality under law.

More intellectual support for this view came from Professor Harry Jaffa, the mentor of Masugi and Marini at Claremont McKenna College. Issues of natural law and Lincoln's treatment of the Declaration of Independence similarly captivated Jaffa. He studied under Leo Strauss, who became, except for John Dewey, the most important American political philosopher of the twentieth century. Strauss emigrated from Germany right before World War II. He and a number of other great German professors set up in New York City what was at first called the University of Exile and later renamed the New School for Social Research. Jaffa justifiably called it "the greatest faculty ever assembled under one roof, courtesy of Adolf Hitler."

Strauss's *Natural Right and History* became a classic of political philosophy. He began the work by quoting the Declaration of Independence, a document for which he had gained a great reverence. He argued that the rejection of natural right had led to "disastrous consequences" in society—in particular, a general confusion over individual rights and public morality. Bloom's *The Closing of the American Mind* is, to a large degree, a brilliant echo of Strauss's work, with obvious similarities in structure and topics.

Jaffa, like Bloom, drew from this Straussian well, applying Strauss's thought to what he saw as the central drama of American history: slavery and the Civil War. In 1946, while studying under Strauss, Jaffa found himself simultaneously reading Plato's *Republic* and the Lincoln-Douglas debates. This, he later concluded, was a "case of divine providence." For, in juxtaposing the two works, "I realized the debates between Lincoln and Douglas paralleled the differences between Socrates and Thrasymachus." His studies gave birth to a book, *Crisis of the House Divided,* and numerous follow-up works exploring the same themes.

Whence did natural right derive in the American tradition? Jaffa located it in the Declaration of Independence, and he saw Lincoln as its chief spokesman when he argued "that the enjoyment of rights enunciated in the Declaration was a goal to be pursued and not a fact to be assumed." Moreover, the notion of "all men are created equal" was meant to include blacks as well as whites. Otherwise, Jaffa claimed in subsequent works, Americans are bound to the cold reasoning of the *Dred*

Scott decision. In this 1857 case, Chief Justice Roger Taney wrote that the Framers of the Constitution did not intend to extend the same rights to blacks as to whites. If Taney is right, Jaffa concluded, the basic legitimacy of the nation's political institutions is in question. Masugi and Marini were Jaffa disciples, and they touted his work to Thomas. Thomas read *Crisis of the House Divided* in 1987 and soon was invoking Jaffa's name in speeches.

Thomas heard counterarguments from William Bradford Reynolds, Charles Cooper, Michael Carvin, and other Justice Department lawyers who maintained that the Constitution should be interpreted strictly according to the intentions of the Framers. They believed that to consult the intentions of the Declaration signers, or to subscribe to evolving standards of legal interpretation (i.e., Jaffa's application of the "all men are created equal" provision to blacks), would allow judges to amend the Constitution at will. There would then be no check on their power. The acerbic Jaffa, for his part, fired back, dismissing such theorists, including Judge Robert Bork of the D.C. Circuit Court of Appeals, as "Confederate jurists." Masugi remembered that Thomas "didn't like what I would call the Southern conservatism that was coming out of the Justice Department."

In the debates that occasionally occurred when Cooper or Carvin came over for a brown-bag lunch at EEOC, the Justice lawyers would take the "Borkean" position and Masugi and Marini would argue the "Jaffa" position. Thomas's overriding concern in these discussions was, "How can you support original intent and be opposed to slavery at the same time, given that the slaveholders signed onto the Constitution?" It was a fair question for which there was no easy answer.

Thomas opted to go with Jaffa's central principle concerning constitutional interpretation. "So when we use the standard of 'original intention,' we must take this to mean the Constitution in light of the Declaration," he said. "With the Declaration as a backdrop, we can understand the Constitution as the Founders understood it—to point toward the eventual abolition of slavery." The problem, of course, was that the Founders had no such clear understanding. Nevertheless, in an article in the *Howard Law Journal,* which Masugi drafted, Thomas repeated this view that the Declaration of Independence is the lodestar for interpreting the Constitution on matters of race.

"Now I realize this is just a beginning of a project, but I hope it is of some use," Thomas said of his productive obsession with Lincoln, the Declaration, and the African-American experience. This "project" would become the most important politico-legal endeavor of his life.

—•—

In July 1987 Thomas took note of Lieutenant Colonel Oliver North, who stood ramrod straight in his green Marine uniform as he took the witness oath before a bank of cameras on Capitol Hill. He then fired a fusillade of rhetoric at rows of astonished congressmen and senators. The public gravitated to the embattled soldier's insolence and charisma. The swelling public support culminated in a pro-North song that played on radio stations in the heartland.

North was living out one of Thomas's ultimate fantasies: blasting Democratic politicians on the Hill and scattering them like so many pigeons. North's ability to turn the nation against Congress "fascinated" Thomas, according to Masugi. He recalled Thomas's analysis: "If you really got to the heart of what people were thinking, why Oliver North received such a positive response, people really do regard Congress with great suspicion. And . . . what North did just confirmed people's worst suspicions about Congress." Thomas took note of his performance and the public's reaction, and carefully saved those pearls of wisdom for another day.

At the same time that the Iran-contra hearings were filling the airwaves in the summer of 1987, Justice Lewis Powell announced his resignation from the Supreme Court. Reagan then made known his intention to nominate Judge Robert Bork to fill Powell's seat. Bork was a dour intellectual with a close-cropped, square-block beard of the old Puritan variety. He was also, by conservative consensus, the most impressive sitting jurist who subscribed to originalism, the school of thought that held, like Reynolds and his followers at Justice, that judges should interpret the Constitution consistent with the intentions of the Framers. Originalism, if fully implemented, would have required the reversal of scores of major Supreme Court rulings on the hottest social issues of the day: abortion, prayer in school, pornography, rights of criminal defendants and prisoners. To the political left, a single such reversal would have been a calamity.

Democrats in the Senate and liberal interest groups rightly sensed the formidable intellectual and political enemy they would face if Bork joined the court. Indeed, over the coming years this web of political allies would display, time after time, a keen ability to intuit which Republican judicial nominees posed serious threats to their power. They would then scramble effectively to defeat them.

The million-dollar advertising campaign launched by People for the American Way and other liberal lobbies distorted Bork's writings and record through commercials on television and radio and in the print media. The administration launched no concerted counterattack. By the time Bork appeared for his confirmation hearings in September, public opinion already was shifting against him. Bork painstakingly explained his beliefs to the Senate Judiciary Committee; his intellectual honesty sealed his fate. After the Senate rejected Bork, conservative writers, and subsequently other journalists, transmuted his name into a verb. "To bork" came to mean roughly "to defeat a political nominee through unscrupulous means."

Thomas was horrified by the treatment accorded his former law professor, condemning the spectacle as a "tragedy for the rule of law." In a March 1988 speech to the Federalist Society chapter at the University of Virginia, Thomas further expressed his outrage. "After Bob Bork's defeat, Joe Biden [chairman of the Senate Judiciary Committee] crowed that he believed his rights were inalienable ones.... At that moment, conservatives should have known that they were not using their best arguments. They had in fact surrendered the moral high ground to those who least understood it." While he savored the moment, Thomas would come to regret this goading of Biden and the Senate Democrats—and in relatively short order.

Thomas's own relations with Congress deteriorated further. In December 1987 he learned of yet another administrative debacle at EEOC, this one occurring on his watch. Jim Troy, EEOC's director of program operations, walked into Thomas's office to inform him that he had made an unfortunate discovery: a large number of age discrimination cases in which the statute of limitations had passed before the agency had taken any action.

"How could this happen?" Pamela Talkin demanded.

Thomas's immediate reaction showed the maturation of his political skills. "We've got to tell the Hill," he declared. "We're gonna have to get this fixed. We're gonna have to tell people that this has happened. Let's find out the magnitude of it."

Thomas directed Troy to assess the damage. Within a day or two, Troy reported back that the botched cases numbered in the hundreds.

Thomas sent out a scathing memo to the agency's district offices. He said that the lapsed cases were "absolutely inexcusable" and "tantamount to a dereliction of duties." He stated he would "not tolerate such mishandling of even one case" in the future. Thomas gave 7 of 23 district directors poor performance evaluations as a result and warned them they would be fired if there were additional problems. Eventually, EEOC identified approximately nine hundred charges for which the two-year statute of limitations had expired.

Thomas spun the problem back at Congress as well as he could. He pointed out that the Democrats in Congress had cut the Reagan administration's budget request for EEOC every year he had worked there. The money Congress had not appropriated, Thomas noted, would have gone toward upgrading staff and computer systems. His statements to the press were pugnacious: "The people doing the complaining participated in the mugging and in tying our hands and in putting millstones around our necks, and then complain when we can't run the mile in four minutes." He also noted that under the old Norton regime, such age cases were "routinely dumped" and not prosecuted in any event.

Notwithstanding this spin control, on January 29, 1988, Thomas frankly accepted the blame for the age-discrimination disaster before the House Select Committee on Aging. The *New York Times* called his statements an "unusual assessment by a chief executive of his own agency," and described Thomas as visibly angry as he recounted the agency's mishaps. Thomas told the committee chairman, Edward R. Roybal of California, "We are assessing the damage in each case. We will present a full report. No responsible person would miss the statute. We deserve harsh criticism for this occurrence. It will not happen again."

On January 30, the *Chicago Tribune* praised Thomas's handling of the matter in an editorial entitled, "Without Doubt, a Thomas of Merit"—apparently the first of innumerable times that a variation of the phrase "doubting Thomas" would make its way into a Thomas-related headline in the coming years. The editorial began: "A special award honoring government officials who say the right thing in plain English should be created in the name of Clarence Thomas, chairman of the Equal Employment Opportunity Commission." The editors noted that he fully accepted the blame with "no cop-out" and "no excuses, no bellyaching about the other guy." The encomium ended, "Bless you, Mr. Thomas, for straight talk in an age of waffling."

In 1988, EEOC's financial accounting systems finally met the standards of the General Accounting Office. This was the first time in its twenty-two-year history that the agency had managed to accomplish this. From 1982 to 1988, the number of court actions initiated by EEOC rose from 241 to 555. No longer the turkey farm, EEOC was becoming known throughout the federal bureaucracy as one of the nation's better-run agencies.

Thomas demanded that the administration accord EEOC the higher respect he believed it had earned. He urged the White House to approve better office space for the agency. He learned that plans were afoot to move EEOC headquarters to Buzzard's Point, a bleak area in southwest Washington near the Naval War College. "I'm not going to Buzzard's Point!" he repeatedly vowed to his staffers. Talkin recalled that he lobbied for nicer quarters "so that the EEOC would be in the high-rent district." He believed "an agency of blacks and Hispanics and women shouldn't be relegated to Buzzard's Point. . . . Just because it was a civil rights agency didn't make it a second-class citizen." In September 1988 his persistence was rewarded, as EEOC moved into new offices at 1801 L Street. They were lavish by federal standards, with a red marble facade and a cost of $33 a square foot—one-third more than other rental properties in the area. *Time* magazine ran a small piece on the new offices, entitled "Bureaucracy; Putting on the Ritz." This mattered little to Thomas in comparison with the chorus of gratitude that came from the newly exalted EEOC employees.

Thomas was far more active in the presidential campaign of George Bush than he had been for Ronald Reagan. For one thing, he had not really been a conservative in 1984, particularly on affirmative action. In 1988 he was better acquainted with Bush than he had been with Reagan. And Bush placed a greater emphasis on racial diversity than

had Reagan. Perhaps simple ambition ignited Thomas's interest at this
time; but whatever the reasons, he plunged with relative gusto into the
Bush-Quayle campaign. He was a member of the caucus team at the
GOP national convention in August, and campaigned for Bush at black-
oriented events across the country.

On October 29, at the People of Color Rally in Cincinnati, Thomas
sounded a call to his fellow African-Americans that grew out of his
own, proven success in the Reagan-Bush administration. "There is room
at the inn," he told the audience. "And I am here to sound the welcome
bell." He noted that Bush had headed the United Negro College Fund
drive in 1948. While a congressman, Bush had voted for fair housing
legislation in 1968 despite "intense anger and criticism" back in Texas.
"I am here today to ask for your support of George Bush," he told them.
A few days later, Bush won in an electoral landslide.

Once again, as throughout his political career, Thomas had picked
the right horse. His years of loyal service and his new, self-constructed
conservatism positioned him well for the opportunities that were sure
to arise in the incoming administration.

CHAPTER SEVENTEEN

Cloistered, Again

His gigantic and often conflicting dreams had propelled Clarence Thomas to Washington. Now, as the decade of Reagan drew to a close and his vice president, George Bush, rose to take his place, Thomas found that many of these goals were within his grasp. There was but one major catch: he would finally be forced to choose among them.

Thomas could look back upon his work at EEOC with extraordinary pride and satisfaction. The chairman had indeed "finished the job." The best illustration of EEOC's progress under his leadership was the new esteem in which its previously woebegone financial department was held. Willie King remembered that after EEOC brought its financial house in order, other agencies, such as the Consumer Product Safety Commission, "were sending their workers over to EEOC, believe it or not, to figure out how to handle their financial problems." Though many had aided his efforts, Thomas had demonstrated that even in a recalcitrant bureaucracy, one man could make a difference.

With his work completed at EEOC, that old, elusive quarry, money, now dashed onto the scene again. Thomas recalled that at the dawn of the Bush administration, his objective was straightforward: "Pure and simple, I wanted to be rich." Ricky Silberman, who had become a close friend of Thomas's, shared the same recollection. "He wanted to make a lot of money. He wanted to go into the corporate world." She added that other factors disturbed this simple plan. "There was a part of him that required intellectual stimulation."

His financial opportunities were numerous and inviting. Marini recalled, "I'm sure he could've made a lot of money. And he mentioned he could've made a lot of money." Dick Leon, then practicing corporate law in Washington, estimated that Thomas "easily" could have earned $500,000 a year as an attorney, "not counting corporate boards." Leon pointed to other major public figures, such as Vernon Jordan, who had taken this route and amassed a fortune. By deciding to do otherwise, Leon observed, "he was turning his back on a road that would've led to great financial independence."

Thomas appears to have considered going into politics. Marini thought "that was what he was planning. It was a matter of timing." Armstrong Williams, on the other hand, thought Thomas was "too shy" to run for office. When asked in an interview if he wanted to run for public office, Thomas did not dismiss the notion. "I don't think we'd ever win," he replied. "Certainly the blacks won't vote for you—at least not now." In light of subsequent Republican successes in his home state, it is not hard to envision Thomas in 1989 returning to Georgia and enjoying a successful political career there.

At least this much was settled: Thomas would remain in government. He told John Marini, "I don't think I ever want to go back to the private sector. I want to be involved in public things." Yet as always, his aspirations soared. After Bush's inauguration in early 1989, a friend asked Thomas what position he might seek from the new regime. He responded by voicing the ambition shared over a decade before with a St. Louis reporter: "A seat on the Supreme Court."

Thomas's relationship with George Bush was the cornerstone of his hopes. One high official in the new administration said that Bush was committed both to Thomas and, more generally, to racial diversity in appointments. "President Bush actually kind of had something of a mindset of wanting to find good minority candidates for positions," the official noted. "I think that he wanted to show that he was a good guy on those kinds of issues." This "desire to show he wasn't a racist—kinder, gentler, whatever"—made him "conscious of Thomas in that regard." Moreover, Bush "had met him on a couple of occasions and talked to him during the campaign and transition about ways of engaging in outreach to blacks." Thomas became for Bush something he had not been for Reagan: a distinct, well-known entity. In government, as in politics generally, name identification mattered.

The many years of service and self-promotion were paying off. Large and small things coalesced to form a good impression: his public support for repealing federal racial preferences at the wholesale level,

Masugi's blizzard of letters to the editor at the retail level. These and other actions earned him attention, respect and reciprocal loyalty within the Reagan and Bush administrations. Ricky Silberman, who was well connected in both administrations, said of Thomas's ascension to the judiciary: "It came about from his work at the EEOC, his stand on repeal of the executive order, and then Clarence is a very savvy guy. And he spent four years of the second Reagan administration doing what ambitious young people do in any administration, and that is making friends and getting known. And he was very, very visible."

The many friends he had acquired came to his aid. Michael Uhlmann, an attorney and a prominent figure in the Reagan White House, was one. He directed the Justice Department's transition team for Bush, and had Thomas firmly in mind for promotion. After the election, he met with Thomas three or four times. Uhlmann initially suggested Thomas for the position of deputy attorney general, the number two position in the Justice Department. Although Thomas was interested, the new attorney general, Richard Thornburgh, preferred to make his own selection. Uhlmann then looked for a deputy slot in another agency, such as the Department of Transportation. The new secretary there also had his own deputy in mind.

"It was clear to me that Clarence wanted to serve, but it was also clear that he had not given much thought to any particular job," Uhlmann stated. "It wasn't until well into the conversation that I brought up the circuit [court]." That Thomas was quiet about his judicial aspirations spoke well of him; he accepted the generosity of friends without presuming to direct their efforts. Finally, however, as various doors closed, Uhlmann opened one that led to a unity of opportunity and desire. There were two openings on the U.S. Court of Appeals for the District of Columbia Circuit. Uhlmann thought the president should appoint Thomas to one of them.

A lunch meeting followed, at which C. Boyden Gray of the White House Counsel's Office raised the subject with Thomas. Gray, like so many others in the administration, thought highly of Thomas. So did Lee Liberman, another top attorney in the counsel's office. One of the founders of the Federalist Society, Liberman was, like Bolick, a libertarian. Bolick remembered of the time, "I definitely helped sell Lee on his libertarian instincts, which were very important to her." Bolick made special mention of Thomas's devotion to Ayn Rand. As it turned out, Thomas's philosophy—his own conservative concoction—happened to mirror reasonably well the contemporary political reality: the loose coalition of traditional conservatives and libertarians that constituted the better part of the Republican Party.

Thomas hesitated. In a conversation with Leon, he listed his concerns about accepting the judgeship: he was too young; the lifestyle of a judge was too monastic; it was "not a springboard job." Ricky Silberman, on the other hand, thought the position suited Thomas well, and she urged him to accept it. Her husband, Laurence Silberman, was a judge on the D.C. Circuit, and he concurred with her. Silberman had served as under secretary of labor in the Nixon administration and had helped devise the original goals and timetables for minority employment in the federal government (handiwork he later repudiated as "fundamentally unsound policy"). A libertarian jurist and an advocate of judicial restraint, Silberman's philosophy was similar to Thomas's. He thought Thomas would make an excellent addition to the court and would feel at home there.

The many conflicting signals Thomas sent out to those around him, including the Silbermans, were a function of his indecision, personality and skills. He desired simultaneously several ends that were mutually exclusive: wealth, political power, withdrawal from the public eye. His complex personality added to the confusion: gregariousness mixed with iconoclasm and, often, detachment. Thomas enjoyed a profusion of talents that allowed him to pursue a universe of career goals. The opportunity to join the court of appeals represented a fork in the road, a call to decision, that demanded a final resolution of these competing objectives.

When Thomas asked Danforth for his advice, the senator said simply, "The brass ring doesn't come around very often in life."

Clinching Thomas's decision was his belief that the judgeship would be a stepping stone to the Supreme Court. "When he was appointed to the [D.C.] court by Bush," Marini recalled of his discussions with Thomas, "I got the impression upon talking to him at the time that . . . Bush made it clear to him that he wanted him eventually on the [Supreme] Court. I remember him saying he would never just, if it wasn't the Supreme Court, I don't think he would've taken it. If he thought that was the end. I think he wanted to be in a position to be on the Supreme Court or running for political office." Recounting his conversation with Bush, Thomas said the president indicated "basically, 'I want you on the court. You need experience, and then . . .'"

Thomas met with Bush on July 8. Three days later, the president announced his intention to nominate him to the court of appeals. Thomas called Leon shortly before the news was made public and asked him to come over to his office. When Leon arrived, Thomas told him, "I'm going to be nominated to the U.S. Court of Appeals for the D.C. Circuit. I've decided I'm going to do it. I'd like your help." Thomas added, "They wanted me to be deputy attorney general, but I didn't want to"—an account contradicted by Uhlmann.

Thomas foresaw a tough fight. Liberman and John Mackey of the Department of Justice spearheaded the daily work of the confirmation campaign. Leon assisted with the voluminous requests for documents that came from Senate Democrats on the Judiciary Committee. John Roberts, an attorney in Washington, and Michael Luttig, an attorney with the Department of Justice, conducted the "murder boards," or practice sessions for the hearings. They hurled at Thomas questions they expected Democrats on the committee to ask him.

His nomination provoked the predictable opposition. On October 31, the Alliance for Justice, a liberal legal interest group, released a letter signed by multiple affiliated lobbies alleging that Thomas lacked the requisite "commitment to equal justice, the qualifications and the judicial temperament" for the position. A larger consortium of liberal pressure groups similarly had accused Bork of lacking "judicial temperament," by which they meant he did not share their philosophy. The letter also accused Thomas of "lax enforcement and active circumvention" of civil rights laws while chairman of EEOC. Cited in support of this proposition was the age-discrimination case debacle, the off-and-on effort to "water down" UGESP, and his decision to "gut" class-action suits and to emphasize individual cases instead. As for judicial temperament, the group noted his "record of hostility towards Congress." The organizations signing the letter were a fairly ominous collection: American Federation of State, County and Municipal Employees, National Education Association, People for the American Way, and several feminist groups including the National Abortion Rights Action

League (NARAL), the National Organization for Women, and the National Women's Political Caucus.

Conspicuously absent from this conglomeration were black organizations. This was largely because of a letter of endorsement from William T. Coleman Jr., the former transportation secretary under President Ford and millionaire African-American attorney in Washington (he had taken the private enterprise route to wealth that Thomas, by accepting this nomination, had eschewed). Coleman was also the father of Lovida Coleman, a friend of Thomas's from Yale. In a one-page letter to Bush, Coleman wrote that Thomas would make a "fine appointment and that Mr. Thomas will add further luster and judicial ability to the Court." Because Coleman had served as head of the NAACP Legal Defense and Educational Fund, his credibility with many civil rights organizations helped to stave off opposition from these groups.

On January 10, 1990, Senator Biden sent over the Judiciary Committee's document request to Mackey. In a cover letter, Biden asked that the administration respond to the request within twelve days. It was a ten-page, single-spaced battery of questions that dealt with a kitchen sink of issues: EEOC's employment of Hispanics, Frank Quinn, age-discrimination cases, agency-authorized class-action suits. The *Wall Street Journal* published the entire list on its op-ed page to publicize the onerous discovery request. An accompanying editorial, interestingly entitled "The Next Lynching," warned that Thomas "is being prepared for a political lynching," a fate similar to that of "other uppity blacks" who have sought to "leave the Liberal Plantation."

On the morning of February 6, the first day of the hearings, Thomas was nervous. He remembered "being tired, being anxious, being afraid of what could be done to me before the Senate Judiciary Committee." He went with Ginni and Jamal to pray in a church. Thomas said he offered a brief prayer "as Jesus prayed in the Garden of Gethsemane." When they left the church, he felt he had "turned so much of the burden over to God."

Senator Sam Nunn, Democrat of Georgia, introduced the native Georgian to the committee. Danforth then spoke and vouched for his former staffer. When Thomas addressed the panel, he thanked his grandparents and the nuns of St. Benedict, without whom, he said, "I wouldn't be here." It was an opening statement of only 182 words, terse for the talkative lawyer.

Although conservatives had lampooned Biden in the Bork hearings for his poor grades in law school, he asked the most penetrating questions of Thomas of any senator. From the tone of Biden's inquiries, it quickly became evident that the Democrats on the committee were resigned to Thomas's accession to the court.

Biden first asked Thomas what he would do if he heard a case governed by a Supreme Court ruling with which he disagreed. Thomas stated that "in that circumstance, I think by obligation, as it is in all circumstances, is to follow the Supreme Court precedent, not to establish law on my own." This was merely a truism of the law.

Biden followed up. "Suppose you had a case where the Supreme Court precedent with which you disagreed is not exactly on point, but its underlying principle applies to the case before you. Would you attempt to read the precedent narrowly by limiting it to its facts or decide the case upon the ground?"

"Again, without having a specific set of facts and a specific case before me, Mr. Chairman, I feel I'm answering a general hypothetical," Thomas responded.

"That's why I'm not speaking to any specific case."

"I think that a job of the circuit court judge or any lower court judge is to faithfully adhere to the Supreme Court decision on point, and to faithfully and honestly and as professionally as possible read that decision and apply it to the facts in the particular case before the court, not to torture a case to reach a preconceived notion of what the results should be."

Then Biden turned to natural law. He discussed Thomas's recent writings, which maintained that the Declaration of Independence and natural law underlie and inform the Constitution. "When you say that the Constitution reflects principles of natural law, are you endorsing the idea that the Constitution protects fundamental, though possibly unenumerated, rights?" Biden sought to determine, in other words, whether Thomas intended to do unto the left what they had done to the nation through judicial rulings, i.e., hold that a higher law compelled certain conservative court decisions irrespective of the history or text of the Constitution.

Thomas dealt with this issue nimbly. "In writing on natural law, as I have," Thomas said, "I was speaking more to the philosophy of the founders of our country and the drafters of our Constitution. I was also speaking to an issue that was of significant importance to me, and that is the philosophical basis for doing away with slavery." He insisted that he would not use free-standing notions of natural rights in interpreting the Constitution: "In applying the Constitution, I think I would have to resort to the approaches that the Supreme Court has used. I would have to look at the texture of the Constitution, the structure. I would have to look at the prior Supreme Court precedents on those matters. And as a lower court judge, I would be bound by the Supreme Court decision."

Orrin Hatch asked some of the sharpest questions from the Republican side. While prone to lengthy monologues culminating in questions that served almost as afterthoughts, he proved the most capable defender of the nominee. Frequently, he would set up Thomas with friendly questions, then comment himself on the soundness of Thomas's answers. Hatch pointed out that even while the Justice Department, in 1983 and 1984, had opposed the use of goals and timetables, Thomas had enforced the EEOC's decision to utilize such remedies. He recalled that during this time, Thomas had met with Attorney General Smith and senior officials in the White House, who had tried to bring EEOC into line on the issue. "I know all of this because I had some conservatives complain about you to me," he added, not naming names.

"Well, a lot of people were not happy with me," Thomas said.

"That is right. Well, I think that episode, though, is an example of your ability to apply the law on a Commission policy, even though you personally disagreed with what the Commission policy was at the outset." Thomas's earlier independence on racial preferences was proving to be an enormous asset.

Then it was Howard Metzenbaum's turn. His previous duels with the evasive and insubordinate Thomas appeared to have whetted his appetite for the occasion. In Metzenbaum, Thomas would meet his most visceral opponent, one in whom philosophical and personal differences came together in a bonfire of hostile passions. The senator returned to the issue of goals and timetables, wondering why, in 1985, the commission briefly ceased to use goals and timetables as a remedy in litigation.

Thomas replied, "I believe during my reconfirmation hearings in 1986, very much the same question was raised and there was similar discussion and I think it led you to request our general counsel to send to you routine reports." A few follow-up queries from Metzenbaum went nowhere. He would try his luck again after lunch.

Charles Grassley, Republican of Iowa, explored Thomas's views on constitutional law. Thomas outlined his basic constitutionalism very lightly, but enough to reveal himself as an originalist. He noted again that, as an appellate court judge, he would be bound by Supreme Court precedent. But he also said that for his part, he would look to "the text of the document, to the history, to the debates at the signing or in the ratification process."

Thomas then asserted, "I have not been someone who has had the opportunity or the time to formulate an individual, well thought-out constitutional philosophy." As Brad Reynolds, Armstrong Williams and others could attest, this statement was disingenuous, and strangely, needlessly so. Indeed, his nonconformity and fervid interest in the law had virtually compelled him to fashion his own judicial philosophy in the 1980s.

The committee then heard from a panel of witnesses. One was Frank Quevedo, chairman of the board of the Mexican-American Legal Defense and Education Fund, who had worked as executive assistant to Tony Gallegos in 1982. Quevedo praised Thomas for his "work ethic, integrity, his intellectual curiosity, honesty, and toughness." He described Thomas as someone who "possesses a deep commitment to making victims of discrimination whole and bringing the full force of the law on those recalcitrant employers who violate the law." He urged the committee to confirm Thomas. Thomas's personal charm and prescient outreach toward Hispanics while on the commission helped him to secure this critical endorsement.

After a recess for lunch, Thomas returned to the microphone to face more grilling from Metzenbaum. This time, the senator unwisely tried to draw blood on an arcane topic on which he tripped up only himself. The issue was whether an EEOC official was required to be present when a person waived his right to sue under the Age Discrimination in Employment Act. Metzenbaum asked what Thomas's position was in light of a Supreme Court ruling stating that EEOC must supervise such waivers.

"The EEOC has never supervised waivers," Thomas replied author-itatively. He then discussed in impressive detail the history of EEOC's proposed rulemaking on the subject.

Metzenbaum returned to the subject after an interlude in which two Republicans questioned Thomas. "Let me go back to this point: In the *Lorillard* case, the Supreme Court said that you may not use unsuper-vised waivers. Notwithstanding that, you proposed that unsupervised waivers be authorized, and my first question is how do you explain that?"

Thomas again did not budge. "Senator, I have never proposed that unsupervised waivers be authorized." He explained that EEOC's gen-eral counsel had suggested that the agency promulgate rules allowing unsupervised waivers in EEOC litigation. The courts, he noted, had upheld such waivers.

"At that point, you proposed it?" Metzenbaum asked.

"I did not propose anything."

"Who did propose it?"

For the third time, Thomas explained: "The proposal started with the general counsel and the legal counsel, as do most of our regulatory rulemakings."

Again, Metzenbaum misstated the history of the esoteric issue. He concluded: "In other words, you went forward with the rulemaking, even though your general counsel told you it was not possible to do, you should not do, the Supreme Court had held to the contrary. How do you explain that?"

"Senator, you are confusing two things." Thomas related that the courts had uniformly upheld the waivers, and the general counsel rec-ognized the need for rulemaking in that area of the law.

The colloquy degenerated further.

Metzenbaum: "You are talking about the rulemaking and I am talk-ing about what the rule contains, and I am saying that your general counsel said you could not include certain things in your rules and you are saying—"

Thomas: "The general counsel never said that. The general counsel said—"

Metzenbaum: "What does this mean? What does it mean?"

Thomas: "Which memo are you reading from, Senator?"

And so it went: Metzenbaum haplessly bringing up trivial subjects about which he knew painfully little, against an adversary whose understanding of the issues was probably unparalleled. Metzenbaum bottomed out when he quizzed Thomas about EEOC work-sharing agreements with state and local equal employment agencies. He did not seem to comprehend that EEOC lacked control over state EEO agencies. In any event, as Thomas explained, people filing age discrimination complaints had the right to present those claims at either a local EEOC office or a state agency with a worksharing agreement with EEOC.

The senator from Ohio audaciously stated, in remarks quoted by the *New York Times*, that he would oppose Thomas's nomination because he had "displayed an alarming lack of knowledge" about federal age discrimination laws.

On February 22, the Judiciary Committee recommended Thomas's confirmation by a vote of 12 to 1. Metzenbaum was the sole holdout. On March 6, the full Senate confirmed Thomas.

He would later compare the hearings to "eleven months of having stitches pulled out" or, alternatively, "eleven months of root canals." On another occasion, he drew a parallel to Dante's *Inferno*.

Thomas's elevation was a staggering loss for EEOC. He had served as chairman of the agency longer than any of his predecessors. More importantly, he had rescued the agency from criminality and ridicule, and had done nothing less than transform it from an interagency joke into one of the jewels of the bureaucracy. The employees of EEOC knew that his replacement could not possibly fill his shoes.

Willie King recalled one older woman's reaction to Thomas's farewell. The woman, who was in her sixties and hobbled by phlebitis in her legs, entered the agency through the clerical pool. Thomas learned that she, like King, was from Georgia. When Thomas made his regular rounds, he would faithfully ask, "How is my lady from Georgia?" As Thomas made his last walk-through before departing for the court of appeals, the woman, said King, "broke into tears." "Don't leave me!" she cried, as she tugged forlornly on his suit.

In June, the employees of EEOC invited Thomas back to his old headquarters for a ceremony. They unveiled a gold plaque in his honor, to hang prominently in the lobby of the building. It read:

Clarence Thomas
Chairman of the
U.S. Equal Employment Opportunity Commission

May 17, 1982 - March 8, 1990

IS HONORED HERE
BY THE COMMISSION AND ITS EMPLOYEES
WITH THIS EXPRESSION OF OUR RESPECT AND PROFOUND
APPRECIATION FOR
HIS DEDICATED LEADERSHIP
EXEMPLIFIED BY HIS PERSONAL INTEGRITY AND
UNWAVERING COMMITMENT TO
FREEDOM, JUSTICE AND EQUALITY OF OPPORTUNITY AND TO
THE HIGHEST STANDARDS OF GOVERNMENT SERVICE

The plaque hangs there to this day.

———

The E. Barrett Prettyman U.S. Courthouse was, for the power it wielded, one of the less pretentious structures in Washington. Built on the erstwhile home site of Chief Justice John Marshall, the building was a pedestrian rectangle of light gray granite. Long, dark slats of windows at various intervals were the only feature that interrupted the dull façade. The combined effect of these stripes of dark glass against the plain, lightly hued building suggested either prisoner's garb or a bar code on the side of a cereal box—depending, perhaps, on the reason for the person's visit to the courthouse. Within the courthouse were the U.S. District Court and Court of Appeals for the D.C. Circuit. This jurisdiction of the federal courts principally handled the many issues arising from the new regulations streaming forth from the busy agencies around the city.

Tour buses en route to Capitol Hill and other vehicles belched exhaust into the air as they drove past Third Street and Constitution Avenue. This and other pollution had settled on the already drab courthouse to render it even homelier. A chartreuse statue of Sir William Blackstone, the great English jurist, faced Constitution Avenue. Bearing an eighteenth-century wig and resolved countenance, and holding an enormous tome of law, the soot-covered Blackstone resembled not so much a grave lawgiver as an oddly attired chimney sweep.

Thomas's new chambers were on the east side of the courthouse. He could look out at massive magnolia trees that offered shade to his quarters and remember Georgia. Light oak paneling and the requisite rows of case-law books in floor-to-ceiling bookshelves covered the walls of his chambers. He possessed both a standard-issue polished wooden desk and a stand-up desk, where the active young judge sometimes preferred to do his work. He could peer out onto the street below and watch the files of criminal defendants emerge in shackles from federal buses for their day in court. Thomas would find himself saying "almost every day, 'But for the grace of God there go I.'"

Thomas was happy with the "sublime isolation" he had entered on the court. He concluded that "the cloistered life is more suited to my personality." While friends such as Danforth thought of Clarence as a "people person" unsuited for such a "bookish" existence, the other side of Thomas's personality thrived in the new environment. More than twenty years before, he had sought a virtually monastic lifestyle as a seminarian in the cornfields of Missouri. Now, he had much the same seclusion but with the liberty he craved. He lifted weights in the court's basement gym, smoked cigars as he read briefs, and answered to no boss. "He was happy as a clam," said William Bradford Reynolds, who stayed in touch with Thomas and remained a friend.

The new judge was responsible for hiring his own staff. "Professionally, we operate as if we're independent law firms," Laurence Silberman observed. His managerial talents were constricted to selecting three clerks a year, plus two full-time clerical assistants. Clerks were the court's workhorses. They conducted the legal research and wrote at least first drafts of the vast majority of court opinions. Second-year law students began applying in late January for clerkships that would begin one and a half years later. Thomas received between 300 and 400 applications, and selected a small fraction of these applicants "based almost exclusively on grades, the difficulty of their courses, and their writing experience." All boasted straight A's from "top tier law schools," among whose ranks Thomas included Harvard, Yale, the University of Chicago, the University of Virginia, and Duke. Of the eleven law clerks whom he employed or who accepted a job offer from him, three were women (including one African-American) and one was Asian-American.

His clerks and the other employees throughout the courthouse soon found themselves as charmed by Thomas as the employees at EEOC. One clerk for another judge on the court of appeals remembered, "I think the clerks, even those with various and sundry other points of view, liked him. He was very accessible, very friendly, and people in general really liked him." One security guard said, "He'd talk to you, then see you two, three days later and pick up the conversation where you left off." At his new venue, the Dallas Cowboys' rivalry with the Washington Redskins became twice-a-year fodder for good-natured harangues. On one occasion, Thomas was leaving the courthouse and called out to one of the guards, "You want a hot dog? I'm going to get some lunch." As recounted by another guard who was present, "The guy gave him a whole list of things he wanted. And the judge came back with the food without missing a beat."

At forty-two, Thomas became the youngest judge on the D.C. Circuit. His colleagues on the bench soon took note of his work ethic. Enjoying lifetime tenure within the federal bureaucracy, a judge's work habits sometimes slackened rapidly. Thomas, however, worked long hours and was highly conscientious. His fellow judges also observed that he "listens as well as he talks," and displayed "remarkable equanimity in handling his oral arguments." Other adjectives applied were "businesslike, judicious, and quiet."

His jurisprudence was true to the beliefs he shared with friends during the 1980s. Ricky Silberman, full of spousal pride, believed that "his jurisprudential views evolve and come from his experience with my husband." Like Larry Silberman, she said, Thomas was "very independent, he's strong-willed, and he doesn't take crap from anybody." This description of Thomas's personality was accurate, but the credit given to Judge Silberman was not. Judge Silberman himself remarked that Thomas "absolutely" was an independent thinker. "We did not always agree on particular cases, specific cases," he noted. "If I had influence on Clarence Thomas's role as a judge, it was more in emphasizing to him early on that it was crucially important that he look at each case and think about, the first question he should ask in respect to any question is, What is my appropriate role as a judge? That's advice I would've given any new appointee to the court who came from the policy world."

It is not clear if this advice was necessary, as Thomas had subscribed to a philosophy of judicial restraint years before joining the court. Judge

Silberman remarked, "I think he embraced it [judicial restraint] more as a judge than some people thought he would," given his background as a policymaker and his views on natural law.

In the 145 cases in which Thomas participated at the court of appeals, his experience and philosophy forged his jurisprudence. Many of the cases in which Thomas wrote opinions were criminal cases. New judges on the D.C. Circuit, like rookie attorneys at the Missouri Attorney General's Office, received many such assignments; thus did the wheel of life turn for Thomas. One of the first was *United States v. Poston,* heard on March 20. Prior to his arrest, the defendant, W. J. Poston, had been talking with three men in a Southeast Washington parking lot. One man, Anthony Young, approached the group and purchased PCP from one of Poston's companions. When Poston announced that he was leaving, Young asked if he could "get a ride to Anacostia to serve 'White Boys.'" Poston agreed despite knowing that Young was going to distribute PCP. Police officers broke up the deal; after Young fled and escaped capture, they arrested Poston. He was convicted of aiding and abetting the possession of PCP with intent to distribute.

On appeal, Poston argued the conviction should be overturned because merely giving Young a ride to the site of his intended drug dealing was not a crime. Writing for a three-judge panel that included Silberman and Ruth Bader Ginsburg, Thomas agreed with this position. He noted, however, that the facts were not so simple. Poston did not merely give Young a ride. He remained at the site of the transaction after Young stepped out of his truck. He circled around the block, then stopped at the corner. He behaved, in short, as a lookout. Based on these facts, the court upheld Poston's conviction and mandatory minimum sentence of five years in prison. Thomas subsequently mentioned this case in a speech to Jamal's high school as a warning against associating with the wrong crowd.

In *United States v. Rogers,* Thomas took up another appeal of a drug conviction. Police officers spotted a group of men gathered on Fourth Street S.E., near St. Thomas More School. The area, Thomas noted, "resembles an open-air drug bazaar" (and the proximity of a Catholic school to this environment obviously did not bode well for the defendant). Defendant John Fitzgerald Rogers, a convicted drug dealer, was among the men assembled there. He sat on a wall next to a gym bag.

Upon spying the police, someone said, "Get the bag." Rogers grabbed it and ran off toward the school, tossing the bag into a sewer along the way. When an officer arrested Rogers, they found a telephone beeper on him. The police located and searched the gym bag, discovering fifty-five grams of cocaine, worth approximately $5,500. At trial, Rogers testified that he thought the bag contained something illegal, but not crack. Prosecutors introduced evidence of his prior drug-dealing conviction to rebut his claim. Rogers was convicted of possession of more than fifty grams of crack with intent to distribute.

Rogers argued on appeal that the lower court erred in admitting the evidence of his prior ownership of a beeper and distribution of crack on the same city block. Rogers said the evidence was designed to show he had the "character of a drug dealer," rather than merely to rebut his testimony that he did not know the bag was bulging with crack. Such character evidence generally was inadmissible in criminal trials.

In his opinion, Thomas rejected these claims. He noted that the evidence showed "knowledge, intent, and the absence of mistake." This made the evidence of prior bad acts admissible. He added that overall, there was "[a]mple, and convincing, evidence [that] supported the jury's verdict."

Another criminal case brought Thomas face to face with a more controversial constitutional issue. *United States v. Halliman* involved a group of drug dealers who rented two or three hotel rooms at a time and switched rooms frequently, thereby avoiding the police and search warrants. The police eventually showed up with a warrant for three rooms, but found that the defendant, Hugh Halliman, had moved to a fourth one, Room 900. They knocked on the door. Halliman took his time in opening it. When the police heard the toilet being flushed, they concluded he was destroying evidence, so they broke down the door and found cocaine in the bathroom and elsewhere. Halliman was convicted of possession of cocaine and crack with intent to distribute.

Halliman argued that the evidence obtained from Room 900 should not have been admitted against him. He contended the police had violated his Fourth Amendment right against unreasonable searches and seizures by entering Room 900 without a warrant specifying that room. He invoked the exclusionary rule, a doctrine created by the Supreme

Court which held that evidence obtained in violation of the Fourth Amendment cannot be used in court.

Writing for the court, Thomas upheld the conviction. He found that the police's warrantless entry was justified, and that the evidence could be admitted, because the search and seizure fell within the exigent circumstances exception to the exclusionary rule. Because the police, upon hearing the toilet, reasonably concluded that evidence was being destroyed, they had probable cause to enter and search the room. Thomas observed:

> the police were neither lazy nor inattentive to the Fourth Amendment's warrant requirement; on the contrary, the police carefully investigated the suspicious hotel guests for more than a week and sought warrants for all the rooms that they could link to Halliman. Halliman tried to frustrate the warrant process by hopping from room to room.... Although the police could have obtained an additional warrant prior to the search, their decision not to do so was reasonable under the circumstances.

Thomas balanced this dedication to public order by showing concern for important individual liberties. In *United States v. Long*, he showed that he was willing to reverse a criminal conviction when basic rights were violated. Keith Long appealed his convictions for possession of cocaine with intent to distribute and for using a firearm in the commission of a drug crime. Several D.C. police officers, executing a search warrant, had entered a one-room apartment where they found Long and three other persons. The apartment, in Thomas's words, "brimmed with evidence" of illegal drug use. The officers also saw a .22-caliber revolver between the cushions of a sofa.

The court of appeals upheld Long's conviction for cocaine possession, but overturned his conviction on the firearms charge. In one of his better-written opinions, which was joined by Judge Silberman, Thomas recognized, "As an appellate court, we owe tremendous deference to a jury verdict." Even so, the court could not fulfill this "duty through rote incantation of these principles followed by summary affirmance." After reviewing the record in the case, Thomas concluded that "the government failed to provide any evidence to support a reasonable inference that Long 'used' the revolver." Thomas pointed to several critical facts. When he was arrested, "Long was ten to fifteen feet away from the revolver." There was no evidence that he was trying to reach the gun "or that he even knew of its existence." The apartment was not his residence or property. To uphold the conviction, he wrote, "would obliterate any remaining limits on the meaning of the word 'use.'" Thomas's emphasis on the text of the criminal statute presaged his overall approach to constitutional and statutory interpretation.

Not everything was blood and guts. Thomas also tackled some more technical questions, such as antitrust law, and dealt with the rights of federal employees—a cause, or at least an issue, close to his heart—in *National Treasury Employees Union v. United States*. Federal employees and their unions had filed suit, alleging that the Ethics Reform Act of 1989 violated their First Amendment rights. The act prohibited honoraria for delivering speeches, making appearances, and writing articles for compensation. They sought a preliminary injunction halting enforcement of the ban. Thomas might well have been personally torn; he was no lover of employee rights, yet for one who had considered writing a book or two, the ban may have hit close to home. Thomas and the other two judges ended up siding with the government on the narrow issue of the injunction. The court held that there was no need for an injunction pending a final decision by the district court on the merits of the case.

As a new judge, Thomas was assigned many of the less interesting cases, i.e., ones lacking constitutional issues. This would turn out to be a blessing, as he avoided entanglement in sticky constitutional questions that might have generated an adverse paper trail that would haunt him in the future. A large number of the D.C. Circuit's cases originated in federal agencies. Thomas's management experience at two major federal agencies both lent him helpful background and sharpened his interest in the administrative law cases that came his way. In a speech in February 1991, Thomas said he believed that his years at EEOC provided "tremendous preparation" for the D.C. Circuit. He added, "I say this in retrospect with nothing to gain."

The panels on which Thomas participated would hear oral argument on three or four cases per sitting. At oral argument, Thomas generally was quiet. After reviewing his performance up to mid-1991, *Legal*

Times said of Thomas, "he has often remained silent on the bench." This was consistent with the pattern of his life, stretching back to his days as a new student in high school, college and law school. He knew that it was easier to learn while silent, and that by being silent, he ran far less risk of saying something silly. Throughout his life, every time he rose to a higher level of intellectual competition, Thomas would hold back in public—even when it meant forgoing a prime opportunity to argue and play devil's advocate.

There were notable exceptions to this pattern. In October 1990 his panel took up the case of Clarence Morales, an eighteen-year-old who had pleaded guilty to conspiracy to distribute cocaine base. Morales sought a reduction of the fifty-one-month sentence that was imposed pursuant to federal sentencing guidelines. The policy statement accompanying those guidelines provided that the age and socio-economic status of defendants were irrelevant to sentencing decisions.

Morales' background was much like Thomas's. His father abandoned him. A stepfather who entered the picture insisted that the teenage Morales be sent elsewhere—in his case, a home for juveniles. One notable difference was the death of his mother, who fell off a roof. Morales believed his stepfather threw her off. The stepfather later threatened to kill him.

The assistant U.S. attorney argued that the district court was right not to deviate from the sentencing guidelines. He asserted there was no need to lessen Morales' sentence merely because he was young when he committed his crime and had endured a violent, tragic upbringing. The attorney made the mistake of going so far as to argue that no trial judge would find such a tragic history unusual.

"Wait a minute," Thomas said. "Doesn't that depend on where the judge is—whether he's in suburban Fairfax County or Washington, D.C.?"

One observer recalled that Thomas's statement riveted the courtroom. It was the only question he asked during oral argument. However, Morales' court-appointed lawyer recalled, "he cut straight to the heart of the issue."

Thomas joined the other two judges on the panel in reversing the district court in part. The panel upheld the court's refusal to depart from the sentencing guidelines on the basis of Morales' age, but also ruled that the lower court had erred in concluding it could not consider Morales' "special circumstances."

The case that appears to have provoked Thomas's most extensive participation at oral argument involved racial preferences. *Lamprecht v. Federal Communications Commission* dealt with a policy of the FCC that gave preferential treatment to women applying for television station licenses. Thomas questioned the attorney for the FCC, C. Grey Pash, passionately and at length.

Thomas challenged the presumption that female station owners would offer programming different from that of male owners. "I am left in a quandary or at least at a point where it seems as though we are promoting diversity for diversity's sake, without an explanation as to what effect it will have on the operation of the stations," he told the FCC lawyer. "At least in the case of minorities, there was documented evidence that there was a difference in programming." He noted that female owners do not necessarily use their programming to discuss so-called women's issues.

Pash stated that female owners would have their own "viewpoint and perspective."

"OK. Now, what is that based on?" Thomas asked.

"That is based on the expectation that, because women and other groups—but in this case we are talking about women—have been historically subject to societal prejudices and particular societal attitudes that they ..."

"So, does that mean they will have a different point of view as a result of the prejudice, or they don't own stations because of the prejudice?"

"No," Pash continued, "that means that there is an expectation that, in the aggregate, they will have a different perspective on questions, not on every question, not in every case, but ..."

"Based on what, though? I mean how can you conclude they will have a different perspective?"

"Well, I guess this is going to sound circular, but you can conclude they will have a different perspective, because, historically, they have been subject to prejudice and different societal attitudes, and this has led to their playing a different role in society. They are being treated differently, subject to stereotypes and so forth, and that the expectation is—and I would ... refer you to ... the report of the Civil Rights Commission in 1977 and 1979, in which they talked about how this led to the lack of female participation in broadcast stations, led to different programming, led to programming that maintained stereotypes of women, and ..."

"But how is this expectation any different from a stereotype, if it doesn't have any basis in fact?" Coming from Thomas, the question stung.

"Well, I am not saying it does. I am saying it doesn't have any basis in fact. I am saying that this record doesn't provide factual evidence for it. There certainly is basis in fact that women and minorities have been subject to historical prejudice, have been discriminated against and ..."

"But there is also, with respect to minorities, there is evidence that there is at least a difference in programming in the stations owned by minorities," Thomas noted.

"Well, there is some evidence the Supreme Court said that corroborates it, but we don't read the Supreme Court decision as saying that sort of evidence is necessary."

"OK. Fine. But is there any evidence that there is a difference between the stations owned by women and owned by men?"

"No, there is no evidence in this record...."

"What are women's issues? ... I am at a loss as to what the difference is. You keep referring to diversity. It is diversity in ownership, yes, if you have different people who own radio stations—then there is diversity in ownership. My question goes to what are the consequences of that diversity in ownership, or are we simply using diversity as a proxy for representation in ownership? So, is there some consequence from the difference in ownership?"

"The consequence is that there is an assumption that programming would be different...."

The *Lamprecht* oral argument showed Judge Thomas at the top of his rhetorical game.

As his stature grew, Thomas seemed to treasure all the more his friendships and roots. On November 1, Thomas was preparing to leave for lunch with a couple of clerks. The telephone rang. His secretary told him that Anita Hill was on the line. "I'll get back to her," Thomas said. When Thomas returned her call, they asked each other how they were enjoying their new positions—he with the federal judiciary, she with the University of Oklahoma Law School. She invited him to come and give a speech at her institution.

Two weeks later, he returned to Savannah State College to deliver a speech on what the college denominated "Founders' Day." "My roots are all here," he told the students. "When I look out over the marshes—when I see the magnificent oaks, laden with moss, I can't help but think of the tradition and the values of the people" where he had grown up. He urged them to hone their study skills and shun television, noting that many young people avoid the library "as though it were the Temple of Doom." He asked them to estimate how much time they spent in the library compared with the number of hours frittered away watching TV, "including MTV, soaps and sports. You may exclude all educational and news programs from this estimate." The standard he urged was to spend at least ten "productive hours" in the library every week and forty hours a week of study outside the classroom, and to read one book a month that was not assigned by an instructor.

These were rigors that Thomas expected his own son to meet. In June 1991, Jamal graduated from Bishop Ireton High School, a Catholic school in Alexandria, Virginia, with a B average. This was surely a disappointment to Thomas, but then the goals he had staked out for Jamal to meet, since his infancy, had been wildly unrealistic. A friend of Thomas's remembered Jamal as "a very polite kid" who "seemed very proud of his dad." She added, "He was not always as studious as Justice Thomas would like."

Jamal had matured into a man who resembled his father, with dark skin, full cheeks, and a naturally solid build. Thomas would not permit Jamal to wear an earring, which was becoming fashionable among young men of the time; nor did he approve of rap music, which he termed an "oxymoron."

His classmates liked Jamal so well that they selected him as one of their two graduation speakers. His mother, Kathy Ambush Thomas, flew to Washington to attend the event. Jamal's choice in colleges was quite unusual and suggested some prodding from his eccentric father. He decided to attend the Virginia Military Institute—a curious selection for a young black man. VMI was best known as the old grounds of Thomas J. "Stonewall" Jackson, the school's most famous professor, and the training center for much of the Confederate high command for the Civil War.

In early June, around the time of Jamal's graduation, Thomas entered a ten-kilometer race in Washington to raise money for breast cancer research. He and Boyden Gray of the White House Counsel's Office saw each other and struck up a conversation as they ran shoulder to shoulder down Pennsylvania Avenue. They discussed the ongoing negotiations between the White House and Congress on recent civil rights legislation. Democrats had introduced legislation to restore the legal status quo prior to several recent Supreme Court decisions governing racial quotas and preferences. Bush had called the legislation a "quota bill" the previous year and had vetoed it—the first time a president had refused to sign a civil rights bill. The ensuing criticism greatly bothered the president, who, as Thomas knew, was no enemy of blacks. After a while, Thomas and Gray ceased running and walked together for an hour, talking over the matter. Thomas told Gray he believed the proposed legislation would hurt blacks by encouraging dependency on government and racial preferences.

That Gray thought highly enough of the young judge to seek out his counsel in such a manner was a good sign indeed for Thomas. Administration insiders and informed conservatives knew what Thomas was too modest to admit: He was on the short list for the president's next nomination to the Supreme Court. *National Review,* the nation's leading conservative magazine, openly speculated after Thomas's confirmation to the court of appeals that the D.C. Circuit was merely a way station. The appointment, the magazine said, moved Thomas "closer to a Supreme Court nomination that will doubtless come when Justice Marshall's body goes the way of his mind."

Already within the administration, there was talk about a promotion to the highest court of the land when a vacancy came up. Bush had considered nominating Thomas to the position that opened up in July 1990. The president decided that Thomas needed some seasoning on a lower court and appointed David Souter instead. But Thomas was well placed for the next opening. As Vice President Quayle recalled of Thomas's preparation for the Supreme Court, "Everyone knew what was going on. He was being groomed."

In conversations with friends, Thomas dismissed such analysis and rumors. In January 1991 he wrote a note to Duane Benton, an attorney in Missouri and friend from his days at the Attorney General's Office, mentioning that he had seen himself listed in an article as a potential Supreme Court nominee. "I had hoped that the media would forget about me," Thomas stated. Given his relationship with the media and desire for privacy, these sentiments may well have been sincere.

He demurred similarly in a conversation with Fletcher Farrington, one of his old bosses during his summer of legal work in Savannah. Farrington came to Washington to do some research and depositions in a case and dropped by to see Thomas in his chambers. They visited for about an hour.

Farrington recalled that Thomas "sort of downplayed the idea" of his being elevated to the Supreme Court. He dismissed "all of this stuff you hear about me going over to the big house." Thomas even said he sometimes wondered if he would have served the cause of civil rights better if he had practiced law in Savannah—as Farrington put it, "down here with us in the trenches." Farrington told him "he was nuts," that he was clearly "in the right place."

On June 8, 1991, Thomas returned to Holy Cross for his twentieth class reunion. As he smoked a cigar and reminisced outside the reception, one of his classmates told him, "You're going to be up there on the Supreme Court soon." Thomas laughed. "That's not going to happen," he assured him.

Other classmates, he later recalled, "pummeled" him with questions about the topic. His response was consistent. "I assured them to a moral certainty that no such thing would ever happen."

They and political observers in Washington knew otherwise. Preparation, talent and timing had placed Thomas in an excellent position to see his dreams realized, his vision for the nation written into law. But as his name began to streak across the heavens, another star would rise with his. This one was misshapen and of an odd luminescence; it followed a bizarre trajectory not of its own making. The two unlikely orbs would collide in one of the most spectacular political dramas in American history.

PART FIVE

Accused

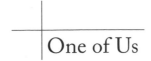

CHAPTER EIGHTEEN

One of Us

Brer Fox tried time and time again to catch Brer Rabbit, and he came mighty near catching him, but time and time again Brer Rabbit got away.

By the summer of 1991, time finally had claimed one of the giants of the civil rights movement, Thurgood Marshall. As counsel for the NAACP, Marshall had argued the winning side in *Brown v. Board of Education.* A little over a decade later, President Lyndon Johnson appointed him to the Supreme Court, making him the first black man to hold a seat there. Even while sitting silently in oral argument, he was an imposing man, with owlish eyes, strong nose and pursed lips that seemed to suggest a continuing disdain for the course of national affairs. Marshall became a reliable liberal on the court, although court insiders noted that as age set in, he became more a fan of daytime television than of grinding out court opinions.

On June 27, Marshall finally deferred to failing health, announcing in a letter that he was resigning from the court. The justice's secretary delivered the letter to the White House at around lunchtime. This set off a commotion and, in short order, a well-coordinated search to find a replacement. That led very quickly to Clarence Thomas.

As Marshall's letter was arriving at the White House, Thomas was shopping with Jamal for some training shoes. He went to his chambers afterward, then left for a late lunch with a former law clerk. Upon returning to the courthouse, one of his clerks informed Thomas of the news: Marshall had announced his retirement; Boyden Gray had called and asked Thomas to attend a meeting at the Justice Department at 4:30 that afternoon.

Thomas arrived at the designated time and, as he recalled, was soon "spirited to the situation room at the Justice Department." It was "a bizarre feeling," Thomas said, to find himself sitting in these sound-proof quarters. At the meeting were Attorney General Thornburgh and Assistant Attorney General Mike Luttig. Since his last service to Thomas in the confirmation battle for the D.C. Circuit Court of Appeals, Luttig likewise had received a promotion: Bush had nominated him to the Fourth Circuit Court of Appeals. They queried Thomas about personal issues that they thought might cause problems, such as his divorce and marijuana use. Thomas also was asked, "Has anyone criticized you and your wife because of interracial marriage?" The meeting lasted approximately forty-five minutes. Luttig's impression of Thomas—accurate, as it turned out—was that he was "scared."

As Thomas was submitting to the first of several such private grillings, John Sununu, Bush's chief of staff, called Tom Jipping of the Free Congress Foundation. Jipping handled legal and judicial affairs for the conservative interest group, which had weighed in on past nominees and had built up a network of grassroots supporters. Sununu informed Jipping that the president's advisers would meet the following morning to recommend a candidate to fill the Marshall seat. Sununu asked that Jipping fax him a memorandum by eight o'clock that evening listing his top three picks and assessing the merits of each.

The year before, Bush had chosen David Souter for his first appointment to the high court. Sununu acknowledged that Bush had settled on Souter to avoid expending the substantial political capital that would have been necessary to confirm a known conservative nominee. Souter was selected with the understanding that the next appointment would be more bold, and therefore would stir up, in Sununu's words, a "knock-down, drag-out, bloody-knuckles, grassroots fight."

With the administration strapping on its armor, Jipping did not allow such a historic opportunity to slip away. He stated unambiguously in his memo which potential nominee most energized conservatives: "Judge Thomas is our first choice." He added, "the *entire* conservative movement not only supports him, but *believes* in him."

Other influential voices from the right spoke up for Thomas. "Once we heard that Marshall was going to step aside, Clarence Thomas was my choice from the very beginning," Dan Quayle recalled, even though the administration "knew it would be a big fight" if the president tapped Thomas. Early in the morning on June 28, Quayle called Jack Danforth

right: Portrait of George Michael Troup at the Georgia Capitol. *(Office of the Secretary of State/Georgia State Capitol)*

below: The King family and their plantation house. *(Midway Museum)*

bottom: This "corn crib," built in 1880, is similar to the cabins that the Thomas family lived in before and after emancipation. This structure today stands approximately two miles from the Thomas sharecropping land near Lovett, Georgia.

above: The hillock of shells behind the Varn factory, descending into the marshes of Pin Point.

right: Myers Anderson, "the strongest man in the world." *(Steven Bisson/Savannah Morning News)*

below: The Anderson house in Savannah, where Clarence and Myers Thomas grew up.

above: Junior class photo from St. John Vianney Minor Seminary, 1966. *(Archives of the Diocese of Savannah)*

left: "Is this high enough, Coach?" was the caption accompanying this photo of Thomas dunking the basketball in his 1967 high-school yearbook. *(Archives of the Diocese of Savannah)*

below: Thomas portraying Simon of Cyrene, the African who helped Christ carry the cross, in a high-school production of the passion play. *(Archives of the Diocese of Savannah)*

above: Photo of Thomas that appeared in his Holy Cross yearbook (the same photo, transposed, appeared in Yale Law School publications). *(Steven Bisson/ Savannah Morning News)*

left: Larry Thompson, Thomas's best friend in St. Louis (photograph from 2001). *(John Disney/Fulton County Daily Report)*

below: Thomas at one of his "whuppings," testifying to a congressional committee in December 1984. *(AP/Wide World Photos)*

above: Ginni and Clarence Thomas in 1991. *(AP/Wide World Photos)*

left: Anita Hill testifying to the Senate Judiciary Committee. *(AP/Wide World Photos)*

above: Thomas responds to Hill's charges, with Senator Danforth (left) and Ginni (right) behind him. *(AP/Wide World Photos)*

right: Cousin Abe Famble and his demonic Anita Hill poster, used in the pro-Thomas march in Pin Point.

right: Clarence and Ginni meet the press outside their home on the night of his confirmation to the Supreme Court. *(AP/Wide World Photos)*

below: Thomas gives a thumbs-up at his swearing-in ceremony at the White House. His son, Jamal (left), and mother, Leola Williams (right), stand with him on the platform. *(AP/Wide World Photos)*

above: "Welcome home" celebration in Pin Point in May 1993. Emma Mae Martin, Thomas's sister, sits second from the right (their mother, Leola Williams, is seated at the far right). In Emma's lap is Mark Martin, the great-nephew Thomas would later rear as his grandfather had reared him. *(Abraham Famble)*

below: Thomas speaks to the American Enterprise Institute in February 2001. The bust of Lincoln given to him stands in the foreground. *(AP/Wide World Photos)*

at his house in Washington. He alluded to the extensive lobbying that Warren Rudman, Republican senator from New Hampshire, had done on behalf of Souter, a native of the Granite State. "Will you do for Clarence Thomas what Warren Rudman did for David Souter?" he asked Thomas's old patron and best friend in the Senate. Danforth assured him that he would.

Later in the day, Thomas remembered, "I was spirited to the White House, by way of a tunnel from the Treasury building." Thomas said it was "kind of clandestine, surreptitious ... sort of like a James Bond movie." Thomas sat in the White House for "a number of hours." Eventually, he was told that if he was not appointed that day, he could assume he would not be offered the nomination. "So I kept my fingers crossed that I wouldn't be nominated," Thomas recalled, with unconvincing self-deprecation.

Before flying up to the family compound in Kennebunkport, Maine, for the weekend, Bush met with Quayle, Thornburgh, Sununu and Gray. Thornburgh said he was impressed with Thomas, but feared a likely backlash from civil rights groups. He also thought the American Bar Association would issue a low rating and milquetoast recommendation. The advice split along racial lines: Thornburgh and Sununu pushed for a Hispanic nominee, Quayle and Gray for Thomas. Bush, Quayle remembered, "went through a great deal" of painstaking deliberations.

On Saturday, June 29, Thomas and Ginni traveled to Annapolis, Maryland, to "celebrate" his not being nominated. The celebration, to the extent it was truly that, would be short-lived. As Bush played golf in Maine, Thornburgh and Gray called him to discuss further the Supreme Court pick. Bush solidified his choice. Pending some final background checks, including a fuller inquiry into his divorce, he was resolved to go with Thomas.

Thomas went in to his chambers on Sunday. Undoubtedly, he did so to lose himself in some work and chase away the blues. After a while, the telephone rang. "Kennebunkport is on the line," one of his clerks informed him.

Thomas picked up the receiver. Soon he was speaking to the man who, by constitutional authority, held the young judge's future in his hands.

The phraseology of the president's invitation was unmistakably Bush. "Clarence," he said, "I haven't figured out the Supreme Court thing. Would you join me for lunch if you're not busy?" Thomas joked years later that his first reaction was to say, "You know, I'm really busy that day."

The next day, Thomas flew out of Andrews Air Force Base with Thornburgh, Sununu and Gray, bound for Kennebunkport. At the D.C. Circuit, Judge Silberman knew of Thomas's travel plans and was thrilled, and in Thomas's absence, he devised a plan to thwart any internal intelligence operations about the trip. The most partisan liberal Democrat on the court, Chief Judge Abner Mikva, had many friends in the press and hoped to be the first to leak the information of Thomas's nomination. Mikva, Silberman recalled, was "intensely curious as to what was happening." As Thomas was en route to Maine, Silberman told Thomas's secretary to keep his door closed. Whenever anybody asked where he was, she was to say, "He's in a meeting." Mikva poked his head in three times, only to receive the disinformation on each occasion.

It was the ninetieth birthday of the president's mother. A large gathering of family members and aides filled the house. The guests overflowed into the yard, where sea breezes gently stroked those who were trying their hand at horseshoes. Barbara Bush spotted Thomas soon after he arrived and welcomed him in her placid, matriarchal voice with a word that said it all: "Congratulations."

With that, Thomas said, "my heart sank. And from then on, it was surreal . . . an out-of-body experience."

President Bush led Thomas upstairs to the master bedroom on the second floor and asked him two questions.

"Can you and your family make it through the confirmation process?"

"If you make it to the court, can you call them as you see them?"

Thomas's response to both was, "Yes."

Bush assured Thomas several times that if he would be confirmed, "I will never criticize a single opinion of yours publicly." The brief, perfunctory interview completed, Bush formally gave him the good news. "Let's go have lunch. I will appoint you to the court at two o'clock today."

The two men emerged from the bedroom for a lunch of crabmeat salad—an improbably appropriate main course for a man whose mother had shucked crabs for a living. As they rejoined the festivities, the assembled well-wishers applauded.

A tall man with a fine, firm chin and a genial smile that was the trademark of successful politicians, Bush led Thomas out from the guest house. His arm rested lightly around the nominee's wide shoulders. It was as if the years of weightlifting, like the years of professional preparation in the law, all had been for this moment. Thomas's jacket swelled from the muscles of his powerful upper body; he very much resembled a retired fullback from his beloved Dallas Cowboys. As Bush stepped to the bank of microphones, Thomas stood behind him, his hands clasped in front of him in the well-trained manner of an altar boy.

"I am very pleased to announce that I will nominate Judge Clarence Thomas to serve as Associate Justice of the United States Supreme Court," Bush told the journalists. He listed the highlights of Thomas's legal career, and offered an observation about Thomas that indicated both the length of their relationship and Bush's skill at judging people:

> I have followed this man's career for some time, and he has excelled in everything that he has attempted. He is a delightful and warm, intelligent person who has great empathy and a wonderful sense of humor. He's also a fiercely independent thinker with an excellent legal mind, who believes passionately in equal opportunity for all Americans. He will approach the cases that come before the court with a commitment to deciding them fairly, as the facts and the law require.

The president concluded, "Judge Thomas's life is a model for all Americans, and he's earned the right to sit on this nation's highest court. And I am very proud, indeed, to nominate him for this position, and I trust that the Senate will confirm this able man promptly."

Then Thomas stepped forward, holding several white pages that flapped slightly in the wind. He had arrived in Maine with some prepared remarks, just in case.

"Thank you, Mr. President," he began. "I'm honored and humbled by your nomination of me to be an Associate Justice of the Supreme Court of the United States.

"As a child, I could not dare dream that I would ever see the Supreme Court—not to mention be nominated to it. Indeed, my most vivid childhood memory of a Supreme Court was the 'Impeach Earl Warren' signs which lined Highway 17 near Savannah. I didn't quite understand who this Earl Warren fellow was, but I knew he was in some kind of trouble.

"I thank all of those who have helped me along the way and who helped me to this point and this moment in my life, especially my grandparents, who are—"

Here, Thomas choked up momentarily.

"—especially my grandparents, my mother, and the nuns—all of whom were adamant that I grow up to make something of myself. I also thank my wonderful wife and my wonderful son."

Thomas then invoked his signature patriotism. "In my view, only in America could this have been possible. I look forward to the confirmation process and an opportunity to be of service once again to my country and to be an example to those who are where I was and to show them that, indeed, there is hope."

In these brief remarks, Thomas already foreshadowed the strategy he would plan and execute for his confirmation battle. His so-called handlers would call it the "Pin Point strategy"—an emphasis on his humble childhood growing up under Jim Crow. Thomas was a far better politician than most of these handlers; he had seen how his life story had spellbound audiences across the country during the many speeches he delivered in the EEOC days. While others would try to arrogate credit for this confirmation strategy, these earliest remarks by Thomas made clear that the "Pin Point strategy" was the creation of the nominee himself.

After the speeches came the first interrogation session from the press. Many of the questions this day were rude. The first was typical: "Mr. President, last year you vetoed the civil rights bill, saying it could lead to quotas. Today you've made a nomination that could be easily seen as quota-based. How do you explain this apparent inconsistency?"

"I don't even see an appearance of inconsistency, because what I did is look for the best man," Bush said. He struggled to find the right words. "I don't accept that at all. The fact that he is black and a minority had nothing to do with this in the sense that he is the best qualified at this time." Many reporters and critics of Thomas would chuckle at this assertion, or even call it mendacious. Bush parried follow-up questions along the same lines.

Thomas was asked his opinion of Earl Warren, whom he had mentioned. Thomas begged off, again demonstrating the caution that had served him well in Washington: "Well, I think that many of the questions that I will be asked during my confirmation process will perhaps bring that comparison out, and I think, out of respect for that process, I'll have to refrain from making that sort of comparison at this time."

"Not even a personal reflection, sir, on what the Warren Court did for minorities?"

"Not even a personal reflection," the nominee said coolly.

Another question directed at Thomas was mean-spirited. "What do you say to critics who say the only reason you're being picked is because you're black?"

Thomas seemed taken aback, bristling slightly. "I think a lot worse things have been said," he replied. "I disagree with that, but I'll have to live with it."

"Refer them to the president," Bush quipped. "How about that for an answer?"

The press corps laughed.

Race, of course, had figured prominently in Bush's decision. Even Thomas's friends and admirers did not bother to try to deny this. Edwin Meese, who remained a friend of Thomas, remembered the reaction to Bush's remarks:

> I do know that a lot of people who are friends of mine and Clarence's at that time thought that perhaps the president was gilding the lily a little bit [in saying Thomas was "best qualified" for the position]. Because they knew that Clarence was very good. But to say that he was the best person was perhaps, some of them thought the president might be stretching it. Or let's put it this way: that the president was influenced somewhat by putting a minority on the court. Because this was Thurgood Marshall's spot.

In private conversations, Thomas acknowledged the discomfort attendant to being Marshall's heir. Not only was he being asked to replace a living legend, but the subtext of race in his appointment was manifest. One friend recalled that Thomas would have preferred that the seat he took not be Marshall's. Thomas "didn't want there to be an appearance—you know, did George Bush pick him because he's black?" In the end, the young judge was left with the opportunity before him—

an extraordinary opportunity that, most likely, would not come around again. In the end, he would not push the nomination away like a wrong order in a restaurant.

Leola Thomas Williams worked two jobs back in Savannah, as an aide at Candler General Hospital and at a nursing home. Between jobs, she returned to her house on June 30 and heard the telephone ringing. "Turn on channel 6. Your son's on it!" a female voice told her. She complied, and soon saw her son standing behind President Bush. A message flashing across the screen informed viewers that he had been nominated to the Supreme Court. Said the nominee's proud mother, "I screamed so loud I dropped the phone."

Journalists fanned out across the country to research the reclusive judge's past. Sister Virgilius Reidy, living at a retirement convent in New Jersey, received a telephone call from a reporter within half an hour of the announcement in Kennebunkport. A "feeding frenzy," in the words of the college's archivist, ensued at Holy Cross. The Maryland court that granted the divorce decree for Clarence and Kathy Thomas did a brisk business.

His fellow judges at the D.C. Circuit congratulated Thomas upon his return. Judge Harry T. Edwards, a liberal Carter appointee, was the only other black member of the circuit. On July 1, he presented Thomas with a cake to celebrate his good fortune.

In private, Thomas admitted that a great apprehensiveness was beginning to descend upon him, ruining the joyful occasion. His immense pride and reputation now faced concerted attacks by powerful enemies, and from multiple angles of approach. He called Alex Netchvolodoff and confided that he had "this fear in the pit of my stomach." At dinnertime, Danforth borrowed the telephone in the Shrine Club of Kirksville, Missouri, to call and congratulate Thomas. The nominee said he was grateful for the honor, but worried about how his opponents might assail him. Danforth suggested that he read the twelfth chapter of Romans: "Repay no one evil for evil, but take thought for what is noble in the sight of all.... Never avenge yourself, but leave it to the wrath of God.... If your enemy is hungry, feed him; if he is thirsty, give him drink."

Danforth recalled of the advice, "I was not able to follow it myself." Nor, it turned out, was Thomas—to his professional betterment.

The gloom settled in more fully in the days that followed. Thomas told Ginni and close friends that he was possessed of the strong feeling that "someone was trying to kill" him. Danforth remembered that Thomas's description of his fears "resembles an extended nightmare or perhaps a scene from a movie thriller." Thomas explained, "The feeling is as though you're waiting in the wilderness for someone with guns to find you and kill you. And that's the way I felt all summer. I felt under siege the entire summer."

At this time, Thomas actually peered through the windows of his house to scour the surrounding countryside for assassins. He surveyed the decks of nearby houses for indications of threats to his life. His behavior would conjure up the famous photograph of one of his heroes, Malcolm X, holding a rifle as he looked carefully out a window for possible—and ultimately very real—menaces. Thomas's conduct, Danforth noted, "may seem paranoid" unless one bears in mind the past racist violence in the South with which Thomas was familiar.

Thomas faced other, broader threats that gave a certain context to his otherwise bizarre actions. By virtue of his nomination to the Supreme Court, he was fully enmeshed in the two most polarizing social issues of his day: race and sex. The main public policies related to these issues were affirmative action and abortion rights. Thomas had staked out strong stands on both, publicly in the case of the former, privately in regard to the latter (as his foes rightly suspected).

Mike Luttig, observing that Thomas "truly treasures his privacy," recounted that Thomas would tell him the reproaches of his adversaries left him feeling "violated." Luttig assured him that the clash of wills over his nomination was purely a "political debate."

"You just don't understand," Thomas insisted adamantly. "These people are after me personally."

On July 4, Thomas and Ginni attended the first of many strategy sessions for his nomination. It was held at Mike Luttig's townhouse in McLean, Virginia. The participants were close confidants of Thomas respected for their political acumen and status in the administration. They included Lee Liberman, Bill Kristol, the new chief of staff to Vice President Quayle, and Ricky Silberman. Under the nominee's auspices, the group divvied up various assignments. Kristol would work with conservative columnists to ensure that the media did not ignore Thomas's message. Kenneth Duberstein, a Washington lobbyist, would coordinate lobbying efforts and arrange the mock hearings to prepare the nominee. Thomas himself would court prominent blacks and black organizations.

Three groups of advisers sprang up subsequently. A large coterie of administration officials met two or three times a week at 9 A.M. on the second floor of the West Wing of the White House. Duberstein chaired the meeting. Attendees included officials from the White House offices of counsel, communications, and public liaison, Quayle's office, and the Justice Department. These larger meetings were mostly to disseminate instructions on how to implement the administration's nomination strategy on such matters as mobilizing grassroots support. Some participants became part of a second circle of advisers that met with Thomas personally and formulated the administration's strategy. These included Luttig, Kristol, Liberman and Mark Paoletta of the White House Counsel's Office, and Ginni Thomas. They met almost every day, often into the evening, on the fifth floor at the Department of Justice building. This group preferred a more muscular public relations effort than the easygoing, insider approach to the nomination adopted by Duberstein. Thomas especially believed they should aggressively work to win over the black community, which he saw as his natural political base. The third cell was a rump group of informal advisers, including Ricky Silberman and other friends, who worked independently of the White House. The last two groups were on the periphery, outside the firm control of the White House. Their more autonomous endeavors reflected conservatives' lingering frustration over the Bork fiasco and their resolution not to be outmaneuvered again.

Thomas's opponents, as the nominee had feared, were hard at work as well. On the day Bush announced his nomination of Thomas, lawyers with the National Abortion Rights Action League (NARAL) stayed up all night poring over the nominee's speeches and writings. Kate Michelman, NARAL's leader, was a woman as intense as her red hair; she had procured an abortion for herself many years before and seemed unable to rest until the remainder of the nation's women followed suit. Patricia Ireland, president of NOW, enlisted Robert Bork's surname in vow-ing shortly after the Kennebunkport announcement, "We're going to bork him." Flo Kennedy, another NOW leader, parroted Ireland: "We have to bork Thomas.... We're going to kill him politically. This little creep, where did he come from?"

Black Americans, by and large, embraced the Thomas nomination. They recognized that he was the only black who was likely to receive the nod from Bush. Quite simply, they preferred a black justice opposed to affirmative action to no black justice at all. Arch Parsons, the veteran black reporter in the Washington bureau of the *Baltimore Sun*, observed tartly, "There is a hell of a difference between a black conservative and a white conservative." Parsons even volunteered to Clint Bolick to serve as a conduit to Benjamin Hooks, the executive director of the NAACP.

Hooks shared the desire to see an African-American on the Supreme Court. At the NAACP convention in Houston in early July, Hooks helped to persuade the organization to defer a decision on Thomas's nomination until its board could meet face to face with the nominee. This decision forestalled any formal opposition from the nation's most prestigious civil rights organization for the critical first month of Thomas's nomination campaign. The delay also stymied the Leadership Conference on Civil Rights, an important cog in the anti-Bork machine, which could not act without a go-ahead from the NAACP.

John Jacobs of the Urban League likewise expressed the common aspiration that blacks be represented on the court. He told the *New York Times*, "I'm trying to deal with the nomination in the context of what our realities are. If Judge Thomas is not selected, what the Administration has proven is that, standing in the wings are a bunch of other folks who are not African-American, who have not had the kinds of life experience that Judge Thomas has had, but who have the same philosophical traits that we criticize in him."

Other black public figures were much less generous. Black Harvard Law insurgent Derrick Bell offered the opinion on the television program *Nightline* that Thomas "looks black" but "thinks white." Carl Rowan, a widely syndicated columnist, appeared on *Inside Washington* and compared Thomas to a former Ku Klux Klan leader who had run for office in Louisiana: "If you gave Clarence Thomas a little flour on his face, you'd think you had David Duke talking." Eleanor Holmes

Norton said on the *MacNeil/Lehrer Newshour* that Thomas lived outside the "black experience in America" (her historically incompetent reign at EEOC did not shame her sufficiently to give Thomas a pass). Spike Lee, the film director then working on his movie biography of Malcolm X, opined that Malcolm X would have called the judge "a handkerchief head, a chicken-and-biscuit-eating Uncle Tom."

Still, polls showed solid black support for the nomination. In a July 5 poll in *USA Today*, 54 percent of blacks supported Thomas's nomination, and only 17 percent disapproved—despite the fact that 52 percent said that Thomas did not represent the views of most blacks. A Gallup poll taken later in the month found that a higher percentage of blacks (57 percent) favored his nomination than whites (52 percent).

Thomas's personal lobbying offensive in the Senate, under the watchful eyes of Duberstein and Danforth, was well under way by the first week of July. Danforth served as escort and facilitator among his Senate colleagues. Joseph Biden, the chairman of the Judiciary Committee, was the first member on whom the pair made a courtesy call. It would be the first of some sixty such visits.

Thomas then met with Strom Thurmond, the committee's ranking Republican. They posed for a photo-op, at which Thomas praised the civil rights movement for helping him to rise to his current opportunity. Sitting next to Thurmond in his Senate office, Thomas told the reporters present that he had "benefited greatly from the civil rights movement, from the justice for whom I am nominated to succeed."

Thurmond handed a pamphlet copy of the Constitution to the nominee and said, "Follow that, and that's all I would ask you to do."

"Thank you, Senator; here is my old copy," Thomas said deftly, pulling out his own pamphlet version from his breast pocket.

When Danforth and Thomas met with Paul Simon, the Illinois senator came away, like so many others, thinking highly of Thomas's personality and demeanor. As Danforth and his charge started to leave Simon's office, Danforth leaned over to Simon and told him, "You'll never get a better nominee from this administration."

The maestro of these operations was Duberstein. Former chief of staff to Reagan in his second term, he had begun his own political consulting and lobbying firm in Washington, which was prospering. The White House, with Thomas's blessing, asked him to "quarterback," in his words, the nomination fight. He had guided Souter through the Senate with relative ease. But Souter was no conservative. Moreover, unlike Bork and Thomas, Souter had left behind no paper trail that could be used to "bork" him. (After a couple of years, Bush got what he paid for in tapping Souter: another Republican Supreme Court nominee defecting to the left, as Earl Warren and many others had done.) Thomas's stated, provocative views posed a far more formidable challenge for Duberstein.

The old Washington hand urged a cautious, cordial campaign designed to ingratiate Thomas with Senate Democrats and the media. At public events, he would offer Thomas impromptu advice. On one occasion, as Thomas walked past a cluster of cameras, Duberstein told him, "Give them a thumbs up." The deferential judge promptly followed the suggestion.

All these gestures of good will did not prevent an ideologically adverse media from zestfully inspecting the conservative nominee. Members of the Washington press corps were overwhelmingly liberal, particularly on social issues such as abortion, issues at ground zero for Supreme Court nominations. Bush's selection of Thomas produced waves of negative stories that crashed against the nominee's pride. In a speech years before, Thomas had praised Louis Farrakhan, the anti-Semitic leader of the Nation of Islam. When reporters uncovered these remarks, Jeff Zuckerman tried to smooth things over by calling Abraham Foxman, the national director of the Anti-Defamation League of B'nai B'rith. Foxman gave him specific instructions as to what Thomas should say to distance himself from Farrakhan. Zuckerman called Bill Kristol and relayed the information. The next day, July 13, Thomas was quoted in the papers making the very statement Foxman had urged. This was still insufficient to gain the ADL's support. Foxman backed away, telling the *New York Times* that Thomas's repudiation of Farrakhan "was welcome, but unfortunately did not go far enough."

For most of July, the nation's newspapers virtually dedicated a column of their front page to unfriendly revelations about Thomas. One was a preemptive strike from the administration itself. The White House leaked to the newspapers that Thomas had smoked marijuana in college. This admission surprised Thomas's close friends from those days, who considered him a wallflower in such matters. *Newsday* reported that Thomas had been slapped with a federal tax lien; the White House explained that this was because of a mathematical mistake on a complicated tax form. "On Monday I was an anti-Semite, on Tuesday I was a pothead, and on Wednesday I was a scofflaw," Thomas complained to a friend after this initial battering.

His first marriage also drew attention. *Time* twice reported that his marriage ended in a "bitter divorce." It offered no evidence and apparently had none, as both Thomas and Kathy remained silent on the subject, and evidence to substantiate such a charge still had not come to the fore over a decade later. Many reporters listened to the tape of their divorce proceedings in the Rockville, Maryland, courthouse; one journalist described the seven-minute tape as "unilluminating." Other reporters staked out Kathy Ambush Thomas's home in Boston, but were granted no interview.

Feminist trepidation over Thomas's apparent anti-abortion leanings ignited concern over his natural law beliefs. St. Thomas Aquinas made a very rare appearance in a national weekly, being featured in a *U.S. News* article entitled, "A higher law for the high court: Would Justice Thomas put God on the bench?"

The hearings promised to be even more taxing. When Antonin Scalia was nominated to the Court in 1986, he refused to answer virtually any questions about the law. But Republicans then were in control of the Senate. After the Democratic takeover later that year, and following Bork's doomed seminar on constitutional law in 1987, there was no turning back for Thomas.

In preparing for the hearings, Thomas labored seven days a week over the briefing books he received from Luttig and the White House Counsel's Office. He met with Luttig in the afternoon and early evening, often for two-to-five-hour stretches; the meetings were either at the Justice Department or, usually, at Thomas's house. On weekends, he camped out in the garage, wearing his standard casual attire of T-shirt and shorts, hunched over his stack of books. Thomas also spent large blocs of time viewing videotapes of the Bork and Souter hearings, studying them and taking notes. When he had trouble sleeping, which was often, he would rise from his bed, insert a tape into his VCR, and escape once again into his work.

Duberstein, Danforth, Luttig and others participated in the "murder boards." Held in Room 180 of the Old Executive Office Building, the mock hearings featured lawyers from the White House and Justice Department seated around a large, horseshoe-shaped conference table. Thomas held the seat of honor in the middle. The panel bombarded him with hostile questions, mining his writings for the most offensive passages.

Luttig was "amazed" at all the vituperation against Congress and praise for Ollie North in Thomas's old speeches. Like Duberstein, he importuned Thomas not to let this happen again. "Voice your anger to me, not to the public," Luttig urged. "Hit me with it. Just let me have it. Just take it all out on me." These verbal sparring matches were intended not only to help him anticipate likely questions, but to deaden the pain that these assaults would inflict on his pride and, possibly, his reputation. Luttig thought these mock grilling sessions important to "smooth the edges of what in front of national television could be perceived as a rougher personality."

The questions Luttig and the other panelists lobbed at Thomas fell into six categories. The main one was "Supreme Court/Constitutional Issues." One-third of the questions in this category related to respect for precedent and the Supreme Court as an institution. Another third addressed natural law and the right to abortion/privacy. The other categories were Thomas's record at OCR; his record at EEOC; affirmative action; criticism of Congress (including his paeans to Colonel North and barbs at Biden); and "personal/miscellaneous," including Thomas's remarks about his sister's welfare dependency.

One question in these sessions displayed an extraordinary presentiment. Duberstein asked Thomas, "Have you ever expressed your views to anyone regarding your views on abortion, either as a policy matter or as a constitutional matter?"

Thomas answered that he had not.

The participants were incredulous. Duberstein pressed him, asking if he had ever discussed the subject even with Ginni. Thomas held firm, insisting he had not and did not have a position on the subject. While he had been present when the subject of abortion had arisen, he had never debated or discussed it or stated a personal view on the matter.

"Oh, come on!" Duberstein and others exclaimed.

"No, I'm telling the truth," Thomas insisted.

Thomas's representations were, of course, inaccurate. He had discussed abortion throughout his adult life with various friends and associates: Mike Boicourt at the Missouri Attorney General's Office, Brad Reynolds, Armstrong Williams and Ken Masugi at EEOC, and presumably many others.

Luttig was dumfounded. "Okay," he asked himself. "What [do] you do with that fact?" If Thomas truly had never discussed abortion, they could not urge him to offer testimony before Congress that was false. They ended up letting the matter go and hoping for the best—but knowing the public would greet these claims as skeptically as they had.

"OK. Not great," was one observer's evaluation of Thomas's performance at the murder boards. "A little bit too cautious, probably." These sessions would prove a faithful predictor of Thomas's testimony when it was finally showtime.

Thomas's talent for politics had its dark side—a disingenuousness that sometimes seeped into dishonesty—but also lent itself well to the task at hand. It was Thomas's idea to employ the "Pin Point strategy" of stressing his impoverished origins in the segregated South. He advocated a further extension of this strategy, a divide-and-conquer effort in which he would curry favor with influential black public figures and lawyers in individual settings. Thomas believed, moreover, that a wedge could be driven between the black community and the nation's liberal civil rights leadership over his nomination. By using the media to go over the heads of these leaders, Thomas and his supporters could reach and appeal to the people who had always been his base: working-class black folk.

Thomas would lead this particular multipronged effort personally. One important gambit was a meeting in midsummer at the home of Connie Newman, a black friend of Thomas's from EEOC. She invited Louis Sullivan, secretary of health and human services, Rev. Joseph E. Lowery of the Southern Christian Leadership Conference and two other SCLC board members, and Walter Fauntroy, the District of Columbia's congressional delegate. The meeting lasted almost three hours.

Lowery and the others were given the opportunity to ask questions of the nominee. They homed in on Thomas's record at EEOC and the court of appeals. Thomas defended and clarified his positions, and assured them he would be an ally once on the Court. According to Lowery, Thomas told them they "would not be disappointed with his stewardship record if he was confirmed."

"I believe in the things you and Dr. King have stood for," Thomas told them. "I have drunk from the bitter cup of racial discrimination." He said he embraced the principle of affirmative action. He mentioned his past sympathies with the Black Panthers.

"I have suffered discrimination," he said. "I know what it means to be black."

The bravura lobbying effort worked. Lowery, for one, concluded that "it would be a mistake politically for him to be confirmed and not to have dialogue with him." He and SCLC, Dr. King's civil rights organization, ended up making the "pragmatic decision," as Lowery put it, to support Thomas's nomination.

The Urban League was neutralized at around the same time. On July 21, the group announced it would not take a position on the Thomas nomination.

Thomas presented his case to the NAACP leadership in the third week of July, meeting in Washington with Hooks and several board members. The nominee declined to discuss specific legal issues that might come before him. Still, with that careful tap dance, Thomas "came across as being a brother," in the words of one person present.

Ultimately, the NAACP's opposition could not be averted. But to counter its expected vote against the nomination, the independent pro-Thomas forces worked with the administration to muddy the news cycle. On July 31, the NAACP board of directors was scheduled to meet in Washington and deliver a lopsided vote against Thomas—but they would have to contend with a show of solidarity from Thomas's folks back home.

Clint Bolick and his Landmark Center for Civil Rights chartered a bus to carry Thomas supporters from Georgia to the nation's capital. Many were his old friends from Pin Point and Savannah. Roy Allen, a childhood friend from St. Benedict's who had been elected a Democratic state legislator, led the delegation. Forty-seven people made the ten-hour bus ride. Over a breakfast of scrambled eggs, they gathered in Thomas's honor, hugging him, posing for pictures. One House waiter requested Thomas's autograph on a napkin, saying he already had Thurgood Marshall's.

"I couldn't go home, so you all brought home to me," Thomas said repeatedly. They regaled him with stories of picking scuppernongs and tying barbed wire out on the farm in Liberty County. Senator Nunn appeared and made some brief, noncommittal remarks. The group later went to the Senate to buttonhole senators on behalf of their old friend. Asked by Senator Herbert Kohl why Thomas should be confirmed, Jackson Fuller, a ninety-one-year-old distant relative, said of Thomas, "He's a fine, obedient young man." When the NAACP voted 50–1 against Thomas later in the day, and the AFL-CIO announced its opposition two hours later, news of the Georgia contingent helped to offset these damaging developments.

Thomas managed to peel off individual NAACP chapters around the country in defiance of the national organization's position on his nomination. Chapters in Compton, California; East St. Louis, Illinois; and Liberty County, Georgia, announced their support for Thomas's nomination. Compton NAACP president Royce W. Esters explained, "We need to move away from the belief that American owes me something or else I'm going to steal." The national headquarters threatened to suspend the rebellious local officials if they did not rescind their decisions. After some negative publicity about the intimidation, the national headquarters backed down.

Thomas also wooed black attorneys in Washington and elsewhere. The *Washington Post* noted on August 9 that Thomas had personally launched a "carefully orchestrated" campaign of meetings "with a broad spectrum of America's black lawyers." As a result, his nomination had "torn the usually tight-knit community asunder." Thomas sought out meetings, lunches, or telephone conversations with prominent African-American lawyers. Most who supported him mimicked Lowery's explanation, offering what the *Post* called the "give-the-brother-a-chance" rationale.

This view ultimately did not carry the day at the National Bar Association, the nation's oldest association of black attorneys. The group's indecision reached the level of self-parody: The judicial selection committee voted against Thomas, 6–5; the board of governors then voted in favor of Thomas, 23–21; finally, the NBA convention rejected his nomination by a vote of 128 to 124. All of the close votes and flip-flops underscored Thomas's strength among black professionals and the black community overall.

William Coleman, for his part, struck an agreement with his daughter Lovida and the White House. He would not take a position on Thomas's nomination if Lovida would do the same, and if the Thomas forces would not bring up his complimentary letter from 1989 in support of Thomas's nomination to the court of appeals.

These efforts solidified Thomas's critical standing among blacks. A *Business Week* poll in early September found 56 percent of blacks supporting Thomas, 31 percent opposed. Thomas's support had solidified over the summer.

The majority support Thomas received from the black community split the liberal coalition that had defeated Bork. With civil rights organizations divided over his nomination, Thomas could focus on defeating the other, potent portion of the liberal opposition: feminist organizations.

In the emerging struggle over Thomas's nomination, feminist leaders were unwilling to subordinate their agenda to that of blacks and civil rights organizations amicable to Thomas.[*] Both groups had

---

[*]The resulting black-feminist schism over the Clarence Thomas nomination was not the first of its kind, but rather a reprise of a similar breach after the Civil War, when women and blacks bitterly competed for power in a postwar society dominated by white men.

Before the war, blacks and women's suffragists were united. Frederick Douglass attended the Seneca Falls Convention in 1848 and seconded the motion by Elizabeth Cady Stanton to proclaim the goal of women's suffrage. He also championed the cause indefatigably in his newspaper, the *North Star*. After the South's surrender, Congress tailored the Fifteenth Amendment to safeguard the right to vote for blacks but not for women. A nasty falling-out ensued.

The prior alliance of blacks and suffragists came undone. Stanton announced her opposition to the amendment, saying it "cannot with justice be passed" because it failed to include suffrage for women. In 1869, at the annual meeting of the Equal Rights Association in New York, Douglass pleaded for feminist support for the amendment. He made his case powerfully: "When women, because they are women, are dragged from their houses and hung upon lamp-posts; when their children are torn from their arms, and their brains dashed upon the pavement; when they are objects of insult and outrage at every turn; when they are in danger of having their homes burnt down over their heads; when their children are not allowed to enter schools—then they will have an urgency to obtain the ballot equal to our own."

requested and received affirmative action; there was some inherent tension in vying for greater portions of this pie. Most obviously in the Thomas hearings, feminists also fought to preserve sexual rights obtained from Supreme Court rulings, especially the right to an abortion established in *Roe v. Wade.*

On this issue, civil rights groups and, according to polls, most blacks parted company with them. Timothy Phelps, a reporter for *Newsday* who covered the Thomas nomination, reflected on the times, "There was a sense of desperation in the women's rights movement when Clarence Thomas was nominated" because of the looming threat to *Roe.* Civil rights groups, on the other hand, were unwilling to join in a crusade for abortion rights. Phelps explained, "Many of the ministers active in the NAACP were fervently opposed to abortion.... As a whole, the liberal coalition was not about to spring into a battle led by women's groups under the banner of abortion."

Feminists decided to set their own course and seek to derail Thomas themselves. NARAL, Phelps reported, "mounted the strongest lobbying effort" of any organization, spending in excess of $100,000 on TV commercials that discussed the threat to abortion rights but not Thomas by name. Abortion rights groups also badgered Senate Democrats. One Democrat on the Judiciary Committee, Dennis DeConcini, recalled that opposition to Thomas came more from feminist groups than from black or civil rights organizations.

Thomas knew where his most deep-seated enemies lay, which was why he had been so careful and deceptive on the subject of abortion. Pro-*Roe* lobbies thought they had found a smoking gun in Thomas's kind words about the Lewis Lehrman *American Spectator* article on the

---

A person in the audience shouted, "Is that not all true about black women?"

Douglass replied, "Yes, yes, yes; it is true of the black woman, but not because she is a woman, but because she is black."

The suffragists resorted to bigoted invective. Susan B. Anthony said the cause of blacks had to take second place to that of women. She argued, "if intelligence, justice, and morality are to have precedence in the government, then let the question of women be brought up first and that of the Negro last." Women's rights advocates cast slurs such as "Sambos" and "ignorant barbarians" upon their erstwhile friends to describe black men who would receive the vote instead of them. Before the adjournment of the 1869 meeting, the suffragists voted to dissolve the Equal Rights Association and form a new, separate National Women's Suffrage Association.

right to life in his 1987 speech to the Heritage Foundation. Danforth quickly countered, on behalf of the nominee, that these remarks were merely a "throwaway line," intended to express good wishes to his host for the occasion. Danforth said he had discussed the matter with Thomas, who "assured me that he has not prejudged any case that might come before the Supreme Court, and that he has formulated no views on the relationship between natural law and abortion." The Lehrman article would resurface in the hearings.

One ally of the pro-*Roe* groups did Thomas a favor by attacking Thomas's past Catholicism. Governor L. Douglas Wilder of Virginia told the media, "The question is, 'How much allegiance is there to the Pope?'" Wilder, who was black, said that the Senate hearings should pay attention to Thomas's position on abortion because "he has indicated he is a very devout Catholic." Wilder apologized for the comment soon after it turned into a national flap. Sister Virgilius Reidy, Thomas's spirited middle-school principal, called the statement a "stupid remark" and upbraided Wilder to a reporter as a "silly man."

Thomas also was fortunate in the enemies arrayed against him on the Judiciary Committee. Many of the Democrats were not exactly choir boys. Ted Kennedy, so effective in leading the drive against Bork, was politically neutralized this time because of his recent, sex-related misadventures in Palm Beach, Florida; his nephew, William Kennedy Smith, had been accused of raping a woman on the same night that Senator Kennedy was observed walking along the beach naked from the waist down. Joe Biden had done poorly in law school, and had dropped out of the 1988 presidential race after a videotape surfaced showing he had plagiarized part of a speech and even biographical material from Neil Kinnock, the leader of the British Labour Party. The Senate Ethics Committee had criticized Dennis DeConcini of Arizona for improperly lobbying federal regulators on behalf of financier Charles Keating, from whom he had received $81,000 in campaign contributions. Howard Metzenbaum, ever accompanied by a cloud of suspicion, had accepted a $250,000 "finder's fee" for locating a buyer for a Washington hotel. He returned the money after the story broke, but denied any wrongdoing.

This ethically challenged opposition was a windfall to Thomas, one that he would greatly need. At the end of August, the American Bar

Association released its rating of Thomas: twelve members of the committee voted him qualified; two voted not qualified; one did not participate. It was the lowest rating received by a Supreme Court nominee since 1955. Marlin Fitzwater, the president's spokesman, spun the issue well, saying only that the administration was "very pleased that the [ABA] has found Judge Thomas qualified to be an Associate Justice of the United States Supreme Court."

Meanwhile, the pro-Thomas forces lined up some impressive endorsements. Formal letters of support came in from a number of law enforcement organizations grateful for Thomas's rulings on the court of appeals: International Association of Chiefs of Police, National Sheriffs' Association, National District Attorneys' Association, D.C. Black Police Caucus. Ginni's old employer, the U.S. Chamber of Commerce, came through for him, as did the Knights of Columbus, a Catholic fraternal order. The National Association of Criminal Defense Lawyers, on the other hand, opposed Thomas because of, among other things, his "dangerous 'natural law' philosophy" and its possible effects on *Roe v. Wade*.

Conservative lobbies also geared up for the fight. Paul Weyrich, a former journalist who had helped establish the Heritage Foundation and who gave Jerry Falwell's Moral Majority its name, lent a hand from the Free Congress Foundation. Other organizations became involved, many of them religious. They included Gary Bauer and the Family Research Council, Phyllis Schlafly's Eagle Forum, Concerned Women for America, and Rev. Louis Sheldon's Coalition for Traditional Values. Bauer and Bill Kristol hatched the idea of funding independent ads in the manner the left had used to good effect against Bork. Under Bauer's leadership, the Citizen's Committee to Confirm Clarence Thomas raised half a million dollars for this purpose, funds used largely on television ads in deep Southern states to turn up the heat on crucial Southern Democrats in the Senate. Bauer and Bolick joined forces in this crusade—one a Christian conservative, the other a libertarian, united in affection for a nominee they believed would represent their views effectively and faithfully. Rev. Pat Robertson's Christian Coalition also chipped in more than $1 million for TV commercials.

On the eve of the hearings, Thomas was indeed in a commanding position. He and his supporters had marshaled substantial resources for the pending fray, including energized grassroots support and money for national advertising. Most important, Thomas had brought much of the civil rights community over to his side and held a solid majority of support among African-Americans in public opinion polls. Things were breaking the right way.

Even as he further scattered his divided foes, their criticism roiled his soul. Ginni observed that the charges "devastated" him. He was convinced his opponents were trying to "destroy" him. He "took each charge personally; each one was affecting him in a deeper and more personal way than she expected."

And the hearings had not even begun.

CHAPTER NINETEEN

Into the Quagmire

Then one day, Brer Fox went to work and got him some tar. He took the tar and he mixed it with some turpentine, and he fixed up a contraption that he called a Tar-baby.

On the day Thomas accepted the nomination at Kennebunkport, Susan Hoerchner, a workers' compensation judge in Norwalk, California, returned home from work and turned on the television. She learned of his nomination from the TV news. Hoerchner's thoughts quickly turned to her friend from Yale Law School, Anita Hill. She remembered a conversation with Hill from around the time Hill began working for Thomas at the Department of Education, in which Hill complained that Thomas had pressured her to date him. She distinctly recalled Hill using the term "sexual harassment" in describing her boss's behavior. Hoerchner decided to try to locate her old friend in Oklahoma.

With the help of directory assistance, Hoerchner reached Hill at her home in Norman. She asked if Hill had heard of Thomas's nomination, and expressed her own outrage, pointedly referring to Thomas as a "pig." She tried to determine if Hill intended to come forward and tell her story. Hill was evasive.

Hoerchner next asked if Hill would object to her relating the story to others. To this, Hill assented.

Three weeks later, Hill called another friend from Yale, Gary Liman Phillips, who was practicing law with the Federal Communications Commission back in Washington. In the course of a casual conversation, Phillips asked Hill what she thought of her former boss's nomination to the high court. Hill replied that she had left EEOC and Washington because Thomas had sexually harassed her.

Thus Anita Hill set into motion the forces that would make her a reluctant national celebrity and ruin the latter half of Clarence Thomas's life.

Hill's furtive allegations of sexual harassment bubbled through the Washington social circuit over the summer. At a dinner party, either Phillips or an associate mentioned Hill's story to leaders of the Alliance for Justice. This liberal interest group had opposed Thomas's placement on the court of appeals and now was working to defeat his latest promotion. The Alliance for Justice officials passed the information along the anti-Thomas grapevine to a staffer for Howard Metzenbaum. Gail Laster, an attorney on Metzenbaum's staff, was directed to follow up and investigate. Ricki Seidman, a staffer for Ted Kennedy, also caught wind of Hill's accusations and pursued them separately.

Laster spoke to Hill by telephone on September 5. "Do you know anything about allegations of harassment at the EEOC?" Laster asked. "We have heard rumors to that effect."

Laster specifically raised the issue of whether Thomas had harassed female employees. She did not ask Hill directly if Thomas had harassed her. Hill encouraged Laster to investigate the charge of sexual harassment, and left it at that. She offered no information about Thomas or her dealings with him.

The next day, Seidman followed up. She reached Hill and asked her about rumors that Thomas had harassed her. Hill would neither confirm nor deny the allegations, but instead asked for more time to think about the sexual harassment issue. On September 9, Seidman called again, assuring Hill that the committee "could accommodate her request for confidentiality." Apparently realizing that her gossip was spreading beyond her control, Hill asked Seidman if she could refer her to an expert in sexual harassment law. Seidman suggested that she speak to James Brudney, an attorney on Metzenbaum's staff. Seidman may have known that Brudney had been a year ahead of Hill at Yale, and that Hill and Brudney had socialized together in the early 1980s while both of them worked in Washington.

The next morning, as the curtain rose on the confirmation hearings, Brudney would be hard at work on behalf of Senator Metzenbaum.

After amassing and dissecting some eight hundred pages of articles, speeches and other writings by and about the nominee, Senate Democrats gathered with their Republican brethren on September 10 to commence the nomination hearings for Clarence Thomas. These would be held in the historic Senate Caucus Room, a place whose last great moment of national fame had occurred four years earlier, when Ollie North delighted Thomas by going on offense against his congressional hosts. The Caucus Room was in the Russell Senate Office Building, an edifice with which Thomas was very familiar, having worked there for Danforth during his days as a Senate staffer. The Caucus Room itself, with its thirty-five-foot ceiling and large Corinthian columns of black-veined marble, gave a certain Greco-Roman feel suggestive of a gladiator pit.

Thomas strode into the hearing room arm in arm with Strom Thurmond. His attire was a patriotic medley of a dark blue, two-piece suit, crisp white shirt and red tie. He followed Duberstein's advice and shook hands with each member of the committee. Then he took his place at the long witness table, which was covered with bouquets of microphones. Beneath the sound equipment was a green felt cloth, intended to muffle sounds other than the testimony. Behind Thomas were Ginni, Jamal, and his mother, brother and sister.

Biden banged the gavel and brought the hearings to order. He was a bright, engaging and loquacious man with thinning brown hair and a flawless, ear-to-ear smile so rapid and reflexive as to resemble a tic. To Biden's left sat the committee's seven Democrats; to his right were the Republicans. Committee staffers, mostly recent college or law school graduates, sat in a row behind the senators, their backs to the ornate wall. Aside from offering a youthful backdrop for the hearings, they would be seen occasionally passing notes with advice or messages to their bosses.

Thomas stood and sternly raised his right hand.

"Judge Thomas, do you solemnly swear to tell the truth, the whole truth, and nothing but the truth, so help you God?" Biden asked.

"I do," he said.

Thomas returned to his seat and delivered an opening statement consistent with the Pin Point strategy: "Much has been written about my family and me over the past 10 weeks. Through all that has happened throughout our lives and through all adversity, we have grown closer and our love for each other has grown stronger and deeper. I hope these hearings will help to show more clearly who this person Clarence Thomas is and what really makes me tick." He spoke of life under poverty and Jim Crow. In his arresting baritone voice, he described his hardscrabble childhood: his days in Pin Point playing in the creeks and marshes, life with his mother and the Savannah tenement, the nuns and the Catholic schools, his grandparents and the racial indignities he saw them suffer. He praised Marshall for "knock[ing] down barriers that seemed so insurmountable to those of us in the Pin Point, Georgias, of the world." The nominee also paid homage to Martin Luther King Jr., the NAACP, and Rosa Parks. He added: "A judge must not bring to his job, to the court, the baggage of preconceived notions, of ideology, and certainly not an agenda, and the judge must get the decision right. Because when all is said and done, the little guy, the average person, the people of Pin Point, the real people of America will be affected not only by what we as judges do, but by the way we do our jobs."

Senator Biden, after thanking him for a "moving statement," then commenced the questioning, some of the most incisive the nominee would face.

Biden first brought up a speech Thomas had made to the Pacific Research Institute. In it, he noted, Thomas had said he found "attractive" the arguments of Stephen Macedo, a professor at Harvard, recommending judicial activism from the right and urging the federal courts to strike down laws that unduly restrict property rights. Biden apparently neglected to read on: Later in the speech, Thomas said he disagreed with such activism.

Instead of pointing out that the remarks were taken out of context, Thomas promptly began his day-long practice of distancing himself from his old writings. "I found Macedo interesting and his arguments interesting, as I remembered," Thomas stated. "Again, it has been quite some time."

"You indicated that you find the arguments—not interesting—

attractive," Biden countered. The chairman pressed Thomas as to what about them he found attractive.

Thomas leaned into the microphone. "As I indicated, I believe, or attempted to allude to in my confirmation to the Court of Appeals, I don't see a role for the use of natural law in constitutional adjudication. My interest in exploring natural law and natural rights was purely in the context of political theory."

When Biden asked why he had cited these thinkers, Thomas's explanation went to the heart of his worldview and jurisprudence: "My purpose was this. . . . You and I are sitting here in Washington, D.C., with Abraham Lincoln or with Frederick Douglass, and from a theory, how do we get out of slavery? There is no constitutional amendment. There is no provision in the Constitution. But by what theory? Repeatedly Lincoln referred to the notion that all men are created equal. And that was my attraction to, or beginning of my attraction to this approach. But I did not—I would maintain that I did not feel that natural rights or natural law has a basis or has a use in constitutional adjudication."

Biden asked the same question another way, trying to finagle testimony more responsive to his concerns about natural law. Thomas replied by bringing up the discriminatory laws that held his grandfather and mother down to low wages. In doing so, Thomas was advancing the Pin Point strategy by weaving it into his testimony, even while simultaneously ducking the hard questions.

Biden's voice rose slightly, betraying some annoyance. "But he [Macedo] doesn't argue about any of those things, Judge."

"I understand that," Thomas said. "I read more explicit areas. I read about natural law even though my grandfather didn't talk about natural—"

"But, I mean, isn't it kind of—I guess I will come back to Macedo."

Rebuffed, Biden next turned to a statement Thomas had made in a speech to the American Bar Association. Thomas had argued that economic rights merit protection from the courts just as much as other civil liberties. Biden noted that this was in error as a matter of positive law. The Supreme Court had held that laws restricting economic rights were subject to a rational basis test, rather than a tougher standard of judicial review such as strict scrutiny, which was reserved for limitations of other civil liberties. "Can you tell me, can you enlighten me on how this was just some sort of philosophic musing?" Biden asked, some-what vaguely.

Thomas again explained that his "interest in this area started with the notion, with a simple question: How do you end slavery? By what theory do you end slavery? After you end slavery, by what theory do you protect the right of someone who was a former slave or someone like my grandfather, for example, to enjoy the fruits of his or her labor?" Thomas emphasized that this was a political theory that would not influence his interpretation of the Constitution. Once again, he managed to work his grandfather into the discussion. Later on, Biden would feel compelled to invoke his "grandfather Finnegan" to even things out.

Eventually, Biden reached the main course. "Now, Judge, in your view, does the liberty clause of the 14th amendment protect the right of women to decide for themselves in certain instances whether or not to terminate pregnancy?" This would be the first of some seventy questions about *Roe v. Wade* asked in the hearings.

"My view is that there is a right to privacy in the 14th amendment," Thomas replied. This position was significant: Conservatives generally would not concede this much, believing instead that the right to privacy (which is not mentioned in the Constitution) is purely a judicial invention.

Biden then asked whether Thomas thought that within this right was a constitutional right to an abortion.

"I do not think that at this time that I could maintain my impartiality as a member of the judiciary and comment on that specific case," Thomas said in what would become a mantra. This was a dodge—by logical extension, no constitutional issues ever could be discussed—but one that convention had decreed to be acceptable in such hearings.

Biden brought up the Lehrman article. Thomas parried. He said that his analysis of the article was not relevant from "a constitutional adjudication standpoint."

The chairman tried another tack. The 1986 Working Group on the Family, on which Thomas served, had criticized the Supreme Court's decisions over the last twenty years concerning the right to privacy. He asked for the nominee's thoughts.

Thomas again skirted the issue, this time with testimony that frayed his credibility. He had attended a number of "informal meetings" of the

Working Group, he said, and had focused on low-income families. Only in regard to low-income families and the problems confronting them had Thomas submitted his "views" to the group for publication in its final paper.

"Did you ever read the report, Judge?"

"The section that I read was on the family. I was only interested in whether they included my comments on the low-income family."

"But at any time, even after it was published?"

"No, I did not."

Biden's skepticism showed. "You haven't to this moment read that report?"

"To this day, I have not read that report." Thomas said he had merely "provided a significant memo, I believe, on low-income families and families that I felt were at risk in the society. . . . I do not remember there being any discussion of the final draft."

"Well," Biden replied, "I have much more to ask you, Judge. . . . But, quite frankly, at this point you leave me with more questions than answers. . . ."

Thomas's responses to Biden's queries about the Working Group were the first of many that week that would dent his reputation as a forthright man.

Friendly questions from Republicans gave Thomas further opportunity to display his sharp political skills. In response to a question from Strom Thurmond on restricting death penalty appeals, Thomas gave an even-handed, populist answer worthy of any member of the political chamber he was addressing: "I would be concerned, of course, that we would move too fast, that if we eliminate some of the protections that perhaps we may deprive that individual of his life without due process. So I would be in favor of reasonable restrictions on procedures, but not to the point that individuals—or I believe that there should be reasonable restrictions at some point, but not to the point that an individual is deprived of his constitutional protections."

Thomas's response to Thurmond's question about victims' rights showed equal adroitness: "I think that there are concerns on both sides. From the standpoint of the victims, that is important. But there are also the constitutional rights of the criminal defendant."

When the committee and the nominee took a brief recess, Danforth headed for "the stakeout," the cluster of reporters and TV cameras where partisans for and against Thomas would offer their "spin" on the testimony just heard. Jipping and Ricky Silberman also were there. They pointed out that Biden had lifted the Macedo quotation out of context.

Paul Simon stepped outside the Caucus Room, where he met an indignant Rosa Parks. She took strong exception to Thomas's praise of King. "With what he stands for, he shouldn't be permitted to use Martin Luther King's name that way!" she exclaimed.

Thomas needed the break as much as anyone. For all his rhetorical footwork, he seemed nervous throughout the initial round of questioning. He paused often and sometimes labored to piece together the right sentences. The murder boards had predicted this, as well as bleaker moments still to come.

On the same day that Thomas was sworn in as a witness, Anita Hill's old friend from Yale, Jim Brudney, called her. A former law clerk for Justice Harry Blackmun (author of the *Roe* opinion) and one of Metzenbaum's most trusted warhorses, Brudney was a man on a mission. The two reacquainted themselves before turning to the business at hand.

Hill began by stressing she did not want her allegations to become public knowledge. Brudney would not be denied so easily. In order to help, he said, he needed specifics of Hill's charges against Thomas—topics and language he used, as well as certain graphic scenes. Brudney said he thought the disclosure might "ruin" Thomas. Her story, he opined, might "quietly and behind the scenes" force Thomas to withdraw his nomination.

Hill gave him some tantalizing details. Brudney said in response that he recognized the seriousness of her allegations. He offered assurances that the matter could be handled discreetly, perhaps in a closed session of the Judiciary Committee.

After hanging up the telephone, Brudney scurried down from his fourth-floor office in the Dirksen Senate Office Building to the Senate Caucus Room. He called two Metzenbaum aides out of the room and informed them of the latest developments.

Brudney later would claim to a Senate investigator that he never mentioned Hill's name to Metzenbaum. Hill would categorically deny this. Brudney, she said, "reported our conversation to Senator Metzen-baum, who told him to refer me to Senator Biden as chair of the committee."

The following morning, Brudney spoke to Harriet Grant, the Judiciary Committee nominations counsel. He told her that a former female employee at Education and EEOC stood ready to allege that Thomas had committed sexual misconduct against her. He wondered if she would call Hill. Grant refused. Standing committee guidelines required that a person with a complaint against a nominee initiate communications with the committee. Brudney telephoned Hill later in the day and told her that she would need to call Grant to trigger this review process.

As Hill was being drawn further into the quagmire of her own making, Brudney's boss led off the questioning shortly after 10:00 A.M.

"Good morning, Judge Thomas. Nice to see you again," Metzen-baum fairly snarled through a taut, forced smile. "Judge, I have made no secret of the fact that I have serious concerns with many of the things in your record," he added. Thomas had handed him, at last, some powerful ammunition. The senator went over Thomas's contortions from the day before—on *Roe* and the right to privacy, on not reading the Working Group report. "And I will be frank; your complete repudiation of your past record makes our job very difficult."

Thomas responded by noting that he had indeed granted many interviews and written many things in the course of his public career. Ginni, he related, had said to him that "to the extent that Justice Souter was a 'stealth nominee,' I am 'Bigfoot.'"

The judge tried to placate the committee with a questionable pledge. "I can assure you—and I know, I understand your concern that people come here and they might tell you A and then do B. But I have no agenda. . . . I don't have an ideology to take to the Court to do all sorts of things."

Senator Dennis DeConcini was less confrontational. Consistent with the demographics of his native Arizona, he questioned Thomas about the attention he had paid to Hispanic issues while at EEOC. Here, the sailing was easier. Thomas could enumerate the many special outreach efforts he had made: new satellite offices in predominantly Hispanic communities, bilingual public service announcements, posters and brochures. He omitted from the list the affirmative action hiring of Hispanics he had once urged.

The senator who drew the most blood from the nominee, through sheer doggedness, was Patrick Leahy of Vermont. A pale and balding man with a smooth demeanor, Leahy came prepared to focus almost single-mindedly on Thomas's views on *Roe*. By the time he had finished, Leahy succeeded in doing what so many others could not: finally pin him down on abortion.

Leahy followed up on questions about the Lehrman article, asking Thomas if he had read it.

"I think I skimmed it, Senator." Thomas added that he had not re-read it for the hearings. This was the first sign of trouble.

Leahy asked whether Thomas discussed or debated *Roe* at Yale Law School after it was handed down.

Thomas replied: "The case that I remember being discussed most during my early part of law school was I believe in my small group with Thomas Emerson may have been *Griswold*, since he argued that, and we may have touched on *Roe v. Wade* at some point and debated that, but let me add one more point to that. Because I was a married student and I worked, I did not spend a lot of time around the law school doing what the other students enjoyed so much, and that is debating all the current cases and all the slip opinions. My schedule was such that I went to classes and generally went to work and went home."

Leahy would not accept this. "Judge Thomas, I was a married law student who also worked, but I also found, at least between classes, that we did discuss some of the law, and I am sure you are not suggesting that there wasn't any discussion at any time of *Roe v. Wade*?"

"Senator, I cannot remember personally engaging in those discussions."

"OK." Leahy continued his line of attack. "Have you ever had discussion of *Roe v. Wade*, other than in this room, in the 17 or 18 years it has been there?"

"Only, I guess, Senator, in the fact in the most general sense that other individuals express concerns one way or the other, and you listen and you try to be thoughtful. If you are asking me whether or not I have ever debated the contents of it, that answer to that is no, Senator."

"Have you ever, in private gatherings or otherwise, stated whether you felt that it was properly decided or not?"

"Senator, in trying to recall and reflect on that, I don't recollect commenting one way or the other. There were, again, debates about it in various places, but I generally did not participate. I don't remember or recall participating, Senator."

"So you don't ever recall stating whether you thought it was properly decided or not?"

"I can't recall saying one way or the other, Senator."

Arguably, Thomas already was being inconsistent. He stated on the one hand that he had never "debated the contents of it." Yet he went on to say he did not recall whether he had ever expressed an opinion on *Roe*—which would mean he could not remember debating the contents of it. Either he did or did not remember; a consistent answer was not supplied.

Leahy pressed on. "Well, was it properly decided or not?"

"Senator, I think that that is where I just have to say what I have said before; that to comment on the holding in that case would compromise my ability to—"

"Let me ask you this: Have you made any decision in your own mind whether you feel *Roe v. Wade* was properly decided or not, without stating what that decision is?"

"I have not made, Senator, a decision one way or the other with respect to that important decision."

Then Thomas, perhaps out of simple fatigue, shed his normal caution and strolled right into the very middle of this quicksand. "Senator," he offered, "your question to me was did I debate the contents of *Roe v. Wade*, the outcome in *Roe v. Wade*, do I have this day an opinion, a personal opinion on the outcome in *Roe v. Wade;* and my answer to you is that I do not." Even when he cited the case in his writings, Thomas said, he "did not and do not have a position on the outcome." As predicted at the murder boards, these representations about *Roe* proved a laughingstock.

Seeing Leahy's success, Biden tried to pile on. He asked about *Eisenstadt v. Baird,* the 1972 case which struck down a law regulating the retail distribution of contraceptives. Given that it was an archaic case unlikely to come before the Court, Biden believed Thomas owed the committee an explanation of his position on the case.

Thomas again claimed he could not answer. He said, "I think that for a judge to sit here without the benefit of arguments and briefs, et cetera, and without the benefit of precedent, I don't think anyone could decide that."

"Well, Judge, I think that is the most unartful dodge that I have heard," Biden retorted.

Thomas recovered somewhat as the day went on. Simon asked him to explain an ostensible contradiction in his persona. Simon said that he saw "two Clarence Thomases. One who has written some extremely conservative and I would even say insensitive things—maybe you wouldn't agree with that description—and then I hear the Clarence Thomas with a heart. . . . How do I put those two Clarence Thomases together, and which is the real Clarence Thomas?"

"Senator, that is all a part of me," Thomas said with a resonant, yet somewhat tired, voice. "You know, I used to ask myself how could my grandfather care about us when he was such a hard man sometimes. But, you know, in the final analysis, I found that he is the one who cared the most because he was honest and straightforward with us, as opposed to pampering us, and prepared us for difficult problems that would confront us."

This recovery was not enough to salvage his performance that day, which even his friends recognized as abysmal. Thomas later complained of having to "play sort of rope-a-dope," an analogy recalling the great boxer Muhammad Ali's strategy of absorbing blows simply to tire out the opposition. He later reflected on his testimony with a candor that deserted him at the time, admitting, "There is an inherent dishonesty in the system. It says, don't be yourself. If you are yourself, like Bob Bork was, you're dead."

Many of Thomas's supporters gave harsh reviews of his testimony. Paul Weyrich remembered that Thomas had expressed an opinion on at least abortion in prior meetings with him. He found Thomas's lack of candor "disingenuous" and "nauseating." A man of probity who recently had been instrumental in sinking John Tower's nomination to be secretary of defense over the nominee's adultery, Weyrich seriously considered withdrawing his support of Thomas. Jipping talked him out of it, arguing that Thomas's responses were cagey but not false. Other Thomas friends, including Larry Silberman and Larry Thompson, thought his answers seemed robotic and inauthentic for a man who enjoyed the rhetorical back-and-forth of such settings.

Thomas had not provably lied under oath; there could be no perjury prosecutions for his slippery answers. Later, Thomas critics would distort his testimony and allege he had denied ever "discussing" *Roe* with anybody. He did not say this, and he would have perjured himself if he had. He was careful to say he had never "debated" the case—in other words, discussed it with a person of opposing viewpoint. No witnesses would emerge in the hearings or subsequent decade to contradict this narrow claim. He also denied having an opinion on *Roe* "this day." This was a subjective matter that could not be disproved, and that therefore was beyond the rebuke of Anglo-American criminal law.

Still, in his desire to avoid any entanglement with *Roe,* the issue that most threatened his nomination, Thomas had offered strained and misleading testimony that would cost him. He had embraced the tar-baby that his opponents had set before him. "His credibility was destroyed, and he needed that credibility later on," observed Clint Bolick. Thomas foes took out an advertisement in *Legal Times* asking people with whom Thomas had discussed abortion to come forward. Fortunately for the beleaguered nominee, no one emerged.

The day after Thomas's *Roe* meltdown, Anita Hill was taking steps that would similarly unravel her credibility. On September 12, she called Harriet Grant and emphasized yet again that she wished to offer her allegations anonymously. She hoped, however, to "remove responsibility" from her shoulders and hand it over to the committee to investigate. When Grant conferred with Biden, he declined her request. He would not circulate "some anonymous charge," in his words. Committee rules required that Hill drop her demand for anonymity.

Brudney did his best to pressure her. He called her thirteen times in as many days between September 10 and September 23. Throughout, he urged her to comply with Biden's terms and, to the extent necessary, come forward publicly.

On September 16, witnesses lined up for and against Thomas in the

Senate Caucus room. The intellectual elite he had been regularly assailing in his speeches formed the mass of opposition. Included in these platoons were a representative of the ABA and professors from Ivy League law schools. In Thomas's camp were people such as Roy Allen, Margaret Bush Wilson, and Griffin Bell, former attorney general in the Carter administration.

Hill, meanwhile, called Susan Hoerchner and asked her to contact Harriet Grant. Hoerchner spoke to Grant the next day and confirmed that Hill had complained to her of sexual harassment at work in the spring of 1981. Like her friend, Hoerchner requested anonymity.

Pro- and anti-Thomas witnesses continued their procession into the Caucus Room on September 17. Sister Virgilius Reidy, Father John Brooks of Holy Cross, and representatives from NAACP chapters in Compton, California, and Liberty County, Georgia, testified. Guido Calabresi of Yale Law School broke ranks with his fellow liberals and volunteered to testify for Thomas. He said later he was "very angry that many people were saying Clarence Thomas was dumb" in the context of the affirmative action debate. He considered this "stereotyping" that was "the liberal equivalent of Willie Horton."

In response, more Ivy League law professors arrived to bolster the anti-Thomas forces. Most eminent was Erwin Griswold, former dean of Harvard Law School. Also, the first wave of feminist activists took their place at the witness table. One was Judith Lichtman, the president of the Women's Legal Defense Fund.

Lichtman also was active behind the scenes with Hill. At Brudney's instigation, Hill had sought the counsel of Susan Deller Ross of Georgetown Law Center. Ross then, with Hill's permission, conferred with Lichtman. Two feminist reporters described Ross and Lichtman respectively as a "well-known feminist" and a "feminist leader." Both women were ardently opposed to Thomas (the nominee's evasions on *Roe* only deepened their concerns). Ross prodded Hill to press the Judiciary Committee about its inaction on her complaint.

On September 19, as the hearings wound to a scheduled close, a frustrated Hill called Grant again. She informed Grant that she was willing to relinquish her demand for anonymity. Hill inquired about the next step in the process. The next day, the last day of scheduled hearings, Grant told Hill that her allegations, though confidential, would be reported to the FBI for investigation. This again spooked Hill, who hesitated. She decided to ponder her next move again. It quickly was becoming apparent that her overriding concern was attacking Thomas anonymously without subjecting herself to exposure.

As the day ended—what he thought was the last day of his ordeal—Thomas and Ginni left for a weekend away from Washington, staying in a hotel on the eastern shore of Maryland, then taking a ferry to Cape May, New Jersey. Senator DeConcini later estimated that as of that moment, Thomas would have had above sixty votes, enough to break a filibuster.

Over the weekend, Hill talked to Shirley Wiegand and Leisha Self, fellow professors at Oklahoma Law School. Hill had "quiet convictions about women's rights," Wiegand later recalled in assessing her politics. Hill also sought more counsel from Ross, who thought that if she did present her allegations publicly, Hill should prepare a written statement documenting the details. By Sunday night, having consulted her new feminist advisers and Brudney, Hill decided to do so.

The next morning, after a night of sleep she described as "fitful," Hill arose early. She spent four hours typing a factual summary, which she intended to be an affidavit. True to her work product over the years, the document contained typographical and grammatical errors, which Hill later blamed on the stress of having to "relive" Thomas's behavior. She failed also to draft an affidavit competently. Although the document began with the words, "I swear," she failed to have it notarized. As a result, posterity would be constrained to refer to the hybrid document awkwardly as a "statement." She faxed it to the Judiciary Committee later that Monday.

By evening, Hill returned home to her three-bedroom ranch-style house of pink bricks to find a message on her answering machine from the Oklahoma City office of the FBI. Two FBI agents, one male and one female, arrived at her home subsequently and interviewed her for forty-five minutes.

Thomas, in the meantime, knew nothing of Hill's machinations. He would have but two more comparatively restful nights of sleep.

On Wednesday, September 25, at 9:45 A.M., Lee Liberman picked up the telephone and called Thomas from the White House. Biden had alerted the administration regarding the FBI investigation. After reading the FBI report of its interview with Hill, Liberman told Thomas he needed to contact the bureau regarding certain allegations that had been made. Despite Thomas's urgent questions, she would not go into details so as not to compromise the investigation. "Don't worry about it," she assured him. "Just answer it honestly and we will talk about it afterward."

Thomas's reaction, in a word, was "panic."

Five minutes later, he called Mark Paoletta at the White House Counsel's Office—"really upset," in Paoletta's recollection. Although Thomas knew he could not ask about the allegations, he was desperate for a friendly voice to talk to. "He just seemed destroyed," Paoletta said.

Thomas called to arrange a meeting with the FBI. Two FBI agents came to his home two hours later. After the three were seated, the interview was conducted between Thomas's front door and the dining room table.

"There's an allegation of sexual harassment," the male agent said. He told him his accuser was Anita Hill.

"Anita?" Thomas said. "You've got to be kidding. This can't be true."

As the agent read Hill's statement, every accusation was a lash that ripped into his reputation. "I could have cried, I was so hurt," he remembered. It was, he said, "like my own child accusing me of something."

The agents asked him about every allegation. Thomas recalled that he had been dating another woman when the harassment allegedly occurred. Hill had stayed in contact with him after she left EEOC, Thomas mentioned. He had helped her obtain her position at ORU Law School. She had even given him a ride in her Peugeot when he visited ORU several years later.

Butch Faddis, a friend of Thomas's from Missouri, arrived at his house right after the FBI agents departed. A shell-shocked Thomas told him that a former employee had accused him of sexual harassment. "Butch, I'm as low as a hog's belly," Thomas said.

Faddis, after learning more about the allegations, thought it was not a major matter.

"You don't understand," Thomas insisted. "You don't understand what these people will do to me.... For a black man, a single black man, this is the ultimate way to destroy ... It's a smear that you can't get off." As Thomas worried about the stain to his good name, Faddis was struck by the fact that "there was never a waver"—nothing in Thomas's response to suggest that the allegations might be true.

Danforth called Thomas after he heard the FBI had finished the interview. Thomas again denied Hill's allegations. Danforth said ominously that whether or not the charge was true, he would support Thomas "to the end."

Thomas and Faddis went out to the patio, reminisced, and barbecued hamburgers. They took a long drive down to the Potomac and sat on its bank, where they talked about their lives. Faddis recalled they discussed the problems in Faddis's life as much as the tempest now enveloping Thomas. When Thomas did discuss Hill's allegations, Faddis found two things especially noteworthy. Thomas never denigrated Hill. And he asserted, "If Gil Hardy was here, this wouldn't be happening right now."

With the investigation under way, Thomas said, "I started destroying myself." He checked through a mental inventory of his moral inadequacies. The list he came up with was deeply revealing about how he viewed his own life. He censured himself for drifting from religion after leaving the seminary; for breaking his marital vows and divorcing his first wife; for watching pornographic movies as a law student; for having "dated quite a bit" in the mid-1980s. Such a bill of particulars showed a very keen sensibility about morality and an unusual ability to detach himself and render such judgments objectively. He even wondered if the ordeal besetting him was a punishment for past sins.

On the morning of Friday, September 27, Thomas received another dose of bad news. *Legal Times* published an article about the *Lamprecht* case, in which Thomas had been an active and impressive participant at oral argument. Thomas had drafted and circulated an opinion in the case in June, several weeks before Bush nominated him to the Supreme Court. Thomas's draft opinion, the newspaper reported, would have overturned the FCC's decision to bestow an FM radio station license on a female owner in Maryland. The FCC had awarded her the license in an effort to promote diversity in ownership. Thomas found this policy inconsistent with a Supreme Court decision handed down the year before striking down certain racial preferences. The article suggested that Thomas purposely had held the opinion back to prevent an accretion to his paper trail.

The leak of Thomas's draft opinion to the media could only have come from a fellow judge on the circuit or a court employee. By far the most likely culprit was Abner Mikva, a partisan liberal who would later leave the bench to serve in the White House Counsel's Office under President Bill Clinton. He was a dissenter in the case and therefore had access to Thomas's opinion. He also contributed articles regularly to *Legal Times*. Mikva admitted talking to the paper, but supposedly only after the reporter had possession of Thomas's opinion. Judge Silberman and five other judges called for an internal investigation at the court of appeals; no such probe took place. Even from the fraternal confines of the judiciary, hard, low blows were being thrown at the nominee.

As senators on the Judiciary Committee began to peruse the Hill statement and FBI report, some of Thomas's allies were understandably alarmed. Arlen Specter, Republican senator from Pennsylvania and supporter of *Roe,* was a key Thomas backer whose confidence now was somewhat shaken. When he learned of the twin looming threats to Thomas—the Hill accusations and the *Legal Times* article—he asked Danforth to arrange for Thomas to meet with him. In Danforth's office, Thomas flatly denied Hill's charges and insisted he had not intentionally withheld the *Lamprecht* opinion. Thus assured, Specter returned to the committee and voted in favor of his nomination.

At around 11:30, Biden stepped out of the Judiciary Committee meeting to inform the nominee he was a "no" vote. It was based on a purely political calculus, Biden said: He could not risk placing another conservative on the court. Biden pledged that if Hill's accusations or the *Lamprecht* opinion became an issue, he would be Thomas's "most adamant and vigorous defender." The Hill allegations, Biden said, had "no merit" in his eyes.

The committee deadlocked on Thomas's nomination, casting a 7–7 tie vote. DeConcini was the only Democrat to join Republicans in voting for Thomas. Biden did as promised and joined the anti-Thomas half. But he added magnanimously, given the accusations swirling behind the scenes, "For this senator, there is no question with respect to the nominee's character, competence, credentials or credibility."

Thomas and the White House had expected to fare better than a tie vote. Now, they had lost some of their momentum going into the vote of the full Senate. They did not then realize that even with this unwelcome development, they had yet not come close to bottoming out.

———

In the first week of October, Thomas's opponents grew desperate. A vote of the full Senate was pending, possibly as early as that Friday, October 4. Metzenbaum convened a meeting in his offices on Wednesday, October 2. Kennedy and Simon attended, along with staffers, to discuss a final strategy to defeat the nomination.

Afterwards, hushed hallway conversations between senators, their aides, and friendly lobbyists obliquely raised the "Oklahoma thing." Simon and Kate Michelman had such a conversation; so did Brudney and Wade Henderson of the Washington office of the NAACP. Henderson would later admit being uncomfortable with the Hill allegations, saying he believed they played to a "racist stereotype." Lichtman raised with Ross the possibility of delivering the story to Nina Totenberg, a fellow feminist who was a journalist and commentator on National Public Radio.

George Mitchell and Bob Dole, the Senate majority and minority leaders, tried to schedule a vote. They worked to fashion a unanimous consent of the chamber's members for a full Senate vote on the nomination by the end of the week, before the Senate broke for a ten-day recess. Metzenbaum, seeking delay, objected to and thwarted the unanimous consent request. "In this business, it's never over till it's over," he told one reporter.

On the same day that the last-minute strategy session was held in Metzenbaum's office, Timothy Phelps, a reporter with *Newsday*, received a note while sitting in the Senate press gallery. A senator wished to speak to him. Phelps had been pursuing the Hill story since mid-July, when he heard of the rumors from Alliance for Justice lobbyists and Senate staffers. He promised the source who gave him Hill's name that he would not ask her directly about the sexual harassment charges. Phelps called Hill several times to try to establish rapport. She did not volunteer the information, and Phelps was left with what limited information he already had.

His conversation with the senator on October 2 changed everything. The senator, whom he identified as an opponent of Thomas's, had summoned Phelps to give him a tip about a possible negative story on Thomas. Phelps asked the senator if he had any hopes of defeating Thomas's nomination.

"Not unless someone with important information who is insisting on keeping it confidential comes forward publicly," the senator told him.

"You mean the law professor from Oklahoma?" Phelps asked.

The senator's eyes "opened in amazement," Phelps recalled. "How did you know about that?" the senator asked.

"What exactly is she saying he did?" Phelps followed up. The senator backed away and terminated the conversation, shaking his head to indicate he could not discuss the matter further.

Phelps concluded he was now released from his vow not to ask Hill about sexual harassment. A senator had independently raised the subject, "albeit unintentionally and indirectly." This senator, almost certainly, was Metzenbaum.

Phelps called Hill on October 2 and 3 to ask about her allegations of sexual harassment. Pursuant to advice from Charles Ogletree, a law professor at Harvard who was now advising her, Hill told Phelps that she would not discuss the subject until he could prove he had a copy of her statement. This strategy, designed to prevent reporters from bluffing her, made it imperative that Phelps or another journalist capture the statement itself.

On Saturday, October 5, the senator with whom Phelps had spoken previously proposed to break the logjam by simply leaking Hill's allegations to him. The senator proposed the following scheme: Phelps would call Hill and ask her to call the senator, and then she would give the senator permission to share the information. The gambit failed when Hill refused to go along. Late in the afternoon, after this effort proved unsuccessful, a "trustworthy" source—presumably the same senator—informed Phelps of the essence of Hill's charges. The behavior of this unnamed offender again suggested someone with tarnished ethics and a deep animus toward Thomas—the most likely candidate, again, being Metzenbaum.

Nina Totenberg had been working separately on the same story. She had the advantage of being someone, in Hill's words, whose "voice I had heard many times over the radio" on NPR, a liberal, publicly funded radio network. Totenberg tried to establish common ground with Hill by bringing up the allegations of sexual harassment she had leveled while working at the *National Observer* years before. Totenberg left out the fact that an editor at the *Observer* had discharged her not for making allegations of sexual harassment, but for plagiarizing from an article in the *Washington Post*.

The charm offensive from Totenberg met a brick wall. As the two reporters jostled to break the story first, Hill remembered Totenberg as exhibiting "exasperation" with her, while Phelps remained more pleasant.

On the morning of October 5, a frustrated Totenberg called Ricki Seidman. Hill's statement, she told Seidman, had become indispensable for obtaining Hill's cooperation. Seidman called Brudney and told him that Hill would not speak to Totenberg unless she first produced evidence that she had Hill's statement. Brudney had elicited from Hill his own copy of her statement on September 25. He told her this was preparatory to writing a memorandum to Metzenbaum on the matter.

Meanwhile, Hill called her old colleague from Education and EEOC, Michael Middleton, in Missouri. She asked if he had heard anything about possible press stories. He had not. He then learned from Hill, for the first time, of her allegations against their former boss.

Within an hour of calling Seidman, Totenberg had received Hill's statement by fax. She was soon on the telephone again with Hill, reading her statement to her. At that point, Hill relented and granted Totenberg one of the interviews of the century.

The chain of events and available evidence would leave little doubt that Brudney, with the knowledge and backing of Metzenbaum, faxed Hill's statement to Totenberg. When asked a decade later who had leaked the Hill statement to the media, one prominent Democrat stated flatly, "It was Metzenbaum." This Democrat explained, "My staff, his staff, and enough staff people knew exactly who it was. His staff did it." This witness further expressed the belief that this act could not have been the work of a rogue Metzenbaum staffer, especially given the bad blood between the senator from Ohio and the nominee. "Metzenbaum," as Hatch later noted, "really couldn't tolerate a conservative African-American."

Thomas already was shattered. His good name, according to Danforth, was his "most prized possession." He knew it would soon be lost forever. Even so, there was some rough justice, or at least predictability, in the way events would unfold. Three of Thomas's greatest shortcomings of character were his inflated pride, questionable relations with women as his marriage was coming apart, and penchant for stretching the truth. Hill, who had come to know him during the most troubled period in his life, would make allegations that struck right at this Achilles' heel.

The many traditional Christians and Jews who enthusiastically supported Thomas's nomination might have found in their creed a divine hand or explanation behind these developments. Thomas himself believed that Hill's destruction of his reputation represented punishment for sins past. Others might have concluded that Thomas's sins were ongoing. Under hostile questioning, Thomas had retreated from the religion of his youth on crucial issues. He had refused, for example, to defend the sanctity of life in the womb, as defined by the Judeo-Christian tradition. He might well have lost his nomination fight had he answered honestly; the continued support of blacks likely would have determined the outcome. Regardless, by this spiritual theory, Thomas had denied his Maker and the natural laws in which he was instructed. So, too, would Thomas now be denied.

CHAPTER TWENTY

Soul Food

"You just took and jammed yourself on that Tar-baby without waitin' for any invitation," said Brer Fox; "and there you are and there you'll stay till I fix up a brush pile and light it on fire, cause I'm going to barbecue you this day, for sure."
Then Brer Rabbit talked mighty humble.

The weekend began cheerfully enough for the nominee. Duberstein authorized Thomas to drive his Corvette again (for weeks, Thomas had mothballed it in the garage to fend off questions about his lifestyle). "We have the votes," Duberstein had assured him—60 to 65 by his tally. The day would end in a very different spirit.

Early in the evening, Lee Liberman called Thomas to inform him that *Newsday* had the Hill story. A crestfallen expression came over Thomas's face as he gripped the receiver to his ear. After the call ended, he commenced a chain reaction of panicked calls: to Duberstein, Liberman again, Paoletta, Gray. Agony soon subsided enough to permit consideration of his next move. Even in the midst of this storm, Thomas seized upon a smart and forceful response. He told the White House that he wanted them to release to the media a list of the other women who had worked for him—women he believed would be anxious to speak kind words for their ex-boss. Thomas himself drew up a list. The administration decided to hold it for the time being.

The following morning, Sunday, October 6, National Public Radio aired Totenberg's exclusive interview of Hill. The Sunday television talk shows, so important for shaping public opinion, were abuzz with this latest, scandalous twist in the Thomas confirmation fight. Thomas believed he should issue a written statement categorically denying Hill's allegations. Duberstein talked him out of it. Guided by optimism later proved preposterous, Duberstein asserted that such a statement would "give the story legs."

By that point, the story already had "legs" the size of those that once supported the Colossus of Rhodes. In fairness, other experienced Washington observers also miscalculated the impact of these developments. The latest issue of *Newsweek*, fresh off the presses, carried an intriguing item that gave grounds for cautious hope. Below an openly anti-Thomas article entitled, "Supreme Conservatism," which featured side-by-side photographs of a burning cross and anti-abortion protestors angrily pointing at some unseen provocation, was a smaller piece, "A Problem for Clarence Thomas." It reported the Hill allegations that had just broken, but questioned whether they would do any lasting damage. The article even ended sympathetically: "The whole matter may blow over as a sordid chapter in Washington hardball. But nothing has ever been easy for Clarence Thomas."

As the crisis entered its second week, Ginni noticed that Thomas had largely ceased to eat. He was surviving on an apple a day. "The humiliation factor," as she described his plight, was "killing him." Over and over, he repeated to her and other intimates, "Why are they trying to destroy me?"

From the time of his nomination, Thomas had apprehended that something terrible—something mortal, in his eyes—lay in the bushes, awaiting an opportunity to waylay him. "These people are going to try to kill me," he had said. "I hadn't done anything to them, but they are going to try to kill me. And so I was always waiting to be killed. I mean literally waiting to be destroyed in some way."

Early in the afternoon, Paoletta came over to watch football with Thomas. To reach the house, he had to brave the roadblock of news vans and satellite dishes lining the street. At one point during his stay, a photographer peered through the window.

The Clarence Thomas hunkered down inside was no longer the fun-loving man with the "big, booming laugh." Instead, Paoletta observed, "he was just totally very sad, like he had lost all hope." A "listlessness/hopelessness" cast a pall over him and his guests. It assumed various forms: Thomas would sit silently, then pace, then doze off for some spell in front of the tv. Paoletta ate two bowls of Ginni's chili while

Thomas ate none. They sat mostly in silence until Paoletta's wife picked him up at around eight o'clock that evening.

The following Monday morning, October 7, Senator Hank Brown of Colorado called Hill to investigate the charges himself. The senator had what he described as an "extended conversation" with Thomas's accuser. What Brown heard was not the emotionally charged story that one would expect to hear from the victim of traumatic events. Rather, he listened quizzically to an articulate woman dryly reciting the components of a sexual harassment claim. He recalled:

> She went through the story in detail, meticulously, like a lawyer would, like she was reading from a brief. And the reason I say that is because she went through the elements like a law student would recite the elements of a crime. It was obviously very lawyerlike and very thorough and very organized. It wasn't like an emotional event had happened to you. It was a very formal recitation.

Brown further described Hill's account as "almost mechanical." Brown, a savvy lawyer and politician, noted, "In talking about an event that occurs in somebody's office, you very seldom hear someone think about or describe it in terms of the elements of a crime." Hill's odd manner raised questions in Brown's mind about her allegations.

The Senate Democratic Caucus met and debated its posture on the Hill affair. Biden was straightforward and deferential to the wishes of his fellow Democrats. He asked the caucus, "What do you want to do? Do we want to string this out? Do we want to move it along?" He advised expediting matters. Other Democrats disagreed, stating cynically, "Let's stretch it out. This is a good issue." Their hope, recalled DeConcini, was to "defeat [Thomas] and stick it to the White House and the president." Alan Dixon of Illinois then spoke. Dixon had promised Quayle, a friend since their days together in the Senate, to support Thomas. Consistent with this pledge, he argued that the Senate "should act right away." He stated, "This is serious. We should act right away and be decisive." The caucus ended up deciding in favor of a "quick re-hearing" devoted to Hill's charges and Thomas's response.

At 11:00 A.M., Hill held a press conference in a classroom at OU Law School. Students and fellow teachers served as a friendly backdrop. She added little in the way of new information, but demonstrated that she was an impressive and believable speaker. Ginni watched the news conference and came away thinking Hill looked credible. She agreed with Thomas that he should issue a public statement. Again, however, Duberstein, Danforth and others in the White House vetoed the idea.

Two events would occur on this otherwise grim day to give hope to Thomas and his backers. Paoletta began to follow through on Thomas's idea of calling other female employees. He thumbed through his Rolodex and called women who had worked with Thomas over the years. The first twenty to twenty-five women he called were unanimous in their disbelief and dismay at Hill's allegations. They were willing to come forward and defend Thomas publicly. A counterattack was taking shape.

Old telephone logs also were dug up at EEOC and the court of appeals. They offered evidence that, for many Americans, would greatly undermine Hill's story. Carbon copies of telephone message slips documented the fact that Hill had called Thomas eleven times from 1984 to 1990. Furthermore, the content of the messages themselves did not suggest any queasiness about being around Thomas. Hill left such messages as, "Just called to say hello. Sorry she didn't get to see you this week." One message mentioned his new marriage. Another left the telephone number of the hotel where she was staying while in Washington.

In these message slips, the Thomas forces possessed hard, unassailable evidence directly undermining Hill's claims. Duberstein's first preference was to deliver the logs to the *Washington Post* confidentially and allow the paper to run an article about them. The *Post* refused to do so, however, unless it could report that it received the documents from the White House and Thomas supporters. This was a peculiar demand, as the *Post* and all other major newspapers routinely published articles based on confidential information without revealing their sources. The White House judged this a double standard; worse still, Duberstein feared the *Post* might convert the story about the logs into an article on administration efforts to smear Hill.

Duberstein opted for another approach. Alan Simpson, Republican senator from Wyoming, was to be interviewed that evening on ABC's *Nightline*. He would appear opposite Totenberg. A tall, lanky cowboy with an avuncular manner and a tendency to offer rambling, if good-humored, malapropisms, he would become one of Thomas's most strenuous supporters on the Judiciary Committee. At Duberstein's request, he agreed to raise the issue of the logs on the air in his debate with Totenberg. The program and subsequent row outside the TV studios became a metaphor for the passions that ruled in both the Senate and the press over Thomas's nomination.

The first portion of the show was devoted to a brief rehashing of how Hill's allegations came to light. As the canned segment discussed Totenberg's success in bringing down an earlier Reagan nominee to the Supreme Court, Douglas Ginsberg, over his use of marijuana, Simpson could see Totenberg on a studio monitor. He took notice of what he judged a "smug expression." He proceeded to lambaste her on the air for attack journalism and ambushing Thomas with last-minute, unproven allegations. As journalists were not used to being on the receiving end of such televised exchanges, Totenberg was not amused.

Following the program, as he walked out of the studio, Simpson saw Totenberg speaking to Senator Simon and his wife. "I want to tell you something, Nina," he said, interrupting their cordial conversation. "What I said in there, don't take it lightly. I meant every word of it."

She let loose with a string of obscenities, then entered a waiting car and sped off, leaving in her wake a signal lesson in press bias.

Clarence and Ginni spent Monday night and all the following day at the four-story Georgetown house of Larry and Ricky Silberman. The refrigerator was stocked with champagne bought in anticipation of a happier occasion. As Thomas's appetite periodically recovered, his hosts offered to order Chinese food or takeout fried chicken. Inevitably, the telephone would ring with more bad news for the nominee. He would lose his appetite again, and the cycle would repeat.

Thomas's grief over the loss of his reputation had not diminished. "Why, Ricky?" he asked of his friend. "You know how I am. Why would anyone do this to me?"

It was a version of the anguished, urgent query he would raise with countless people over the next ten years. Why, indeed, was Hill doing this? Subsequent testimony and events would make clear that her story was riddled with inconsistencies and falsehoods. While Thomas was not a markedly candid man himself, as his earlier testimony had demonstrated, few chinks, by contrast, would emerge in his testimony over her specific allegations.

Hill's possible motivations were plentiful. Thomas had shunted her aside at EEOC when she failed to prove her worth in the tottering agency he inherited, while others such as Allyson Duncan prospered at her expense. Hill was left flailing about in meetings, shuffling his papers, trying futilely to make herself look useful when she plainly was not. Eventually, she parlayed her connection with Thomas into substantial professional advancement—a law professorship with better income, status, work hours, and proximity to home. But the resentment over her fall from grace in Washington probably simmered.

Hill was a feminist. Professor Self, her friend at OU Law School, described her as such, and said she harbored "quiet convictions about women's rights." Early press accounts erroneously described her as a Republican with conservative tendencies. She was, in fact, a registered Democrat and a typical liberal law professor. Thomas was a severe threat to *Roe* and other prominent liberal and feminist causes.

Her career revealed a pattern of blaming her job failures, which mounted over time, on racial and sexual discrimination and harassment. This pattern apparently first cropped up in her conversation with Hoerchner in 1981. At ORU Law School, Hill attributed student complaints about her unpreparedness for class to racism. She would level similar recriminations at OU several years later, when she left amid much smoke and fire. Throughout her career, Hill would make such charges to deal with employment troubles as a squid emits ink to ward off prey. "Anita's whole life revolved around racial or sexual discrimination," observed a law professor and former visiting faculty member at OU. "Everything was sexism or sexual harassment, she was obsessed with it.... Every failure in her life was due to discrimination. She would say she left Washington because she was sexually harassed. And she would say she was racially discriminated against at Oral Roberts."

Hill may have told Hoerchner in 1981 what she thought was a harmless lie. She might have intended for the falsehood to excuse her professional failings to date or to engender sympathy; maybe Thomas had been inattentive or brusque to her that particular day. By this theory, the lie metastasized into something she had not anticipated. Unquestionably, she did not wish to be dragged into the national spotlight, but sought to torpedo Thomas's nomination from the shadows. Still, this explanation could not account for everything—for example, her casual statement about Thomas harassing her to Gary Liman Phillips shortly after the nomination. This latter rumor-mongering was not necessary for her to save face, and appears to have been premeditated.

Of course, many motives may have been at work. One of the most obvious explanations for her conduct was simple jealousy. She was only a few years behind Thomas at Yale. Thomas had used his Yale law degree as the launching pad for a legal career that led to a nomination to the Supreme Court. Her career had been a disappointment. She had bounced around among jobs; her indolence and prickly personality had forced her to rely on the beneficence of friends—Gil Hardy, Clarence Thomas—to obtain new positions when she wore out her welcome. By attacking Thomas, she would lose an employment reference and helpful contact. But by the time the dust had settled, she would be a national celebrity, and would no longer need him.

On Tuesday, October 8, the Senate had to decide how to deal with a situation that was rapidly mushrooming into a national spectacle. Biden had retreated into a fully defensive posture. As he walked by some reporters on his way from the Senate floor, he declared, "The Judiciary Committee did not screw up on anything." Other Democrats similarly ran for cover. Most Democrats who were previously "yes" votes were peeling off. Duberstein estimated 47 votes for confirmation as the day began.

The Thomas camp executed the first stages of a counterattack. Danforth called a press conference to release and highlight the telephone logs discussed by Simpson the night before. A letter from Phyllis Berry Myers also was distributed. She disputed Hill's bizarre claim at her press conference the day before that she did not know Myers and vice versa. Both were on Thomas's small personal staff at the same time, Myers noted, and they attended staff meetings together.

The White House also released an affidavit by Thomas that flatly denied Hill's charges. Thomas's statement was the product of extensive revisions and discussions earlier in the day. Thomas's first draft specifically addressed Hill's allegations. Working with Larry Silberman and a half-dozen senators and staffers on the other end of the phone line, Thomas edited the affidavit, reducing it to a general denial. Nevertheless, by afternoon, the number of solid votes for confirmation had plummeted from 60 to 41.

Danforth and other senators met in late afternoon in Senator Mitchell's office to reach an agreement on how to handle the Hill controversy. Normally an unflappable man, Danforth erupted at the latest chicanery as he referred to his tireless work to broker a compromise between the White House and Senate Democrats on a new civil rights bill. Danforth noted that the same moderate Democrats who were withholding votes expected him to take the lead in facilitating this agreement. He angrily told them, "this makes me really mad. . . . Senators threatening not to vote or vote no unless we have the delay are the ones who say to me every time I come on the floor of the Senate, How's the civil rights bill coming, Jack? What are you doing for us on the civil rights bill? You guys rely on me to save you on the civil rights bill and to work out something that is acceptable to you and then you treat me like this?" Danforth stared at Metzenbaum's staffers in the room— "those I believed to be the leakers," he later wrote.

"St. Jack" threw in some profanity for good measure. Strom Thurmond was so taken aback that he admonished Danforth afterwards. "You are a minister," he said. "You shouldn't take the Lord's name in vain."

The two parties were coming to an accord on how to treat Hill's charges. As decided in their caucus meeting, the Democrats requested a delay in the confirmation vote to investigate matters. Republican senators met separately in Senator Dole's office. Dole urged a delay. The votes simply were not there, he concluded.

Thomas spent much of the afternoon roaming dejectedly around the Silbermans' pool, smoking cigars and fielding calls from Danforth on his mobile telephone. Danforth finally called to relate the bad news about the vote count, and said that he and other Republicans thought Thomas's nomination would be defeated if the vote was held that day. The Republicans were resolved that the vote should be postponed, to allow for an investigation of Hill's charges.

Thomas again became agitated. "What are they doing to me?" he demanded. He announced that he did not think that he could take it anymore.

After he terminated the call, Thomas turned to Ginni and Larry Silberman and told them of the emerging consensus in favor of a Senate investigation. Silberman urged Thomas to agree to a delay. Otherwise, he believed, it would look as if the nominee feared an inquiry and was guilty of the alleged misconduct. He implored Thomas to forget about confirmation and focus instead on defending his reputation.

Republican senators on the committee called to check in with the nominee. Hatch tried his best to boost Thomas's spirits. Simpson, fresh from his dogfight with Totenberg, was in no mood for self-pity. Thomas started in with his complaints. "I am exhausted. I'm washed out," he told the senator.

"Buckle up your guts, pal, and get on the field and forget all the other stuff," Simpson bluntly chided him. Simpson thought it no time for weakness. "Look, if somebody did this to me and it was all a lie, I'll tell you what I'd do, Clarence, and if you can't do that, I won't vote for you." It would prove to be excellent advice, the verbal equivalent of smelling salts.

Another spine-stiffening phone call came in from Allen Moore, a friend from Danforth's staff. Moore, like the rest of Thomas's partisans, urged him to stand and fight for his rapidly shredding reputation.

Thomas finally called Danforth to respond to the request for a delay. "I have to clear my name, Jack," he told him. He asked that the Republicans seek a postponement of the vote. Danforth announced Thomas's request on the Senate floor. Both parties readily assented.

Thomas began to recruit friends and allies for the coming conflict. That afternoon, Thomas spoke to his old friend from Missouri, Larry Thompson. Since taking Thomas's advice and moving to Georgia, Thompson had become a major figure in the Atlanta legal community, serving as a U.S. attorney and becoming a partner at King & Spaulding. When Thomas called, Thompson was preparing to fly to Los Angeles for a crucial meeting in a large federal case he was working on involving the Charles Keating financial scandal.

Thomas "was really down" when he called, Thompson recalled. "More down than I've ever, ever heard him in all the years that we've known each other."

Thomas told him, "I really need some help. This thing has gotten crazy."

"Obviously, I'll help you," Thompson replied. "What do you want me to do?"

Thomas "really couldn't articulate what he really wanted me to do. And obviously, I didn't really know how I could help."

Thompson explained his situation and his imminent travel to Los Angeles. "I'll come up next week," he pledged.

Thomas did not try to hide the disappointment in his voice. "Well, man, I appreciate that, but it'll be too late," he told Thompson.

Thompson vowed to "see what I can do." Shortly thereafter, he obtained a postponement of his meeting in California, and was flying north to Washington instead.

As the day wound down and the sun swept across the American heartland, those in Hill's camp also were making plans for the coming clash. Judith Resnick, a law professor at the University of Southern California, called Emma Jordan, a law professor at Georgetown, to discuss assembling a "dream legal team" to come to Hill's aid. They sought to enlist a cadre of the brightest feminist lawyers and leaders in the nation. Some were already on board, others would join within the next twenty-four hours—an array of premier lawyers and law professors stretching from coast to coast. Also drawn to the fray were current or former officials with leading feminist lobbies such as NARAL and Emily's List. Few blacks would join Hill's team. Instead, she would draw from the ranks of feminists determined to defend *Roe*, who saw in her their last realistic chance to vanquish Thomas.

That night, Biden called Hill to provide an update and to offer sympathies. He informed her that hearings were being scheduled to look into her charges. He also related what he understood to be Thomas's likely defenses, including the female employees lining up to testify for him. Hill told Biden she had not secured legal counsel. This claim was inaccurate; Ross and Ogletree were advising her pro bono, and a national dream team was being formed with her knowledge and consent. Biden replied, "Aw kiddo I feel for you. I wish I weren't the chairman, I'd come to be your lawyer."

At the Silbermans' house, there were more fruitless deliberations over whether to order Chinese food. Thomas finally declared that he simply wanted to go home. Before he and Ginni departed, Danforth called. After Thomas completed his discussion with Danforth, the senator handed the telephone over to Duberstein. Larry Silberman and others had led Thomas to realize he had appeared far too programmed in the earlier hearings. Pent up with rage, Thomas unleashed some of his fury on the person he blamed for the earlier, misbegotten public relations strategy.

"Now wait a minute," Thomas barked. "We'll talk tomorrow. But I want you all to understand one thing. I did it your way last time; I'm doing it my way this time. They're going to see me, the unvarnished me, and if that's not good enough, so be it."

"I will write the statement," Thomas added, referring to his testimony to the committee. "I'm going to go home and write the statement, nobody's going to have anything to do with that."

Thomas later would state that the worst part of the confirmation hearings was the suffering Ginni endured. Maybe time distorted his memory. For Thomas, the most difficult aspect of the experience unquestionably was the public desolation of his reputation, in which his enormous pride was invested.

Insomnia again tortured Thomas after he and Ginni returned home. At 12:25 A.M., on the morning of Wednesday, October 9, Thomas asked Ginni to call some friends—Kay Coles James and Elizabeth Law and their husbands, Charles James and Steven Law. Kay James had known Thomas through the "conservative black network," as she termed it, and Ginni through a Bible study group. At her husband's request, Ginni called the Laws first, then the Jameses, to ask if they could come over at 8:30 the next morning to pray with him.

Good Christians all, the foursome honored this inconsiderate midnight request and visited the Thomas house eight hours later. Jones could see that Thomas had not slept. He was, she observed, "a broken human being." Ginni confided that he had lain the night before in the fetal position. For the next three hours, the group prayed, read the Bible, and talked about the spiritual dimensions of the battle raging around them. Over and over, Thomas looked down, shook his head, and wailed, "Why are they doing this to me?"

Kay James told the group of how she had coped with learning she had a tumor. She concluded the question pressed by such occasions was, "Either you believe in God or you don't."

Thomas responded, "I do."

"Well, then, if you do, you have to figure out what this means for your life. Those are the kinds of things we need to be thinking about and not despairing," she said.

Someone reminded Thomas that Christians must lean on God.

"No, no, no," he replied. "You don't understand. I've been leaning on God all summer—this time God has to lift me up."

When they parted, the Laws left behind "praise tapes" so that Christian music could fill the Thomas home. The group had spoken of the reality of evil and spiritual warfare, and how his confirmation battle had become a theater of that war. Thomas agreed with this theological interpretation of his straits. "I can see that this is bigger than me. This is about where the country is going. This is about the course of America."

Across the Potomac, Republican senators were trying to divide up the duties for the confirmation hearings, which were to begin in two days. Dole, Thurmond, Danforth, Hatch and Brown met to parcel out these assignments. One of the biggest issues was selecting a person to question Hill. Republicans, at Hatch's suggestion, thought it best to delegate this exercise to one person, who could follow through with a series of logical, probing questions. Otherwise, Hatch feared, the hearings would become an "absolute fiasco," with parallel charges and countercharges leveled and nothing resolved. Democrats took the opposite tack, allowing each Democrat on the committee to ask questions of Thomas willy-nilly. They would come to regret the lack of coordination.

Hatch thought the best person to question Hill was Specter. He was low-key but persistent, and a supporter of *Roe*. He was also a former district attorney from Philadelphia with substantial skills as a trial lawyer. Specter was pompous even by the standards of a body with considerable egos; his fellow Republicans knew how to appeal to him in summoning him to duty. Danforth called Specter and repeatedly urged a variation of, "We are really counting on you, Arlen."

Danforth drove to Thomas's house later in the day to pick up the nominee for a trip to the White House. He found Thomas in the family room, wearing a white shirt, suit pants and suspenders. Thomas, Danforth recalled, hugged him with the "desperate clinging of a lost soul." He sat on a couch, Danforth on a chair next to him. He rested his head in his hands and sobbed unrestrained. He kept saying, "I don't know what to do."

"Clarence, what do you want to do?" Danforth asked.

Thomas composed himself enough to list four intelligent options. The first was retrospective: He noted he could have permitted the Senate to vote the day before. He would have lost, but the matter would have been behind him.

Second, he could still withdraw his nomination. Danforth asked if Thomas wished to do so. "No," he replied.

Third, he could appear before the Judiciary Committee "on the committee's terms," and come away further abused.

Fourth, he could go on the offensive against the Senate and his accusers and take his case to the American people.

Thomas resolved to pursue the fourth alternative. "That's what I want to do," he told Danforth. For all his melancholy and self-doubts, he had firmly resolved to fight. Danforth took Thomas's hand and prayed that God would grant Thomas the strength for the approaching hearings.

Danforth drove Thomas and Ginni to the White House for a photo-op. Bush thought the press should see him with his nominee, lest Thomas's enemies believe he was being abandoned. The president and Thomas and Mrs. Bush and Ginni left the Oval Office in pairs for separate walks around the White House grounds. Bush was very supportive of Thomas, criticizing Congress for its handling of the matter. He questioned Thomas about Hill and her motives. A reporter asked Thomas, who was making his first public appearance since Hill's allegations became public, whether he would "stick it out." Thomas said only, "Yup."

Bush never wavered in his confidence in Thomas. "He went all out for him," Quayle remembered. "That meant talking to senators, making sure the press knew we had full confidence in him." In their morning meetings in the Oval Office, Bush told Quayle, "Clarence is a good man. The only reason he's being pilloried is because he's conservative and black." Bush, Quayle concluded, was "determined to win."

In his meetings with Quayle, Thomas told the vice president that Hill's allegations were "outrageous and offensive." Quayle recalled, "What he said publicly, he told us privately."

Hill soon would receive support from unexpected quarters: Angela Wright, the volatile former EEOC employee whom Thomas had fired. Wright had since landed a job as an assistant metropolitan editor at the *Charlotte Observer* in her native North Carolina. Aspiring to become a columnist, she wrote a sample column about Anita Hill, sharing what she said were her own recollections about Thomas's misconduct toward her. Somebody with access to the draft article—presumably a foe of Thomas's at the *Observer*—informed the Senate Judiciary Committee of her writings. One of Biden's staff attorneys on the Judiciary Committee called Wright to determine if she would share the column with the committee or come to Washington. She refused both entreaties. Later, the male attorney called back, this time accompanied by a female attorney on the committee. Together, they convinced her to give a statement to the committee the following day.

Even as his enemies multiplied, Thomas kept up a brave front in public. Privately, he was as despondent as ever. He told his old childhood friend, Lester Johnson, "I've never felt this bad in my whole life." He compared his trials to the worst indignities of his youth. "I've been through days when they called me nigger, told me I was thick-lipped and had nappy hair, but this affects my whole family. This is the worst thing anybody could ever do." He added, "The only thing that's been keeping me up is God."

Thomas had been surviving on one hour of sleep a night. He had lost fifteen pounds in two weeks. That night would be no different. The tossing and turning awakened Ginni. She saw her husband climb down and lie on the floor. To Ginni, it was

> like something was inside of him, physically, like there was this battle going on inside of him. Like it's not over yet. Like those prayers aren't enough. There's something else.... What it felt like is that Clarence still had some sin in his life and he had to get that out in order to be open to the Holy Spirit and that he had a vestige of sin, that he was in this furnace and God wasn't going to let him keep going without eliminating this vestige of sin.

Thomas too instinctively latched onto a religious explanation for the adversity. In his many hours of introspection, he had reviewed his life carefully. He came away with an altered, perhaps annealed view of himself. "I don't think that I had truly repented for the way I had conducted myself since 1968," he concluded. "In some sense, I felt that this punishment was being visited upon me" for past sins. Thomas saw this process as a spiritual purging, a mortification of the flesh and soul of the sort that the early Christians would have recommended for a troubled spirit. The Hill allegations were the first major professional hardship Thomas had ever faced in his otherwise steady ascent of the American political regime. The experience forced him to look within:

> I thought that in a sense that going through this, total accountability, and then having to directly confront any indiscretion that I might have made or engaged in my life required me to become a better person . . . than I was before, to be more accountable to not only myself—it's hard because I'm really hard on myself—but to God. . . . And it was the first time, I think, since the sixties that I have just opened up and not just asking God for help, but opened up and asked Him to take charge of my life, and also to connect myself to following His will. And it was in that sense that I became a better person and purged myself of what I had done before and refined myself and became close to what Jesus was.

The next morning, at eight o'clock, the Laws returned. This time, their stay was brief, as Thomas had to attend a morning strategy meeting. Thomas was more lively than before, but still not his old self. He acknowledged he had been too concerned about his own reputation and name; he kept hearing himself saying, "*My* reputation. I have got to clear *my* name . . . *my, my, my.*" He realized he had been far too self-centered throughout the recent tribulations.

At nine, Thomas arrived at his chambers at the court of appeals. He met with Luttig to prepare for the hearings into Hill's allegations, which were to begin the following morning. As soon as he had closed the door to his chambers, Thomas again broke down. He cried what Luttig called "loud tears." As he grew weary from his mourning, Luttig helped him over to the conference table. Thomas wept for fifteen minutes. "These people have destroyed my life," he repeated.

After comforting his friend, Luttig returned his attention to the business before them. He pressed Thomas in detail about Hill's allegations. Could there have been some misunderstanding? he wondered. Luttig ran into categorical denials. "Mike, this has all been made up," Thomas insisted. Luttig interrogated him about other private aspects of his life. Danforth noted that Thomas, no longer a Catholic, treated this meeting as an opportunity for confession. From these free disclosures, Luttig came away confident that Thomas was telling the truth.

Other information he received was less heartening to Luttig. Thomas said he planned to confront the committee about its handling of the affair, to go on the offensive. Luttig considered this a grave mistake. By this point, however, Thomas was not to be swayed. The only remaining issue was the matter of choosing the right tactics for executing this revised, militant strategy.

The day progressed with Angela Wright offering her contribution to the drama. Lawyers with the Judiciary Committee gathered around a speaker phone in a committee office to interview her under oath. Wright testified that Thomas commented on her anatomy several times. On one occasion he came by her apartment at night, "unannounced and uninvited." In a conversation with her, Thomas turned the subject to the prospect of his dating her. "You need to be dating me," he would say. "I think I'm going to date you."

Wright said Thomas made comments about the female anatomy "quite often." At one out-of-town seminar, Thomas complimented her dress and asked about the size of her breasts. Wright said she told Phyllis Berry Myers about this, and that Myers' reply was, "Well, he's a man, you know, he's always hitting on everybody." Myers denied this allegation, and the comment scarcely sounded like something a close friend of Thomas would have said.

Wright testified that when Thomas fired her, he said one reason for the discharge was that he did not appreciate her failure to wait for him outside his office after work. Wright suggested that her rejection of his advances might have contributed to his decision to terminate her.

When questioned by an attorney for the Republicans on the committee, Wright denied that she believed Thomas had sexually harassed her. "I am a very strong-willed person and at no point did I feel intimidated by him," she stated. A Biden staffer then asked, "Do you mean sexually harassed in a legal sense?" Wright reversed herself, saying she did think it "fit the legal definition, yes." Later in the day, Wright was told she would be subpoenaed to testify in Washington.

Committee staffers also interviewed Rose Jourdain, the former speechwriter. She said Wright came into her office to complain about comments Thomas had made about her body, breasts and legs, and how she looked in certain dresses and suits. On one occasion, Jourdain said, Wright entered her office crying because of such statements. Jourdain denied that Wright was flirtatious—a claim that was later contradicted almost universally by Wright's co-workers at EEOC and other work sites.

Both Wright and Jourdain, of course, had a score to settle—Thomas had fired them on the same day. Wright's firing was for incompetence, and it was not the first job she had left behind in flames. She had accused her previous employer in the federal bureaucracy of racism. Given the near-unanimous opinion of staffers that Wright was flirtatious and sexually assertive, and Wright's own, convincing claim that she was a "very strong-willed person," Jourdain's testimony also was unpersuasive. Wright enjoyed angling for Thomas's attention and that of other men; the notion that she cried when and if she received it was not credible. No other EEOC employee at the time of Wright's employment would step forward to corroborate Wright's complaints of sexual harassment by Thomas or resulting distress. Wright's role in the coming hearings would provide a fascinating subplot.

At noon, Danforth hosted his second press conference of the week, this one featuring seventeen women who had worked for Thomas and stood ready to vouch for him. They appeared before microphones and television cameras, sharing their stories and praise of Thomas, and reflecting by their hues and beliefs the diverse races and faiths that Thomas had attracted to his staff. Some spoke with tears streaming down faces. Pam Talkin's appraisal of Thomas was typical. She described the embattled nominee as "almost puritanical."

Larry Thompson arrived at Thomas's house at around the same time. Thomas was dressed in his typical casual attire: a long-sleeved pullover sport shirt, shorts, and jogging shoes. When Danforth joined them that afternoon, the three bowed their heads in prayer and beseeched God's intervention. Thompson would come away from his dealings with

Danforth touched by his spiritual approach to professional matters. "Up until that time, I had really never brought prayer into my practice," he acknowledged years later. "Jack did that, and that's something that I've actually used and have continued since then. So that was sort of a real significant point for me in my own personal and professional life."

Thompson was amazed that so little had been done to prepare for the hearings. "What I saw as a trial lawyer from Atlanta, Georgia, was ... this wasn't the advise and consent process—this was a plain old-fashioned fist fight," Thompson recalled. He viewed the hearings as akin to a trial—except that nobody had properly prepared the witnesses for Thomas, something that any trial lawyer would have done. "A lot of what we did was just engage in old-fashioned witness preparation," he said. As Thompson asserted this crucial leadership, Dick Leon assisted in speaking to the witnesses and going over their anticipated testimony.

The six Republicans on the Judiciary Committee held a final strategy session in Thurmond's office in the Russell building that evening, with Danforth and Duberstein joining them. They finalized their plan to let Hatch and Specter take the lead in questioning Thomas and Hill. Each would play to his strengths: Hatch lobbing loquacious softballs to Thomas, Specter carefully grilling Hill.

As the night wore on, his guests departed, leaving Thomas to ruminate over the day to come—the biggest in his life. Thomas paced, thought out loud, and wrote down ideas for his testimony. Later, he dictated them to Ginni. He was secretive about his remarks. He spoke to Duberstein but refused to accept suggestions for his speech. Luttig called several times to try to pry Thomas's remarks out of him. Thomas gave him the gist of his remarks—a belligerent approach of which Luttig still disapproved—but made it clear he did not care to discuss specifics.

These and other telephone calls were his major distractions. One turned out to be not only welcome, but crucial to his strategy and speech. The call came from an old friend, Ted Wells. His old sparring partner from Holy Cross had gone on to become one of the nation's premier trial lawyers. Unlike Thomas, he had chosen wealth over public service, opting for a lucrative private practice in New York. His clients ranged from Michael Milken to Exxon to the NAACP. The great flair he displayed as a nascent criminal defense attorney at Holy Cross blossomed into grand success as a lawyer; these included acquittals for two Cabinet secretaries facing criminal prosecutions, Ray Donovan in the 1980s and, subsequently, Mike Espy in the 1990s. Wells also was active in the Democratic Party.

For all their continuing philosophical differences, the racial implications of the media spectacle Hill had touched off greatly troubled Wells. The suggestion that black men could not control their sex drives fueled the destructive stereotype of the black-man-as-sex-fiend. He and Thomas discussed how, throughout U.S. history, such assumptions were often the kindling for lynchings and racial persecutions. From this conversation with an old and crafty adversary, Thomas would collect the seed for the most memorable line he would offer the following day.

Thomas finally went to bed at 11:30. Virginia remained awake for a while, trying to synthesize the ideas left on the potpourri of notes and yellow pads covering the dining room table. After a spell, Thomas came downstairs.

"Take all these things away," he said.

Ginni cleared the table and left him with a blank pad and pen.

"Well, let me just think. Let me open up to the Holy Spirit," Thomas muttered. Then he sat down and began to write. Ginni input his remarks page by page into the computer upstairs. He finished at 4:45. After perhaps ten minutes of rest, he rose to face his enemies.

Unraveled

"I don't care what you do with me, Brer Fox," he said, "just don't fling me into that brier patch. Roast me, Brer Fox," he said, "but don't fling me into that brier patch."

Thomas called Senator Danforth at 6:30 A.M. on Friday, October 11, to read him his prepared statement. Danforth suggested a couple of very minor changes. Luttig called Thomas one last time to find out what he had written. He asked Thomas if he had prepared his statement. "Yes," replied Thomas. He then refused to read it to him.

A deputy federal marshal picked up the Thomases and drove them to the Russell Senate Office Building. Along the way, Ginni listened to religious music through earphones. Thomas gazed out the window and collected his thoughts and courage. They arrived at Danforth's office at nine. They would have an hour to make final preparations for the ten o'clock hearing.

The hallway outside Danforth's office was crowded with boisterous supporters of Thomas. Black church members hailed him as he approached. Inside the office, other well-wishers were assembled, including many of the women who had worked for Thomas and come to Capitol Hill to defend him. Danforth led his wife, Sally, and the Thomases into his office for some privacy. They sat on adjacent couches.

After discussing the hearings, the two couples held hands and prayed. Again, Danforth supplicated God to impart strength to Thomas, "for he has none." He prayed that Thomas might be freed of the burden of wanting to be on the Supreme Court, and that he seek only to do God's will. Afterwards, they rose from their seats.

"This is going to sound a little hokey," Danforth said, and asked that they follow him. The senator led the three to his office bathroom, the only place he believed to be wholly out of earshot from the crowds out-side. A tape player sat on the washstand; the tape inside was cued to play a song.

After Danforth closed the door, the four formed a tight circle inside the cramped quarters. They clasped hands as Danforth pressed the play button. The tape player filled the little room with the strains of a classic Christian hymn, "Onward, Christian Soldiers." Danforth noted that Thomas's head was bowed, his eyes closed, his feet beating time to the music.

After two verses, Danforth pressed the stop button. He placed his hands on Thomas's shoulders and said, "Go forth in the name of Christ, trusting in the power of the Holy Spirit."

The four emerged from Danforth's office and parted the sea of supporters in the lobby and hallway. They walked the halls Thomas once had traversed as a young staffer for Danforth, bursting with dreams. Thomas felt "armed for battle," he said later. He was confident that his statement would strike the right tone. He believed "God had given me these words, and that I was going to speak these words."

As they entered the Caucus Room, Thomas walked to his seat, his ice-cold eyes locked on Metzenbaum's. Whereas before, Thomas had approached the committee rostrum to shake the members' hands, now he simply glared at them. Thomas later said that he looked upon them as "petty little thieves sitting up there," and the journalists to his rear as a "cabal" eagerly awaiting his demise.

Biden commenced the proceedings with a lengthy explanation and defense of the committee's handling of the controversy. Thomas privately was fuming over Biden's refusal to honor his vow to defend him against Hill's accusations. As he awaited his opportunity to speak, Thomas wrote five words repeatedly on the outside of a brown file folder: "In the name of Christ."

When Biden had completed his long self-justification, it was Thomas's turn.

"Mr. Chairman, Senator Thurmond, members of the committee, as excruciatingly difficult as the last two weeks have been, I welcome the opportunity to clear my name today. No one other than my wife and Senator Danforth . . . has seen or heard the statement, no handlers, no advisers.

"The first I learned of the allegations by Professor Anita Hill was on September 25, 1991, when the FBI came to my home to investigate her allegations. When informed by the FBI agent of the nature of the allegations and the person making them, I was shocked, surprised, hurt, and enormously saddened.

"I have not been the same since that day. For almost a decade my responsibilities included enforcing the rights of victims of sexual harassment. As a boss, as a friend, and as a human being I was proud that I have never had such an allegation leveled against me, even as I sought to promote women, and minorities into non-traditional jobs."

Thomas said he had been "wracking my brains and eating my insides out trying to think of what I could have said or done to Anita Hill to lead her to allege that I was interested in her in more than a professional way, and that I talked with her about pornographic or X-rated films. . . . Contrary to some press reports, I categorically denied all of the allegations and denied that I ever attempted to date Anita Hill, when first interviewed by the FBI. I strongly reaffirm that denial."

He incorporated one Duberstein idea into his speech, issuing a general disclaimer about a possible misunderstanding. "[I]f there is anything that I have said that has been misconstrued by Anita Hill or anyone else, to be sexual harassment, then I can say that I am so very sorry and I wish I had known. If I did know I would have stopped immediately and I would not, as I have done over the past two weeks, had to tear away at myself trying to think of what I could possibly have done." This would be his only concession the entire day. "I have not said or done the things that Anita Hill has alleged. God has gotten me through the days since September 25 and He is my judge."

The "high honor" of being nominated, Thomas said in a deep and emotional voice, "has been crushed. From the very beginning charges were leveled against me from the shadows—charges of drug abuse, anti-Semitism, wife-beating, drug use by family members, that I was a quota appointment, confirmation conversion and much, much more, and now, this."

He declared, "I have complied with the rules. I responded to a document request that produced over 30,000 pages of documents. And I have testified for five full days, under oath. I have endured this ordeal for 103 days. Reporters sneaking into my garage to examine books I read. Reporters and interest groups swarming over divorce papers, look-ing for dirt. Unnamed people starting preposterous and damaging rumors. Calls all over the country specifically requesting dirt. This is not American. This is Kafka-esque. It has got to stop. It must stop for the benefit of future nominees, and our country. Enough is enough."

As he neared the conclusion of his speech, Thomas skillfully injected the Pin Point strategy. "Mr. Chairman, in my forty-three years on this Earth, I have been able, with the help of others and with the help of God, to defy poverty, avoid prison, overcome segregation, bigotry, racism, and obtain one of the finest educations available in this country. But I have not been able to overcome this process.... No job is worth what I have been through, no job. No horror in my life has been so debili-tating. Confirm me if you want, don't confirm me if you are so led, but let this process end. Let me and my family regain our lives."

He lamented that there was "nothing this committee, this body or this country can do to give me my good name back, nothing." The nom-inee then gave the senators a taste of things to come later in the day: "I will not provide the rope for my own lynching or for further humil-iation. I am not going to engage in discussions, nor will I submit to rov-ing questions of what goes on in the most intimate parts of my private life or the sanctity of my bedroom. These are the most intimate parts of my privacy, and they will remain just that, private." If ever a single word could capture a man's personality, surely the last word of Thomas's opening statement did so.

After a moment of silence, in which Thomas's resonant words sank in, the haste and disorganization of the hearings became apparent. The committee promptly crumbled into factions quarreling over procedu-ral matters. Biden announced that Hill had requested that her state-ment not be used in the hearings. Hatch and other Republican senators raged.

Hatch angrily insisted, "I intend to use that statement, because it is fair to use it. I do not want to hurt—"

"Senator, let me—" Biden interrupted.

"Let me finish."

"No; I will not."

"Yes, you will. Yes, you will."

The procedural wrangling finally led to a brief recess, during which the committee members moved into Senator Kennedy's nearby office to discuss things further. During the break, Ginni Thomas and Timothy Phelps, who was seated behind her, stood up. When he began to say something, she said sternly, "D-O-N'-T T-A-L-K T-O M-E," stretching out the words for emphasis. After she repeated it a second time, Phelps sat back down. Later, he would write that he could not blame her for her hard feelings.

After the committee members filed back in, Biden announced that the committee had decided to permit Hill to testify first. After being escorted by a Capitol police officer, she would enter the Caucus Room with a self-confident stride and dressed in an attractive turquoise business suit. Gone were the big glasses, pony tail, and frumpy attire of the EEOC years. The Hill who appeared before national television wore mascara that tastefully accentuated her large eyes, as well as other complimentary makeup. The cameras became her greatest ally.

Hill began her testimony with her own, thumbnail version of the Pin Point strategy. Behind her sat her parents and family, visually bolstering her life story. She discussed her own humble beginnings, growing up poor and black in rural Oklahoma. She noted the "solid family affection" shown by her parents and the "religious atmosphere in the Baptist faith" in which she was reared.

For the first three months in which she worked for Thomas, Hill stated, "my working relationship with Judge Thomas was positive. I had a good deal of responsibility and independence. I thought he respected my work and that he trusted my judgment."

Things then changed, as he began a campaign of pressuring her into dating him. She declined. He asked her several more times over the coming weeks, and insisted that she explain the reasons for her refusal. "These incidents took place in his office or mine. They were in the form of private conversations which would not have been overheard by anyone else."

Subsequently, Thomas would call her into his office to discuss work, or suggest that they share lunch at a government cafeteria. He would then speak explicitly about vulgar sexual matters. He talked about "acts that he had seen in pornographic films involving such matters as women having sex with animals, and films showing group sex or rape scenes.

He talked about pornographic materials depicting individuals with large penises, or large breasts involved in various sex acts.

"On several occasions Thomas told me graphically of his own sexual prowess." Her efforts to change the subject, she said, "were rarely successful."

Why did she follow Thomas to EEOC? Hill stated that when Thomas was made "Chair of the EEOC, I needed to face the question of whether to go with him. I was asked to do so and I did. The work itself was interesting, and at that time, it appeared that the sexual overtures, which had so troubled me, had ended." Also, she said she "had no alternative job. While I might have gone back to private practice, perhaps in my old firm, or at another, I was dedicated to civil rights work and my first choice was to be in that field." There was also the fear that the Reagan administration would succeed in its vow to abolish the Department of Education.

During the fall and winter of 1982, Thomas badgered her about why she did not go out with him. He made discomfiting remarks about her personal appearance. Once, while she was in his office, Thomas was drinking a Coke. Thomas looked at the can and asked, "Who has put pubic hair on my Coke?" In February 1983 Hill was hospitalized for five days for acute stomach pain that she attributed to stress on the job.

Relief arrived in the spring of 1983. At that time, "an opportunity to teach at Oral Roberts University opened up. I participated in a seminar, taught an afternoon session in a seminar at Oral Roberts University. The dean of the university saw me teaching and inquired as to whether I would be interested in pursuing a career in teaching, beginning at Oral Roberts University. I agreed to take the job, in large part because of my desire to escape the pressures I felt at the EEOC due to Judge Thomas."

When she informed Thomas that she was leaving EEOC, he told her she no longer had an excuse not to go out with him. He asked if he could take her out to dinner as a professional courtesy and not as a social invitation. They went to a restaurant near their offices. Thomas told her over dinner "that if I ever told anyone of his behavior that it would ruin his career."

Hill then turned to the issue of the telephone logs. She downplayed them, saying she had had "minimal contacts with Judge Clarence Thomas since" leaving Washington. She had seen him only twice, once "to get a reference from him and on another, he made a public appearance at Tulsa."

Regarding her motives for stepping forward, she stated, "I declined any comment to newspapers, but later when Senate staff asked me about these matters, I felt that I had a duty to report." She concluded by saying, "I took no initiative to inform anyone. But when I was asked by a representative of this committee to report my experience, I felt that I had to tell the truth. I could not keep silent."

As in her telephone conversation with Senator Brown, Hill's delivery was dispassionate and calm. She proved a highly articulate and assertive speaker, as one would expect of a Yale Law graduate; she also made a very favorable visual impression on the nation via television. But by day's end, her testimony would come apart, and her allies on the committee would be on the run.

Biden walked Hill chronologically through her experiences. He began by asking her questions about her job at Wald, Harkrader, her original law firm. In describing her work duties, Hill stated, "most of my work was basically what was available and when I had time available to do it." This suggested that she was overwhelmed with work, something that, years later, she would admit was not the case.

"Did someone approach you and say there's another job you might like, or did you indicate that you would like to leave the law firm to seek another job?" Biden asked.

"I was interested in seeking other employment. It was never suggested to me at the firm that I should leave the law firm in any way." She went on to say that she departed because "I thought that I would be more personally fulfilled if I pursued other fields of the law." A partner at Wald, Harkrader, would emerge to challenge Hill's testimony on this point. In subsequent writings, Hill would partially corroborate this partner's testimony by acknowledging that she left the firm after realizing she was not on partnership track.

Biden then asked why she had followed Thomas to EEOC.

"My understanding from him at that time," replied Hill, "was that I could go with him to the EEOC, that I did not have—since I was his special assistant, that I did not have a position at the Office for Education, but that I was welcome to go to the EEOC with him.

"It was a very tough decision, because this behavior occurred. However, at the time that I went to the EEOC, there was a period—or prior to the time we went to the EEOC, there was a period where the incidents had ceased, and so after some consideration of the job opportunities in the area, as well as the fact that I was not assured that my job at Education was going to be protected, I made a decision to move to the EEOC."

Biden followed up, "Were you not assured of that, because you were a political appointee, or were you not assured of it because—tell me why you felt you weren't assured of that."

"Well, there were two reasons, really," replied Hill. "One, I was a special assistant of a political appointee, and, therefore, I assumed and I was told that that position may not continue to exist. I didn't know who was going to be taking over the position. I had not been interviewed to become the special assistant of the new individual, so I assumed they would want to hire their own, as Judge Thomas had done.

"In addition, the Department of Education at that time was scheduled to be abolished. There had been a lot of talk about it, and at that time it was truly considered to be on its way out, and so, for a second reason, I could not be certain that I would have a position there."

These assertions were unconvincing. Federal employees were famous for having a Talmudic understanding of their rights, and knowing in particular whether or not they were civil service employees (and therefore protected from unfair termination). Hill was a Schedule A attorney, not a Schedule C, or unprotected political, employee. The head of the personnel office at OCR subsequently stated that he personally briefed Hill on her rights as a Schedule A attorney when she was hired. Andrew Fischel told her that she could be dismissed only for cause and that her job was not contingent on her supervisor. If she truly was worried about her job security due to Reagan's plan to eliminate the department, it was unclear why she accepted the job at Education in the first place.

Biden asked other unremarkable questions that elicited remarkable answers. He asked where Thomas had made these lewd comments. Hill said this occurred in her office or his. Allyson Duncan, no Thomas partisan, later would state that this did not jibe with her recollection, as

Thomas rarely went into the offices of his staffers and largely kept to himself.

Hill mentioned that Thomas had referred to a man with a very large penis in certain pornographic materials he had viewed. The name, which would become through Hill's testimony part of popular culture, was named Long Dong [Hill said "John" at first] Silver.

Then came the Republicans' turn. Arlen Specter homed in with an Ichabod Crane-type intensity and earnestness, beginning by stating that he did not regard the hearings as "an adversary proceeding," but rather a quest for the truth. Nevertheless, he would demonstrate his superb skills as a trial lawyer, and would prove in the process that his considerable ego was not without some basis.

Specter roved from topic to topic, at times seemingly without a coherent reason for doing so. Hill's testimony presented such a target-rich environment, it was indeed hard to choose. Specter started by asking her about a conversation she had had with two old Thomas friends, Carlton Stewart and Stanley Grayson, at the ABA convention in Atlanta the prior summer. Hill had told them it was "great" that Thomas had been nominated, and stated "how much he deserved it."

Hill replied she had stated merely that it was a "great opportunity" for her old boss. Both men later would contradict her testimony.

Specter asked about Hill's claim, made at her press conference and quoted in the *New York Times,* that she did not know Phyllis Berry Myers. A reporter had related to her Myers' belief that Hill was disappointed in Thomas's lack of sexual attraction to her. In a flash of temper, Hill had unwisely snapped, "Well, I don't know Phyllis Berry and she doesn't know me." Myers, Specter noted, had released a statement saying that she had known Hill. Moreover, many people could testify that they knew each other.

Hill contended she meant solely that they were "not close friends." That was clearly, however, not what she had said.

Specter asked why she had given more specifics in her testimony to the committee as opposed to her interview with the FBI. He referred particularly to what he delicately called the "Coke incident."

Hill stated the FBI agent had told her "it was regular procedure to come back and ask for more specifics if it was necessary. And so, at that time, I did not provide all of the specifics that I could have." She also claimed the "FBI agent made clear that if I were embarrassed about talking about something that I could decline to discuss things that were too embarrassing, but that I could provide as much information as I felt comfortable with at that time." The agent asked her to "describe the kinds of incidents that had occurred as graphically as I could without being embarrassed."

Both agents, one of whom was female, would soon contradict her testimony on these points via fax machine. Years later, Hill herself would contradict her own testimony. She would write that she had not offered the FBI agents more details because "I thought that what I had said was more than enough to convey the nature of what had happened. I still did not trust their role in the process. Moreover, their inquiry was not a demanding or probing one."

Specter asked about Hill's conversation with Jim Brudney. Hill said that the "content of the conversation was really" an attempt to elicit from Brudney a "legal conclusion" as to whether Thomas's conduct, in his opinion, constituted sexual harassment. When Hill wrote about this conversation years later, she mentioned three topics she discussed with Brudney—keeping her charges private, the mechanics of any ensuing investigation, and whether any other women had come forward with similar complaints against Thomas. She mentioned nothing about a discussion of sexual harassment law.

The Pennsylvania senator followed up with a question about a *USA Today* article on October 9 that said, "Anita Hill was told by Senate staffers her signed affidavit alleging sexual harassment by Clarence Thomas would be the instrument that 'quietly and behind the scenes' would force him to withdraw his name." The newspaper attributed the comment to Keith Henderson, a ten-year friend of Hill's and a former staffer with the Senate Judiciary Committee.

Hill's response and demeanor betrayed fear. "I do not recall. I guess— did I say that? I don't understand who said what in that quotation."

Specter: "Well, let me go on. He said, 'Keith Henderson, a ten-year friend of Hill and former Senate Judiciary Committee staffer, says Hill was advised by Senate staffers that her charge would be kept secret and her name kept from public scrutiny.' Apparently referring again to Mr. Henderson's statement, 'they would approach Judge Thomas with the information and he would withdraw and not turn this into a big story,

Henderson says.' Did anybody ever tell you that, by providing the state-ment, that there would be a move to request Judge Thomas to with-draw his nomination?"

Hill resorted to selective amnesia. "I don't recall any story about pressing, using this to press anyone," she replied.

Specter was puzzled. He noted that this would have happened within the last month.

Hill allowed, "We were discussing this matter very carefully, and at some point there might have been a conversation about what might happen."

"Might have been?"

"There might have been, but that wasn't—I don't remember this specific kind of comment about 'quietly and behind the scenes' press-ing him to withdraw."

Specter asked Hill about what might have been discussed in addi-tion to that phrase. Hill denied there was any suggestion that the charges might result in Thomas's withdrawal. She then added, "There might have been some conversation about what could possibly occur." Later she asserted that her recent conversations with Senate staff "have become much more blurry, but these are vivid events that I recall from even eight years ago when they happened...."

Specter responded by pointing out that the prospect of forcing a Supreme Court nominee to withdraw was "something that is very, very vivid, stark, and you are talking about something that occurred within the past four or five weeks...."

Hill retreated to pleading memory loss in response to further ques-tions along these lines. "I don't recall a specific statement, and I cannot say whether that comment would have stuck in my mind. I really can-not say that," she stated. Later in the day and through the hearings, Specter would have much more to say about this implausible testimony.

Friendly questioning from Senator Leahy yielded additional pecu-liar answers. Hill stated that she could not remember the name of the restaurant where Thomas had taken her out to dinner on the night he told her she could "ruin" his career by disclosing his harassment. She could not even recall the type of restaurant or kind of food they ordered.

In response to another of Leahy's questions, Hill claimed that Thomas had asked her for dates "five to ten times." This would prove arguably her most incredible statement of the day. Anybody who knew Thomas even superficially knew that a man of such immense pride would not repeatedly abase himself with an unreceptive woman.

When Specter was allotted more time, he asked Hill about her failure to take contemporaneous notes of Thomas's harassment. By contrast, Hill acknowledged she had taken notes to "document my work." She logged in every work assignment and the dates she completed them "in order to protect myself," she said, as she feared "being fired."

This, again, was odd. Hill could only be fired for cause. As both she and Thomas knew, much to his vexation, it was virtually impossible to discharge even a provably incompetent Schedule A employee. Indeed, her note-taking was the sort of thing that a floundering Schedule A employee typically did to try to ward off a poor rating by a supervisor (this behavior suggested, moreover, that she knew the panoply of rights invested in her by virtue of being a civil service employee).

Specter noted another problem with Hill's explanation. "Well, when you comment about documenting your work to protect yourself because of concern of being fired, wouldn't the same precise thought about documentation have led you to document Judge Thomas's statements to you?"

"Well, I was documenting my work so that I could show to a new employer that I had in fact done these things," Hill replied. "I was not documenting my work so that I could defend myself or to present a claim against him."

This second explanation for her work logs was inconsistent with her prior explanation given only a minute before—that she had wanted to protect herself from being "fired." This was one of the few inconsistencies that would escape Specter. Instead, he was content to observe that a new employer typically would not want a log of all the work she had done, but merely a "finished product." Hill stated, unpersuasively, that she wished to show that she could churn out work "in a very fast-paced job situation." Her contention that she planned to impress a prospective employer with her work logs from EEOC defied the everyday experience of millions of Americans.

Specter moved on. He discussed the 180-day statute of limitations period for sexual harassment claims under Title VII, noting that the period is so short because such claims are hard to defend against. Hill had to agree. She offered no credible explanation for her failure to press her claims earlier, or for following her alleged harasser from job to job and continuing to extract professional benefits from her relationship.

"Professor Hill, do you know a man by the name of John Doggett?" Specter asked subsequently.

"Pardon me?"

"A man by the name of John Doggett?"

"John Doggett?"

"John Doggett III."

"Yes, I have met him."

"I ask you this, Professor Hill, in the context of whether you have any motivation as to Judge Thomas. What was your relationship with Mr. Doggett?"

Hill panicked, clearly fearing an ambush. "I don't recall. I do not recall. We were friends, but I don't—it wasn't anything. I just don't know."

Specter paused and said he would give her an opportunity to read Doggett's statement. Doggett would turn out to be a counterproductive witness for Thomas, which made Hill's discomfiture all the more extraordinary in retrospect.

Specter next questioned her about her time at ORU Law School, and the statement by Dean Charles Kothe that she once had volunteered to drive Thomas to the airport.

"I really don't recall that I voluntarily agreed to drive him to the airport," she replied. "I think that the dean suggested that I drive him to the airport, and that I said that I would." Kothe would contradict this in testimony over the weekend. "But at any rate, one of the things that I have said was that I intended to—I hope to keep a cordial professional relationship with that individual, and so I did him the courtesy of driving him to the airport."

"Well, when you say you wanted to maintain a cordial professional relationship, why would you do that, given the comments which you represent Judge Thomas made to you, given the seriousness of the comments, given the fact that they violated the Civil Rights Act? Was it simply a matter that you wanted to derive whatever advantage you could from a cordial professional relationship?"

"It was a matter that I did not want to invoke any kind of retaliation against me professionally. It wasn't that I was trying to get any benefit out of it." This statement was arguably inconsistent with Hill's own prior statement, and made little sense, because Thomas was no longer her employer. Years later, she would admit she was trying to obtain professional advantage from her association with Thomas at the time. She wrote, "I refused to let his bad behavior cheat me of every benefit of my good work."

After a brief interlude, Specter asked some frivolous questions about John Doggett, then returned to more favorable terrain.

"I am informed, Professor Hill, that you were a Schedule A attorney and in that capacity could stay at the Department of Education. Is that incorrect?"

"I believe I was a Schedule A attorney . . . ," she stated. "At the time I understood that my job was going to be lost. That was my understanding." This contradicted her earlier statement that she thought she *might* lose her job.

She testified that she did not know she could remain at OCR and made no effort to inquire about the matter. She said Thomas had told her she could not stay at OCR after he left, and she relied on his assertion. This testimony raised more questions (why would she have simply taken the word of her alleged persecutor?) and would be contradicted by multiple witnesses. The Republicans attempted to introduce an affidavit by Harry Singleton, Thomas's friend and successor at OCR, contradicting Hill's claim on this matter. Metzenbaum objected, and Biden ruled the document inadmissible. (Singleton subsequently said that he discussed with Hill whether she wanted to remain at OCR. He explained, "We both went to Yale, and it is a small network." He expressed his desire that she stay at Education. She responded, "Oh, no, I'm going with Clarence.")

Specter brought up the telephone logs and Hill's public avowals about them. He read her part of a *Washington Post* article, which quoted her as saying the logs were "garbage," and "that she had not telephoned Thomas, except to return his calls."

"No, I did not say that," Hill stated. She insisted she had told the reporter merely that she had not "talked to Clarence Thomas ten or eleven times over that period of time. . . . I think there was miscommunication in the entire interview." Specter did not follow up on this incoherent answer. To some degree, he did not need to. As it stood, it was Hill's word versus that of one of the nation's most prestigious newspapers.

Specter returned to her September 9 conversation with Brudney. "Mr. Brudney said to you that the nominee, Judge Thomas, might not wish to continue the process if you came forward with a statement on the factors which you have testified about?"

"Well, I am not sure that that is exactly what he said. I think what he said was, depending on an investigation, the Senate, whether the Senate went into closed session and so forth, it might be that he might not wish to continue the process."

"So Mr. Brudney did tell you that Judge Thomas might not wish to continue to go forward with his nomination, if you came forward?"

"Yes."

Noting that, with this testimony, Hill had recanted her earlier testimony, Specter later would rightly question whether Hill had committed perjury. He could have made the same claim about many of her other statements.

Liberal Democrats on the committee ignored these shifting and unbelievable answers, pausing mostly to honor Hill. Kennedy told the witness, "I just want to pay tribute to both your courage in this whole procedure and for your eloquence and for the dignity with which you have conducted yourself...." Veritably basking in the hearings, which were his illicit handiwork, Metzenbaum commended Hill for her "valor." He stated that the "women of this country, I am certain, owe you a fantastic debt of gratitude for bringing this issue of sexual harassment to the fore."

When his turn came, Alan Simpson introduced affidavits from Agents John B. Luton and Jolene Smith Jameson, who both contradicted Hill's account of her FBI interview. Luton stated that he apologized to Hill for the sensitivity of the matter, but advised her to be "as specific as possible and give details." Hill also was told that if the questions were too embarrassing, Luton would leave the room and she could speak to the female agent, Jameson, alone. Specter later noted in summary that Hill had given three statements about Thomas's alleged misconduct, all of them successively expansive.

Hank Brown brought up a fascinating series of questions that, from the standpoint of historians, would be cut off all too quickly. "My impression at the time was that she was very much pro-choice," Brown later observed of Hill. During his minutes of questioning, he inquired about Hill's conversations with Thomas regarding abortion rights and *Roe*.

"With regard to the judge himself, you clearly, in working with him as you had, were familiar with a portion of his philosophy. Do you find you were in agreement with his philosophy on most issues proposed? What can you share with us on that?"

Hill replied, "I can say that during the times that we were there, worked together, there were matters that we agreed on and some that we did not agree on and we had discussions about those matters. But I am not really certain what his philosophies are at this point."

"Would that be the case with regard to, say, abortion or *Roe v. Wade*?"

"That I am not sure of his philosophies?"

"Sure of his philosophy or do you perceive a significant difference between the two of you in that area?"

"Yes." Brown's question was somewhat vague, and so the meaning of Hill's response was unclear.

Brown then asked what those differences were. Before Hill could answer, Biden disallowed the question, stating that the hearings were about Hill's charges of sexual harassment, not abortion. This was a fair point which Brown did not protest. But if Biden and the other Democrats had known his reason for asking the question, they might not have intervened so quickly, or at all. Brown subsequently explained his train of logic:

> The reason I asked the question was, it struck me as somewhat unusual that Clarence Thomas would never have even expressed an opinion on the court decision to people. Regardless of where you are on the issue, it struck me as unusual that a Yale attorney would not have expressed a viewpoint on it. And Anita Hill obviously had significant contact with him. So the reason I asked her the question was to find out if they had talked about *Roe*. If he had, it might've been inconsistent with his earlier statements.

Given the lack of credibility in her earlier testimony, Hill's affirmations about Thomas's comments on *Roe* could not have been taken at face value. Still, fate and Chairman Biden seemingly were on Thomas's side when Brown was diverted from this tantalizing line of questioning.

After a protracted self-justification, in which he defended the manner in which the hearings were conducted, Biden told Hill, "I admire you," and excused the witness. She returned to the meeting rooms of the Rules Committee, where she was reunited with her lawyers, family and friends. They held hands while a minister said a prayer, giving thanks for God's strength. Back in Norman, Oklahoma, the local florists delivered to her office so many flowers and plants from well-wishers that the law school administrative offices, in her words, "smelled like a perfumery."

Prayers were going up from both sides in this battle. But as Lincoln observed of the Civil War, which was fought over a similarly contentious underlying issue (slavery instead of abortion), both parties in the controversy invoked God, but both could not be right. Hill had made specific allegations that Thomas had denied in full. One person was lying under oath.

By the time Specter finished his cross-examination of Hill, the evidentiary record and subsequent events would leave little doubt as to which witness was more credible. In a compressed period of question time, and with only a couple of days to prepare for the hearings, Specter nevertheless had succeeded in demolishing Hill. She was thoroughly discredited, gasping for answers, spinning yarns as she went along. Following her Senate testimony, she would never again expose herself to unrestricted questions about her allegations.

Conservatives remained wary of Specter even after this important service. He supported *Roe* and abortion rights, and he would prove too unreliable on other important causes. But his cross-examination of Anita Hill would serve as both roadmap and foundation for all subsequent analysis of Hill's charges.

Even so, for several hours on October 11, 1991, Hill captivated the nation. Her beauty and speaking skills transfixed television viewers and the senators before her. Throughout the day, Democrats on the committee fawned over her, and Republicans apologized or sought to justify their inconvenient questions of her.

As dusk began to settle in over Washington, the anti-Thomas forces were full of optimism. During a brief recess in the hearings, right before Hill concluded her testimony, Tom Brokaw of NBC News interviewed Senator Howell Heflin about Hill's well-received testimony. With a

somewhat incongruous smile, Heflin reminded Brokaw and his viewers that the day was not over, that Thomas would be returning to testify. "I don't want to hang somebody before the trial is over, or neither
turn 'em loose before the trial is over," he said with a grin.

Never would a member of the Senate eat his words more spectacularly.

The Empty Noose

Of course Brer Fox wanted to hurt Brer Rabbit as bad as he could, so he caught him by the hind legs and slung him right in the middle of the brier patch. There was a considerable flutter where Brer Rabbit struck the bushes, and Brer Fox sort of hung around to see what was going to happen.

L ike a willful youngster plugging his ears, Thomas had refused to watch or listen to Hill's testimony. After he left the Caucus Room and returned to Danforth's office, he told Allen Moore, "I'm not watching it. I don't need to see those lies. I know what she is going to say. I just want to go home." So he did. Upon arriving at his house, Thomas procured a cigar, turned on his stereo, and idled away the day conversing with the deputy marshal assigned to protect him.

Later, Thomas said he did not listen to Hill's testimony because he "couldn't take it." His years in Washington had not toughened his skin much, if at all; even if they had, the mortification was overwhelming. But he did keep tabs on Hill's testimony by calling Larry Silberman at his chambers every thirty to forty-five minutes and soliciting a report. He also asked Ginni for regular updates. This was odd but predictable behavior for an extraordinarily proud and sensitive man.

At 5 P.M., Thomas returned to Capitol Hill. Peering into Danforth's office, he saw on the television that Hill still was testifying. "I'm not watching it," he declared. At that point, Danforth turned off the TV and cleared the room. Thomas and Luttig remained alone. Fortunately for Thomas, the resourceful Luttig had made notes of Hill's testimony. He reviewed her allegations with Thomas. As Luttig went over the charges, Thomas would periodically interrupt with new cries of "Why would she be doing this?" and other anguished comments about the humiliation he was suffering. Luttig once again counseled the nominee against attacking the committee.

After Thomas's meeting with Luttig, Ginni and others noticed that he looked exhausted. His eyes were red, his movements languid. Ginni suggested that he try to sleep. Danforth turned out the lights in his office and offered his couch to the nominee.

Instead, he sat and talked with Danforth in the dimly lit room. He paced, sat, paced some more, fuming all the while about his ordeal. Hatch came by and found Thomas pacing like a caged animal, "mad at everybody, mad at everything." He gave the nominee a pep talk, saying, "Don't take crap from anybody, including me. And be yourself. Above all, be yourself. Clarence, they're gonna love you."

Thomas began to consider more concretely what he would say to the committee. The specter of a lynching, which had been in his opening statement, pervaded his thoughts. As he sat on the couch in Danforth's office, he remarked, "You know what this is, Jack? This is a lynching. This is a high-tech lynching."

"Clarence, if that is how you feel, then go upstairs and say it," Danforth replied.

He further suggested that Thomas make a note of the sentiment. Thomas jotted it down.

"Men are whipped oftenest who are whipped easiest," Frederick Douglass once observed. Douglass knew whereof he spoke, having fought off a cruel overseer and assistant as a young slave, thereby sparing himself further whippings. Thomas would act consistent with this wisdom. Metzenbaum and Hill's other allies would hurl at him their best Washington hardball. He now was ready to knock the cover off it.

When he left Danforth's office, observers noted that Thomas had a "big, beaming smile."

Back in Dublin, Georgia, Evelyn Thomas, the nominee's cousin, and Ada Snell were watching the hearings at a convenience store they operated near Interstate 16. As Thomas prepared to appear again before the committee and rebut Hill's charges, they hoped for a display of strength. Referring to his paternal grandfather, the minister who grew stern when provoked, Evelyn wanted to see the "November coming out in him."

Ken Masugi also awaited Thomas's response. He recalled his discussions with Thomas at EEOC after Ollie North had turned the tables on Congress. Since those hearings, congressional scandals had filled the newspapers: congressmen raising their own pay and kiting checks at the House bank. Masugi recalled, "As soon as I knew it came down, that he had this situation" with Anita Hill and Congress, "I felt very confident he would do the right thing ... and take the offensive, just as North did."

Dennis DeConcini, like the other members of the Judiciary Committee, recognized the high stakes confronting the nominee. He observed, "He needed to attempt to put on the defensive those who were trying their best to not confirm him. And when you get to the wall, as he was, you do things that you might not do or say if this was just a love-fest."

<hr>

At 9:00 P.M., during "prime time"—the peak hours for television viewing—Thomas walked into the Caucus Room with Ginni and Danforth, who sat down behind him, chatting and smiling. All the despair Thomas had suffered in private now was nowhere in evidence. The witness who appeared was a statue of cold defiance.

The evening's events began with Biden asking the nominee, somewhat inanely, "Do you have anything you would like to say?"

"Senator," Thomas replied, "I would like to start by saying unequivocally, uncategorically [sic] that I deny each and every single allegation against me today that suggested in any way that I had conversations of a sexual nature or about pornographic material with Anita Hill, that I ever attempted to date her, that I ever had any personal sexual interest in her, or that I in any way ever harassed her.

"Second, and I think a more important point, I think that this today is a travesty. I think that it is disgusting. I think that this hearing should never occur in America. This is a case in which this sleaze, this dirt, was searched for by staffers of members of this committee, was then leaked to the media, and this committee and this body validated it and displayed it in prime time over our entire nation.

"How would any member on this committee or any person in this room or any person in this country would like sleaze said about him or her in this fashion or this dirt dredged up and this gossip and these lies displayed in this manner? How would any person like it?

"The Supreme Court is not worth it. No job is worth it. I am not here for that. I am here for my name, my family, my life and my integrity. I think something is dreadfully wrong with this country, when any person, any person in this free country would be subjected to this. This is not a closed room.

"There was an FBI investigation. This is not an opportunity to talk about difficult matters privately or in a closed environment. This is a circus. It is a national disgrace."

Thomas started to lean back in his chair. Then, he suddenly leaned forward again, as if remembering he had omitted something from his speech—something important.

"And from my standpoint, as a black American, as far as I am concerned, it is a high-tech lynching for uppity blacks who in any way deign to think for themselves, to do for themselves, to have different ideas, and it is a message that, unless you kow-tow to an old order, this is what will happen to you, you will be lynched, destroyed, caricatured by a committee of the U.S. Senate, rather than hung from a tree."

Thomas leaned back again, this time heavily and for good.

For several seconds, the room was utterly still. Seldom if ever had senators been addressed in such a manner. Never had a black man rebuked them in this way on national television.

It fell to Heflin to ask the nominee about the charges. Except for Metzenbaum, the Democrats could not possibly have made a worse choice. Accustomed to amiable waffling, the lead-footed Heflin was ill suited to carefully examining a hostile witness. Even the charming Southern accent no longer sounded so endearing. In the wake of Thomas's statements, he would risk looking like a bigoted Alabama judge circa 1930. To a careful politician used to seeking political cover, this was a genuine nightmare.

Heflin was visibly uncomfortable. He stammered as he tried to change the subject with his first question. "Judge Thomas, in addition to Anita Hill, there have surfaced some other allegations against you."

Heflin then asked about Earl Harper Jr. Harper was a lawyer in EEOC's Baltimore office accused of sexual harassment in the early 1980s. Heflin recited a local television story that had broken the night before, which alleged that David Slate, then the general counsel of EEOC, had recommended in a memorandum to Thomas that Harper be terminated. Thomas did not dismiss him, but instead retained him for eleven more months before he retired.

The senator's facts were wrong, however, and Thomas corrected him with aplomb. Harper's supervisor, Thomas recalled, had recommended suspension or something "less than termination." Thomas insisted that Harper be fired—not a surprising posture, given Thomas's strictness toward bumbling or misbehaving employees generally. But because of the layers of procedural armor enjoyed by civil service employees, Thomas could not simply discharge him. He noted regarding Harper that "there are a number of procedural protections that he had, including a hearing and, of course, he had a lawyer and there was potential litigation et cetera." It was Thomas who insisted that Slate raise the sanction to termination. Harper ultimately was not dismissed because he effectively utilized his rights as an employee. Heflin's questions simultaneously underscored Thomas's talent as a manager, his hostility to sexual harassment, and the rights at Hill's disposal as a Schedule A employee should she truly have feared that he would summarily fire her.

The topic was beside the point as well. Hatch objected to Heflin's wandering line of questioning. Biden agreed, saying, "I do not see where it is relevant."

A chastened Heflin replied, "All right, sir, I will reserve an exception, as we used to say." He nervously played with his pen, rolling it among his fingers. Thomas glared back in stony anger.

"Now, I suppose you have heard Professor Hill, Ms. Hill, Anita F. Hill testify today," Heflin asked.

"No, I haven't."

"You didn't listen?"

"No, I didn't. I have heard enough lies."

"You didn't listen to her testimony?"

"No, I didn't."

"On television?"

"No, I didn't," Thomas said with deep intonation. "I've heard enough lies. Today is not a day that, in my opinion, is high among the days in our country. This is a travesty. You spent the entire day destroying what it has taken me forty-three years to build and providing a forum for that."

A flustered Heflin backtracked. "Judge Thomas, you know we have a responsibility too, and as far as I am involved, I had nothing to do with Anita Hill coming here and testifying. We are trying to get to the bottom of this. And, if she is lying, then I think you can help us prove that she was lying."

Thomas did not give an inch: "Senator, I am incapable of proving the negative that did not occur." The redundancy emphasized his point.

"Well, if it did not occur, I think you are in a position, with certainly your ability to testify, in effect, to try to eliminate it from people's minds."

"Senator, I didn't create it in people's minds. This matter was investigated by the Federal Bureau of Investigation in a confidential way. It was then leaked last weekend to the media. I did not do that. And how many members of this committee would like to have the same scurrilous, uncorroborated allegations made about him and then leaked to national newspapers and then be drawn and dragged before a national forum of this nature to discuss those allegations that should have been resolved in a confidential way?"

"Well, I certainly appreciate your attitude toward leaks. I happen to serve on the Senate Ethics Committee and it has been a sieve."

Thomas again gave no quarter, responding this time with some wry humor. "But it didn't leak on me. This leaked on me and it is drowning my life, my career and my integrity, and you can't give it back to me, and this committee can't give it back to me, and this Senate can't give it back to me. You have robbed me of something that can never be restored."

DeConcini piped up. "I know exactly how you feel," he stated. It was a cloying and self-serving comment from a man who, as a member of the Keating Five, had been embroiled in a political scandal of his own making. (Back home in Arizona, a local political cartoonist routinely depicted him with elfish ears and dollar bills sticking out of his front suit pocket.) Thomas simply let the comment float by. DeConcini was his only Democratic ally on the committee; he knew he would need every vote he could get.

Heflin continued his retreat. He conceded that Hill "could be living in a fantasy world. I don't know." He pointed out that "if you didn't listen to what she said today, then that puts it somewhat in a more difficult task to find out what the actual facts are relative to this matter."

"The facts keep changing, Senator," Thomas responded. "When the FBI visited me, the statements to this committee and the questions were one thing. The FBI's subsequent questions were another thing. And the statements today, as I received summaries of them, are another thing."

Heflin tried to turn things around by pursuing a reliable old line of attack against the conservative judge.

"Judge, if you are on the bench and you approach a case where you appear to have a closed mind and that you are only right, doesn't it raise issues of judicial temperament?"

Thomas slapped down the "judicial temperament" charge as quickly as it was raised. "Senator, there is a difference between approaching a case objectively and watching yourself being lynched. There is no comparison whatsoever."

Heflin wanted no more of this. "Judge, I don't want to go over this stuff but, of course, there are many instances in which she has stated, but—and, in effect, since you didn't see her testify I think it is somewhat unfair to ask you specifically about it." He concluded: "I would reserve my time and go ahead and let Senator Hatch ask you, and then come back."

Biden next recognized Hatch, who, after noting that Hill was "very impressive," added, "And I hate to go into this but I want to go into it because I have to." Then he took Thomas through Hill's allegations one at a time.

"At any time did you say to Professor Hill that she could ruin your career if she talked about sexual comments you allegedly made to her?"

"No."

"Did you say to her in words or substance that you could ruin her career?"

"No."

Hatch went on. "Did you ever say in words or substance something like there is a pubic hair in my Coke?"

"No, Senator."

"Did you ever refer to your private parts in conversations with Professor Hill?"

"Absolutely not, Senator."

As Hatch asked about his alleged discussions of sex and his pressuring her to date him, Ginni swept her hand beneath her eyes to wipe away the streams of tears. Later, she would pull out a tissue from her pocket as the tears flowed freely.

Hatch asked Thomas for his opinion of the charges.

"Senator, if any of those activities occur, it would seem to me to clearly suggest or to clearly indicate sexual harassment." But, Thomas noted, he was not guilty of them, and Hill's account of the matter did not make sense. Hill could have reported his alleged misconduct to an EEO officer at the Department of Education. She also could have informed an EEO officer at EEOC while she worked there, an officer whose work Thomas had no power to review.

Thomas confirmed that Hill did not have to accompany him to EEOC because she was a Schedule A attorney. "If she was concerned about job security, I could have certainly discussed with Harry Singleton what should be done with her. He is a personal friend of mine. He is also, or was, a personal friend of the individual who recommended Anita Hill to me, Gil Hardy."

He made some other critical points in his defense. Hill, he observed, might have felt slighted because he gave her less attention at EEOC, whose "enormous management problems" preoccupied him. Thomas also noted that the phone log of Hill's calls to him "reflects only those calls where she was unsuccessful in reaching me." There were more calls than she had admitted making.

Hatch finished with a question well suited for the self-indulgence of the era: "How do you feel right now, Judge, after what you have been through?"

The query punctured a dam of self-pity. "Senator, as I indicated this morning, it just isn't worth it. And the nomination is not worth it, being on the Supreme Court is not worth it, and there is no amount of money that is worth it, there is no amount of money that can restore my name, being an associate Justice of the Supreme Court will never replace what I have been robbed of, and I would not recommend that anyone go through it.

"This has been an enormously difficult experience, but I don't think that that is the worst of it. I am forty-three years old and if I am not confirmed I am still the youngest member of the U.S. Court of Appeals for the D.C. Circuit. And I will go on. I will go back to my life of talking to my neighbors and cutting my grass and getting a Big Mac at McDonald's and driving my car, and seeing my kid play football. And I will live. I will have my life back. And all of this hurt has brought my family closer together, my wife and I, my mother, but that is not—so there is no pity for me."

"I think the country has been hurt by this process. I think we are destroying our country. We are destroying our institutions. And I think it is a sad day when the U.S. Senate can be used by interest groups, and hatemongers, and people who are interested in digging up dirt to destroy other people and who will stop at no tactics, when they can use our great political institutions for their political ends, we have gone far beyond McCarthyism. This is far more dangerous than McCarthyism. At least McCarthy was elected."

The spotlight returned to Heflin, and he acquitted himself no better than he had before. He started to go through the same checklist of superficial questions he had asked of Hill to such mirth earlier in the day. This time, he ran into a brick wall.

Typical was Thomas's response to Heflin's query about whether Hill was a "zealous civil rights supporter": "Senator, I cannot characterize her that way. I have not thought about her that way. But I would like to address what you said before that. I think you have more than an obligation to figure out why she would say that. I think you have an obligation to determine why you would allow uncorroborated, unsubstantiated allegations to ruin my life."

By the time Heflin reached his question about whether Hill was trying to be a "martyr," Thomas simply sighed. "Senator, I can't answer all those questions."

Heflin twice solicited a psychological profile, asking if she showed "signs" of "being out of touch with reality" or that she "lived in a fantasy world or anything?"

To the second inquiry, Thomas replied wearily, "Senator, again, I don't know. I am not a psychiatrist or psychologist. I was a busy chairman of an agency."

Heflin ultimately declared, "I believe that is all," and threw in the towel for the night. The committee adjourned a few minutes later, at 10:34 P.M. Danforth placed his right arm around Thomas as they and Ginni strode away from the cameras and out of the Caucus Room.

The "high-tech lynching speech" would prove the turning point of the confirmation fight. Immediately after the speech, John Cochran of NBC News told viewers that White House officials said they had known the content of Thomas's speech in advance. This was false. As one high-level administration official recalled, "I think everyone [at the White House] was just stunned by it." The instant consensus among the journalists covering the speech was that Thomas had helped his cause immensely.

Thomas backers across the country judged the speech a rousing success. Ed Meese remembered it as "a decisive moment." Back in Pin Point, Abe Famble, Thomas's cousin, told his wife, "You're doggone real. That's what it is. A high-tech lynching." Ada Snell in Dublin, Georgia, declared, "Thank God. It's about time." She believed "the speech—that turned the tide."

The next day, Saturday, October 12, brought news that the hearings the night before had reaped some of the highest ratings in the history of television. The proceedings had earned a rating two and a half times that of an American League baseball playoff game played opposite them. In banner headlines across the country, the term "lynching" was nearly ubiquitous and prominent. That meant a net win for Thomas.

On his way back to the Senate that morning, Thomas saw firsthand the evidence of his speech's effect on the American people. Motorists who recognized him honked their horns in approval or gave him a thumbs-up.

Leahy was given the first share of question time. He was not nearly the same voracious senator who had exacted from Thomas his damaging testimony about *Roe*. He asked about Hill's allegations concerning a private farewell dinner with him.

Thomas said he did not recall ever going out to dinner with Hill. He denied ever discussing pornographic films with her. He spoke of his staff as his "personal charges" whom he sought to aid professionally.

Leahy asked Thomas, ". . . why would she do this?"

"Senator, you know, I—I have asked myself that question, as I told you. I have not slept very much in the last two and a half weeks. I have thought unceasingly about this, and my wife simply said, 'Stop torturing yourself.'

"I don't know why family members turn on each other. I don't know why a son or a daughter, or a brother or sister would write some book that destroys a family. I don't know. All I can tell you is that from my standpoint I felt that I did everything I could toward Professor Hill in the same way that I would do with my other special assistants to discharge my responsibilities. I don't know. I do not have the answer."

Hatch focused on issues involving racial stereotypes. The day before, he had told Thomas he would pursue this topic; Thomas strongly approved and was ready. Some of Hatch's questions betrayed either a lack of understanding of such stereotypes or inadequate preparation. Thomas nevertheless used the questions as starting points for strong answers.

Thomas mentioned that in the 1970s, he had studied the history of lynchings in some detail. He noted that throughout this blood-soaked history, "there is invariably or in many instances a relationship with sex—an accusation that that person cannot shake off. That is the point that I am trying to make. And that is the point that I was making last night that this is a high-tech lynching. I cannot shake off these accusations because they play to the worst stereotypes we have about black men in this country."

Hatch discussed portions of Hill's testimony, asking if certain allegations were a "stereotype." Often, Thomas answered frankly, "No." Later, however, Thomas assumed control of the dialogue and offered his own highly charged assessment of the matter.

"I have been harmed worse than I have ever been harmed in my life," he stated. "I wasn't harmed by the Klan, I wasn't harmed by the Knights of Camelia, I wasn't harmed by the Aryan Race, I wasn't harmed by a racist group, I was harmed by this process, this process which accommodated these attacks on me. . . . I would have preferred an assassin's bullet to this kind of living hell that they have put me and my family through."

These remarks resonated powerfully among black Americans. Unlike the vast majority of whites, many blacks actually knew who the Knights of Camelia were. The reference to an "assassin's bullet" also was inflammatory.

Hatch scrutinized some other aspects of Hill's testimony. He informed the committee he had learned of a recent civil rights case from

Kansas in which the character "Long Dong Silver" was discussed. He observed that the book *The Exorcist* contained a reference in the dialogue to pubic hair in a Coke. Privately he declared of the matter, "This is just too cute."

After the lunch break, Danforth slipped Thomas a note right before he continued his testimony. The note gave him an update on the telephone calls coming in to Danforth's office: of the fifteen samples taken, 100 percent were in favor of the embattled nominee.

Biden asked some questions, none of which dented Thomas's story. He tried to establish rapport with the nominee by using a football analogy—comparing Thomas to a 280-pound lineman and himself to a 130-pound flankerback. The audience laughed, but Thomas was unmoved.

"In order to attempt to seek the truth," Biden continued, "I am accepting, for the sake of this discussion, the assertions that you never said anything in the workplace or out of the workplace to Ms. Hill. Let's, as we lawyers say, stipulate to that for the moment."

"Senator, you stipulated to my character earlier," Thomas said acidly, referring to Biden's broken pledge to defend him against Hill.

"I did, and I have again," Biden replied falsely, even as he described Hill a few seconds later, with awkward emphasis, as an "incredibly credible woman."

Before beginning his questioning, Specter went over Hill's testimony regarding the *USA Today* article and the clandestine attempts it reported to force Thomas to withdraw his nomination. He noted that Hill had changed her testimony from a feigned lack of recollection regarding Brudney's assertions on this matter, to an acknowledgement, in the afternoon, that he did tell her that Thomas might withdraw if she came forward.

"Now, Judge Thomas, what do you make of that change of testimony?"

"Senator," Thomas replied, "I think that the individuals such as Jim Brudney, Senator Metzenbaum's staffer on the Education and Labor Committee, should be brought to hearings like this to confront the people in this country for this kind of effort, and I think that they should at some point have to confront my family."

Metzenbaum interrupted at that point, stating that Brudney "was performing his responsibilities as a member of my staff."

After Thurmond jumped in to urge an FBI investigation of the leak, Specter directed the committee's attention away from those "collateral issues." He then averred, "it is my legal judgment, having had some experience in perjury prosecutions, that the testimony of Professor Hill in the morning was flat-out perjury, and that she specifically changed it in the afternoon when confronted with the possibility of being con-tradicted, and if you recant during the course of a proceeding, it is not perjury, so I state that very carefully as to what she had said in the morning."

After noting the problems in Hill's testimony regarding her status as a Schedule A employee and her comments to the *Washington Post*, Specter trained his critical eye on Thomas for a change. "I was a little disappointed, maybe more than a little disappointed, that you did not watch the proceedings yesterday," he noted, and asked why not.

"Senator, the last two and a half weeks have been a living hell and there is only so much a human being can take." He said he "didn't see any reason to suffer through more lies about me. This is not an easy experience."

Specter observed that "it just struck me a little peculiarly that you had not wanted to see what she had said. . . . I just was concerned that you had taken that course, in light of the seriousness, the importance, and the gravity of the matter."

"Senator, I wish there was more for me to give, but I have given all I can," was the self-pitied reply.

Shortly thereafter, Metzenbaum again stood up for Brudney. "I want to make it clear that Mr. Brudney was doing what he should have done, and had he done less he would have been irresponsible. And had this Senator and this committee done less, it would have been irresponsi-ble. Sexual harassment is too important an issue to sweep under the rug."

Thomas shot back, "Senator, it was not swept under the rug. This issue was investigated by the FBI and then leaked to the press, and I do not share your view that this was not concocted. This has caused me great pain—and my family great pain, and God is my judge, not you, Senator Metzenbaum."

Heflin haplessly asked more questions. This time, he compared the Thomas-Hill scenario, with its lack of corroborating witnesses, to a typical date rape case. Hatch objected to the question on the grounds of relevance, and for suggesting improperly that Thomas had committed date rape. Heflin would later clarify and retract any suggestion that he had accused Thomas of date rape. When Heflin asked Thomas about an equally sensitive topic—his divorce—Thomas stiff-armed him, refusing to answer his question because it was "irrelevant."

"All right, I will respect you," Heflin said compliantly. "Whatever you want to state and however you want to answer it."

After more back-and-forth from other senators, Alan Simpson raised the subject of Angela Wright. "Angela Wright will soon be with us, we think, but now we are told that Angela Wright has what we used to call in the legal trade, cold feet." He asked Thomas, "Did you fire her and if you did, what for?"

"I indicated, Senator, I summarily dismissed her and this is my recollection. She was hired to reinvigorate the public affairs operation at EEOC. I felt her performance was ineffective, and the office was ineffective. And the straw that broke the camel's back was a report to me from one of the members of my staff that she referred to another male member of my staff as a faggot."

"As a faggot?"

"And that is inappropriate conduct, and that is a slur, and I was not going to have it."

"And so you just summarily discharged her?"

"That is right."

Simpson went on, "That is kind of the way you are, isn't it?"

The question was too treacly for Thomas, who answered merely, "That is the way I am with conduct like that, whether it is sex harassment or slurs or anything else. I don't play games."

Of course, the precipitating reason for Thomas's firing of Wright was her failure to invite Tony Gallegos to a press conference. The remark about the homosexual staffer was a significant demerit in his eyes; in the hearings, however, Thomas assigned the comment more importance than he had at the time of her discharge. He recognized that the "faggot" comment would put the Democrats even more on the defensive.

Wright waited all day in the Washington office of her attorney for her chance to testify. Hill's advisers ended up deciding they did not want Wright to testify because of her erratic work history and temperament, and their fear that she might damage Hill's cause in other ways.

By the time Thomas finished testifying early in the evening, he had held up well both physically and analytically. His denials and explanations were consistent, his story coherent. There would appear no gaping contradictions or shifting explanations, as plagued Hill's testimony. His Republican defenders were thrilled with his performance. Hill would later write, "By Saturday afternoon, after the 'high-tech lynching' claim, it appeared as though none of the members of the committee were my allies."

Dole and Hatch decided that Thomas should be seen in a public place following the latest round of testimony. Hatch told the nominee, "Clarence, I want to take you and Virginia to dinner." Hatch and his wife would entertain the Thomases and Danforths at Morton's, one of Thomas's favorite steakhouses. "He's a robust eater, and he loved Morton's," Hatch recalled. The restaurant was located in Tysons Corner, Virginia, a suburb in heavily Republican northern Virginia.

The three couples were seated at a large table in the middle of the restaurant. Their conversation ranged broadly. They talked about the divisions that the confirmation fight had exposed between feminists and blacks, and how this alliance was not in the interests of blacks. Danforth noted that this was especially apparent in the negotiations over the pending civil rights bill. Throughout dinner, people approached Thomas and encouraged him. At one point, five young women walked up to the table and told Thomas to "hang in there."

Thomas also saw Robert Bork and his wife dining at another table with Ted Olson, a prominent Washington attorney and Thomas friend from the Reagan administration, and his future wife, Barbara. Thomas walked over to greet his former professor and similarly assailed judicial nominee. Bork asked how Thomas was doing.

"I'm hanging in there," Thomas replied.

"I know what you're going through," Bork told him. "My heart goes out to you." Bork urged him to keep fighting.

After polishing off a large porterhouse steak, which represented an end to his weeks-old involuntary fast, the nominee and his entourage stood up to leave the restaurant. (The bill came to $350, which Hatch paid.) The other patrons rose and delivered an impromptu standing ovation.

"He walked out of there ten feet off the ground," Hatch said. "And I think that was one of the things that helped him to weather the calumny.... He walked out of there knowing that people were listening to him and were believing him, that they liked his candor."

—•—

The committee reconvened on Sunday, October 13, for its final day of hearings into the Hill charges. The day led off with a panel of Hill supporters: Susan Hoerchner; John W. Carr, a New York lawyer who had dated Hill when she was at EEOC; Ellen M. Wells, a friend of Hill's; and Joel Paul, a law professor at American University in Washington.

Hoerchner, Carr and Wells testified that Hill had told them in or around the time frame in which she worked for Thomas that her boss was harassing her. Hoerchner had told committee staffers several days before her Senate testimony that Hill had informed her of this harassment in the spring of 1981. Hill was not then working for Thomas at Education. Hill's lawyers asked for a break. After stepping outside for a brief conference with them, Hoerchner returned and told the staffers that she could not recall exactly when Hill had told her of the harassment, but that she believed Hill mentioned that the harasser's name was Clarence. In her testimony to the Judiciary Committee, Hoerchner stated more firmly that Hill had mentioned Thomas's first name, in apparent contradiction of her earlier, more tenuous avowals.

In an exchange with Simpson, Hoerchner was further discredited and narrowly avoided her own perjury troubles. She denied that she had ever filed a sexual harassment charge. When Simpson confronted her with a document indicating she had filed a sexual harassment claim against a fellow workers' compensation judge in California, she was forced to concede the inaccuracy of her earlier testimony.

Ellen Wells stated that in the fall of 1982, Hill had complained of "inappropriate" behavior by Thomas. Hill did not provide details, Wells said, except to say that the behavior was "sexual in nature." However, in an interview with Senate staffers several days before, Wells had stated she was not certain the behavior complained of was sexual. Under such circumstances, Hill's complaint could have included Thomas's icy indifference to lackluster subordinates or her poor work assignments.

John Carr said he had developed a "social relationship" with Hill during the first part of 1983, while he was attending Harvard University, and that they spoke several times by telephone during this time. Hill told him once during this time that her supervisor was harassing her and making sexual advances. She cried during the conversation. Carr concluded she was referring to Thomas, although he admitted, under cross-examination by Specter, that he could not remember if she referred to Thomas by name. But he did recall that he told Hill it was "appalling" that the "head of the EEOC" would engage in such conduct. This conversation was during the same period when Duncan was eclipsing Hill at the agency and Hill was otherwise visibly losing ground at her job.

Joel Paul recalled a conversation with Hill in July 1987, when she was conducting research at American University. During lunch at a university cafeteria, Paul asked about Hill's professional background and innocently inquired why she had left EEOC. Paul testified that Hill seemed "embarrassed that I had raised the subject by asking her why she had left the EEOC." She replied that her supervisor at EEOC had sexually harassed her. Paul could not recall if she mentioned Thomas's name. Like her conversation with Carr, this discussion with Paul provided support for the conclusion that Hill lied to cover up her career failures. Paul said she appeared embarrassed when he inquired about her work history; he had unintentionally stumbled onto an uncomfortable topic. Hill then said she left the agency—a departure that, she feared, might suggest a failure on her part—because of sexual harassment.

Paul's testimony provided the strongest confirmation that Hill leveled false harassment charges against Thomas to deflect attention from her career failures. Why would she discuss such a thing with a complete stranger, in response to an unremarkable question about a career change over lunch, yet not tell family or close friends? Why would she tell Paul in 1987 but not report such gross misconduct to appropriate law enforcement agencies, or for that matter to the Senate when Thomas was up for confirmation to the EEOC chairmanship the year before or to the court of appeals three years later?

While these supporters of Hill were testifying, partisans of both sides were moving their fight into the realm of pseudo-science. Hill submitted to a polygraph test. The person who administered it could find no evidence she was not telling the truth. Meanwhile, through separate channels, Republicans were learning of two psychiatrists, Jeffrey Satinover of Connecticut and Park Dietz from California, who had advanced the belief that Hill might think she was telling the truth because she suffered from erotic delusions. Larry Thompson questioned Satinover and advocated offering this analysis as an explanation for Hill's self-confident performance.

Committee members also sparred over collateral issues. Republicans sought to subpoena Hill's employment records to impeach her testimony about her experience at Wald, Harkrader. Democrats wished to explore Thomas's past interest in pornography. Ultimately, both sides agreed to set those matters aside.

As the afternoon progressed, Thomas watched the Redskins game on television, calling Larry Silberman every hour or so to ask for a synopsis and analysis of the testimony, which he himself still refused to watch. "Clarence, I'm watching the game the same as you are," Silberman kept telling him, to little avail. The White House switchboard called Thomas to patch through a call from the widow of slain Egyptian President Anwar Sadat. She had called to tell Thomas that he was an international hero. There was little evidence, however, to back up this extravagant, albeit encouraging, claim.

Wright still wished to testify. The Republicans wanted her to, believing it would bolster Thomas. Hill's supporters and many Democrats viewed her as a wild card. Biden's main concern was that he not be perceived as refusing to allow a harassed woman to testify. As the Judiciary Committee met in Kennedy's office, a committee staff member called Wright's lawyer. Wright agreed to a compromise: She would not testify, but her statement and that of Rose Jourdain would be entered into the record. Sukari Hardnett wrote an affidavit attesting that Thomas showed special interest in employees who were "young, black, female and reasonably attractive." She could not, however, corroborate Hill's or Wright's claims.

On Sunday night, a panel of female supporters of Thomas testified during prime time. Diane Holt, J. C. Alvarez, Nancy Fitch, and Phyllis

Berry Myers all sided with Thomas over Hill. Myers noted that Hill lied in stating at her press conference that she did not know her. (Myers herself had little reason to lie, as Thomas had discharged her several years before for bizarre behavior at work.)

Alvarez, a former special assistant, was especially articulate and impressive. A burly woman with large, dark eyes, she referred to herself as "John Q. Public," and said she had flown in to Washington because "I am just a real American from Middle America who will not stand by and watch a crime being committed and walk away." Her description of Hill was devastating:

"I don't know how else to say it but I have to tell you that it just blew my mind to see Anita Hill testifying on Friday. Honest to goodness, it was like schizophrenia. That was not the Anita Hill that I knew and worked with at EEOC. On Friday, she played the role of a meek, innocent, shy Baptist girl from the South who was a victim of this big, bad man.

"I don't know who she was trying to kid. Because the Anita Hill that I knew and worked with was nothing like that. She was a very hard, tough woman. She was opinionated. She was arrogant. She was a relentless debater. And she was the kind of woman who always made you feel like she was not going to be messed with, like she was not going to take anything from anyone. She was aloof. She always acted as if she was a little bit superior to everyone, a little holier than thou. I can recall at the time that she had a view of herself and her abilities that did not seem to be based in reality. For example, it was sort of common knowledge around the office that she thought she should have been Clarence's chief legal advisor and that she should have received better assignments.

"And I distinctly remember when I would hear about her feeling that way or when I would see her pout in office meetings about assignments that she had gotten, I used to think to myself, 'Come on, Anita, let's come down to Earth and live in reality.' She had only been out of law school a couple of years and her experience and her ability couldn't begin to compare with some of the others on the staff. But I also have to say that I was not totally surprised at her wanting these assignments because she definitely came across as someone who was ambitious and watched out for her own advancement. She wasn't really a team player, but more someone who looked out for herself first. You could see the same thing in her relationships with others at the office."

Alvarez added that she herself had been sexually harassed, and she could not conceive of following a harasser to another job.

Hatch asked Diane Holt, Thomas's personal secretary for six years, about the telephone logs and calls from Hill. Holt said they were "always cordial" calls. Hill had called Thomas another five or six times and reached him, thus negating the need for a written message on those occasions (Hill, in other words, had called Thomas more times than the logs indicated). This contradicted another key portion of Hill's testimony. Both Holt and Hill testified that they were good friends and had often gone to lunch together. Holt, however, said she "never" saw anything unusual occur between Thomas and Hill. When Thomas announced he would be leaving Education to head EEOC, Holt recalled of herself and Hill, "We were both enthusiastic about going to EEOC." The two women agreed that "this man is a rising star and we wanted to be there with him."

Hatch asked the four, "Do any of you believe her testimony here?"

All of them replied in the negative. In perhaps the single most damning phrase of the proceedings, Holt, Hill's friend, stated flatly, "I do not believe a word, not one word."

After eleven o'clock, Stanley Grayson, Carlton Stewart, John M. Doggett III and Charles Kothe appeared. Grayson and Stewart confirmed that Hill had told them at the ABA convention that she thought Thomas's nomination was "great" and that he deserved it. This again contradicted Hill. Doggett, a tall, intense black man with a beard, large, expressive eyes, and a proclivity to expressive hand gestures, offered a self-absorbed opening statement about his own life and travails. Doggett then testified that he attended a going-away party for Hill when she left Washington for ORU. At the party, Hill sought him out and asked to talk to him in private. She told him, "I'm very disappointed in you. You really shouldn't lead women on, or lead on women, and then let them down." Doggett testified that he had no interest in Hill and had never expressed any, and was surprised by her statement. He concluded, "Ms. Hill's fantasies about my sexual interest in her were an indication of the fact that she was having a problem with being rejected by men she was attracted to."

Doggett was in for a rough night. Biden pointed out shortly thereafter that his contretemps with Hill was an easily explainable misunderstanding between two members of the opposite sex. Biden and Leahy relished noting the absurdity of Doggett's erotomania analysis. Lost in the exchange, however, was what Doggett's testimony did show: Hill was not credible when she testified she did not remember Doggett. She surely remembered him well, and had denied remembering him to avoid dredging up an episode she knew could only prove embarrassing.

Kothe, the former dean of ORU law school, also cut a striking figure. With his large, Coke-bottle glasses, white hair, and a certain charisma reserved for the elderly when they speak with great animation, Kothe contradicted Hill, stating that he did not offer her a job after watching her teach. He had merely asked her in conversation over lunch whether she might be interested in coming to ORU to teach. Like many white, Christian conservatives, Kothe was enchanted with Thomas and spoke highly of his character, saying he had "never ever heard this man use a profane word. And like I am experienced with other lawyers and other men and in a long discourse inevitably there is a story somebody wants to tell. I never heard him tell a dirty story, so to speak, or make an off-color remark. It just has to be that this man in the situations I have seen him in would have to be the greatest actor in history to have disguised this part of his nature that has been described here...."

Late in the evening, eight other women who had worked with Thomas testified. All of them found it inconceivable that he could have harassed Hill. Pamela Talkin described him as "a man who looked at his shoes when other men were craning their necks to look at a woman."

Other activities, many related to polygraphs, were occurring off camera. Senator Brown sought out his own expert on polygraphs. The expert thought little of the polygraph Hill had passed, judging that the questions were phrased so poorly that she could be evasive but literally truthful. Moreover, the control questions and readout of the polygraph were not available for inspection, and the person who read her tape was judged a political polygraph taker, not an independent expert. Ironically, the committee's liberal lions—Kennedy, Metzenbaum and Simon—previously had spoken out against admitting polygraph test results in court, declaring them unreliable.

Still, Thomas's supporters feared that Hill's passing of her polygraph examination would prove a critical public relations victory. Larry Thompson took the initiative in preparing for Thomas to counter Hill's successful test. He arranged for a polygraph expert to fly in from North Carolina the following morning. Thompson later said he wept after making the call, seeing that his friend had been reduced to such a predicament. He told Sally Danforth that he could not ask Thomas to take the test. Sally agreed to ask him instead.

When she called Thomas and broached the subject, he did not waver. "No, I will not take a polygraph test," he told her. He repeated this when Luttig asked him separately—and again a third time, when Thompson mustered the courage to ask as well. Thomas believed it would set a terrible precedent for people seeking high office in the United States.

There would be no polygraph test for Clarence Thomas. Yet he could not resist telling Thompson, "You tell them I'll be next in line if they take one as to who leaked."

Joy in the Morning

By-and-by he heard somebody call him, and way up the hill he saw Brer Rabbit sitting cross-legged on a chinkapin log combing the pitch out of his hair with a chip of wood. Then Brer Fox knew that he had been fooled mighty badly. Still Brer Rabbit was pleased to fling back some of his sass, and he hollered out:

"Bred and born in the brier patch, Brer Fox—bred and born in the brier patch!"

Polls taken over the weekend showed that the public overwhelmingly believed Thomas over Hill. The margins ranged from 47 to 24 percent (*USA Today*) to 51 to 25 percent (*Los Angeles Times*) to 53 to 29 percent (ABC News–*Washington Post*). After weeks of agony, things were finally going Thomas's way.

Thomas and Hill both were flawed witnesses. For years, Thomas had demonstrated a penchant for exaggerating or trimming the truth in the manner of a successful politician. This defect of character came to the fore at the worst possible time for him, during his testimony on *Roe* earlier in the hearings. Yet Hill faced her own set of problems. She was, as it were, the plaintiff, and as such she bore the burden of proof. The citizens of the legalistic nation to which she spoke grasped this. Moreover, Hill had to overcome a pervasive skepticism arising from the way her allegations had come to light. Her failure to report the alleged behavior at the time and her willingness to exploit her relationship with Thomas subsequently damaged her credibility gravely. Most important, her own story was shredded by Specter's questioning.

Another critical development in Thomas's favor was his growing support among black Americans. Blacks still backed his confirmation by a wider margin than whites. The ABC News–*Washington Post* poll found 70 percent of blacks supporting Thomas, and only 50 percent of whites. *USA Today* found that 63 percent of blacks stood by Thomas, compared with 55 percent of whites. The high-tech lynching speech appeared to have stimulated a significant rise in support over the weekend. In one poll, 61 percent of blacks backed Thomas, an increase from 55 percent the previous month. White support in the same poll was only 50 percent.

Interviews of African-Americans showed a common sentiment. Doshie Palmer, an elderly resident of South Central Los Angeles, stated frankly, "I don't think blacks should be against blacks." The *Atlanta Journal and Constitution* conducted informal canvasses of blacks in the city after the media reported Hill's charges. Some who had not supported Thomas previously now endorsed him, complaining, as one person put it, of his "public castration."

In the Democratic caucus on the eve of the Senate vote, members circulated polls of black Americans concerning the Thomas nomination. These polls solidified the votes of Georgia Democrats Sam Nunn and Wyche Fowler, two critical votes for Thomas. A third Democratic senator told his colleagues that he was going to vote for Thomas specifically because of these polls. The surveys also greatly influenced other Southern Democrats, who counted on strong black support for their reelection fights. Of the eleven Democrats who ended up voting for Thomas, eight were from the South, and were uniformly anxious to retain their critical African-American electoral base.

In the end, the proud nonconformist who bucked racial solidarity would find his political salvation in the black community, which considered him a wayward son. As a result, a moral debt was repaid. As Thomas had stood with his fellow blacks at Holy Cross in the walkout of 1969, so would his fellow blacks stand with him at his moment of maximum peril. Their support would prove decisive.

<hr />

On Monday, October 14, Danforth and Thomas's partisans labored for one last day to shape public opinion. St. Jack, now a hardened warrior deep in the mire, released an affidavit from a partner at Hill's old law firm challenging her testimony about her work history. Danforth also batted around theories of erotomania suggested by Satinover and Dietz.

By then, however, after the longest hearings in the history of Supreme Court nominations, public opinion largely had congealed.

The White House shifted its battle plans to focus on the swing voters in the Senate. Bush and Quayle personally lobbied some 10 to 12 senators, mostly Southern Democrats. Early in the nomination fight, Quayle had obtained private assurance from Alan Dixon that he would vote for the nominee. This would prove vital to Thomas's nomination, as would all pledges of Democratic support. The following day, Tuesday, October 15, Alabama's Richard Shelby gave more encouragement when he announced on the *Today* show that he would vote in favor of Thomas later in the day.

One of the most moving demonstrations of support for Thomas came far to the south. The Savannah area had followed the travails of its favorite son closely. The black-owned *Savannah Tribune* essentially turned over its weekly newspaper to the Hill crisis, carrying five front-page photos of Thomas and declaring, "The Tribune Family Salutes Judge Thomas." In Pin Point, a reporter for the *Los Angeles Times* found that his support among the hamlet's residents had held as firm as "an ancient wall of rocks." The prior Sunday, many of them had attended Sunday services at Thomas's childhood place of worship, Sweet Field of Eden Baptist Church. Afterwards, they conducted a small-scale version of the old civil rights protests that once swept through the area. Some three hundred people picked up handmade signs and marched to the town's community center. During the march, which was nearly a mile in length, the people of Pin Point sang spirituals, including "Jacob's Ladder."

They strode down the sandy road known formally as Pin Point Avenue, past the grounds where Thomas's first home once had stood. Around many of the massive, moss-draped live oaks that formed the landscape of his childhood, yellow ribbons now appeared as signs of support. The residents had designed and purchased T-shirts in honor of the nomination. These depicted the modest skyline of Pin Point and stated below, "Pin Point, Ga. Home of Judge Clarence Thomas." The slogans on the signs were as defiant as the nominee. One quoted Thomas himself: "I'd Rather Die Than Withdraw." Abe Famble, Thomas's cousin and childhood companion, carried a sign depicting a demonic Anita Hill.

On the day of the Senate vote, the streets of the village were almost deserted. The hub of activity was Famble's trailer, which hosted most of the residents for what they hoped would be a victory party. Media vans clogged up much of the sandy semicircle that allowed ingress into Famble's Cove, the collection of homes where Famble and his extended family lived.

The guest of honor was Leola Thomas Williams. The week before, Hill's allegations and the ensuing national drama had left her bedridden. Now, she told the reporters assembled around her how it pained her to see "my son criticized and not be able to do anything about it." She added, "I know my child didn't do what they said he said. If my child had done something like that, I'd jump up in that courtroom and box his mouth." As for Hill's treatment of Thomas, "He helped somebody and this is what he got in return."

As the Senate prepared to vote, Famble's guests fanned out around his large-screen TV. Williams tightly clutched her Bible. She alternately closed her eyes, raised her arms, and prayed with greater intensity as the vote approached. Loud boos went up when Senator Kennedy was mentioned. For some time, the vote held at 49 in favor of confirmation and 46 against. Inexplicably, the TV's audio suddenly went silent. Famble located the remote control and switched to another channel with sound.

A few minutes later, the voting ended. Vice President Quayle, presiding over the Senate, announced the final numbers: 52 senators had voted in favor of Thomas, 48 against. Thomas was confirmed.

Williams and others leaped up from the couch. "We made it! We made it! We made it!" she cheered. Gospel hymns drowned out the television commentators. "Thank you, Jesus!" Williams cried. "We got the victory. God had the last word." She fell to her knees to render thanks and praise. "Oh, my God, what they did to my boy."

The cultural fault lines evident in the battle over Thomas's nomination were equally plain in the national reaction to his confirmation. A bar at Grand Central Station in New York became something of a microcosm for the country. As the television announced the vote total, most of the whites in the bar cursed and wailed. "They believed him," several women cried in disbelief. The half a dozen blacks in the establishment greeted the news altogether differently. They stood up and cheered. Then they raised their glasses to the new Supreme Court justice.

Thomas had watched little of the Senate debate preceding the vote. He had declined an invitation to join President and Mrs. Bush for the occasion, stating that he preferred to remain at home. As the voting neared, he went to take a shower. After the vote, a friend called to inform Ginni of the news. Ginni then told Thomas, who was emerging from the shower, of his confirmation. Thomas shrugged.

Friends of the Thomases soon began to descend on their home. The Danforths, Laws, and others arrived. They joined hands in the living room and gave thanks to God. Allen Moore encouraged Thomas to write a short statement to read to the media, which were preparing to decamp at last from outside his house. Senator Thurmond pressed Thomas to speak as well.

Wearing a suit and black overcoat, and holding a large, black umbrella to shield Ginni and himself from the cold rain, Thomas walked the short distance from his front door to the throngs of journalists waiting along the street. Thurmond accompanied him. Ginni offered her pretty, good-natured smile as a backdrop to the nominee, as he spoke to the media and, through them, the nation.

"This is a time for healing, not a time for anger or animus or animosity," he said. "We have to put these things behind us and go forward." Thomas thanked "all who helped me, all my friends, all those people who prayed for me, those whom I knew, those whom I didn't know, all the people who sent cards and letters and flowers and candy and all sorts of things, but most of all who sent love and who sent support." He offered a heartfelt patriotic flourish: "I'd like to thank America, for the things it stands for. And I'd like to think that at least in my life, in our lives, that we can uphold those ideals."

Thomas also evidenced a rekindling of religiosity. He offered one of the stronger professions of faith by a high-ranking American public official in many years: "I'd also like to make it unequivocally clear that throughout this process, and especially the last painful week, that I give God thanks for our being able to stand here today and I give God thanks for our ability to feel safe, to feel secure, to feel loved, and I give God thanks that the Senate approved me in this process."

Inside, Thomas shook his head back and forth when discussing all that had occurred. He told Sally Danforth what he would tell friends and strangers alike for the next ten years—but always in private: "I just always will be absolutely baffled at what made this thing happen and what made her do this. She was always a very nice person. We always had a fine time together. We were friends. I just cannot understand it. She was a tough woman, but she was a good person. It just baffles me."

The 52 to 48 confirmation vote was the narrowest margin of victory for a Supreme Court nominee in the twentieth century. Five days after his confirmation, on October 18, President Bush hosted Thomas and his supporters at the White House for a swearing-in ceremony. A brilliant sun warmed the crowd of approximately a thousand people. The Marine band played on the Truman balcony, their patriotic tunes blaring above the heads of many politicians and Thomas partisans who had suddenly become nationally renowned. Representatives of the Compton NAACP attended. A number of Thomas's advocates wore buttons saying, "I take a stand so Clarence can take a seat." Senators Biden and DeConcini were the only Democrats from the Judiciary Committee to come to the event. Sylvester Stallone and Reggie Jackson, the famous actor and the baseball player, also were there. Stallone told a reporter, "Considering his humble background, I think he'll be a real representative of the common man."

Also attending was a man neither Thomas nor his mother had seen much of for forty years. After joining the D.C. Circuit, Thomas had found and reestablished relations with his father. M.C. Thomas was still living in Philadelphia. The two men visited each other's homes; Thomas introduced Jamal to his grandfather. Thomas had taken the initiative, and M.C. had reciprocated only slightly. "I didn't want to be hangin' around. I'm not qualified for that," he later explained. Thomas made certain that his father was invited to the event along with his mother. She privately objected to M.C.'s presence. In fact, neither parent had done much for their newly famous son, and Thomas recognized that both had a roughly equal right to share in the occasion.

Bush spoke and praised Thomas's character. "Clarence Thomas has endured America at its worst and he's answered with America at its best. He brings that hard-won experience to the high court and America will be the better for it."

He added, "So let me say to everyone here: Don't be overawed by the solemnity of this moment. Celebrate this day. See what this son of Pin Point has made of himself. See how he makes us proud of America, proud of all that is best in us."

Justice Byron R. White, clad in his black robe, rose to administer the oath. It would not be the judicial oath, which marks the beginning of a Supreme Court justice's tenure. The chief justice alone administered this oath, and the current chief justice, William Rehnquist, was unavailable, his wife having recently passed away. The oath used this day was the standard avowal taken by federal employees. It was an ersatz oath for this occasion, but curiously appropriate given the years Thomas had spent toiling in the federal bureaucracy.

White mentioned that he stood in the place of Rehnquist, who could not attend. He noted politely that the oath he was able to administer was legally meaningless: "When at ten o'clock on November 1, you take the judicial oath that is required by statute, you will become the 106th justice to sit on the Supreme Court, and we look forward to that day." Thomas placed his left hand on a Bible that Ginni held. He raised his right hand and recited the oath read to him by White. "It's a great pleasure, Judge Thomas," White told him upon completing the oath.

Thomas flashed a thumbs-up afterwards, then walked to the lectern. "Wow, this is wonderful," he said. Thomas expressed condolences for the loss of Rehnquist's wife before thanking the crowd for their support.

"Since that bright sunny day in Kennebunkport, July 1, there have been many difficult days as we all went through the confirmation battle, and I mean we all. But on this sunny day in October, at the White House, there is joy. Joy in the morning."

The crowd applauded. Thomas's allusion to Psalm 30:5 reflected his recent stirring of faith. "I thank Almighty God, I thank those who stood along the road of 43 years of my life from Pin Point to the Supreme Court, from 1948 to 1991." He had not thanked the Almighty in his speech at Kennebunkport; he took pains to remedy that omission now. He finished: "Only in America could this day have been possible. I thank you all and may God bless you."

On November 1, Rehnquist swore in Thomas officially in an oak-paneled conference room at the Supreme Court. Only Ginni and Danforth attended. It was the first time in fifty years that this ceremony had taken place in private. Such seclusion was the first of many signs that the Thomas who emerged from his confirmation hearings was an emotionally scarred man.

Ten years later, when a high-school student asked him to describe the typical career path of a Supreme Court justice, Thomas laughed. He replied that his own career plans had gone "down the drain." He then summoned from his well of prudent wisdom a durable instruction that captured well his own experience: "You do well what's before you. And don't stop dreaming and hoping and thinking."

The confirmation hearings were a travesty with no redeeming features, Danforth would state ten years later. When asked if Thomas had become more religious because of the hearings, he replied categorically, "There is nothing good that could be said for what happened." This was a remarkable statement coming from a Christian minister. Danforth came to describe the confirmation ordeal as yielding a "resurrection" of Thomas, but he meant this in a vague, secular sense.

Thomas himself recognized that he had come out of the hearings fundamentally transformed, and, he believed, a "better person." He felt the brutal hearings had been "God's will." Many Hill sympathizers would praise the hearings for providing a national seminar on sexual harassment; Danforth and most of Thomas's other friends and advisers would condemn the hearings with equal force. What all of them missed was the greatest dividend of the hearings, at least from Thomas's perspective. By his own reckoning, he had grown closer to his God.

PART SIX

Defender of the Framers

The Stillness of Wounded Pride

On the day he joined the Supreme Court, Clarence Thomas instantly became, far and away, the most famous of the nine justices. Indeed, he was the most famous justice since Earl Warren, who provoked the angry signs that Thomas had noticed along Georgia highways as a child. The televised hearings into Anita Hill's allegations ensured that the public eye would stare at Thomas for the rest of his life. This steady gaze would transform his life and singe his soul. He would complain about being recognized not only in hardware stores near his home, but on the streets of London. Even under the best of circumstances, the obsessively private Thomas would have found fame terribly bothersome after the novelty quickly faded. The supernova of negative notoriety he had experienced proved a far worse burden, one he could not bear.

And yet ignominy was part of the deal. The stares, the giggles, the occasional jabs from late-night comedians—they would become as essential an aspect of his existence as his black robe. Thomas would confront this new adversity predictably: with pride, work ethic, withdrawal and bitterness.

One of his first acts was not in keeping with the entrenchment and seclusion that were to come. He and Ginni granted an extensive and highly personal interview to, of all publications, *People* magazine, a periodical devoted largely to fawning profiles of and gossip about celebrities. The magazine made the exclusive interview its cover story. Ginni shared in the interview that she had been sexually harassed at a previous job before she met Thomas. ("I think Clarence would have killed him.") She also compared Hill to the deluded Glenn Close character in the movie *Fatal Attraction,* adding, "I always believed she was probably someone in love with my husband and never got what she wanted."

Word leaked out of the high court that some of Thomas's fellow justices were miffed at this interview. They were right that *People* was scarcely the periodical of record for Supreme Court justices. Still, the nation benefited, if only because Thomas would grant so few other interviews in the years to come. Except for occasional, prepared speeches to friendly audiences, the voice that once resonated so strongly and defiantly throughout the Senate Caucus Room and national airwaves was about to grow silent.

He moved into chambers described by one of his clerks as "very small," in keeping with those normally reserved for the newest justice. Within a year, he would relocate into the more spacious chambers formerly occupied by Byron White. The accommodations were typical for the Court. The thick wooden door and paneling were of American quartered white oak, stained dark. Shelves full of Supreme Court case-law books covered one wall. A fireplace took a square bite out of another. Above it hung a portrait of Booker T. Washington. A third wall featured photos and paintings of black history and of Savannah during the 1950s. Thomas would move these decorations around from time to time. On the wall behind his desk, surrounded by an ornate silver-and-gold frame, was a black-and-white sketch of Frederick Douglass.

The fireplace became a focal point in the room. Thomas said that his "rule" was to use the fireplace instead of the central heating when the temperature outside dropped below 50 degrees. "It makes me feel like I'm on the farm or something," he explained. Above the sleek black mantle, Thomas placed various objects of affection. There were photographs of Ginni and Jamal, one of which showed his son posing in his handsome gray VMI uniform. Later, Thomas would place on the mantle a black bust of Churchill, which the Claremont Institute would bestow upon him. Ginni gave him a second bust that evoked still greater sentimentality, and that Thomas placed on one of his bookshelves—a small bronze bust of his grandfather. Inscribed below was one of Myers Anderson's more memorable epigrams: "OLD MAN CAN'T IS DEAD. I HELPED BURY HIM."

A huge, dark mahogany desk dominated the office space. Placed on top were miscellaneous items of utility and expression: a green banker's lamp, a silver cup holding pens, a Rolodex stuffed with names of friends. As at the court of appeals, a standing desk was placed to the side for those occasions when Thomas chose to rise from his leather chair. There was also a computer—which, as one Thomas clerk put it, "he actually uses." On his desk and mantle would appear, over the years, signs to pronounce his views and injunctions. They displayed the bellicosity, droll humor, and obsession with privacy that overwhelmed him post–Anita Hill. They read, "SAVE AMERICA, BOMB YALE LAW SCHOOL"; "NO WORD SPOKEN HERE IS EVER REPEATED OUTSIDE THESE WALLS"; "Please do not emanate into the penumbra," mocking the language from *Griswold v. Connecticut* that provided the raw jurisprudential material for *Roe.* On his blue leather couch was a pillow that Sally Danforth made for him, its woven message saying, "He ain't heavy, he's my brother."

Through the massive oak door that separated his office from the world was a foyer. Seated at desks outside were his two secretaries, both of them African-American. Two of his clerks sat in a room off the foyer; the other two clerks sat in an office upstairs (the pairs would trade places in the middle of the court's annual term). Paintings in the foyer depicted rural black life: cotton bales being unloaded from a riverboat, laborers working in a cotton field.

Despite lifetime tenure, Thomas continued to follow his grandfather-inculcated regimen of rising before daylight to begin his work. He typically awakened at 4:00 A.M. By 5:30, he and Ginni (with whom he carpooled to work) would drive down Interstate 66 past the Beltway, then across the Potomac toward the Capitol. Arriving at the court at around 6:00 or 6:30, he shed his business attire to work out in the court gymnasium. He often listened to "oldies" music (rock-and-roll from his childhood) as he rode an exercise bicycle or lifted free weights. He no longer jogged around Capitol Hill, something he had enjoyed before the confirmation hearings took away his anonymity.

He entered his chambers at around 7:00 or 7:30, ready for work. Unless oral argument spilled over into afternoon or an extended lunch date appeared on his calendar (his favorite haunt was the Monocle, a restaurant near the Capitol), he left for home at around 1:00 P.M. for the rest of the workday. The advent of faxes and, subsequently, the Internet allowed Thomas this flexibility; he became the first justice to have his house wired for telecommuting. For the remainder of the day, he communicated with his clerks by telephone or e-mail. Thomas sometimes retired to his study in the early evening to complete the day's labors.

Prior to joining the Court, Thomas believed it to be fractured personally as well as professionally along ideological lines. He noted, "What I had read suggested there were different and apparently warring camps among the justices." Now he tirelessly repeated how wrong this misconception had been—and how grateful he was for the cordiality he encountered. Almost a decade later, Thomas would affirm that he had yet to hear an "unkind word" from his fellow justices. He would hold up the Court as a "model of civility."

He attributed this comity to institutional necessity. He once remarked, "You decide these cases with eight other people and not like them and see how hard that is." The cultural fissures that his nomination deepened could easily have alienated the more liberal members of the Court. Thomas detected no such revulsion. Still, the other eight justices were a brilliant and intimidating group.

He found Chief Justice William Rehnquist a "wonderful, fair" man. A tall, somewhat awkward man, Rehnquist was known to be short with attorneys who did not show proper deference to the Court or respect for the Court's time in oral argument. In conference with his fellow justices, Rehnquist was a bit more gentle. He would nudge colleagues who digressed from or belabored the topic at hand by saying, "So what's your vote?" Thomas referred to him as "Chief." Soon after joining the Court, Thomas confided in Rehnquist that he felt "a bit out of place," given the great lawyers who had preceded him. Rehnquist replied, "Clarence, in the first years you wonder how you got here. After that you wonder how your colleagues got here."

Other friendships took root with several of his fellow associate justices. Sandra Day O'Connor, the first female justice, became, in his words "a dear, dear friend on the court." Reserved and aloof, O'Connor gained among attorneys back in her native Arizona the nickname "The Ice Maiden" for her demeanor and toughness on criminals while she was a state-court judge. She was kind to Thomas when he joined the Court, and he reciprocated. By decade's end, the Thomases and O'Connors would vacation together in O'Connor's home state of Arizona.

Thomas also came to cherish his relationship with Lewis Powell, a recently retired justice. Like O'Connor, Powell was a justice whose jurisprudence lacked firm philosophical moorings. Thomas judged the graceful, elderly Virginian a "wonderful, decent man." Powell and Thomas were the two Southerners on the Court. Thomas insisted that Powell was from the "upper South," while he hailed from the "deep South." Only Southerners would have quibbled over such a distinction.

Also retaining chambers in the Supreme Court building was Thurgood Marshall. At their first meeting, which took place after Thomas's confirmation, he and Marshall spoke for over two hours, with Marshall sharing stories from his days as a civil rights lawyer and justice. But in subsequent speeches, Thomas would not refer publicly to any warm personal conversations he had had with the justice he replaced. Thomas's clerks later confirmed that the two men were not close. Given that Marshall had been privately opposed to Thomas's nomination, this was to be expected.

His closest friend on the Court during the first year was Byron White. The man who stood in for Rehnquist at the *faux* swearing-in ceremony at the White House was, by some measures, an unlikely Thomas intimate. He had been appointed to the Court in 1962 by a Democrat, John F. Kennedy. The two dissimilar justices did, however, share a passion for sports. White had accomplished what Thomas had only dreamt of as an athlete: he had been a star running back for the University of Colorado football team, where he earned the nickname "Whizzer." He went on to play professional football, also becoming a Rhodes scholar, Yale Law School graduate, and decorated Navy veteran of World War II. Thomas and White played basketball once or twice a week with a handful of clerks on a court right above the main courtroom—a floor known by the irreverent nickname "The Highest Court in the Land."

In White, Thomas found not only a sports hero, but a teacher. The Thomas who ran EEOC frequently delighted in skewering his opponents with hard-edged rhetoric. In his Supreme Court opinions, Thomas by and large would avoid such declamations. A major reason for this shift was the influence of White. One of Thomas's clerks observed, "Thomas tries to model his opinions off Justice White. He was one of his mentors, even though they were on the Court together only a short time." Thomas thereafter would strive to write measured opinions in the mold of White.

This was quite unlike another justice who would loom over Thomas's career. Antonin Scalia would become widely known as something of an intellectual puppet master of Thomas, an unfair but foreseeable allegation. A diminutive Italian-American with a ready, acerbic wit, Scalia was a brilliant intellect and the best writer on the Court since Oliver Wendell Holmes. Unwilling to subordinate his wicked pen to something as uninspiring as collegiality, he enjoyed provoking his intellectual opponents just as Thomas had enjoyed jousting with his political foes in the 1980s. Thomas's clerks confirmed that Scalia's barbs caused a "long breach" between him and O'Connor.

Thomas and Scalia, on the other hand, had much in common. Both were conservative appointees of Republican presidents; both enjoyed being provocateurs; Scalia was ardently Catholic, Thomas waywardly so. These similarities invited comparisons, and journalists came to dismiss Thomas as a Scalia "clone," advancing the notion that Thomas merely followed Scalia's lead. These accusations were some of the toughest blows that the fiercely independent Thomas had to absorb during his time on the Court.

The Supreme Court was not a tightly knit social network. The chambers of the nine justices were dispersed throughout the large, unnaturally quiet building. Even mere conversation among the justices was relatively rare, confined mostly to formal conferences and occasional lunches. This was a disappointment to the garrulous Thomas. He would describe life on the Court as "isolated" and "sedentary." The justices conducted their daily business, he observed, in "virtual isolation, even within the Court. It is quite rare that the members of the Court see each other during those periods when we're not sitting or when we're not in conference. And the most regular contact beyond those two formal events are the lunches we have on conference and court days." On another occasion, he observed, "It's like an old big refrigerator there, lonely and cold."

On Monday mornings, Thomas's adamant stride could be heard striking the marble floors en route to the robing room on the first floor. He and the other justices draped themselves with the standard black robe of a Supreme Court justice, then emerged at ten o'clock through openings in a large, red velvet curtain to enter the main courtroom, or Court Chamber, for oral argument. The courtroom rose to a forty-four-foot ceiling and was lined with Ionic columns of white Italian marble. Above the columns were friezes of eminent lawgivers: Moses, King John (the reluctant signer of the Magna Carta), Blackstone. Confucius and Mohammed lent some cultural and religious diversity to the art, perhaps to keep the ACLU from filing suit against the Supreme Court itself. Ionic columns stood behind the justices, who sit in high-backed, svelte black leather chairs. Microphones were provided for all nine. Thomas almost never needed his.

After oral argument, the justices would meet in private conferences to discuss and vote on the cases. The Court sat for oral argument on Monday, Tuesday and Wednesday mornings. The Monday cases were discussed at conferences on Wednesday afternoons, the Tuesday and Wednesday cases on Friday mornings. Before each conference, Thomas would read the briefs submitted by the attorneys, the petition for writ of certiorari or "cert petition," and the opinions of the lower courts. Also, he held extensive discussions with his clerks in chambers before drafting an outline giving the reasons for his decision. He summed up his preparation for the conferences as "reading, writing, and thinking."

The conferences began with a handshake. This was a tradition that Thomas deemed a "sign of mutual respect." The justices discussed one case at a time, going around the large wooden table, starting with the chief justice, then in descending order of seniority. Each justice offered both a vote and an explanation. "We don't have the luxury of saying, 'Well, I feel that this should be the answer.' We have to explain why you think it's the answer," Thomas noted.

Being the newest member of the Supreme Court carried advantages and disadvantages. At the D.C. Circuit, the junior judge was required to express his views first at conferences—"and the others could sort of chop away," Thomas recalled. At the Supreme Court, however, the newest justice voted last. That made things "quite a bit easier. I get to see all the other arguments and by the time it gets to me, virtually everything that is going to be said on any side of the issue has been said—except when I differ with all eight, then you feel a bit like a brat."

With his rookie status came certain obligations, which constituted a very mild form of hazing. He was required to open the door and keep the minutes of the conferences. David Souter, who handed these duties over to Thomas, gave him what Thomas called some "on-the-job training as to what that really meant and how to record the votes and how to report. He literally sat next to me and allowed me to be his apprentice for several weeks before he turned it over."

Critical to the Supreme Court's operations were the clerks. Each justice could hire four. They were the workhorses who prevented the justices from being submerged in paperwork, much of it frivolous. In 1972, the justices started a "pool" arrangement to deal with the burgeoning caseload of an increasingly litigious society. They decided that the clerks would review incoming petitions for writ of certiorari. A clerk reviewing a petition would write a "cert memo" to all the justices in the pool. This memo would summarize the case and recommend whether the Court should grant or deny "cert"—that is, accept or reject the case. The justices then would vote based on the clerk's memorandum. Only John Paul Stevens did not participate in this arrangement.

Typically, the Court accepted around one hundred cases each term. Thomas, like the other justices, also enlisted his clerks to write a "bench memo" for his eyes only, discussing the merits of the case. Like the clerks for the other justices, Thomas's clerks would write the first drafts of his Court opinions. By the time Thomas's opinions were published, however, they would usually bear the distinct imprint of his own forceful style, consistent with his writings before he joined the Court.

No justice could boast of greater loyalty from his clerks. Thomas came to refer to them alternately as his "family" or "kids." Thomas's clerks were drawn from the same general background. All were in the top 1 or 2 percent of their law school class, and all came from elite institutions. More than half came from three law schools: Harvard, Yale, and the University of Chicago. Thomas privately stated his belief that these schools offered the most rigorous programs; that the first two were the most prestigious and the last the most conservative of the nation's top ten schools surely were factors in his eyes as well. Over the years, Thomas selected a higher percentage of minorities as clerks (14 percent) than any other justice save for Stevens, who tied him for this distinction. This would come as no surprise to his diverse former colleagues at EEOC. Nor was it at all odd that the female clerks he selected were, as one of them put it, a "pretty tough group of women."

Prospective clerks were required first to clerk for a year on a U.S. court of appeals. The "feeder judges" for whom they worked served as a filter through whom only the premier clerks passed to the Supreme Court. Thomas's friend Larry Silberman enjoyed the best rate for placing his clerks on the Supreme Court. Thomas routinely selected one clerk a year from Silberman's chambers and another from the chambers of friend and former aide-de-camp Mike Luttig, who sat on the Fourth Circuit Court of Appeals. An interview for a Thomas clerkship had two stages. First, the current Thomas clerks would interview the applicant. As one clerk recounted, this first interview was a "very rigorous interview to make sure you understand where he [Thomas] stands on the issues." Afterwards, the applicant enjoyed what this clerk described as a "nice conversation" with Thomas himself. Thomas's hard-nosed management style still found an outlet at the Court: He smartly delegated the unpleasantness of ideological vetting to subordinates.

Thomas oversaw only four clerks and a couple of secretaries and a messenger. "He's a very good administrator," one clerk recalled. "I think that comes from his years in the executive branch." He selected one of his clerks each term to serve as the chief clerk. In practice, this honorific meant the designated clerk was responsible for certain administrative tasks, such as keeping track of the deadlines for submission of bench memos and opinions. "He liked to run a tight ship," said one clerk. "He wanted to finish things with plenty of time. He liked to have a bench memo written so that each clerk could see it."

There was a reason for this policy. Thomas circulated the bench memos to the other clerks before convening a meeting of the clerks in his chambers. The four clerks then debated how he should vote on pending cases. These meetings were called clerk conferences. Most justices preferred merely to review a bench memo from a single clerk before deciding how to vote. Thomas desired and invited a wide-ranging discussion by his clerks so that he might consider every possible factor. Not one to let talent go to waste, he sought to tap the collective intelligence of the crew of young lawyers at his disposal. As at EEOC, he also seemed to revel in presiding over such intellectual skirmishes. While he was not the only justice to hold clerk conferences—Scalia and O'Connor also did so—his conferences were the most uninhibited and wide-ranging on the Court. One clerk explained, "I think there are justices who don't really want to hear too much debate. In other chambers, I got the sense that too much discussion was not really, that clerks were hesitant to sometimes press a point. But in our chambers, it was, 'Say whatever you want, duke it out,' and the justice liked listening to that."

For the clerks, as for the justice, these clerk conferences were one of the highlights of their service on the Court. One Thomas clerk summed up well the prevailing sentiment among the clerks in stating that this "free-for-all argument with him about how his opinion should come out" was "the most remarkable thing about the clerkship." Another clerk described the clerk conferences as a "knockdown, drag-out fight for two hours or more." In the early part of a term, Thomas held back on offering his own views so as not to discourage robust debate. "He hated yes people," one clerk stated. "He wanted people to air their views. Then when they got more comfortable, the dynamic would change." Another clerk observed of the conferences that "there were no sacred cows. Maybe it's the iconoclastic nature of the justice that trickles down to his clerks."

Broad guidelines governed such conferences. For all the strong opinions the clerks expressed on the major issues before the Court, the clerk conferences were always, in one clerk's words, a "very good-natured, professional exchange of views." If the conversation veered into an area that he thought too far afield, Thomas would prod the clerk back to the subject at hand with a comment such as, "No, we're not going that way." Some topics were off limits only because of time constraints. One clerk noted as an example that it was "not productive" to "reargue the constitutionality of the death penalty." When Thomas felt that the subject had been exhausted, he would declare, "We're done now."

The clerks tended to fall into two ideological camps. This duality reflected the divergent wings of the conservative coalition that Thomas straddled so well and naturally: traditionalists, known in the law as originalists, and libertarians. Originalists believed the Supreme Court should interpret the Constitution by consulting the intentions of the Framers. Libertarians asserted that the federal judiciary should use its power to curb excessive government regulations and increase economic liberty. These twin impulses competed constantly for the fidelity of Thomas's heart. In the clerk conferences, both typically found their champions. One clerk noted, "He's willing to go back to the very beginning on constitutional issues, figure out the original understanding, track the case law and figure out a point where the case law" began to depart from the will of the Framers. Yet he was also attuned to libertarian concerns. In either case, if doing the right thing meant overturning long-settled Court opinions, Thomas was not averse to doing so. One clerk noted that in the conferences as well as in his opinions, "Nothing is taken for granted."

From these and other experiences, Thomas's clerks would come away with a conception of their boss strikingly similar to that held by Thomas's many former subordinates in the executive branch. Typical was the assessment of one female clerk: "He's just the greatest guy in the world. If he told me to walk across burning coals for a mile, I'd ask which direction to go. . . . He's one of a handful of people, and handful is probably an overestimation, who I can honestly say has never disappointed me, has never let me down in any way."

In addition to the clerk conferences, Thomas's clerks enjoyed a closer relationship with their justice than clerks in any other chambers. Some clerks saw their justices rarely, and then only in a very formal setting. Some clerks were "bummed out," in the words of one Thomas clerk, because their justice had forgotten their names. Other justices were quite austere compared with Thomas. One Thomas clerk contrasted him with O'Connor: "I think you feel very much on your p's and q's around her." Similarly, while Justice Scalia was described as a "great guy," one clerk noted, "He doesn't kind of goof around with his clerks." With Thomas, on the other hand, "He's so unpretentious and down-to-earth that you feel like you can joke around with him. That you can smile and tell a joke and it will be well received."

Thomas would chat with his clerks about their families, personal lives, and current events, making the clerkship experience, in the words of one clerk, like being "part of a family." Frequently, he invited his clerks to join him for lunch in the Senate cafeteria near the Court. "It was fun to see people drop their food trays when they realized who he was," recalled one participant. He enjoyed teasing the clerks, handing out nicknames based on, for example, a point of view they repeatedly voiced. Such humble mingling with and concern for his clerks was, in one clerk's experience, "unique" on the Court. As a result, his clerks became "terrifically loyal to him."

At the beginning of the term, Thomas would invite the new clerks over to his house for dinner and a screening of his favorite movie, *The Fountainhead*. The stilted acting tended to evoke groans and jokes from the young, critical audience. "A lot of people think the movie is bad," one clerk remembered. "People tease him and rib him" because of it. But, the clerk added, "You just can't imagine sitting in a living room of, say, Justice O'Connor and making fun of her" in the same manner.

— —

Within the giant white walls of the Supreme Court building, Thomas was able to cocoon himself in a tranquil world disconnected from the hurly-burly outside; such was the prerogative of judges with lifetime tenure. Yet the emotional wounds inflicted by the Anita Hill ordeal were deep, painful and lasting. Signs quickly began to emerge that for all the solace he gained from life in the most obscure and secretive of the three branches of government, all was not well. He began the construction of a vast moat of privacy designed to protect him from his detractors.

Soon after he joined the court, he and Ginni moved to a wooded, five-acre lot with a large house in suburban Fairfax County, Virginia. The large, red-brick house they purchased stood at the end of a long, paved driveway on the edge of dense woods. The structure featured five bedrooms and a large wooden deck, which blended into the sylvan landscape behind the house. Even at such a secluded location, however, Thomas was not beyond the reach of his tormentors. Picketers led by Rev. Al Sharpton would protest outside his home later in the decade. Shortly after he and Ginni moved in, unidentified vandals destroyed their mailbox.

Thomas grew bitter at the high price he had paid for his seat on the Supreme Court, later describing himself as a "wounded bear those first few years" on the Court. He was too proud to discuss Anita Hill's charges publicly. In private settings, however, he felt an abiding need to share his frustrations and feelings, even with strangers. In lunches with clerks of other justices, Thomas brought up the subject of the confirmation battle himself. "He clearly wanted to talk about what happened," one clerk told a newspaper reporter. "He really wants people to agree with him that something outrageous happened."

The same pattern replicated itself in conversations Thomas held over lunch or at parties in and around Washington. He would either raise the subject of the Hill hearings himself or eagerly discuss the topic if raised. The common theme to such catharses was that Hill's charges were "crazy." The impetus behind these comments was a desire for others to appreciate the trauma he had experienced. This was a message that also would tincture many of his speeches throughout the decade— though none of them would mention Hill. One friend recalled that every time they met for lunch after the hearings, he would "rehash the confirmation hearings."

The tragic effects of the Anita Hill hearings were profound and barely below the surface. One person close to Thomas described the transformation that the hearings wrought: "I think it just destroyed him. I think it changed him for life. It was a horribly sad thing on all sorts of levels. It just ruined him. It just ruined the second half of his life. He'll never get over that attack on him. And it's colored his thinking." This friend described the confirmation ordeal as "something he can't forget and can't forgive." The attack of his "reputation for integrity and dignity" was too much for him to endure without bitterness.

Many Thomas friends acknowledged that the confirmation ordeal made him a far more steadfast conservative. One friend said: "I think much of what he does now is not a payback, that's too crass, but is just a natural reaction to the pain they put him through. I think he would not be as conservative on the Court if not for those confirmation hearings. The Clarence that I knew, that I used to talk to about things, was not as conservative." Thomas's thinking process was described as: "I'm gonna live long enough; I'm gonna stay on the Court long enough; and I'm gonna write the decisions that will get them. I don't think that's his conscious thinking, but that's his way of getting revenge." In short, "He's very angry. It shouldn't affect his thinking on the Court, but it does."

Jeff Zuckerman, Thomas's chief of staff at EEOC, also sensed a change in ideology—which he applauded. The Anita Hill hearings provided the last fillip Thomas required to make him the unwavering conservative so many of his friends and allies hoped he would become. Zuckerman explained:

> The Clarence Thomas before the Anita Hill escapade was not the same person as the Justice Thomas who came out of that escapade. My take

is that Chairman Thomas, Court of Appeals Judge Thomas, . . . to whatever degree he disagreed with the civil rights organizations, I think he nonetheless accepted them as good people. He could disagree with them, but still think they're decent people. I think that the Anita Hill escapade . . . shocked him into believing that these were basically evil people. He'd been doing a lot of reading over the years, and not just Sowell, without really fully buying into it, I think. But I think the shock of that whole experience, to see who were his friends and who was out to destroy him as a human being, I think kind of pushed him into a camp, pushed him really firmly.

Zuckerman noted, "In 1984, even 1986 when I left, I believe he was personally conservative, but not a real strong, self-assured kind. But I think today," Zuckerman added with a chuckle, "he's a real, real conservative."

In comments both public and private, Thomas let it be known that he would pursue a policy of retribution through longevity. He vowed to stay on the Court for forty years. This would mean he would retire when he was eighty-three, the same age as Thurgood Marshall when he left the Court. At one meeting with black reporters, Thomas said, "I'm going to be here for 40 years. For those who don't like it, get over it." He repeated this to friends and audiences throughout the 1990s. His advice to Glenn Loury, a friend and black academic, was, "I want you to start exercising and watch your diet so you'll be around when I step down from the Court in 2034. They can say what they want to say, but I'm going to be making law for a long time."

The emotional scars showed in other ways. Thomas began to tell people that he did not watch TV news or read the newspapers aside from viewing sports programming or reading the sports pages. "I occasionally stumble into the news," he told one audience. "I read newspapers very quickly. I read the *New York Post,* usually. It has a fabulous sports page." Such an explanation of "stumbling into the news" was embarrassingly labored and typical of his orientation toward the media. His peculiar behavior apparently prompted even Ginni to question him about it. "My wife says she is amazed at how much news I am aware of, and I don't know where I get it. . . . But I do keep up with it. I don't read about the Court. I don't read about people who write about the Court. . . . But I somehow get the news." He has admitted to reading the *Washington Times,* the city's more conservative newspaper, and to listening to Rush Limbaugh, who became a good friend in the 1990s. The same Thomas who, as a child, had squinted at the newspapers wall-papering his house as he learned to read now shunned such journals with equal intensity.

The most publicly visible change in Thomas was his silence during oral argument. The man who was described in his senior yearbook as someone who "loves to argue"; who held forth as a voice crying in the wilderness in the Black Students' Union at Holy Cross; who surrounded himself with people of different ideological stripes at EEOC, largely for the pleasure of debating: this man did not survive the confirmation process. In his place was a man demonstrably fearful of participating in oral argument. Seldom did he say anything at all in the chamber; almost never did he ask a question. As one of his clerks noted, "There's a silence in the chamber when he asks a question, because he asks one so rarely."

Those who had known Thomas over the years found this transformation puzzling. Mike Boicourt, his old friend from the Missouri Attorney General's Office, had seen Thomas make his first oral arguments to the Missouri Supreme Court. "It strikes me as odd," Boicourt observed, "that he has this policy now of not speaking during oral argument. He was certainly outgoing and inquisitive when I knew him and confident of his ability to speak in public." One judge on the D.C. Circuit also noticed the difference. "He's like two different people. He was talkative, gregarious on our court, a real participant. Now he seems to be in a shell."

Thomas would offer various explanations for this policy of silence, none of them persuasive. One was that his refusal to ask questions was an act of self-denial. "I've been criticized for not talking much, but I find it hard to talk and listen at the same time," he said. Put another way to another audience: "If I invite you to argue your case, I should at least listen to you." To his clerks, Thomas would say that he viewed oral argument as largely superfluous. "It's in the briefs," he would tell them; lawyers could add little orally to what they had written in far more detail. On another occasion, when a high-school student asked him why he was so quiet, he replied, "There are lots of reasons." He rattled off several: "One, do you think there are too few questions asked? ... I don't ask for entertainment.... Usually, if you wait long enough, someone else will ask your question.... I've been on the other side of the podium.... I don't want to give them a hard time."

These excuses crumbled with any scrutiny. Oral argument was an old institution at the Court. Such a sweeping dismissal of the entire practice—from a conservative, no less—begged more questions than it answered. That other justices asked questions did not mean that Thomas's were of no value. Giving the attorneys a "hard time" was how a Supreme Court justice made them earn their pay. Throughout his life, Thomas had grown silent when placed in a new and challenging situation, withdrawing until he learned his way around his new environment. On the Supreme Court, Thomas grew quiet and stayed that way, long after he had otherwise become comfortable as a justice. By the end of the 1990s, Thomas was the only justice who almost never said a word in oral argument.

His loyal clerks noted that liberal justices such as Brennan and Marshall rarely asked questions, yet were not criticized for their silence. The difference was that Thomas had joined the high court in the era of Oprah Winfrey and obsessive self-expression, a culture for which he showed some affinity in his speeches and public pronouncements. This was a man who, throughout his life, had lived for the sting of rhetorical battle. If any member of the Court should have hastened and welcomed the free-ranging oral argument that came to the Court in the 1990s, it was Thomas. Instead, he spent oral arguments clearly detached from the proceedings: rubbing his eyes in apparent boredom; slouched in his chair, looking upwards; flipping through papers. His actions betrayed him further: He did not even bother to listen to the attorneys to whom, he insisted, he was deferring.

One positive outcome of the Anita Hill contretemps was a deeper loyalty and commitment to those who stood with him during that trial. Armstrong Williams, who remained a close friend, saw that Thomas became more thoughtful of others after the experience. In the 1990s, Williams suffered a couple of significant personal traumas—when a male employee sued him for sexual harassment and when he and his longtime girlfriend parted ways. In response to the first event, Williams said, "He'd call every day. He'd send me notes. He'd say he was praying for me. He was the best friend I had during that time." Several years later, when he broke up with his girlfriend, Thomas "called every day for several weeks." The Thomas of the 1990s gave back more to his friends than he had previously. Williams concluded, "It shows how much he's grown. . . . He could never have given that of himself during the eighties."

Thomas also rewarded his loyalists more publicly. On November 19, 1991, Thomas appeared on National Empowerment Television to be interviewed by Paul Weyrich of the Free Congress Foundation. In the years before cable TV news channels, Weyrich's group beamed a talk show by satellite to his followers around the country. Thomas told the audience of conservative activists, "We would like to thank everyone and indicate to everyone out there, everyone in this room, around the country, the deep, deep gratitude that we have for the way that you stood up for us and the love that you showed for us." By contrast, Thomas shied from hostile venues. In April 1992 he was scheduled to judge evening moot-court competition at Seton Hall Law School in Newark, New Jersey. After learning that a women's student group was planning a candlelight vigil to protest his presence, Thomas cancelled. This, too, was the start of a pattern.

For some, his lingering bitterness was especially compelling proof that he was innocent of Hill's charges. As one commentator noted, "Deep-set anger is not the emotion commonly associated with guilty men who have beaten the rap." But Thomas's withdrawal from public debate and adverse forums cast an unnecessary pall over his public life that his supporters would struggle for a decade to explain or defend. He would not forgive his enemies or subject his pride to additional incoming fire. For this stubborn policy, he would suffer further, as the pains of the past gnawed at him.

Few would confront him about these shortcomings. After his confirmation to the Court, many of Thomas's friends became literal courtiers. Their professional interest in remaining in his good graces precluded even friendly criticism, especially in such a sensitive area of his life. So it fell to a police officer at the Supreme Court to tell Thomas what he needed to hear. Soon after Thomas joined the Court, this officer "would look at me worn down and he would say, 'Don't let them steal your joy.'" This would prove to be the single best piece of advice Thomas received during his first ten years on the court.

One realm in his life over which Thomas retained total control was his judicial philosophy. The confirmation hearings solidified his philosophical inclinations, but they did not make him a doctrinaire conservative. He had showed this orientation in speeches delivered in the late 1980s, when he was already quoting the Founders in counseling the nation on the best course of collective action.

On the Supreme Court, this reverence for tradition and constancy led Thomas to embrace originalism. Opposing originalism was the "living Constitution" theory of the left, which held that judges must update the Constitution by interpreting it in line with contemporary theories of justice. This meant that judges were free to rule as they pleased, guided only by their conscience. Thomas believed that when the Court voted in this manner, decreeing a public policy without public approval, it was robbing the American people of some of their democratic power. In opposing the antidemocratic jurisprudence of the "living Constitution," originalism, as understood by Thomas, was shorthand for commitment to the rule of law.

Thomas's originalism became evident almost immediately. As when he started at the Missouri Attorney General's Office and then the D.C. Circuit, his workload was initially freighted with commercial, statutory and criminal cases. In *Doggett v. United States*, for example, the Supreme Court considered the appeal of a man who, after being indicted on federal drug charges, left the country for Panama, then later returned to America and avoided arrest for over eight years. The Court held that by taking so long to arrest and prosecute him, the federal government had violated Doggett's Sixth Amendment right to a speedy trial. In a dissent joined by Rehnquist and Scalia, Thomas wrote that the Court should have upheld his conviction. Thomas surveyed the history of the Speedy Trial Clause, finding that it was not meant to bar such prosecution. He concluded that Doggett had suffered no harm from the delay, but in fact benefited to the extent that he had turned his life around in the interim, leading the judge to give him a lighter sentence because of his subsequent reformation. "Today's opinion, I fear, will transform the courts of the land into boards of law enforcement supervision," Thomas wrote.

The omen articulated in this last sentence would find a striking parallel in Thomas's most famous opinion of his first term. In *Hudson v. McMillian,* an inmate in Louisiana, Keith Hudson, sued prison officials for physical abuse he suffered while in custody. Two correctional officers beat Hudson while a supervisor told them "not to have too much fun." A federal magistrate who reviewed the case described the injuries Hudson sustained as "minor." Nevertheless, these included minor bruises, facial swelling, loosened teeth, and a cracked partial dental plate. Hudson filed suit under federal civil rights statutes, alleging that prison officials violated the Eighth Amendment's prohibition on cruel and unusual punishments.

In a 7–2 decision, the Supreme Court, breaking with earlier rulings, upheld Hudson's right to sue prison officials for these injuries. Under its previous decisions, inmates were permitted to sue only if they could prove that they had suffered a serious injury. In an opinion written by O'Connor, the Court held that the use of excessive physical force against a prisoner may constitute cruel and unusual punishment even if an inmate does not suffer serious injury. Prison officials, the Court ruled, automatically violate the Eighth Amendment if they use "unnecessary and wanton" physical force to cause harm, if they use force "maliciously and sadistically to cause harm," or if their actions are "repugnant to the conscience of mankind."

In a dissenting opinion joined by Scalia, Thomas penned one of his most controversial opinions. He summarized his view at the outset: "In my view, a use of force that causes only insignificant harm to a prisoner may be immoral, it may be tortious, it may be criminal, and it may even be remediable under other provisions of the Federal Constitution, but it is not cruel and unusual punishment."

Thomas offered an extensive history of the Cruel and Unusual Punishments Clause. The Framers, he observed, clearly had not intended for the clause to proscribe such conduct by prison officials as Hudson had suffered:

> Surely prison was not a more congenial place in the early years of the Republic than it is today; nor were our judges and commentators so naïve as to be unaware of the often harsh conditions of prison life. Rather, they simply did not conceive of the Eighth Amendment as protecting inmates from harsh treatment. Thus, historically, the lower courts

routinely rejected prisoner grievances by explaining that the courts had no role for regulating prison life.

Subsequent Court interpretations of the amendment reflected this original understanding. "Until recent years, the Cruel and Unusual Punishments Clause was not deemed to apply at all to deprivations that were not inflicted as part of the sentence for a crime," he noted. "For generations, judges and commentators regarded the Eighth Amendment as applying only to torturous punishments meted out by statutes or sentencing judges, and not generally to any hardship that might befall a prisoner during incarceration.... It was not until 1976—185 years after the Eighth Amendment was adopted—that this Court first applied it to a prisoner's complaint about a deprivation suffered in prison." That case was *Estelle v. Gamble.* Thomas argued that the Court should not extend *Estelle* to allow suits by inmates who could not prove serious injuries. He pointed out that the inmate could have sued prison officials under state law instead.

Thomas ended his opinion with an expression of sympathy alloyed with cold reason:

> Today's expansion of the Cruel and Unusual Punishments Clause beyond all bounds of history and precedent is, I suspect, yet another manifestation of the pervasive view that the Federal Constitution must address all ills in our society. Abusive behavior by prison guards is deplorable conduct that properly evokes outrage and contempt. But that does not mean that it is invariably unconstitutional. The Eighth Amendment is not, and should not be turned into, a National Code of Prison Regulation.

Scalia joined this opinion without comment. In doing so, he departed from the view he had endorsed only a year before, in *Wilson v. Seiter,* that the Eighth Amendment covered prison conditions in addition to merely criminal punishment per se. Interpreted broadly, Thomas's bold opinion stood for the proposition that the Eighth Amendment did not apply to prisons at all.

Thomas's firm approach to criminals also was evident in *Dawson v. Delaware.* David Dawson had escaped with three other inmates from a prison in Delaware. Dawson stole a car and burglarized a house. He then went to a second house, where he found Madeline Kisner, murdered her, then stole her car and some money. Dawson was subsequently apprehended and convicted of first-degree murder. In the sentencing phase of the trial, the Court considered various aggravating and mitigating factors, pursuant to earlier Supreme Court rulings, in deciding whether to impose the death penalty. The prosecution introduced, as an aggravating factor, the fact that Dawson was a member of the Aryan Brotherhood, a white supremacist prison gang. After Dawson was sentenced to death, he argued on appeal that the admission of this prison-gang evidence violated his constitutional rights.

In an opinion by Rehnquist, the Supreme Court held 8–1 that the admission of this evidence violated Dawson's First and Fourteenth Amendment rights. The Court ruled that the evidence concerning his beliefs and associations was irrelevant to the sentencing. Moreover, the admission of the evidence violated Dawson's First Amendment right to be a member of a social group—in this case, a prison gang. Accordingly, the Court overturned Dawson's death sentence.

Thomas was the only dissenter. He argued that the evidence was relevant because a Delaware statute allowed the admission of evidence demonstrating the "character and propensities" of a defendant. Dawson had introduced evidence that he hoped would demonstrate good character, such as membership in the Green Tree Program (a drug and alcohol program) and various therapy groups. Delaware sought to rebut this character evidence by establishing his membership in a racist prison gang. "I do not consider the evidence of Dawson's gang membership irrelevant to his character," Thomas noted sardonically. "The Court's opinion suggests that the Constitution now imposes a double standard for determining relevance: a standard easy for defendants to satisfy, but difficult for prosecutors.... The Court nowhere explains why courts and juries may consider some First Amendment protected activities when assessing character, but they cannot consider others." He added, "Although we do not sit in judgment of the morality of particular creeds, we cannot bend traditional concepts of relevance to exempt the anti-social."

Thomas's first race case was *United States v. Fordice.* The central issue was whether the state of Mississippi still was upholding segregation in its institutions of higher education. Mississippi underwrote financially both the old state universities and the traditionally black colleges in the state. In an 8–1 decision, the Court ruled that if state policies rooted in Mississippi's previous, *de jure* racial discrimination were encouraging segregation, the state was required to reform those policies to the extent practicable and consistent with sound educational practices.

Thomas wrote a brief concurring opinion that applauded the majority's decision. Having fought for the survival of black colleges while at the Department of Education, he took up the same project on the high court. Thomas noted that the majority opinion was a departure from prior Court rulings on desegregation, and that "because [the decision] does not compel the elimination of all observed racial imbalance, it portends neither the destruction of historically black colleges nor the severing of those institutions from their distinctive histories and traditions." Moreover, "we do not foreclose the possibility that there exists 'sound educational justification' for maintaining historically black colleges *as such*." Thomas concluded, "It would be ironic, to say the least, if the institutions that sustained blacks during segregation were themselves destroyed in an effort to combat its vestiges."

The most controversial case of Thomas's first term was *Planned Parenthood v. Casey*, in which the Court considered restrictions on the right to an abortion enacted by the state of Pennsylvania. *Casey* was the long-awaited opportunity for the Court to reconsider *Roe*. Thomas's feminist foes would learn in short order they were right to discern in Thomas an opponent of *Roe*. The Court ruled 5–4 to uphold the right to an abortion. O'Connor, Kennedy and Souter joined to author an opinion that scrapped *Roe*'s "trimester" formula, which had divided the nine months of pregnancy into three phases for analytical purposes. But the core right remained: States could restrict the right to an abortion only as long as the regulations did not constitute an "undue burden" on the right to abort a pregnancy before the baby became "viable," or capable of life outside the womb. Thomas, White and Scalia joined Rehnquist's dissenting opinion, which called for the reversal of *Roe*'s constitutional right to an abortion.

The media's reaction to Thomas's rulings varied by case. His defense of historically black colleges in *Fordice* drew praise. But his votes in *Hudson* and *Casey* elicited strong criticism from liberal journalists and columnists. It was not hard for Thomas's critics to mischaracterize his principled defense of the rightful scope of the Eighth Amendment as indifference to the torture of inmates. The title of a *New York Times* editorial lambasting Thomas said it all when it labeled him "The Youngest, Cruelest Justice." William Raspberry, an African-American syndicated columnist with the *Washington Post,* wrote his column in the style of a letter addressed to the incorrigible justice. "Come on, Clarence," he said. "Conservative is one thing; bizarre is another."

Years later, Thomas still complained about the media's treatment of his *Hudson* dissent. He said in one speech, "I must note in passing that I can't help but wonder if some of my critics can read. One opinion that is trotted out for propaganda, for the propaganda parade, is my dissent in [*Hudson*]. The conclusion reached by the long arms of the critics is that I supported the beating of prisoners in that case.... How one can extrapolate these larger conclusions from the narrow question before the Court is beyond me, unless, of course, there's a special segregated mode of analysis."

Rev. Joseph E. Lowery was one of many Americans who wished to have a word with Thomas after the *Hudson* decision. He wrote Thomas a letter and mailed it to his home to "remind him about our conversation" during his confirmation campaign. Lowery, for some reason, was under the misimpression that Thomas's stated fidelity to the traditional desires of blacks mandated that the Eighth Amendment be interpreted in a certain manner. Thomas never responded to the letter.

Still, Lowery saw in Thomas's first year of jurisprudence concrete signs that the ugliness of the confirmation hearings had served to "freeze his antipathy toward the left." Lowery had hoped that lifetime tenure on the Supreme Court would allow Thomas to be "'free at last,' free to be a brother from Pinpoint, Ga. who had tasted the bitter dregs of racism." But the freedom Thomas now cherished, much to Lowery's dismay, would allow him to defend rigorously the Framers of the Constitution, no matter how disconcerting this was to the journalists and civil rights professionals who continued to oppose him.

Homecoming

A year after the confirmation hearings, Anita Hill remained a rally-ing point for feminist media executives and reporters. The pro-ducers of *Murphy Brown* and *Designing Women*, two popular TV comedies, offered pro-Hill episodes as part of this campaign. The offer-ing on the latter show was entitled "The Strange Case of Clarence and Anita"; one of the program's producers described it as a "valentine to all the women who believed Anita Hill was treated unfairly." *60 Min-utes* devoted a feature to Hill. Throughout the interview, Hill was eva-sive and churlish. "I can't say enough that we need to get beyond those hearings," she declared at one point. "We need to move beyond that." Still, the interview provided free and generally sympathetic publicity. For all her protestations, the hearings made her famous and relatively wealthy. She garnered $10,000 to $12,000 per speaking appearance, often to rapt audiences at Ivy League universities.

The favorable media treatment burnished Hill's public image in a rapid and extraordinary manner. Polls at the time of the hearings showed that the public believed Thomas over Hill by a two-to-one margin. A year later, public opinion performed a somersault. Polls showed that Hill's credibility now either equaled Thomas's or exceeded his by up to ten points. The reversal of public opinion on Anita Hill would provide conservatives with their best case study of the power of adverse media bias. One black writer not aligned with conservatives noted in the *Wash-ington Post* what was plain: "If there has been a shift in public opinion since a year ago, one can attribute it to a year of pro–Anita Hill effu-sions from white media feminists, including the producers of popular sitcoms."

The elections in November also seemed a national repudiation of Clarence Thomas. Alan Dixon of Illinois, one of Thomas's supporters, lost his reelection bid for the Senate to Carol Moseley-Braun, a black woman and critic of Thomas. California elected two Democratic female senators, Dianne Feinstein and Barbara Boxer, the latter having trooped over to the Senate from the House of Representatives during the hearings to show solidarity for Hill. After Oliver Stone included a gratuitous swipe at Arlen Specter in his new movie *JFK,* Lynn Yeakel, a previously unknown female Democrat, nearly defeated him in his Senate reelection campaign in Pennsylvania. Forty-six women were elected to the House of Representatives, a record. Bill Clinton, a year ahead of Thomas at Yale, was elected president after his wife Hillary publicly lauded Hill for her courage.

One of the very few bits of good news Thomas encountered on Capitol Hill during this time was his meeting with Patricia Cornwell, the best-selling crime novelist. Orrin Hatch, a friend of both Thomas and Cornwell, was the conduit for this exchange. Hatch had tried to persuade Cornwell of the justice of Thomas's cause. Cornwell, a Democrat and feminist, insisted that she did not find him credible.

"Patricia," Hatch told her, "I'm willing to bet that if you met Clarence Thomas, within ten minutes you'll believe he's one of the most honest people you've ever met."

"Oh, no," she replied. "I'll never believe that Anita Hill wasn't telling the truth."

When Cornwell subsequently came to Washington to visit Hatch, he said he would invite Thomas over to meet her. She agreed. When the two met, Hatch recalled, they promptly "locked horns." Cornwell grilled him on the hearings. "It was like a tennis match," he said. "She really went at him and he just matter-of-factly answered all her questions." After "about ten minutes," by Hatch's calculation, Cornwell turned to the senator. "Damn it, you're right," she told Hatch. "He couldn't have done that."

By and large, however, 1992 was a grim year for Thomas. He coped with the negativity swirling about him by concentrating on his jurisprudence.

In the main prisoners' rights case of the term, it was Scalia's turn to sign on to a Thomas opinion. This one called for overturning yet another precedent of several decades' vintage. In *Helling v. McKinney,* an inmate sued prison officials over his exposure to second-hand smoke from his cellmate's cigarettes, alleging that such exposure threatened his health in the future. The Court ruled 7–2 that the inmate had brought a viable claim under the Eighth Amendment. In another expansion of *Estelle v. Gamble,* the court held the inmate merely had to demonstrate that prison officials were deliberately indifferent to his future health, not only his current health.

Joined solely by Scalia in dissent, Thomas noted that in *Hudson,* the Court had held that an inmate could sue for only minor injuries. Now, the Court was expanding the Eighth Amendment to encompass the "mere risk of injury." Thomas reiterated his view, first stated in *Hudson,* that deprivations suffered in prison were not part of a criminal sentence, and therefore not cruel and unusual "punishment" under the Eighth Amendment. Thomas's dissent offered the fullest exhibition yet of his system for determining the intentions of the Framers. He examined, in order, the text of the Eighth Amendment, the history of the right, the debates in the Constitutional Convention and ratifying conventions in the states, and the courts' subsequent interpretation of the right.

Thomas began by looking at the accepted definition of "punishment" at the time of the framing of the Constitution. He consulted dictionaries of the era, including *Webster's* and *Black's Law Dictionary.* He traced the history of the right against cruel and unusual punishment back to the English Bill of Rights, which was adopted a century before Madison drafted the U.S. Bill of Rights. Thomas then scrutinized James Madison's notes from the Constitutional Convention, the records of the ratifying conventions in the states, and the Delaware Constitution of 1792, which was enacted one year after the Bill of Rights.

He also reviewed early prison jurisprudence, finding that courts had uniformly rejected "conditions of confinement" claims by prisoners until well into the twentieth century. Indeed, he remarked, "this Court did not so much as intimate that the Cruel and Unusual Punishments Clause might reach prison conditions for the first 185 years of the provision's existence. It was not until the 1960s that lower courts began applying the Eighth Amendment to prison deprivations . . . and it was not until 1976 . . . that this Court first did so."

His analysis led him to reject the inmate's claim. Thomas observed that "although the evidence is not overwhelming, I believe that the text and history of the Eighth Amendment, together with the decisions interpreting it, support the view that judges or juries—but not jailers—impose 'punishment.'" Going beyond his criticism of *Estelle* in *Hudson,* he went out of his way to state that if the issue were presented "squarely," "I might vote to overrule *Estelle.*" Scalia, by comparison, had not previously expressed or even suggested such a radical view; yet he joined Thomas's opinion.

In *United States v. James Daniel Good Real Property,* Thomas evinced his longstanding concern for property rights and due process of law. Police officers in Hawaii raided James Daniel Good's home and found drugs and drug paraphernalia. He pled guilty to promoting a harmful drug in violation of Hawaii law. Four and a half years later, the federal government filed a civil action against him as well. Arguing that Good had used his house and land as a base for committing or facilitating federal drug crimes, the government applied for forfeiture of his real estate. After an *ex parte* proceeding at which Good was not present, a federal magistrate authorized seizure of the property. On appeal, Good claimed that the government had deprived him of due process of law. The Supreme Court agreed. It held that except in exigent circumstances, the government must accord such property owners notice and a meaningful opportunity to be heard before their real estate can be seized under civil forfeiture laws.

Thomas was pleased that the Court had risen to the defense of due process rights for property owners. He also expressed substantial concerns about civil forfeiture statutes generally. But he added, "Although I concur with both of these sentiments, I cannot agree that Good was deprived of due process of law under the facts of this case."

All those hours of childhood work for his grandfather forged the respect for property rights he outlined:

> Like the majority, I believe that "[i]ndividual freedom finds tangible expression in property rights." . . . In my view, as the Court has increasingly emphasized the creation and delineation of entitlements in recent years, it has not always placed sufficient stress upon the protection of individuals' traditional rights in real property. Although I disagree with the outcome reached by the Court, I am sympathetic to its focus on the protection of property rights—rights that are central to our heritage. . . . And like the majority, I am disturbed by the breadth of new civil forfeiture statutes . . . which subjects to forfeiture *all* real property that is

used, or intended to be used, in the commission, or even the *facilitation,* of a federal drug offense.

Given the evolution in this area of the law, Thomas wrote, "it may be necessary—in an appropriate case—to reevaluate our generally deferential approach to legislative judgments in this area of civil forfeiture." Still, he concluded that Good had received due process before the property was confiscated, and therefore the forfeiture was warranted. Good had been duly convicted of drug offenses. Accordingly, he received due process in the earlier criminal proceedings. Thomas observed, "Notice, of course, is provided by the conviction itself."

Thomas's opinion was a supple examination of several complex, related issues: property rights, civil forfeiture laws, due process concerns. He explored each nuance separately and fully. By the end of the 1992–93 term, those who questioned the independence or adequacy of Thomas's intellect either had not read his opinions or preferred to ignore or mischaracterize them.

As Anita Hill's public image improved, Thomas sought to rehabilitate his own tattered reputation. He knew this would be a long-term undertaking. Thomas told his friends that he thought it would take ten years for him to recover what he called, rightly, his erstwhile "good name." Less than a year after joining the Court, he embarked on a campaign of public speeches to accomplish this transformation. Many of these speeches would be aired on C-Span, the cable TV channel devoted to public affairs.

He was careful to select friendly audiences. His first speech after ascending to the Court was delivered in September 1992 to a group of federal judges and lawyers in Bolton Landing, New York. Composed of people whose careers Thomas could damage with a negative vote, such an audience was unlikely to indulge in boos and placards. They received him kindly.

For his first major public address, Thomas decided to return to the most comfortable environs he had ever known—Georgia. He accepted Mercer Law School's invitation to speak at their annual Law Day on May 1. He also agreed to speak at a dinner for the Georgia Public Policy Foundation, a conservative organization based in Atlanta. Larry

Thompson, ensconced as a partner at King & Spaulding in Atlanta, was instrumental in securing his consent for both commitments. Thomas also swept down to the sea for a triumphant return home to Pin Point.

Before Thomas arrived in Macon for the Law Day celebration, Philip Shelton, dean of Mercer Law School, distributed a memorandum to the students. Shelton wrote he had assured Thomas that Mercer would provide "a civil, respectful and hospitable environment." A makeshift platoon of local police officers and U.S. marshals patrolled the lobby and ballroom of the Radisson Hotel, where the speech was to take place. Bomb-sniffing German shepherds from a nearby Air Force base also made the rounds. On the morning of the event, Thomas, accompanied only by one marshal, slipped away from his hosts to enjoy breakfast at one of his old haunts, a restaurant called Huddle House, one of a chain of squat, rectangular greasy spoons that appeared at regular intervals along the highways of Georgia. (The chain's motto was "Best Food Yet.")

Thomas's speech was the biggest thing to happen at the sleepy Southern law school in memory. Some nine hundred students, roughly half of the Mercer student population, attended, more than had come to hear former President Carter several years before. After learning that C-Span intended to film the speech, the university constructed a special podium and four mini Greek columns for a set. Griffin Bell, the former U.S. attorney general and fellow Georgian, introduced Thomas to the audience in the ballroom. Having recently torn his Achilles tendon playing basketball with his clerks, Thomas gamely hobbled onto the stage with crutches.

He was greeted with enthusiastic applause. Clearly grateful for the respite from protests and venom, Thomas choked up, thanking the crowd profusely for their warm reception. "I have looked forward to this day . . . for a long time," he told the crowd with the deep voice that always compelled attention.

He thanked Georgians for their support during his confirmation fight, and then addressed the nation's cultural slide. After noting the decline in manners and morality throughout the country, Thomas recalled of his childhood: "The families poorest in means were often the richest in manners." Part and parcel of this degeneration, Thomas said, was the rise of what he branded the "new intolerance." Thomas asserted that terms such as "tolerance" or "sensitivity" are "merely trotted out as justifications in an attempt to intimidate and silence those who dare to question popular political, social or economic fads." As evidence of this chilling effect on free speech, he cited the many people who had approached him in airports, restaurants, or elsewhere to say how much they agreed with him—in a whisper. Clearly they feared being seen to transgress an enforced uniformity of thought, which he compared to the racism and prejudice of his youth.

Though not one of his better speeches, it earned what one reporter called "thunderous standing ovations." After shaking hands with some members of the audience, he left the ballroom and headed by car to Atlanta, refusing to be interviewed afterwards or to provide copies of his speech. The fear and disdain of the press that would largely define his public persona throughout the decade had begun to surface.

The following day, Thomas addressed the Georgia Public Policy Foundation. He first spoke to a group of about thirty people at the exclusive Buckhead Club, at which he shared some off-the-record stories about the inner workings of the Court. Later, he went to the Doubletree Hotel for a reception and dinner before a much larger crowd. On a beautiful, sunny day in which large, puffy clouds floated by, Thomas mingled with guests on a patio that overlooked a lovely pond with sparkling fountains.

Thomas took an interest in a jazz band from a middle school in Atlanta, which was performing at the event. All of the dozen or so members of the band were black. For ten to fifteen minutes, Thomas sat down with the boys and girls. He talked to each of them, asking about their goals. "You could see, their eyes were like saucers, a couple of these kids," recalled Matthew Glavin, president of the host foundation. Thomas told them, "I want you to promise me that you're gonna stay in school." He later referred to the children in his formal remarks.

Another guest who came away with a different, albeit equally arresting, memory of the occasion was Jeff Dickerson. A black conservative who had formerly written for the editorial page of the *Atlanta Journal and Constitution,* Dickerson had come to know Thomas during the 1980s. The newspaper's management recently had tapped Dickerson to start a new section of the paper, called "City Life." When he told Thomas of his new post, Dickerson recalled, "He gave the impression that the liberal press was going out of its way to silence a strong black conservative voice. And I didn't feel that way at all. I felt I was doing something different—I could go back to it [editorial writing] if I wanted to." Dickerson thought Thomas's assumption odd: "I usually ascribe conspiracy theories to the other side. You know, Dick Gregory and those guys. But it almost had that ring to it. It was as if there was this liberal conspiracy out there to silence black conservatives." Years later, Dickerson recalled, "His words stuck with me." Even when among his people in Georgia, the bitterness and paranoia of the confirmation experience bubbled just below Thomas's surface.

At the dinner, the Georgia Public Policy Foundation presented Thomas with its Georgia Freedom Award. The organization had hired a local artist to create the award, a brass eagle mounted on Georgia granite. Larry Thompson introduced Thomas to the crowd of around seven hundred guests. Thomas's remarks were essentially the same as those delivered in Macon the day before, and they received an equally warm response. "He wanted his coming out to be in his home state," Glavin remembered. "He said that night, 'I'm glad to be home.'"

The next day, all of Thomas's careful efforts to thwart a media assault proved for naught. The *Atlanta Journal and Constitution* published an article questioning whether, by appearing at an annual fundraiser dinner for the conservative organization, Thomas had violated the ethics code for federal judges. The *New York Times* would note evenhandedly two weeks later that justices ranging from William Brennan to Scalia had spoken routinely at such fundraiser dinners.

Even so, Glavin was mortified. Receiving a telephone call from Thomas, who was then en route by car to Savannah, he abjectly apologized. Thomas reassured him: "Calm down, Matt. I've just gone through a thousand times worse than that." Glavin would gratefully remember Thomas's reaction as "very gracious."

The third leg of Thomas's trip was the hero's welcome that awaited him in Pin Point. The town had changed greatly in the years since his childhood. The Varn seafood processing plant had closed down and was slowly decomposing. Yet the great national prosperity enjoyed in the years since Thomas's childhood had remade Pin Point's residences; trailers now replaced many of the older, homemade structures. On another gorgeous day, his kin and former neighbors gathered around the Pin Point Community Center to celebrate his long, arduous climb to the high court.

With the continuing aid of crutches, he made his way to the little stage put together in front of the structure. His autograph suddenly had become valuable, and well-wishers thrust paper and pen in front of him to solicit the coveted signature. Marshals combed the paths on which Thomas had played with his brother and cousins as a boy, looking for possible dangers to the new justice lurking in the woods.

When Thomas spoke to the small crowd, he thanked the members of his hometown for their expressions of solidarity during his recent trials. Although frequently wooden in formal speeches, Thomas was especially loose and vibrant this day as he addressed his family and friends in front of the community center. He confessed at long last to having filched candy from the neighborhood store as a boy. Referring to the marshals, he said, "I can admit it now. I have protection."

He elicited additional knowing laughter when he spotted and teased his childhood friend, "Little" Richard Wiggins, in the crowd. Wiggins had borrowed money from Thomas in adolescence and never repaid him. Thomas drew guffaws when he pointed to Wiggins: "Hey, Richard, where's that money you owe me?" Abe Famble, Thomas's cousin and longtime Pin Point resident, observed of the townspeople, "They knew exactly what he was talking about."

In September, Thomas returned to St. Louis, another former place of residence, to speak to a meeting of the Missouri State Bar. But even this ostensibly amicable venue was the setting for a minor flap. A black lawyers' association in St. Louis threatened to boycott Thomas's speech, and then opted for a lesser discourtesy, deciding simply not to host a reception for him. Judge Theodore McMillian, a black judge on the U.S. Court of Appeals for the Eighth Circuit, did not attend the speech for a reason that he said "has something to do with Thomas." When asked by a local reporter, he declined to explain: "I'd better take the Fifth."

Speaking at the Adam's Mark Hotel downtown, Thomas tried to give the impression that his suffering was behind him. "I have had many, many reasons to hate and to resent: poverty, racism, segregation, discrimination, unfairness," he stated. "With God's help, I have been able to overcome the temptation to do so." Yet he also alluded to a recent, negative article about him in a way that showed the pain was still there. An article by Jeffrey Toobin, "The Burden of Clarence Thomas," had appeared a few weeks earlier in the *New Yorker* magazine. It reported Thomas's lingering bitterness, aversion to speaking appearances before hostile gatherings, and heightened conservatism since joining the Court. Toobin also alleged that Thomas's fellow justices remained "distant" from him and that he relied inordinately on his clerks to handle much of his workload—claims that were inaccurate. Thomas once had read the *New Yorker* in the segregated Carnegie Library in Savannah and dreamt of being sophisticated enough to understand it fully. Now, he found the magazine an outlet for yet another unflattering profile of himself. This was too much for him to bear in silence. In his speech, he stated, "I have seen many who have suddenly become experts on me. . . . [T]hey all tend to be consistently and unanimously wrong, especially those who insist that I remain bitter about my life's experiences." The article reporting Thomas's speech in the next day's *St. Louis Post-Dispatch* captured the self-refuting essence of his talk: "I'm Not Bitter Anymore, Justice Thomas Says Here."

On November 30, Thomas spoke at an annual dinner hosted by the Claremont Institute in Los Angeles. The proceedings were in honor of Sir Winston Churchill, who had earned Thomas's admiration for his resolution and principles. "He epitomizes someone who stood by his convictions even when all seemed to be against him," Thomas told the assembled guests. The institute gave Thomas a bust of Churchill. A photograph of Thomas taken at the event shows him holding the bust while wearing an extraordinary, beaming smile, suggesting that such handsome awards meant much to him.

The theme of the speech was personal responsibility. As so often before, Thomas focused on his grandfather, particularly Myers Anderson's decision to evict him from his house after he left the seminary. Thomas said that from this harsh edict, he learned "'the other side of freedom'—those duties and obligations that, when fulfilled, make personal freedom possible and sustain it through life." Quoting Churchill, Thomas declared, "The price of greatness is responsibility." He explored a thesis that he would defend repeatedly in subsequent speeches: Americans were eschewing responsibility in favor of victimhood. "We relieve individuals of accountability for their exercise of freedom by some ever-present theory of determinism," Thomas explained. "People all become victims of something. Any problem or lack becomes society's fault or one's parents' fault. In no case can it be that the individual simply failed to undertake successfully the responsibilities of freedom." For rejecting such views, Thomas said, his grandfather today would find himself an "anachronism."

Although this speaking tour was well received, the event in 1993 that most strengthened Thomas's reputation was the publication of a book. *The Real Anita Hill* by David Brock added to Thomas's good name by subtracting from Hill's. A writer for the conservative magazine the *American Spectator,* Brock followed up on information and leads about Hill that came to the Senate Judiciary Committee during the hearings, but which Republican staffers could not fully investigate because of time constraints. Brock contended that what he termed the "Shadow Senate"—the "loose coalition of special-interest lobby groups, zealous Senate staffers, and a scandal-hungry press corps"—had pushed a reluctant Anita Hill into the national spotlight. His strongest chapter fleshed out Specter's line of questioning and rebutted Hill's tangled testimony point by point. To believe Hill's account, Brock noted, required disbelieving seventeen other witnesses, many of whom had no conceivable reason to lie. "Alternatively, all of these individuals could have been correct, and Hill could have made more than a dozen false statements under oath." Brock also established that Hill was no conservative Republican, as some journalists had suggested at the time, but rather a conventional feminist in her views.

Brock got away with a number of errors. He misidentified Jim Brudney, Metzenbaum's staffer, and Paul Simon as the "villains" who leaked Hill's allegations and statement to the press. (Metzenbaum, Thomas's old and sly enemy, was the one responsible.) He tendentiously dismissed the credible corroborating testimony of several pro-Hill witnesses before the Judiciary Committee, ascribing purely political motives to their allegations. He was unconvincing in arguing that Hill's contemporaneous complaints to these individuals might have been references to another EEOC "supervisor." (Thomas was always her supervisor.) "Everyone who knew both Thomas and Hill believed Thomas, not Hill," he claimed—an overstatement of his case. (Brock did not interview former colleagues of the two who sided with Hill.) Yet *The Real Anita Hill* received praise from unlikely sources—namely, book reviewers with the liberal *New York Times* and *Washington Post*—and the book became a national bestseller.

As the confirmation hearings continued to resonate in the popular culture, Thomas found he had lost not only his reputation, but even the barest measure of privacy. One of his preferred destinations on weekends was Hechinger's, a hardware chain store in the Washington area. When Thomas told one audience in Ohio that he was unable to visit the store without being recognized, a reporter noted that "there was an edge to the comment." In a later speech, Thomas recalled an incident one Saturday morning when he ventured out to Hechinger's to purchase some washers in order to fix a sink or toilet. He noticed a man staring at him. Finally, the man summoned the courage to approach him. "Are you that there judge?" the man asked Thomas. Thomas replied curtly that he was, in fact, "that there judge." The man, Thomas said, then "got confused and left."

"You literally can't do anything," Thomas bemoaned before one audience. "My wife and I were on the streets of London, we figured we were safe. 'Hey, Justice Thomas! Let's take a picture.' We were recognized three or four times there I think."

To insulate himself further from the demands of the madding crowds, Thomas began to avoid shopping at malls and other such stores. If he wished to purchase or obtain some new music—gospel choirs, blues and Motown were among his favorites—he enlisted Armstrong Williams for the effort. Williams typically would receive a call from Thomas while the judge was in his car, listening to music on the radio. "Do you hear that? Do you hear that?" Thomas would say on his cellular telephone. "Boy, I like that. Good music." Williams would take the hint and either buy him a new CD or cassette or make a copy for him.

By 1994, the *Washington Post* described Thomas as "the most media-shy of all the current justices." Some of this reticence was part of a calculated media relations strategy. Williams believed that frequent interviews with the press would dilute his star power, with the result that his speeches would not be covered as extensively. Thomas agreed and rarely spoke to the press. As for Thomas friends who showed loose lips in dealing with the media, one Thomas intimate summed up the policy: "Part of how you remain a close friend of Clarence is you don't talk about him."

—•—

The decisions handed down in 1994 would further establish Thomas as a growing intellectual force on the Court. Cases involving criminals' rights continued to provoke opinions from him. In yet another major prison case, *Farmer v. Brennan,* Dee Farmer, a transsexual inmate, sued federal prison officials after another inmate beat and raped him. Farmer filed suit for being placed in an environment with a history of inmate violence, despite authorities' knowledge that he "projects feminine characteristics" and was particularly vulnerable to sexual assaults. Farmer contended that such placement by prison officials constituted cruel and unusual punishment.

In an opinion by Souter, the Court held that prison officials can be held liable for deliberate indifference to an inmate's health or safety if the officials know an inmate faces substantial risks of serious harm and disregards that risk by failing to take reasonable countermeasures. The prisoner must prove the officials were subjectively aware of the risk.

Thomas voted with the majority, but he offered a concurring opinion to set forth his own reasoning. He began with a proclamation that offered no concessions to critics of his *Hudson* dissent: "Prisons are necessarily dangerous places; they house society's most antisocial and violent people in close proximity with one another.... Today, in an attempt to rectify such unfortunate conditions, the Court further refines the 'National Code of Prison Regulation,' otherwise known as the Cruel and Unusual Punishment Clause."

He applauded the Court's decision to "tak[e] a step in the right direction by adopting a restrictive definition of deliberate indifference." However, he would not accept the "constitutional predicate of the Court's analysis," namely, that the Eighth Amendment applies to prisons. As in *Hudson* and *Helling,* Thomas remarked that "Conditions of confinement are not punishment in any recognized sense of the term, unless imposed as part of a sentence.... As an original matter, therefore, this case would be an easy one for me: Because the unfortunate attack that befell petitioner was not part of his sentence, it did not constitute 'punishment' under the Eighth Amendment." He reiterated his critique of *Estelle* and its progeny, stating that the "logical result" of divorcing the Eighth Amendment from its history "is to transform federal judges into superintendents of prison conditions nationwide." Once again, he remonstrated that the Court should "reconsider *Estelle* in light of the constitutional text and history."

In criminal cases, Thomas would balance two scales—one weighed down by his abiding regard for public safety, the other by his deep-seated concern for the rights of the individual. The latter consideration dominated in *Staples v. United States*. Federal law prohibited possession of an unregistered "firearm," including "machine guns." The statute defined a "machine gun" as a weapon that automatically fires more than one shot with single pull of the trigger. When Harold Staples was found in possession of such an firearm, he was arrested and charged with violating the National Firearms Act. At trial, Staples testified that he had never fired the weapon automatically and did not know that the gun could be fired in such a manner. He was convicted nevertheless.

In a 7–2 decision, the Supreme Court overturned his conviction, with Thomas writing the opinion for the majority. The Court held that the federal government was required to prove beyond a reasonable doubt that Staples knew his rifle had the characteristics that brought it within the statutory definition of a machine gun. Traditionally in Anglo-American law, Thomas noted, the state was required to prove *mens rea* ("guilty mind") to sustain a criminal conviction. In other words, the government must establish that the individual acted with a wrongful or criminal purpose. In interpreting criminal statutes, courts generally disfavored offenses with no *mens rea* requirement. Given this historical and legal background, Thomas observed, Staples should not be subject to up to ten years of imprisonment simply for not knowing that his semi-automatic weapon was fully automatic. He explained: "In short, we conclude that the background rule of the common law favoring *mens rea* should govern interpretation of [the statute] in this case. Silence does not suggest that Congress dispensed with *mens rea*. . . . Thus, to obtain a conviction, the Government should have been required to prove that petitioner knew of the features of his AR-15 that brought it within the scope of the Act."

The subject of race provoked Thomas's best work of the term. The court in *Holder v. Hall* considered a challenge by black voters to a sole-commissioner form of government in a county in Georgia. They asserted that Section 2 of the Voting Rights Act of 1965 mandated that the county commission have five members, so that the county's blacks residents could have more influence. Otherwise, they argued, the county's laws unlawfully "diluted" the voting power of minorities. The Court held in a 5–4 decision that the size of local governing body was not subject to challenge under the Voting Rights Act as a dilutive practice.

Thomas wrote a concurring opinion. Joined by Scalia, this was one of the longest separate opinions in the history of the Court. Thomas agreed with the Court's opinion insofar as it held that "the size of a governing body is not a 'standard, practice, or procedure' within the terms of the Act." But he urged the Court to go further. "In my view, however, the only principle limiting the scope of the terms 'standard, practice, or procedure' that can be derived from the text of the Act would exclude, not only the challenge to size advanced today, but also challenges to allegedly dilutive election methods that we have considered within the scope of the Act in the past."

Taking aim at the entire concept of "dilutive" practices, Thomas argued that interpreting the phrase "standard, practice, or procedure" to include such claims "is at odds with the statute and has proved utterly unworkable in practice." To determine whether electoral practices dilute the voting power of minorities, "we have immersed the federal courts in a hopeless project of weighing questions of political theory.... Worse, in pursuing the ideal measure of voting strength, we have devised a remedial mechanism that encourages federal courts to segregate voters into racially designated districts to ensure minority electoral success. In doing so, we have collaborated in what may aptly be termed the racial 'balkaniz[ation]' of the Nation."

He denounced the "disastrous misadventure in judicial policymaking" on which the Court had embarked by misinterpreting the Voting Rights Act in this manner. The Court, he averred, should hold that the size of a government body is not a "standard, practice, or procedure" because "those terms reach only state enactments that limit citizens' access to the ballot." The crux of the problem was the Court's 1986 decision in *Thornburg v. Gingles*. This decision found that the "essence" of a vote dilution claim under Section 2 is that "a certain electoral law, practice, or structure interacts with social and historical conditions to cause an inequality in the opportunities enjoyed by black and white voters to elect their preferred representatives." Thomas argued that the Court should overturn *Gingles* and abandon vote "dilution" claims entirely.

Thomas conducted a sweeping study of the relevant legal history to support his argument. "If one surveys the history of the Voting Rights Act," Thomas observed:

> ... one can only be struck by the sea change that has occurred in the application and enforcement of the Act since it was passed in 1965. The statute was originally perceived as a remedial provision directed specifically at eradicating discriminatory practices that restricted blacks' ability to register and vote in the segregated South. Now, the act has grown into something entirely different. In construing the Act to cover claims of vote dilution, we have converted the Act into a device for regulating, rationing, and apportioning political power and racial and ethnic groups.

In reviewing the intentions behind the act, Thomas examined its effects on voter registration by blacks as well as the earliest judicial interpretations of the act. These benchmarks, he reasoned, offered no succor for *Gingles*.

> Once one accepts the proposition that the effectiveness of votes is measured in terms of the control of seats, the core of any vote dilution claim is an assertion that the group in question is unable to control the "proper" number of seats—that is, the number of seats that the minority's percentage of the population would enable it to control in the benchmark "fair" system. The claim is inherently based on ratios between the numbers of the minority in the population and the numbers of seats controlled.

This result had no basis in law or history. The Voting Rights Act guaranteed equal access to the ballot, not equal outcomes based on race.

That the Court had become, in Thomas's estimation, a band of philosopher-kings was not his only concern. "The dabbling in political theory that dilution cases have prompted, however, is hardly the worst aspect of our vote dilution jurisprudence." He explained:

> Far more pernicious has been the Court's willingness to accept the one underlying premise that must inform every minority vote dilution claim: the assumption that the group asserting dilution is not merely a racial

or ethnic group, but a group having distinct political interests as well. Of necessity, in resolving vote dilution actions we have given credence to the view that race defines political interest. We have acted on the implicit assumption that members of racial and ethnic groups must all think alike on important matters of public policy and must have their own "minority preferred" representatives holding seats in elected bodies if they are to be considered represented at all.

Such a policy requires "segregating the races into political homelands that amounts, in truth, to nothing short of a system of 'political apartheid.'" Such assumptions were "repugnant to any nation that strives for the ideal of a color-blind Constitution."

The text of the act and related history made it clear that Section 2 was not meant to countenance "proportional allocation of political power according to race." *Gingles* and its rotten fruit must fall. "In my view, our current practice should not continue. Not for another Term, not until the next case, not for another day.... The 'inherent tension'— indeed, I would call it an irreconcilable conflict—between the standards we have adopted for evaluating vote dilution claims and the text of the Voting Rights Act would itself be sufficient in my view to warrant overruling the interpretation of § 2 set out in *Gingles*."

The sheer scope of this discourse on the language and history of the Voting Rights Act, combined with his jeremiads against racial separatism, ensured that Thomas's opinion in *Holder* would not be disregarded. The *New York Times* described it as a "remarkable dissent" and an "extraordinary document." Paul Gigot, a conservative columnist for the *Wall Street Journal,* hailed it as "seismic" and a "tour de force."

What lent the opinion its silent power was the fact that it flowed from the heart of a black man maligned by his own people for holding such views. Thomas's entire adult life had been devoted to proving the thesis of this opinion: Blacks do not all think alike. His concurrence in *Holder* was an eloquent argument in behalf of this truth.

1787, a Wonderful Year

Fame conferred on Thomas privileges as well as troubles. As a celebrity, he was allowed to mingle with other celebrities, the most important to him being professional sports heroes. The Dallas Cowboys were a special focus of his affections. He came to know the team's owner, Jerry Jones, who showered him with blessings: a Super Bowl ring, permission to roam on the Cowboys' practice field while wearing a Cowboys jersey, a seat in his luxury box high atop Robert F. Kennedy Stadium when the Cowboys came to Washington to play the archrival Redskins.

Basketball was another prime interest. In December 1994, when superstar forward Charles Barkley and the Phoenix Suns traveled to D.C. to play the Washington Bullets, Barkley spent four hours with Thomas at the Supreme Court, a visit arranged by Armstrong Williams. Each man gave of himself: The two played basketball on the "highest court in the land," but also talked politics. Barkley was, like Thomas, a political iconoclast—a black, self-described Republican who at the time was considering a future run for governor of his home state of Alabama. "I think I'm smart, but I was learning on the go talking with him," Barkley said of the visit. "He's achieved true greatness." Thomas's basketball skills were another matter. "He thinks he can play," Barkley said wryly. In a later conversation with his friend Dick Weiler back in Missouri, Thomas complained of referee bias in professional basketball: "As good as Michael Jordan is, he doesn't need any help from the referees."

Life was full of such unfairness, a fact that Thomas knew better than most people. Two clouds, in particular, still hung over him at the time. One was the growing, stereotypical assumption that he was a mere follower, or even "clone," of Scalia. (Black commentator Carl Rowan first used the term in a syndicated column in July 1993.) A year later, a front-page article in the *Washington Post* asserted, "their pattern on opinions is that Scalia writes it up and Thomas signs it. That has spawned criticism that Thomas is a pawn of Scalia."

It was true that Thomas and Scalia often voted in tandem. But as Thomas's former clerks and defenders would point out, liberal justices in the Court's recent history also behaved similarly. In his book *First Principles,* Scott Douglas Gerber assessed Thomas's first five years on the Court. Gerber's statistical analysis found that Thomas and Scalia voted the same in 80 percent of cases and Ginsburg and Breyer in 76 percent of cases. Souter and Breyer, two of the Court's liberals, were the most likely to vote together, at 84 percent. For all of these justices, the consistency lay in a joint adherence to a common belief system: originalism for Thomas and Scalia, "living Constitution" liberalism for justices left of center.

Thomas's independence of mind was clear as early as his *Hudson* dissent, and unmistakable by the end of his first full term. In the 1992 term, Thomas joined Scalia in five concurring opinions, one dissent, and one opinion concurring in part and dissenting in part. This was a very small fraction of the 107 total cases that yielded full Court opinions. Thomas wrote six concurrences of his own and one dissent, which Scalia joined. Thomas was more likely to join Rehnquist in dissent (twice) or other members of the Court (thrice) than Scalia. In 81 of the 107 cases, Thomas voted with the majority, as did Scalia a comparable percentage of the time. Thomas wrote the majority opinion in 11 cases. Indeed, Court insiders indicated that Thomas persuaded Scalia to change his vote on an at least one important case during this period.

By 1995, Thomas's corpus of opinions showed he had become the most faithful originalist on the Court, and, *ipso facto,* the most conservative justice. Across a broad horizon of constitutional issues—federalism, criminal justice, freedom of religion—Thomas consistently planted his flag to the right of Scalia. He had also become the second most prolific opinion writer on the Court and the author of some of the longest separate opinions in the Court's history.

A second thorn piercing Thomas's side was his ruptured relationship with black opinion leaders, and to some degree the black community generally. Civil rights leaders and black journalists, the vast majority of whom were liberal, had taken Thomas to task for his opinions. Thomas tried to mend this schism through personal outreach. At Williams' suggestion, he called a highly unusual press conference with selected black journalists and opinion leaders on October 26, 1994. During a wide-ranging discussion, Thomas declared in an unfortunate Nixonian formulation, "I am not an Uncle Tom." The *Washington Post* amplified this assertion by making it part of its headline in the next day's edition. Yet Thomas's charm remained formidable, and it moved at least one of the attendees. Activist and future Al Gore campaign director Donna Brazile told the *Post*, "As a young African American woman on my first visit to the court, I was very moved by some of his statements." Brazile subsequently was harangued by civil rights leaders, who asked if she had "taken leave of [her] senses."

Another effort to address this breach was a sentimental speaking appearance a month later at Tuskegee University. Booker T. Washington, a hero to both Myers Anderson and his famous grandson, helped found Tuskegee in 1881 and served as its first teacher. Tuskegee became one of the nation's most storied black colleges. The university did not formally invite Thomas to deliver a speech; rather, a Tuskegee college bowl team visited Thomas's chambers earlier in the year and asked him informally. He accepted readily.

Thomas flew into Birmingham, Alabama, and on November 18 made the two-hour drive to Tuskegee. Despite the lack of a formal invitation, the college took measures to ensure basic Southern hospitality. Midday classes were cancelled to allow students to attend the event. About two thousand did.

"This is a dream come true," Thomas told the crowd with evident emotion. "It's an honor to be at the school built by Booker T. Washington." He recalled how his grandfather always had called him "Booker T.," and how the great apostle of black self-help was an awe-inspiring figure in "the entire small world of my youth."

The construction of Thomas's address at Tuskegee differed from that of his typical speech. Absent were the long, lawyerly sentences that formed the bulk of his other speeches. Instead, a simple repetition supplied a cadence. His voice rose and fell as he intoned his remarks:

> Many of you are the first in your family to go to college. I was there. Some of you have grown up in rural areas. I was there. Some of you were raised by one or neither parent. I was there. Some of you have

barely or never seen your fathers. I was there. Some of you only have one pair of shoes. I was there. Some of you will be heavily in debt when you leave college. [The students cheered.] I finished paying my student loans two years ago. So I was there. Some of you may be frustrated. Some of you may be angry. Some of you may be confused. I was there.

He had come to Tuskegee, he related, on a "mission of love." He added: "I am no better than you-all. I'm no smarter than you-all. I'm no more talented than you-all. I've never been No. 1 in my class. I'm scared to death of aerospace, engineering, and physics."

Two major books about Thomas appeared in 1994. His patron in the Senate, John Danforth, wrote by far the best first-hand account of the confirmation hearings. *Resurrection* described the anguish that overwhelmed Thomas after Hill came forward with her allegations. The senator related how Thomas had subdued these emotions only days before the pivotal "high-tech lynching" speech. Thomas granted Danforth a bitter interview; throughout, the new justice came across as so angry over the ordeal as to be spitting nails with every punctuation mark. The book related many private details about Thomas and his reaction to Hill's charges that otherwise would have been lost to history.

Far more heralded in the media was the publication of a second book on the hearings, *Strange Justice*. Written by Jane Mayer and Jill Abramson, two reporters with the *Wall Street Journal*, the book told the life stories of Thomas and Hill and the circumstances of their clash before the nation. To distinguish their work from others in the marketplace, Mayer and Abramson resorted to drawing every possible negative conclusion or implication about Thomas.

Strange Justice was far more ambitious than David Brock's *The Real Anita Hill*. Mayer and Abramson covered much more ground, combining biography with political reporting (while Brock interviewed dozens of people, the two reporters said they interviewed hundreds). They also scrutinized Thomas's professional ambitions and veracity more thoroughly. In addition, they found additional witnesses (namely, Brad Mims and Cathy Thompson) to support some of Hill's complaints about Thomas at the time she worked for him. Not surprisingly, Nina Totenberg gave the book a glowing review. Writing for the *Los Angeles Times*, she described the authors as having "no ax to grind," as opposed to Brock, whose work was "so factually flawed that his book ... is not

viewed seriously in either the academic or journalistic communities"—
those communities being liberal. Left unexplained was why Totenberg,
a partisan actor in the confirmation drama, felt it ethically proper to
review the book.

Throughout *Strange Justice,* there was a liberal sprinkling of mean-
spirited asides about the justice. Mayer and Abramson cruelly refer to
his first, family-built house in Pin Point as a "shack." They blithely suggest that Thomas was a bastard, which was provably false. The authors'
discussion of Thomas's relationship with his sister, Emma Mae Martin, so disturbed her that she refused to grant any other interviews for
the next six years. Although Mayer and Abramson sifted meticulously
through Thomas's past experiences with pornography, they came up
with little new information. They resorted to publishing accusations
that other liberal reporters had refused to report because of concerns
about their accuracy. Sukari Hardnctt, one of the three women who
came forward at the hearings to make charges against Thomas, described
one portion of the book discussing her as an "absolute bunch of crap."
In the paperback edition, a sentence stating that White House lawyer
Mark Paoletta's actions may have violated a federal anti-lobbying act
was deleted after he protested the inaccuracy to the publisher.

Mayer and Abramson stopped short of accusing Thomas of perjury.
They stated, nevertheless, that the preponderance of the evidence suggested that Hill, not Thomas, was telling the truth—although the transcripts of the hearings impeached this position. Still, such conclusions
and the shrill, negative tone of the book appealed to the authors' friends
and fellow feminists in the media. Many embraced the book uncriti-
cally. The authors appeared on ABC's *Nightline, Good Morning America, Larry King Live* and an hour-long edition of ABC's *Turning Point.*
The *Wall Street Journal* and *Newsweek* ran excerpts. Mayer appeared
with Danforth on *Nightline,* but otherwise, Mayer and Abramson refused
to appear anywhere alongside defenders of Thomas. Howard Kurtz of
the *Washington Post* noted, "The media embrace of 'Strange Justice'
contrasts sharply with the chilly reception accorded David Brock's best-
selling 1993 book, 'The Real Anita Hill.' . . . That book generated few
news stories, and the TV shows that invited Brock insisted that he appear
with an advocate for Hill." Most remarkably, *Strange Justice* was nominated for a National Book Award before it was even published.

The 1994 term featured some of the most important and far-reaching cases to come before the Supreme Court in decades. It was also the moment at which Thomas began to assert an increasingly bold jurisprudence—perhaps in response to the intellectual challenge at hand. On November 8, almost as if indicating the intensified role he intended to play, Thomas spoke from the bench during oral argument for the first time in more than eighteen months. This earned a mention in *USA Today*, which reported that his fellow justices "seemed startled when Thomas's deep voice resounded from the right side of the bench."

United States v. Lopez, the most important case of the term, caused a seismic shift in the constitutional landscape. The Court struck down the Gun-Free School Zones Act on a 5–4 vote. By passing this legislation, Congress had made it a federal crime to knowingly possess a firearm in a school zone. The Court ruled that Congress had exceeded its powers under the Commerce Clause, which authorizes it "[t]o regulate Commerce … among the several states." This was the first time since the New Deal that the court had nullified federal legislation on these grounds.

Writing for the majority, Chief Justice Rehnquist observed, "To uphold the Government's contentions here, we would have to pile inference upon inference in a manner that would bid fair to convert congressional authority under the Commerce Clause to a general police power of the sort retained by the States." The Court, he stated, would not "proceed any further" down that road.

Even the majority's dramatic reversal of course was not enough to satisfy Thomas. He wrote a lengthy concurring opinion explaining why he thought the Court had not gone far enough. "I write separately to observe that our case law has drifted far from the original understanding of the Commerce Clause," Thomas began. Then he observed, "it seems to me that the power to regulate 'commerce' can by no means encompass authority over mere gun possession, any more than it empowers the Federal Government to regulate marriage, littering, or cruelty to animals, throughout the 50 States. Our Constitution quite properly leaves such matters to the individual States."

Thomas examined the original understanding of the Commerce Clause through a familiar prism. He looked at the accepted definitions of "commerce" in 1787, the year the Constitution was adopted. He also pored over the debates at the Constitutional Convention, the *Federalist Papers,* and early court cases interpreting the clause.

His comprehensive review of the relevant history led him to what he deemed the source of recent judicial confusion over the Commerce Clause. He believed the substantial effects test was the suspect, and he called on the Court to discard it. "I am aware of no cases prior to the New Deal that characterized the power flowing from the Commerce Clause as sweepingly as does our substantial effects test," Thomas noted. "My review of the case law indicates that the substantial effects test is but an innovation of the 20th century." Such a statement, penned on the eve of the twenty-first century, was a quaint declaration of a man whose worldview, in many respects, was anchored in an earlier era.

He took issue with Stevens' contention in dissent that the Court's ruling was "radical," a claim he denied, but not very persuasively. The majority's decision was, of course, quite radical. By Thomas's measure, however, it was not radical enough. "If anything," he insisted, "the 'wrong turn' was the Court's dramatic departure in the 1930's from a century and a half of precedent."

Thomas left himself some wiggle room. "This extended discussion of the original understanding and our first century and a half of case law does not necessarily require a wholesale abandonment of our most recent opinions," he wrote near the conclusion of his opinion. A footnote following this statement offered a disclaimer: "Although I might be willing to return to the original understanding, I recognize that many believe that it is too late in the day to undertake a fundamental reexamination of the past 60 years. Consideration of *stare decisis* and reliance interests may convince us that we cannot wipe the slate clean." This was a fair and prudent point: Citizens might have relied on the existing constitutional order in making personal or business decisions, making summary deracination of these cases unjust. Nevertheless, one sensed in this footnote an attempt to have it both ways intellectually—an audacious opinion seasoned with comforting rhetoric in defense of the status quo.

Having made this limited concession, Thomas betrayed his true desire: launching a full-scale rebellion against the rulings of the New Deal era. The Court, he said, must resist the "blank check" of power given to the federal government. He concluded, "At an appropriate juncture, I think we must modify our Commerce Clause jurisprudence. Today, it is easy enough to say that the Clause certainly does not empower Congress to ban gun possession within 1,000 feet of a school."

Vying with *Lopez* for significance this term was *U.S. Term Limits, Inc. v. Thornton*. The case centered on whether states could vote to limit the number of terms their representatives could serve in Congress. The people of Arkansas, as part of a national term-limits movement, amended their state constitution to prohibit members of Congress from being elected to more than three consecutive terms in the House of Representatives or two terms in the Senate. In a 5–4 decision, the Court struck down the Arkansas law.

Thomas wrote a massive dissent joined by Rehnquist, O'Connor and Scalia. It ran eighty-one pages in the U.S. Reports, a length suggesting a justice determined not to be outdone in thoroughness or devotion to the Framers, whom Stevens cited in his majority opinion. Indeed, thoroughness was called for, as the Framers' views on the subject were not entirely clear.

Thomas summarized his conclusion: "Nothing in the Constitution deprives the people of each State of the power to prescribe eligibility requirements for the candidates who seek to represent them in Congress. The Constitution is simply silent on this question. And where the Constitution is silent, it raises no bar to action by the States or the people." His analysis rested on the original understanding of the federal system of government. When the Constitution was adopted, Thomas observed, "the people of each State surrendered some of their authority to the United States." Under the Tenth Amendment, the states and the people retained whatever power they did not expressly delegate to the federal government. "In short, the notion of popular sovereignty that undergirds the Constitution does not erase state boundaries, but rather tracks them."

Those wishing to invalidate the Arkansas law carried a burden of proof. In light of the history of the framing of the Constitution and the Tenth Amendment, such advocates should be required to "point to something in the Federal Constitution that deprives the people of Arkansas of the power to enact such measures." Opponents of the Arkansas term limits measure could not meet this burden.

Thomas's survey of the constitutional history led to familiar sources. He reviewed the text of the Constitution, particularly the Qualifications Clauses; the debates at the Convention, including an earlier draft of the qualifications provision by the Committee of Detail; and the ratification debates. He also quoted Jefferson, who believed that the power to set disqualifications for Congressmen resided with the states. The early Court cases, Thomas concluded, supported his view that states could impose term limits. He looked to the Court's 1819 decision in *McCulloch v. Maryland* and subsequent case law. He acknowledged the contrary views on the subject by Justice Joseph Story in his celebrated *Commentaries on the Constitution of the United States*. Thomas would say of the former justice that while he was a "brilliant and accomplished man," his commentaries were written a half-century after the framing: "Rather than representing the original understanding of the Constitution, they represent only his own understanding." This was one of his few intellectual evasions (Thomas, in fact, quoted Story often in his own opinions when it suited his purposes).

Thomas's exhaustive dissent lacked the scathing wit and entertaining verve of one of Scalia's opinions. But what the opinion lacked in aplomb, it made up for in scope and dedication to originalism. Coming from a black man, moreover, such a defense of states' rights required considerable intellectual audacity.

In another case, Thomas finally applied originalism to freedom of speech. He also spurred Scalia to do the same; neither justice had done so previously. *McIntyre v. Ohio Elections Commission* generated an opinion from each justice that laid out the analytical differences of their originalist jurisprudence.

Margaret McIntyre had run afoul of school officials in Westerville, Ohio, by distributing leaflets outside a school meeting that advocated defeat of a proposed tax levy. Some of the handbills identified her as the author; others said they expressed the views of "Concerned Parents and Tax Payers." A school official gallantly filed a complaint with the Ohio Elections Commission, saying the leaflets violated state law by failing to identify the author. The commission fined her $100.

By a 7–2 vote, the Supreme Court held that the Ohio law prohibiting distribution of anonymous campaign literature violated the First Amendment's freedom of speech. In his opinion for the majority, Stevens asserted that the right to publish anonymously lay within this First Amendment guarantee. The opinion did not consult the intentions of the Framers or the history of the First Amendment.

In a concurring opinion, Thomas sought to provide some historical balance. He proposed "a different methodology" to reach the same outcome. He wished to determine "whether the phrase 'freedom of speech, or of the press,' as originally understood, protected anonymous political leafleting." He added, "I believe that it did." Quoting language from old, frequently ignored cases, Thomas set forth the starting point for his discussion. "When interpreting the Free Speech and Press Clauses, we must be guided by their original meaning, for '[t]he Constitution is a written instrument. As such its meaning does not alter. That which it means when adopted, it means now.'"

He could find no record of discussions of anonymous political expression in the First Congress or the state conventions that ratified the Bill of Rights. "Thus, our analysis must focus on the practices and beliefs held by the Founders concerning anonymous political articles and pamphlets." Thomas's treatment roved from Colonial times to post-Convention writings. He considered the trial of John Peter Zenger as well as the many revolutionary and early U.S. tracts that conscripted the names of great Romans (Publius, Cato, Brutus, et al.) as noms de guerre. He also scrutinized the debate between Federalists and Anti-Federalists over anonymous political speech.

Unlike the majority, which had neglected to consult this history, Thomas concluded from these and other sources that the First Amendment encompassed a right to write anonymously:

> The majority fails to seek the original understanding of the First Amendment, and instead attempts to answer the question in this case by resorting to three approaches. First, the majority recalls the historical practice of anonymous writing from Shakespeare's works to the Federalist Papers to Mark Twain. . . . Second, it finds that anonymous speech has an expressive value both to the speaker and to society that outweighs public interest in disclosure. Third, it finds that [the Ohio statute] cannot survive strict scrutiny because it is a content-based restriction on speech.

He disposed of these arguments in order:

> I cannot join the majority's analysis because it deviates from our settled approach to interpreting the Constitution and because it super-

imposes its modern theories concerning expression upon the constitutional text. Whether "great works of literature" by Voltaire or George Eliot have been published anonymously should be irrelevant to our analysis, because it sheds no light on what the phrases "free speech" or "free press" meant to the people who drafted and ratified the First Amendment. Similarly, whether certain types of expression have "value" today has little significance; what is important is whether the Framers in 1791 believed anonymous speech sufficiently valuable to deserve the protection of the bill of rights. And although the majority faithfully follows our approach to "content-based" speech regulations, we need not undertake this analysis when the original understanding provides the answer.

Like the majority, however, Thomas concluded that the Ohio law violated the right to anonymous speech, and had to be overturned.

In his dissent, with Rehnquist joining, Scalia decried the Court's voiding of anonymous-speech laws in forty-nine states, and questioned the feasibility of determining the original understanding of a right to anonymous speech. Scalia offered a different guidepost: "Where the meaning of a constitutional text (such as 'the freedom of speech') is unclear, the widespread and long-accepted practices of the American people are the best indication of what fundamental beliefs it was intended to enshrine." The laws against anonymous speech had existed for a sufficient period of time for Scalia to uphold the Ohio law based on this tradition.

This analysis did not persuade Thomas. These statutes dated back only one hundred years, not to the framing of the First Amendment. Thomas responded in his concurrence, "While, like Justice SCALIA, I am loath to overturn a century of practice shared by almost all of the States, I believe the historical evidence from the framing outweighs recent tradition." In Thomas's view, Scalia's review of the relevant history had not gone back far enough.

Scalia, furthermore, had not shown the same deference to long-standing state laws in his earlier First Amendment jurisprudence. He had, for example, joined the majority in *Texas v. Johnson* in striking down the laws of all fifty states that banned flag burning. By his reasoning in *McIntyre*, these laws should have been upheld rather than swept away.

Scalia acknowledged this disparate treatment. "It can be said that we ignored a tradition as old, and almost as widespread, in *Texas v. Johnson*," he noted. Scalia nevertheless contended that *Johnson* stood "for the proposition that postadoption tradition cannot alter the core meaning of a constitutional guarantee." This, of course, begged the question of why flag burning was covered by the "core meaning" of the First Amendment more than Ms. McIntyre's flyers. The strained distinction Scalia drew—that the "bedrock principle" at the heart of the First Amendment safeguarded flag burning but not anonymous pamphleteering—did not convince Thomas, and did not seem to convince even Scalia himself. By any reasonable measure, political literature was far more central to freedom of speech than flag burning. And the latter was hardly a tradition of long standing in 1989, when the Court handed down its *Johnson* decision.

Thomas, in sum, forced Scalia to confront errors in his earlier jurisprudence. Indeed, it is unlikely that Scalia would have felt the need to enunciate his "widespread and long-accepted practices test" if Thomas had not hewed so closely to the intentions of the Framers in *McIntyre*.

The other major First Amendment case of the term dealt with a more predictable source of judicial vexation, religion. In *Rosenberger v. Rector & Visitors of the Univ. of Virginia*, the Court considered a case arising from Jefferson's old institution, the University of Virginia. No longer a citadel of religious liberty, the university had refused to pay for the printing costs of a Christian student newspaper, *Wide Awake*, out of a student activities fund that normally compensated outside contractors for the printing costs of various student publications. The university maintained that the Christian publication violated campus policies, which banned funding for student publications that "primarily promot[e] or manifes[t] a particular belie[f] in or about a deity or an ultimate reality." By a 5–4 vote, the Court held that the university's policy violated the First Amendment right to freedom of speech.

In dissent, Souter reverted to the Warren Court's former practice of quoting constitutional history to lend a veneer of tradition to an antitraditional opinion. Souter pointed to the debate over the Virginia tax assessment bill in 1786. The bill sought to levy a tax to support the clergy of the state. Madison wrote a Memorial and Remonstrance against Religious Assessments that helped defeat the bill. Souter argued that if the author of the First Amendment opposed such legislation, *Wide Awake* was not entitled to a similar subsidy.

By dabbling in originalism, Souter had stepped onto Thomas's turf, and Thomas did not let the challenge go unanswered. His concurring opinion was the first court analysis in decades to examine thoroughly the history of the Establishment Clause. Thomas began:

> I agree with the Court's opinion and join it in full, but I write separately to express my disagreement with the historical analysis put forward by the dissent. Although the dissent starts down the right path in consulting the original meaning of the Establishment Clause, its misleading application of history yields a principle that is inconsistent with our Nation's long tradition of allowing religious adherents to participate on equal terms in neutral government programs.

Thomas noted that the snippets of history Souter cited from the assessment debate "hardly compe[l] the dissent's conclusion that government must actively discriminate against religion. The dissent's historical discussion glosses over the fundamental characteristic of the Virginia assessment bill that sparked the controversy: The assessment was to be imposed for the support of clergy in the performance of their function of teaching religion."

The reason Madison objected, Thomas pointed out, was not because he thought it wrong for the government to support religious enterprises financially. Rather, the assessment did not treat all faiths equally. Madison criticized the "preferential nature of the assessment," fearing that certain denominations might receive special treatment over others. Thomas also looked at Madison's early legislative proposals dealing with support of religious institutions. "Even if Madison believed that the principle of nonestablishment of religion precluded government financial support for religion per se (in the sense of government benefits specifically targeting religion)," he concluded, "there is no indication that at the time of the framing he took the dissent's extreme view that the government must discriminate against religious adherents by excluding them from more generally available financial subsidies."

Thomas then examined the remainder of Souter's dissent. "Stripped of its flawed historical premise, the dissent's argument is reduced to the claim that our Establishment Clause jurisprudence permits neutrality

in the context of access to government *facilities* but requires discrimination in access to government *funds.*" He noted that the same First
Congress that framed the Bill of Rights elected chaplains for both chambers and appropriated salaries for them. The nation's churches had
enjoyed exemptions from property taxes since the Revolutionary War.
"In my view, the dissent's acceptance of this tradition puts to rest the
notion that the Establishment Clause bars monetary aid to religious
groups even when the aid is equally available to other groups. A tax
exemption in many cases is economically and functionally indistin-
guishable from a direct monetary subsidy."

His final twist of the knife was to note that by the dissent's reasoning, churches would be disqualified from receiving protection from
police or fire departments:

> Thus, history provides an answer for the constitutional question posed
> by this case, but it is not the one given by the dissent. The dissent iden-
> tifies no evidence that the Framers intended to disable religious enti-
> ties from participating on neutral terms in even-handed government
> programs. The evidence that does exist points in the opposite direction
> and provides ample support for today's decision.

Souter's history lessons could not escape the central thrust of
Thomas's argument: If the First Amendment truly barred the government from financially supporting religious endeavors, why did it take
two hundred years to divine the Framers' intentions on this matter?
The best Souter could muster, in the end, was to accuse Thomas of
being quixotic. By arguing that the Establishment Clause merely for-
bids governmental preference of one religion over another, Souter said,
Thomas "wishes to wage a battle that was lost long ago" in a string of
earlier Supreme Court decisions. In this, at least, Thomas and the dissenting justices were in agreement.

In conference, Thomas was passionate in discussions about two major
race cases before the Court. In one conference in January 1995, he
implored his colleagues to take into account his experience under Jim
Crow. When the justices considered *Missouri v. Jenkins,* a desegregation case, Thomas pointed out, "I am the only one at this table who
attended a segregated school. And the problem with segregation was
not that we didn't have white people in our class. The problem was that
we didn't have equal facilities. We didn't have heating, we didn't have

books, and we had rickety chairs." He also mentioned the famous footnote in *Brown v. Board of Education* in which the Court struck down
school segregation, in part, because of social science showing that segregation had caused black children to feel inferior to whites. The greater
evil of segregation, Thomas insisted, was that blacks were consigned to
inferior facilities, not that they were unable to attend school with whites.

A week later, the nine justices met to discuss *Adarand Constructors,
Inc. v. Pena,* a case involving racial set-asides in federal contracts. Again,
Thomas invoked his own life as a talking point—an unusual rhetorical
tactic for the intensely private man. He discussed how his grandfather
had not needed affirmative action to obtain contracts for his fuel-delivery
business. Racial preferences, he said, were based on the patronizing
notion that blacks are inherently inferior. Moreover, the Constitution
is color-blind. The government should not be in the business of award-
ing contracts based on race.

The two race cases provoked equally passionate written opinions
from him. *Missouri v. Jenkins* revolved around a controversial ruling by
a federal district court in Missouri. To discourage "white flight" from
inner-city schools, the court imposed on the Kansas City school district the most expensive desegregation program for primary and secondary schools in the nation's history. The court began its supervision
of Kansas City's schools after suit was filed in 1977 alleging continuing segregation. Since then, the court required school officials to fund
a list of extravagant improvements in the schools to make them more
attractive to whites. These remedies included a 2,000-square-foot plan-
etarium, a 25-acre farm, and a model United Nations equipped for language translation. Because the school district could not afford all these
upgrades, the State of Missouri was obliged to underwrite them. Finally,
the court ordered salary increases for virtually all teachers and other
staff in the district. By a 5–4 vote, the Supreme Court stepped in and
drew the line, saying the district court had abused its powers in ordering this salary hike.

Thomas's concurring opinion began with a bracing proclamation.
"It never ceases to amaze me that the courts are so willing to assume
that anything that is predominantly black must be inferior." He felt
compelled to write the concurrence, he stated, so that he could "add a
few thoughts with respect to the overall course of this litigation."

Two "threads" in the Court's recent jurisprudence had led to this "unfortunate situation." First, the Court had endorsed a theory that "black students suffer an unspecified psychological harm from segregation that retards their mental and educational development." Thomas questioned this. "This approach not only relies upon questionable social science research rather than constitutional principle, but it also rests on an assumption of black inferiority."

The second thread was judicial abuse of power. He observed, "we have permitted the federal courts to exercise virtually unlimited equitable powers to remedy this alleged constitutional violation. The exercise of this authority has trampled upon principles of federalism and the separation of powers and has freed courts to pursue other agendas unrelated to the narrow purpose of precisely remedying a constitutional harm."

On the first of these, Thomas argued that the district court had erred grievously in concluding that racial imbalance in the student population, by itself, was unconstitutional. "In effect, the court found that racial imbalances constituted an ongoing constitutional violation that continued to inflict harm on black students," Thomas observed. "This position appears to rest upon the idea that any school that is black is inferior, and that blacks cannot succeed without the benefit of the company of whites." He pinpointed the problem: "The District Court's willingness to adopt such stereotypes stemmed from a misreading of our earliest school desegregation case." The case he referred to was *Brown v. Board of Education.*

Here, Thomas would tread upon one of the Court's most hallowed decisions. After all, Thurgood Marshall had argued the *Brown* case before the Court. For any black man to reconsider *Brown* was an extraordinary intellectual feat; for Thomas to do so was perhaps his bravest act as a justice.

For all his fears of hostile crowds and journalists, Thomas did not shrink from an intellectual fight where it counted most—court opinions. He disputed the *Brown* Court's use of psychological and sociological surveys "that purportedly showed that *de jure* segregation harmed black students by generating 'a feeling of inferiority' in them." In language notably similar to that in speeches and articles penned while at EEOC, he explained:

Segregation was not unconstitutional because it might have caused psychological feelings of inferiority. Public school systems that separated blacks and provided them with superior educational resources—making blacks "feel" superior to whites sent to lesser schools—would violate the Fourteenth Amendment, whether or not the white students felt stigmatized, just as do the school systems in which the positions of the races are reversed. Psychological injury or benefit is irrelevant to the question whether state actors have engaged in intentional discrimination—the critical inquiry for ascertaining violations of the Equal Protection Clause. The judiciary is fully competent to make independent determinations concerning the existence of state action without the unnecessary and misleading assistance of the social sciences.

Desegregation had not been the cure-all for black underachievement that its creators had promised. "Given that desegregation has not produced the predicted leaps forwarding black educational achievement, there is no reason to think that black students cannot learn as well when surrounded by members of their own race as when they are in an integrated environment. Indeed, it may very well be that what has been true for historically black colleges is true for black middle and high schools." Thomas cited his *Fordice* concurrence, in which he had talked of black colleges as a "source of pride to blacks who have attended them and a source of hope to black families who want the benefits of . . . learning for their children."

The second "thread"—abuse of judicial power—generated comparable scorn. Thomas placed in historical context the district court's misuse of its equitable powers. He examined the history of equity in law, the birth of English courts of equity, and the Framers' concerns about such powers. He noted the Framers' "suspicion" of equity; they saw such judicial authority, when unchecked, as a vehicle for tyranny. Thomas quoted Jefferson and Hamilton from the *Federalist Papers* in support of his position.

He concluded with parting shots at both flawed premises. "We must forever put aside the notion that simply because a school district today is black, it must be educationally inferior." And, "The desire to reform a school district, or any other institution, cannot so captivate the judiciary that it forgets its constitutionally mandated role. . . . At some point, we must recognize that the judiciary is not omniscient, and that all problems do not require a remedy of constitutional proportions." With his concurrence, Thomas sought to substitute natural law for social science as the constitutional basis for racial equality.

In *Adarand Constructors, Inc. v. Pena,* Thomas again wrote an opinion true to the statements he had made to his colleagues during conference. A company in Colorado had challenged set-asides for minority-owned enterprises in contracts for federal highway construction. By a 5–4 margin, a splintered court struck down the set-asides. In prior decisions, the Court had held that the Fourteenth Amendment's Due Process Clause, which applied to state governments, required strict scrutiny of all race-based action by state and local governments. Under strict scrutiny analysis, the Court would uphold the policy only if the Court found it to be narrowly tailored to serve a compelling governmental interest. The Court had declined to apply strict scrutiny to the federal government in such cases. In *Adarand,* the Court reversed course and, in an opinion by O'Connor, held that strict scrutiny would apply to federal racial classifications.

Thomas concurred partly with the majority's opinion, but wrote separately to voice strong exception to the dissent. "I agree with the majority's conclusion that strict scrutiny applies to *all* government classifications based on race. I write separately, however, to express my disagreement with the premise underlying Justice STEVENS' and Justice GINSBURG's dissents: that there is a racial paternalism exception to the principle of equal protection." Thomas declared:

> Government cannot make us equal; it can only recognize, respect, and protect us as equal before the law. There can be no doubt that the paternalism that appears to lie at the heart of this program is at war with the principle of inherent equality that underlies and infuses our Constitution. See Declaration of Independence ("We hold these truths to be self-evident, that all men are created equal, that they are endowed by their Creator with certain unalienable rights, that among these are Life, Liberty, and the pursuit of Happiness").

This citation engraved into constitutional law a transmission of natural law philosophy from Leo Strauss to Harry Jaffa to Clarence Thomas.

Years of frustration from seeing his accomplishments second-guessed forged the remaining core of his opinion:

> These programs not only raise grave constitutional questions, they also undermine the moral basis of the equal protection principle.... Inevitably, such programs engender attitudes of superiority or, alternatively, provoke resentment among those who believe that they have been wronged by the government's use of race. These programs stamp minorities with a badge of inferiority and may cause them to develop dependencies or to adopt an attitude that they are 'entitled' to preferences.

He concluded, "In my mind, government-sponsored racial discrimination based on benign prejudice is just as noxious as discrimination inspired by malicious prejudice. In each instance, it is racial discrimination, plain and simple."

Thomas's opinions in *Jenkins* and *Adarand* were departures from originalism, lacking his usual punctilious examination of the intentions of the Framers. The reason was unmistakable. Thomas knew that the Framers of the Fourteenth Amendment and the Equal Protection Clause did not intend to write the core principle of the Declaration of Independence into the Constitution. As Raoul Berger noted in his definitive history of the Fourteenth Amendment, the clause was intended merely to ensure that newly emancipated blacks would be treated equally before the law when others sought to deprive them of their fundamental rights to life, liberty and property. Even if the Framers had incorporated into the clause the sentiments of the Declaration of Independence, they still would not have endorsed racial equality; that was Lincoln's gloss. Indeed, segregation continued unabated for another century after the amendment was adopted. In the last decades of the twentieth century, the Supreme Court interpreted the Fourteenth Amendment as a general equalizer between various classes of people, an approach without historical foundation. From an originalist perspective, Thomas's Jaffa-inspired jurisprudence was no more legitimate than these left-of-center efforts.

In race cases as well as most freedom-of-speech cases, Thomas would stray from originalism. Applying originalism to the Fourteenth Amendment would have required Thomas to admit that the Constitution was, in a fundamental sense, racist in conception. This his patriotism would not allow. "I have felt the pain of racism as much as anyone else," Thomas once remarked (hyperbolically). "Yet I am wild about the Constitution and about the Declaration.... I believe in the American proposition, the American dream, because I've seen it in my own life." The two race cases of the crucially important 1994 term showed that to uphold this dream, he would carve out an exception to originalism.

His cousin Abe Famble and other relatives from Georgia visited him and Ginni annually. On one such trip, Thomas took his guests to Gettysburg and they toured the battlefield and the national cemetery where Lincoln delivered his address. Thomas stood at the same spot where Lincoln had given his oration. He imagined the courage required to declare such sentiments in an era far more racially charged than Thomas's day.

"I always wonder about Pickett's charge," Thomas told one audience subsequently. He had stood on Cemetery Ridge and gazed out across the broad field that the Confederate soldiers had to cross as they marched toward a "certain death." "Who among us knows of any cause for which we will march across a Pickett's field?" he asked. "It takes a lot of courage," he concluded, "a lot more than I think I have." That a black son of Georgia could look with compassion on these fallen warriors of the Old South arguably said more about his commitment to racial forgiveness than any line in his opinions.

Keeping the Faith

Justice Thomas's opinions in the 1994 term, particularly those in *Jenkins* and *Adarand*, drew brickbats and pickets from many black opinion leaders and journalists. In its June 26, 1995, issue, *Time* magazine published an article denouncing Thomas's racial jurisprudence. The title of the piece, "Uncle Tom Justice," was itself a remarkable racial affront.

On September 12, Rev. Al Sharpton, the New York City civil rights activist, led a contingent of four hundred demonstrators to protest on a public road outside Thomas's subdivision in Fairfax County. The participants arrived in chartered buses to find twenty police officers and federal marshals awaiting them. A line of yellow police tape and a helicopter circling overhead further supervised the proceedings. During two hours of speeches, hymns and prayers, they excoriated Thomas as an ingrate and turncoat.

Thomas tried to make light of this vituperation. After attending a speech by Tom Sowell at the American Enterprise Institute, Thomas milled about with some of the attendees. As he often did at public gatherings, he found himself engaged in conversation with a young black man. "You ought to drop by my house sometime," he told the young man. "You can meet Al Sharpton." As Thomas unloaded his booming laugh, the young man, according to one bystander, "didn't quite know what to think."

Despite the attacks against him, Thomas cared deeply about young blacks and the social rapids they had to negotiate. During the summer, he spoke to Glenn Loury in his chambers. "Look at these young brothers dying in the street—the drive-by shootings, the violence," he told Loury. "If dogs were being struck down at the same rate and in the same way, and left bleeding in the gutter, there would be a society of blue-haired women to save our canine friends. But these are young black men bleeding in the gutter, and no one seems to give a damn."

The opportunity to speak to children and young adults was, to Thomas, "one of the wonderful things about the job." The nest at home was empty, leading him to concentrate his paternal energies elsewhere. Jamal was preparing to graduate from VMI. Thomas had enjoined him only to pursue "an honest job and an honest living." But he also expected his son to do as he had done with regard to living arrangements. Upon Jamal's graduation, Thomas would have a message for him like that he had received from his grandfather: "Your address has changed." After graduating, Jamal would begin a career not unlike that of Thomas's brother, Myers, working in corporate management for, among other companies, a prominent bank.

One young black man in Washington, D.C., Cedric Jennings, came to Thomas's attention at around this time and became something of a special charge. Thomas had read in the *Wall Street Journal* about how Jennings, a student at the worst high school in the city, had grown up the son of a violent criminal, living in a small apartment overlooking a drug market. Thomas invited the young man to his chambers. He subsequently took the extraordinary step of allowing Ron Suskind, the reporter who had originally written about Jennings, to accompany the young man and record their exchange.

"You know, Cedric, I sense that you and I are a lot alike," Thomas said to lead off the conversation. "I have a sense of what you've been through."

Asked which college he planned to attend, Jennings told the justice he had decided on Brown University.

Thomas frowned and shook his head. "Well, that's fine, but I'm not sure if I would have selected an Ivy League school," he said, disparaging his own career path. "You're going to be up there with lots of very smart white kids, and if you're not sure about who you are, you could get eaten alive."

Jennings grew quiet, and Thomas, sensing that he had been too rough, tried to lift his spirits.

"It's not just at the Ivies, you understand. It can happen at any of the good colleges where a young black man who hasn't spent much time with whites suddenly finds himself among almost all whites. You can feel lost."

Thomas counseled him to avoid classes and orientation on race relations: "You have to resist that, Cedric. You understand?"

Jennings nodded, saying, "Like, you mean that you have to be your own person."

"That's right! That's it!" Thomas exclaimed, gesturing with his hand for emphasis.

The young man read aloud a poem he had written. It began: "With torch in hand, he always runs into the sunset / Always alone, not knowing his destiny."

Thomas said in a subdued voice, "Oh, yeah. I feel that way sometimes." The reporter thought he detected a moistening of Thomas's eyes.

At the conclusion of the meeting, Thomas walked slowly toward Jennings. "I'm sure you'll do just fine at Brown and after that, too," the justice assured him. "It's just that I understand, in a very personal way, how big a step you're taking. . . . You may find you're never fully accepted up ahead . . . that you've landed between worlds. That's the way I feel sometimes, even now, and it can make you angry. But you just have to channel that anger, to harness it."

The title of Suskind's resulting article in *Esquire,* "And Justice Thomas Wept," seemed to overstate what had happened. Suskind's assertion that Jennings left the meeting "curiously happy to be headed for home" also seemed questionable and below the belt. Yet Suskind rightly discerned in Thomas the continuing nursing of past injustices. In a subsequent interview, Suskind recalled, "He remembers indignities from 30 or 40 years ago with great precision. He felt the hurts deeply, and they have not healed."

There were plenty of lighter moments in Thomas's dealings with youngsters. One of the more notable occurred in April 1996. As part of the Imani project, gifted students, most of them African-American, from the Charlottesville, Virginia, public schools were allowed to travel to Washington to meet Thomas. Thomas hosted one such meeting with fourth-grade participants in one of the oak-paneled conference rooms at the Court.

Beneath oil paintings of former justices, Thomas held a dialogue with the children that would end up fundamentally altering his lifestyle. He went through his standard litany of instructions to the youngsters, urging them to do their homework, work hard, listen to their parents, and read instead of watching television.

Then one particularly assertive boy shot his hand up into the air. When Thomas called on him, the boy asked, "Don't you do things that you like but that aren't really good for you?"

Thomas thought for a moment. Then he replied, "Well, I guess I do. I smoke cigars."

The precocious youngster stood his ground. "Well, if you're going to smoke cigars, why should I give up TV?"

"Buddy," Thomas answered, "if you promise me that you'll cut back on watching television and read more for a year, until I see you next year, I promise you I'll never smoke another cigar."

Thomas extended his hand for a handshake. The boy's eyes widened. "Oh, OK," he said, a bit unnerved by the sudden change of events. The two cemented the deal with a clasp of hands.

His young guests could not have known what a jolt this agreement would give Thomas's lifestyle. Until this promise, he frequently lighted up a cigar by nine in the morning. He savored his cigars as he read briefs. He also was known to blow smoke playfully in the faces of his clerks.

Upon returning to his chambers after his talk, Thomas told his secretary, Dorothy Barry, "Dorothy, I want you to cancel my cigar orders." Thomas then entered his chambers, picked up his cigar box, and threw away the remaining offenders.

The following year, the same boy returned to the Court. "I haven't smoked any cigars—how much TV have you watched?" Thomas asked him. Both parties, it appeared, had kept their side of the bargain.

The major race case before the high court in the 1995 term was *Bush v. Vera*. It involved racial gerrymandering, a topic that came before the Court regularly during the 1990s. A federal court in Texas had scrutinized three oddly shaped congressional districts in that state, and ruled that the three districts were racially gerrymandered in violation of the

Fourteenth Amendment. Five justices of the Supreme Court voted to uphold this ruling.

Thomas's concurrence, which Scalia joined, took issue with O'Connor's majority opinion, which stated that strict scrutiny did not apply to "the intentional creation of majority-minority districts." Thomas wrote that this claim broke faith with the *Adarand* decision of the prior year, whose principle that "all governmental racial classifications must be strictly scrutinized" should be affirmed and extended ("even in the sensitive area of state legislative redistricting, I would make no exceptions"). Thomas would have to hold his fire until the day when he would finally be asked to write an opinion for the Court on the issue of race.

Thomas's most important opinion of the term involved the seemingly lackluster issue of commercial speech. The Court in *44 Liquormart, Inc. v. Rhode Island* considered a Rhode Island statute that barred any advertisements of the retail price of alcoholic beverages. Writing for the Court's unanimous decision, Stevens stated that Rhode Island could not demonstrate that the price advertising it had banned was deceptive or related to unlawful activity. The Court concluded that the state was trying to prevent dissemination of truthful commercial messages simply because it disapproved of them. The Rhode Island statute had to pass the test laid down in an earlier Supreme Court ruling, *Central Hudson Gas & Elec. Corp. v. Public Serv. Comm'n of N.Y.*, which held that the Court must use "special care" in reviewing blanket bans on speech.

Thomas wrote a concurring opinion to advocate stronger safeguards for commercial speech. "In cases such as this, in which the government's asserted interest is to keep legal users of a product or service ignorant in order to manipulate their choices in the marketplace, the balancing test adopted in [*Central Hudson*] should not be applied, in my view. Rather, such as 'interest' is *per se* illegitimate and can no more justify regulation of 'commercial' speech than it can justify regulation of 'noncommercial' speech."

To him, it made no sense to distinguish between commercial and noncommercial speech for First Amendment purposes. Thomas noted that the Court historically had accorded commercial speech less protection under the First Amendment than other forms of speech. This perplexed him:

I do not see a philosophical or historical basis for asserting that "commercial" speech is of "lower value" than "noncommercial" speech. Indeed, some historical materials suggest to the contrary.... Nor do I believe that the only explanations that the Court has ever advanced for treating "commercial" speech differently from other speech can justify restricting "commercial" speech in order to keep information from legal purchasers so as to thwart what would otherwise be their choices in the marketplace.

Central Hudson had to go because it was both insufficiently protective and unwieldy. The Court "has never explained why manipulating the choices of consumers by keeping them ignorant is more legitimate when the ignorance is maintained through suppression of 'commercial' speech than when the same ignorance is maintained through suppression of 'noncommercial' speech." Furthermore, the Court had found it hard to apply *Central Hudson*'s case-by-case balancing test, which is "inherently nondeterminative." The Court, Thomas argued, should reinstate a 1976 ruling which applied the First Amendment to a ban on price advertising regarding prescription drugs.

His concurrence offered little in the way of history, as opposed to his offering in *McIntyre*. Yet he railed against the double standard for freedom of speech that the Court previously had accepted because of distrust of big business. Thomas's concurrence in *44 Liquormart* was one of the staunchest defenses of economic liberty in the Court's history, and an opinion that no doubt would have pleased Ayn Rand immensely.

Another prison case appeared on the docket, *Lewis v. Casey*. Inmates in Arizona filed suit alleging that the state had violated their right of access to the courts. The federal district court agreed, finding the prison law libraries inadequate. The judge then entered a twenty-five-page injunctive order to ensure "meaningful access to the Courts." The order specified "in minute detail" (Scalia's words) the hours of operation for the law library, minimal educational requirements for prison librarians, and the occasions when inmates could visit the library. The ruling was based on the Supreme Court's 1977 decision in *Bounds v. Smith*, in which the Court held that states were obligated to maintain prison law libraries or provide comparable legal assistance to inmates.

The Court in *Lewis* struck down these judicial regulations by an 8–1 vote, finding that the lower court had not given sufficient consideration to the views and expertise of state prison authorities. The injunction also was overbroad. Writing for the Court, Scalia noted zestfully that *Bounds* did not "guarantee inmates the wherewithal to transform themselves into litigating engines capable of filing everything from shareholder derivative actions to slip-and-fall claims."

Thomas again was dissatisfied. He filed a concurring opinion to call for the repeal of *Bounds*. "I find no basis in the Constitution—and *Bounds* cited none—for the right to have the government finance the endeavor" of prison law libraries, he wrote. This time, Scalia did not join him.

Like the prison beating case of *Hudson v. McMillian*, for which Thomas had drawn so much ire, *M.L.B. v. S.L.J.* was another hard case for a faithful originalist. The State of Mississippi had terminated a mother's parental rights to her two minor children. She sought to appeal the order. State law required her to pay, in advance, record-preparation fees of over $2,000. She could not afford the expense, and asked the court to permit her to proceed *in forma pauperis,* or without having to pay the fee. There was no recognized right for her to proceed in that manner in a civil, as opposed to a criminal, appeal. The Mississippi Supreme Court denied her application.

The U.S. Supreme Court voted 6–3 to overturn the Mississippi Supreme Court's ruling. Ginsburg wrote the opinion for the Court. In prior rulings, the Court had held that states could not require criminal defendants to pay for transcripts of trial proceedings as a condition for appeal. Ginsburg extended that analysis to the mother's civil case, which, the justice stated, involved a "fundamental" right. Under the Due Process and Equal Protection Clauses of the Fourteenth Amendment, the mother was entitled to a free transcript at state expense.

Thomas wrote a dissenting opinion. Scalia joined it in full; Rehnquist, true to form, joined it except for the part in which Thomas called for rolling back another hoary precedent. Although he expressed sympathy for the mother—she could easily have been his own impoverished mother or sister—Thomas recognized the problems that the Court's ruling would create:

> The inevitable consequence [of the ruling] will be greater demands on the States to provide free assistance to would-be appellants in all manner of civil cases involving interests that cannot, based on the test established

by the majority, be distinguished from the admittedly important interest at issue here. The cases on which the majority relies, primarily cases
requiring appellate assistance for indigent criminal defendants, were
questionable when decided, and have, in my view, been undermined
since.

In dissenting from this new right to a "due process appeal *gratis*,"
Thomas took aim at *Griffin v. Illinois*, a 1956 decision in which the
Warren Court began its expansions of the rights of criminals and criminal defendants by striking down as unconstitutional an Illinois law
requiring a criminal defendant to purchase the trial transcript for his
appeal. The Court cited the Due Process and Equal Protection Clauses
of the Fourteenth Amendment.

Thomas criticized this reliance on the Fourteenth Amendment. He
wrote that "the Equal Protection Clause shields only against purposeful discrimination: a disparate impact, even upon members of a racial
minority, the classification of which we have been most suspect, does
not violate equal protection." More bluntly, "The *Griffin* line of cases
ascribed to—one might say announced—an equalizing notion of the
Equal Protection Clause that would, I think, have startled the Fourteenth Amendment's Framers." Notably, Thomas consulted the intentions of the Framers of the Fourteenth Amendment—something he
did not do in race cases.

"If this case squarely presented the question, I would be inclined to
vote to overrule *Griffin* and its progeny," Thomas said in a declaration
that was becoming for him something of a mantra. Regardless, he would
not extend the *Griffin* line of precedent to the current case. *Griffin*
involved criminal appeals, which enjoyed special protection under the
Constitution. There was little to prevent the Court from extending the
Griffin analysis to require a waiver of court fees to divorce or foreclo-
sure actions, Indeed, there was no legitimate analytical distinction
between such suits and the case of an appealing mother. "In brushing
aside the distinction between criminal and civil cases—the distinction
that has constrained *Griffin* for 40 years—the Court has eliminated the
last meaningful limit on the free-floating right to appellate assistance."

He concluded by noting that many states already provided for *in
forma pauperis* civil appeals. Some made special allowances for parental
termination cases. "I agree that, for many—if not most—parents, the

termination of their right to raise their children would be an exaction more dear than any other.... I do not agree, however, that a State that has taken the step, not required by the Constitution, of permitting appeals from termination decisions somehow violates the Constitution when it charges reasonable fees of all would-be appellants." This case lay at the conjunction of Thomas's views on welfare, federalism and originalism. For Thomas, all of these considerations inclined toward denying the mother's application, no matter how heartless such a ruling might appear.

Such uncompromising rulings were not without their compensations. By 1996, Thomas had become a genuine hero on the right. His confirmation hearings had galvanized conservatives and rallied them to his cause. Now, he found great warmth at every conservative gathering. He gave several speeches to various meetings of the conservative Federalist Society during the 1990s, and without exception was honored there as one of the great standard-bearers of their cause.

Such affection was especially strong among religious conservatives. On May 11, 1996, Thomas delivered the commencement address at Liberty University, a Christian institution in Virginia founded by Rev. Jerry Falwell. Bob Dole, the Republican presidential nominee, had been scheduled to speak there but cancelled two weeks before the event. Falwell then called Thomas, and the justice gamely agreed to fill in. His speech was devoted to lambasting the "cultural fog" of "self-pity" enveloping the land, an ironic message from a person who often sank into such sentiments himself.

Thomas made many admirers among the people he met while at Liberty. Dwayne Carson, the campus pastor who helped slip Thomas's black robe on him, was one. "He made an incredible impression with all of us that day," he recalled. "He stayed and shook hands with all the graduates." Carson would gush over the "humble, genuine" man who crossed paths with him for the afternoon. He noted particularly the eye contact. Of all the people who had attended past commencement addresses—President Bush, Newt Gingrich, Billy Graham, James Dobson—Thomas, he said, was the most gracious. The justice stayed for an hour, until all of the students' names had been called out, some 1,200 in total.

Carson's "one lasting thought" after Thomas drove away in the black

Lincoln Town Car that transported him to the event was, "Lord, thank You that he is on the Supreme Court—to know that he's up there defending our Constitution and that he's defending it by looking to a Higher Power." Carson added, "I've kept him on my prayer list ever since."

Young conservatives in Washington also revered him. One Republican staffer from Capitol Hill accompanied his boss to see Thomas in his chambers. The staffer described Thomas as "amazingly gracious." He noted, like the pastor at Liberty, the justice's effortless ability to make eye contact equally with boss and underling. He also was impressed with the breadth of his learning: "He was talking about everything from Henry VIII to the drafting of the Declaration of Independence." A rolling bookrack with two shelves of books stood at the ready—his summer reading, Thomas informed the visitors. The conversation, the staffer recalled, was "this great stream of consciousness that touched on all walks of life, from the lofty heights of Margaret Thatcher, William Bennett, English common law, to football, NASCAR." The questions Thomas asked were "more than just superficial questions. They're genuine questions . . . it's more than just a common courtesy that some people do on autopilot." When he returned to his office, this staffer, who was accustomed to meeting many renowned people through his work, was "kind of in a daze" from the experience.

While such stories were common among conservatives in Washington, civil rights leaders were much less impressed. In May 1996, Thomas planned to speak at Texas Wesleyan University Law School. A local group of black ministers protested outside the posh Worthington Hotel in Fort Worth, where Thomas was staying with Scalia and Byron White for a judicial conference. The protestors so upset Thomas that he threatened to call off his speech. The law student who had invited Thomas to speak prevailed upon the preachers to cancel their scheduled protests at the law school itself. Thomas then went forward with his talk.

A more serious dispute that flared into a national controversy occurred back in the D.C. area. In May, the PTA of the Thomas G. Pullen Creative and Performing Arts School invited Thomas to speak. The Pullen School was a magnet school in Prince Georges County, Maryland, an affluent, predominantly black suburban county outside the nation's capital. The occasion for the invitation was a ceremony honoring Pullen's first class to complete all nine years at the school. The invitation prompted three black members of the school board to threaten to protest Thomas's appearance. On May 22, the superintendent of the Prince Georges schools canceled the invitation.

Even Thomas's frequent detractors in the media judged this censorship intolerable. On June 3, the school board, facing a hostile press, backed down and voted 6–4 to overrule the cancellation. Throughout, Thomas did his best not to become emotionally invested in the controversy. On June 5, he asked Armstrong Williams—who was interceding with the press regarding the flap—"Everything okay?"

"You don't need to know," Williams replied.

"Okay, keep it that way," Thomas said.

On the morning of June 5, the principal of the Pullen school called Thomas's chambers to extend the invitation once again. Thomas magnanimously accepted.

The next day, an article appeared in the *Washington Post* with interviews of eighth-graders at the Pullen School. Twelve were interviewed, or 10 percent of the class; eight were black. All thought Thomas should be allowed to speak to them. The comments were poignant. "They should have asked us before disinviting him," said Janelle Taylor. "It's our awards ceremony, not theirs," Christina Johnson said. "We were just trying to make it special," Dorienne Coleman said. "We didn't want to turn it into political." Johnson added that if the adults wanted to protest, they should "go to the Supreme Court."

On June 10, Thomas arrived at 7:00 P.M. for the ceremony. About fifty protestors were assembled outside. Some of the hostile signs read, "No Uncle Tom in our county" and "Uncle Thomas is a traitor." Pro-Thomas forces countered with signs stating, "Say no to hate and bigotry, let Thomas speak." Thomas received a standing ovation. He spoke to the children about their futures, encouraging them to continue to pursue their dreams with hard work and dedication to purpose.

Controversy also descended on the other half of the Thomas household during this stormy period. Ginni had joined the staff of Congressman Dick Armey in 1993. After Republicans gained control of the House of Representatives in 1994, Armey became the House Majority Leader. One of Ginni's major contributions was her suggestion that

House staffers consolidate and track collectively all of the scandals then effervescing in the Clinton administration. These included Whitewater, the firings in the White House Travel Office, the leaking of FBI files. Ginni described the job as "lots of meetings, lots of coordination and trying to get Republicans on the same sheet of music."

In April, she sent out a memo marked "urgent" to House committee chairmen, asking them to help in assembling such information. *Roll Call* subsequently reported that she had prepared an "assault book" on the Clinton administration for Republican congressmen to wield in the fall campaigns—a document brimming with some seventy-five Clinton administration scandals.

Barbara Olson, the wife of Theodore Olson and a friend of the Thomases, said, "Ginni is someone who brings people together. She never says a bad word." Ginni would leave thoughtful notes to inspire or encourage her co-workers, with such sayings as, "Don't let them get you down." Olson described them as "inspirational little notes with a smile on it." Ginni helped Olson land her job at the House as chief investigative counsel on the House Government Oversight Committee.

At one of the committee hearings, Democrats lashed back at what they viewed as a growing conservative female cabal. Jim Moran, a Democratic congressman from Virginia, took note of the two conservative women, pointing first to Barbara Olson, and then to Ginni. Identifying her as "that woman out there in the blue dress," Moran said, "That's Clarence Thomas's wife." "What's Mrs. Clarence Thomas doing here?" he asked. "I really smell a political witch hunt here."

Olson described the experience as "just totally humiliating." Ginni also was devastated, "because she liked to keep a low profile." Female Republican members of Congress dashed off a letter to Moran and fellow Democrat Paul Kanjorski to rebuke them for their "sexist and thoughtless" remarks. The letter stated, "The fact that your remarks tied these women's professional actions to their spouses is outrageous. American women have struggled for decades to be seen as professional equals, and your remarks put these women back in the category of chattel." In addition, 130 female GOP staffers sent a letter of their own expressing outrage.

The most meaningful show of support, however, came from Ginni's husband. When Thomas heard of the exchange, he called Ginni at work and left her a voice mail, singing several lines from Mitch Ryder's classic tune from the 1960s, "Devil with a Blue Dress On."

Amidst these nonstop crises, Thomas found time for an important private moment back at his alma mater when, after almost three decades of estrangement, he returned to the Catholic Church.

He had lived on the fringes of the church since leaving Immaculate Conception Seminary. His correspondence to Tom O'Brien during his first semester at Holy Cross revealed that he never completely turned his back on Catholicism. Yet he struggled to find the right time or circumstances to come back to the fold. During these years of spiritual wandering, Thomas learned that he needed to rely on something outside himself for daily guidance. He explained, "When I put my homemade compass down to explore some of those other experiments, they did not work. They merely substituted aimless autonomy of the individual for true freedom."

The confirmation ordeal had solidified matters. Thomas noted candidly, "one good thing that does come from adversity like that is a firm restoration of religious faith." Moreover, he no longer blamed the Catholic Church for whatever occurred at Conception, or for his own shortcomings. "Years later, I would find out, as you get older, that it was not the religion that was the problem. It was the fallibility and failures and imperfection of man."

"His religion is a very important part of his story," Ricky Silberman observed of her friend. "His religion has changed as his needs have changed." After the confirmation hearings, when life as he had known it was demolished, Thomas felt a call to reconcile with the church that had nurtured him.

The press would speculate that the ordination of Scalia's son Paul as a priest and Thomas's attendance of his first Mass in Virginia were the catalyst for this change. In reality, Thomas's return to Catholicism was more on the order of Bob Dylan's description of his own journey of faith—a slow train coming. On June 8, before he addressed his Twenty-fifth Reunion Banquet at Holy Cross, he received communion for the first time in almost three decades.

Thomas once again became devout. He began to attend St. Joseph's Church on Capitol Hill, an old brownstone church a short walk from the Supreme Court, often showing up for the daily Mass at 12:10 P.M.

One observer noted that when Thomas took a seat, it was "never ostentatiously at the front, but always quietly to the side or somewhere in the back." The observer added, "I think often he just goes by himself." These daily pilgrimages were a metaphor for the manner in which he had returned to the Catholic Church: alone, and with much contemplation along the way.

"I Am a Man, a Black Man, an American"

Over the summer of 1996, Thomas and Ginni traveled to England, where he spent an hour with Margaret Thatcher. The "thing I found intriguing about it was how well read she is," he observed. "She was pulling books off her book shelf that were underlined, highlighted and thought through." During the same trip, Thomas had tea with Paul Johnson, the renowned conservative historian.

The rest of the summer was devoted to simple pleasures: reading, mowing the lawn ("other people don't cut it right"), socializing. In July, Ted and Barbara Olson hosted their annual barbecue for the Federalist Society, inviting law students from Federalist Society chapters in the Washington area and leaders of the ninety-seven other student chapters throughout the country. The cookout, held as usual at their home in Great Falls, Virginia, drew around three hundred people. It had become a regular, all-star gathering of conservative jurists, lawyers and journalists. Attendees included Bork, the Silbermans, members of Congress, and other prominent lawyers and judges.

Thomas was the leading celebrity at the barbecues and the hub of the youthful energy that pulsated through such gatherings. Ted Olson observed, "The young people clearly have great respect for him and want to meet him and express their respect and affection for them." He added, "We finally had to regulate it a little bit because he wasn't getting anything to eat. He was standing there surrounded by fifty young people, and taking the time to listen, standing there sometimes in the heat ... listening, talking, exchanging views with all the students."

Soon after the new term began in October, Thomas celebrated his fifth anniversary on the Court. His clerks organized a celebratory dinner at A.V. Ristorante Italiano on New York Avenue N.W. An establishment favored by Scalia and Rudy Giuliani, the mayor of New York, the restaurant featured an enormous red, white and green awning extending some thirty feet toward New York Avenue, the words "AV," "PIZZA," and "RISTORANTE" glowing in large green-and-white neon signs above. In a back room with red-and-white checkered tablecloths and worn, dark wooden tables, many of Thomas's closest friends assembled: Scalia, the Silbermans and Olsons, current and former clerks. They toasted him and gave "touching tributes," in the words of one participant. Thomas returned the kindnesses with expressions of gratitude to the friends who had stood with him during five trying years. He also made a special point, as he often did, of mentioning Ginni, his "best friend," and affirming before the company how much he loved her.

The lecture circuit again beckoned. On November 21, he spoke to the New England School of Law and called for a renaissance of "just plain good manners" in American society. For examples, he pointed to the decline in such basic pleasantries as "please" and "thank you." He also mentioned professional sports and the spectacle of athletes engaging in "excessive showboating" and "taunting" of opponents. Thomas cited Tocqueville and George Washington's hand-copied "Rules of Civility" in making the case for greater comity in American life. As if to make his point for him, a claque of some thirty-five people protested his speech outside the Westin Hotel in Boston, shouting "Justice Yes, Thomas No."

The following spring, Thomas returned to Savannah. His old friend Lester Johnson had invited him to speak to the Savannah Bar Association. Thomas also had learned that one of his high-school teachers from St. John Vianney, Father Boland, had been named bishop of Savannah. Thomas let it be known that he wished to meet with Boland. The new bishop reciprocated by hosting a luncheon for the prodigal son.

When Thomas arrived at Savannah's Catholic Pastoral Center on April 3, 1997, veterans of his minor seminary met and embraced him outside. Betty Purdy, the former secretary of the now-shuttered institution on the Isle of Hope, was one of the first to greet him. When Thomas saw Boland, he offered a secular confession. "There's one thing I didn't tell you when I took your geometry class," he said. "I'd already taken it before" (at St. Pius).

At once generous, poignant and self-pitying, Thomas's speech touched almost every conceivable emotion in the speaker and his audience. He explained he had not previously sought out Bishop Boland and the Diocese of Savannah because he preferred to wait until he was once again a full member of the church. "I wanted to thank you as a grown-up, as a practicing Catholic with all the benefits of the sacraments, not as a fallen-away Catholic." He expressed gratitude once again to the nuns of St. Benedict and the priests in the diocese who had taught him to "analyze and read and think." He avowed, "But for this diocese, I certainly would not be on the Supreme Court of the United States."

"I've regained something that I left at Holy Cross in 1968," he added (actually, he had left it at Conception). "I have returned to my own faith. Once a Catholic, always a Catholic."

He mourned the loss of the "black Catholic schools [closed] for the sake of the 'pipe dream' of integration." The death of the institutions that had fostered his success was, for him, a source of great regret. "The poor education for blacks that resulted from some of these decisions deeply saddens me. It was very harmful."

There was also a subtext of personal bitterness in his talk. Thomas referred to himself as a "stray dog" during his years at the minor seminary. For the first time in public, he recalled the occasion when he was not allowed to play basketball in the post-supper, pickup game at St. John's. He also brought up affirmative action and related old wounds. "Some people look at me and credit affirmative action for my success. They say, 'You benefited from it.' How? Affirmative action came into being in Philadelphia in 1973." Thomas noted that he graduated from Yale Law School the next year. This history was both inaccurate and disingenuous.

The angry cloud lifted later in the day. After a public speech in the evening, Lester Johnson noted, Thomas was in high spirits. He stayed for two hours afterward to greet people and sign autographs. Such informal pressing of the flesh remained one of his great strengths.

—◆—

As Thomas gained seniority on the Court, more important opinions were assigned to him. The senior justice in the majority and in the minority of a case assigned to one justice within his group the responsibility for writing the opinion for them all. Rehnquist would typically make the assignment on one side, while the senior justice in the opposing bloc—frequently it was Stevens—did the same.

In the 1996 term, Rehnquist assigned Thomas the majority opinion in *Kansas v. Hendricks.* Kansas had passed a Sexually Violent Predator Act to deal with repeat sexual offenders. The legislation provided for the civil commitment of persons likely to commit "predatory acts of sexual violence" because of a "mental abnormality" or "personality disorder." The law allowed state officials to warehouse sex offenders in secure state facilities after their criminal sentences expired if they remained a danger to society.

By a 5–4 vote, the Court upheld the Kansas act. In a lengthy opinion, Thomas examined the history of civil commitments in the United States. He observed, "States have in certain narrow circumstances provided for the forcible civil detainment of people who are unable to control their behavior and who thereby pose a danger to the public health and safety." While noting the disagreement among psychiatrists about what constitutes mental illness, or even whether pedophilia or paraphilias are mental illnesses, Thomas concluded that Leroy Hendricks' admitted lack of volitional control, coupled with his prediction of future dangerousness, distinguished him from those more suited for criminal proceedings.

"The State may take measures to restrict the freedom of the dangerously mentally ill," Thomas wrote. "This is a legitimate non-punitive governmental objective and has been historically so regarded." Thomas rejected Hendricks' claim that the civil commitment constituted a violation of his constitutional rights. The commitment proceedings were not a violation of the Double Jeopardy Clause because they were civil, not criminal. Similarly, Thomas disagreed with the dissent by Justice Stephen Breyer that the commitment amounted to additional punishment in violation of the *Ex Post Facto* Clause. The commitment did not violate this clause because "the Act does not criminalize conduct legal before its enactment, nor deprive Hendricks of any defense that was available to him at the time of his crimes."

Freedom-of-speech cases continued to bend Thomas's originalism like light passing through a glass of water. *Reno v. American Civil Liberties Union,* in which the Court unanimously struck down the federal

Communications Decency Act, demonstrated the shifting, almost *ad hoc* nature of his and Scalia's jurisprudence in this area of the law. The act was meant to address the burgeoning pornography trade on the Internet. The legislation prohibited the knowing transmission of obscene or indecent messages to any recipient under the age of eighteen. The act also forbade the knowing sending or displaying to a minor of any message "that, in context, depicts or describes, in terms patently offensive as measured by contemporary community standards, sexual or excretory activities or organs." This latter provision tracked language from earlier Supreme Court decisions that specified how legislatures could constitutionally regulate obscene or indecent materials.

Despite Congress's efforts to comply with these earlier rulings, the Court voided the act, ruling that it violated the First Amendment. The Court affirmed the body of law it had developed in freedom-of-speech cases involving sexual matters. In an opinion by Stevens, the Court held broadly that "'[s]exual expression which is indecent but not obscene is protected by the First Amendment.'" While there is a "governmental interest in protecting children from harmful materials, that interest does not justify an unnecessarily broad suppression of speech addressed to adults." Stevens' opinion ended with the resounding proclamation, "The interest in encouraging freedom of expression in a democratic society outweighs any theoretical but unproven benefit of censorship."

O'Connor and Rehnquist concurred in the judgment in part but dissented in part. They stated that it was possible for Congress to create "adult zones" on the Internet, but the act had failed to do so properly. The two justices applied the Court's past interpretations of zoning laws, concluding that parts of the act could be salvaged (save for those portions that "substantially interfer[e] with the First Amendment rights of adults"). Thomas and Scalia, by contrast, simply signed on to the Court's evisceration of the act. *Reno* was Thomas's nadir as an originalist during his first ten years on the Court.

Another freedom-of-speech case elicited fuller reflections from Thomas. In *Glickman v. Wileman Bros. & Elliott*, California tree fruit growers, handlers and processors filed suit to challenge marketing orders imposed by the U.S. secretary of agriculture. The marketing orders mandated that they pay money to the federal government to support an advertising campaign promoting "California Summer Fruits." The agricultural concerns claimed that the marketing orders violated the First Amendment.

Stevens again wrote the opinion of the Court, which upheld the orders by a 5–4 vote. Stevens wrote that the orders were constitutional because the advertising did not restrain the petitioners' speech, compel actual or symbolic speech, or advocate a particular message with which the companies disagreed or that was ideological or political.

Thomas filed a dissent, which was joined in part by Scalia. Taking up where he left off in *44 Liquormart,* Thomas said he wished "to note my disagreement with the majority's conclusion that coerced funding of advertising by others does not involve 'speech' at all and does not even raise a First Amendment 'issue.' . . . It is one thing to differ about whether a particular regulation involves an 'abridgment' of the freedom of speech, but it is entirely another matter—and a complete repudiation of our precedent—for the majority to deny that 'speech' is even at issue in this case." He reiterated his call for the overturning of *Central Hudson.* The majority's opinion, as Thomas saw it, was either an erratic departure from past decisions or simply tyrannical.

> What we are now left with, if we are to take the majority opinion at face value, is one of two disturbing consequences: Either (1) paying for advertising is not speech at all, while such activities as draft card burning, flag burning, armband wearing, public sleeping, and nude dancing are, or (2) compelling payment for third-party communication does not implicate speech, and thus the Government would be free to force payment for a whole variety of expressive conduct that it could not restrict. In either case, surely we have lost our way."

A major federalism case of the term was *Printz v. United States.* The Brady Law passed by Congress required the U.S. attorney general to set up a national system for instantly checking the backgrounds of prospective purchasers of handguns. The legislation also mandated that the chief law enforcement officer (CLEO) of each local jurisdiction conduct such checks until this national system was in place. CLEOs in Montana and Arizona challenged the constitutionality of the act. Scalia wrote the opinion for the Court. In a 5–4 ruling, the Court held that the Constitution did not allow the federal government to deputize state law enforcement officials to enforce federal legislation. The Brady Law,

Scalia noted, effectively transferred the president's authority to administer federal laws to thousands of state CLEOs.

Thomas concurred. He joined Scalia's opinion in full, but noted, "I write separately to emphasize that the Tenth Amendment affirms the undeniable notion that under our Constitution, the Federal Government is one of enumerated, hence limited, powers." In his dissent, Stevens referred to Thomas's originalist approach to the Commerce Clause as "revisionist." Thomas responded, "Under my 'revisionist' view, the Federal Government's authority under the Commerce Clause ... does not extend to the regulation of wholly *intra* state, point-of-sale transactions.... Absent the underlying authority to regulate the intrastate transfer of firearms, Congress surely lacks the corollary power to impress state law enforcement officers into administering and enforcing such regulations." Again, Thomas called upon the Court to return to the original understanding of the Commerce Clause.

The Brady Law was constitutionally suspect on additional grounds. "I question whether Congress can regulate the particular transactions at issue here," he stated. Noting that the First Amendment prohibits Congress from abridging freedom of speech or prohibiting free exercise of religion, Thomas wrote, "The Second Amendment similarly appears to contain an express limitation on the Government's authority." Thomas quoted the amendment in support of his argument: "A well regulated Militia, being necessary to the security of a free State, the right of the people to keep and bear arms, shall not be infringed."

"This Court has not had the recent occasion to consider the nature of the substantive right safeguarded by the Second Amendment," Thomas observed. A footnote followed this statement, which pointed out that this issue had not come before the Court since 1939, when the Court declined to address it. "If, however, the Second Amendment is read to confer a *personal* right to 'keep and bear arms,' a colorable argument exists that the Federal Government's regulatory scheme, at least as it pertains to the purely intrastate sale or possession of firearms, runs afoul of that Amendment's protections." A second footnote followed, which mentioned the "impressive array of historical evidence" assembled in recent years indicating "that the 'right to keep and bear arms' is, as the Amendment's text suggests, a personal right." Thomas gave a lengthy string citation of the many books and articles by Second Amendment scholars espousing this view.

"As the parties did not raise this argument, however, we need not consider it here," Thomas continued. "Perhaps, at some future date, this Court will have the opportunity to determine whether Justice Story was correct when he wrote that the right to bear arms 'has justly been considered, as the palladium of the liberties of a republic.'" If nothing else, the opinion made clear that Justice Story had returned to Thomas's good graces.

With this, Thomas became the first justice to clearly suggest that the Second Amendment right to keep and bear arms was an individual, constitutional right that the federal courts should recognize and uphold. He later defended his opinion by saying, "Come the revolution, I don't want to be with the guys who eat Brie. I want to be with the guys with the guns."

———

On May 30, 1997, Thomas and Ginni celebrated their tenth wedding anniversary. As they dined at a local steakhouse, Thomas handed her a small jeweler's box. When Ginni opened it, she found a duplicate of the thin gold wedding band with small diamonds that he had slipped onto her finger a decade before in Omaha.

"With this ring, I thee wed. Will you marry me all over again?" he asked. She answered "yes." They toasted to the anniversary—zinfandel for her and water for him (a Protestant, Ginni was more Catholic than Thomas when it came to adult beverages). She would wear both bands on her finger thereafter.

The pain of the confirmation hearings still lingered. When Abe Famble and other relatives from Pin Point visited Thomas that summer, Thomas took him for a ride in his black Corvette.

"Well, man, looks like things are looking up for you now, since that Miss Hill controversy is over with," Famble said as they drove.

"Yeah, Abe," Thomas replied, "I tell you, I'm glad it's over with, too. I look back over it sometimes. I don't think I would have gone through it if I knew what it was going to be like now. Because it was pure hell."

In October, Anita Hill finally published her own book on the hearings. By then, she had departed from the University of Oklahoma Law

School, leaving in her wake yet another flurry of accusations. She would end up at the Department of Women's Studies at Brandeis University, a more prestigious institution than OU, although her descent from professor of law to the amorphous new discipline of "women's studies" suggested continued career problems. In *Speaking Truth to Power,* she would offer an excuse for her job difficulties at OU and every other point in her peculiar career: It was always discrimination.

The book read in many parts as if it had been edited by a criminal defense attorney. In recounting Thomas's alleged harassment, for example, Hill merely quoted verbatim and at length from her statements and testimony to the Senate, rather than discussing the episode in human terms.

She devoted much of the book to trying to explain her more odd or inconsistent allegations. Why did she not report Thomas's misconduct at the time of its occurrence? She said "that was what I had learned as a young black woman: do your schoolwork or job and don't take biases or insults personally." Hill also claimed, "I believed my professional role included protecting him."

How did she explain calling and keeping in touch with Thomas all those years?

> Once I was no longer under his supervision, I began to bifurcate my feelings about Clarence Thomas psychologically. I was able to think of him as a former employer and even a personal acquaintance with whom I could continue a congenial relationship. I separated that from his mistreatment and I equated this reaction with professionalism.... My sense of professionalism, which some may describe as opportunism, allowed me to divorce my personal feelings from my work interests. That, in retrospect, was a mistake.... Though I had dealt with the situation as I best knew how and had chosen not to rely on him in future employment endeavors, I had performed well as his assistant, and I refused to let his bad behavior cheat me of every benefit of my good work.

This dual explanation—she had "separated" herself psychologically from Thomas but felt entitled to capitalize on her relationship with him— contradicted her testimony to the Senate, in which she claimed she did not seek professional advantages from her relationship with Thomas.

Why did she claim, at her press conference before the hearings, that she did not know Phyllis Berry Myers, a person with whom she had worked on a small staff? "I had found myself wondering who she was, recalling her only vaguely and mostly just by name. Because I could not believe that her comment was being taken seriously, my response was rather casual." This contrived explanation deepened the impression left by the original falsehood.

Why had her testimony changed regarding the *USA Today* article reporting that she was told her affidavit would quietly force Thomas to withdraw? Hill blamed Arlen Specter, who "would repeat the same question until he got the answer he wanted," although in fact his persistence in no way required her to change her testimony. Her allowance that she "might" have discussed Thomas's possible withdrawal was, in retrospect, a "foolish concession." But when Specter pressed her, she admitted that Thomas's possible withdrawal in fact *was* discussed, not "might have been." This was, in fact, the basis of Specter's accusations of perjury.

Other details offered by Hill were inaccurate or contradicted by others. Sukari Hardnett, Hill wrote, had testified that Thomas "attempted to date her and that when she refused, his attitude toward her became less friendly." This was not true. Regarding Jim Brudney: "I knew who he was but we did not socialize together." Her friend Diane Holt contradicted this, as did Armstrong Williams. Hill claimed she refused to sit near Thomas on the airplane flight to Oklahoma because "I could not bear to spend any kind of time in such close proximity to him." But she had no aversion to the familiarity and ongoing contact provided by a telephone.

Then there was this strange aside, in which Hill wrote that on September 23, 1991, after she had faxed her statement to the Senate, she was preparing to leave her house when the telephone rang. The woman on the line said she worked in the same building where Hill's doctor was located. "You hit my car in the parking lot of the medical building," the woman said. She even specified the date of one of Hill's visits to the doctor. Hill related the exchange:

> "What are you talking about?" I asked, genuinely puzzled.
> "I had a friend with the police department trace your tag number," she said.
> Though no visible damage had been done to her car, she claimed that the collision had caused a misalignment of her wheels. I did not recall any such collision and was sure none had taken place. Neverthe-

less, I gave her the name of my insurance agent and asked her to contact him. "I am too distracted and too busy to take care of this myself."

She insisted that she wanted to handle the matter without going to
my insurance company. "I would be willing to settle with you for a new
set of tires," she declared.

"Look, I don't have time to discuss this now. I'd rather you talk with
my insurance agent and let him take care of it," I snapped back.

The conversation then ended—presumably, although Hill does not say
so, with her hanging up on the woman.

This bizarre anecdote was illuminating not only because it confirmed
Hill's bad temper and self-importance, traits remembered by her co-
workers in Washington, but also because of the convenient, if unbelievable, memory lapse: She could not "recall any such collision"?

Elsewhere in her book, she would blame "racist hostility" and "racist
and sexist" retribution for her failures at Oral Roberts and the University of Oklahoma, respectively. David Brock's *The Real Anita Hill* came
in for the same treatment. Brock had relied on "sexual mythology about
black women" and "fabricated and misquoted sources." "As a white male
he is given permission to define me, a black woman, on whatever terms
he chooses, without establishing any credentials to do so.... All of
Brock's false claims, accusations, and theories fall into a void about black
women, another void about women who raise harassment claims, and
still another, even larger void of misogyny."

Reviews of Hill's book were negative. Critics condemned it for perhaps the worst possible sin in a memoir: dullness. The book was described
as "entirely humorless" (*Washington Post*), "the first Valium Nation memoir" (*Los Angeles Times*), a book that "feels like just another lecture"
(*Boston Globe*), and, most biting, "a book whose moment has passed"
(*New York Times*). Television was more kind to Hill, as it had always
been. She received easy treatment on NBC's *Dateline* program and made
other successful stops on the promotion circuit.

As Hill was stirring up bad memories with her book tour, Thomas
and Ginni found solace elsewhere. They were preoccupied with a pending new arrival to their household. During his visits to Savannah and
Pin Point, Thomas had taken notice of a beautiful little boy, of the same
age he had been when he used to play along the sandy paths of Pin
Point. It was Mark Martin, the grandson of his sister, Emma, born on

September 24, 1991—just days before the world heard the phrase "high-tech lynching."

Like Thomas himself, Mark was bright and showed an early interest in reading. He had besieged his grandmother or other relatives daily with books he wanted read to him. He worked to memorize the alphabet and numbers from a chart stapled to Emma's front door. "Little Markie was a very bright young fellow around here," Abe Famble recalled. "And I think the judge detected that."

Thomas had come to a point in his life where he acknowledged, in almost every speech and extended private conversation, the vast debt he owed to his grandfather. He could repay this debt to Myers Anderson only by doing for another what the old man had done for him. Mark's father—Emma's son—had encountered trouble with the law; the boy's parents had divorced. Thomas sought out both of them to inquire if they would have any objection to Mark's coming to live with him and Ginni in Virginia. They consented. In November, the custody papers were signed and the final arrangements were made.

Guiding his relations with Mark was a lesson Thomas had learned from his grandmother, Aunt Tina. He and Ginni were mindful of the nature of their relationship with the child, and careful not to suggest that they had become his father or mother. When introducing Mark to others, Thomas referred to him as his "great-nephew."

Thomas applied the same discipline to the boy that he had used so successfully with Jamal. He read to him and quizzed him on his multiplication tables. Mark's presence filled an important part of Ginni's life as well. At one public appearance in Phoenix, she could be seen instructing Mark not to sit down at the table too quickly. Later in the evening, as the change of time zone took its toll, she rocked the boy to sleep in her arms.

One of the many other perquisites of living with Thomas was the opportunity to meet sports stars. Mark shared the same name as the driver of the number 6 Valvoline car on the NASCAR racing circuit. When Thomas mentioned the driver's name in one of his speeches, little Mark turned and offered a heart-melting, perfect smile to the crowd, thinking he had just achieved immortality.

In a term of relatively tedious cases, *United States v. Bajakajian* stood out as Thomas's most interesting opinion of 1998. Customs inspectors at Los Angeles International Airport had searched the baggage of Hosep Bajakajian, who was bound for Cyprus. Using dogs trained to detect currency by scent, they found $230,000 in cash. When one of the inspectors told Bajakajian he was required to report all money in excess of $10,000 in his possession or baggage, he told officials he had only $8,000 and his wife $7,000. A subsequent, full search yielded $357,144. The inspectors seized the currency and arrested Bajakajian. He was charged with willfully failing to report that he was transporting more than $10,000 outside the United States, making a false material statement to the U.S. Customs Service, and committing an offense requiring forfeiture of the money. He pled guilty to the first count; the second was dismissed. After a bench trial, the district court found that the entire amount of money was to be forfeited because it was involved in the offense.

In his appeal to the Supreme Court, Bajakajian argued that the forfeiture violated the Excessive Fines Clause of the Eighth Amendment. In a 5–4 ruling, the Court agreed and disallowed the forfeiture. The unusual constellation of issues in the case, which pitted law enforcement concerns against libertarian worries about due process and governmental intrusion, produced a peculiar alliance in the Court's voting. Thomas joined the Court's four liberals in forming the majority. Stevens then picked him to write the opinion for the Court.

Thomas came down on the side of property rights, due process, and fear of unbounded governmental power. Notwithstanding his new allies, he wrote the opinion consistent with his originalist approach to the law. Upon reviewing the history of the clause, he observed, "This Court has had little occasion to interpret, and has never actually applied, the Excessive Fines Clause. We have, however, explained that at the time the Constitution was adopted, 'the word "fine" was understood to mean a payment to a sovereign as punishment for some offense.'"

The compelled forfeiture of Bajakajian's currency constituted punishment, Thomas concluded. He traced back the history of the forfeiture statute not to *in rem* forfeitures of "guilty" property—that is, property

used in the commission of a crime—but to *in personam* criminal forfeitures. The latter were punitive measures, and legally had been treated
as such since the Middle Ages. The states at the time of the framing
had not passed laws providing for forfeitures as punishment for crimes.
The First Congress also rejected such punishment for federal crimes.
Congress did not press such laws into service until 1970, when they
were resurrected as part of an effort to combat the rising scourge of illegal drugs. Given this historical and legal background, Thomas judged
that the forfeiture of Bajakajian's money was a "fine" for purposes of
the Eighth Amendment.

He then turned to considering whether the fine was excessive. This,
too, was uncharted territory for the Court. Thomas drew from history
and precedents in constructing a test. "The touchstone of the constitutional inquiry under the Excessive Fines clause is the principle of pro-
portionality: The amount of the forfeiture must bear some relationship
to the gravity of the offense that it is designed to punish," Thomas
wrote. He went on to state expressly, "We now hold that a punitive forfeiture violates the Excessive Fines Clause if it is grossly disproportional
to the gravity of a defendant's offense."

In reaching this standard, Thomas found that the intentions of the
Framers did not provide much guidance in this case. There simply was
not enough recorded history on the question to settle the matter. He
considered the definitions of "excessive" from the time of the framing
in contemporaneous editions of Webster's and Samuel Johnson's dictionaries. But he could find no discussion of the issue by the First
Congress or in the state ratification debates.

As a result, he turned instead to two other considerations. "The first,
which we have emphasized in our cases interpreting the Cruel and
Unusual Punishments Clause, is that judgments about the appropriate
punishment for an offense belong in the first instance to the legislature.... The second is that any judicial determination regarding the
gravity of a particular criminal offense will be inherently imprecise."
The principle he selected was that of gross disproportionality. He culled
this notion from the Court's earlier rulings on the Eighth Amendment's
Cruel and Unusual Punishments Clause. Thomas, of course, had been
quite critical of many of those precedents in other cases; most notably,
he had called for the outright overturning of *Estelle* and *Bounds*. In

groping for a standard to apply in a case of first impression, he relied on the Court's prior interpretations of a companion clause in the amendment.

The large forfeiture in this case, Thomas concluded, violated the Excessive Fines Clause under this standard. It was an enormous fine for a crime that he termed "solely a reporting offense." Bajakajian was, for example, not "a money launderer, a drug trafficker, or a tax evader." The forfeiture was grossly disproportionate to the offense, and therefore unconstitutional.

Kennedy wrote a strong dissent, which was joined by Rehnquist, O'Connor and Scalia. In many ways, Kennedy's dissent read more like a typical Thomas opinion than Thomas's own offering for the majority. "For the first time in its history," Kennedy announced,

> the Court strikes down a fine as excessive under the Eighth Amendment. The decision is disturbing both for its specific holding and for the broader upheaval it foreshadows. At issue is a fine Congress fixed in the amount of the currency respondent sought to smuggle or to transport without reporting.... The Court all but says the offense is not serious anyway. This disdain for the statute is wrong as an empirical matter and disrespectful of the separation of powers.

Kennedy repeatedly called Thomas's opinion and reasoning "novel," as if needling the conservative justice for favoring originality over tradition.

Thomas's deep sensitivity to privacy concerns was manifest in his social life as well as his jurisprudence. He and Ginni traveled through Kansas City around January 1998 and visited some old friends from Conception. Accepting a dinner invitation from Jim Kopp, they arrived one evening accompanied, as always, by U.S. marshals. One stood watch outside Kopp's house; the other remained inside.

The conversation turned to their Conception Seminary days—and their interests in females at the time. Thomas halted the conversation momentarily. He turned and addressed the marshal inside the house.

"Can you go outside?" he asked the marshal.

"No, Justice Thomas, I have to stay inside the facility."

Thomas turned to Kopp. "Do you have a basement?" he asked. Despite Thomas's long record of concern for lesser employees, the marshal soon was dispatched to the household dungeon so that their conversation could continue with intimacy.

The speeches Thomas gave during the summer of 1998 received prominent notice. Writing for *USA Today*, Tony Mauro concluded that they "marked a turning point for Thomas" in his effort to "answer back" to his critics and continue the decade-long project to rehabilitate his public image.

The speeches included comments about weight gain and the profusion of gray in his hair. The latter had happened to his grandfather at around the same age, he insisted—perhaps to deny his enemies the satisfaction of thinking they had inflicted this upon him. He also spoke wistfully of "those of us who are inexorably slipping into the twilight of our mortality."

One of the dominant themes of his addresses—a guaranteed crowd-pleaser with his largely conservative audiences—was the erosion of character and virtue in American society. He spoke of urban neighborhoods being in chaos and the precipitous surge in illegitimacy. Thomas said, "Years ago I gave speeches about the out-of-wedlock birth rate, but of course I was criticized as though I was the one responsible for it."

His most profound critique of America's spiritual malaise came in a speech to a Heritage Foundation conclave in Palm Beach, Florida, on February 1, 1998: "Even as the stock market has soared to unimaginable heights and interest rates have dropped to equally unimaginable depths, we hear much alarming talk about the state of morals and virtue as well as the state of our culture." He talked of misplaced priorities: "In a sense, we become much like Mrs. Jellyby in the Charles Dickens novel *Bleak House*. She was content to throw herself wholeheartedly and enthusiastically into her distant philanthropic projects involving fan-makers and flower girls, but was unconcerned about her unkempt children, her filthy house, neglected husband, or the starving beggar at the door. . . . [W]e find it more comfortable and safer to tackle someone else's problem rather than ours."

In defining "character," Thomas quoted from the Webster's and Oxford dictionaries. He agreed with Aristotle that people learn character through habit—"by practicing the craft." Ultimately, character comes down to individual commitment. "We know it is often difficult to work hard, exhibit politeness, remain honest, and so forth. We are bound to lose our patience with others or show some selfishness on occasion, but vigilance with respect to the small matters of life often demands self-sacrifice." While there had been "much important debate lately about the broader cultural war—the preoccupation with self-indulgence and other vice," he believed it vital that the nation "not lose sight of the fact that each individual has his own battle to wage for control of his own soul and to attain character."

The most poignant speech of his career came on July 29. Thomas's relations with civil rights leaders, and consequently with much of the black community, had worsened during his time on the Court. The abuse reached a new level with a cover story in the November 1996 issue of *Emerge,* the magazine that billed itself as "Black America's Newsmagazine." On its cover was a caricature of Thomas as a lawn jockey standing outside the Supreme Court building. The article was entitled "Uncle Thomas: Lawn Jockey for the Far Right." Inside the magazine was a depiction of Thomas shining Scalia's shoes. It was a shockingly offensive portrayal that would not have been allowed in a black publication if the subject had been anyone other than Clarence Thomas.

In another attempt to bridge the chasm created by such writing and by liberal black opinion leaders, Thomas agreed to speak to the National Bar Association Convention in Memphis. The nation's oldest association of black lawyers, the NBA had formed in 1925 because the American Bar Association at the time did not admit blacks. The NBA's judicial council, composed largely of judges, voted to disinvite him, but the organization's leadership overruled them. William Raspberry also came to Thomas's defense against his would-be censors: "It'll get me in trouble with some of my friends to say so, but Supreme Court Justice Clarence Thomas has managed (again) to wrest the intellectual, ethical and common-sense high ground from his critics."

"The justice is going," Armstrong Williams, Thomas's unofficial press secretary, told one newspaper on June 24. "He's pumped. He's got a message to bring."

On July 29, as he took the stage at the convention, Thomas would hear a heckler behind him calling him an "enemy of the people."

He spoke of the attitudes he faced as a result of his unwillingness to support the orthodoxy of the civil rights establishment. "I have no right to think the way I do because I'm black. Though the ideas and opinions themselves are not necessarily illegitimate if held by non-black individuals, they, and the person enunciating them, are illegitimate if that person happens to be black." African-Americans were a diverse people, he emphasized. He noted the differences between blacks from the rural South and those from Northern cities such as New York and Philadelphia—the same differences he had noticed upon traveling to Holy Cross. Diversity of thought should be expected as well, and would be expected from anyone who was not black.

He stood defiant in defense of his principles: "Despite some of the nonsense that has been said about me by those who should know better, and so much nonsense, or some of which subtracts from the sum total of human knowledge, despite this all, I am a man, a black man, an American. And my history is not unlike that of many blacks from the deep South. And in many ways it is not that much different from that of many other Americans." He added that he, like Frederick Douglass, believed "that whites and blacks can live together and be blended into a common nationality." Separatism was un-American.

"It pains me deeply, or more deeply than any of you can imagine, to be perceived by so many members of my race as doing them harm," Thomas acknowledged, as true a statement as he ever uttered. "All the sacrifice, all the long hours of preparation were to help, not to hurt." And yet he would not stoop to pleading for acceptance. "I have come here today not in anger or to anger, though my mere presence has been sufficient, obviously, to anger some. Nor have I come to defend my views, but rather to assert my right to think for myself, to refuse to have my ideas assigned to me as though I was [sic] an intellectual slave because I'm black. I come to state that I'm a man, free to think for myself and do as I please."

This last statement, which came near the end of his address, was as strong a candidate for his epitaph as anything he had penned in a Supreme Court opinion.

Another speech two months later, on September 12, proved in some ways to be even more emotional and self-revealing. At a forum in Washington sponsored by *Headway* magazine, a journal edited and published by black conservatives, Thomas began by acknowledging people in the room who had stood with him during his career. This eclectic assortment included Strom Thurmond, C. Boyden Gray, Phyllis Berry Myers, Armstrong Williams.

As he spoke, he reflected on other friends who had passed on, particularly Gil Hardy, his best friend from college and law school, who had died several years before in a diving accident. "We made wonderful friends, lifelong friends, lost some friends, lost my dearest of friends. . . ." He paused. "You know there are some friends . . ." He paused again, overcome by grief. The audience applauded in support.

Thomas asked for a drink of water. He dabbed his eyes with a napkin. "I apologize," he said when he continued. "There are some friends you never stop missing."

He went on to mention that "one of those friends is my good friend, Gil Hardy, whose honor, whose integrity, whose goodness was trashed in order to destroy me. That, my friends, is wrong."

It would have been highly inconsiderate for anybody to correct Thomas in the midst of such sorrow. But in fact, Gil Hardy's honor and reputation had not been sullied during the Hill-Thomas hearings. His name barely came up at all. Thomas's sadness had to do with himself.

Thomas recovered when he spoke of the need for firmness and integrity. "Life is not worth living without principles. It's not worth living without backbone. If you don't have a backbone, you slither, you don't walk upright." He quoted Christ's request at Gethsemane—that "this cup pass away"—and even suggested that he too had sacrificed: "I can look my son in the eye, and I can tell him that I laid down my life for him and did the best I could."

Happier times lay in store for him on September 25, when he spoke at St. Vincent College in Pennsylvania. Like Conception, St. Vincent was a Benedictine institution founded right after the Civil War to help the newly freed slaves. Thomas was asked to speak at the Red Mass, an annual invocation of God's blessing on judges and lawyers.

The event could not escape the controversy that dogged Thomas in his public appearances. The Association of Pittsburgh Priests wrote a letter to the bishop of the Greensburg diocese and St. Vincent's Archabbot Douglas Nowicki, criticizing their decision to invite Thomas because he "has consistently voted in favor of the death penalty." Nowicki responded by pointing out that previous speakers had included Isaac Asimov and Carl Sagan, who were atheists.

At 6:30 A.M., Thomas joined the monks for their morning prayer, remaining for their Mass afterward. For the morning, at least, it was as if he had never left Conception Abbey.

In his address, Thomas said the occasion was something of a homecoming for him because of his roots with the Benedictines. Much of the raw material for the speech—which emphasized personal virtue—was similar to the address he had given to the Heritage Foundation. At the luncheon that followed, a young black student at the college paid tribute to Thomas. The young man, Janard Pendleton, was the son of a single mother in Pittsburgh. Pendleton stood and recited from memory "The Negro Mother," a poem by Langston Hughes.

Thomas and Pendleton chatted warmly during the luncheon. Pendleton found him "a very down-to-earth person. Very easy to talk to." They talked mostly about "academic success, his encouraging me to do well in school." Thomas was direct, as usual.

"What are your grades like?" he asked the collegian.

"I'm pretty much all A's and a couple B's."

"All A's," Thomas said emphatically. "We want all A's."

On October 22, Thomas spoke to schoolchildren at an elementary school in Denver. He encouraged the youngsters to jettison their TVs (whether their parents approved of such incitement was unclear). When one boy said he wanted to grow up to be a basketball player, Thomas was abrupt. "You can't make your dreams out of sports," he said, without admitting that he himself had cherished such dreams at the same age and even later. The children were impressed to learn that he was driven in a limousine from place to place and had no boss, and that not even the president could fire him.

When one fifth-grader presented him with a plaque, Thomas responded, "I'm going to keep this on my wall until one of you becomes my law clerk. Who's going to come and take this off my wall?"

"Me!" "Me!" the children shouted.

Later in the day, Thomas fielded questions from students at Denver University Law School. He insisted in advance that no reporters be allowed to attend. "He's goosey about the media," said Jan Laitos, the law professor who arranged his visit.

——

In 1999, the impeachment of President Bill Clinton touched off a historic crisis for American feminism. This crisis arose from feminists' disparate treatment of two graduates of Yale Law School, one year apart: Clinton and Clarence Thomas.

Clinton's false testimony about his relationship with Monica Lewinsky contributed only tangentially to this undoing. More important were allegations attendant to the scandal, which went to the very heart of feminists' standing critique of sexual harassment. Paula Jones, Kathleen Willey and Juanita Broaddrick—supporting actresses in the Lewinsky drama—alleged that Clinton had misused his office to sexually harass and assault them. The same feminist leaders who had quickly rallied to Anita Hill—despite the serious questions surrounding her charges—deserted these three female witnesses against the president.

The graying ladies who had led the fight for sexual equality in the 1960s joined all the president's women in the 1990s. Betty Friedan had branded President Bush and Arlen Specter "Public Enemies No. 1 and 2" for their support of Thomas over Hill. Yet she spoke out in defense of Clinton. The National Organization for Women, so active in fighting Thomas, stood staunchly by Clinton throughout his presidency. Gloria Steinem likewise pledged allegiance to the president. In an op-ed article in the *New York Times,* she distinguished Hill's case from that of Jones and Willey on the ground that "Clinton took 'no' for an answer" (Steinem neglected to note that he had done so only after first touching them crudely without their consent). Steinem dismissed Clinton's assault of Willey on federal property as a "clumsy sexual pass," frankly justifying this double standard by invoking Clinton's support of abortion rights: "If President Clinton were as vital to preserving freedom of speech as he is to preserving reproductive freedom, would journalists be condemned as 'inconsistent' for refusing to suggest he resign? Forget it."

Anita Hill, herself a feminist leader by the late 1990s, shared her thoughts. In a *Newsweek* article published on June 9, 1997, to help promote her forthcoming book, Hill compared her allegations with Jones' sexual harassment case against Clinton. Their situations, Hill wrote, "are quite different." The Thomas confirmation hearings were "a public forum that invited a public conversation. But a pending civil action—even one against the president—does not generally invite that kind of public engagement." Why a Supreme Court nominee merited more

public scrutiny than a sitting president—the person charged with enforcing federal civil rights laws—was left unexplained and, indeed, was a
non sequitur.

Less than a year later, Hill would appear on NBC's *Meet the Press* to
offer further commentary. When asked if feminist leaders were applying a double standard to Clinton's accusers, Hill responded with evasive banalities: "It is a reality that we have to deal with. We live in a
political world, and the reality is there are larger issues other than just
individual behavior." She went on to join Steinem in siding with Clinton because he was reliably feminist on "the bigger issues"—presumably abortion rights. Never would Hill come to the defense of any of
the three women whose accusations against President Clinton were far
more serious than anything she had ever alleged about Clarence Thomas.

Many journalists and politicians who had amplified Hill's allega-
tions with gusto subscribed to the same feminist double standard. The
Washington Post, Newsweek and NBC News held exclusive stories about
Jones, Lewinsky and Broaddrick until others broke the news for them
(in Broaddrick's case, the story was held until after Clinton's impeachment trial—quite unlike the Hill bombshell that exploded prior to the
Senate vote on Thomas's confirmation). Joseph Biden had begun the
Anita Hill phase of Thomas's confirmation hearings by proclaiming,
"Sexual harassment is a serious matter and, in my view, any person guilty
of this offense is unsuited to serve, not only [on] the nation's highest
court, but any position of responsibility, of high responsibility in or out
of government." Yet he would side with Clinton on all counts in the
Senate trial. Indeed, of the 26 senators still serving in the Senate who
had voted against Thomas's confirmation, all 26 voted down the line
for Clinton only seven years later.

In public, Thomas declined to comment on this typhoon of hypocrisy.
On the eve of Clinton's Senate trial, when somebody asked him if the
Constitution permitted the Senate to convict but not remove an
impeached president, Thomas replied, to considerable laughter, "Nice
try." But in private, Thomas was appalled at Clinton's behavior. The
double standards practiced by Democrats also struck a nerve. One friend
of Thomas's recalled, "The thing that was most surprising to him was
the way the Cabinet reacted." Despite overwhelming evidence that
Clinton had committed multiple felonies in office, not one Cabinet

member resigned. To a self-described "law-and-order man" like Thomas, such abdication of responsibility was astonishing.

After Clinton, jokes in the popular culture about Clarence Thomas and sexual harassment would never sound quite right. In the wake of Clinton's behavior, debates over Anita Hill's allegations suddenly became akin to squabbles in the Flat Earth Society after Copernicus. There was an indirect vindication of Thomas in these events, a cornucopia of ironies in which another man might have found a sort of grim satisfaction. But as his friends observed, the pain that still privately crippled him overwhelmed any such ambiguous remedy.

Life, Liberty, and the Open Road

On February 14, 1999, more than a hundred thousand people cheered and hailed Clarence Thomas, Grand Marshal of the Daytona 500. The raucous tribute came in a lavish event that would have been the envy of Tiberius. This honor was the culmination of his long-running interest in race cars and the NASCAR racing circuit. Wearing a leather auto racer's jacket with a checkerboard stripe, Thomas waved to the crowd and basked in the thunderous reception and the warmth of a delightful winter's day in Florida. To him were reserved the honors of saying in his grand baritone voice, "Gentlemen, start your engines."

Thomas had learned the mechanics of automobiles from his grandfather. He became fascinated with professional auto racing later in life. One of his most valued possessions was his black Corvette ZR1. On it the ardent individualist had placed a personalized license plate: REZ IPSA, a variation of the legal phrase *res ipsa loquitur* ("the thing speaks for itself"). His knowledge of NASCAR was substantial and included detailed familiarity with the cars, drivers and tracks around the country. Southern white men were the predominant fans of NASCAR (for this reason, the host of one national sports talk show referred to the sport as "Neckcar"). Thomas told friends that he felt quite comfortable in the company of these fans, calling them "real Americans." Dick Weiler, his old friend from Missouri, said he was delighted to be named grand marshal: "He just thought that was a hoot."

On his speaking tours, Thomas still favored places such as Florida, and relatively obscure educational institutions, most of them in the South and West. An exception to this geographical bias was made for conservative conferences conveniently held in the D.C. area. It was to such an audience that Thomas spoke on February 9, right before his appearance before the throngs of NASCAR enthusiasts to the south.

The occasion was a Lincoln Day celebration, which the Claremont Institute held at the Mayflower Hotel.

Thomas took the opportunity to elaborate on his jurisprudence in race cases. He repeatedly and fulsomely praised Harry Jaffa, acknowledging a clear and important intellectual debt. His words also paralleled, perhaps unconsciously, parts of Lincoln's Gettysburg Address: "It is right and fitting that we should do so [learn from Lincoln]; our words cannot add to the greatness of the man or the depth of the sacrifice that he made."

The core of the speech was a defense of both his constitutional theories on race and the nation he served. "How is it that I, a descendant of slaves, could use the word 'good' in describing a nation that condoned slavery?" Thomas asked. He noted, "Our Founders, after all, did more than just suffer the existence of slavery. They codified it. They protected it. They inscribed it into the fundamental charter of our government: the Constitution of the United States."

Americans should remember "the alternatives that were available to the Founders. For if the Founders had no alternative but to compromise with slavery, we can hardly fault them for failing to accomplish the impossible." Had they not compromised on the issue of slavery, the new nation would have bifurcated in 1787. Thomas commended the Founders' exhibition of what Aristotle called the "virtue of practical wisdom." They saw that "only a union of all the states—even one tarnished by a compromise with slavery—offered the prospect of putting slavery on the course of ultimate extinction."

Lincoln, like the Founders, was not above reproach on the matter of race. Thomas reminded the audience that the sixteenth president had made his own compromises with slavery, rejecting abolitionism and enforcing fugitive slave laws. "By so defending a bad regime, did Lincoln himself become a bad man?" he asked.

Thomas answered in the negative, and based this on Lincoln's ultimate intentions. Preserving the union was essential to extinguishing slavery. By keeping the South within the union, the rest of the nation could work to check the growth of slavery. "For Lincoln, as for the Founders, the moral course, the prudent course, the course most likely to lead to the ultimate abolition of slavery was, in fact, not to join with the abolitionists. Lincoln's lesson for us, however, is even more profound: the realization that prudence is sometimes a compromise with principle, in order, ultimately, to vindicate that principle." "The Virtue of Practical Wisdom," as Thomas entitled his address, was a graceful blueprint to racial healing and a reminder of Thomas's own great intellectual strength: his prudence.

In April, Thomas headed west. He addressed the University of Montana School of Law on April 13, speaking to nearly a thousand people. He criticized the American Bar Association—which had given him a low rating—for becoming "just another interest group." Melissa Harrison, associate dean and professor at the law school, found Thomas himself far more interesting than his speech. "One thing that I admired about Justice Thomas, and I must say I was not prepared, because politically I'm very different, but he was personally a very open, accessible, charming person."

Thomas and Harrison struck up a conversation about religion. "I'm a devout Episcopalian and he's a devout Catholic," she noted, and like Thomas, she had considered becoming a priest. "Justice Thomas and I talked about how we're both drawn to monastic life in some ways. We find it compelling and we both have done retreats [at monasteries]." She concluded that both of them were "drawn to the contemplative life."

Thomas attended two classes at the Montana law school, including Harrison's criminal procedure class. "And his attitude was very much, just throw at me what you want to throw at me," Harrison said. "He really enjoys one-on-one conversation.... My own personal opinion is that he is much better one-on-one in small groups than he is as a speaker in front of a large group. I thought he was much more interesting in front of the students." To ensure a relaxed environment, Thomas banned C-Span, which was there to film his speech, from the classroom, explaining that he wanted to feel "more free" with the criminal-law students.

Harrison was struck by how liberal he sounded in his remarks to her class. He questioned, for example, whether police have the right to stop and frisk suspected criminals absent probable cause. Were the Court to adopt this view, it would mark a significant extension of a major Warren Court decision, the 1968 case of *Terry v. Ohio*. "I think the students and I were very surprised at how liberal his comments were," she stated.

"We also talked about children," Harrison recalled. When he returned to Washington, Thomas sent her a children's book available at the Supreme Court gift shop, which he autographed. The book was *Marshall, the Courthouse Mouse.*

On May 22, Thomas delivered the commencement address at George Mason University in Fairfax, Virginia, not far from his house. He urged each of the graduates to "be a hero" and not surrender to the "cultural atmosphere of victimization and whining." He exhorted them not to "wallow in self-pity and defeatism," although he wallowed in the familiar story of how his fellow Yale Law students had smirked at him when he had trouble finding a job out of law school.

Later in the year, on October 20, Thomas traveled to Chapman University School of Law in Orange County, California. As he was about to enter the law school building, he noticed a catering crew unloading a truck. He went up them and introduced himself, learned their names and engaged in some light conversation for a few minutes. Eight hours later, after giving a short speech and patiently enduring hundreds of requests for autographs and photographs, Thomas emerged from the building. He saw the catering crew again and called out to them by their names, wishing them farewell.

In late November he went to Michigan to commemorate the opening of the Ave Maria School of Law, a school with a traditional Catholic bent, bankrolled by Tom Monaghan, the wealthy former owner of Domino's Pizza and the Detroit Tigers baseball team. After giving a speech devoted to federalism, a perennial Thomas topic, the justice fielded questions from the audience. One observer noted, "Few of the questions afterwards dealt with federalism. Although there were a hundred or so lawyers and their spouses, they had more personal questions." Thomas remained an enigma whose longing for privacy only stoked the public's interest.

In *City of Chicago v. Morales,* handed down in 1999, Thomas again found himself in the minority on the subject of crime control. The City of Chicago passed an anti-gang ordinance that prohibited "criminal street gang members" from "loitering" with one another or with other persons in any public place. In a 6–3 decision, the Supreme Court struck down the ordinance as violating the Due Process Clause. The Court, in an opinion by Stevens, held that the law was "unconstitutionally vague." The ordinance also proscribed much "harmless conduct" and gave excessive discretion to police. In a plurality opinion, Stevens recognized a right to "loiter for innocent purposes." Cited in support of this proposition was the 1972 case of *Papachristou v. City of Jacksonville,* which struck down the nation's vagrancy laws.

Thomas dissented. Joined by Rehnquist and Scalia, his dissenting opinion was a stirring defense of crime-plagued residents of the inner city. "By invalidating Chicago's ordinance, I fear that the Court has unnecessarily sentenced law-abiding citizens to lives of terror and misery," he stated at the outset of his opinion. "The ordinance is not vague. '[A]ny fool would know that a particular category of conduct would be within [its] reach.' . . . Nor does it violate the Due Process Clause. The asserted 'freedom to loiter for innocent purposes,' . . . is in no way 'deeply rooted in this Nation's history and tradition.'"

The Chicago ordinance was vital for combating street gangs. "Gangs fill the daily lives of many of our poorest and most vulnerable citizens with a terror that the Court does not give sufficient consideration, often relegating them to the status of prisoners in their own homes." The preceding year, Thomas noted, the Chicago public schools hired dozens of adults to escort neighborhood children to school, the children having become "too terrified of gang violence to leave their homes alone." He said, "The ordinance does nothing more than confirm the well-established principle that the police have the duty and the power to maintain the public peace, and, when necessary, to disperse groups of individuals who threaten it."

Thomas discussed the relevant constitutional history:

> Laws prohibiting loitering and vagrancy have been a fixture of Anglo-American law at least since the time of the Norman Conquest. . . . The American colonists enacted laws modeled upon the English vagrancy laws, and at the time of the founding, state and local governments customarily criminalized loitering and other forms of vagrancy. Vagrancy laws were common in the decades preceding the ratification of the Fourteenth Amendment, and remained on the books long after.

Another questionable precedent, *Papachristou,* came within the radius of his scythe. "Even assuming, then, that *Papachristou* was correctly decided as an original matter—a doubtful proposition—it does not compel the conclusion that the Constitution protects the right to loiter for innocent purposes." He flatly dismissed the plurality's newly coined right:

> ... there is no fundamental right to loiter. It is also anomalous to characterize loitering as "innocent" conduct when it has been disfavored throughout American history. When a category of conduct has been consistently criminalized, it can hardly be considered "innocent." ... The term "loiter" is no different from terms such as "fraud," "bribery," and "perjury." We expect people of ordinary intelligence to grasp the meaning of such legal terms despite the fact that they are arguably imprecise.

Thomas concluded with an impassioned plea on behalf of the citizens of crime-infested areas:

> Today, the Court focuses extensively on the "rights" of gang members and their companions. It can safely do so—the people who will have to live with the consequences of today's opinion do not live in our neighborhoods. Rather, the people who will suffer from our lofty pronouncements are people like Ms. Susan Mary Jackson, people who have seen their neighborhoods literally destroyed by gangs and violence and drugs. They are good, decent people who must struggle to overcome their desperate situation, against all odds, in order to raise their families, earn a living, and remain good citizens.... But the Court today has denied our most vulnerable citizens the very thing that Justice STEVENS ... elevates above all else—the "freedom of movement." And that is a shame.

In 1999, Thomas finally was asked to write for the Court in a race case. *Hunt v. Cromartie* represented the third time in six years that litigation over North Carolina's Twelfth Congressional District had come before the Court. This time, the Court voted unanimously to overturn a federal district court's ruling that the North Carolina legislature had engaged in unconstitutional racial gerrymandering.

"Viewed *in toto*," wrote Thomas, "appellees' evidence tends to support an inference that the State drew its district lines with an impermissible racial motive—even though they presented no direct evidence of intent." The district court erred in granting summary judgment, however, because there remained genuine issues of material fact to be resolved. Still, Thomas brought together a majority to endorse a statement he had made in his concurrence three years before in *Bush v. Vera:* "Our decisions have established that all laws that classify citizens on the basis of race, including racially gerrymandered districting schemes, are constitutionally suspect and must be strictly scrutinized." With this sentence, racial gerrymandering became clearly subject to strict scrutiny.

In *Saenz v. Roe*, the Court took up the State of California's decision to curtail the welfare benefits of newly arrived residents. California offered its residents higher welfare benefits than most other states. State officials concluded that consequently, the Golden State had become a magnet for out-of-state welfare recipients seeking a raise. California passed legislation that limited welfare benefits for new residents to the level of benefits they received in their state of origin.

The Court voted 7–2 to strike down the California law. Stevens wrote the opinion for the Court, reasoning that California had violated the fundamental "right to travel." This constitutional guarantee "protects the right of a citizen of one State to enter and to leave another State, the right to be treated as a welcome visitor rather than an unfriendly alien when temporarily present in the second State, and, for those travelers who elect to become permanent residents, the right to be treated like other citizens of that State."

The Court grounded its ruling in the Privileges and Immunities Clause of Article IV, Section 2 of the Constitution. This clause provides: "The Citizens of each State shall be entitled to all Privileges and Immunities of Citizens in the several States." In several decisions after the Civil War, known collectively as the *Slaughter-House Cases*, the Court interpreted the clause so narrowly as to divest it of any power. The Court in *Saenz*, however, found that the clause prohibits "discrimination against citizens who have completed their interstate travel."

In his dissent, Thomas expostulated with the majority to undertake a complete review of the Court's past treatment of the Privileges and Immunities Clause. He examined the original understanding of the clause (something he had declined to do for a companion clause, the Equal Protection Clause) and found it at great variance with the Court's jurisprudence of over a century. He would offer the most thorough treatment of the clause in a Court opinion since the *Slaughter-House Cases*.

"In my view," he wrote, "the majority attributes a meaning to the Privileges or Immunities Clause that likely was unintended when the Fourteenth Amendment was enacted and ratified." Thomas pointed out that while the Court had granted "near-talismanic status" to the Equal Protection and Due Process Clauses of the Fourteenth Amendments, it had "all but read the Privileges or Immunities Clause out of the Constitution in the *Slaughter-House Cases.*" He sought to resurrect the clause, but with an outcome very different from that endorsed by the majority. "Unlike the majority, I would look to history to ascertain the original meaning of the Clause." Thomas conceded in a footnote the perplexing ambiguity of the clause: "Legal scholars agree on little beyond the conclusion that the Clause does not mean what the Court said it meant in 1873."

Thomas examined the history of the clause, tracing it back to the 1606 Charter of Virginia. From this historical analysis, he concluded that "the terms 'privileges' and 'immunities' (and their counterparts) were understood to refer to those fundamental rights and liberties specifically enjoyed by English citizens, and more broadly, by all citizens." He cited Justice Bushrod Washington's famous opinion in *Corfield v. Coryell,* which, Thomas observed, "indisputably influenced the Members of Congress who enacted the Fourteenth Amendment." In their debates, congressmen referred explicitly to *Coryell* and stated that the clause was necessary to secure the fundamental rights Washington had listed. Thomas judged that

> their repeated references to the *Corfield* decision, combined with what appears to be the historical understanding of the Clause's operative terms, supports the inference that, at the time the Fourteenth Amendment was adopted, people understood that "privileges or immunities of citizens" were fundamental rights, rather than every public benefit established by positive law. Accordingly, the majority's conclusion—that a State violates the Privileges or Immunities Clause when it "discriminates" against citizens who have been domiciled in the State for less than a year in the distribution of welfare benefit appears contrary to the original understanding and is dubious at best.

Thomas once again challenged the Court to reconsider a long-settled ruling. The target this time was the *Slaughter-House Cases,* precedent that had stood since Reconstruction. Remarkably, Rehnquist joined him in this call. Thomas explained:

> Because I believe that the demise of the Privileges or Immunities Clause has contributed in no small part to the current disarray of our Four-

teenth Amendment jurisprudence, I would be open to reevaluating its meaning in an appropriate case. Before invoking the Clause, however, we should endeavor to understand what the framers of the Fourteenth Amendment thought that it meant. We should also consider whether the Clause should displace, rather than augment, portions of our equal protection and substantive due process jurisprudence. The majority's failure to consider these important questions raises the specter that the Privileges or Immunities Clause will become yet another convenient tool for inventing new rights, limited solely by the "predilections of those who happen at the time to be Members of this Court."

Throughout the latter half of the twentieth century, the Equal Protection Clause had been the wellspring of court interventions on behalf of black Americans. Like his criticism of *Brown v. Board of Education,* Thomas's dissent in *Saenz* was singular in light of this history.

⁓

As Thomas continued to publish distinctive and provocative opinions, the liberal journalists who dominated the national media still tended to view him as a pawn of Scalia. Thomas seethed over this caricature. Increasingly, he began to spar with such detractors in his speeches. In 1998 he had told the National Bar Association:

> ... contrary to suggestions otherwise, [there is no] intellectual or ideological pied piper on the Court.... With respect to my following, or, more accurately, being led by other members of the Court, that is silly, but expected since I couldn't possibly think for myself. And what else could possibly be the explanation when I fail to follow the jurisprudential, ideological and intellectual, if not anti-intellectual, prescription assigned to blacks. Since thinking beyond this prescription is presumptively beyond my abilities, obviously someone must be putting these strange ideas into my mind and my opinions. Though being underestimated has its advantages, the stench of racial inferiority still confounds my olfactory nerves.

A once-aspiring journalist proud of his own writing abilities, Thomas also was sensitive about being measured against the stylish Scalia in this realm. "I know I write some eye-glazing opinions," he admitted, adding, "Someone says I show no personality in opinions. I never thought it was some prose award we were writing for. If I wanted beautiful prose, I could read Faulkner, perhaps I could read Hemingway.... Cute opinions can lead us astray. Glib terms, glib approaches. We are not there to entertain, we are there to decide, to be precise."

As the decade drew to a close, Thomas steadily gained more respect from opinion leaders in the media. A front-page article in the *Washington Post* in May 1999 signaled this shift. Written by Joan Biskupic, the *Post* reporter who covered the Supreme Court, the article built on a premise she had first offered four years before on the same page:

> For the past eight years, Supreme Court Justice Clarence Thomas has walked in the shadow of Justice Antonin Scalia. The pair have voted together more than any other two justices ... inspiring criticism that Thomas is simply a "clone" or "puppet" of the forceful, fiery-tempered Scalia. But increasingly, Thomas has been breaking from Scalia, taking pains to elaborate his own views and securing his position as the most conservative justice on the court.

The article alleged that Thomas's independence was a new development. This was not accurate, but it showed that even in a newspaper that Thomas distrusted, he was starting to be recognized as his own man.

Another segment of the media, the movie industry, was less generous. In 1996, the movie *Jerry Maguire* featured a gratuitous reference to Hill's sexual harassment charges against him. On August 29, 1999, the cable TV movie channel Showtime aired "Strange Justice," a filmed adaptation of Mayer and Abramson's work of the same name. The creation of "composite characters" in place of Bush administration and Democratic officials was one of the lesser liberties taken by the filmmakers. Most egregiously, the movie offered a postmodernist version of the high-tech lynching speech. Thomas is shown marching into the hearing room with "Onward, Christian Soldiers" as the soundtrack. He later rises from his chair, rips off his shirt, and declares, "This is a circus. This is a national disgrace." Standing bare-chested, he tugs upward on his tie in imitation of a noose and shouts, "This is a high-tech lynching!" A reviewer with the *Washington Post* described these scenes as "bizarre," and panned the movie. Larry Thompson, Thomas's old friend and counsel during the hearings, auditioned as a movie critic in the *Wall Street Journal* by describing the film in a review as "another hatchet job on Justice Thomas's character."

Thomas responded to this treatment with peculiar behavior of his own. To minimize his paper trail, he generally did not make copies of his speeches available to the public. A spokesperson at the Supreme Court's public information office acknowledged that Thomas "is not one who readily makes his text available." Upon review of its files, the office found that it had only one of his speeches on hand. (Apparently reflecting the pall that Thomas's aversion to publicity casts over his subordinates, the Court spokesperson declined even to give her last name, saying she did not "want to be cited.") Sometimes, Thomas would work from an outline rather than a prepared address, but he refused even to make the outline public.

This pattern began with his speech in 1993 at Mercer Law School and continued through the end of the decade. When the director of public relations at St. Vincent College innocently asked for a copy of his address at the Red Mass, Thomas declined. "He was very adamant about saying that there were no notes or text available," the official recalled. "I almost got the sense that he didn't do it because he didn't want to be quoted." When officials at Ave Maria School of Law asked if they could publish his speech, he told them he "wanted to think about it." After Thomas gave a widely publicized speech to the National Restaurant Association, the association, through a spokesman, refused to release a copy of his remarks, saying they could do so only with his consent (which was never granted). This odd policy suggested that Thomas was prepared to have the nation revert to an oral tradition for the transmission of knowledge. His approach also was self-serving: He sought the benefits of a speaking tour without adding to his paper trail. The weird end result was, intellectually speaking, half a loaf.

Thomas likewise avoided Ivy League law schools for fear of hostile reception. He judged moot court at Brigham Young University Law School—one of the nation's most conservative law schools—only after a campus women's group was told not to protest his visit. But he declined similar invitations to speak or judge moot court competitions at Harvard and Yale. Charles Fried, a former government colleague and a Harvard law professor in the 1990s, said, "I keep urging him to come, and I keep urging people to invite him.... He's got his reasons. I think he's concerned that he would not find the kind of reception which a Supreme Court justice should expect."

Thomas also shied away from returning to Yale. He based his grudge on Yale's failure to support him adequately during the confirmation hearings. James A. Thomas, associate dean of Yale Law School, confirmed, "He's not been eager to come back here. And I'd say that stems from the negative reaction to the hearings.... I guess his feeling is, if he comes back, there'll be protests and who needs it.... I kind of wish he would come back."

Even friends began to acknowledge that this eccentric behavior threatened to undermine the personal rehabilitation he had sought. Noting his silence at oral argument and other quirks, one nationally known conservative said, "At some point, you gotta say, that looks weird." This observer added, "He could be a powerful public teacher on the conservative side. And he's personally such a powerful figure. You wonder whether, maybe he's right to husband his resources and pick his shots very carefully. But one worries a little that he's not having the impact he could have because of the reticence." Indeed, Thomas's speeches routinely generated news articles by wire services, which were then picked up by newspapers across the country. Those articles usually became the only way of preserving his remarks.

As the ten-year anniversary of his confirmation neared, these speeches still overflowed with bitterness. "I, for one, have been singled out for particularly bilious and venomous assaults," Thomas had told the NBA convention, although he added, not very credibly, "it is rare that I take notice of this calumny." He was cognizant of the Christian injunction to forgive one's enemies. "That is the requirement," he noted. But by decade's end, there was no evidence in the public record—and virtually none among Thomas's intimates—to suggest any real success at compliance with this religious injunction. In his Lincoln Day speech, Thomas mentioned in a telling aside that he had recently reviewed a "small portion of my confirmation hearings. That is not something that I do on a regular basis—I assure you. That is sort of like digging in old wounds."

This resentment flared up starkly in his speech to the Goldwater Institute in Phoenix on November 19. The institute bestowed on him an award named after the late senator from Arizona. "I deeply appreciate receiving the honor in the name of someone who measured liberty so dearly," he declared as he lauded the legacy of Barry Goldwater. His address was a conventional discourse on federalism enlivened by repeated references to personal suffering. At one point, he said with little persuasiveness, "thank God, we have recovered from [the confirmation process]." He closed with a mawkish self-application of Goldwater's most famous line: "I took no bullets in defense of our country. I fought no wars. I have no Omaha Beaches. . . . The least I could do is to accept calumny and libelous insults without complaint. No, my friends, accepting viciousness in defense of liberty is no price at all to pay for our country." The fact that the last two sentences of this monodrama contradicted each other indicated how much his head and heart were still in conflict over this issue.

That Christmas season, Thomas found joy out on the open road. He and Ginni spent some time vacationing with the O'Connors in Arizona. Thomas also took possession of a new and rather striking vehicle: a bus. He had special-ordered it from the manufacturer, requesting what one friend called something on the order of a "moving apartment." The sleek, silver vehicle was described as "the kind rock groups have," and featured a kitchen, bedroom, bathroom and numerous other amenities. The source of this whimsical interest was unclear. Dick Weiler thought it might have been a NASCAR thing: "Those guys [the racers] all drive around in buses."

The new year brought melancholy news that Thomas's brother, Myers, had passed away. He had been running on a Sunday morning, before Mass, when he suffered a heart attack. On January 23, 2000, Myers died at Meadowcrest Hospital in New Orleans at the age of fifty. He left behind a wife and two children.

Myers had been Thomas's constant company during the long hours of work before and after school and in the steamy summers out on the farm. They had been "raised as twins," Thomas later remarked. Grandfather Myers Anderson and the regime he enforced had forged the character of both boys. Their shared adversity under this steely regime created a unique bond. When his brother passed away, Thomas had to search his memory all the way back to their childhood to recollect the last time the two of them had argued.

As Thomas was becoming a national figure, Myers too was following the childhood injunction to succeed. Myers became a C.P.A. after leaving the Air Force. He then joined the corporate management of a succession of hotel chains. Thomas once described him as "the C-plus student who became the A-plus person."

Upon learning of his brother's death, Thomas traveled first to New Orleans to console Myers' family. Subsequently they all flew to Savannah, where the wake was held at their childhood parish, St. Benedict the Moor, at 7 P.M. on January 28. The old neighborhood was not what it had been during their youth. A sign saying "Police Drug Check Point" had been posted along the street only a stone's throw away from his childhood home. The marshals drove Thomas, Ginni, Jamal and Mark in the familiar small caravan of large black cars and vans that now announced their appearance in public.

Several relatives, including Ginni and Myers' daughter, Kimberly, spoke at the evening service. Thomas also stood to offer a short eulogy. He did not speak for very long before he broke down and abruptly ended his remarks.

The funeral was held inside the church the next morning at 11:00 A.M. Mourners filled the church to capacity. Others stood along the back walls and even outside in the inclement weather. As the steady drizzle occasionally hardened into sleet, the mourners drove in procession south down Interstate 17. Myers Thomas was laid to rest in the Palmyra Baptist Church Cemetery near Sunbury. His grave was next to that of his grandparents, and among some of the other great personages of Liberty County.

In a speech three months later to the Federal Bar Association in Tampa Bay, Thomas shared some thoughts about his loss. These reflections were interwoven with a discussion of other topics. Thomas seemed preoccupied throughout. Indeed, whether it was his lingering grief or the heavy press of business at the Court, Thomas's speech was notable for its lack of coherence.

He broadly criticized reporters and analysts of the Court, those who tried to discern the inner workings of the most secretive organ of the federal government. "One of the things, from time to time, when I heard about things that are said of the Court, it's almost as though there are those who are Court watchers trying to keep score. Who does what? How do they vote? Who asks what question? Who's most flamboyant? Who had the glib comments?" He continued:

> You know, think about it just a second. If you were having difficult surgery, would you really care about the score, or who has the glib comments during the surgery? Who happens to travel north or south during

surgery? No. What you're interested in is the surgery being done properly. It is frivolous to talk about scorekeeping in that way. We are deciding issues that will affect the fate of our country, our lives individually
and our lives collectively. Those things are not only unimportant; they're
frivolous.

Thomas took further exception to a recent news account of the
Court's decision concerning tobacco regulation. "One of my clerks said
that there was a report after the announcement of the FDA case involving the authority of the FDA to regulate cigarettes. And it was such an
unimportant point—Who smoked on the Court?" Thomas said of this
reporting, "Not only is it frivolous . . . [it is] destructively frivolous."

Was it truly "frivolous" for journalists to try to make sense of voting
patterns or judicial philosophy in arguably the most powerful branch
of government? Or was this not the most respectful way for observers
to analyze a great institution? Thomas surely knew from his own life
that judges are human beings who vote based on their own lifestyles
and preferences. Moreover, the author of the "Pin Point strategy" was
scarcely in a position to criticize the media for examining his personal
life when he himself had used his biography for self-advancement
throughout his career.

He wandered onto even shakier ground when he brought up his
brother's funeral awkwardly as a rhetorical point:

> As I sat there or stood there in the funeral parlor, having taken away a
> week from work, work became irrelevant suddenly. The things that mat-
> ter—and we know it—are faith, family, friends. Not who's smartest.
> Not which score we have at the end of the day. Not who's written the
> most opinions or the most dissents. Not who's most akin to Oliver Wen-
> dell Holmes. But whether or not we are akin to someone like my brother
> in spirit. We have done the principled thing, we have done the right
> things by our faith, by our families, and by our friends.

Thomas had enjoyed great success over the years with a proven oratorical formula: discussing life on the high court and the law, weaving
in personal details, advancing a theme and then driving it home. But
now he seemed to be employing personal tragedy in an unwieldy attempt
to discourage people from making personal or ideological comparisons
among the justices on the Court. This strange act recalled Al Gore's
use of his sister's death from lung cancer and his son's automobile accident

in speeches to his party's national conventions, cloying acts of opportunism for which conservatives roundly assailed him. Perhaps it was just a poor choice of examples in a rambling speech. Even so, Thomas's attempt to enlist his brother's death to immunize himself from public scrutiny made this otherwise forgettable speech in Tampa Bay the worst of his career.

———

In the Court's 1999 term, the State of Missouri offered its former resident on the high court another opportunity to sharpen his jurisprudential saw. *Nixon v. Shrink Missouri Government PAC* involved a Missouri statute that set a maximum limit on contributions to political candidates in the state. The caps ranged from $275 to $1,075. Opponents of these limits challenged them on First Amendment freedom-of-speech grounds. The case offered a chance to revisit *Buckley v. Valeo*, the 1976 decision in which the Court reviewed and upheld much of Congress's post-Watergate campaign finance reforms. Applying strict scrutiny, the Court in *Buckley* had upheld the $1,000 federal limit on contributions. In a 6–3 decision, the Court reaffirmed *Buckley* and applied it to state campaign finance regulations. However, the Court held that the maximum dollar amounts for contributions need not be "pegged" to those upheld in *Buckley*.

Thomas filed a dissent, which Scalia joined. "In the process of ratifying Missouri's sweeping repression of political speech, the Court today adopts the analytic fallacies of our flawed decision in *Buckley v. Valeo*," Thomas wrote. What was more: "Unfortunately, the Court is not content to merely adhere to erroneous precedent. Under the guise of applying *Buckley*, the Court proceeds to weaken the already enfeebled constitutional protection that *Buckley* afforded campaign contributions. In the end, the Court employs a *sui generis* test to balance away First Amendment freedoms." Thomas asserted, "our decision in *Buckley* was in error, and I would overrule it. I would subject campaign contribution limitations to strict scrutiny, under which Missouri's contribution limits are patently unconstitutional."

Restrictions on campaign contributions, Thomas reasoned, were restrictions on speech. "I begin with a proposition that ought to be unassailable: Political speech is the primary object of First Amendment

protection.... The Founders sought to protect the rights of individuals to engage in political speech because a self-governing people depends
upon the free exchange of political information." He devoted a para-
graph to a very brief treatment of the related history. Thomas judged
Missouri's contribution limits an unlawful abridgment of freedom of
speech because they caused a "suppression of political speech." He concluded by noting the incongruence of the Court's ruling:

> For nearly half a century, this Court has extended First Amendment
> protection to a multitude of forms of "speech," such as making false
> defamatory statements, filing lawsuits, dancing nude, exhibiting drive-
> in movies with nudity, burning flags, and wearing military uniforms.
> Not surprisingly, the Courts of Appeals have followed our lead and con-
> cluded that the First Amendment protects, for example, begging, shout-
> ing obscenities, erecting tables on a sidewalk, and refusing to wear a
> necktie. In light of the many cases of this sort, today's decision is a most
> curious anomaly. Whatever the proper status of such activities under
> the First Amendment, I am confident that they are less integral to the
> functioning of our Republic than campaign contributions.

Thomas's continuing ambivalence over freedom of speech was most
striking in *United States v. Playboy Entertainment Group, Inc.* Federal
law required cable television operators who offered sexually oriented
programming to scramble or block those channels or limit their transmission to hours when children were not likely to be watching television. By administrative regulation, this time period was determined to
be 10 P.M. to 6 A.M. Because scrambling could not ensure that non-
paying viewers would be shielded from all of the lurid images and sounds,
most cable operators simply prohibited any such programming from
airing during two-thirds of the day. Playboy challenged this restriction.

The Court agreed with Playboy and struck down the law as violating the First Amendment. Kennedy wrote the opinion for the 5–4
majority—a majority that included Thomas. The government, Kennedy
stated, had failed to prove a nationwide problem meriting a complete
daytime ban.

Thomas's concurring opinion recalled his slippery speeches on affirmative action in the early 1980s. On the one hand, Thomas said, much
of Playboy's programming was obscene and therefore subject to a complete ban. "It would seem to me that, with respect to at least some of
the cable programming affected by [the statute], the Government has

ample constitutional and statutory authority to prohibit its broadcast entirely," he wrote. "A governmental restriction on the distribution of obscene materials receives no First Amendment scrutiny."

On the other hand, things were more complex than that. Since the Justice Department had not proved the programming was obscene, he felt compelled to join the majority. "I am unwilling, in the absence of factual findings or advocacy of the position, to rely on the view that some of the relevant programming is obscene." In doing so, he did not even quibble with some of Kennedy's sweeping language in defense of Playboy. Indeed, Thomas outdid him to some extent: "I am unwilling to corrupt the First Amendment to reach this result [upholding the law]. The 'starch' in our constitutional standards cannot be sacrificed to accommodate the enforcement choices of the Government."

Anybody who had worked for Thomas would have fully expected his unsparing critique of the Justice Department. Yet the administration's ineptitude or ideology did not explain why Thomas's own analysis was divorced entirely from the original understanding of the First Amendment. Nor did these other factors justify the vigorous prose, and the accompanying attempt to clothe Playboy with Old Glory. It was left to the liberal Breyer, joined in dissent by Rehnquist, O'Connor and Scalia, to point out that the government had in fact shown a nationwide problem justifying the daytime ban, and that other remedies would be ineffective in addressing the problem.

The Fifth Amendment right against self-incrimination generated an important case in this active term, *United States v. Hubbell,* in which Webster Hubbell, a former Justice Department official and prime figure in the Whitewater investigation, appealed his indictment on tax and fraud charges after Kenneth Starr subpoenaed him to appear before a grand jury and produce eleven categories of documents. Hubbell invoked his Fifth Amendment right against self-incrimination and refused to state whether he had documents. Starr then gave him immunity and obtained a court order directing Hubbell to turn over the documents, some thirteen thousand pages in all. After Hubbell did not prove as helpful to prosecutors as they had anticipated, they indicted him on tax and fraud charges based on the documents he had relinquished.

The Court ruled 8–1 that the indictment violated the Fifth Amendment. The majority opinion by Stevens held that a witness does not have to disclose the existence of incriminating documents that the government cannot describe with reasonable particularity. Moreover, the government cannot prosecute a witness if the witness produces the documents after receiving a grant of immunity.

Thomas wrote a concurring opinion joined by Scalia, noting that the Court had utilized the act-of-production doctrine, "which provides that persons compelled to turn over incriminating evidence pursuant to a subpoena *duces tecum* or a summons may invoke the Fifth Amendment privilege against self-incrimination as a bar to production only where the act of producing the evidence would contain 'testimonial' features." While Thomas thought that the Court had properly applied the doctrine, "I write separately to note that this doctrine may be inconsistent with the original meaning of the Fifth Amendment's Self-Incrimination Clause." He noted: "A substantial body of evidence suggests that the Fifth Amendment privilege protects against the compelled production not just of incriminating testimony, but of any incriminating evidence. In a future case, I would be willing to reconsider the scope and meaning of the Self-Incrimination Clause."

Thomas sifted through the history of the Fifth Amendment. The self-incrimination clause provided, "No person ... shall be compelled in any criminal case to be a witness against himself." He focused on the original understanding of the term "witness." The accepted definition of "witness" was a person who gives or furnishes evidence, as opposed to someone who merely testifies. Thomas pored over dictionaries from the period (six in total). His opinion also reviewed the history of the Self-Incrimination Clause, early state constitutional provisions, Madison's drafting of the Fifth Amendment, and subsequent court decisions. Finally, another precedent was placed on the chopping block when Thomas recommended that the Court reconsider its 1976 ruling in *Fisher v. United States*, which held that the government may force a person to surrender incriminating physical evidence.

Though Scalia and Thomas joined each other's opinions, their respective opinions in *Dickerson v. United States* (which upheld *Miranda* in the same term) and *Hubbell* accentuated the differences in their originalism. In his *Dickerson* dissent, Scalia neglected to analyze the history of the Fifth Amendment, even though such a review undoubtedly would have bolstered his argument that *Miranda* found no support in consti-tutional history. Instead, Scalia analyzed the text and feasted on the delicious contradictions of his adversaries. Thomas, by comparison, extensively discussed the history of the right against self-incrimination.

Troxel v. Granville dealt with grandparents' rights, a topic of great interest to Thomas for the obvious reasons. The case originated when the Troxels sought visitation rights with their two grandchildren—the daughters of their deceased son—who had been born out of wedlock. A Washington State statute allowed any person to petition for visita-tion rights at any time. The law authorized state courts to grant such rights whenever a court concluded that the visitation may serve the child's best interest. The mother of the girls did not oppose the visita-tions, only the amount of time requested.

The Court overturned the Washington law. O'Connor, in a plural-ity opinion, wrote that the statute violated the mother's due process right to make decisions concerning the care, custody and control of her daughters. A parent has a fundamental right to make such decisions. The statute granted too much discretion to the courts.

Thomas concurred. He faced a difficult choice: parental rights ver-sus originalism. He believed strongly that the government should defer to parents in matters of child-rearing, yet he recognized that the Due Process Clause of the Fourteenth Amendment was not intended to strike down such state laws. To evade this tough call, Thomas settled for blaming the lawyers for inadequate briefing.

He stated that "neither party has argued that our substantive due process cases were wrongly decided and that the original understand-ing of the Due Process Clause precludes judicial enforcement of unenu-merated rights under that constitutional provision. As a result, I express no view on the merits of this matter, and I understand the plurality as well to leave the resolution of that issue for another day." He contin-ued: "Consequently, I agree with the plurality that this Court's recog-nition of a fundamental right of parents to direct the upbringing of their children resolves this case. . . . Here, the State of Washington lacks even a legitimate governmental interest—to say nothing of a compelling one—in second-guessing a fit parent's decision regarding visitation with third parties."

Thomas recognized that the Court in *Troxel* was greatly expanding the Due Process Clause, far beyond any correspondence with the original understanding of the provision. In case after case throughout the 1990s, he had gone out of his way to dust off old precedents of borderline relevance and advocate their demise. Here, however, he looked the other way and joined the Court's decision.

Abortion attracted the lion's share of public attention in this term. Nebraska, like twenty-nine other states, had banned partial birth abortion. The statute defined this as "an abortion procedure in which the person performing the abortion partially delivers vaginally a living unborn child before killing the unborn child and completing the delivery." In *Stenberg v. Carhart*, the Court held 5–4 that the law was unconstitutional.

Writing for the majority, Breyer stated that the law violated the right to an abortion for two reasons. First, the law lacked a "health exception." Using language from *Casey*, Breyer wrote that there must be an exception to the ban when the procedure is "necessary, in appropriate medical judgment, for the preservation of the life or health of the mother." The statute also ran afoul of *Casey* by imposing an "undue burden" on a woman's ability to procure an abortion. Breyer devoted much of his opinion to addressing points made in Thomas's dissent.

O'Connor and Kennedy, whose alliance in *Casey* was decisive, this time parted company. O'Connor, mindful of her status as the first female justice, clearly did not wish to break ranks with feminists. Kennedy, for his part, was demonstrably upset that the majority had overruled his previous work in *Casey*. That decision, he believed, had been designed to allow the Court to uphold anti-abortion legislation that did not repeal the right to an abortion or place an undue burden on that right. He saw the ban on partial birth abortion as doing neither. The majority's opinion, he wrote, "repudiates this understanding."

Only Rehnquist, Scalia and Thomas called for overturning the constitutional right to an abortion. Thomas's dissent was the lengthiest and widest-ranging of the three. In addition to challenging the right to an abortion coined in *Roe*, he denounced *Casey* as equally flawed, "constructed by its authors out of whole cloth." He remarked, "The standard set forth in the *Casey* joint opinion [O'Connor and Kennedy] has no historical or doctrinal pedigree. The standard is a product of its authors' own philosophical views about abortion, and it should go without saying that it has no origins in or relationship to the Constitution and is, consequently, as illegitimate as the standard it purported to replace."

Then Thomas engaged *Casey* on its own terms. "Even assuming, however, as I will for the remainder of this dissent, that *Casey's* fabricated undue-burden standard merits adherence (which it does not), today's decision is extraordinary." He continued:

> Today, the Court inexplicably holds that the States cannot constitutionally prohibit a method of abortion that millions find hard to distinguish from infanticide and that the Court hesitates even to describe.... This holding cannot be reconciled with *Casey's* undue-burden standard, as that standard was explained to us by the authors of the joint opinion, and the majority hardly pretends otherwise.... Today's decision is so obviously irreconcilable with *Casey's* explication of what its undue-burden standard requires, let alone the Constitution, that it should be seen for what it is, a reinstitution of the pre-*Webster* abortion-on-demand era in which the mere invocation of "abortion rights" trumps any contrary societal interest. If this statute is unconstitutional under *Casey*, then *Casey* meant nothing at all, and the Court should candidly admit it.

He noticed a gap in the Court's jurisprudence, which he sought to fill. "In the almost 30 years since *Roe*, this Court has never described the various methods of aborting a second or third trimester fetus." Thomas subsequently related the testimony of abortionists in describing how a typical "dilation and evacuation" or D&E procedure was performed. Because of the size of the child at this stage, Thomas noted, "the physician will grasp the fetal parts and 'basically tear off pieces of the fetus and pull them out.'... The fetus will die from blood loss, either because the physician has separated the umbilical cord prior to beginning the procedure or because the fetus loses blood as its limbs are removed." At this point, the abortionist will collapse the skull and pull it through the cervical canal. To perform a partial birth abortion, the abortionist places scissors into the base of the skull, spreads them to enlarge the opening, then inserts a suction catheter and sucks out the brains to collapse the skull.

Given these facts, Thomas dismissed the majority's stated concern that the statute could be applied to an ordinary D&E. The statute covered only those abortions in which the physician "partially delivers" the unborn child. This, Thomas noted, "suggests removing an intact unborn child from the womb, rather than pieces of a child." He cited *Webster's Dictionary* in defining the term "deliver." "No one, including the majority, understands the act of pulling off a part of a fetus to be a 'delivery,'" he observed. The statute governed only "partial birth abortion," which was clearly defined.

Thomas sought to force the majority to confront the horror of its ruling. "Although the description of this procedure set forth above should be sufficient to demonstrate the resemblance between the partial birth abortion procedure and infanticide, the testimony of one nurse who observed a partial birth abortion procedure makes the point even more vividly:

> The baby's little fingers were clasping and unclasping, and his little feet were kicking. Then the doctor stuck the scissors in the back of his head, and the baby's arms jerked out, like a startle reaction, like a flinch, like a baby does when he thinks he is going to fall.
>
> The doctor opened up the scissors, stuck a high-powered suction tube into the opening, and sucked the baby's brains out. Now the baby went completely limp.

"The question whether States have a legitimate interest in banning the procedure does not require additional authority," Thomas concluded. "In a civilized society, the answer is too obvious, and the contrary arguments too offensive to merit further discussion." Following this statement, Thomas offered a wry "But see" citation of the Stevens and Ginsburg concurring opinions.

On June 28, when the Court announced its decision in *Stenberg,* the normally reserved Thomas read part of his dissent aloud and with obvious emotion. He quoted from the portions that described the "horrifying" partial birth abortion procedure itself.

His dissent in *Stenberg* reflected his opposition to abortion, something well known to his family and friends. In private, he subtly communicated these beliefs to like-minded persons. The year before, right after his speech to the Goldwater Institute, for instance, Thomas stayed to greet many members of the audience, among them two leaders of Arizona Right to Life. The president of the organization, John Jakubczyk, was wearing a "precious feet" lapel pin—tiny gold feet showing the size of a baby's feet at ten weeks after conception. When

Jakubczyk introduced himself to Thomas, the justice commented on his pin.

"The first time I saw those were on Maureen Scalia," Thomas told him.

"Well, I'm president of Arizona Right to Life," Jakubczyk replied.

"Thank you."

"Thank you for being," Jakubczyk said.

"I know what you mean."

Carolyn Gerster also spoke to Thomas and commended him for his speech. They talked of Truro Episcopal Church, Thomas's former church in Virginia, which Gerster had attended for five years. She also spoke of her activism in defense of the unborn. Before they parted, they hugged. Thomas then told her, "God bless you. Keep the faith. Never, never give up."

Thomas's first decade on the Court thus ended as it had begun: with a terrible fight over abortion. During his confirmation hearings in 1991, feminists had rightly sensed his opposition to their cause; religious conservatives intuited an allegiance to theirs. His votes and opinions showed that for both camps, Thomas had been worth the fight.

In 2000, the press began to take greater heed of Thomas's work. The front page of *USA Today* offered contradictory assessments of his jurisprudence. An article on May 23 discussing recent Supreme Court rulings alleged that Thomas had separated himself from Scalia, "with whom he often moves in step." On July 6, in an article entitled "Thomas Makes His Mark," Tony Mauro gave a more thoughtful analysis. Reporting on "the very interesting year" Thomas had lived through, Mauro called him "the court's most fascinating member—and its most undervalued." After his brother's death, "Thomas carried on, issuing a notable body of opinions that should bury, once and for all, the demeaning rap on him that he is nothing but a rubber stamp for fellow conservative Antonin Scalia." Mauro was even more generous in offering a broader social observation: "To the extent that affirmative action is losing strength in the courts and in public opinion, he is probably as responsible for the shift as much as California-based activist Ward Connerly." In short, "He is no other justice's unthinking sidekick."

The *Chicago Tribune* joined what was becoming something of a band-wagon. A front-page article pointedly dismissed the condescending catchphrase "Scalia-Thomas." Accusations that the two justices vote as a "single entity," wrote Jan Crawford Greenburg, were "misleading because the two can and do see things differently." Greenburg contin-ued: "Scalia and Thomas vote together about 80 percent of the time, but other justices—such as David Souter (chosen by President George Bush) and Ginsburg (chosen by President Clinton)—pair up about as often." The misperception of Thomas as the "intellectual understudy" of Scalia ignored the fact that Thomas "often is boldly independent."

Even one of the nation's leading liberal commentators exalted Thomas. Nat Hentoff wrote, "To the incremental surprise and perhaps discomfiture of some of his critics, Justice Clarence Thomas is grow-ing harder to stereotype." In the 1999 term, just ended, "he has writ-ten as boldly and uncompromisingly in celebration of the First Amendment as did Justices William O. Douglas and William Bren-nan Jr. in days of yore."

Whether such praise bolstered Thomas's spirits was unclear. He con-tinued to refuse to disclose what publications he read. Still, that such praise was rolling in from such unexpected sources showed that his lib-ertarian strain was winning over admirers even on the left. None could credibly assert, however, that he had written his opinions with such an outcome in mind. The only consistent theme that tied together his opinions of 1999–2000 was the fact that he remained a man who stub-bornly thought for himself.

CHAPTER THIRTY

New Horizons

The 2000 presidential election was, to some extent, a referendum on the Supreme Court. With the stock market at a record high, leading economic indicators at their strongest levels in decades, and peace and security at home and abroad, Americans were ensured of food and safety, and therefore free to vote according to other factors, such as values. Abortion was more than ever a battleground. The Supreme Court had become the self-designated arbiter of this right and a growing list of other profound cultural disputes: homosexual rights, euthanasia, gun ownership, racial preferences. The next president, Americans realized, might nominate several justices whose votes could make the difference in cases involving any of these heated conflicts.

In their speeches, Al Gore and George W. Bush brought up Clarence Thomas's name to highlight their differences. Gore promised to appoint justices on the order of Thurgood Marshall instead of Clarence Thomas. Bush said he favored justices from the mold of Scalia and Thomas.

It was perhaps fitting that the courts ultimately decided the presidential contest. After the Florida Supreme Court voted unanimously to change the electoral deadline to allow for recounting in some of the state's counties, the U.S. Supreme Court overturned this decision and remanded the case to Florida on December 4. A county circuit court judge then sided with Bush. Gore returned to the Florida Supreme Court. On December 8, a chastened but still-defiant Florida Supreme Court sided with Gore in a 4–3 vote. They denied Gore's challenge to votes certified in Nassau County and Palm Beach County. But they sustained his petition regarding the nine thousand ballots in Miami-Dade County for which the machines had not detected a vote (so-called undervotes). The court ordered a hand recount of these ballots. The court also directed the circuit court to include in the certified totals 215 and 168 votes from Palm Beach and Miami-Dade Counties that prior manual recounts had identified for Gore, but after the November 26 deadline had passed.

Within an hour of the Florida Supreme Court's decision, Thomas was reading the court's opinion. The next day, Gore's victory began to melt, as Bush's lawyers again trooped back to the U.S. Supreme Court. The justices met for a rare Saturday conference, and voted 5–4 to grant a stay temporarily halting the recount and to accept the case for review. The fault line in this decision was deep and ominous. Five Republican-appointed justices—Rehnquist, O'Connor, Scalia, Kennedy and Thomas—voted for the stay. Four other justices, including the two appointed by Clinton, voted against it. Stevens, the most senior and combative of the Court's liberals, issued an unusual opinion criticizing the stay, which provoked Scalia into publishing his own blunt remarks in opposition.

Oral argument was held on Monday, December 11 for *Bush v. Gore.* As in the first oral argument, Ted Olson, Thomas's old friend, appeared on behalf of Bush. The Court made the audiotape of the session available to television networks less than an hour after the conclusion of oral argument. Cable TV networks played the tape with photographs of the justices on the screen. As each justice spoke, a red or alternatively colored frame around the photograph would light up. As in both oral arguments, the only justice who never asked a question or uttered a comment—and whose photograph remained anomalously unlit—was Thomas. The oral arguments served to publicize, as never before, the singularity of Thomas's reticence.

As the Court worked feverishly to finalize and announce its ruling, Thomas remarked to a colleague on the Court, "I haven't pulled an all-nighter since law school." After what was apparently the most compressed time frame ever for the issuance of a Supreme Court opinion, the Court handed down its ruling on the evening of Tuesday, December 12. The Court tried to mask its internal differences by styling the decision as *per curiam,* meaning "by the court." *Per curiam* decisions usually were unanimous rulings in uncontroversial cases. This old format became in *Bush v. Gore* a device to imply unity when there was none.

The *per curiam* opinion became, in effect, the O'Connor-Kennedy opinion. Every other justice filed or joined a concurring or dissenting opinion.

The *per curiam* opinion held that the lack of uniform standards governing the manual recounts violated the Equal Protection Clause. The Court found the right to vote a fundamental right. The standards for determining voter intent in the manual recounts varied from county to county; this denied voters equal protection of the law. Seven justices concluded that there were constitutional problems with the recount as ordered by the Florida Supreme Court.

Rehnquist filed a concurring opinion, which Thomas and Scalia joined; they agreed with the reasoning in the *per curiam* opinion. This was a stretch for Thomas and Scalia. Applying the Equal Protection Clause to ballot evaluations by county canvassing boards was well outside the original understanding of the clause. Bork, among other conservatives, later would criticize this rationale. But Rehnquist also stated that his trio would have reversed the Florida Supreme Court's ruling on "additional grounds." Namely, they believed that the Florida court had created new standards for resolving presidential election contests after the election was held. The Florida court's rulings thereby violated Article II, Section 1 of the Constitution and a federal election statute.

The four most liberal members of the Court argued that there remained time to conduct a proper manual recount before the meeting of the Electoral College. This could be done if uniform standards were put in place. Stevens, joined in dissent by Ginsburg and Breyer, took issue with Rehnquist, arguing that federal election laws assumed the involvement of the state judiciary in interpreting state election laws. The Florida Supreme Court had made "no substantive change in Florida electoral law," but was merely trying to count all legally cast votes. Stevens ended his opinion with a caustic blast that was widely quoted in the press: "Time will one day heal the wound to that confidence that will be inflicted by today's decision. One thing, however, is certain. Although we may never know with complete certainty the identity of the winner of this year's Presidential election, the identity of the loser is perfectly clear. It is the Nation's confidence in the judge as an impartial guardian of the rule of law."

As the majority had hoped, the ruling settled the election. With

Republicans in control in the Florida legislature and secretary of state's office, and his judicial avenues closed, Gore conceded the following evening. But in trying to resolve the election in the same magisterial fashion with which it had tried to broker compromises in other societal quarrels, the Court finally revealed plainly the partisanship previously obscured in less political cases. The liberal justices supported Gore, while the Court's conservatives and Republican swing votes sided with Bush. The oracles at Delphi, it turned out, were human. Blacks, over 90 percent of whom had voted for Gore, were particularly outraged. Thomas later said he wished the Court could have avoided taking the case.

The day after the Court announced its opinion, Thomas appeared at a previously scheduled event covered by C-Span. The occasion was another of his frequent talks to youngsters—this time to a group of honor students from high schools in Salisbury, Maryland, and Erie, Pennsylvania. In the East Conference Room, Thomas paced vivaciously in front a large fireplace, gesturing strongly with his meaty hands. His talk was widely quoted by newspapers still devouring the national election story.

"The last few weeks have been exhausting," he told the students. "But in a lot of ways, it shows the strength of our system of government." Thomas found new relevance for an observation he had been making for years: "I can still say, after the events of this week and all the turmoil, that in nine plus years here, I've yet to hear the first unkind word."

"I plead with you that, whatever you do, don't try to apply the rules of the political world to this institution; they do not apply," he stressed. "The last political act we engage in is confirmation." This was not true, of course. The Court was intensely partisan, cleft by vast ideological differences that exposed themselves most clearly when the liberals saw a chance to pick a Democratic president and the Republicans and conservatives seized the opposite opportunity.

Whatever the stresses of the preceding days, Thomas was in impressive form. He commented good-naturedly once again about gaining weight and the gray hair he had acquired since joining the Court. ("Now I have only a few hairs, and what I have of that is gray.") As he spoke of Churchill and Nazi tanks sweeping across Europe, his massive hand

glided in front of the transfixed youngsters. He praised the children—
"That is a very good question"—to encourage them, especially the black
and female students who raised their hands.

Some of the students were good enough budding journalists to knock
the practiced justice off stride. One young woman asked, "Why did you
agree to do an interview with us?" She had unknowingly touched on a
sore point. Thomas searched for the right words. "Well, I have, I do
quite a bit—I don't think it's necessarily an interview," he finally said.

As December closed, Bush began to announce his nominees for
Cabinet positions. The name that drew the most fire was Thomas's old
colleague from the Missouri Attorney General's Office, John Ashcroft.
On Election Day, Ashcroft had earned a mention in the history of political curiosities by losing his reelection bid for the U.S. Senate to a
deceased opponent, Governor Mel Carnahan (who had died in an airplane crash several weeks before the election). Bush then tapped Ashcroft
to serve as U.S. attorney general.

At the time of his nomination, Ashcroft already had blazed an
extraordinary political career. After being elected attorney general of
Missouri, he had served two terms as governor of the state and a term
in the U.S. Senate. He remained what he had been twenty-five years
before when he repeatedly and unsuccessfully invited Thomas to his
home for dinner: a devout evangelical Christian and deeply conservative attorney. These qualities shook the keen antennae of the political
left, ever vigilant for a threat to their power base in the judiciary.

The same forces once galvanized by Thomas's nomination to the
Supreme Court again went into battle mode. Democratic leaders in the
Senate and leaders of liberal interest groups told the *Washington Post*
soon after Bush picked Ashcroft that they viewed the coming hearings
as a "warm-up" for a Supreme Court confirmation fight, should Bush
nominate someone of his ideological stripes for the high court. Pro-
abortion activist Kate Michelman sprang back into action, as did Ralph
Neas, who had left the Leadership Conference on Civil Rights to become
president of People for the American Way. Unlike Thomas, Ashcroft
would not enjoy black support. The election still rankled most African-
Americans. Many also took exception to the leading role Ashcroft played
in defeating the nomination of Judge Ronnie White, a black member
of the Missouri Supreme Court, to a federal district court judgeship.

Ashcroft had criticized White for his ruling in a death penalty case, calling him soft on crime. The NAACP announced that it would treat the vote on Ashcroft as a "near-litmus test on civil rights."

Ashcroft's testimony before the Senate Judiciary Committee suggested a debt to Thomas's earlier successful trips to Capitol Hill. He tap-danced as much as possible around inflammatory issues and offered various concessions to the left in an attempt to dampen Democratic opposition. Race and sex continued to be the flash points of judicial appointments. On January 16, 2001, Ashcroft addressed the latter by affirming before the Senate Judiciary Committee, "I accept *Roe* and *Casey* as the settled law of the land." The "settled law of the land" approach was the identical dodge that Thomas had used to such good effect fifteen years before during his reconfirmation hearings to the EEOC—in his case, regarding affirmative action rulings. That Thomas had arrived at this strategy at such a young age, and without the extensive political experience and success Ashcroft had gained by 2001, underscored Thomas's great political instincts and the critical role they played in his rise to power.

A familiar procession of liberal senators on the committee gazed once again at new prey. Even Ashcroft's former membership in the Senate did not spare him harsh words. Kennedy distorted Ashcroft's record much as he had Bork's, accusing his old colleague of deliberately obstructing voluntary desegregation plans in St. Louis. Leahy, who had been so effective with Thomas, drew some blood from Ashcroft as well. He noted that Ashcroft had opposed Bill Lann Lee, Clinton's nominee to head the civil rights division of the Justice Department, because he thought he lacked a "capacity to have a balanced view" in making decisions. Ashcroft stated that he had feared Lee would not enforce Supreme Court rulings on affirmative action in government contracts. Leahy was incredulous. "He said he would uphold it," Leahy replied. "I mean, what more could he say?"

Reporters noticed that Ashcroft appeared taken aback. The *New York Times* observed that the former senator "seemed stunned by the ferocity of the questioning." As the hearings began, the *Times* noted, "The room swirled with expectations that his confirmation hearings seemed likely to be the nastiest ideological battle since the hearings to confirm Clarence Thomas as a Supreme Court justice nearly a decade ago."

Ashcroft weathered the Senate storm, but, like Thomas, emerged from the harrowing ordeal a changed man. The Judiciary Committee approved his nomination 10–8 in a near-party-line vote. On February 1, the Senate confirmed him by a vote of 58–42. The 42 votes represented the most negative votes for any attorney general nominee since 1925. Later that day, Ashcroft and his wife drove to the Supreme Court. There, in a private ceremony (even photographers were banned from the historic occasion), Clarence Thomas administered the oath of office to his old colleague. The two bruised souls at last had a common bond.

With the blessing of the administration, Ashcroft selected two Thomas friends as his top aides: Larry Thompson as deputy attorney general and Ted Olson as solicitor general. But Ashcroft would trim his ideological sails thereafter. He declined to attend a Conservative Political Action Conference in February, even though the group intended to bestow on him its most prestigious award. Ashcroft informed them that the ethics office at the Justice Department (still controlled by a Clinton appointee) had counseled him not to attend the event.

In this respect, at least, the borking of Ashcroft was more successful than that of Thomas. In continuing to attend—and, indeed, favoring—friendly conservative forums, Thomas upheld the old political maxim of dancing with the ones who had "brung" him to power.

―――

As the ten-year anniversary of his confirmation hearings approached, Thomas gave perhaps the rawest display yet of his unremitting bitterness over the experience. On February 13, 2001, he delivered the keynote address to an annual dinner of the American Enterprise Institute, a prestigious conservative think tank. The 1,600 guests who gathered at the Washington Hilton to hear his speech constituted a who's who of the conservative movement. Vice President Dick Cheney and Scalia were among the many notable attendees. AEI presented Thomas with an enormous bust of Lincoln, some three feet in height. A man who proudly collected busts of personal heroes, Thomas was visibly pleased by the award.

Dressed smartly in a well-fitted tuxedo, Thomas was, on the surface at least, at the top of his oratorical form. Elongating his sentences with his resonant baritone voice, he conflated the philosophical with the personal. "It is very tempting to confine my talk tonight to the subject that I am most familiar with: the law and my years at the Court," he said at the outset. "But, even though straying from that narrow ground may be hazardous, I am going to speak more broadly tonight—as a citizen who believes in a civil society, and who is concerned because too many show timidity precisely when courage is demanded."

The theme of his speech was the need for public servants to show moral courage. It was an audacious thesis for an audacious man. He quoted from Hamilton's *Federalist* No. 78, and commented, "The trait that Hamilton singles out—fortitude—is fundamental to my philosophy of life, both as a judge and, more fundamentally, as a citizen of this great nation." Recycling some material used in earlier speeches, Thomas spoke passionately of his life and beliefs. The justice who craved privacy more than any other, and who took such extreme and awkward steps to safeguard his sanctuary, seemed oblivious to the irony of his remarks:

> We all share a reasonable and, in many ways, admirable reluctance to leave the safety and peacefulness of private life to take up the larger burdens and challenges of active citizenship. The price is high, and it is easier and more enjoyable to remain within the shelter of our personal lives and our local communities, rather than the larger state. To enter public life is to step outside our more confined, comfortable sphere of life, and to face the broader, national sphere of citizenship.

Woes and complaints then cascaded over the speech, coming in trenchant succession. "In my humble opinion, those who come to engage in debates of consequence, and who challenge accepted wisdom, should expect to be treated badly." "It does no good to argue ideas with those who will respond as brutes. Works of genius have often been smashed and burned, and geniuses have sometimes been treated no better." "Even if one has a valid position, and is intellectually honest, he has to anticipate nasty responses aimed at the messenger rather than the argument." "[A]ctive citizens are often subjected to truly vile attacks; they are branded as mean-spirited, racist, Uncle Tom, homophobic, sexist, etc."

These remarks were obviously autobiographical. They also served to remind discerning listeners that Thomas could not live up to his own exhortations. He ended the speech by invoking Pope John Paul II's moving injunction to those who once had lived under communism: "Be not afraid."

Thomas's speech proved that he still made good copy for the press. Newspapers across the country reported on the event. Yet the address was, at bottom, an elegant and particularly audacious exercise in self-pity. After the Anita Hill hearings, the magma of resentment inside Thomas had hardened into unforgiving wrath. He had all but withdrawn from public life, save for amicable gatherings such as this where he could fulminate against his enemies and receive sympathetic and exuberant applause. Even as he pressed others to "be not afraid," Thomas neglected to heed his own counsel.

"How do I want to be remembered?" he replied to a question from an audience of high-school honor students in December 2000. "Oh, gosh, maybe I won't be remembered. . . . You know, I'm the 106th member of the Court. . . . Most are not remembered." The answer he finally came up with seemed sincere: "That I did my job and I did it fairly and conscientiously and honestly. That's all you can hope for."

With his first decade on the Supreme Court drawing to a close, Clarence Thomas's ten-year campaign to rehabilitate his public image also was winding down. At a speech in May 2000 to the Richmond Bar Association, Thomas acknowledged that he was cutting back on his speaking engagements. The speech, he told his audience, was something of a "last hurrah for me."

Would he heed a call to a larger public role in the years to come? The one issue that seemed capable of prodding him back onto the national stage was race. "The issue of race is the one major albatross around the neck of this country," he had observed in 2000. While unforgiving of personal enemies, Thomas was equally adamant about turning the other cheek to white people. "From the minute they put the first slave on the first ship, they violated God's law," Thomas observed in a conversation with Armstrong Williams. He continued:

From the first drop of the venom of racism to the slave codes to the Jim Crow law, they broke God's law. If I raise my hand in hatred or revenge against them, then I break God's law. If I type one word at my word processor in one opinion against them, I break God's law. Whether it is my opinion or a concurring opinion, I break God's law. If I write racism into law, then I am in God's eyes no better than they are.

He placed this struggle in historical and religious perspective. "A tremendous burden has been placed upon the righteous black man of today to rise above the wrongs done to him and help right America. Because of the history of suffering of black people—and there is redemption in suffering—black people have a critical role in bringing to fruition the promise of 1776." As for the Framers, "The signatories of the Constitution had the ideas, but never the courage to carry them forward for all mankind. We must have more strength than they had to do what is right."

Such views ensure that Clarence Thomas will continue to stir up passionate opposition, particularly from members of his own race. Yet this same divergence of opinion is a striking vindication of his faith in the Constitution and the American experiment—for such plurality of beliefs would not be possible in a less tolerant regime. This tension between Thomas and the African-American people also will continue to place his life in stark relief. By putting his head down and charging through life as an independent moral agent, guided only by his own internal compass, Thomas has ensured that he will not be remembered merely as a casualty of the culture wars, a sort of Nathan Hale of modern conservatism. Whatever else they may say of him, his detractors will have to confront the irrevocable fact that he is, and will remain, a free man.

Author's Note

The seed for this book was an article I wrote about Clarence Thomas for the August 30–September 6, 1999, issue of the *Weekly Standard*. Entitled "America's Leading Conservative," the article reviewed in brief Thomas's life and work on the Supreme Court. It praised him for his moral courage and independence and his de facto leadership of the conservative movement.

Clarence and Ginni Thomas were informed of the article right before publication. Both responded enthusiastically. Ginni mailed copies of the article to some of Thomas's close friends.

Upon learning that readers had reacted favorably to the article, and that no full-length biography of Thomas had been written, I decided to proceed with a book myself. In September 1999 I wrote a letter to Thomas to broach the idea. I admitted frankly that I doubted the endeavor would be successful without his cooperation. I enclosed a copy of the article and asked him to consider my idea. A couple of weeks later, I followed up with a telephone call to his chambers. His secretary, Dorothy Barry, confirmed that he had received my correspondence.

Thomas never responded to my letter or telephone call.

I learned that he was scheduled to speak to the Goldwater Institute in Phoenix, where I live, on November 19. Mutual friends attempted to arrange a meeting between the two of us. When Thomas was asked whether he would be interested in such a meeting, he responded viscerally, protesting that he was very tired and overscheduled; that he had planned on enjoying a leisurely trip to Arizona; that he did not warrant a biography because he was a relatively young man.

Thomas added that he had a "set policy" against granting interviews for books or articles. I later learned that this was inaccurate. He has granted several such interviews since joining the Supreme Court. Thomas also claimed, as he would later on, that he had never read my article.

Several days later, Dorothy Barry communicated to a mutual friend that Thomas was not willing to meet with me before or after his speech. He would meet me at the reception, she said, but not for an interview. Barry also informed this friend that Thomas was "not enthusiastic that a biography is being written about him." The next day, I called Thomas's chambers and confirmed these statements.

By this point, it was clear that Thomas preferred not to meet with me. It appeared, moreover, that he felt mutual friends had cornered him into a social obligation. I thought it best not to meet with him under these circumstances. Accordingly, I attended the speech but did not force myself on him.

Despite Thomas's opposition, I ultimately decided to proceed with the project. While conducting interviews for the book, I learned that Thomas at first actively discouraged people from cooperating. After a while, his resistance became more passive and subtle. For example, a number of Thomas's old friends who called him to seek clearance to speak with me did not have their phone calls returned. As the project wound down in early 2001, Thomas appeared to grow more comfortable with—or at least more resigned to—the idea of this book. A number of interviews I conducted during this time would not have occurred without at least his tacit consent.

Fortunately, many of Thomas's relatives and friends cared enough about his life story and reputation to grant interviews. I am deeply grateful for their assistance.

Although Thomas has been visited with more public scrutiny than any other justice in the history of the Supreme Court, most of this attention has been devoted to his relationship with Anita Hill. As a result, I found that large swaths of his life had been neglected or overlooked entirely. In my travels to Georgia, New England, Washington, D.C., Missouri and Texas, I came across important people and materials that had not been given their due. These people included Thomas's father, M.C. Thomas, who had not been interviewed before; the Thomas family in Georgia; and many other relatives and friends across the country. I also learned of important facts about Thomas's childhood in Pin Point and other Georgia locales, the reasons for his decision not to become a priest, and his years as a college student and young lawyer in Missouri. The archives of the Diocese of Savannah, College of the Holy Cross, Yale Law School, and the George Bush Presidential Library yielded fascinating articles and speeches written by Thomas that had never been published, as well as memoranda, newspaper articles, photographs, and other important documents previously overlooked.

In interviews of friends and co-workers from his days in the Reagan administration, I became aware of Thomas's tremendous talents as a political actor and manager, but also his captiousness and occasionally ruthless treatment of subordinates. I found new and significant details about Anita Hill, the deliberations of Senate Democrats, and the genesis of the high-tech lynching speech. In assessing Thomas's Supreme Court years, I benefited from the first in-depth interviews granted by his former clerks, as well as the insights of relatives and friends.

I am grateful for the assistance of the following individuals and institutions, whose generous support made this book a reality: William Kristol of the *Weekly Standard;* Michael S. Joyce and Michael M. Uhlmann of the Lynde and Harry Bradley Foundation; Roland and Betsy Nehring of the Nehring Foundation; Gary Schmitt of the New Citizenship Project; and Peter Collier of Encounter Books, my editor and publisher.

I am also indebted to the following for their research assistance and the resources they made available to me: The Roman Catholic Diocese of Savannah, Georgia; Kaye Kole (for her genealogical research in Savannah); Seabrook Village in Midway, Georgia (Liberty County); Conception Seminary in Conception, Missouri; College of the Holy Cross; Yale Law School; the University of Missouri; Arizona State University; and the George Bush Presidential Library. Ken Masugi, John McConnell, and Sister Virgilius Reidy shared with me their files of correspondence, clippings, and other materials about Clarence Thomas.

It is not possible to adequately thank the hundreds of people who granted interviews for the book—those who volunteered to drive me down the back roads of rural Georgia; who spent hour after hour painstakingly explaining the minutiae of the federal bureaucracy; who, as members of high-priced law firms, forfeited billable hours to share their stories and reflections. Many of these kind souls are acknowledged in the notes and bibliography (others asked for anonymity, and I honored their request).

Other than my editors at Encounter Books, the only persons to read the manuscript before publication were my father, James A. Thomas, my Aunt Helen Carter, and my wife, Ann Estrada Thomas. Their diverse critiques were extremely helpful. Special thanks go to my wife and three children, who enveloped me with the sounds of domesticity, understood the late-night trips to In-N-Out Burger, and provided a constant reminder right outside my door that there is far more to life than the written word.

It is my hope that this book will permit a more complete understanding of Clarence Thomas, a remarkable public figure who is, for all his shortcomings, anything but dull.

Selected Bibliography

Trrue to the principles espoused by Clarence Thomas, this bibliography discriminates on the basis of individual merit. That is, this is a selected bibliography. It lists only the primary sources of information for this book, works that have significantly influenced Thomas's life, and Thomas's own more important works. Each category of sources or works has its own form of abbreviation, which is noted to the left. Cases are abbreviated by recognizable surname, as is the practice in the law. Other sources and works are cited in full the first time they appear in the notes, then are abbreviated in recognizable form thereafter. String citations, which are commonly used in law cases, are utilized in an attempt to combine brevity with thoroughness.

Published Works

BOOKS

Blo. Bloom, Allan. *The Closing of the American Mind: How Higher Education Has Failed Democracy and Impoverished the Souls of Today's Students.* New York: Simon & Schuster, 1987.

Dan. Danforth, John C. *Resurrection: The Confirmation of Clarence Thomas.* New York: Viking, 1994.

Doug. Douglass, Frederick. *Life and Times of Frederick Douglass.* New York: Collier Books, 1962.

DuB.Fam. Du Bois, W. E. B., ed. *The Negro American Family.* New York: Negro Universities Press, 1969.

DuB.Land. ———. "The Negro Landholder of Georgia." In *Contributions by W. E. B. Du Bois in Government Publications and Proceedings,* edited by Herbert Aptheker. Millwood, New York: Kraus-Thomson Organization Ltd., 1980.

Hill Hill, Anita. *Speaking Truth to Power.* New York: Anchor, 1997.

Jaf. Jaffa, Harry V. *Crisis of the House Divided: An Interpretation of the Issues in the Lincoln–Douglas Debates.* Chicago: Univ. of Chicago Press, 1982.

Phe. Phelps, Timothy M. and Helen Winternitz. *Capitol Games: Clarence Thomas, Anita Hill, and the Story of a Supreme Court Nomination.* New York: Hyperion, 1992.

Rand Rand, Ayn. "The Objectivist Ethics." In *The Virtue of Selfishness: A New Concept of Egoism.* New York: Signet, 1964.

Str.   Strauss, Leo. *Natural Right and History*. Chicago: Univ. of Chicago Press, 1952.

Sow.   Sowell, Thomas. *Race and Economics*. New York: David McKay Co., 1975.

R.W.BB   Wright, Richard. *Black Boy*. New York: HarperCollins, 1993.

R.W.NS   ————. *Native Son*. New York: Harper & Row, 1989.

Wash.   Washington, Booker T. *Up from Slavery*. In *The Booker T. Washington Papers*, vol. 1., edited by Louis R. Harlan and John W. Blassingame, Urbana, Ill.: Univ. of Illinois Press, 1972.

X   Malcolm X and Alex Haley. *The Autobiography of Malcolm X*. New York: Ballentine, 1992.

ARTICLES

Kap.   Kaplan, David A., Bob Cohn, et al. "Supreme Mystery." *Newsweek*, 16 September 1991, pp. 18ff.

Kauf.   Kauffman, Bill. "Clarence Thomas." *Reason*, November 1987, pp. 29–33.

Rob.   Roberts, Steven V., Jeannye Thornton and Ted Gest. "The Crowning Thomas Affair." *U.S. News & World Report*, 16 September 1991, pp. 24–30.

Ros.   Rosen, Jeffrey. "Moving On." *New Yorker*, 29 April–6 May 1996, pp. 66–73.

Sus.   Suskind, Ron. "And Justice Thomas Wept." *Esquire*, July 1998, pp. 70–73, 146.

Th.1   Thomas, Clarence. "It's About Time." *The Pioneer*, November–December 1966, p. 3.

Th.2   ————. "Black Viewpoint Sees Walkout As a Chance for Liberation." *The Crusader*, 19 December 1969, p. 12.

Toob.   Toobin, Jeffrey. "The Burden of Clarence Thomas." *New Yorker*, 27 September 1993, pp. 38–51.

Will.   Williams, Juan. "A Question of Fairness." *Atlantic Monthly*, February 1987, pp. 70-82.

CASES

Adarand Constructors, Inc. v. Pena, 515 U.S. 200, 115 S.Ct. 2097 (1995); 115 S.Ct. at 2119 (Thomas, J., concurring in part and concurring in the judgment)

Bush v. Gore, 121 S.Ct. 525 (2000)

Bush v. Vera, 517 U.S. 952, 116 S.Ct. 1941 (1996); 116 S.Ct. at 1972–74 (Thomas, J., concurring)

City of Chicago v. Morales, 119 S.Ct. 1849 (1999); 119 S.Ct. at 1879–87 (Thomas, J., dissenting)

Dawson v. Delaware, 503 U.S. 159, 112 S.Ct. 1093 (1992); 112 S.Ct. at 1100–05 (Thomas, J., dissenting)

Dred Scott v. Sandford, 60 U.S. (19 How.) 393 (1857)

Farmer v. Brennan, 511 U.S. 825, 114 S.Ct. 1970 (1994); 114 S.Ct. at 1990–91 (Thomas, J., concurring

44 Liquormart, Inc. v. Rhode Island, 517 U.S. 484, 116 S.Ct. 1495 (1996); 116 S.Ct. at 1515–20 (Thomas, J., concurring in part and concurring in the judgment)

Glickman v. Wileman Bros. & Elliott, 521 U.S. 457, 117 S.Ct. 2130 (1997); 117 S.Ct. at 2155–56 (Thomas, J., dissenting)

Griswold v. Connecticut, 381 U.S. 479 (1965)

Holder v. Hall, 512 U.S. 888, 114 S.Ct. 2581 (1994); 114 S.Ct. at 2591–2619 (Thomas, J., concurring)

Hudson v. McMillian, 503 U.S. 1, 112 S.Ct. 995 (1992); 112 S.Ct. at 1004–11 (Thomas, J., dissenting)

Hunt v. Cromartie, 119 S.Ct. 1545 (1999)

Kansas v. Hendricks, 521 U.S. 346, 117 S.Ct. 2072 (1997)

Lewis v. Casey, 518 U.S. 343, 116 S.Ct. 2174 (1996); 116 S.Ct. at 2186 (Thomas, J., concurring)

McIntyre v. Ohio Elections Commission, 514 U.S. 334, 115 S.Ct. 1511 (1995); 115 S.Ct. at 1525-30 (Thomas, J., concurring)

Missouri v. Jenkins, 515 U.S. 70, 115 S.Ct. 2038 (1995); 115 S.Ct. at 2061–73 (Thomas, J., concurring)

M.L.B. v. S.L.J., 519 U.S. 102, 117 S.Ct. 555 (1996); 117 S.Ct. at 570–78 (Thomas, J., dissenting)

Nixon v. Shrink Missouri Government PAC, 120 S.Ct. 897 (2000); 120 S.Ct. at 916–27 (Thomas, J., dissenting)

Planned Parenthood v. Casey, 505 U.S. 833, 112 S.Ct. 2791 (1992)

Printz v. United States, 117 S.Ct. 2365 (1997); 117 S.Ct. at 2385–86 (Thomas, J., concurring)

Reno v. American Civil Liberties Union, 521 U.S. 844, 117 S.Ct. 2329 (1997)

Roe v. Wade, 410 U.S. 113 (1973)

Rosenberger v. Rector & Visitors of the Univ. of Virginia, 515 U.S. 819, 115 S.Ct. 2510 (1995); 115 S.Ct. at 2528–33 (Thomas, J., concurring)

Saenz v. Roe, 119 S.Ct. 1518 (1999); 119 S.Ct. at 1535-38 (Thomas, J., dissenting)

Staples v. United States, 511 U.S. 600, 114 S.Ct. 1793 (1994)

Stenberg v. Carhart, 120 S.Ct. 2597 (2000); 120 S.Ct. at 2635–56 (Thomas, J., dissenting)

Troxel v. Granville, 120 S.Ct. 2054 (2000); 120 S.Ct. at 2067–68 (Thomas, J., concurring)

United States v. Fordice, 505 U.S. 717, 112 S.Ct. 2727 (1992); 112 S.Ct. at 2744–46 (Thomas, J., dissenting)

United States v. Hubbell, 120 S.Ct. 2037 (2000); 120 S.Ct. at 2050–54 (Thomas, J., concurring)

United States v. James Daniel Good Real Property, 510 U.S. 43, 114 S.Ct. 492 (1993); 114 S.Ct. at 515–17 (Thomas, J., concurring in part and dissenting in part)

United States v. Lopez, 514 U.S. 549, 115 S.Ct. 1624 (1995); 115 S.Ct. at 1642–57 (Thomas, J., concurring)

United States v. Playboy Entertainment Group, Inc., 120 S.Ct. 1878 (2000); 120 S.Ct. at 1894–95 (Thomas, J., concurring)

U.S. Term Limits, Inc. v. Thornton, 514 U.S. 779, 115 S.Ct. 1842 (1995); 115 S.Ct. at 1875–1914 (Thomas, J., dissenting)

Government Publications

Flem.R. *Report of Temporary Special Independent Counsel*, 102d Cong., 2nd Sess. (1992) (report of Peter Fleming Jr.).

Hear.86 *Hearing before the Committee on Labor and Human Resources on Clarence Thomas, of Missouri, to Be Chairman of the Equal Employment Opportunity Commission*, 99th Cong., 2nd Sess. (1986).

Hear.90 *Confirmation Hearing on Clarence Thomas to Be a Judge on the U.S. Court of Appeals for the District of Columbia*, 101st Cong., 2nd Sess. (1990).

Hear.91   *Nomination of Judge Clarence Thomas to Be Associate Justice of the Supreme Court of the United States: Hearings before the Committee on the Judiciary, United States Senate,* 102nd Cong., 1st Sess., 4 vols. (1991).

Unpublished Works

INSTITUTIONS

BushL   George Bush Presidential Library. The files utilized were those of Lee Liberman, Mark Paoletta and John Sununu.

CSArc.   Conception Seminary Archives

DioSav.   Diocese of Savannah Archives

HCArc.   College of the Holy Cross Archives

INTERVIEWS (TITLES OMITTED)

AF	Abraham Famble	JIZ	Jeffrey I. Zuckerman
AJC	Antonio J. Califa	JK	Jon Kyl
AKD	Allyson K. Duncan	JL	John Lyons
AM	Andrew McDonald	JM	John Marini
AW	Armstrong Williams	JP	Janard Pendleton
BBO	Barbara B. Olson	JS	John Stevens
BL	Blanche Lambert	JTK	James T. Kopp
BP	Betty Purdy	KB	Kevin Boland
BTN	Benedict T. Neenan	KM	Ken Masugi
CB	Clint Bolick	LD	Laura Devendorf
CF	Charles Fried	LDT	Larry D. Thompson
CS	Charles Shanor	LLO	Lee Liberman Otis
DBP	Dorothy Barnes-Pelote	LHS	Laurence H. Silberman
DD	Dennis DeConcini	LT	Lonnie Thomas
DN	Douglas Nowicki	LTW	Leola Thomas Williams
EJ	Eddie Jenkins	MB	Michael Boicourt
EM	Edwin Meese III	MCT	M.C. Thomas
EMM	Emma Mae Martin	MD	Merry Devendorf
ET	Evelyn Thomas	MG	Matthew Glavin
FF	Fletcher Farrington	MH	Melissa Harrison
GC	Guido Calabresi	MJH	Michael J. Horowitz
GHWB	George Herbert Walker Bush	MM	Michael Middleton
HB	Hank Brown	MNJ	Malcolm N. Joseph III
HJ	Harry Jaffa	MVR	Mary Virgilius Reidy
IB	Ivalene Beacham	NNB	Neil N. Bernstein
JAT	James A. Thomas	NJP	Ned J. Putzell Jr.
JCD	John C. Danforth	NT	Nina Totenberg
JC	Jeff Dickerson	OH	Orrin Hatch
JDQ	J. Danforth Quayle	PBL	Philip B. Lyons
JEB	John E. Brooks	PDS	Philip D. Shelton
JEL	Joseph E. Lowery	PS	Paul Simon
JF	John Fitzpatrick	PT	Pamela Talkin

QJ	Quintin Johnstone	SH	Sukari Hardnett
RGS	Ricky Gaull Silberman	TBO	Theodore B. Olson
RJL	Richard J. Leon	TJO	Thomas J. O'Brien
RW	Richard Weiler	WBR	William Bradford Reynolds
SBT	Scott B. Thompson	WK	Willie King

OTHER MEDIA

Cas.Conv. "A Casual Conversation, Part I." Kay Coles James' Interview of Clarence Thomas. 10 September 1996. Obtained from www.neopolitique.org website; look under Archives: Interviews.

C-Span 2000 Justice Clarence Thomas, Questions and Answers to Students from Salisbury, Maryland, and Erie, Pennsylvania, C-Span, 13 December 2000.

SPEECHES

Sp.ASPA Speech to the American Society for Public Administration, National Capital Area Chapter. Washington, D.C. 5 December 1983.

Sp.Act. "Religion and the Constitution of Liberty." Speech to the Acton Institute. Grand Rapids, Michigan. 5 May 1994.

Sp.Casc. Speech to the Cascade Employers Association. Portland, Oregon. 13 March 1985.

Sp.Cato Speech to the Cato Institute. Washington, D.C. 23 April 1987.

Sp.Cent. Speech to the Centenary U.M.C. 17 June 1984. This speech has not been published previously, perhaps because of the confusion about where it was delivered. At the top of the copy of the speech on file at the Bush Library is written, in Thomas's distinctive handwriting, "Centenary U.M.C." This cryptic abbreviation may have referred to a Centenary United Methodist Church, of which there are at least four in the United States. The location remains unclear.

Sp.Chur. Speech to the Churchill Dinner Proceedings, Claremont Institute. Los Angeles, California. 20 November 1993.

Sp.Clark Speech to Clark College. Atlanta, Georgia. 23 August 1983.

Sp.Comp. Speech to Compton Community College. Compton, California. 14 February 1986.

Sp.Fed.Bar Speech to the Federal Bar Association, Tampa Bay Chapter. Tampa Bay, Florida. 22 April 2000.

Sp.Fed. "Victims and Heroes in the 'Benevolent State.'" Speech to the Federalist Society's Ninth Annual Lawyers Convention. Washington, D.C. 22 September 1995.

Sp.Fran. Speech to the Franciscan Sisters Tribute. Savannah, Georgia. 5 April 1986.

Sp.Ga.So. Speech to Georgia Southern College. Statesboro, Georgia. 24 February 1987.

Sp.Geor. Speech to the Georgetown Law Center EEO Symposium. Washington, D.C. 20 February 1986.

Sp.Gold. Speech to the Goldwater Institute. Phoenix, Arizona. 19 November 1999.

Sp.HHS Speech to the Department of Health and Human Services Personnel/EEO Management Conference. 16 November 1983.

Sp.Head. Speech to *Headway* Magazine's National Leadership Conference. Washington, D.C. 12 September 1998.

Sp.Her.87   Speech to the Heritage Foundation. Washington, D.C. 18 June 1987.

Sp.Her.98   "Character." Speech to the Heritage Foundation. Palm Beach, Florida. 1 February 1998.

Sp.HC94   "Education: The Second Door to Freedom." Speech to College of the Holy Cross. Worcester, Massachusetts. 3 February 1994.

Sp.HC96   Speech to College of the Holy Cross 25th Reunion Banquet. Worcester, Massachusetts. 8 June 1996.

Sp.Kiw.   Speech to the Kiwanis Club. Washington, D.C. 14 January 1987.

Sp.Lin.   "The Virtue of Practical Wisdom." Speech to the Lincoln Day Colloquium and Dinner, Claremont Institute. Washington, D.C. 9 February 1999.

Sp.Merc.   Speech to Mercer University Walter F. George School of Law, Law Day. Macon, Georgia. 1 May 1993.

Sp.NBA   Speech to the National Bar Association Convention. Memphis, Tennessee. 29 July 1998.

Sp.NewC   Speech to the New Coalition. Chicago, Illinois. 17 August 1983.

Sp.St.P.   Speech to St. Paul's Lutheran Church Laity Day. Washington, D.C. 12 August 1990.

Sp.Sav.C.   Speech to Savannah State College, Commencement Address. Savannah, Georgia. 9 June 1985.

Sp.Sav.F.   Speech to Savannah State College, Founders' Day. Savannah, Georgia. 16 November 1990.

Sp.Syr.   Speech to Syracuse University College of Law, Commencement Address. Syracuse, New York. 19 May 1991.

Sp.T.Bar   Speech to the Tulsa Bar Association Prayer Breakfast. Tulsa, Oklahoma. 21 November 1986.

Sp.U.Va.   Speech to the University of Virginia. Charlottesville, Virginia. 19 October 1983.

Reference Notes

CHAPTER ONE: Two Plantations in Georgia

7 "To understand": *Doug.* 161.

7 "We Afro-Americans": Speech at Black History Month Celebration, U.S. Dept. of Labor, 18 February 1983, p. 1.

7 Black family history: All levels of government have done a deplorable job of maintaining records relevant to African-American family history. When this writer attempted on several occasions in 2000 to research the records of the Augusta and Savannah branches of the Freedmen's Savings and Trust Company, he found them to be not merely in disarray, but gone. Only one microfilm existed of these documents, and it was missing, its whereabouts unknown to the courteous but baffled library personnel. In late 2000, as this book was being written, bipartisan legislation was introduced in Congress that would appropriate a small amount of federal money to microfilm the crumbling, extant paper records from the Freedmen's Bureau field offices. These efforts are to be commended.

8 Clarence Thomas is a descendant: AS; SBT; BL. Ada Snell and Scott Thompson are unofficially the premier black and white historians of Laurens County. The Snells were very close to the Thomas family. Ada Snell stated definitively that November Thomas's family came from the Thomas plantation. She based this on the family stories about slavery and local families that she heard as a child from her great-grandmother and grandparents. Thompson said that almost all of the black Thomases in Laurens County, particularly in the northern part of the county whence Clarence Thomas's father and grandfather came, are descendants of the Thomas slaves. Snell referred to the estate that they came from as the Thomas plantation; Thompson called it the Thomas Crossroads plantation. The former term is used throughout this work if only in the interest of brevity. M.C. Thomas stated that his father was born in Johnson County. This is only a couple of miles north of the land that the Thomas family sharecropped in Lovett. He did not know more of the family history. Other members of the Thomas side of the family declined to cooperate without the approval of Justice Thomas. He declined to grant such approval even for genealogical research.

Blanche Lambert, a relative of Clarence Thomas, was able to trace his family tree on his mother's side, by name, back to the King plantation in Liberty County.

8 "peculiarly self-reliant": *DuB.Land* 98–99.

9 Ibos: Donald L. Grant, *The Way It Was in the South: The Black Experience in Georgia* (New York: Birch Lane Press, 1993), p. 48.

9 Fort Mose: Philip S. Foner, *History of Black Americans,* vol. 1 of 3 vols. (Westport, Conn.: Greenwood Press, 1975), pp. 19, 263.

9   Revolutionary War: Grant *Way* 12–14, 26–27; John W. Blassingame, *The Slave Community: Plantation Life in the Antebellum South* (New York: Oxford Univ. Press, 1972), p. 122 (quoting Andrew Jackson).

10   Douglass on Georgia: *Doug.* 41.

10   Agriculture of Laurens and Liberty Counties: U.S. Dept. of Agriculture, Soil Conservation Service, *Soil Survey of Johnson and Laurens Counties, Georgia* (Washington: October 1991); U.S. Dept. of Agriculture, Soil Conservation Service, *Soil Survey of Liberty and Long Counties, Georgia* (Washington: October 1982); Interview of Jack Holt, Georgia Dept. of Agriculture.

10   Thomas plantation: SBT; Scott B. Thompson, "Thomas Crossroads: An Ancient Landmark of Laurens," *Dublin Courier Herald*, 11 March 1998; Bertha Sheppard Hart, *The Official History of Laurens County, Georgia, 1807–1941* (Athens, Ga.: Agee Publishers, 1987), pp. 12–13.

11   Troup: A. L. Hull, "George Michael Troup," in *Men of Mark in Georgia*, ed. William J. Northen (Spartanburg, S.C.: Reprint Co., 1974), vol. 2, pp. 432–41; Scott B. Thompson, "George Troup: A Premier Statesman," *Dublin Courier Herald*, 29 July 1997, p. 4a.

12   Thomas plantation under Troup: SBT; Interview of Irene Cordell. An arsonist burned the Thomas-Troup plantation house to the ground in 1995.

13   Du Bois and Kemble on Liberty County: *Du.B.Land* 185; Frances Anne Kemble, *Journal of a Residence on a Georgian Plantation in 1838–1839* (Chicago: Afro-Am Press, 1969), p. 323.

13ff Liberty County history: Robert Long Groover, *Sweet Land of Liberty: A History of Liberty County, Georgia* (Roswell, Ga.: W. H. Wolfe Associates, 1987), pp. 35–39; LD.

13ff Myers and C. C. Jones: Robert Manson Myers, ed., *The Children of Pride: A True Story of Georgia and the Civil War* (New Haven: Yale Univ. Press, 1972), pp. 8, 10–11.

14   Tasks: MD.

14   "not Tara": LD.

14   "malaria and a decline": George A. Rogers and R. Frank Saunders Jr., *Swamp Water and Wiregrass: Historical Sketches of Coastal Georgia* (Macon, Ga: Mercer Univ. Press, 1984), pp. 62, 157.

16   Miscegenation: Groover *Sweet* 38; Rogers *Swamp* 111; *DuB.Land* 185.

16   "double-jointed": BL.

17   Slaves as babies and children: Kemble *Journal* 31, 174, 312; John Brown, *Slave Life in Georgia: A Narrative of the Life, Sufferings, and Escape of John Brown, a Fugitive Slave*, ed. F. N. Boney (Savannah, Ga.: Beehive Press, 1991), pp. 7–8.

17   Slave auctions: Brown *Slave* 11, 100.

17   Slave childhood: Kemble *Journal* 200, 269; *Wash.* 217.

18   Slave marriages: Kemble *Journal* 15, 228, 167 (Kemble was speaking of a slave woman violated by a male slave; the man was a driver, and the right to rape was effectively a fringe benefit of this position); J. William Harris, *Plain Folk and Gentry in a Slave Society: White Liberty and Black Slavery in Augusta's Hinterlands* (Middletown, Conn.: Wesleyan Univ. Press, 1985), p. 47.

18   Slave meals: Brown *Slave* 14; Kemble *Journal* 134, 389. As Roswell King supervised the Pierce plantations where Kemble lived, the regime described there was undoubtedly very much like that of the King plantation.

   One oft-cited authority maintained that the food given slaves was "coarse but abundant," including cornmeal, bacon, and sometimes molasses, vegetables, and fish. Ralph Betts Flanders, *Plantation Slavery in Georgia* (Cos Cob, Conn.: John E. Edwards, 1967), p. 156. Written long before desegregation and chock-full of lingering Confederate resentment, this book sometimes pops up as a resource work on slavery (even Philip Foner cites Flanders; see Foner *History*, vol. 1, p. 616). Flanders' work drips with racist revisionism, including such assertions as, "Undoubtedly, from the standpoint of the health of the Negro the institution of slavery was beneficial to him." (pp. 170–71). The book is unreliable and should be shunned.

19 Slave clothing: Brown *Slave* 8; Charles Ball, *Fifty Years in Chains* (New York: Dover, 1970), p. 369.

19 Slave dwellings: Thomas plantation: SBT; "Oliver Edmond: A Voice from the Past," *Laurens County News*, 25 February 1976, p.1 (describing the slave cabins at a nearby Laurens County plantation owned by Troup). King plantation: William S. Pollitzer, *The Gullah People and Their African Heritage* (Athens, Ga.: Univ. of Georgia Press, 1999), pp. 168–70.

19 Slave work: Clarence Thomas: Sp.Comp.

19 Daily regimen: Brown *Slave* 4, 13; Kemble *Journal* 65.

19 Thomas slaves: SBT; Pollitzer *Gullah* 94.

20 King slaves: Charles Joyner, *Remember Me: Slave Life in Coastal Georgia* (Atlanta: Georgia Humanities Council, 1989), p. 6; MD.

20 Slave punishment: Thomas Plantation: "Oliver Edmond."

21 Stephens: Harris *Plain* 168.

21 Brown: Brown *Slave* 25–28.

21 Ball: Ball *Fifty* 340, 349, 366–67.

22 Glasgow and experiments: Brown *Slave* 33–38, 40–43.

22 Masters: Brown *Slave* 166; Ball *Fifty* 363; Doug. 76, 78; Kemble *Journal* 98.

23 Elderly slaves: Kemble *Journal* 303.

23f Slave religion: Ibid. 221; Harris *Plain* 48, 61, 52.

24ff "The Weeping Time": Charles Johnson and Patricia Smith, *Africans in America* (New York: Harcourt Brace, 1998), pp. 431–38.

26 Federal gunboats: Letter from Rev. C. C. Jones to Lt. Charles C. Jones Jr., 28 April 1862, in Myers *Children* 885–89.

26f Cain and slave weddings: Clarence L. Mohr, *On the Threshold of Freedom: Masters and Slaves in Civil War Georgia* (Athens, Ga.: Univ. of Georgia Press, 1986), pp. 74, 82–83.

27ff Sherman: Burke Davis, *Sherman's March* (New York: Random House, 1980), p. 26; William Tecumseh Sherman, *Memoirs of General W. T. Sherman* (New York: The Library of America, 1990), pp. 627, 684.

28 Sherman in Laurens County: Hart *Laurens* 88; SBT; "Oliver Edmund"; AS.

28f Illinois soldier: Davis *Sherman's* 45.

29 Sherman in Liberty County: Groover *Sweet* 48; LD; Rogers *Swamp* 69; Letter from Laura E. Buttolph to Mrs. Mary Jones, 30 June 1865, in Myers *Children* 1279; Cornelia Jones Pond, *Life on a Liberty County Plantation* (Darien, Ga.: The Darien News, 1974), p. 134.

29 "no more bondsmen": Letter from Mrs. Mary Jones to Gen. James H. Wilson, U.S.A., 1 August 1865, Myers *Children* 1285.

30 Black landowners in Liberty County: MD; Grant *Way* 90.

CHAPTER TWO: Furnaces of the Will

31f Peonage: John Dittmer, *Black Georgia in the Progressive Era, 1900–1920* (Urbana, Ill.: Univ. of Illinois Press, 1977), p. 79; SBT.

32ff Racial violence: Grant *Way* 104–7; Jonathan M. Bryant, "'We Have No Chance of Justice before the Courts': The Freedmen's Struggle for Power in Green County, Georgia, 1865–1874," in *Georgia in Black and White: Explorations in the Race Relations of a Southern State, 1865–1950,* ed. John C. Inscoe (Athens, Ga.: Univ. of Georgia Press, 1986), pp. 21, 26; Hart *Laurens* 57.

32f Legislature: Grant *Way* 108–11; Scott B. Thompson, "George Linder: A Respected Gentleman," *Dublin Courier Herald,* 24 February 1998, p. 4a.

33f Law enforcement: SBT; Numan V. Bartley, *The Creation of Modern Georgia* (Athens, Ga.: Univ. of Georgia Press, 1983), p. 140.

34 Lynchings: Bartley *Creation* 124–31.

34 "inhuman conditions": Sp.Bl.Hist. 4.

34 great-great-grandparents: Speech to the American Newspaper Publishers Association, 27 April 1983, p. 1.

35 James Audley Maxwell King: Letter from Mrs. Mary Jones to Mrs. Mary S. Mallard, 19 November 1867, in Myers *Children* 1406.

35 Harry Allen land: Deed and documents of real property obtained from Liberty County Courthouse, Hinesville, Georgia.

35 Allen farming, Lutricia Allen, Seabrook community: JS; LD; BL; Georgia Writers' Project, *Drums and Shadows: Survival Studies among the Georgia Coastal Negroes* (Athens, Ga.: Univ. of Ga. Press, 1940), pp. 112–13.

36 Du Bois on the black church: *DuB.Land* 130.

37ff Atlanta Riots: Charles Crowe, "Racial Violence and Social Reform: Origins of the Atlanta Riot of 1906," *Journal of Negro History,* July 1968: 234–56; Charles Crowe, "Racial Massacre in Atlanta, September 22, 1906," *Journal of Negro History,* April 1969: 150–73; W. E. B. Du Bois, "The Economic Revolution in the South," in *The Negro in the South: His Economic Progress in Relation to His Moral and Religious Development* by Booker T. Washington and W. E. B. Du Bois (New York: Citadel, 1970), p. 115.

39 Norman "November" Thomas: MCT; death certificate of Norman Thomas; interview of Rex Jackson; AS; SBT; Grant *Way* 211.

39f Race relations: AS. On the other hand, Snell judged race relations in rural Laurens County to be good, and far better than in the cities. In her part of the countryside, whites and blacks would draw water from the same well. Her family helped to feed a poorer white family who lived nearby.

40 Clarence Thomas on November Thomas: Speech to the Yale Law School Black Law Students Assn. Conference, New Haven, Conn., 7 April 1984, p. 1.

40ff November Thomas as a man: AS; IB; LT.

40 Dennen Barron: LT; IB.

40 Food: Bo Whaley, "He's 90, Going Strong," *Dublin Courier Herald,* 22 August 1979, p. 7 (regarding Will Thomas); AS.

41 Shelter: AS (confirming Du Bois' descriptions of rural black life at the time).

42f Myers Anderson: LTW; JS.

43f Paul Jackson, Sue Bowens, Emma Jackson: JS; BL; FP.

44 Thomas versus Du Bois on the black family: Speech to the U.S. Navy, Afro-American Day Celebration, 28 October 1986, p. 7; *DuB.Fam.* 29, 37, 151–52, 130.

44 Leola Thomas Williams: LTW; JS; BL; FP.

45 Clarence Thomas on Gullah influence: Sp.Head.; Sp.Gold.

45 Gullah: John W. Blassingame, *The Slave Community: Plantation Life in the Ante-bellum South* (New York: Oxford Univ. Press, 1972), pp. 23–24; MD.

46f African influence: Eugene D. Genovese, *Roll, Jordan, Roll: The World the Slaves Made* (New York: Pantheon, 1974), p. 395.

47 Clarence Thomas on oral traditions: Sp.Bl.Hist. 3.

CHAPTER THREE: A Phoenix Rises in Pin Point

51 Birth of Clarence Thomas: LTW; AF; Interview of Odessa Famble; Speech to the National Black Nurses Assn. Conference, 10 August 1985, p. 1.

52 Movement of Thomas family: Hart *Laurens* 134; MCT; LTW. Many members of the Thomas family declined to be interviewed without Justice Thomas's approval.

52f Bethesda: Grant *Way* 10; George Whitefield, Letter III in *Three Letters from the Reverend Mr. G. Whitefield* (Philadelphia: Franklin, 1740), pp. 13–16, 13–14; EMM; interview of Bill F. McIlrath Sr.

53f Pin Point: Paula Reed Ward, "Pin Point: Solitude and Shellfish," *Savannah Morning News,* 14 February 2000, p. 1B; *Drums* 82–83; AF; BushL (Informal Biography of Clarence Thomas, Liberman files, pp. 1–3).

54f M.C. and Leola: LTW; MCT; AF; EMM; AS; *Phe.* 31.

55 "Like so many": Speech to Edison Electric Institute, 23 March 1983, p. 23.

56 "walked away": Sp.Cent. 6.

56 Devoes: EMM; AF; LTW.

57ff Play: AF; Sp.T.Bar 1–2; Sp.Cent. 10.

60f School: Sp.Yale.Bl. 1; Sp.HC94 2; Grant *Way* 375 (Georgia's reaction to *Brown*); Ros. 66.

61 Clothing: Will. 71; AF.

61 Dorothy Barnes-Pelote: DBP.

62 Fire: EMM; AF.

62ff Savannah: Pin Point interviews by the author; AF; Sp.T.Bar. 2–3; Sp.Edis. 26; BushL (Bio. 4); Will. 73; Rob. 25; Sp.Kiw. 3.

64 Moving in with grandparents: Sp.T.Bar 2–3; Will. 73; MM. Leola Thomas Williams told *Newsweek* reporters, "Then one day, I came by and mother said, 'They know you're their mother, but can I keep them all the time? You just come and get them when you want.' I didn't have no other choice." Kap. Williams later said to other reporters that she simply decided, "you need a man over your boys." John Lancaster and Sharon LaFraniere, "Thomas: Growing up Black in a White World," *Washington Post,* 8 September 1991, p. A1. This author was unable to ask her about this event. Thomas's account appears to be more reliable.

64 "son of his grandfather": MM.

64 "statistic waiting": C-Span2000.

CHAPTER FOUR: The Strongest Man in the World

65 "greatest single influence": Dinesh D'Souza, "Clarence Thomas on Law, Rights and Morality," *Wall Street Journal,* 2 July 1991, p. A12.

65f Myers Anderson's business: Kap.; Charlotte Grimes, "Clarence Thomas: From Humble Start, He Set High Goals," *St. Louis Post-Dispatch,* 7 July 1991, p. 1A; Speech to the Pacific Research Institute, 10 August 1987, pp. 3–4; *Phe.* 34–35.

The Kaplan *Newsweek* story about the watch did not name its source. The stable hand story appeared in the Grimes article and was told by Frank Mathis, director of the Office of Black Ministry for the Diocese of Savannah. The two may be reconcilable to some degree. It is possible that Anderson experienced both indignities in succession; the stable hand incident may have happened in Liberty County or very early in his career in Savannah. It is also possible that neither occurred. Anderson undoubtedly experienced significant racism and discrimination in both Liberty County and Savannah. On the other hand, his own ambition played a key role in his successful entrepreneurship.

66 Anderson's daily regimen: Sp.Head. 12; Speech to the U.S. Chamber of Commerce, Nat'l Chamber Litigation Center Forum, 27 May 1983, p. 1; BushL (Bio. 7); Speech to the Nat'l Assn. of Black MBAs, 6 October 1983, p. 4; Sp.Am.News. 1–2; Sp.Merc. 10.

67 Myers' sayings: Sp.Syr. 11; Sp.Chur. 4; Sp.Her.98 8; Sp.Cent. 4; Sp.St.P. 2; Sp.Kiw. 2; Sp.Navy 4.

67 Christine Anderson: Sp.Am.News 1; Sp.Kiw. 2; EMM; BushL (Bio. 9–10); Sp.Head. 16; Sp.St.P. 2; Sp.Bl.Nurses 2.

67 Discipline: Rob.; EMM; *Phe.* 39; Sp.Merc. 9.

68 House: EMM; Lancaster, "Growing."

68 Neighbors: Sp.Her.98; BushL (Bio 8); Sp.Head. 16.

69 Enrollment at St. Benedict: Sp.Fran. 2; Martin Gottlieb and Peter Applebome, "Jim Crow's Ghost," *New York Times,* 8 August 1991, p. A1.

69f Franciscan nuns: MVR; Sp.Fran. 11; Jingle Davis, "'Prepared to Compete in a White World,'" *Atlanta Journal and Constitution,* 21 July 1991, p. A13; Rob.; Barbara King, "Justice Thomas Thanks Church for Its Support," Catholic News Service article, DioSav.

70 Discipline at school: Sp.Fran. 5; Christopher Sullivan, "Friends Say Supreme Court Nominee 'Hasn't Forgotten His Roots,'" Associated Press wire story, 3 July 1991; *Phe.* 38.

70 Daily routine: Sp.Fran. 2–3; MVR.

71 Succession of nuns: Sp.Fran. 2–4; MVR.

71 Curriculum: MVR; Sp.Fed. 2.

71 Attendance: Sp.HC94 2; Sp.Kiw. 5, 12; Sp.Head. 12; BushL (Bio 9).

72 School performance: David Margolick, "Judge Portrayed As a Product of Ideals Clashing with Life," *New York Times,* 3 July 1991, p. A1; MVR; Cas.Conv.

72 Guard and altar boy: MVR; David, "Prepared"; "Clarence Thomas: The Making of a Black Conservative," *Orlando Sentinel,* 7 July 1991, p. A1.

72 Grandparents' faith: Sp.Cent. 4; Sp.T.Bar 4; Sp.Kiw. 1; Sp.Navy 4.

72f Work with grandfather: Sp.Act.; Sp.Comp. 2; Sp.Bl.Nurs. 5; Sp.Comp. 3; Will. 74; Sp.Gold. 8; BushL (Bio 6).

74 Library and reading: Sp.HC94 3; Speech to Bishop Ireton High School, BushL (Liberman file); Sp.BlNurs. 3; Will. 73; Rosalind Resnick, "From 'Hatred and Love' to a Successful Career," *National Law Journal,* 15 July 1991, p. 29; EMM; Sp.Syr. 7.

74 Play: Hear.91 1:594; Sp.HC94 2; Sp.Syr. 7; Sp.Gold. 3.

75 ABC: Will.

75 Visiting Thomas family: AF; AS.

75f Visiting Liberty County: Sp.Edis. 23; Sp.NBA; Sp.Pac. 4–5; BushL (Bio 6–7); Sp.Sav.F. 11–12; WK (co-worker); FP; Interview of Florence Roberts; JS; EMM; MD.

76f Savannah history: AM.

77 "nightmare": Sp.Edis. 26.

77 Segregation in Savannah: Speech to the Capital Press Club, 19 September 1983, pp. 1–4; Sp.Kiw. 2; Sp.Navy 3; Sp.Ireton; Sp.Merc. 6; *Phe.* 36; Chester A. Higgins Sr., "'We Are Going to Enforce the Law!'" *The Crisis,* February 1983, pp. 50–56, 60; Gary Wray McDonogh, *Black and Catholic in Savannah, Georgia* (Knoxville, Tenn.: Univ. of Tennessee Press, 1993), p. 57.

78 Wanda Lloyd: Wanda Lloyd, "Growing up Black in Savannah," *USA Today,* 30 July 1991, p. 8A.

78f Myers Anderson and discrimination: Sp.Bl.MBA 3–4; BushL (Bio 5–6); Will.; Kauf. 29; Sp.Comp. 2; Sp.Merc. 7.

79 Civil rights movement in Savannah: AM; McDonogh *Catholic* 56; Gottlieb, "Jim Crow"; Carl Gillard, "Giving Hosea Williams His Due," www.savannah-online.com/columns; Grant *Way* 416–18.

80 St. Pius exam: MVR; Barbara King, "But for This Diocese … ," *Southern Cross,* 10 April 1997, p. 1, Dio.Sav.; Sp.Act.

80 St. Pius classes: Sp.Fran. 4; Sp.HC94 1.

80 St. Pius basketball: Kevin Cullen, "Twice a Crusader May Be Enough," *Boston Globe,* 28 July 1991, Focus section, p. 71.

80 Decision to become priest: Sp.T.Bar. 4; Sp.Chur. 3; KB.

81 Telling Famble and Johnson: AF; *Phe.* 43.

81 Investiture: "Investiture at the Minor Seminary Demonstrates Spiritual Fruitfulness," *Golden Key,* December 1964, Dio.Sav.

CHAPTER FIVE: Black Spot on the White Horse

83 "cemetery": Sp.Ireton.

83 History of Benedictines: Jerome Oetgen, "The Benedictines in Savannah," *Georgia Historical Quarterly* 53 (1969): 165–83.

83 History of St. John Vianney Minor Seminary: AM; KB; Dio.Sav.

83 Philosophy of Education: "Welcome to St. John's Seminary 1964," Dio.Sav.

84 Only black, departure from home: Sp.Sav.C. 14; Sp.Edis. 24. Thomas erred in stating that this was his first opportunity to associate with whites. He forgot about the Franciscan nuns.

84 Purdy and Boland: BP; KB.

84f Daily regimen: Dio.Sav.; AM; Higgins, "Enforce"; Lancaster, "Growing."

85 Classes: Dio.Sav.; Sp.HC94 3; MVR; BushL (Bio 10); Sp.HC94 3.

85 Quiet in class: KB; JF.

85 "self-conscious": C-Span2000.

85 Proving himself: Sp.Ga.So. 6; *The Fairmont Papers: Black Alternatives Conference* (San Francisco: ICS, 1981), pp. 81–82.

86 Sports: KB; JF; Dio.Sav.

86f Writing: JL; Clarence Thomas, "A Freshman's Thoughts," *The Pioneer,* September-October 1966, p. 1 (Dio.Sav.); Th.1 (Dio.Sav.).

87f Drama and Project Sandfly: JF; Mark Everson, "Project Sandfly," *The Pioneer,* January-February-March 1967, p. 3.

88 Visiting home: BP; AF; Interview of Isaac Martin; Higgins, "Enforce."

89 Loneliness: Sp.Kiw. 8; Sp.NBA; King, "Diocese"; Dio.Sav.

89   Challenges to inherent equality: Sp.Kiw. 8; Higgins, "Enforce."

89   "24 hours a day": Sp.Sav.C. 14.

89   Racial insults: Speech to the National Institute for Employment Equity, 26 May 1984, p. 15; Sp.Ga So. 6; Will. 74.

89f Jibes escalated: Lancaster, "Growing"; "Clarence Thomas '71: 'Old Man Can't Is Dead,'" *Crossroads*, March-April 1984, p. 1 (HCArc.).

90   St. Jude statue: Sus. 72.

90   Basketball: King, "Diocese."

90   Withdrawal from classmates: Will.; *Fairmont Papers* 81.

90   King note: "Old Man Can't."

91   NAACP meetings: Sp.Edis. 24; Sp.Sav.F. 10; Higgins, "Enforce."

91   Students and faculty recollections: Rosalind Resnick, "From 'Hatred and Love' to a Successful Career," *National Law Journal*, 15 July 1991, p. 29; KB; Lancaster, "Growing."

92   Reading: Sp.Kiw. 8; Higgins, "Enforce."

92   Wright: Kauf.;, *R.W.NS* 68; *R.W.BB* 113; Will. 74.

92   Reading about lynchings: Sp.Her.87 7; Sp.Ga.So. 3; Speech to the Black Caucus Seminar, 26 September 1987, p. 2.

92   Frost: Sp.NewC 17.

92   "crisis of faith": Sp.T.Bar 5.

93   grandfather's financial sacrifice: Sp.HC94 3.

93   Application for college seminary: KB.

93   First to graduate high school: Higgins, "Enforce."

93   "helped me to learn": King, "Justice Thomas Thanks Church for Its Support," Catholic News Service article, Dio.Sav.

CHAPTER SIX: Dreams Denied

95   Trip to Missouri: Sp.Merc. 5

96f First day: JTK; TJO.

97   "The aim": *Immaculate Conception Seminary Bulletin*, 1967–68, p. 11 (CSArc.).

97f Classes and grades: BTN: JTK.

98   Laugh: JTK; CB; interview of John McConnell (re woofer).

98ff Changes at Conception: BTN; JTK; CSArc.

100 "though we were isolated" and "my faith": Sp.HC96 2.

101 "brokest guy": TJO.

101 Sports: TJO; BN.

101f Fitting in: BTN; Lancaster, "Growing"; JTK; TJO.

102f Trips to Kansas City: TJO; JTK. In a speech in 1988, apparently delivered in the Kansas City area (the speech's text does not provide its location), Thomas once spoke of being thrown out of Shakey's Pizza for having "too much 3.2 beer and good cheer." (Speech to the Heartland Labor and Employment Law Institute, 28 October 1988.) Thomas, like most successful men, was not one to insult a friendly business audience by dredging up unpleasant or hostile anecdotes. It appears he changed the facts of the Shakey's incident to avoid giving offense.

103ff Monique: TJO.

105 Thomas on King assassination: Sp.T.Bar 5–6; "Old Man" (re white seminarian); Hear.91 1:366; Will.; Sp.NBA.

105 Sr. Ryan's account: Robert Holton, "Critics to Judge: Once a Catholic, Always a Catholic," *Our Sunday Visitor,* 21 July 1991, p. 3 (Dio.Sav.).

106 Why Thomas left seminary: Ibid.; BTN; TJO.

107 Conception alumni: CSArc.

107 Anger with church: Sp.NBA.

107 "How could I stay": Sp.HC94 3, 1.

108 Univ. of Missouri: Sp.HC96 2.

108 "After a minor dispute": Sp.Chur. 3.

108 Nina Simone: Sp.Edis. 25.

109 Job in Savannah: Responses to Questions submitted by the Senate Judiciary Committee, 1991, pp. 2–4, BushL (Liberman file) [hereinafter Resp.Quest.].

109 Application to Holy Cross: "Old Man": Sp.HC96 2.

109 Fewer than twenty black students: HCArc.

109 Acceptance by Holy Cross: Sp.HC96 2.

109 "with no hope": Sp.HC94 4.

CHAPTER SEVEN: Years of Rage

113 Trip to Holy Cross: Sp.HC94 3; Speech to the Connecticut Business and Industry Assn., 12 December 1985, p. 1; Higgins, "Enforce."

113 Holy Cross history: Sp.HC94 3; JEB; Interview of Mark Savolis.

114 Worcester: JEB; Kevin Cullen, "Thomas in College: Complex Activist," *Boston Globe,* 23 July 1991, p. A1; EJ; MNJ.

114 *Manchester Union Leader:* Letter to the Editor and Response, "On Importing Black People," *Manchester Union Leader,* 28 March 1969, HCArc.

115 Racial incidents at Holy Cross: Jim O'Neill, "Clarence Thomas: A Man of Conviction and Contradiction," *Providence Sunday Journal,* 8 September 1991, HCArc.; Cullen, "Complex"; H. James Bush, "Situation of Blacks at Holy Cross Analyzed," *The Crusader,* 25 April 1969, p. 1.

115 "Lonely, miserable and cold": Aaron Epstein, Gary Blonston, and Christopher Scanlan, "Thomas' Conservative Views Rooted in Rural Georgia, Yale," *Orange County Register,* 6 July 1991, p. A1.

115 "cold, isolated": "Old Man."

115 *New York Times:* Timothy J. Connolly, "Reputation for Independent Thinking," *Worcester Sunday Telegram,* 8 September 1991, p. A1.

115 Meeting people in cafeteria: RJL.

115 Independence and abrasiveness: JEB; EJ; MNJ.

116 Poor: Cas.Conv.; EMM; RJL.

116 1 percent of population: Bush, "Situation."

116 "The biggest thing": Higgins, "Enforce."

117 Separatism: Bush, "Situation"; JEB.

117 Black corridor: "Black Corridor Set for Healy," *The Crusader,* 25 April 1969, p. 2 (HCArc.); EJ; Rob.

118 Grades: TJO.

118 Classes: "Old Man"; Sp.HC94 4, 8.

118 Silence in class: Cullen, "Complex"; O'Neill, "Conviction"; Margolick, "Judge"; Sus.

119 Mixers: RJL; interview of Anna Maria official; Bush, "Situation."

119 Self-esteem regarding women: TJO; Lancaster, "Growing"; *Phe.* 48.

119 Kathy Ambush: EJ; Wayne Woodlief, "Former In-Law Thomas Is Supreme," *Boston Herald,* 4 July 1991, p. 1; interview of Anna Maria official.

119 Holy Cross in 1969: RJL; MVR; Sp.HC96 3; Cullen, "Complex."

119 "I was truly": Cas.Conv.

120 Thomas's politics in 1969: EJ; Rob.

120 Thomas's religion in 1969: TJO. The letter actually bears the date 1968 instead of 1969. Thomas was attending Conception in 1968 and would not have written such a letter in that year. It is obvious (and O'Brien agreed) that the year was in error—a common error, as a new year had just begun.

121 GE protest: Thomas Myers, "RSU Blocks Student Interviews with GE," *The Crusader,* 12 December 1969, p. 1; "Black Departure Forces College Crisis," *The Crusader,* 19 December 1969, p. 1 (HCArc.).

121 BSU response: MNJ; EJ. Twenty-five years later, Thomas offered an account of BSU's actions that differed from those of other black students present. He stated that one of his closest friends was disciplined for protesting the on-campus recruiting of a corporation that did business in South Africa. When the black protestors were singled out for disciplinary purposes, he said, "This injustice was proof positive for me that Blacks could never be treated fairly on a predominantly White campus—or in a White society for that matter. I had finally had enough. Most of my fellow Black students felt the same way; so we decided to leave." Sp.HC94 5. In fact, GE's dealings in South Africa were not the motivation for the protests and appear to have played no role in them. In later years, as Thomas was criticized for being disloyal to the causes of blacks, he was not above gilding stories to demonstrate a longstanding opposition to racism—even when, as in this case, the protests had nothing to do with the anti-apartheid movement. Thomas, moreover, was very reluctant to leave campus. His account here glosses over this fact.

123 Robert Bliss: Lee Hammel, "Thomas Is 1971 HC Grad," *Worcester Telegram & Gazette,* 2 July 1991, p. A1.

123 "As I packed": Sp.HC94 5–6.

124 Walkout strategy: Brian C. Mooney and Walter V. Robinson, "Peers Recall Nominee's Conservative Leanings," *Boston Globe,* 2 July 1991, p. 12; EJ.

125 Thomas's apologia: Ibid.

126 BSU meetings: EJ.

126 "Remember why we're here": O'Neill, "Conviction."

126 Additional BSU demands: Clarence Thomas, "Blacks Discuss Change with President Swords," *The Crusader,* 28 February 1969, p. 2 (HCArc.)

126 "my radical days": Sp.Edis. 26.

126 "my rebellious stage": Cas.Conv.

126 Thomas on Black Panthers: Kauf.

127 "those who beckoned": Sp.Ga.So. 3.

127 Free breakfast program: O'Neill, "Conviction"; Timothy J. Connolly, "Reputation for Independent Thinking," *Worcester Sunday Telegram,* 8 September 1991, p. A1; EJ.

127 Music, attire, war: Sp.HC94 3; Kap.; Resnick, "Hatred"; Cullen, "Complex"; TJO.

128 Philosophy: TJO; Cas.Conv.

128 Malcolm X: *X* 239–44, 271–274.

128 Black Muslims: Kauf.; EJ.

128 Visits in Savannah: EMM; Sp.Fed. 10; Sp.Act.

128 Changes in 1970: RJL.

129 "It seemed that no tradition": Sp.HC94 3–5.

129 "nihilistic fog": Sp.NBA.

130 "Cooz never": *Phe.* 48.

130 Jenkins on marijuana: Connolly, "Reputation."

130 Poem: EJ; Richard Lacayo, "A Question of Character," *Time,* 21 October 1991, p. 43.

130 Track: Connolly, "Reputation"; O'Neill, "Conviction."

131 Weightlifting: RJL; *Phe.* 46.

131 BSU election: EJ; Cullen, "Complex."

131 Thomas considers leaving: "Old Man"; JEB. There is some confusion as to when Thomas seriously considered leaving Holy Cross. Father Brooks thought this occurred in the fall of 1969. A *Washington Post* article quoted friends as saying Thomas grew "tired of school" and considered departing in the spring of 1970. Lancaster, "Growing." Neither seems quite right. Thomas's explanation to Father Brooks about his reasons for leaving—that the brothers were "fighting among themselves"—were almost identical to the words he used in the BSU election meeting. Moreover, such a devastating experience would seem far more likely to cause such a personal crisis than anything in the fall of 1969, when he had just met Kathy Ambush and fallen in love. It is possible, of course, that Thomas considered leaving Holy Cross several times for various reasons.

132 Gil Hardy: Sp.Head. 17; MNJ.

133 Engagement to Ambush: Woodlief, "Former In-Law": O'Neill, "Conviction"; Hammel, "Thomas."

133 Applying to Yale: O'Neill, "Conviction"; Connolly, "Reputation."

133 Choosing Yale: "Clarence Thomas: Off to Law School, then Back Home to 'Help People'," *Crossroads,* May, 1971 (HCArc.); Sp.Syr. 2.

134 Leonard Cooper: Hammel, "Thomas."

134 Graduation: JEB; EMM; Sp.Syr. 2; HCArc.; Lancaster, "Growing"; Resp.Quest.

134 Wedding: Interview of Clyde Cox (re All Saints); "Kathy G. Ambush Wed in Church," *Worcester Sunday Telegram,* 6 June 1971, p. 5D.

CHAPTER EIGHT: The Monkey on His Back

135 Black Panthers at Yale: John Taft, *Mayday at Yale: A Case Study in Student Radicalism* (Boulder, Colo.: Westview Press, 1976); Robert Brustein, *Revolution As Theatre: Notes on the New Radical Style* (New York: Liveright, 1971).

135 Thomas apartment: The address was 386 Prospect, Apt. B5. It was listed in the 1974 New Haven City Directory, New Haven City Library.

135 "depressing" summer of '71: Sp.NBA.

135 Civil rights work in summer of 1971: Sp.Edis. 26; BushL (Bio. 11); Resp.Quest. 2.

136 Attire: JAT; QJ; EMM; Carole Bass, "A Portrait of Thomas at Yale," *Legal Times,* 15 July 1991, p. 1. Harry Singleton insisted it was a denim rather than a wool

hat. He said both he and Thomas wore overalls out of "solidarity with the little man out there." Bass, "Portrait." Johnstone remains adamant that it was a wool cap, a view shared by James A. Thomas. Emma Mae Martin thought the suspenders were inspired by his grandfather, Myers Anderson.

137 Studying: QJ; Rob.

137 Classes: QJ; Will.; JM.

137 Quiet in class: QJ; Will. Thomas said that he remained quiet and sat toward the back in an effort to hide his "blackness." Thomas had a lifelong pattern of falling silent at the outset of new professional situations. His explanation for his silence at Yale is vague and not particularly credible.

137 "good grades": Will.

138 Clinton, Rodham: JM; GC.

138 200 alumni: Sherry R. Sontag, "Classmates: 'Clarence Is Just Clarence,'" *National Law Journal,* 15 July 1991, p. 29.

138 Confederate flag: Carole Bass, "A Portrait of Thomas at Yale," *Legal Times,* 15 July 1991, p. 1.

138 Friends: QJ; JAT; RJL.

139 Singleton and Washington: Sontag, "Classmates"; *Phe.* 50–51; Rob.

139 Football: Rob.; Bass, "Portrait."

139 Legal aid office: AJC; Bass, "Portrait."

140 Affirmative action at Yale: JAT; Letter from Guido Calabresi to Senator Arlen Specter, 6 September 1991, in Hear.91 2:257–58. The Supreme Court struck down a quota system in the University of California system very similar to Yale's original affirmative action program in *University of California Regents v. Bakke,* 438 U.S. 265 (1978).

140 Thomas "clearly recognized": Neil A. Lewis, "On Thomas's Climb, Ambivalence About Issue of Affirmative Action," *New York Times,* 14 July 1991, p. 1.

140 Clarence Thomas supporting affirmative action: JAT.

141 "Clarence always professed": John King, "Thomas' Trail: From Student Activist to Self-Help Advocate," Associated Press wire story, 4 July 1991.

141 "worst experience": Juan Williams, "Black Conservatives, Center Stage," *Washington Post,* 16 December 1980, p. A21.

141 Yale professor criticizing affirmative action: Lewis, "Climb." Winters noted the inferior academic records of black applicants to Yale at the time in Sharon LaFraniere, "Despite Achievement, Thomas Felt Isolated," *Washington Post,* 9 September 1991, p. A1. Winters initially agreed in writing to be interviewed for this book. He subsequently did not respond to a follow-up telephone request for an interview.

141 Ricky Silberman: Richard Whitmire and Rochelle Sharpe, "Thomas Arrived at Yale a Liberal, Left a Conservative," Gannett News wire story, 3 July 1991.

141 Henry Cornelius Terry: *Phe.* 49.

141 "I was never": C-Span2000.

142 "You had to prove": Williams, "Black Conservatives."

143 "liberal mainstream": Bass, "Portrait."

143 Singleton on conversion: Epstein, "Rooted."

143 Lenny Cooper: Hammel, "Thomas."

143 Singleton on "real transformation": Sontag, "Classmates."

144 "I never gave up": D'Souza, "Thomas."

144 "I wandered aimlessly": Sp.T.Bar 6.

144 Pornography: *Phelps* 51; Lacayo, "Question."

145 Bobby Hill as "hero": Sp.Sav.F. 13.

145 Thomas at Hill, Jones & Farrington: FF.

146 Carl Junior Isaacs: Tony Mauro, "A Judicial Career Forever Marked with an Asterisk?" *The Recorder,* 11 December 1995, p. 8; description of murders from *Isaacs v. Kemp,* 778 F.2d 1482 (11th Cir. 1985).

147 "didn't work out": Cas.Conv.

148 Interviews in Georgia: Sp.Merc. 5; Sp.Sav.F. 1; Sp.Syr. 4.

148 Interviews elsewhere: Cas.Conv.; Commencement Speech, University of North Dakota Law School, 1998 Commencement Speech, *North Dakota Law Review* 74 (1998): 435–439, 436.

148 Dissertation: Testimony of Guido Calabresi, Hear.91 2:249–56; GC; QI. Calabresi would not confirm that Johnstone was the professor who gave Thomas the low grade. However, since Johnstone stated that he sponsored Thomas and Hardy's paper, the inference is clear.

149 Hiring by Danforth: GC; JCD; Sp.Sav.F. 13–14; Sp.N.Dakota 436.

149 Interviews in Missouri: MB; Claudia MacLachlan, "Judge Thomas' Early Career," *National Law Journal,* 15 July 1991, p. 30; Karen Tumulty, "Court Path Started in the Ashes," *Los Angeles Times,* 7 July 1991, p. A1; Jill Lawrence, "The Product of a Classic Rags-to-Riches Tale," Associated Press wire story, 2 July 1991.

149 "I accepted that offer": Sp.KCBar 1.

150 Jamal: Charlotte Grimes, "Clarence Thomas: From Humble Start, He Set High Goals," *St. Louis Post-Dispatch,* 7 July 1991, p. 1A; Sontag, "Classmates."

150 Classmates "smirked": Sp.N.Dak. 436.

150 Yale law degree: Sp.Head. 16; Cas.Conv.

CHAPTER NINE: Apostle to the Rednecks

151 Danforth and Wilson: Hear.91 1:600 (testimony of M. B. Wilson).

151 "broken-down Volvo": RW.

152 "if you ever": Kauf.

152 Apartment: RW.

152 Danforth's election: JCD; RW; NNB. Missouri election information provided by the Missouri Secretary of State's Office.

153 First impressions: RW; MB.

153 First black attorney: JCD; MB. Given that the State of Missouri imposed segregation for almost a century after the Civil War and excluded blacks from the University of Missouri Law School, it is scarcely conceivable that another black attorney worked in the office before Thomas.

154 "$11,000 a year": Margolick, "Judge."

155 Office conditions: RW; Robert L. Koenig, "Danforth Powerhouse Grew in Leaky Cellar," *St. Louis Post-Dispatch,* 8 July 1991, p. 1B.

155 Thomas's office: MB.

155 Flag: NNB; MM; Robert L. Koenig, "Confederate or Georgian? Thomas' Flag Is Subject for Speculation," *St. Louis Post-Dispatch,* 16 July 1991, p. 9A; MacLachlan, "Judge." Wilson, "a southerner myself," said he asked Thomas about the desk flag. Thomas held out the flag so that Wilson could see the blue field and shield of the State of Georgia along the left-hand side of the flag. Thomas told Wilson,

"This flag flies from every courthouse, school and public building in my home state. Every black child in Georgia has to grow up under this flag. Think about that." Letter from S. Joel Wilson to the *New York Times,* 11 July 1991. This was obviously a different flag from the full-length Confederate flag that many witnesses saw in both Thomas's apartment at Yale and in his office in Missouri.

155 First oral argument: BushL (Bio. 13); Cas.Conv. 4.

155 Criminal appellate practice: Resp.Quest. 18–19.

156 *Missouri v. Torrence:* 519 S.W.2d 360 (Mo. App. 1975). The Senate Judiciary Committee requested that Thomas list his most important cases from the Missouri Attorney General's Office. One of the cases Thomas mentioned was *Torrence.* Resp.Quest. 18–19.

157 *Missouri v. Collins:* 519 S.W.2d 362 (1975).

157 "wonderful, deep voice": MB.

157 Boicourt and Weiler: MB; RW; Kap.; Speech to the Disabled Black Americans Conference, 11 February 1987, pp. 1–3.

158 Ashcroft: RW; MC; NNB. There is no evidence to support the allegation made in Jane Mayer and Jill Abramson's book *Strange Justice* (p. 68) that Thomas taunted Ashcroft with profanity. The quotations provided in *Strange Justice* do not support this claim. The only alleged source for this assertion is an interview of Andy Rothschild, an assistant attorney general at the time. Rothschild subsequently complained to journalist David Brock that he had been misquoted; the text of *Strange Justice* suggests that he was. Rothschild did not return telephone calls seeking an interview.

Others at the office strongly disputed Mayer and Abramson's account. Michael Boicourt, one of Thomas's closest friends in the office, said he could not recall any occasion when Thomas used profanity. He was certain he had not done so in Ashcroft's presence. Neil Bernstein, now a law professor at Washington University, said that although he occasionally heard Thomas use a curse word, such language was neither inordinate nor inappropriate for the company in which it was spoken. He greatly doubted that Thomas would have used profanity in Ashcroft's presence. Thomas, he said, would have known it to be "deeply offensive" to a powerful rising star in the office.

Ashcroft at first agreed to an interview for this book as long as the questions were submitted in writing. He subsequently declined to answer them. This writer served as an intern for then-Governor Ashcroft in the summer of 1986 while a student at the University of Missouri.

159 Snake story: RW.

160 Entertainment after hours: RW; MB.

160 Friends at work: MB; RW.

161 Christmas 1974: *Dan.* 6; JCD.

162 Sowell: Kauf.; Sp.Head. 11. Alex Netchvolodoff, one of Danforth's chief aides, told one reporter that Thomas became acquainted with Sowell at Yale. Netchvolodoff said that by the time Thomas arrived at Jefferson City, "much to our interest, he was already a disciple of Thomas Sowell." MacLachlan, "Career." Thomas also talked of being handed Sowell's book *Black Education* while at Yale, but of pitching it in the trash unread. Kauf. Thomas was at least familiar with Sowell by the time he arrived in Missouri. The discrepancy between Thomas's and Netchvolodoff's recollections on this point is curious. Netchvolodoff did not respond to a telephone request for an interview.

162 Review by Novak: Michael Novak, "Shattering the Cliches of Race," *Wall Street Journal,* 4 September 1975, p. 10.

162 "intellectual manna": Sp.Cato 7.

163 *Race and Economics: Sow.* v–vii, 10, 33, 98–100, 87–88,144–45, 201, 204.

164 Contacting Sowell: Kauf.; Sp.Head. 11.

164 "When I read": Cas.Conv.

164 Independent voting for Ford: Sp.Head. 12. One article reported that Thomas registered Republican in 1974. This information was either in error or based on different information provided by Thomas. Howard Kurtz, "Clarence Thomas; Skirting the Controversy of Civil Rights Policy," *Washington Post,* 22 September 1986, p. A15.

164 Thomas's politics: JCD; MB.

165 Thomas on race relations, Great Society: MB; RW.

165 Thomas on abortion: MB.

165 Representing dept. of revenue: RW.

166 *McKay Buick v. Spradling:* 529 S.W.2d 394 (Mo. 1975).

166 *L&R Distributing v. Missouri Dept. of Revenue:* 529 S.W.2d 375 (Mo. 1975).

166 *Missouri ex rel. Dyke v. Spradling:* 536 S.W.2d 839 (Mo. App. 1976).

166 Background on litigation strategy: Resp.Quest. 22; RW.; JCD.

167 Reputation as attorney: MB; NNB.

167 Record as attorney: Tom Charlier, "In Missouri, Young Thomas Won Respect, Shaped Law," *Memphis Commercial Appeal,* 8 July 1991, p. A1.

167 Lincoln Univ.: RW; Grimes, "Thomas."

167 Kathy: RW; MB; Sp.Head. 15 (Jamal had been in "private schools from the age of 2 on").

167 Walking to work "before dawn": Sp.Syr. 6.

167 Jamal: RW; Kap.; EMM.

167 "financially strapped": Sp.Syr. 5–6.

167 "It's time to pay off": Kap.

CHAPTER TEN: Money Isn't Everything

169 Putzell: NJP.

170 Duesenberg: Remarks of Richard Duesenberg, Transcript, Briefing on the Nomination of Clarence Thomas by the Washington Legal Foundation, 3 September 1991.

170 Pay at Monsanto: LDT.

170 Work at Monsanto: LDT; Resp.Quest. 15–18.

171 Quality of Thomas's work: NJP; LDT.

171 Reading self-help books: Sp.Syr. 10–11.

171 Thompson: LDT.

172 Holy Cross: JEB; Hear.91 2:62.

172 Black failure rate at Holy Cross: "Affirmative Action: Cure or Contradiction?" *The Center,* November-December 1987, pp. 20–28, 25.

173 St. Louis desegregation: AKD.

173 Discussions about race relations: LDT.

173 Thomas's reflections on 1970s: Speech to the State of Missouri Human Rights Conf., 20 May 1983, pp. 9–11.

173 "At a point": Kauf.

174   Complaints about work: LDT.

175   "I've got better things": Ibid.

175   Leaving Monsanto: NJP.

175   "I made a decision": Cas.Conv.

176   Senate Judiciary question: Resp.Quest. 39.

CHAPTER ELEVEN: The Coattails of St. Jack

177   Thomas's Senate office: EJ.

177   Work duties: Resp.Quest. 16.

177   "great job": Cas.Conv.

178   "What is the right": Sp.Syr. 5.

178   "clearly the most popular": *Dan.* 7.

178   Alvarez: Hear.91 2:8.

178   Hatch, Bush: OH; EJ. When asked how he came to know Thomas, Bush replied:
        "I came to know Clarence as his name began surfacing for the Supreme Court. I
        knew him by reputation before that." GHWB. Jenkins and a senior White House
        official in the Bush administration offer a different and more persuasive account.
        They gave a timeline that suggests Thomas came to know Bush slightly during
        his tenure with Danforth, and then far better during Bush's 1988 presidential
        campaign.

179   Singleton: AJC. The conversation took place after Singleton succeeded Thomas at
        the Dept. of Education.

179   Farrington: FF.

179   Parties in Washington: EJ.

179   *St. Louis Post-Dispatch:* Grimes, "Thomas."

180   Jay Parker: Sp.Head. 10–12; Kap.; biographical information on Parker in "Black
        America under the Reagan Administration: A Symposium of Black Conserva-
        tives," *Policy Review,* Fall 1985, pp. 27–41, 29.

180   "Goodbye, Clarence": JCD.

180   Invitation to Fairmont Conf.: Sp.Her.87 1–6; Sp.Head 12.

181   Juan Williams: Juan Williams, "Black Conservatives, Center Stage," *Washington
        Post,* 16 December 1980, p. A21.

181   "wandered in the desert": Sp.Her.87 6.

181   Thomas's remarks at Fairmont: *Fairmont Papers* 81–83.

182   Sister on welfare: Williams, "Black"; EMM.

182   "accurate, but unfortunate": Memorandum from Clarence Thomas to Fred
        Abramson, 12 October 1989, Paoletta Master Briefing Book, p. 13 (BushL).

183   "the most interesting": Will.

183   "All of a sudden": Kauf.

183   "resulting outcry": Sp.Her.87 6–7.

184   Meese: EM.

184   Memo of 12/22/80 to Parker: Liberman file, BushL.

185   Offer for OCR: WBR.

186   Thomas "insulted": Sp.Her.87 6–7; Kauf.

186   "eaten crow": Memo to Abramson, BushL.

187 Hill biographical info.: *Hill* 15–47. Through her secretary at Brandeis University, Hill declined to be interviewed for this book. The author also asked Hill by e-mail if there were any relatives, friends, or associates Hill believed the author should interview, and, if so, could she provide their names and telephone numbers or e-mail addresses. Hill did not respond to this e-mail.

187 Hill at law firm: Ibid., 55–60; David Brock, *The Real Anita Hill* (New York: Free Press, 1993), pp. 219–24 [hereinafter *Bro.*] (partners' recollections of Hill). Thomas' "bad breath" comment was in *Dan.* 37. When this memorable halitosis first made its presence known is unclear; the narrative assumes that this was Thomas' first impression, as first impressions last.

CHAPTER TWELVE: Call It Stormy Monday

193 Theodore White: Theodore H. White, *America in Search of Itself: The Making of the President 1956–1980* (New York: Harper & Row, 1982), pp. 5, 130–35.

193 OCR data: Resp.Quest. 3; Hear.91 1:334.

193 Middleton: MM.

195 Califa: AJC.

195 Hill: *Hill* 68; Resp.Quest. 43. Thomas has stated that he vaguely remembers Gil Hardy telling him—and Hill subsequently confirming—that she was experiencing sexual harassment at Wald, Harkrader when she decided to leave. His recollection was that a partner wanted to have a personal relationship with her outside the office; she refused; the partner responded by withholding good work assignments and giving her work negative reviews. Diane Holt had a similarly murky recollection. *Dan.* 35. Hill may well have made these allegations; her life was basically a stream of frivolous complaints against former employers and associates. Still, she does not mention this mistreatment in her book, even amid plenty of other criticisms of the firm. One also wonders why, if she mentioned this, Thomas—then one of the nation's leading civil rights enforcers—did not urge her to file a civil rights complaint against her former employer.

196 "Within a month": Sp.Clark 4.

197 "I refused": Ibid. 5.

197 Bilingual education: MM; AJC.

197 Mentally retarded: Speech to the Urban League, 18 June 1985, p. 5.

197 *Adams v. Bell: Women's Equity Action League v. Cavazos*, 906 F.2d 742, 744 (D.C. Cir. 1990); see also *Adams v. Matthews*, 536 F.2d 417 (D.C. Cir. 1976); *Adams v. Bell*, 711 F.2d 161 (D.C. Cir. 1983). Excerpts from Thomas's deposition taken from Terence Moran, "When Clarence Thomas Defied a Judge," *Legal Times*, 19 August 1991, p. 1.

198 Compliance with *Adams:* Hear.91 1:331–35; "Adams v. Bell Litigation," Master Briefing Book for Senate Judiciary Committee Minority Staff (Paoletta file, BushL).

198 Questioning of Thomas: Moran, "Defied."

200 Ride home for Califa: AJC.

200 Meetings with Reynolds, Horowitz: WBR; MJH; MM.

202 "The emphasis": Sp.Her.87 8–9.

202 Voting Rights Act: Charles R. Babcock, "White House Delays Taking Stand on Voting Rights Act Extension," *Washington Post*, 30 June 1981, p. A7; Sp.Her. 9–10.

203 Action against Alabama: 5 January 1982 news release (Paoletta file, BushL); Charles R. Babcock, "U.S. to Press Alabama on College Desegregation," *Washington Post*, 6 January 1982, p. A21.

204 Bob Jones U: Sp.Her.87 9–10; Lee Lescaze and Charles R. Babcock, "Reagan Submits Bill Denying Tax Breaks to Segregated Schools," *Washington Post*, 19 January 1982, p. A1; *Bob Jones University v. United States*, 461 U.S. 574 (1983).

204 "Fiasco": Interview with Clarence Thomas, "'Job Discrimination Is Still Very, Very Serious,'" *U.S. News & World Report*, 14 March 1983, pp. 67–68.

205 Thomas's management style: MM; AJC. Califa's memory of Thomas's management skills and work ethic differed sharply from Middleton's. "He wasn't a workaholic at Education," Califa said. He called him "very disengaged," and thought he spent a good deal of time "working out at the gym." Weightlifting still was a strong avocation of Thomas's; he typically would work out at the nearby NASA gym over the lunch hour, then grab a takeout lunch or have his secretary procure lunch, then eat it at his desk. But Califa is the only person to have accused Thomas of such laziness during his time with the federal government. Most of the time, Thomas was accused of the opposite extreme—obsessive overwork.

It is likely that Califa's own discouragement at not being promoted by Thomas influenced his recollections. Also, Thomas was holed up in his office frequently; few except for Middleton saw enough of him to assess his daily routine. Both are possible explanations for this disparate view of his work habits.

205 "isolated": Sp.T.Bar. 7.

206 Hill at OCR: Hear.91 4:36–40; *Hill* 68; *Dan.* 36; *Hill* 70.

207 Meeting with Benjamin Hooks: MM. Thomas' aides in later years heard him tell the story of how, early in his tenure with the Reagan administration, he once kicked representatives of the NAACP out of his office. Middleton never heard this anecdote and doubted its accuracy. While Thomas might have cut a meeting short with a group that he thought was being overly critical of him, Middleton could not imagine that he would have "stood up and said, 'Get out.'" The story appears to have been an embellishment.

207 "cacophony": Sp.T.Bar 7.

207 "Here's a strange black": Kim Masters, "EEOC's Thomas: Ready to Sing a Different Tune?" *Legal Times*, 24 December-31 December 1984, p. 2.

208 Reaction to media: Sp.Her.87 8, 11.

208 Legal Times *reporter: Masters, "Ready."*

208 Charles Murray: *Losing Ground: American Social Policy, 1950–1980* (New York: Basic Books, 1984), p. 220.

209 Discussions of welfare, Supreme Court: MM. Samuel Pierce, the secretary of Housing and Urban Development, was actually the highest-ranking black official in the Reagan administration with a law degree.

210 William Bell: Herbert H. Denton, "Reagan EEOC Nominee under Attack," *Washington Post*, 4 November 1981, p. A1; Terence Moran, "Clarence Thomas, Fitting No Mold," *Legal Times*, 16 October 1989, p. 1; EM.

210 "My reaction": Sp.Casc. 1.

210 Staff meeting on EEOC appt.: AJC; *Dan.* 38 (re Holt and Hill).

210 Thompson: LDT.

CHAPTER THIRTEEN: A New Sheriff in Town

211 First day at EEOC: Sp.Casc. 1.

212 "shambles": Sp.ASPA 2–10; Sp.Casc. 2.

212 Work conditions: Ibid.; PBL.

213 Files in ceiling and telephone directory: PBL.

213 OMB analysis: Sp.ASPA 9–10.

214 GAO Report: Comptroller General, Report to the Chairman, Committee on Labor and Human Resources, United States Senate, "Continuing Financial Management Problems at the Equal Employment Opportunity Commission," 17 May 1982, pp. i-iii.

214 First meeting: Moran, "Fitting."

214 Executive director: Sp.ASPA 12–13.

214 Personal staff: AKD; MM;

215 "the first person I hired": Higgins, "Enforce."

215 Hill's work: Hear.91 4:53–54, 166, 36–40.

215 Duncan's work: AKD.

217 Alvarez on Thomas's advisers: Hear.91 2:9.

217 Willie King: WK. Her role as amanuensis for Martin Luther King is mentioned in Taylor Branch, *Parting the Waters: America in the King Years, 1954–63* (New York: Simon & Schuster, 1988), p. 744.

218 Agency goals: Sp.ASPA 16–20; Sp.HHS 22.

219 Relations with employees: WBR; CS; JIZ; AW; WK.

220 Leadership skills: MM.

221 Videotapes of early speeches: *Phe.* 94.

221 "Clarence is like a 1960s student": Masters, "Ready."

221 "I don't fit in": Ibid.

222 "monastic recluse": Sp.Casc. 16.

222 Social awkwardness: MM; AKD.

222 Lillian McEwen: AKD.

223 Rapid charge system: Sp.Casc. 7–11.

223 "strict law and order": Sp.KCBar 15, 23.

224 "civil rights statutes will not": Speech to the American Bar Assn. EEO Cmte., Sarasota, Fla., March 1983, p. 10.

224 Treble damages: Sp.Cap.Press 12.

224 "As you can expect": Sp.Geor. 11–13.

224 Denial of access to civil rights groups: JM.

224 "Crying on shoulder" of grandfather: Ros.

224 Talk with grandparents about Republicans: Unidentified speech, Liberman file, BushL. The time and place where Thomas gave this speech are unclear. Apparently, he delivered it to a Republican gathering, either in 1984 or, more likely, 1988. The speech is written in Thomas's distinctive and beautiful handwriting.

225 Armstrong Williams: Phil McCombs, "The Jester Weeps for King," *Washington Post*, 15 January 1983, p. C1; AW.

226 First year statistics: Sp.ASPA 15–16.

226 "Doesn't sound very exciting": Sp.Casc. 5.

CHAPTER FOURTEEN: Turkey Shoot

227 "Turkey farm": MM.

227 $4,000 employee: *Phe.* 93.

227 Civil service rules: The laws governing civil service protections are scattered throughout the United States Code and the Code of Federal Regulations. Some of the more relevant provisions are 42 U.S.C. 4303 *et seq.* and 5 C.F.R. 1201 *et seq.*

228 Thomas's management style: MM; AW.

228 "Walk and shock": AW.

229 Criticizing union and civil service system: Sp.Casc. 6, 10–11.

229 Frank Quinn: Hear.90 351; Aric Press, Phylis Malamud, Diane Camper, and Peggy Clausen, "Quotas under Attack," *Newsweek,* 25 April 1983, p. 95.

229 Thomas on competence: CS; other interviews by the author.

230 Sowell lectures: AKD.

230 Improvements at agency: Talking Points, 4 November 1983, in Liberman file, BushL; Speech to the National Assn. of Black MBAs, 6 October 1983, p. 6.

230 Myers Anderson: Sp.Cent 4–5 ("I am satisfied"); Sp.Bl.Nurses 5; death certificate of Myers Anderson; funeral bulletin provided by Leola Thomas Williams.

231 "No levee": Sp.St.P. 2.

231 Reaction to Anderson's death: Sp.T.Bar 8; Sp.Bl.Nurses 5.

231 Religious experience: Sp.T.Bar 8–9.

232 "God is all right": Will.

232 "When the civil-rights people": Ibid.

233 Hill's skills at EEOC: Hear.91 4:166–69, 220–22; MM.

233 Hill's indolence: *Dan.* 38; interviews by the author.

233 Trying to win attention from Thomas: AW; *Bro.* 307.

233 Tension and debates with Hill: Hear.91 4:166–69, 358 (Berry Myers); AW.

234 Alvarez: Hear.91 4:359–60, 337–42.

234 Hill portraying special relationship with Thomas: Ibid.; WK.

234 Hill vs. Duncan: AKD. Duncan stated that during her years of working with Thomas, she saw no evidence of what she would consider sexual harassment by Thomas.

235 Pitting employees against one another: AKD; SH.

235 Hill losing to Duncan: WK; *Bro.* 316–17.

235 Keeping a log: *Dan.* 39.

235 Hill and Reynolds: WBR.

236 Hill and Kothe: Hear.91 4:90, 169; *Hill* 80–81; Letter from Gilbert E. Hardy to Charles A. Kothe, 13 May 1983, Liberman file, BushL; Letter from Clarence Thomas to Charles A. Kothe, 31 May 1983, Liberman file, BushL.

237 Williams' warning regarding Hill: *Dan.* 38–39.

237 *Williams v. City of New Orleans:* 729 F.2d 1554 (5th Cir. 1984).

238 Controversy over *Williams* amicus brief: TBO; JIZ; MJH; WBR; "EEOC Seeks to Avoid Future Freezeout by Justice," *Legal Times,* 18 April 1983, p. 7; Barbara Rosewicz, "EEOC Chief Defends His Independence," U.P.I. wire story, 27 October 1983.

238 "the only conflict": Rosewicz, "EEOC Chief."

238 Fried: CF.

239 Thomas vs. Reynolds: AW; MM; WBR.

239 Urban League Panel discussion: Juan Williams, "EEOC Chief Faults Administration on Curbing Bias," *Washington Post*, 3 August 1983, p. A2.

239 "Don't tell me": Will.

239 "saving yourself for": MJH. At the conclusion of several discussions with the author, Horowitz added the following explanation for this remark to Thomas: "In all those years I dealt with him, as I would urge him to be a more overt change agent, and there would often be a cautious resistance, what is now clear to me is that a central issue for Clarence Thomas was that nobody was ever going to lynch him.... When he did that [made this remark], it had nothing to do with saving himself [for advancement]. It was just that nobody was going to lynch him or manipulate him." This disclaimer is unpersuasive for several reasons. The remark was not, "Clarence, what are you saving yourself *from*"—a comment that might be construed as consistent with this explanation. It was clearly a rebuke to Thomas for placing his own political self-preservation above the administration's agenda. Moreover, it was well known to Jeff Zuckerman, Middleton, and other high-level sources in the administration and EEOC that Thomas and Horowitz had a frosty relationship that became quite contentious in late 1984. Horowitz's disclaimer, in the author's estimation, is disingenuous.

240 "the hounds": Sp.Casc. 3.

240 "perception problem": "E.E.O.C. Chief Cites Trouble in Resolving Some Job Bias Cases," *New York Times*, 2 June 1983, p. B9.

240 Justice Dept. affirmative action plan: "Justice, EEOC Wrangle over Jobs Plan," Associated Press, 7 September 1983.

241 James Watt: Elizabeth Neus, "EEOC Chairman Says Watt's Comment Symptomatic of Washington Problem," U.P.I. wire story, 7 October 1983.

241 "a lot of racists": Will.

242 Public statements on affirmative action: David E. Anderson, untitled U.P.I. wire story, 31 March 1982; "The Conservative at the EEOC," *Business Week*, 9 August 1982, pp. 54–55; Interview with Clarence Thomas, "'Job Discrimination Is Still Very, Very Serious,'" *U.S. News & World Report*, 14 March 1983, pp. 67–68; Sp.Chicago 15; Sp.Census 5.2.83 19; Sp.HHS11.16.83 14; Speech to the Litigation Programs Conference, 13 January 1983, pp.14–15, 20.

242 Thomas Sowell on racial resentment: Thomas Sowell, *The Economics and Politics of Race* (New York: William Morrow, 1983), pp. 253–54.

244 Thomas a "conservative": Sp.KCBar 13; Speech to the National Chamber Litigation Center, 17 January 1985, p. 3; Cas.Conv. (denying that he is a conservative).

244 Observations about Thomas's views: AW; RGS; WBR.

245 "training film": KM.

245 Rand's objectivism: *Rand* 23–33.

246 Thomas's conservatism: Sp.KCBar 13.

246 Thomas's early legal philosophy: WBR; AW.

247 Thomas on Framers' racial views: Sp.Columbia 1–2.

247 *Dred Scott:* Sp.U.Va. 3.

248 "zapped": Sp.ANPA 14.

248 Shyness: AW.

248 Lighter-skinned blacks: MM; interviews by the author. Sowell's discussion is in *Sow.* 40–41.

249 Bennett vs. Thomas: Phil McCombs, "NEH Chief Rejects Job Rules," *Washington Post*, 19 January 1984, p. D1; JIZ.

249 Slate vs. Thomas: Juan Williams, "Improper Handling of EEOC Cases Charged," *Washington Post,* 8 February 1984, p. A5; JIZ. Slate did not respond to a telephone request for an interview.

250 Congressional hearings: *Bro.* 91–92 (quoting Bolick); Merrill Hartson, "Civil Rights Figure Explains Refusal to Testify," Associated Press wire story, 13 March 1984.

250 Vagrant: "Old Man Can't."

251 Divorce: Woodlief, "Former In-Law"; Hammel, "Thomas" ("wonderful friend"); EJ; Allen Moore, "The Clarence Thomas I Know," *Washington Post,* 16 July 1991, p. A19.

CHAPTER FIFTEEN: Running for a Second Term

253 Alvarez and Gallegos: CB.

253 References to Hispanics in speeches: Speech at EEO Conference in the Caribbean, 9 May 1984, p.6; Speech at EEOC Senior Executive Seminar, 12 September 1983, p. 3; Speech at EEOC Seminar, Denver, Colo., 12 September 1984, pp. 5–6.

254 Commission meetings: CS; RGS; CB.

255 Father's Day speech: Sp.Cent.

257 Zuckerman: JIZ.

258 GOP Convention: AW; Sandra Evans and Tom Sherwood, "Blacks Seek to Make Presence Felt, Build Party Alternative," *Washington Post,* 22 August 1984, p. A6.

258 Thomas and Reagan: EM; RW.

259 Pre-election speech: Speech to the National AEP Conference, 22 October 1984, pp. 6–7.

259 "moan and whine": Juan Williams, "EEOC Chairman Blasts Black Leaders," *Washington Post,* 25 October 1984, p. A7.

260 November meeting in White House: WBR; MJH; MM. Horowitz stated that he did not remember the meeting with Thomas. However, he said he held several meetings at around that time encouraging bold action in the new administration. The substance of his talks remained the same. Reynolds remembered the meeting distinctly. The account of the meeting combines Horowitz's standard, post-election "pep talk" with Reynolds' account. Thomas also related the gist of the meeting to Middleton. Middleton remembered it well; indeed, he left EEOC because of the announced change in Thomas's public policy.

261 Middleton's departure: MM. Sukari Hardnett said Middleton told her before he left EEOC of Thomas' fateful meeting at the White House and the ensuing change in policy.

261 "Survival": Jacqueline Trescott, "Issues amid Festivities," *Washington Post,* 21 January 1985, p. C3.

262 Legal Times: *Masters, "Ready."*

262 Interest groups notice change: Howard Kurtz, "Clarence Thomas; Skirting the Controversy of Civil Rights Policy," *Washington Post,* 22 September 1986, p. A15.

262 *New York Times* article: Robert Pear, "Changes Weighed in Federal Rules on Discrimination," *New York Times,* 3 December 1984, p. A1.

263 National Chamber speech: Sp.Chamber 3–4, 15.

264 *Meritor Savings Bank v. Vinson:* 477 U.S. 57 (1986).

265 Thomas's lobbying efforts re *Vinson:* CF.

265 Angela Wright: WK; Memorandum from Angela Wright to Kate Semerad, Liberman file, BushL; *Bro.* 260–62 (Diane Holt); AW. Wright did not respond to a telephone request for an interview.

266 Firing of Angela Wright: PT; AW; CB; interviews of other EEOC employees; 1 March 1985, letter from Thomas to Wright, Liberman file, BushL.

267 Rose Jourdain: *Phe.* 362; JIZ; Speech to the Southwestern Legal Foundation, 18 October 1985, pp. 15–16.

267 Anita Hill's entreaties: JIZ.

267 Critique of racial preferences: Sp.Southw. 23–24.

268 Savannah State College: Sp.Sav.C.

269 Convent now halfway house: Sp.Syr. 7.

269 Comparable worth: "'Comparable Worth' Theory Loses Ground," Associated Press wire story, 6 January 1985, p. C14; Carol Kleiman, "Changes at EEOC Spell Trouble, Attorney Says," *Chicago Tribune,* 26 August 1985, p. C17.

269 Review of UGESP: Speech to the American Bar Assn., 3 May 1984, p.16; JIZ.

270 Proposed repeal of Executive Order 11246: Howard Kurtz, "Affirmative Action Policy Gains a Reprieve," *Washington Post,* 25 October 1985, p. A1.

270 Business support of affirmative action: Anne B. Fisher, "Businessmen Like to Hire by the Numbers," *Fortune,* 16 September 1985, p. 26.

271 Cabinet council meeting: Kurtz, "Affirmative"; JIZ.

271 Clint Bolick: CB.

271 Thomas on lazy employees: Sp.Southw. 14.

272 "Some heads are gonna roll!": JIZ. In *Strange Justice,* Mayer and Abramson state that Zuckerman was Thomas's sidekick when he made such announcements in the hallways. (p. 141). Zuckerman described this as "claptrap," and explained persuasively that Johnny Butler accompanied Thomas. Zuckerman recalled: "Basically, what he did was, he would go wandering around the agency, just chatting with people. The last thing in the world that he could've used in his trips around the agency was this white guy who was reputed to be Brad Reynolds' henchman as his accompaniment. I understood that. That didn't hurt me. He would come back and tell me what people had said.... The notion that I would go around the halls with him is absolutely nuts."

272ff Sukari Hardnett: SH.

274 Jamal's question about career: Speech to the EEO Coordinators Assn., 10 July 1985, p. 3.

275 Discussion with Danforth: Hear.90 25; *Dan.* 7. In his Senate testimony during Thomas's nomination to the court of appeals, and his 1994 book *Resurrection,* Danforth gave two slightly different versions of Thomas's response to his question about remaining at EEOC. Danforth's memory on incidental details such as this has proved fuzzy. As the latter response by Thomas is more similar to what Thomas told Dick Leon and others, it is the one chosen for the text.

275 Discussion with Leon: RJL.

276 Registered Republican: Resp.Quest. 7.

276 Letter to Reagan: Letter from Clarence Thomas to President Reagan, 6 February 1986, Liberman file, BushL.

279 Senate rejection of Reynolds *et al.:* Glen Elsasser, "Reagan's Nominee Rejected," *Chicago Tribune,* 28 June 1985, p. C1; Howard Kurtz, "Reagan Pick for Judgeship Is Rejected," *Washington Post,* 6 June 1986, p. A1.

280   Clarence Pendleton: "This Clarence is the One with the 'Bor-r-ring' Style," *Los Angeles Times*, 24 April 1986, part 1, p. 31; Sp.Casc. 17.

281   *Legal Times* on affirmative action: Masters, "Ready." The 1979 case was *United Steelworkers of America v. Weber*, 443 U.S. 193 (1979).

281   Quayle on Metzenbaum: JDQ.

282ff Reconfirmation hearings: Hear.86 1, 8–10, 44–46, 55–56.

284   Reconfirmation vote: Lena Williams, "Equal Employment Official Wins Approval for 2d Term," *New York Times*, 7 August 1986, p. A19.

CHAPTER SIXTEEN: Thomas Becomes a Conservative

285   "The best thing": Sp.T.Bar 6.

285   Second swearing-in: Will.; interviews of EEOC employees. Williams stated that he left EEOC for unrelated reasons.

286ff Masugi: PBL; KM.

288   Masugi memo re Marini: Memorandum from Ken Masugi to Clarence Thomas, 5 February 1987, Masugi file.

288   Marini: KM; JM.

289   Talkin: PT.

289   Diversity of staff: Resp.Quest. 43.

290   Thomas on staff meetings: Sp.Chur. 3; Sp.Merc. 14.

290   Openness to ideas: PBL.

290   Reading: PT; JM.

291   ADL Conference: JIZ.

291   Virginia "Ginni" Lamp: JIZ; CB; Laura Blumenfeld, "The Nominee's Soul Mate," *Washington Post*, 10 September 1991, p. F1.

292   "black female friends" and "pool of butter": Ed Henry, "Virginia Thomas: Escaping Her Husband's Shadow," *Roll Call*, 20 May 1996.

293   "in love": Blumenfeld, "Nominee's"; David Margolick, "Nuns' Push Set Thomas on Road to Achieving," *New York Times*, 5 July 1991, p. A1.

293   Reaction to relationship: Michael Hedges and Jerry Seper, "Clarence Thomas: Winning over Skeptics on Job, in Life," *Washington Times*, 4 July 1991, p. E1; Blumenfeld, "Nominee's"; interview of former staffer for Nebraska congressman.

293   Nat'l Press Club speech: Memoranda in Masugi file; Isaiah J. Poole and Thomas D. Brandt, "EEOC Chairman Rips Republicans for Ignoring Blacks," *Washington Times*, 20 November 1986, p. A1.

294   Working Group on Family: White House Working Group on the Family, *The Family: Preserving America's Future*, December 1986, Liberman file, BushL.

295   Juan Williams: Will.

295   Thomas on J. Williams: Sp.Head. 13.

296   Editorial: "The EEOC Is Thriving," *Washington Post*, 1 August 1987, p. A22.

296   Lyons: PBL.

297   "You don't see": Masters, "Ready."

297   Jamal and Ginni: Blumenfeld, "Nominee's."

298   "I was not yet ready": Memorandum from Thomas to Fred Abramson, 12 October 1989, in Paoletta Master Briefing Book, p. 13, Paoletta file, BushL.

298   Myers Anderson's philosophy: JM.

298 Thomas's philosophy: CB; KM.

298 Thomas on Bloom: Sp.Pac. 1.

299 Distrust of government: Sp.Cato 5–8.

300 Economic liberty: Sp.Pac. 4.

300 Business and tax codes: KM; PBL.

301 Individual rights: Sp.Chicago 6; Sp.Ga.So. 4

301 Too many rights: Sp.Pac. 6–10.

301 Speeches: Sp.Cato; Sp.Her.87.

302 Yale Law article: Clarence Thomas, "Affirmative Action Goals and Timetables: Too Tough? Not Tough Enough!" *Yale Law & Policy Review,* Spring/Summer 1987, pp. 402–11.

303 Review of Bolick book: Clarence Thomas, "A Second Emancipation Proclamation," *Policy Review,* Summer 1988, p. 84–85.

303 *Reason* interview: Kauf.

305 Stanley Grayson: Cullen, "Complex."

306 Thomas on natural law: Sp.Ga.So. 6; Sp.Her.87 23; Sp.Pac. 12–13.

306 Early thoughts on Dec. of Indep.: Sp.ANPA 4.

306 Jaffa: HJ.

307 Strauss's *Natural: Str.* 1–3.

307 Jaffa's *Crisis: Jaf.* 2–3.

308 Jaffa on *Dred Scott:* Harry Jaffa, *Original Intent and the Framers of the Constitution: A Disputed Question* (Washington: Regnery, 1994), pp. 13–54.

308 *Howard Law Journal:* Clarence Thomas, "Toward a 'Plain Reading' of the Constitution: The Declaration of Independence in Constitutional Interpretation," *Howard Law Journal* 30 (1987): 691–703.

309 "Now I realize": Sp.Pac. 15.

309 Thomas on North: KM.

309 Thomas on Bork: Sp.Pac. 15–16.

310 Age cases: PT.

311 Scathing memo: Jim Schachter, "900 Age Bias Cases Botched by U.S. Agency," *Los Angeles Times,* 8 January 1988, part 1, p. 1.

311 "unusual assessment": "900 Age Cases Died Wrongly, Agency Chief Says," *New York Times,* 29 January 1988, p. A36.

311 *Chicago Tribune:* Editorial, "Without Doubt, a Thomas of Merit," *Chicago Tribune,* 30 January 1988, p. C8.

312 EEOC finances: "EEOC: 1982 to the Present," December 1988, p.7, Masugi file; Litigation Performance, FY 1982, 1986 and FY 1989, table in Hear.90 339.

312 New offices: PBL; PT; "Bureaucracy: Putting on the Ritz," *Time,* 26 September 1988, p. 31.

313 Speech to People of Color Rally: Paoletta file, BushL.

CHAPTER SEVENTEEN: Cloistered, Again

315 Willie King: WK; Hear.90 150.

315 "Pure and simple": Sp.Gold 4.

315 Financial dreams and prospects: RGL; JM; RJL.

316 Entering politics: JM; AW; Kauf.

316 "A seat": Kap.

317 Uhlmann: David Brock, "Strange Lies," *American Spectator,* January 1995, pp. 30–41 (confirmed in e-mail from Uhlmann to the author).

317 Opportunity on D.C. Circuit: RGS; LLO; CB.

318 Thomas weighs the offer: RJL; RGS; LHS. Silberman repudiated his earlier work on goals and timetables in Laurence H. Silberman, "The Road to Racial Quotas," *Wall Street Journal,* 11 August 1977.

318 Stepping stone to Supreme Court: JM; Resp.Quest. 41. In an interview, Bush said he did not recall conversations with Thomas "relating to his nomination to the appeals bench." However, Bush also admitted a lack of memory generally about his relationship with Thomas.

319 Alliance for Justice letter: Liberman file, BushL.

320 Coleman letter: Ibid.

320 Biden letter and document requests: Ibid.; "Sen. Biden Checks a Judicial Nominee" and "The Next Lynching," *Wall Street Journal,* 17 January 1990, p. A20.

320 Morning of February 6: Sp.St.P. 3.

320ff Confirmation hearings: Hear.90 27–30, 36–37, 47–48, 165, 175–78, 181–95.

325 "alarming lack of knowledge": Neil A. Lewis, "Metzenbaum Weighs in against Court Nominee," *New York Times,* 22 February 1990, p. A18.

325 "eleven months": Speech at Wiley, Rein & Fielding luncheon, 29 June 1990, p. 1, Liberman file, BushL.

325f Thomas's departure: WK.

327 "But for the grace of God": Hear.91 1:260.

327 "Sublime" and "cloistered": Sp.Ec.Club 1; Sp.Wiley 2.

327 "people person": JCD.

328 Interviewing clerks: Sp.Ireton.

328 Racial and gender breakdown: Resp.Quest. 44.

328 Relationship with clerks and guards: Interviews of clerks and guards.

328 Fellow judges' impressions: "How ABA Came to Call Thomas 'Qualified,'" *Legal Times,* 23 September 1991, pp. 12–13.

328 Jurisprudence: RGL; LHS.

329 *United States v. Poston:* 902 F.2d 90 (D.C. Cir. 1990).

329 *United States v. Rogers:* 918 F.2d 207 (D.C. Cir. 1990).

330 *United States v. Halliman:* 923 F.2d 873 (D.C. Cir. 1991).

331 *United States v. Long:* 905 F.2d 1572 (D.C. Cir. 1990).

332 *National Treasury Employees Union v. United States:* 927 F.2d 1253 (D.C. Cir. 1991).

332 Thomas's caseload: LHS; interviews of clerks.

332 "tremendous preparation": Sp.Ec.Club 12.

333 Generally quiet in oral argument: Interviews of clerks; Verbatim, "'Promoting Diversity for Diversity's Sake,'" *Legal Times,* 15 July 1991, pp. 10–12.

333 Clarence Morales: Terence Moran, "Reconciling Nominee's Values and Experience," *New Jersey Law Journal,* 11 July 1991, p. 4; *United States v. Lopez,* 938 F.2d 1293 (D.C. Cir. 1991).

334 *Lamprecht* oral argument: Verbatim, "Promoting."

335 Anita Hill conversation: *Dan.* 66; telephone logs in Liberman file, BushL; interviews by the author.

336 Savannah State: Sp.Sav.F. 1–8.

336 Jamal and his graduation: Tumulty, "Court Path"; Woodlief, "Former In-Law"; *Dan.* 151; WK; FF.

337 Conversation with Gray: *Phe.* 1–3.

337 National Review: "Off the Record," *National Review,* 19 March 1990, p. 64.

337 Quayle: JDQ.

338 Benton: Tom Charlier, "In Missouri, Young Thomas Won Respect, Shaped Law," *Memphis Commercial Appeal,* 8 July 1991, p. A1.

338 Farrington: FF.

338 Holy Cross reunion: RJL.

338 "moral certainty": Sp.HC 96 1.

CHAPTER EIGHTEEN: One of Us

341 Epigraphs at the beginning of the chapters in Part Five are from Joel Chandler Harris, "The Wonderful Tar-Baby Story," in *Brer Rabbit: Stories by Uncle Remus* (New York: Harper & Row, 1941), pp. 6–11. The original nineteenth-century dialect has been modified slightly for clarity.

341 News of Marshall's resignation: *Dan.* 1.

341 Meeting at DOJ: Ibid., pp. 2–3; Joan Biskupic, "Thomas Recalls His Reluctant Journey," *Washington Post,* 2 August 1999, p. A17.

342 Sununu-Jipping communications: Thomas L. Jipping, "'Judge Thomas Is the First Choice': The Case for Clarence Thomas," *Regent University Law Review* 12 (1999–2000): 397–401; Interview of Thomas L. Jipping. Jipping has noted that both David Brock and Mayer and Abramson misinterpreted these communications. Jipping, "'Judge Thomas,'" pp. 398–99 n.10. Brock alleged that Jipping's memo was "likely written in a self-serving manner, designed to foster the impression that…Jipping was more powerful than he was." Brock, "Strange Lies," p. 37. He also claimed that "inside" legal advisers already had made the decision to nominate Thomas. The allegations of self-flattery are unkind and misplaced. Sununu specifically solicited the memo from Jipping. The claim that Thomas's nomination was wholly preordained also is inaccurate. Quayle, Gray, Liberman and others have made clear that Bush did not make his decision until several days after Marshall's announcement, and after much internal wrangling. Whatever assurances Bush had given Thomas previously about a promotion to the Supreme Court, his subsequent deliberations over the appointment appear to have been sincere.

Mayer and Abramson contrived that Thomas's nomination was part of an "unusual IOU" that the White House owed Jipping. Bush and Sununu, in consulting Jipping and appointing Thomas, were "making good" on that "deal." Mayer and Abramson, *Strange Justice,* pp. 11–14. Jipping dismisses this convincingly as "almost laughable." Instead of fulfilling a quid pro quo, Sununu was merely following the administration's own, self-dictated political strategy—which Sununu had candidly shared with Jipping the year before—of enlisting help from Free Congress Foundation and other grassroots organizations for the tough confirmation fight that lay in store for any staunchly conservative nominee.

Jipping, for his part, errs in arguing that his organization was critical to Thomas's confirmation. The assistance was helpful but certainly not indispensable. African-American support was decisive for Thomas's confirmation. Bush was not beholden to a relatively obscure lobby such as Free Congress Foundation for anything, certainly not something as important as a Supreme Court nomination.

342   Quayle-Danforth communication: JDQ; JCD; Dan Quayle, *Standing Firm* (New York: HarperCollins, 1994), p. 267.

343   Trip to White House: Biskupic, "Thomas Recalls."

343   Bush's meeting with advisers: *Phe.* 4–5.

344   Call from Bush: Biskupic, "Thomas Recalls"; Sp.Gold. 4.

344   Disinformation to Mikva: LHS. Mikva did not respond to a telephone request for an interview.

344   Meeting at Kennebunkport: Biskupic, "Thomas Recalls"; Margaret Carlson, "Marching to a Different Drummer," *Time,* 15 July 1991, p. 19; *Phe.* 13; Sp.Gold. 4–5.

345ff   Press conference: Transcript of same.

347   Meese: EM.

347   Thomas friend re Marshall seat: Interview of Thomas friend.

348   Leola Thomas Williams: Paula Chin and Gail Wescott, "The Making of a Judge," *Time,* 22 July 1991, p. 40.

348   "feeding frenzy": Interview of Mark Savolis.

348   Edwards' cake: Interview of John McConnell (recounting story from Arnon Siegel, Thomas clerk). Edwards did not respond to a telephone request for an interview.

348   "fear in the pit": Rob.

348   Call from Danforth: *Dan.* 8.

349   Fear of being killed: Ibid., pp. 10–11.

349   July 4 meeting: Interviews by the author.

350   Three pro-Thomas groups: *Phe.* 71–72; *Dan.* 15; interviews by the author.

350   NARAL and NOW: *Phe.* 18; *Bro.* 61.

351   Giving up the news: *Dan.* 11.

351   Arch Parsons: *Phe.* 7.

351   Hooks and NAACP: *Phe.* 7–12, 29–30.

351   John Jacobs: Steven A. Holmes, "Black Quandary over Court Nominee," *New York Times,* 4 July 1991.

352   Polls of blacks: Tom Squitieri, "Poll: Blacks Split on Thomas," *USA Today,* 5 July 1991, p. 1A; Larry Hugick, "Gallup Poll ... ," *St. Louis Post-Dispatch,* 21 July 1991, p. 4B.

352   Thomas and Thurmond: James Rowley, "Thomas Lauds Civil Rights Drive, Meets Members of Senate Panel," *Boston Globe,* 10 July 1991.

352   Thomas and Simon: Paul Simon, *Advice and Consent: Clarence Thomas, Robert Bork and the Intriguing History of the Supreme Court's Nomination Battles* (Washington: National Press Books, 1992), p. 81.

352   Duberstein: Interviews by the author; *Dan.* 20.

353   Farrakhan: JIZ; Robert Pear, "Despite Praising Farrakhan in 1983, Thomas Denies Anti-Semitism," *New York Times,* 13 July 1991, p. 7.

354   "bitter divorce": Carlson, "Marching"; Chin and Wescott, "Making."

354   "unilluminating": *Phe.* 17.

354   Aquinas article: Ted Gest and Jeffery L. Sheler, "A Higher Law for the High Court: Would Justice Thomas Put God on the Bench?" *U.S. News & World Report,* 22 July 1991, pp. 50–51.

355   "rougher personality": *Dan.* 26–27.

355 Questions asked at murder boards: Paoletta file, BushL.

355 Discussion of abortion: Ibid. (abortion question); *Dan.* 23–24.

356 Meeting with Lowery et al.: JEL; "Amen Corner" article faxed by Lowery. In an interview, Walter Fauntroy said he could not remember much about the meeting. He suggested that the author "go with" Lowery's account, as he was confident it would be accurate. Sullivan and Newman did not respond to written requests for interviews.

357 Meeting with Hooks and NAACP: *Phe.* 76.

357 Charter bus from Georgia: CB; Sharon LaFraniere, "Hometown Wellwishers Take Bus to Breakfast with a Favorite Son," *Washington Post,* 1 August 1991, p. A4; Dawn Ceol, "Hometown Folks Say Thomas' Detractors Don't Know the Man," *Washington Times,* 1 August 1991, p. A1.

358 Compton NAACP chapter: "Has the Civil Rights Movement Gone 'Terribly Wrong'?" *Business Week,* 16 September 1991, pp. 32–33.

358 Targeting black lawyers: Gary Lee, "Nominee Finds No Middle Ground," *Washington Post,* 9 August 1991, p. A4.

359 *Business Week* poll: "Has the Civil."

360 Black-feminist split after Civil War: Philip S. Foner, introduction to *Frederick Douglass on Women's Rights,* ed. Foner (Westport, Conn.: Greenwood Press, 1976), pp. 12–40; Benjamin Quarles, *Frederick Douglass* (Washington: Associated Publishers, 1948), pp. 244–47.

360 "sense of desperation": *Phe.* 19.

360 "Many of the ministers": *Phe.* 135.

360 Feminist lobbying: DD.

360 Lehrman article: Lewis E. Lehrman, "The Declaration of Independence and the Right to Life," *American Spectator,* April 1987, pp. 21–23; Ruth Marcus, "Danforth: Thomas Speech Didn't Reflect Abortion View," *Washington Post,* 19 July 1991, p. A4.

361 L. Douglas Wilder: "Wilder Apologizes on Thomas Remark," *New York Times,* 5 July 1991, p. A9; John P. Gallagher, "Thomas' Teacher Defends Prize Pupil," files of Sister Virgilius Reidy.

362 Endorsements: Hear.91 1:514–15.

362 Criminal defense lawyers: Hear.91 2:490.

362 Conservatives gear up: EM; CB; *Phe.* 134; interview of Len I. Munsil.

363 Attacks "devastated" him: *Dan.* 15.

CHAPTER NINETEEN: Into the Quagmire

365 Hoerchner-Hill communications: Hear.91 4:271–333; *Bro.* 30–31. Throughout the narrative discussing Hill's allegations against Thomas, the author has relied on the testimony and other sources that are most persuasive. For example, although Hill was not a credible witness before the Judiciary Committee, she alleges in her book, *Speaking Truth to Power,* that Metzenbaum staffer James Brudney briefed Metzenbaum early on about her allegations. Brudney denied this claim to a Senate investigator. Hill's book is cited in support of the conclusion that Brudney told Hill that he had in fact informed Metzenbaum, contradicting his later statements to the investigator. Hill had no discernible reason to prevaricate about this, while Brudney did (i.e., protecting his boss). Metzenbaum's personal role in the Hill affair tips the balance in favor of believing Hill on this point.

366 Hill-Phillips conversation: *Bro.* 31–32.

366 "Do you know": *Hill* 105.

366 Laster-Hill communication: Ibid. 107; Hear.91 4:36–58; Flem.R. 11–12.

366 Seidman-Hill communication: Hear.91 4:36–58; Flem.R. 12–13.

368 Thomas's opening statement: Hear.91 1:109–10.

368ff Hearings on Sept. 10: Ibid. 1:111–16, 127–33.

372 Rosa Parks: Simon *Advice* 83.

372 Hill-Brudney communications: Ibid. 4:58–137; *Hill* 110–11.

373 Hearings on Sept. 11: Hear.91 1:177–380.

374 Thomas's responses to Leahy: In *The Real Anita Hill,* Brock defends Thomas's credibility on the matter of *Roe.* He states:

"Thomas never said that he had had no discussions about *Roe.* He simply sidestepped Leahy's question altogether by saying he had never 'debated the contents of it.' This construction had a precise meaning among lawyers: Thomas was saying he had not debated the legal contents, or the jurisprudence, of *Roe.* In other words, Thomas may have discussed abortion or even *Roe* in layman's terms while expressing no critique of the ruling's legal basis. That Thomas would have done so seemed odd only to laymen; lawyers know that few are really able to debate the ruling's arcane jurisprudence." *Bro.* 97–98.

Brock's analysis is in error. First, he selectively quoted Thomas's testimony. He did not quote the most damning portion, in which Thomas stated categorically, "Senator, your question to me was did I debate the contents of *Roe v. Wade,* the outcome in *Roe v. Wade,* do I have this day an opinion, a personal opinion on the outcome in *Roe v. Wade;* and my answer to you is that I do not." Hear.91 2:223. Thomas testified not only that he had never debated *Roe;* he denied even possessing an opinion on the case that day. Thomas's claim, while not provably false as a matter of criminal law, was not credible.

Moreover, the "construction" Thomas offered—saying that he had not "debated the contents" of *Roe*—did not carry the "precise meaning among lawyers" that Brock claimed. There is no such term of art in the law. Thomas's best defense is that there is no available evidence that he ever technically "debated" *Roe* with a person in disagreement with him.

375 *Eisenstadt v. Baird:* 405 U.S. 438 (1972).

376 "Rope-a-dope": *Dan.* 27.

376 "inherent dishonesty": *Dan.* 27.

376 Weyrich: *Phe.* 194–95.

377 Silberman and Thompson: LHS; LDT.

377 Bolick on credibility: *Bro.* 92.

377 Hill-Grant communications: Flem.R. 16–17; *Bro.* 119–20; *Phe.* 211–13.

377 Brudney-Hill communications: Flem.R. 17–18; *Bro.* 121.

378 Hoerchner-Grant communications: *Bro.* 123; *Hill* 113.

378 Calabresi: GC.

378 "Two feminist reporters": Mayer and Abramson, *Strange,* p. 239.

378 Hill-Ross communications: Flem.R. 16–17; *Bro.* 125–26; *Hill* 114–15.

378 Hill-Grant communications: Flem.R. 16–17; *Bro.* 125–27; *Hill* 113–14.

379 DeConcini: DD.

379 Weigand and Self: *Phe.* 216.

379 Writing her statement: *Hill* 115.

380 Thomas learns of FBI investigation: *Dan.* 32–33.

380 FBI interview of Thomas: Ibid. 34–35; *Phe.* 218.

380 Conversation with Faddis: *Dan.* 42.

381 Past sins: Ibid. 44.

381 *Lamprecht: Bro.* 103–4; interviews by the author.

382 Thomas's conversations with Specter, Biden: *Dan.* 48.

383 Litchman and Totenberg: Ibid. 144

384 Metzenbaum's objection: Ibid. 146–47.

384 Phelps' conversation with senator: *Phe.* 229–30. Handing off negative tidbits to
reporters was consistent with Metzenbaum's modus operandi. Metzenbaum was
also Thomas's bitterest foe and the one with the shadiest ethics.

Brock would blame Simon for this conversation (which he unfairly characterized as a "leak"). Simon, however, was not known for playing such hardball.
Republican senators uniformly vouched for Simon after the hearings. Brown
described him as having "outstanding character," and said he would be "very surprised" if Simon was responsible for the initial disclosures about Hill. HB.

In contrast, Republicans on the committee instantly suspected Metzenbaum as
the man behind the dissemination of Hill's allegations. Hatch mentioned Metzenbaum specifically after learning about it. Peter Fleming, the special independent counsel, subsequently concluded that the senator who spoke to Phelps had
seen Hill's statement but not the FBI report. Flem.R. 32–35. This would suggest
Metzenbaum, as Simon unquestionably had access to the FBI report, but Metzenbaum apparently did not. Fleming's conclusion also is consistent with Phelps'
account. Phelps said he *called* Simon on Wednesday, October 4.

Of course, muddling things further is the fact that even a senator without
access to the FBI report could have spoken to somebody else who did, and then
simply lied about how he obtained the information. For that matter, Phelps could
be lying. His accounts are inconsistent in some respects. His story in *Capitol
Games* of an in-person unintentional disclosure by a senator differs from the
account he gave to Seidman on September 3. In this discussion, Phelps told her
he thought he "might be on to something" based on Simon's silence on the telephone when he mentioned Hill's name. Flem.R. 24.

Fleming's conclusion that the senator who spoke to Phelps had seen the Hill
statement but not the FBI report was, in Brock's estimation, "based on political
convenience rather than the evidence." This was because Fleming was "a Senate
employee." *Bro.* 421–22 n.23. By this reasoning, however, the entire Fleming
report, on which Brock relies heavily, should be discounted, including Fleming's
strong suggestion that Brudney provided Hill's statement to Totenberg.

In an interview with the author, Simon denied leaking information about Hill
to the media. He said he confirmed the essence of Hill's statement only when
contacted by Nina Totenberg and Tim Phelps on October 5, while he was
attending a board of trustees meeting at Dana College in Nebraska. At that
point, Simon stated, "I don't know that I confirmed it, but I certainly didn't lie
about, and indicated yes, I knew about the affidavit." There was no point in denying information that the reporters had obtained independently, he said. Simon
declined to grant an interview to Brock; he stated he considered him unreliable in
light of his article on Anita Hill in the *American Spectator* (in which Brock
alleged that Simon's wife, a devoted feminist, was behind the leak). "He's the only
reporter I've ever done that to my whole political life," Simon stated.

Metzenbaum did not respond to a telephone or written request for an interview. When contacted by telephone and asked for an interview, Metzenbaum
asked that this author first send him a written request. He specifically wished to

be informed of the author's "slant." When the author asked Metzenbaum for his address, Metzenbaum provided an inaccurate one. The author obtained the correct address from his secretary. He never responded to the letter.

Both senators have denied wrongdoing. Given Metzenbaum's character and vendetta against Thomas, the balance falls in his direction.

385   Totenberg: *Hill* 121–22; *Bro.* 158; NT; Albert R. Hunt, "Tales of Ignominy, Beyond Thomas and Hill," *Wall Street Journal,* 17 October 1991, p. A22. Nina Totenberg requested written questions, then declined to answer many of them. Among these were questions regarding the identity of the leaker.

385   Prominent Democrat re Metzenbaum: Interviews by the author. Brock pins the blame for the faxing of Hill's statement on Brudney alone. This rogue staffer theory is unrealistic. It also ignores Metzenbaum's deep disdain for Thomas and the senator's well-known Machiavellian ethics. A prominent Democrat well positioned to know the truth also disputes Brock's conclusion. Brudney did not respond to an e-mail request for an interview.

386   "conservative African-American": OH. Hatch did not state who he believed to be the senator(s) responsible for the leak of Hill's statement.

386   "most prized possession": *Dan.* 39.

CHAPTER TWENTY: Soul Food

387   Corvette, Liberman call: Ibid. 49–50, 55–57.

388   *Newsweek* article: "A Problem for Clarence Thomas," *Newsweek,* 14 October 1991, p. 56.

388   "humiliation factor": *Dan.* 57.

388   Paoletta: Ibid., pp. 57–58.

389   Brown-Hill communication: HB. Brock wrote that this call took place on October 8, not October 7. Brown stated that it occurred on the Monday morning after the Hill allegations broke, making the latter date the accurate one.

389   Democratic caucus: DD.

390   Simpson-Totenberg exchange: "Personalities," *Washington Post,* 9 October 1991, p. C3; *Dan.* 68–69. Totenberg says that Simpson later apologized, which was consistent with his general backtracking after the hearings.

391   "Why, Ricky": *Phe.* 274.

392   Hill's politics: Ibid. 247–48, 260.

392   "Anita's whole life": *Bro.* 338–39.

393   Biden on Judiciary Committee: *Phe.* 263.

393   Phyllis Berry Myers: Letter of Phyllis Berry Myers, 7 October 1991, Liberman file, BushL.

394   Danforth erupts: *Dan.* 81–83.

395   Larry Silberman's advice: LHS.

395   Simpson's advice: *Dan.* 76–77.

395   Thomas-Thompson call: LDT.

396   Hill's team comes together: *Phe.* 285–86, 295–96.

396   Biden-Hill communication: *Hill* 156.

397   Thomas chides Duberstein: *Dan.* 86. Danforth stated of the conversation, "Ken has no recollection of the ensuing discussion and concludes that someone else must have been on the phone." By all indications, this is a classic example of the selective amnesia that befouls many of the nation's brightest minds in Washing-

ton when a clear memory might be professionally hazardous. Ricky Silberman heard the Thomas end of the conversation, and her account, as stated in Danforth's book, is persuasive.

397 Prayer sessions with Laws and Jameses: Ibid. 87–89.

398 Choosing Specter: Ibid. 92–93; OH; JCD.

399 Thomas with Danforth: Ibid., pp. 96–97.

399 Thomas with Bush: Ibid., pp. 100–1; *Phe.* 288.

400 Quayle: JDQ.

400 Thomas-Johnson call: *Phe.* 289.

400 Thomas on floor: *Dan.* 106.

400 Spiritual purging: Ibid., pp. 106–7.

401 Thomas-Luttig meeting: Ibid., pp. 108–10.

403 Thompson's arrival: LDT.

404 Republican strategy session: *Phe.* 290; *Dan.* 120–21.

404 Ted Wells: Jan Hoffman, "Outsider? Insider? A Lawyer Wins as Both," *New York Times*, 12 January 2000, p. B2.

405 Wells-Thomas communication: Interviews by the author. Danforth wrote that Thomas received a call from a Tony Welters, "perhaps late on Friday night," in which the issue of sexual stereotypes came up. *Dan.* 151. The call actually was from Ted Wells—a phonologically similar name—on Thursday night, and the general issue of lynchings was the subject.

405 Thomas writes speech: *Dan.* 125–26.

CHAPTER TWENTY-ONE: Unraveled

407 Events before hearings: Ibid. 126–30; Hear.91 4:5–10.

408ff Thomas's speech: Hear.91 4:5–10 (beginning).

411 Ginni Thomas and Phelps: *Phe.* 307.

411ff Hill's testimony: Hear.91 4:36–137.

414 Head of OCR personnel office: *Bro.* 173–74.

415 Hill's contradiction re FBI agents: *Hill* 118.

416 Hill's conversation with Brudney: Ibid. 110–11.

420 "I refused to let": Ibid. 84.

420 Hill's conversation with Singleton: *Bro.* 174.

420 Brown's reason for *Roe* questions: HB. Brown disputed an account in Mayer and Abramson's *Strange Justice* about this series of questions. The authors asserted that John Mackey of the Justice Department drafted for Brown his questions about abortion (p. 295). "That was absolutely inaccurate," Brown said in an interview. "The questions were mine." They also quoted a Brown aide—but not Brown himself—as stating, "We had to destroy the argument that she had no motive." Brown's response follows: "The entire statement is completely inaccurate. First of all, I drafted the question myself. I did not have any help from staff. It was solely my own idea. And secondly, the characterization of the purpose involved [i.e., establishing that Thomas and Hill disagreed about abortion] is totally inaccurate as well. And lastly from a scholarship point of view, the authors never even bothered to talk to me about it. And further, in terms of the quote from the staff member, I can't imagine any staff member making that statement. First of all, what is said is wholly inaccurate. And so I can't imagine anybody carrying that viewpoint."

423   "smelled like a perfumery": *Hill* 3–4.

423   Brokaw interview of Heflin: NBC News videotape, BushL.

CHAPTER TWENTY-TWO: The Empty Noose

425   Thomas before speech: *Dan.* 137–42.

426   Thomas-Hatch conversation: OH.

426   "Men are whipped": *Doug.* 384.

426   Evelyn Thomas, Masugi, DeConcini: ET; AS; KM; DD.

427ff Testimony: Hear.91 4:157–270

434   John Cochran: NBC News videotape, BushL.

439   Hill's advisers re Wright: *Phe.* 354.

439   "Hill would later write": *Hill* 217.

439   Dinner at Morton's: OH; BBO; TBO; *Dan.* 157.

440   Hoerchner: Hear.91 4:271–333; *Bro.* 209–14.

440f Wells: Hear.91 4:271–333; *Bro.* 250–51.

442   Erotic delusions: LDT.

442   Discussions with Silberman, Sadat: Ibid. 171–72.

442   Wright's non-testimony: Ibid. 174–75; *Phe.* 368.

445   Polygraph analysis: *Dan.* 180; *Bro.* 283.

446   Thomas on polygraph: *Dan.* 181–83.

CHAPTER TWENTY-THREE: Joy in the Morning

447   Polls of blacks: Sandra Sanchez, "Public Support for Thomas Follows Party Lines," *USA Today,* 14 October 1991, p. 2A; George E. Curry, "Black Support for Nominee Rises," *Chicago Tribune,* 15 October 1991, p. 4C.

448   Informal polls in Atlanta: Angela Tuck and Holly Morris, "The Clarence Thomas Hearings: Nation Reacts; Georgia Reaction," *Atlanta Journal and Constitution,* 12 October 1991, p. A9.

448   Polls of blacks in Democratic caucus: DD; PS.

449   White House lobbying: GHWB; JDQ.

449   "ancient wall of rocks": Lee May, "Hometown Support Is Rock-Solid," *Los Angeles Times,* 12 October 1991, p. A6.

450   Celebration at Famble house: AF; DBP; "We made it": Marcus Holland, "We've Got Victory," *Savannah Morning News,* 16 October 1991, p. 1A; Mark Mayfield, "Pin Point, Ga.: 'Thank you, Jesus,'" *USA Today,* 16 October 1991, p. 2A.

450   Reaction to confirmation elsewhere: Joyce Price, "From Pin Point to Boston, Jeers . . . and Cheers," *Washington Times,* 16 October 1991, p. A7.

450   Bar at Grand Central: Charles Laurence, "America Holds Its Breath for the Final Act of a Real-Life TV Thriller," *Daily Telegraph,* 16 October 1991, p. 1.

451   Thomas during vote: *Dan.* 195.

451   Thomas's speech outside house: James Gerstenzang, "Bush Warned Thomas: Politics, Not Merit," *Los Angeles Times,* 16 October 1991, p. A7.

452   Conversation with Sally Danforth: *Dan.* 196.

452   History of confirmation votes: R. W. Apple Jr., "Senate Confirms Thomas, 52–48, Ending Week of Bitter Battle," *New York Times,* 16 October 1991, p. A1.

452f Swearing-in ceremony: Paul Bedard, "'America at Its Best': Bush Lauds Thomas at Swearing-In," *Washington Times*, 19 October 1991, p. A1; Ann Devroy, "'There Is Joy,' Thomas Tells Crowd," *Washington Post*, 19 October 1991, p. A8.

452 M.C. Thomas: MCT; interviews by the author.

454 High-school student: C-Span2000.

454 Danforth's reflections on confirmation: JCD.

454 Thomas's reflections on confirmation: *Dan.* 195–99.

CHAPTER TWENTY-FOUR: The Stillness of Wounded Pride

457 *People* article: "Breaking Silence," *People*, 11 November 1991, pp. 108–16.

458 Thomas's chambers: Interviews of Thomas clerks. The "SAVE AMERICA" sign and foyer were described in Sus.

458 "rule" re fireplace: Tony Mauro, "Thomas Speaks," *Legal Times*, 14 September 1992, p. 9 (quoting from interview given to internal Supreme Court newsletter).

459 Thomas's daily regimen: Interviews of Thomas clerks; Marc Fisher, "The Private World of Justice Thomas," *Washington Post*, 11 September 1995, p. B1; Karen Testa, "Supreme Court's Thomas Opens Up," Associated Press, 9 December 1997.

460 "warring camps": Sp.Act.

460 "unkind word": C-Span2000.

460 Rehnquist: Sp.Gold. 1.

460 O'Connor: Ibid.

461 Powell: Sp.Head. 14.

461 Marshall: Juan Williams, *Thurgood Marshall: American Revolutionary* (New York: Times Books, 1998), pp. 392–94.

461 White: Interviews of Thomas clerks.

461 Scalia: Ibid.

462 "virtual isolation": Sp.NBA.

462 "big refrigerator": Joan Biskupic, "'I Am Not an Uncle Tom,' Thomas Says at Meeting," *Washington Post*, 28 October 1994, p. A1.

464 Percentage of minority clerks: Tony Mauro, "Corps of Clerks Lacking in Diversity," *USA Today*, 13 March 1998, p. 12A.

465 Thomas's preparation for conferences: Interviews of Thomas clerks; C-Span2000.

465 Discussions in conferences: C-Span2000; Sp.NBA; Mauro, "Thomas Speaks."

466 Clerk conferences: Interviews of Thomas clerks.

467 Relations with clerks: Ibid. His clerks also did not detect in him any evidence of the character flaws Anita Hill had alleged. Those interviewed uniformly spoke of Thomas as "prim" or a "clean liver." One volunteered that he never heard him use profanity of any kind. Hill's allegations, when repeated to Thomas clerks, evoked only indignation and utter disbelief.

468 House in Virginia: Interviews by the author.

468 "wounded bear": Sp.Gold. 5.

468f Thomas's private discussions about Hill: Interviews by the author.

470 Live for 40 years: Joan Biskupic, "'I Am Not an Uncle Tom,' Thomas Says at Meeting," *Washington Post*, 28 October 1994, p. A1; Tom Barton, "Thomas Proves You Can Go Home Again," *Savannah Morning News*, 6 April 1997; Ros. (conversation with Loury).

470 Thomas on avoiding the news: Speech to the Ashbrook Center for Public Affairs, February 5, 1999 (answers to questions following speech); Glen Elsasser, "Thomas' Courtly Silence May Mask Anger," *Chicago Tribune,* April 29, 1994, p. 1.

471 Thomas in oral argument: Interviews of Thomas clerks; MB; David G. Savage, "In the Matter of Justice Thomas," *Los Angeles Times Magazine,* 9 October 1994, p. 14.

471 Quiet in oral argument (putative act of self-denial): Sp.Gold. 3, Alan Cooper, "Thomas: Internet Offers New Issues," *Richmond Times-Dispatch,* 20 May 2000, p. B3.

471 Quiet in oral argument ("It's in the briefs"): Interviews of Thomas clerks.

471 Quiet in oral argument (potpourri of excuses): C-Span2000.

472 Armstrong Williams: AW.

473 "Deep-set anger": David Andrew Price, "Twisting Thomas," *Forbes MediaCritic,* 1996, pp. 31–39.

473 "steal your joy": Ros.

474 *Doggett v. United States:* 505 U.S. 647, 112 S.Ct. 2686 (1992); 112 S.Ct. at 2694–2701 (Thomas, J., dissenting).

475 *Hudson v. McMillian:* 503 U.S. 1, 112 S.Ct. 995 (1992); 112 S.Ct. at 1004–11 (Thomas, J., dissenting). The citation for Estelle v. Gamble is 429 U.S. 97, 97 S.Ct. 285 (1976).

476 *Dawson v. Delaware:* 503 U.S. 159, 112 S.Ct. 1093 (1992); 112 S.Ct. at 1100–05 (Thomas, J., dissenting).

477 *United States v. Fordice:* 505 U.S. 717, 112 S.Ct. 2727 (1992); 112 S.Ct. at 2744–46 (Thomas, J., dissenting).

478 *Planned Parenthood v. Casey:* 505 U.S. 833, 112 S.Ct. 2791 (1992).

479 Articles on *Hudson:* "The Youngest, Cruelest Justice," *New York Times,* 27 February 1992, p. A24; William Raspberry, "Confounding One's Supporters," *Washington Post,* 28 February 1992, p. A23.

479 "I must note in passing": Sp.NBA.

479 Lowery: JEL.

CHAPTER TWENTY-FIVE: Homecoming

481 Polls and one black writer: Ishmael Reed, "Feminists v. Thomas," *Washington Post,* 18 October 1992, p. C1.

482 Patricia Cornwell: OH. Cornwell, through an assistant, at first agreed to be interviewed, but later declined.

482 *Helling v. McKinney:* 509 U.S. 25, 113 S.Ct. 2475 (1993); 113 S.Ct. at 2482–85 (Thomas, J., dissenting).

484 *United States v. James Daniel Good Real Property:* 510 U.S. 43, 114 S.Ct. 492 (1993); 114 S.Ct. at 515–17 (Thomas, J., concurring in part and dissenting in part).

485 Ten-year campaign to recover "good name": AW.

486 Shelton's memo at Mercer: PDS; Toob.

486 Huddle House: PDS.

486 Speech at Mercer: PDS; Sp.Merc.

487 "thunderous standing ovations": Bill Rankin, "Clarence Thomas Hits Intolerance," *Atlanta Journal and Constitution,* 2 May 1993, p. D2

487 Declining to be interviewed: Jodi White, "Thomas Urges 'Civility' in Law Day Speech," *Macon Telegraph,* 2 May 1993, p. A1.

487 Georgia Public Policy Foundation speech: MG.

488 Jeff Dickerson: JD.

488 Flap over fundraiser: MG; Bill Rankin, "Thomas's Atlanta Talk Raises Ethics Questions," *Atlanta Journal and Constitution,* 7 May 1993, p. A1; Linda Greenhouse, "What Justices Do off the Bench," *New York Times,* 21 May 1993, p. B9.

488 Trip to Pin Point: AF.

489 Boycott in St. Louis: Daniel R. Browning, "Black Lawyers Group Denies Plan to Boycott Thomas' Speech," *St. Louis Post-Dispatch,* 7 August 1993, p. 3B.

489 Speech in St. Louis: Tim Poor, "I'm Not Bitter Anymore, Justice Thomas Says Here," *St. Louis Post-Dispatch,* 30 September 1993, p. 1A; Toob.

490 Speech to Claremont: Sp.Chur.

491 David Brock: *Bro.* 36, 203, 380.

492 "edge to the comment": Elsasser, "Courtly Silence."

492 "that there judge": Sp.Ashbrook 11.

492 London visit: Ibid.

492 Buying music: AW.

492 "most media-shy": Biskupic, "Uncle."

492 Reason for few interviews: AW.

493 "Part of how": Interviews by the author.

493 *Farmer v. Brennan:* 511 U.S. 825, 114 S.Ct. 1970 (1994); 114 S.Ct. at 1990–91 (Thomas, J., concurring).

494 *Staples v. United States:* 511 U.S. 600, 114 S.Ct. 1793 (1994).

495 *Holder v. Hall:* 512 U.S. 888, 114 S.Ct. 2581 (1994); 114 S.Ct. at 2591–2619 (Thomas, J., concurring). Other cases cited therein are *Shaw v. Reno,* 509 U.S. 630, 113 S.Ct. 2816 (1993); *Thornburg v. Gingles,* 478 U.S. 30, 106 S.Ct. 2752 (1986).

497 Media regarding *Holder:* Linda Greenhouse, "Voting Rights...," 1 July 1994, p. A18; Paul Gigot, "Why Liberals Should Thank Clarence Thomas," *Wall Street Journal,* 8 July 1994, p. A10.

CHAPTER TWENTY-SIX: 1787, a Wonderful Year

499 Cowboys: Marc Fisher, "The Private World of Justice Thomas," *Washington Post,* 11 September 1995, p. B1; AW.

499 Barkley: Greg Boeck, "Sir Charles' Capitol Idea," *USA Today,* 8 December 1994, p. 3C; Tony Mauro, "Courtside," *The Recorder,* 23 December 1994, p. 10.

499 "Clone": Carl T. Rowan, "Conservative Clone," *Louisville Courier-Journal,* 7 July 1993, p. 11A; Joan Biskupic, "Scalia, Thomas Stand Apart on the Right," *Washington Post,* 24 June 1994, p. A1.

500 Gerber: Scott Douglas Gerber, *First Principles: The Jurisprudence of Clarence Thomas* (New York: NYU Press, 1999), p. 209, Table 2.

500 107 cases in first term: Analysis and interviews by the author.

500 Meeting with black journalists: Biskupic, "Uncle"; Fisher, "Private."

501 Trip to Tuskegee: Interview of J. J. Johnson of Tuskegee; Ros.; Scott Thurston, "Thomas preaches self-help," *Atlanta Journal and Constitution,* 19 November 1994, p. A3.

502 *Resurrection* quotation: Dan. *208.*

502 Totenberg: Nina Totenberg, "A Question That Won't Go Away," *Los Angeles Times,* 13 November 1994, book review section, p. 2.

503 "absolute bunch": SH. Hardnett was referring to a passage on page 137, which discussed a group of black professionals in the Washington area (of which she was a member) and their trip to Martha's Vineyard. Mayer and Abramson also misidentified her as a law clerk.

503 Paoletta: David Streitfeld, "Book Report," 27 August 1995, p. X15.

503 Kurtz: Howard Kurtz, "Is Thomas Harassed?" *Washington Post,* 11 November 1994, p. D1.

504 Thomas speaks at oral argument: Tony Mauro, "Heads Turn As Thomas Asks a Question," *USA Today,* 9 November 1994, p. 13A.

504f *United States v. Lopez:* 514 U.S. 549, 115 S.Ct. 1624 (1995); 115 S.Ct. at 1642–57 (Thomas, J., concurring).

506 *U.S. Term Limits, Inc. v. Thornton:* 514 U.S. 779, 115 S.Ct. 1842 (1995); 115 S.Ct. at 1875–1914 (Thomas, J., dissenting). The citation for *McCulloch v. Maryland* is 4 Wheat. 316, 4 L.Ed. 579 (1819).

507ff *McIntyre v. Ohio Elections Commission:* 514 U.S. 334, 115 S.Ct. 1511 (1995); 115 S.Ct. at 1525–30 (Thomas, J., concurring).

510ff *Rosenberger v. Rector & Visitors of the Univ. of Virginia:* 515 U.S. 819, 115 S.Ct. 2510 (1995); 115 S.Ct. at 2528–33 (Thomas, J., concurring).

512 Conferences about race cases: Ros.; interviews by the author.

512 Missouri v. Jenkins: *515 U.S. 70, 115 S.Ct. 2038 (1995); 115 S.Ct. at 2061–73 (Thomas, J., concurring).*

513ff Adarand Constructors, Inc. v. Pena: *515 U.S. 200, 115 S.Ct. 2097 (1995); 115 S.Ct. at 2119 (Thomas, J., concurring in part and concurring in the judgment).*

517 Raoul Berger: Raoul Berger, *Government by Judiciary: The Transformation of the Fourteenth Amendment* (Cambridge, Mass.: Harvard Univ. Press, 1977), pp. 166–92.

518 "wild about the Constitution": D'Souza, "Thomas."

518 Gettysburg: AF.

518 Pickett's charge: Sp.Ashbrook.

CHAPTER TWENTY-SEVEN: Keeping the Faith

519 *Time:* Jack E. White, "Uncle Tom Justice," *Time,* 26 June 1995, p. 36.

519 Sharpton: Eric Lipton, "400 Activists Protest outside Justice's Home," *Washington Post,* 13 September 1995, p. D3.

519 AEI conference: PBL.

519 Loury: Ros.

520 "one of the most wonderful": Tony Mauro, "Thomas Speaks," *Legal Times,* 14 September 1992, p. 9.

520 Jamal: AF; WK.

520 Cedric Jennings: Sus.

521 "He remembers indignities": David G. Savage, "Justice Thomas Defined by His Roots, and Distance from Them," *Los Angeles Times,* 22 June 1998, p. A5.

522 Giving up cigars: Interviews by the author.

522 *Bush v. Vera:* 517 U.S. 952, 116 S.Ct. 1941 (1996); 116 S.Ct. at 1972–74 (Thomas, J., concurring).

523 *44 Liquormart, Inc. v. Rhode Island:* 517 U.S. 484, 116 S.Ct. 1495 (1996); 116 S.Ct. at 1515–20 (Thomas, J., concurring in part and concurring in the judgment). The citation for *Central Hudson Gas & Elec. Corp. v. Public Serv. Comm'n of N.Y.* is 447 U.S. 557, 100 S.Ct. 2343 (1980).

524 *Lewis v. Casey:* 518 U.S. 343, 116 S.Ct. 2174 (1996); 116 S.Ct. at 2186 (Thomas, J., concurring). The citation for *Bounds v. Smith* is 430 U.S. 817, 97 S.Ct. 1491 (1977).

525f *M.L.B. v. S.L.J.:* 519 U.S. 102, 117 S.Ct. 555 (1996); 117 S.Ct. at 570–78 (Thomas, J., dissenting). The citation for *Griffin v. Illinois* is 351 U.S. 12, 76 S.Ct. 585 (1956).

527 Liberty University: Interview of Dwayne Carson.

528 Republican staffer: Interview of Republican staffer.

528 Texas Wesleyan: April M. Washington, "Thomas Decries Affirmative Action," *Dallas Morning News,* 8 May 1996, p. 1A.

529 Pullen School flap: David Montgomery and Lisa Frazier, "P. G. School Tries Again with Thomas," *Washington Post,* 6 June 1996, p. B1; Steve Twomey, "Kids Not Blind to Injustice," *Washington Post,* 6 June 1996, p. B1.

530 Ginni's briefing book on Clinton: Interview of Kyle McSlarrow; Ed Henry, "Armey Aide Writes Briefing Book on Clinton Scandals for Members," *Roll Call,* 30 September 1996.

530 Ginni's confrontation with Moran: BBO; Jennifer Senior, "GOP Women Charge Dems with Sexism," *The Hill,* 15 May 1996, p. 24.

531 "Devil with a Blue Dress On": BBO.

531 "homemade compass": Sp.Act.

531 "one good thing": Sp.Head. 16.

531 "Years later": C-Span2000.

531 Ricky Silberman: RGO.

531 Receives communion: Sp.HC96 4.

531 Attending Mass at St. Joseph: Interviews by the author.

CHAPTER TWENTY-EIGHT: "I Am a Man, a Black Man, an American"

533 Thatcher: Cas.Conv.

533 Paul Johnson: JM.

533 Mowing the lawn: Tom Barton, "Thomas Proves You Can Go Home Again," *Savannah Morning News,* 6 April 1997.

533 Federalist barbecues: TBO; interviews by the author.

533 Fifth anniversary: Ibid.

534 N.E. School of Law: Speech to the New England School of Law, 21 November 1996, published in *New England Law Review* 31 (Winter 1997): 515–21. Protestors discussed in Peter S. Canellos, "Thomas Urges 'Plain Good Manners,'" *Boston Globe,* 22 November 1996, p. B2.

534 Return to Savannah: BP; interview of Barbara King.

534f Speech to Savannah diocese: King, "Diocese"; Dio.Sav.

536 *Kansas v. Hendricks:* 521 U.S. 346, 117 S.Ct. 2072 (1997).

536 *Reno v. American Civil Liberties Union:* 521 U.S. 844, 117 S.Ct. 2329 (1997).

537 *Glickman v. Wileman Bros. & Elliott:* 521 U.S. 457, 117 S.Ct. 2130 (1997); 117 S.Ct. at 2155–56 (Thomas, J., dissenting).

538ff *Printz v. United States:* 117 S.Ct. 2365 (1997); 117 S.Ct. at 2385–86 (Thomas, J., concurring).

540 "Come the revolution": Interviews by the author.

540 Tenth wedding anniversary: Peggy Noonan, "After Anita Hill," *Good Housekeeping,* September 1997, p. 216.

540 Famble: AF.

540 Anita Hill: *Hill* 69–70, 83, 181–82, 190, 253, 108, 80, 115–16, 89, 335, 281–83.

543 Reviews of Hill's book: Christopher Hitchens, "The Wrong Questions," *Washington Post,* 9 November 1997, p. X4; Susie Linfield, "The True Story of a Reluctant Participant," *Los Angeles Times,* 26 November 1997, p. E3; Patricia Smith, "Hill's Tell-All Feels Like Just Another Lecture," *Boston Globe,* 25 November 1997, p. D3; Margaret Talbot, "Talking Back," *New York Times,* 26 October 1997, sect. 7, p. 7.

543f Mark Martin: EMM; AF.

545ff *United States v. Bajakajian:* 524 U.S. 379, 118 S.Ct. 2028 (1998). Theodore Olson brought this case to the author's attention.

547 Dinner at Kopp house: TJO.

548 Mauro: Tony Mauro, "Thomas Spent Time off in Public Eye," *USA Today,* 5 October 1998, p. 4A.

548 Chaos and illegitimacy: Sp.Ashbrook.

548 Heritage Foundation: Sp.Her.98.

549 *Emerge:* "Uncle Thomas: Lawn Jockey for the Far Right," *Emerge,* November 1996, pp. 38–48.

549 Raspberry: William Raspberry, "Justice on the High Ground," *Washington Post,* 3 August 1998, p. A21.

549 "The justice is going": Tony Mauro, "Thomas Still Plans Memphis Speech," *USA Today,* 24 June 1998, p. 4A.

549 "enemy of the people": Sp.Head. 16.

550 NBA speech: Sp.NBA.

550f *Headway* speech: Sp.Head.; Steven A. Holmes, "In Speech, Justice Thomas Talks of 'Backbone' and Beliefs," *New York Times,* 13 September 1998, sect. 1, p. 45.

551f St. Vincent controversy: Dwayne Pickels, "Catholic Group Unhappy about Talk by Justice," *Pittsburgh Tribune-Review,* 25 September 1998, p. B1.

552 Speech at St. Vincent: DW; JP.

552 Trip to Denver: Bill Scanlon, "Toss TV and Study, Study, Study," *Rocky Mountain News,* 23 October 1998, p. 4A.

553 Steinem: Gloria Steinem, "Feminists and the Clinton Question," *New York Times,* 22 March 1998, sect. 4, p. 15.

553 Hill on Clinton: Anita Hill, "The Paula Problem," *Newsweek,* 9 June 1997, p. 38; Associated Press, "Anita Hill Says Clinton's Policies Are More Important Than Conduct," *St. Louis Post-Dispatch,* 23 March 1998, p. A11.

554 Biden: Hear.91 4:2.

554 "Nice try": Questions following Sp.Ashbrook.

555 Thomas on Clinton: Interviews by the author.

CHAPTER TWENTY-NINE: Life, Liberty, and the Open Road

557 Daytona 500: RW; JK; interviews by the author.

558 Lincoln Day speech: Sp.Lin.

559 Montana: MH; interview of Ed Eck. The citation for *Terry v. Ohio* is 392 U.S. 1, 88 S.Ct. 1868 (1968).

560 George Mason U: Jacqueline L. Salmon, "Thomas Exhorts Law Grads to Be Heroes," *Washington Post,* 23 May 1999, p. C3.

560 Chapman U: Speech at Chapman Univ., 20 October 1999; interviews by the author.

560 Ave Maria: George Bullard, "New Law School Touched by Thomas," *Detroit News,* 20 November 1999, p. 1C; interview of Joseph Falvey.

560ff *City of Chicago v. Morales:* 119 S.Ct. 1849 (1999); 119 S.Ct. at 1879–87 (Thomas, J., dissenting). The citation for *Papachristou v. City of Jacksonville* is 405 U.S. 156, 92 S.Ct. 839 (1972).

562 *Hunt v. Cromartie:* 119 S.Ct. 1545 (1999).

563f *Saenz v. Roe:* 119 S.Ct. 1518 (1999); 119 S.Ct. at 1535–38 (Thomas, J., dissenting). The citation for the *Slaughter-House Cases* is 16 Wall, 36, 21 L.Ed. 394 (1872); that of *Corfield v. Coryell* is 6 Fed. Cas. 546 (No. 3, 230)(CCED Pa. 1825).

565 Comparisons with Scalia: Sp.NBA; Sp.Ashbrook; Sp.Lin.

566 Biskupic: Joan Biskupic, "After a Quiet Spell, Justice Finds Voice," *Washington Post,* 24 May 1999, p. A1. In September 1999, after this author's article on Thomas appeared in the *Weekly Standard,* Biskupic called the editor of the *Standard* to complain about the analysis of her May 24, 1999, article. She alleged that insufficient credit had been given her for challenging the conventional wisdom that Thomas was a follower of Scalia. The fundamental premise of Biskupic's analysis, however, was that Thomas had broken away from Scalia's spell only recently. This was inaccurate.

566 "Strange Justice" on Showtime: Ken Ringle, "Not Quite Doing 'Justice' to History," *Washington Post,* 28 August 1999, p. C1; Larry Thompson, "TV: Reliving a 'Strange Justice,'" *Wall Street Journal,* 23 August 1999, p. A13.

567 Copies of speeches at Supreme Court: Interview of Dorothy Barry; interview of Patricia of the Supreme Court's public information office. Barry declined to make copies of his speeches available. The spokesperson in the public information office did allow that her first name was Patricia, and that she was the "only Patricia in the office."

567 Refusal to hand out written remarks: Interview of Don Orlando (St. Vincent); interview of Joseph Falvey (Ave Maria); interview of Susan Kessler (Nat'l Restaurant Assn.).

567 Moot court: CF; JAT; QJ; interviews by the author.

568 "I, for one": Sp.NBA.

568 "That is the requirement": Sp.Head. 16.

568 Goldwater: Sp.Gold.

570 Funeral of Myers Thomas: EMM.

570f Tampa Bay speech: Sp.Fed.Bar.

572 *Nixon v. Shrink Missouri Government PAC:* 120 S.Ct. 897 (2000); 120 S.Ct. at 916–27 (Thomas, J., dissenting). The citation for *Buckley v. Valeo* is 424 U.S. 1, 96 S.Ct. 612 (1976)(per curiam).

573 *United States v. Playboy Entertainment Group, Inc.:* 120 S.Ct. 1878 (2000); 120 S.Ct. at 1894–95 (Thomas, J., concurring).

574f *United States v. Hubbell:* 120 S.Ct. 2037 (2000); 120 S.Ct. at 2050–54 (Thomas, J., concurring). The citation for *Dickerson v. United States* is 120 S.Ct. 2326 (2000); *Fisher v. United States* is 425 U.S. 391, 96 S.Ct. 1569 (1976).

576 *Troxel v. Granville:* 120 S.Ct. 2054 (2000); 120 S.Ct. at 2067–68 (Thomas, J., concurring).

577ff *Stenberg v. Carhart:* 120 S.Ct. 2597 (2000); 120 S.Ct. at 2635–56 (Thomas, J., dissenting).

579 Arizona Right to Life leaders: Interviews of John Jakubczyk and Carolyn Gerster.

580 *USA Today:* Richard Willing, "High Court Sides with Playboy," *USA Today,* 23 May 2000, p. 1A; Tony Mauro, "Thomas Makes His Mark," *USA Today,* 6 July 2000, p. 15A.

581 *Chicago Tribune:* Jan Crawford Greenburg, "Thomas and Scalia: 2 Justices, 2 Viewpoints," *Chicago Tribune,* 7 June 2000, p. 1.

581 Hentoff: Nat Hentoff, "First Friend," *Legal Times,* 3 July 2000, p. 62.

CHAPTER THIRTY: New Horizons

584ff *Bush v. Gore:* 121 S.Ct. 525 (2000); *Bush v. Palm Beach County Canvassing Bd.,* 121 S.Ct. 471 (2000).

586 Speech to high-school students: C-Span2000.

587 Ashcroft a "warm-up": Eric Pianin and Thomas B. Edsall, "3 Cabinet Nominees Will Face Hill Fight," *Washington Post,* 4 January 2001, p. A1.

588 Ashcroft testimony: "Excerpts from Senate Hearing on Ashcroft Nomination for Attorney General," *New York Times,* 17 January 2001.

588 Comparison to Thomas hearings: David Johnston and Neil A. Lewis, "Ashcroft Pledges to Enforce Laws as Hearings Open in Senate," *New York Times,* 17 January 2001, p. A1.

589 Ashcroft avoids CPAC conference: Robert Novak, "Lott Bolts at Bush Appointments," *Chicago Sun-Times,* 4 March 2001.

589 AEI speech: Speech to the American Enterprise Institute, 13 February 2001.

591 "want to be remembered": C-Span2000.

591 "last hurrah": Alan Cooper, "Thomas: Internet Offers New Issues," *Richmond Times-Dispatch,* 20 May 2000, p. B3.

591 Conversation with Armstrong Williams: Armstrong Williams, "An Exclusive Conversation with Clarence Thomas," 31 October 1995, disseminated on wire services.

Index